PEARSON CUSTOM **SOCIAL WORK**

Dynamics of Poverty
Buffalo State College
Dr. Christopher B. Aviles

PEARSON

Senior Vice President, Editorial: Patrick F. Boles
Editor: Ana Díaz-Caneja
Development Editor: Abbey Lewis
Editorial Assistant: Hannah Coker
Operations Manager: Eric M. Kenney
Production Manager: Jennifer Berry
Art Director: Renée Sartell
Cover Designer: Renée Sartell

Cover Art: "Tierradentro" by Ignacio Auzike, courtesy of Getty Images; "Watermelons Series" by Segundo Huertas, courtesy of Getty Images; abstruse background, courtesy of Roberto A. Sanchez/iStockPhoto; squares abstract painting, courtesy of Phillip Jones/iStockPhoto; painted background, courtesy of Andrea Haase/iStockPhoto.

Printed in the United States of America.

V3NL

Please visit our website at *www.pearsonlearningsolutions.com*.

Attention bookstores: For permission to return any unsold stock, contact us at *pe-uscustomreturns@pearson.com*.

Pearson Learning Solutions, 501 Boylston Street, Suite 900, Boston, MA 02116
A Pearson Education Company
www.pearsoned.com

ISBN 10: 1-256-58365-0
ISBN 13: 978-1-256-58365-3

Table of Contents

Social Policy and the American Welfare State

© Jeff Greenberg/The Image Works

Social welfare policy is best viewed through the lens of political economy (i.e., the interaction of economic, political, and ideological forces). This chapter provides an overview of the American welfare state through that lens. In particular, it examines various definitions of social welfare policy, the relationship between social policy and social problems, and the values and ideologies that drive social welfare in the United States. In addition, the chapter examines the effects of ideology on the U.S. welfare state, including the important roles played by conservatism and liberalism (and their variations) in shaping welfare policy. An understanding of social welfare policy requires the ability to grasp the economic justifications and consequences that underlie policy decisions. As such, this chapter contains a brief introduction to Keynesianism, free market economics, socialism, and communitarianism, among others.

American social welfare is in transition. Starting with the Social Security Act of 1935, liberals argued that federal social programs were the best way to help the disadvantaged. Now, after 70 years of experimenting with the **welfare state,** a discernible shift has occurred. The conservatism of U.S. culture—so evident in the Reagan, Bush (both Bushes), and even Clinton presidencies—has left private institutions to shoulder more of the welfare burden. For proponents of social justice, the suggestion that the private sector should assume more responsibility for welfare represents a retreat from the hard-won governmental social legislation that provided essential benefits to millions of Americans. Justifiably, these groups fear the loss of basic goods and services during the transition in social welfare.

The political trajectory shifted with the 2008 election. The election of Barack Obama as the 44th President of the United States not only broke a racial barrier but also swept away the strident conservatism that had defined the presidency of George W. Bush. Winning 52 percent of the vote and increasing Democratic majorities in both chambers of Congress, the Obama victory heartened liberals who anticipated an expansion of government social programs. Obama's platform was crafted to appeal to middle-class voters who had lost ground economically during the second Bush presidency and included the following objectives:

- Increase capital gains taxes on individuals making more than $250,000 per year while providing tax credits for couples earning less than $200,000 annually.
- Jump-start the economy through a $700 billion stimulus package that included $25 billion for infrastructure projects as well as $25 billion for state and local governments.
- Introduce progressivity in the withholding tax by adding a tax of 2 to 4 percent for individuals whose incomes exceed $250,000 a year.
- Require that all children have health insurance, prohibit insurance companies from refusing to insure people with pre-existing conditions, and mandate that employers provide health insurance to workers or pay into a health insurance fund.
- Spend $10 billion to expand and improve pre-school education and $12 billion for higher education in the form of a $4,000 refundable tax credit in exchange for 100 hours of community service.[1]

While liberal pundits hailed the resurgence of "a vast new progressive movement,"[2] structural limits would certain restrain Obama's ambitions. Massive deficits left by the second Bush administration compounded by a looming recession mean that economic issues will not only trump other priorities, but that reduced tax revenues will impede the ability of the government to meet existing obligations let alone expand social programs. Moreover, the Republicans can filibuster Democratic initiatives in the Senate that are perceived as being particularly generous. Obama's centrist inclinations will help build bipartisan support for his legislative agenda. This was evident in his understanding of welfare reform. Acknowledging that "conservatives—and Bill Clinton—were right" to scrap the Aid to Families with Dependent Children program, Obama also recognized that welfare reform had "swelled the ranks of the working poor." Consequently, he argued that a post-welfare reform anti-poverty policy must entail increasing the Earned Income Tax Credit for low-income working families, but also expanding community-based health and education as well as law enforcement.[3] Clearly, economic and political circumstances will test the new president's leadership in managing domestic affairs and therein social welfare.

Despite the Democratic victory in 2008, structural features of the American welfare state militate against a major expansion of government, per se. A pluralistic mix of private and public services is an overriding feature of U.S. social welfare. As in other realms, such as education, in social welfare private institutions coexist alongside those of the public sector. U.S. social welfare has a noble tradition of voluntary citizen groups taking the initiative to solve local problems. Today, private voluntary groups provide important services to **AIDS** patients, the homeless, immigrants, victims of domestic violence, and refugees.

Social welfare has become big business. During the last 30 years, the number of human service corporations—for-profit firms providing social welfare through the marketplace—has increased dramatically. Human service corporations are prominent in long-term nursing care, health maintenance, child day care, psychiatric and substance abuse services, and even corrections. For many welfare professionals, the privatizing of social services is troubling, occurring as it does at a time when government has reduced its commitment to social programs. Yet human service corporations will likely continue to be prominent players in shaping the nation's social welfare policies. As long as U.S. culture is democratic and capitalistic, entrepreneurs will be free to establish social welfare services in the private sector, both as nonprofit agencies and as for-profit corporations.

The **mixed welfare economy** of the United States, in which the voluntary, governmental, and corporate sectors coexist, poses important questions for social welfare policy. To what extent can voluntary groups be held responsible for public welfare, given their limited fiscal resources? For which groups of people, if any, should government divest itself of responsibility? Can human service corporations care for poor and multiproblem clients while continuing to generate profits? Equally important, how can welfare professionals shape coherent social welfare policies, given the fragmentation inherent in such pluralism? Clearly, the answers to these questions have much to say about how social welfare programs are perceived by human service professionals, their clients, and the taxpayers who continue to subsidize social programs.

The multitude of questions posed by the transition of social welfare in this country is daunting. Temporarily satisfied by the draconian 1996 welfare reform bill (and the dramatic cuts in the nation's public assistance rolls), conservatives later shifted their attention to "reforming" social insurance programs such as Social Security and Medicare through privatization. Yet past advocates of social justice such as Jane Addams, Whitney Young Jr., and Wilbur Cohen, to name a few, interpreted the inadequacy of social welfare provision and the confusion of their times as an opportunity to further social justice. It remains for another generation of welfare professionals to demonstrate the same imagination, perseverance, and courage to advance social welfare in the years ahead. Those accepting this challenge will need to be familiar with the various meanings of social welfare policy, differing political and economic explanations of social welfare, and the multiple interest groups that have emerged within the U.S. social welfare system.

Definitions of Social Welfare Policy

The English social scientist Richard Titmuss defined **social services** as "a series of collective interventions that contribute to the general welfare by assigning claims from one set of people who are said to produce or earn the national income to another set of people who may merit compassion and charity."[4] Welfare policy, whether it is the product of governmental, voluntary, or corporate institutions, is concerned with allocating goods, services, and opportunities to enhance social functioning.

William Epstein defined social policy as "social action sanctioned by society."[5] Social policy can also be defined as the formal and consistent ordering of human affairs. **Social welfare policy,** a subset of social policy, regulates the provision of benefits to people to meet basic life needs, such as employment, income, food, housing, health care, and relationships.[6]

Social welfare policy is influenced by the context in which benefits are provided. For example, social welfare is often associated with legislatively mandated programs of the **governmental sector,** such as **Temporary Assistance for Needy Families (TANF).** In the TANF program, social welfare policy consists of the rules by which the federal and state governments apportion cash benefits to an economically disadvantaged population. TANF benefits are derived from general revenue taxes (often paid by citizens who are better off). But this is a simplification of benefits provided to those deemed needy.

Benefits provided through governmental social welfare policy include cash, along with noncash or in-kind benefits, including personal social services.[7] Cash benefits can be further divided into social insurance and public assistance grants.

In-kind benefits (provided as proxies for cash) include such benefits as food stamps; Medicaid; housing vouchers; Women, Infants, and Children (WIC) coupons; and low-income energy assistance. Personal social services are designed to enhance relationships between people as well as institutions, such as individual, family, and mental health treatment; child welfare services; rehabilitation counseling; and so forth. Although complicated, this classification reflects a common theme—the redistribution of resources from the better-off to the more disadvantaged. This redistributional aspect of social welfare policy is generally accepted by those who view social welfare as a legitimate function of the state. Governmental social welfare policy is often referred to as "public" policy because it is the result of decisions reached through a legislative process intended to represent the entire population.

But social welfare is also provided by nongovernmental entities, in which case social welfare policy is a manifestation of "private" policy. For example, a nonprofit agency with a high demand for its services and limited resources may establish a waiting list as agency policy. As other agencies adopt the same strategy for rationing services, clients begin to pile up on waiting lists and some are eventually denied services. Or consider the practice of "dumping," a policy that has been used by some private health care providers to abruptly transfer uninsured patients to public hospitals while they are suffering from traumatic injuries. Patients can—and sometimes do—die as a result of private social welfare policy.

Because U.S. social welfare has been shaped by policies of governmental and nonprofit agencies, confusion exists about the role of for-profit social service firms. The distinction between the public and private sectors was traditionally marked by the boundary between governmental and nonprofit agencies. Profit-making firms are "private" nongovernmental entities that differ from the traditional private voluntary agencies because they operate on a for-profit basis. Within private social welfare, it is therefore important to distinguish between policies of for-profit and of nonprofit organizations. A logical way to redraw the social welfare map is to adopt the following definitions: *Governmental social welfare policy* refers to decisions made by the state; *voluntary social welfare policy* refers to decisions reached by nonprofit agencies; and *corporate social welfare policy* refers to decisions made by for-profit firms.

Social Problems and Social Welfare Policy

Social welfare policy often develops in response to social problems. The relationship between social problems and social welfare policy is not linear, and not all social problems result in social welfare policies. In many instances, existing social welfare policies are funded at ineffectual levels. For example, the Child Abuse Prevention and Treatment Act of 1974 was designed to ameliorate the problem of child abuse, yet underbudgeting left Child Protective Service (CPS) workers in a catch-22 situation. The act required CPS workers to promptly investigate child abuse reports, but agencies had inadequate staff resources to deal with the skyrocketing number of complaints. Caught in a resources crunch, many CPS workers were unable to properly investigate allegations of abuse, resulting in many children dying or undergoing serious injury.

Social welfare is not merely an expression of social altruism; it contributes to the maintenance and survival of society. In this respect, social welfare policy helps hold together a society that may fracture along social, political, and economic stress lines. Social welfare policy is also useful in enforcing social control, especially as a proxy for more coercive measures such as law enforcement and the courts.[8] When the basic minimum needs of the disadvantaged are met, they are less inclined to revolt against the unequal distribution of resources. Social welfare policies also subsidize employers, because welfare benefits supplement low and nonlivable wages, thereby maintaining a work incentive. If wages are insufficient to meet basic food, clothing, and shelter needs, little incentive exists for workplace participation. Without social welfare, like earned income tax credit (EITC), employers would have to raise wages and prices for consumers. Social welfare also supports important industries, such as agriculture (food stamps), housing (Section 8 and various other housing programs), and health care (Medicaid and Medicare). If social welfare benefits were suddenly eliminated, a segment of U.S. business would collapse and prices for commodities and services would rise dramatically. Social welfare benefits help maintain stable price structures and economic growth.

Social welfare policies also relieve the social and economic dislocations caused by the uneven nature of economic development. For example, one of the main features of capitalism and economic globalism is a constantly changing economy where jobs are created in one sector and lost (or exported) in another. The result is large islands of unemployment as workers transition from one employment sector to the other or are lost in the shuffle. Myriad social welfare programs, such as unemployment insurance and food stamps, help soften the transition. Without such social benefits, fundamental questions would also arise about the moral nature of U.S. society. Finally, social welfare policies are a means for rectifying past and current injustices. For example, affirmative action was designed to remedy the historical discrimination that denied large numbers of Americans access to economic opportunities and positions of power. School breakfast and lunch programs, teacher incentive pay, and other policies are designed to help ameliorate the unequal distribution of resources between underfunded inner-city and better-funded suburban school systems.

Social Work and Social Policy

Social work practice is driven by social policies that dictate how the work is done, with whom, for how much, and toward what ends. For example, a social worker employed in a public mental health center may have a caseload of well over 200 clients. Given that caseload size, it is unlikely that the worker can engage in any kind of sustained therapeutic intervention with clients because the size of the caseload permits little more than case tracking. Or consider the worker who must find employment for mothers on public assistance about to lose benefits because of the imposition of time limits, but who are unlikely to locate adequate work because of high area unemployment. In these instances, economic (i.e., underfunding) and political factors contribute to policies that determine the ability of the worker and agency to accomplish their jobs.

An ideological preference among policymakers for private sector social services has resulted in less funding for public agencies. The conservative focus on cutting taxes—evident in the dramatic tax cuts of the last Bush administration—led to reductions in public revenues and hence reductions for social programs. In response to diminishing revenues, public agencies adjust in predictable ways, such as cutting qualified staff and expecting existing staff to do more with less, utilizing less-qualified and lower-paid staff, promoting short-term or group interventions designed to cheaply process more clients, and freezing or reducing the salaries and benefits for professional staff. Combined, these strategies help shape an agency geared to processing more clients rather than helping individual ones. Hence, what a trained social worker can accomplish depends, in part, on the available resources within the agency.

Although not obvious at first glance, many social workers in private practice who depend on managed care for reimbursement experience similar constraints. Specifically, managed care plans dictate how much a social worker will be paid and how often they will see a client; accordingly, care management dictates the kinds of interventions that will be practical in the allotted time. In fact, these policies have as much impact on what social workers do in their day-to-day work as the microlevel theories taught in much of social work education. Accepted agency policy also helps to dictate what is taught in direct social work practice.

Values, Ideology, and Social Welfare Policy

Social welfare policies are shaped by a set of social and personal values that reflect the preferences of those in decision-making capacities. According to David Gil, "Choices in social welfare policy are heavily influenced by the dominant beliefs, values, ideologies, customs, and traditions of the cultural and political elites recruited mainly from among the more powerful and privileged strata."[9] Charles Prigmore and Charles Atherton list no fewer than 15 values that influence social welfare policy: achievement and success, activity and work, public morality, humanitarian concerns, efficiency and practicality, material comfort, equality, freedom, external conformity, science and secular rationality, nationalism and patriotism, democracy and self-determination, individualism, racism and group superiority, and belief in progress.[10] How these values are played out in the realm of social welfare is the domain of the policy analyst. Despite the best of intentions, social welfare policy is rarely based on a rational set of assumptions and reliable research.

One view of a worthwhile social policy is that it should leave no one worse off and at least one person better off, at least as that person judges his or her needs. In the real world of policy that rarely occurs. More often than not, policy is a zero-sum game, in which some people are advantaged at the expense of others. In fact, it can be argued that major social policies are based on values, not on the careful consideration of alternative policies.

Of course, there are serious consequences when social welfare policy is determined to a high degree by values. Since the late 1970s, social welfare policy has been largely shaped by values that emphasize self-sufficiency, work, and the omniscience of the marketplace. Because policymakers expected disadvantaged people to be more independent, supports from government social programs were significantly cut. Although these reductions saved money in the short run, most of the beneficiaries whose supports fell to the budget ax were children. Eventually, cuts in social programs may well lead to greater expenditures, as the generation of children who have gone without essential services begin to require programs to remedy problems associated with poor maternal and infant health care, poverty, illiteracy, and family disorganization. Although in 2006 the U.S. ranked fourth internationally in purchasing power parity (what a family income can actually buy in a given country), it ranked 22nd in public spending on family benefits.[11]

Social values are organized through the lens of ideology. Simply put, an **ideology** is the framework of commonly held beliefs through which we view the world. It is a set of assumptions about how the world works: what has value, what is worth living and dying for, what is good and true, and what is right. For the most part, these beliefs are rarely examined and are simply assumed to be true. Hence, the ideological tenets around which society is organized exist as a collective social consciousness that defines the world for its members. All societies reproduce themselves partly by reproducing their ideology; in this way, each generation accepts the basic ideological suppositions of the preceding one. When widely held ideological beliefs are questioned, society often reacts with strong sanctions. Ideological trends influence social welfare when

adherents of one orientation hold sway in decision-making bodies.

Ideology even more strongly influences social welfare policy during periods of threat, such as the current "War on Terror." In this instance, social welfare policy fades into the background as the perceived need for personal and national security takes center stage. U.S. social history has been intermittently shattered when oppressed groups assert their rights in the face of mainstream norms. Such periods of social unrest strain the capacity of conventional ideologies to explain social problems and offer solutions. Sometimes social unrest is met with force, as during the period of the great labor strikes of 1877. In other instances, such as the Great Depression, social unrest is met with expanding social welfare programs.

The Political Economy of American Social Welfare

The term **political economy** refers to the interaction of political and economic theories in understanding society. The political economy of the United States has been labeled **democratic capitalism**—an open and representative form of government that coexists with a market economy. In that context, social welfare policy plays an important role in stabilizing society by modifying the play of market forces and softening the social and economic inequities that the market generates.[12] To that end, two sets of activities are necessary: state provision of social services (benefits of cash, in-kind benefits, and personal social services) and state regulation of private activities to alter (and sometimes improve) the lives of citizens. Social welfare bolsters ideology by helping to remedy the problems associated with economic dislocation, thereby allowing society to remain in a state of more or less controlled balance.

As noted earlier, the U.S. welfare state is driven by political economy. Ideally, the political economy of the welfare state should be viewed as an integrated fabric of politics and economics, but in reality, some schools of thought or movements contain more political than economic content, and vice versa. For example, most economic schools of thought contain sufficient political implications to qualify them as both economic and political dogmas. Conversely, most political schools of thought contain significant economic content. It is therefore often difficult to separate political from economic schools of thought. For the purposes of this chapter, though, we will organize the political economy of U.S. welfare into two separate categories: (1) predominantly economic schools of thought and (2) predominantly political schools of thought. The careful reader will find a significant overlap among and between these categories.

The U.S. Economic Continuum

In large measure, economics forms the backbone of the political system. For example, we would not have the modern welfare state without the contributions of economist John Maynard Keynes. Conversely, we would not have the conservative movement without the contributions of classical or free market economists such as Adam Smith or Milton Friedman. Virtually every political movement is somehow grounded in economic thought. The three major schools of economics that have traditionally dominated American economic thought are Keynesian economics; classical or free market economics (and its variants); and, to a lesser degree, democratic socialism.

Keynesian Economics

Keynesian economics drives liberalism and most welfare state ideologies. John Maynard Keynes' economic theories formed the substructure and foundation of the modern welfare state, and virtually all welfare societies are built along his principles. Sometimes called demand or consumer-side economics, this model emerged from Keynes's 1936 book, *The General Theory of Employment, Interest and Money*.

An Englishman, Keynes took the classical model of economic analysis (self-regulating markets, perfect competition, the laws of supply and demand, etc.) and added the insight that macroeconomic stabilization by government is necessary to keep the economic clock ticking smoothly.[13] He rejected the idea that a perfectly competitive economy tended automatically toward full employment and that the government should not interfere in the process. Keynes argued that instead of being self-correcting and readily able to pull themselves out of

John Maynard Keynes is best known as the economic architect of the modern welfare state.

recessions, modern economies were recession prone and had difficulty providing full employment.

According to Keynes, periodic and volatile economic situations that cause high unemployment are primarily caused by instability in investment expenditures. The government can stabilize and correct recessionary or inflationary trends by increasing or decreasing total spending on output. Governments can accomplish this by increasing or decreasing taxes (thereby increasing or decreasing consumption) and by the transfer of public goods or services. For Keynes, a "good" government is an activist government in economic matters, especially when the economy gets out of full employment mode. Keynesians believe that social welfare expenditures are investments in human capital that eventually increase the national wealth (e.g., by increasing productivity) and thereby boost everyone's net income.

Keynes's doctrine emerged from his attempt to understand the nature of recessions and depressions. Specifically, he saw recessions and depressions as emerging from businesses' loss of confidence in investments (e.g., focusing on risk rather than gain), which in turn causes the hoarding of cash. This loss of confidence eventually leads to a shortage of money as everyone tries to hoard cash simultaneously. Keynes's answer to this problem is that government should make it possible for people to satisfy their economic needs without cutting their spending, which prevents the spiral of shrinking incomes and shrinking spending. Simply put, in a depression the government should print more money and get it into circulation.[14]

Keynes also understood that this monetary policy alone would not suffice if a recession got out of control, as in the depression of the 1930s. In a depression, businesses and households will not increase spending regardless of how much cash they have. To help an economy exit this trap, government must do what the private sector will not—namely, spend. This spending can take the form of public works projects (financed by borrowing) or of direct governmental subsidization of demand (welfare entitlements). To be fair, Keynes saw public spending only as a last resort to be employed if monetary expansion failed. Moreover, he sought an economic balance: Print money and spend in a recession; stop printing and stop spending once it is over. Keynes understood that too much money in circulation, especially in times of high production and full employment, leads to inflation. Although relatively simple, Keynes's theories represent one of the great insights of twentieth-century economic thought.[15] These ideas also formed the economic basis for the modern welfare state.

Conservative or Free Market Economics

Whereas liberalism is guided by Keynesian economics, the conservative view of social welfare is guided by free market economics. It is predicated on a belief in the existence of many small buyers and sellers who exchange homogeneous products with perfect information in a setting in which each can freely enter and exit the marketplace at will.[16] None of these assumptions hold in the real world of economics. For instance, the free market model does not address the dominance of distribution networks by a single retailer like Wal-Mart. There is nothing in the free market model that addresses the lack of equitable distribution of knowledge, experience, opportunity, and access to resources enjoyed by buyers and sellers. The free market model ignores theft, fraud, and deception in cases like Enron, and it ignores the competitive advantages that accrue through lobbying and special interest negotiations like Halliburton's no competition bids for Iraq reconstruction projects. It also ignores the power of large retailers in controlling the market by

instituting late shopping hours or even 24/7 businesses that make it impossible for small family-owned businesses to compete.

The ascendance of the conservative economic (and social) argument accelerated after 1973, when the rise in living standards began to slow for most Americans. Conservatives blamed this economic slowdown on governmental policies—specifically, deficit spending, high taxes, and excessive regulations.[17] In a clever sleight of hand, government went from having the responsibility to address economic problems (à la Keynes) to being the cause of them.

Milton Friedman, considered by some to be the father of modern conservative economics, was one of Keynes's more ardent critics. In opposition to Keynes, Friedman argued that using fiscal and monetary policy to smooth out the business cycle is harmful to the economy and worsens economic instability.[18] He contended that the Depression did not occur because people were hoarding money; rather, there was a fall in the quantity of money in circulation. Friedman argues that Keynesian economic policies must be replaced by simple monetary rules (hence the term *monetarism*). In effect, he believes that the role of government is to keep the money supply growing steadily at a rate consistent with stable prices and long-term economic growth.[19]

Friedman counseled against active efforts to stabilize the economy. Instead of pumping money into the economy, government should simply make sure enough cash is in circulation. He called for a relatively inactive government in economic affairs that did not try to manage or intervene in the business cycle. For Friedman, welfare spending existed only for altruistic rather than economic reasons.[20] To the right of Milton Friedman is Robert Lucas, 1994 Nobel Prize winner and developer of the "theory of rational expectations." Lucas argued that Friedman's monetary policy was still too interventionist and would invariably do more harm than good.[21]

Developing outside of conventional economics, **supply-side economics** enjoyed considerable popularity during the early 1980s. Led by Robert Barth, editorial page head of the *Wall Street Journal*, supply-siders were journalists, policymakers, and maverick economists who argued that demand-side policies and monetary policies were ineffective.[22] They maintained that the incentive effects of reduced taxation would be so large that tax cuts would dramatically increase economic activity to the point where tax revenues would rise rather than fall. (Former president George H. W. Bush referred to this as *voodoo economics* in 1980.[23]) Specifically, supply-siders argued that tax cuts would lead to a large increase in labor supply and investment and therefore to a large expansion in economic output. The budget deficit would not be problematic because taxes, increased savings, and higher economic output would offset the deficit. In the early 1980s, supply-siders seized power from the Keynesians and mainstream conservative economists, many of whom believed in the same things but wanted to move more slowly.[24]

Although some supporters preferred to think of supply-side economics as pure economics, the theory contained enough political implications to qualify as a political as well as an economic approach. Supply-side economics provided the rationale for the punishing cuts in social programs executed under the Reagan administration.

Despite their popularity in the early years of the Reagan administration, supply-side ideas fell out of favor when it became evident that massive tax cuts for the wealthy and corporations did not result in increased capital formation and economic activity. Instead, the wealthy spent their tax savings on luxury items, and corporations used tax savings to purchase other companies in a merger mania that took Wall Street by surprise. Other corporations took advantage of temporary tax savings to transfer their operations abroad, further reducing the supply of high-paying industrial jobs in the United States. For these and other reasons, the budget deficit grew from about $50 billion a year in the Carter term to $352 billion a year in 1992.[25] Although the term "supply-side economics" fell out of favor by the late 1980s, many of its basic tenets, such as massive tax cuts and cuts in social welfare spending, were adopted by the G. W. Bush administration. The result mirrored the earlier effects of supply-side policies: huge federal and state budget shortfalls, corporate hoarding, greater economic inequality, and stagnant wages.[26]

Conservative economists argue that large social welfare programs—including unemployment benefits and public service jobs—are detrimental to the society in two ways. First, government social programs erode the work ethic by supporting those not in the labor force. Second, because they are funded by taxes, public sector social welfare programs divert money that could otherwise be invested in the private sector. These conservative economists believe that economic growth helps everyone because overall prosperity creates more jobs, income, and goods, and these eventually filter down to the poor. For conservative economists, investment is the key to prosperity and the engine that drives the economic machine. Accordingly, many conservative economists favor tax breaks for the wealthy based on the premise that such breaks will result in more disposable after-tax income freed up for investment. High taxes are an impediment to economic progress because they channel money into "public" investments and away from "private" investments.

In the neoconservative paradigm, opportunity is based on one's relationship to the marketplace. Thus, legitimate rewards can occur only through marketplace participation. In contrast to liberals who emphasize mutual self-interest, interdependence, and social equity, conservative economists argue that the highest form of social good is realized by the maximization of self-interest. In the conservative view (as epitomized by author Ayn Rand[27]), the best society is one in which everyone actively pursues their own good. Through a leap of faith, the maximization of self-interest can somehow be transformed into a mutual good. This premise was proved false by the 2008 global economic crisis. This premise was proved false by the 2008 global economic crisis.

Conservative economists maintain not only that high taxation and government regulation of business serve as disincentives to investment, but that individual claims on social insurance and public welfare grants discourage work. Together these factors lead to a decline in economic growth and an increase in the expectations of beneficiaries of welfare programs. For conservatives, the only way to correct the irrationality of governmental social programs is to eliminate them. Charles Murray has suggested that the entire federal assistance and income support structure for working-aged persons (Medicaid, the former Aid to Families with Dependent Children [AFDC], food stamps, etc.) should be scrapped. This would leave working-aged persons no recourse except to actively engage in the job market or turn to family, friends, or privately funded services.[28]

Many conservative economists argue that economic insecurity is an important part of the entrepreneurial spirit. Unless people are *compelled* to work, they will choose leisure over work. Conversely, providing economic security for large numbers of people through welfare programs leads to diminished ambition and fosters an unhealthy dependence on the state. Conservatives further argue that self-realization can occur only through marketplace participation. Hence, social programs harm rather than help the most vulnerable members of society. This belief in the need for economic insecurity forms the basis for the 1996 welfare reform bill that includes a maximum time limit on welfare benefits.

Some conservative economists are influenced by "public choice" theory. The **public choice school** gained adherents among conservative analysts as faith ebbed in supply-side theories. Not widely known outside academic circles until its major proponent, James Buchanan, was awarded the Nobel Prize for economics in 1986, the public choice model states that public sector bureaucrats are self-interested utility-maximizers, and that strong incentives exist for interest groups to make demands on government. The resulting concessions from this arrangement flow directly to the interest group and their costs are spread among all taxpayers. Initial concessions lead to demands for further concessions, which are likely to be forthcoming so long as interest groups are vociferous in their demands. Under such an incentive system, different interests are also encouraged to band together to make demands, because there is no reason for one interest group to oppose the demands of others. But while demands for goods and services increase, revenues tend to decrease. This happens because interest groups resist paying taxes directed specifically toward them and because no interest group has much incentive to support general taxes. The result of this scenario is predictable: Strong demands for government benefits accompanied by declining revenues lead to government borrowing, which in turn results in large budget deficits.[29] Adherents of public choice theory view social welfare as a series of endless concessions to disadvantaged groups that will eventually bankrupt the government.

The Global Economic Crisis and the Flaws in the Free Market Argument

In a rare occurrence in 2008, Alan Greenspan, the former 18-year Federal Reserve chairman, admitted he "made a mistake" in trusting free markets to regulate themselves without government oversight. He also conceded a serious philosophical flaw in his thinking. Namely, that an unfettered free market is an essential part of a superior economy. Greenspan further admitted that "I made a mistake in presuming that the self-interests of organizations, specifically banks and others, were . . . capable of protecting their own shareholders and their equity in the firms."[30] This was an amazing series of admissions from the man known as the "oracle"—or the one thought of as being almost infallible in his economic acumen. More importantly, Greenspan's admissions repudiated the belief that largely unregulated free markets inevitably yield superior economic gain.

The initial event triggering the 2008 global economic crisis was the collapse of the U.S. housing market and the realization that domestic and foreign banks and investment houses and institutions were holding hundreds of billions of dollars of subprime mortgages (i.e., mortgages given to less creditworthy borrowers) that were essentially toxic debt with little hope of repayment. Moreover, investors realized that many subprime mortgages were underpriced in terms of risk. Specifically, the higher interest rate charged to credit-challenged borrowers was below the real interest rate that would have been required to justify the higher risk. Underpricing risk has been a major factor in the subprime mortgage crisis.

It is overly simplistic to blame the economic crisis solely on subprime loans or on families who took out mortgages they could not repay. Multiple factors converged to create the economic crisis, including the largely unregulated derivatives market and various other forms of dodgy financial instruments. Derivatives are used by major banks and businesses to hedge risk or engage in speculation. They are financial instruments whose value depends on that of an underlying commodity, bond, equity, or currency. Investors purchase derivatives to bet on the future (or as a hedge against the potential adverse impacts of an investment), to mitigate a risk associated with an underlying security, to protect against interest rate or stock market changes, and so forth. Derivatives are sold by hedge funds, investment houses, insurance companies, and banks. Derivatives are used in a variety of areas. For example, credit derivatives can involve a contract between two parties that allows one of them to transfer their credit risk to the other. The party transferring the risk pays a fee to the party that assumes it.

All forms of derivatives are risky investments since they are basically big bets made in amounts (often in the billions) that are astounding even to financially sophisticated investors. Like all forms of gambling, derivatives only work if the casino has the money to meet their obligation to bettors. In turn, the system collapses if the house lacks the cash (i.e., it has a liquidity problem) to pay winners. The 2008 economic crisis was partly precipitated by the derivatives market (which hedged bets on portfolios that included subprime mortgages) and the resulting liquidity problem.

Trying to Save the Economy The precursor to the massive federal bailout of Wall Street and the banking industry began in February 2008 when former president G. W. Bush signed the $168 billion stimulus package giving tax rebates to more than 130 million households.[31] Bush administration officials hoped the tax package would be sufficient to kick-start the economy and steer it away from a full-blown recession. He was obviously wrong.

Shortly thereafter, federal loans and bailout proposals came at an almost dizzying pace. In March 2008, the Federal Reserve enticed JP Morgan with a $29 billion credit line to take over the failing Bear Stearns investment house.[32] One financial institution after another failed or was taken over. Later in 2008, Bank of America bought Countrywide Mortgage (the largest U.S. mortgage lender with assets of $209 billion) for a paltry $4.1 billion in stock. Fearing that Merrill Lynch was next, CEO John Thain quickly sold out to Bank of America. In another stunning move, JP Morgan Chase (the third largest U.S. bank) bought Washington Mutual (WaMu), the nation's largest thrift bank, after it was seized by federal regulators. Meanwhile, Wells Fargo was busy acquiring Wachovia Bank for $15.1 billion in stock.[33]

When Freddie Mac and Fannie Mae were facing a bankruptcy that threatened to further destabilize an already devastated housing market, the Feds came to the rescue by buying up to $200 billion of stock (including bad mortgage debt). Since Freddie Mac and Fannie Mae guarantee $5.4 trillion in outstanding mortgage debt, the costs of the bailout could eventually run even higher, especially given the 1.3 million homes in foreclosure in 2008.[34]

While the Feds let the investment banking house Lehman Brothers die (the largest bankruptcy in U.S. history), they relented with American International Group (AIG)—the world's largest insurer—by providing a two-year $85 billion line of credit. In return, the federal government took control of some of AIG's equity and assets. In September 2008, the Central Bank lent AIG an additional $37.8 billion. In total, by late 2008 the U.S. government had put about

$123 billion at AIG's disposal.[35] Not wanting to be left out of the party, U.S. automakers also pressed for taxpayer subsidized loans.[36]

After much jockeying, Congress finally approved a $700 billion (a number that swelled to $825 billion) bailout for Wall Street in September 2008. Despite this bailout, world markets continued to convulse with uncertainty. Frightened by increased market instability, the Federal Reserve further cut the U.S. prime rate, a strategy that seemed to have little effect. Taken together, these bailout obligations added up to more than $1 trillion, barring a few billion here and there.

With the exception of Bush's tax stimulus package, the bailouts and financial help were largely directed at the supply side of the economy.[37]

Can the U.S. Government Pay the Bill? To put things into perspective, the proposed $825 billion bailout (inflated by pork) was more than the U.S. government spent on defense ($549 billion), Social Security ($581 billion), or Medicare and Medicaid ($561 billion) in 2007.

Much of the money to pay for the bailouts will come from foreign investors who purchase U.S. Treasury bills. As long as foreign investors are confident in the ability of the United States to solve its problems, the country can borrow. All bets are off if their faith in the United States is shaken, or if foreign investors begin to prefer hard assets like cheap buildings, land, or factories over paper.

Foreign investors are closely watching U.S. economic data. In 2008, the U.S. gross domestic product (GDP) was $14 trillion—the highest in the world. However, the International Monetary Fund (IMF) predicted U.S. economic growth to be 0.6% in 2008 or half that of other industrialized nations like Germany, the UK, France, Spain, Japan, and Canada.[38] Moreover, the 2008 U.S. budget deficit was $410 billion, an amount that significantly added to the existing national debt of $10 trillion.[39]

By 2009, government spending on bailouts and loans could exceed $1.4 trillion or about 10 percent of the GDP, adding 13 percent to the national debt. The national debt could total a whopping 81 percent of the GDP. If Wall Street is not properly regulated, or if the structural problems are deeper than anticipated, current bailout attempts will likely fail.

The 2008 economic crisis led to profound consequences for the nation and its social welfare system. The semi-nationalization of large chunks of the U.S. banking system calls into question the long-term belief in the sanctity of the marketplace and the viability of laissez-faire capitalism. Even more amazing is that the semi-nationalization of the banking system occurred under the former Bush administration. Regardless, the financial crisis will also prove a punishing experience for nonprofit human service organizations that depend on individual and foundation philanthropy as well as government agencies that rely on tax revenues. Not surprisingly, the collapse of Wall Street will chill any subsequent debate around privatizing Social Security.

Democratic Socialism

After a long dormant period, the cobwebs of socialism were dusted off in the 2008 presidential election when John McCain falsely accused Barack Obama of being a socialist. Democratic socialism (as opposed to old Soviet-style socialism) is based on the belief that radical economic change can occur within a democratic context. While eschewing capitalism, democratic socialists, such as the late Michael Harrington, have a fundamental belief in the democratic process.

Democratic socialism sharply veers from Keynesianism and conservative economics. Specifically, Keynesians basically believe in the market economy but want to make it more responsive to human needs by smoothing out the rough edges. Conservatives believe that the economy should be left alone except for a few minor tweaks, such as regulating the money flow. Other conservative economists argue that the market should be left totally alone. On balance, both Keynesians and economic conservatives have a basic faith that capitalism can advance the public good and be made compatible with human needs. In that sense, Keynesians and economic conservatives have more in common with each other than Keynesians have with socialists.

Proponents of **socialism** argue that the fundamental nature of capitalism is anathema to advancing the public good. Socialists contend that a system predicated on pursuing profit and individual self-interest can lead only to greater inequality. The creation of a just society requires a fundamental transformation of the economic system, and the pursuit of profit and self-interest must be replaced by the collective pursuit of the common good. Not surprisingly, socialists rebuff Keynesians because of their inherent belief that economic problems can be fixed by simple technicalities instead of major institutional change. Socialists differ from conservatives for obvious reasons, such as the primary importance they place on markets, their belief in subordinating individual interests to market forces, and their overall social conservatism.

Left-wing theorists maintain that the failure of capitalism has led to political movements that have pressured institutions to respond with increased social welfare services. They believe that real social welfare must be structural and can be accomplished only by redistributing resources. In a just society where goods, resources, and opportunities are made available to everyone, all but the most specific forms of welfare (health care, rehabilitation, counseling, etc.) would be unnecessary. In this radical worldview, poverty is directly linked to structural inequality: People need welfare because they are exploited and denied access to resources. In an unjust society, welfare functions as a substitute, albeit a puny one, for social justice.[40]

Some socialists argue that social welfare is an ingenious arrangement on the part of business to have the public assume the costs caused by the social and economic dislocations inherent in capitalism. According to these theorists, social welfare expenditures "socialize" the costs of capitalist production by making public the costs of private enterprise. Thus, social welfare serves both the needs of people and the needs of capitalism. For other socialists, social welfare programs support an unjust economic system that, in turn, continues to generate problems requiring social programs. For these radicals, social welfare programs function like junk food for the impoverished: They provide just enough sustenance to discourage revolution but not enough to make a real difference in the lives of the poor. Within this radical framework, social welfare is seen as a form of social control. Frances Fox Piven and Richard Cloward summarize the socialist argument:

> Relief arrangements are ancillary to economic arrangements. Their chief function is to regulate labor, and they do that in two general ways. First, when mass unemployment leads to outbreaks of turmoil, relief programs are ordinarily initiated or expanded to absorb or control enough of the unemployed to restore order; then, as turbulence subsides, the relief system contracts, expelling those who are needed to populate the labor markets.[41]

In place of liberal welfare reforms, the radical vision proposes that the entire social, political, and economic system undergo a major overhaul. In the radical context, real welfare reform (i.e., a complete redistribution of goods, income, and services) can occur only within a socialist economic system.

The U.S. Political Continuum

Various understandings of the political economy produce differing conceptions of the ultimate public good. Competition among ideas about the public good and the welfare state has long been a knotty issue in the political economy of the United States. Because shifts in government policy are driven largely by an ideologically determined view of the public good, any policy analysis must be based on whose definition is being examined. In a democratic capitalist society, beliefs about the public good often vary depending on the proponent's position in the social order.

The major American ideologies, (neo)liberalism and (neo)conservatism, hold vastly different views of social welfare and the public good. Conservatives believe that the public good is best served when individuals and families meet their needs through marketplace participation. Accordingly, conservatives prefer private sector approaches over governmental welfare and advocate for smaller government social welfare programs. Conservatives are not antiwelfare per se; they simply believe that government should have a minimal role (i.e., serve as a "safety net") in ensuring the social welfare of citizens. Traditional liberals, on the other hand, view government as the only institution capable of bringing a measure of **social justice** to millions of Americans who cannot fully participate in the U.S. mainstream because of obstacles such as racism, poverty, and sexism. Traditional liberals therefore view governmental social welfare programs as a key component in promoting the public good. One of the major differences between conservatives and liberals lies in their differing perceptions of how the public good is enhanced or hurt by welfare state programs.

The understanding of "the public good" is lodged in the political and ideological continuum that makes up the U.S. political economy. An appreciation of this requires an understanding of the interaction of schools of political thought and how they evolved. These ideological tenets also shape the platforms of the major political parties and can be divided into two categories: (1) liberalism and left-of-center movements, and (2) traditional conservatives and the far right.

Liberalism and Left-of-Center Movements

Liberalism Since Franklin Delano Roosevelt's **New Deal,** advocates of liberalism have argued for advancing the public good by promoting an expanding economy coupled with the growth of universal, non-means–tested social welfare and health programs. Traditional liberals used Keynesian concepts as the economic justification for building the welfare state. As such, the general direction of policy from the 1930s to the early 1970s was for the federal government to assume greater amounts of responsibility for the public good.

American liberals established the welfare state with the passage of the Social Security Act of 1935. Harry Hopkins—a social worker, the head of the Federal Emergency Relief Administration, a confidant of President Roosevelt, a co-architect of the New Deal, and a consummate political operative—developed the calculus for American liberalism: "tax, tax; spend, spend; elect, elect."[42] This liberal approach was elegant in its simplicity: The government taxes the wealthy, thereby securing the necessary revenues to fund social programs for workers and the poor. This approach dominated social policy for almost 50 years. In fact, it was so successful that by 1980 social welfare accounted for 57 percent of all federal expenditures.[43]

By the mid-1960s, the welfare state had become an important fixture in America's social landscape, and politicians sought to expand its benefits to more constituents. Focusing on the expansion of middle-class programs such as Federal Housing Administration (FHA) home mortgages, federally insured student loans, Medicare, and veterans' pensions, liberal policymakers secured the political loyalty of the middle class. Even conservative politicians respected voter support for the middle-class welfare state, and not surprisingly, the largest expansion of social welfare spending occurred under Richard Nixon, a Republican president.

Yet the promise of the U.S. welfare state to provide social protection similar to that in industrialized European nations never materialized. By the mid-1970s, the hope of traditional liberals to build a welfare state mirroring those of northern Europe had been replaced by an incremental approach that narrowly focused on consolidating and fine-tuning the programs of the Social Security Act. One reason for this failure was the ambivalence of many Americans toward centralized government. "The emphasis

■ *Barack Obama was elected president of the United States in 2008.*

consistently has been on the local, the pluralistic, the voluntary, and the business-like over the national, the universal, the legally entitled, and the governmental," observed policy analyst Marc Bendick.[44]

Liberalism lost ground for another reason. The Social Security Act of 1935—the hallmark of American liberalism—was primarily a self-financing social insurance program that rewarded working people. Public assistance programs that contained less political capital and were therefore a better measure of public compassion, were rigorously means tested, sparse in their benefits, and operated by the less than generous states. For example, although Social Security benefits were indexed to the cost of living in the mid-1970s, AFDC benefits deteriorated so badly that about half its value was lost between 1975 and 1992. At the same time that Social Security reforms reduced the elderly poverty rate by 50 percent, the plight of poor families worsened.

Neoliberalism By the late 1970s, the liberal belief that the welfare state was the best mechanism to advance the public good was in retreat. What remained of traditional liberalism was replaced by a **neoliberalism** that was more cautious of government, less antagonistic toward big business, and more skeptical about the value of universal entitlements.

The defeat of Jimmy Carter and the election of a Republican Senate in 1980 forced many liberal Democrats to reevaluate their party's traditional position on domestic policy. This reexamination, which Charles Peters christened "neoliberalism" to differentiate it from old-style liberalism, attracted only a small following in the early 1980s.[45] However, by the mid-1990s, most leading Democrats could be classified as neoliberal. Randall Rothenberg charted signs of the influence of neoliberalism on the Democratic domestic policy platform as early as 1982, when he observed that the party's midterm convention did not endorse a large-scale federal jobs program, did not endorse a plan for national health insurance, and did not submit a plan for a guaranteed annual income.[46]

In the late 1980s, a cadre of prominent mainstream Democrats established the Democratic Leadership Council (DLC). In part, their goal was to wrest control of the Democratic Party from traditional liberals and to create a new Democratic Party that was more attuned to the beliefs of the traditional core voters. In 1989 the DLC released *The New Orleans Declaration: A Democratic Agenda for the 1990s,* which promised that Democratic Party politics would shift toward a middle ground combining a corporatist economic analysis with Democratic compassion. Two of the founders of the DLC were Al Gore and Bill Clinton, who chaired the DLC just before announcing his presidential candidacy.[47] President Obama's campaign platform and cabinet-level appointments point to him also being largely in the neoliberal camp.

Compared to traditional liberals, neoliberals were more forgiving of the behavior of large corporations and were opposed to economic protectionism. Grounded in *realpolitik,* neoliberals viewed the New Deal approach (with the exception of Social Security) as too expensive and antiquated to address the mood of voters and the new global realities. Consequently, neoliberals distanced themselves from the large-scale governmental welfare programs associated with Democrats since the New Deal. Like their neoconservative counterparts, they called for reliance on personal responsibility, work, and thrift as an alternative to governmental programs. Accordingly, their welfare proposals emphasized labor market participation (workfare), personal responsibility (time-limited welfare benefits), family obligations (child support enforcement), and frugality in governmental spending. They argued for reduced governmental spending while encouraging businesses to assume more responsibility for the welfare of the population.

Former Secretary of Labor Robert Reich advocated a postliberal formulation that replaced social welfare entitlements with investments in **human capital.** Public spending was divided into "good" and "bad" categories: "Bad" was unproductive expenditures on welfare and price supports; "good" was investments in human capital, such as education, research, and job training.[48]

Neoliberalism altered the traditional liberal concept of the public good. Instead of viewing the interests of large corporations as antithetical to the best interests of society, neoliberals argued for free trade, less regulation, and a more laissez-faire approach to social problems. They also viewed long-time Democratic Party supporters, such as labor unions, with caution. For example, when labor unions fought to stop NAFTA (the North American Free Trade Agreement), former President Clinton continued to endorse it, despite labor's threats to oppose his reelection bid in 1996. The same was true for the GATT (General Agreement on Tariffs and Trade) agreement. In both instances, Clinton was firmly aligned with conservative Democrats and Republicans. Traditional liberal Democrats found themselves alone, bereft of support from the first Democratic White House in 14 years. In effect, the new shapers of the public good had systematically excluded key actors of the old liberal coalition.

The neoliberal view of the public good reflects a kind of postmodern perspective. For neoliberals, the public good is elusive, and its form is fluid. Definitions of the public good change as a social order evolves and new power relationships emerge. Thus, neoliberals do not define the public good as tethered to industrial era allegiances but look to a postindustrial society composed of new opportunities and new institutional forms.

Neoliberalism, then, is more a political strategy and pragmatic mode of operation than a political philosophy embodying a firm view of the public good. This is both its strength and its weakness. Specifically, the strength of neoliberalism lies in its ability to compromise and therefore to accomplish things. Its weakness is that when faced with an ideological critique, neoliberals are incapable of formulating a cogent ideological response. When G. W. Bush argued for staying the course in 2004, voters knew exactly what he meant even if they disagreed with him. When Clinton argued for staying the course in 1994, the public were unsure of the course.

In the American and British contexts, neoliberalism represents a "third way." Anthony Giddens offers a philosophical rationale for neoliberalism: "We should speak of a *positive welfare,* to which individuals and other agencies besides government contribute—and which is functional for wealth creation. The guideline for investment is *human capital* wherever possible, rather than the direct provision of economic maintenance. In place of the welfare state, we should put the *social investment state,* operating in the context of a positive welfare society."[49]

The Self-Reliance School A perspective gaining influence in economically distressed areas and in developing countries is the **self-reliance school.**[50] This school maintains that industrial economic models are irrelevant to the economic needs of poor communities and are often damaging to the spiritual life of people.[51] Adherents of self-reliance repudiate the emphasis of Western economic philosophies on economic growth and the belief that the quality of life can be measured by material acquisitions. These political economists stress a balanced economy based on the real needs of people, production designed for internal consumption rather than export, productive technologies that are congruent with the culture and background of the population, the use of appropriate and manageable technologies, and a small-scale and decentralized form of economic organization.[52] Simply put, proponents of self-reliance postulate that more is less and less is more. The objective of self-reliance is the creation of a no-poverty society in which economic life is organized around issues of subsistence rather than trade and economic expansion. Accepting a world of finite resources and inherent limitations to economic growth, proponents argue that the true question of social and economic development is not what people think they want or need but what they require for survival. The self-reliance school accepts the need for social welfare programs that ameliorate the dislocations caused by industrialization, but it prefers low-technology and local solutions to social problems. This contrasts with the conventional wisdom of the welfare state, which is predicated on a prescribed set of programs on a national scale, administered by large bureaucracies using sophisticated management systems.

Classical Conservatives and the Far Right

Classic Conservatism Former conservative political leaders such as Nelson Rockefeller, Richard

■ *Senator John McCain was defeated by Barack Obama in the 2008 presidential election.*

Nixon, and Barry Goldwater represented traditional conservatism. Few traditional conservatives occupy important leadership positions in the Republican party, as most have been replaced by cultural conservatives. Other conservatives like John McCain have had to spin their message to try to gain the approval of cultural conservatives.

On one level, all conservatives agree on important values relating to social policy. Beneath this agreement, however, important differences exist among various conservative factions.

Older, traditional conservatives diverge with the newer cultural conservatives on a range of social issues. First, as strict constitutionalists, traditional or classical conservatives believe strongly in the separation of church and state. They see prayer and religion as personal choices in which government has no constitutional right to intervene. Second, although both classical conservatives and cultural conservatives supposedly advocate for a weaker federal government, cultural conservatives also demand that the federal government use its power to implement their domestic agenda in areas they consider immoral, such as abortion and homosexuality.

Third, classical conservatives are more socially liberal than their cultural counterparts. For example, the late Barry Goldwater, a conservative icon and former U.S. senator and 1964 presidential candidate, stated that "I have been, and am still, a traditional conservative, focusing on three general freedoms—economic, social, and political. . . . The conservative movement is founded on the simple tenet that people have the right to live life as they please, as long as they don't hurt anyone else in the process."[53] Following that line of reason, Goldwater's outspoken support of homosexuals in the military was directly opposed to the principles of neoconservatives. Regarding reproductive freedom, classical conservatives might challenge cultural conservatives on various measures that limit or ban abortions.

From the late 1970s onward, factions within the conservative movement became more pronounced. Old-style conservatives such as Nelson Rockefeller, Barry Goldwater, and William Cohen, who were more concerned with foreign policy than with domestic issues, were replaced by a new breed of cultural conservatives, such as Dick Armey, Newt Gingrich, Phil Gramm, and Sam Brownback. These cultural conservatives were committed to reversing 50 years of liberal influence in social policy. How the cultural conservatives came to shape social policy warrants elaboration, although it is first important to examine neoconservatives, the forerunners of cultural conservatism.

Neoconservatism Before the 1970s, conservatives were content to merely snipe at welfare programs, reserving their attention for areas more consistent with their traditional concerns such as the economy, defense spending, and foreign affairs. However, by the mid-1970s, younger conservative intellectuals recognized that the conservative stance toward social welfare was myopic because welfare was too important to be lightly dismissed. Consequently, **neoconservatives** sought to arrest the growth in governmental welfare programs while simultaneously transferring as much welfare responsibility as possible from government to the private sector.[54] They faulted government programs for a breakdown in the mutual obligation between groups; the lack of attention to how programs were operated and benefits awarded; the dependency of recipients; and the growth of the welfare industry and its special interest groups, particularly professional associations.[55] To counter the liberal goals of full employment, national health care, and a guaranteed annual income, neoconservatives maintained that high unemployment was good for the economy, that health care should remain in the private marketplace, and that competitive income structures were critical to productivity. They argued that income inequality was socially desirable because social policies that promote equality encourage coercion, limit individual freedom, and damage the economy.[56]

The neoconservative attack on the welfare state was so well crafted because many neoconservatives, among them Irving Kristol and Norman Podhoretz, were former liberals who had developed misgivings about the welfare state and joined the conservative movement in protest. Neoconservatives were effective in critiquing the welfare state, in large measure because they were so familiar with its philosophical origins. (One commentator classified them as liberals who had been mugged.) Despite their opposition to the welfare state, former liberals found their new conservative home anything but tidy. Born out of an urban environment, neoconservatives fashioned themselves as cosmopolitan intellectuals and free thinkers. Social issues such as abortion, school prayer, and the like were not a hot button item for this movement.

By the late 1970s, the position occupied by neoconservatives in the conservative movement began to be usurped by the emerging cultural conservatives. Although the neoconservatives provided the intellectual wedge that fractured the liberal consensus around the welfare state, cultural conservatives, such as Trent Lott and Tom DeLay, attained the leadership positions necessary to take down what was left of the institutional structure of liberal public philosophy. Properly understood, neoconservatism is at odds with the culturally conservative Republican agenda. The rift between the more urbane neoconservatives and the cultural conservatives was illustrated by John McCain's choice of Sarah Palin as his vice presidential running mate in 2008. Neoconservatives such as David Brooks, David Frum, Christopher Buckley, and others abhorred the choice of Palin whom they saw as unqualified but also as representing the culturally conservative faction of the party that believed in creationism, and were opposed to abortion regardless of the circumstances.

Cultural Conservatism The neoconservative assault on liberal social policy was soon taken over by cultural conservatives, who raged against governmental intrusion in the marketplace while simultaneously attempting to use the authority of government to advance their social objectives in the areas of antiwelfare planks, sexual abstinence, school prayer, abortion, and antigay rights proposals. Cultural conservatives cleverly promoted a dual attitude toward the role of government. Mimicking their classical conservative predecessors in demanding a laissez-faire approach to economics, they steadfastly refused to translate that orientation to social affairs. Instead, cultural conservatives argued for social conformity and a level of governmental intrusion into private affairs that made most classical conservatives gag. In contrast to the classical conservative skepticism about blending religion and politics, cultural conservatives opportunistically embraced the rising tide of fundamentalist religion. As a measure of their success, this cobbled-together coalition of economic conservatives, right-wing Christians, and opportunistic politicians had by the late 1980s virtually decimated what remained of Republican liberalism, whose adherents had become an endangered species like liberal Democrats.

Cultural conservatives view the state as the cause of rather than the solution to social problems. With the exception of protecting people (police and defense) and property, cultural conservatives argue that the very existence of the state is antithetical to the public good because government interferes with the maximization of individual self-interest. Hence, their posture toward government is adversarial, except when the state is used to further their social agenda. Even though cultural conservatives argue for a minimalist state, they have been willing to compromise these libertarian leanings by adopting the agenda of traditionalists in myriad social issues such as school prayer, abortion, sexual orientation, and drug testing.

The conservative agenda of the 1980s was fourfold: (1) end the liberal hegemony in social policy, (2) reroute public policy through the private sector, (3) curtail costly social programs that lessen profits and restrict the global competitiveness of corporations, and (4) preclude the possibility of a resurgence in social programs. In tandem with this agenda, conservative presidents such as Reagan and the two Bushes prohibited the future growth of the welfare state by employing multiple strategies such as tax policy and federal budget deficits that precluded any form of significant public spending. As such, few responsible politicians would argue for increased social welfare spending given the 2008 federal debt of around $10 trillion.

In 1994, frustrated voters seemed ready to give cultural conservatives control of the Senate and the House. Cultural conservatives had learned from past mistakes. Instead of toying with incremental policies, they proposed bold new social initiatives that were incorporated into the Contract with America

spotlight 1

Two groups that exemplify the differences between liberal and conservative political movements are the Green Party and the Moral Majority.

The Green Party

Ten key values serve as guiding principles for the Green Party—grassroots democracy, social justice and equal opportunity, ecological wisdom, nonviolence, decentralization, community-based economics and economic justice, feminism and gender equity, respect for diversity, personal and global responsibility, and future focus and sustainability. To learn more about these key values, go to the Green Party's website at **www.gp.org/tenkey.html.**

The Moral Majority

Traditionalists are characterized by conservative evangelical groups such as the Moral Majority. The Moral Majority and other traditional groups believe that God's laws must be translated into politics, and "higher laws" must become the laws of the state. Traditionalists are highly critical of governmental social programs, which they associate with a liberal social philosophy that is eroding traditional social institutions, particularly the family and the church. To learn more about the Moral Majority platform, visit the group's website at **www.faithandvalues.us.**

(designed to alter most of the safety net programs within a two-year period), a document signed by more than 300 House Republicans in 1994.[57] The crowning victory of the conservative movement occurred with the passage of the Personal Responsibility and Work Opportunity Reconciliation Act (PRWORA) in 1996.

Libertarianism Libertarians reflect another perspective. Specifically, this school of thought believes in virtually no government regulation.

> We, the members of the Libertarian Party, challenge the cult of the omnipotent state and defend the rights of the individual. We hold that all individuals . . . have the right to live in whatever manner they choose, so long as they do not forcibly interfere with the equal right of others to live in whatever manner they choose. We . . . hold that governments . . . must not violate the rights of any individual: namely, (1) the right to life— accordingly we support the prohibition of the initiation of physical force against others; (2) the right to liberty of speech and action—accordingly we oppose all attempts . . . [at] . . . government censorship in any form; and (3) . . . we oppose all government interference with private property. . . .[58]

Libertarians argue that governmental growth occurs at the expense of individual freedom. They also believe that the proper role for government is to provide a police force and a military that possesses only defensive weapons. Libertarians are highly critical of taxation because it fuels governmental growth. Apart from advocating minimal taxation earmarked for defense and police activities, they oppose the income tax. Because libertarians emphasize individual freedom and personal responsibility, they advocate the decriminalization of narcotics and believe that government should intercede in social affairs only when an individual's behavior threatens the safety of another.

The Welfare Philosophers and the Neoconservative Think Tanks

Many welfare professionals envisioned a U.S. welfare state based on a European model.[59] This vision was shared by virtually every social welfare scholar writing in the late 1960s and early 1970s.[60] In turn, most social workers supported a liberal welfare philosophy grounded in a system of national social programs that would be deployed as more citizens demanded greater services and benefits. This framework was informed by European welfare states, especially the Scandinavian variant that spread health care, housing, income benefits, and employment opportunities equitably across the population.[61] It also led Richard Titmuss to hope that the welfare state, as an instrument of government, would eventually lead to a "welfare world."[62]

For U.S. welfare philosophers, government programs that restricted the caprices of capitalism were both desirable and inevitable. In their classic *Industrial Society and Social Welfare,* Harold Wilensky and Charles Lebeaux suggested that "under continuing industrialization all institutions will be oriented toward and evaluated in terms of social welfare aims. The 'welfare state' will become the 'welfare society,' and both will be more reality than epithet."[63]

Despite the widespread acceptance of this liberal vision, an alternative vision arose that questioned the fundamental nature of welfare and social services. Throughout the 1970s and 1980s, conservatives (especially right-wing **think tanks,** or conservative policy institutes) busily made proposals for welfare reform. In fact, no conservative policy institute could prove its mettle until it produced a plan to clean up "the welfare mess." The Hoover Institution at Stanford University helped shape the early conservative position on welfare. "There is no inherent reason that Americans should look to government for those goods and services that can be individually acquired," argued Hoover's Alvin Rabushka, who listed four strategies for reforming welfare: (1) let users pay, (2) contract for services, (3) fund mandated services through the states, and (4) emphasize private substitution.[64] Martin Anderson, a Hoover senior fellow and later a domestic policy adviser to the Reagan administration, elaborated the conservative position on welfare in terms of the need to (1) reaffirm the need-only philosophical approach to welfare and state it as explicit national policy; (2) increase efforts to eliminate fraud; (3) establish and enforce a fair, clear work requirement; (4) remove inappropriate beneficiaries from the welfare rolls; (5) enforce support of dependents by those who have the responsibility and are shirking it; (6) improve the efficiency and effectiveness of welfare administration; and (7) shift more responsibility from the federal government to state and local governments and private institutions.[65] These recommendations formed the backbone of the 1996 PRWORA.

Another conservative think tank, the American Enterprise Institute (AEI), commissioned sociologist Peter Berger and theologian Richard John Neuhaus to prepare a theoretical analysis of U.S. society. Berger and Neuhaus's *To Empower People: The Role of Mediating Structures in Public Policy* identified the fundamental problem confronting the culture, such as the growth of megastructures (big government, big business, big labor, and professional bureaucracies), and the corresponding diminution in the value of the individual. The route to empowerment was to revitalize "mediating structures," among them the neighborhood, family, church, and voluntary associations.[66] In a subsequent analysis, an AEI scholar recategorized the corporation from a megastructure to a mediating structure, thus leaving the basic institutions of liberal social reform—government, the professions, and labor—as the sources of mass alienation.[67]

Not to be outdone, the Heritage Foundation featured *Out of the Poverty Trap: A Conservative Strategy for Welfare Reform* by Stuart Butler and Anna Kondratas.[68] Following along the same lines, the Free Congress Research and Education Foundation proposed reforming welfare through "cultural conservatism;" that is, by reinforcing "traditional values such as delayed gratification, work and saving, commitment to family and to the next generation, education and training, self-improvement, and rejection of crime, drugs, and casual sex."[69]

A handful of other works also served as beachheads for the conservative assault on the liberal welfare state. George Gilder's *Wealth and Poverty* argued that beneficent welfare programs represented a "moral hazard" that insulated people against risks essential to capitalism and thus contributed to dependency.[70] Martin Anderson concluded that income calculations should include the cash equivalent of in-kind benefits, such as food stamps, Medicaid, and housing vouchers, thus effectively lowering the poverty rate by 40 percent.[71] Taken together, these ideas and recommendations provided a potent critique of liberal governmental welfare programs. Unlike classical conservatives of an earlier generation, neoconservatives not only did their homework on social welfare policy but they also prepared proposals for welfare reform.

As Peter Kindle earlier pointed out in a supplement to this text, perhaps the most enduring change engineered by the conservative movement is what Jacob Hacker calls the "Great Risk Shift."[72] The private ownership of property and the acceptance of personal responsibility have long been core American values, which partly explains why opposition to former President Bush's "ownership society" has not materialized until recently. In *The Great Risk Shift*, Hacker exposes Bush's ownership society and the Republican Party's emphasis on personal responsibility as the code for shifting economic risk away from government and corporations and onto the back of the American family.

Simply put, private and public support mechanisms have fallen behind the pace of change in contemporary society. Almost half of marriages end in divorce. Over a third of employed Americans say that they are frequently worried about losing their jobs. Structural changes in the nature of employment, primarily seen in a shift away from manufacturing to the lower-paying service sector, have left many without the skills needed for new jobs or the resources to retrain. The likelihood of family income dropping 50% has almost tripled since the 1970s; personal bankruptcies and home foreclosures have increased by a factor of five; and over any two-year period more than 80 million Americans go without health insurance coverage.[73] During a 30-year period in which middle-class incomes have been stagnant, the need for increased economic security has been met by neglect from private and public institutions.[74]

The risk shift is happening in almost all sectors. Corporate retirement programs are shifting away from defined benefit plans in which retirees are guaranteed a set retirement income to defined contribution plans in which retirement depends on the investment savvy of the employees' investments. Whether these changes will help or hurt the individual depends on many factors, but it is clear that it is a shift in risk from corporation to the individual worker.

The absence of universal health care has underscored the importance of employer-provided health insurance; however, the increasing instability of employment often means that job transitions are accompanied by the inability to acquire health coverage. Conservatives have proposed Health Savings Accounts as a means of activating market forces to control health costs, but they reflect another risk shift from the corporation to the individual worker. The former Bush administration suggested the elimination of employer-provided health insurance in favor of tax deductions for health insurance premiums, yet another shifting of risk from corporations to the individual or family.[75] An important implication of Hacker's argument is that good social welfare policy analysis can no longer be restricted to a focus on income; it also must attend to the shifting dynamics of risk. As such, progressive social welfare policies must help to mitigate the degree of risk the individual family must bear.

Conclusion

John Judis and Michael Lind argue that "Ultimately American economic policy must meet a single test: Does it, in the long run, tend to raise or depress the incomes of most Americans? A policy that tends to impoverish the ordinary American is a failure, no matter what its alleged benefits are for U.S. corporations or for humanity as a whole."[76] To this we would add: "What are the effects of an economic policy on the social health of the nation?" Researchers at Fordham University's Institute for Innovation in Social Policy contend that the nation's quality of life has become unhinged from its economic growth. "We really have to begin to reassess this notion that the gross domestic product—the overall growth of the society—necessarily is going to produce improvements in the quality of life."[77] Constructing an Index for Social Health that encompassed governmental data from 1970 to 1993, researchers found that in six categories—children in poverty, child abuse, health insurance coverage, average weekly earnings adjusted for inflation, out-of-pocket health costs for senior citizens, and the gap between rich and poor—"social health" hit its lowest point in 1993. These indicators have worsened in the years since 1993, and we presume that the downward trend continues.

A corollary question is "What's the economy for, anyway?" In other words, do we exist to serve the economy or should the economy serve us? Economists often talk about the gross national product (GNP) or gross domestic product (GDP), productivity, and overall economic growth as if they were religious truths. Discussions typically revolve around how to best grow the economy, not whether the economy should grow. Meanwhile, too little of the economic discussion involves environmental sustainability or quality of life issues. John de Graaf has addressed these issues in *Affluenza* (the film and the book) as have other authors in various forms. (See Spotlight 2.)

As this chapter has demonstrated, social welfare in the United States is characterized by a high degree of diversity and is not a monolithic, highly

spotlight 2

What's The Economy For, Anyway?

by *John de Graaf*

In the global economy, it seems *everyone* is dissatisfied and looking for different models. One by one, Latin American countries are moving from Right to Left. On the other hand, in Europe, the parties of social democracy have been losing ground to the Center (Europe's "right-wing" parties would be Centrist or Left in the United States), one after another.

All of this frenetic searching begs the fundamental question: What's the Economy for, Anyway? How much stock can we take in the Dow Jones? Is the Gross Domestic Product the measure (the grosser the better), and stuff the *stuff*, of happiness? Is the good life the *goods* life?

If so, then there's little doubt that the freer-market regimes win big. U.S. per capita GDP is still 30 percent higher than the average in Western Europe, just as it was a generation ago. We've got bigger homes, bigger cars, and more high-definition televisions. On the other hand if we measure success by the happiness, health, fairness and sustainability of economies, the picture looks very different.

I've been doing a little number-crunching lately, comparing data from such sources as the 2007 OECD (Organization for Economic Cooperation and Development) Fact Book, the World Health Organization, and the UN (United Nations) Human Development Index, trying to see how countries are doing in real, empirical terms when it comes to health, quality of life, justice, and sustainability. The results, I'm afraid, would come as a shock to those who look to the United States as the model of economic success.

Let me do a few of the numbers: compared, for example, to western European nations, the United States ranks *worst* or next-to-worst when it comes to child welfare, health care, poverty, income equality, pollution, CO_2 emissions, ecological footprint, personal savings, income and pension security, balance of payments, municipal waste, development assistance, longevity, infant mortality, child abuse, depression, anxiety, obesity, murder, incarceration, motor vehicle fatalities, and leisure time. We do slightly better in education. Our unemployment rate looks pretty low, unless you count those 2.3 million people we've got behind bars, an incarceration rate 7 to 10 times as high as Europe's.

Since 1970, Europeans have traded a portion of their productivity gains for free time instead of stuff, a trade that pays off in many ways. New studies show that long working hours, the norm in the United States, contribute to poor health, weakened family and community bonds, *and* environmental damage. Americans, far less healthy than Europeans, spend twice as much for health care per person. In fact, we spend nearly half the world's *total* health care budget, an amount that will reach 20 percent of our GDP by 2010—with the worst outcomes. Yet, all of that spending counts as a *plus* when it comes to GDP. The leisure that Europeans enjoy, the long meals and café conversations, the long walks and bike rides, count only as wasted time, adding not a single point to GDP. *La dolce vita,* by that measure, is for losers.

But which countries come out on *top* in measures of quality of life? It's the northern European nations, those that combine a strong social safety net with shorter working hours, high but progressive tax rates and strong environmental regulations. *The pattern is as clear as can be.*

I have found no one who refutes these figures. They simply explain them away by saying that the United States can't be like Europe. Why not?

One argument for why the United States can't even have such things as paid maternity leave—a reality in every country on the globe except the United States, Swaziland, Lesotho, Liberia, and Papua New Guinea—is that we're so affected by *globalization*. But with its massive domestic market, the United States is just about the *least* affected by globalization of all industrial countries.

American conservatives argue that Europeans can't continue to compete in the global economy. But according to the World Economic Forum, over the past few years, four of the six most globally competitive countries have been in Europe. Even American businesses invest five times as much each year in Germany as they do in China and more in Belgium than in India. And they make money doing it.

When all else fails, there's the final appeal: the United States may not be very healthy, fair or sustainable, but it's "the land of opportunity," where *anyone* can make it big if they're willing to work hard enough. Yet a recent study finds that Americans actually have only about one-half to one-third as much chance as Europeans of escaping low-income lives and rising to the top.

The steady drone from some European business leaders about the American economic miracle masks what should be obvious—they'd like to join our CEOs in making 400 times as much as their average workers, instead of the miserable 30 to 40 times as much they now make. Their voices speak louder than those of the average European citizen, who enjoys his or her six weeks of vacation, restful meals, family leave, health care, sick pay, free college education, and secure pension plan.

Since Ronald Reagan declared that "government cannot be the solution because government is the problem," indices of American quality of life, fairness, economic security, and environmental sustainability have all fallen sharply in comparison with those in Europe. The conservative economic revolution has produced a *gush-up* instead of a "trickle-down." For most of us, the "ownership society," emphasizing privatization, deregulation and massive tax cuts for the wealthy, is really a *"you're on your owner*ship" society.

To make America better, our President tells us, we must do even *more* of these things, making tax cuts for the wealthy permanent, for example. But the working definition of insanity is to keep doing the same things hoping for a different result.

If we want to build societies that really work for people, we need to ask, "What's the Economy for, Anyway?" And then we need to separate the real results from the myths, shed a little of our American hubris and start looking at how other countries are actually edging us out by providing policies that succeed. That way lies a happier, healthier, more just and sustainable world.

John De Graaf is a documentary filmmaker and coauthor (with David Wann, Thomas Naylor, and Vicki Robin) of *Affluenza: The All-Consuming Epidemic* (San Francisco Berrett-Koehler, 2005)

---

centralized, well-coordinated system of programs. Rather, a great variety of organizations provide a wide range of benefits and services to different client populations. The vast array of social welfare organizations contributes to what is commonly called "the welfare mess." Consequently, different programs serving different groups through different procedures have engendered an impenetrable tangle of institutional red tape that is problematic for administrators, human service professionals, and clients.

The complexity of U.S. social welfare policy can be attributed to several cultural influences, some of which are peculiar to the American experience. For instance, the U.S. Constitution outlines a federal system whereby states vest certain functions in the national government. Although the states have assumed primary responsibility for social welfare through much of U.S. history, this changed with Franklin Delano Roosevelt's New Deal which ushered in a raft of federal programs. Over subsequent decades, federal social welfare initiatives played a dominant role in the nation's welfare effort. Still, states continued to manage important social welfare programs, such as mental health, corrections, and social services. Over time, the relationship between the federal government and the states has changed. From the New Deal of the 1930s through the Great Society of the 1960s, federal welfare programs expanded, forming the American version of the "welfare state." Beginning in the 1980s, the Reagan administration sought to return more of the responsibility for welfare to the states, a process called devolution.[78] This devolution was furthered by the Clinton administration with the signing of the PRWORA.

A second confounding element can be attributed to the relatively open character of U.S. society. Often referred to as a melting pot, the national culture is a protean brew of immigrant groups that competed with one another to become an established part of national life.[79] A staggering influx of

Europeans in the late nineteenth century gave way to waves of Hispanics and Asians entering the United States a century later.[80] Historically, social welfare programs have played an important role in the acculturation of these groups. At the same time, many ethnic groups brought with them their own fraternal and community associations, which not only provide welfare benefits to members of the community but also serve to maintain its norms. Other groups that have exerted important influences on U.S. social welfare are African Americans, the aged, women, and Native Americans. The very pluralism of U.S. society—a diverse collection of peoples, each with somewhat different needs—contributes to the complexity of social welfare.

Third, the economic system exacerbates the complexity of social welfare. The U.S. economy is predominantly capitalist, with most goods and services being owned, produced, and distributed through the marketplace. In a capitalist economy, people are expected to meet their basic needs in the marketplace through labor force participation. When people are unable to participate fully in the labor market, social programs are deployed to support these groups. These programs take various forms. Many are governmental programs. Private sector programs often complement those of the public sector. Within the private sector, two organizational forms are common—nonprofit organizations and for-profit corporations. Often these private sector organizations coexist, proximate to one another.[81]

Finally, various religious or faith-based organizations strongly influence social welfare in the United States. This is seen most clearly in the range of faith-based agencies that offer social services, such as Jewish Family Services, Lutheran Social Services, Catholic Charities, and the Salvation Army. In many cases, religious-based agencies provide services to groups that would not otherwise receive them. Today many faith-based agencies receive federal funds for various services they provide to the public. It is likely that this trend will grow.

The complexity of social welfare in the United States helps account for changes in welfare policies and programs. For example, since 1980 a convergence of social, political, and economic forces has led to a reappraisal of welfare. Liberal and conservative scholars have questioned the dominance of government programs in welfare provision. At the same time, a

firestorm of fundamentalism has swept across the nation, attracting the allegiance of groups associated with evangelicalism. The traditionalist movement flexed its muscles through the elections of Ronald Reagan, the two Bush administrations, the installation of a Republican Senate in the early 1980s and a conservative House of Representatives in 1994, and an effective grassroots mobilization that challenged government policies on issues ranging from the family to affirmative action. By the early 1990s, social conservatism had begun to influence Democratic party leaders, traditional supporters of government welfare programs. To reestablish credibility in an increasingly conservative political milieu, liberals distanced themselves from the large-scale government welfare programs they had been associated with since the New Deal. In place of these programs, many liberals called for a reliance on personal responsibility, work, and thrift.

Conservative public sentiment has served as a backdrop for the debate on the future of welfare policy.[82] An ascendant conservatism has not only checked further expansion of federal social programs, but the unprecedented tax cuts engineered by the former Bush administration threatened to dry up the revenues upon which social programs are dependent. The magnitude of this cannot be overstated: The tax cuts of the George W. Bush presidency eliminated the federal surplus; after September 11, 2001, Social Security and Medicare funds that had been set aside for retiring baby boomers were diverted to national security. As a result, the unfunded obligations of Social Security and Medicare and those of the federal retirement programs totaled $16.7 trillion in 2007.[83] The impact of this on social programs is profound, and the future solvency of social insurances for retirees would require a 91 percent increase in the withholding tax or an 81 percent increase in the income tax paid by individuals. If future workers reject such tax increases, pressure will build to convert Social Security and Medicare to means-tested, welfare programs. "This is the death trap of the welfare state," concluded Paul Samuelson, "here and in Europe and Asia."[84] Given these developments, welfare professionals face a formidable challenge: How can basic goods and services be brought to vulnerable populations within a context of such complexity and uncertainty?

Discussion Questions

1. According to the authors, American social welfare is undergoing a transition. Which ideologies, schools of political economy, and interest groups within social welfare stand to gain most from this transition?

2. Ideology tends to parallel schools of political economy. How would classical conservatives and liberals address current social welfare issues such as health care, long-term care for the aged, and substance abuse? How would neoconservatives and neoliberals diverge from traditional conservatives and liberals on these issues?

3. Which schools of political, social, and economic thought discussed in this chapter would come closest to being classified as moderate? Why?

4. The chapter argues that in large measure social policy dictates social work practice. Do you agree with that premise? Explain your position. Can you think of any instances (historic or otherwise) in which social work practice has led to changes in social welfare policy?

5. In your opinion, which schools of economic and political thought are the most compatible with social work practice? Why? What are the incompatibilities in the various schools of thought with macro- and micro-level social work and practice?

Notes

1. Glenn Kessler and Amy Goldstein, "A Guide to the Candidates' Positions," *Washington Post* (November 3, 2008), pp. A10–A11.

2. E. J. Dionne Jr., "The Opening Obama Saw," *Washington Post* (November 3, 2008), p. A21.

3. Barack Obama, *The Audacity of Hope* (New York: Three Rivers, 2006), pp. 256–257.

4. Richard Titmuss, *Essays on the Welfare State* (Boston: Beacon Press, 1963), p. 16.

5. Contained in personal correspondence between David Stoesz and William Epstein, April 2000.

6. Education would logically be included here, except that in the American experience it has been treated separately.

7. See Alfred Kahn, *Social Policy and Social Services* (New York: Random House, 1979).

8. Frances Fox Piven and Richard Cloward, *Regulating the Poor* (New York: Vintage, 1971).

9. David Gil, *Unraveling Social Policy* (Boston: Shenkman, 1981), p. 32.

10. Charles Prigmore and Charles Atherton, *Social Welfare Policy* (Lexington, MA: D.C. Heath, 1979), pp. 25–31.

11. World Development Indicators Database, World Bank, September 2007. Retrieved 2008, from http://siteresources.worldbank.org/DATASTATISTICS/Resources/GNIPC.pdf; and OECD Family Database, Social Policy Division, Directorate of Employment, Labour and Social Affairs, Public Spending on Family Benefits, January 1, 2007. Retrieved March 29, 2008, from www.oecd.org/dataoecd/45/46/37864391.pdf

12. Claus Offe, *Contradictions of the Welfare State* (Cambridge, MA: MIT Press, 1984).

13. John Maynard Keynes, *The General Theory of Employment, Interest and Money* (London: Macmillan, 1936).

14. Paul R. Krugman, *Peddling Prosperity: Economic Sense and Nonsense in the Age of Diminished Expectations* (New York: W.W. Norton, 1994).

15. Ibid.

16. In their book *Economics for Social Workers: The Application of Economic Theory to Social Policy and the Human Services* (New York: Columbia University Press, 2001), Michael Anthony Lewis and Karl Widerquist identify four conditions that must hold for a free market to exist.

17. Ibid.

18. Milton Friedman, *Money Mischief: Episodes in Monetary History* (New York: Harcourt Brace, 1992).

19. Milton Friedman, *Capitalism and Freedom* (Chicago: University of Chicago Press, 1962).

20. Ibid.

21. Robert E. Lucas, *Studies in Business Cycle Theory* (Cambridge, MA: MIT Press, 1981).

22. Krugman, *Peddling Prosperity*.

23. Ibid.

24. Ibid.

25. Congressional Budget Office, *The Economic and Budget Outlook: Fiscal Years 1993–1997* (Washington, DC: Congressional Budget Office, 1992), p. 28.

26. See Beth Shulman, *The Betrayal of Work: How Low Wage Jobs Fail 35 Million Americans* (New York: The

New Press, 2003); Lawrence Mishel, Jared Bernstein, and John Schmitt, *The State of Working America 2000/2001* (Ithaca, NY: Cornell University Press, 2001); and Jared Bernstein, "Economic Growth Not Reaching Middle- and Lower Wage Earners," January 28, 2004, retrieved 2004, from www.epinet.org/content.cfm/webfeatures_snapshots

27. See Ayn Rand, *The Fountainhead* (New York: New American Library, 50th Anniversary Edition, 1996); *Atlas Shrugged* (New York: Signet Book; 35th Anniversary Edition, 1996).

28. Charles Murray, *Losing Ground* (New York: Basic Books, 1984), pp. 227–228.

29. *Privatization: Toward More Effective Government* (Washington, DC: U.S. Government Printing Office, 1988), pp. 233–234.

30. Michael Grynbaum, "Greenspan Concedes Error on Regulation," *New York Times*, October 23, 2008, p. 1.

31. CNN News, "Taxpayers Would Get Checks under Economic Stimulus Plan," January 24, 2008. Retrieved October 25, 2008, from http://edition.cnn.com/2008/POLITICS/01/24/economic.stimulus/

32. Edmund L. Andrews, "Fed Acts to Rescue Financial Markets," *New York Times*, March 17, 2008, p. 4.

33. Mark Landler, "U.S. Is Said to Be Urging New Mergers in Banking," *New York Times*, October 20, 2008, p. 18.

34. Greg Morcroft, "Treasury Set to Bail Out Fannie Mae, Freddie Mac," *MarketWatch*, September 6, 2008. Retrieved October 25, 2008, from www.marketwatch.

35. Matthew Karnitschnig, Deborah Solomon, Liam Pleven, and Jon E. Hilsenrath, "U.S. to Take Over AIG in $85 Billion Bailout," *Wall Street Journal*, September 16, 2008, p. 10; The Associated Press, "AIG Borrows $90.3 Billion from Federal Reserve," *BusinessWeek*, October 24, 2008, p. 2.

36. Paul Wallis, "$25 Billion Fed Loan to Car Industry; It's Not a Bailout, Says Detroit," *Digital Business Journal*, September 29, 2008. Retrieved October 25, 2008, from www.digitaljournal.com/article/260441

37. Uwe E. Reinhardt, "Does the Democrats' Stimulus Package Make Economic Sense?" *New York Times*, October 24, 2008, p. 16.

38. Subir Lall, "World Economic Outlook: IMF Predicts Slower World Growth Amid Serious Market Crisis," *IMFSurvey*, April 9, 2008. Retrieved October 23, 2008, from www.imf.org/external/pubs/ft/survey/so/2008/RES040908A.htm

39. Associated Press, "2008 U.S. Budget Deficit Bleeding Red Ink First 4 Months of Budget Year at Nearly $88B, Double Amount Recorded For Same 2007 Period," CBS News, February 12, 2008. Retrieved October 24, 2008, from www.cbsnews.com/stories/2008/02/12/national/main3822385.shtml

40. Jeffry Galper, "Introduction of Radical Theory and Practice in Social Work Education: Social Policy."

Mimeographed paper, Michigan State University School of Social Work, ca. 1978.

41. Piven and Cloward, *Regulating the Poor*, pp. 3–4.

42. Harry Hopkins, *Spending to Save: The Complete Story of Relief* (Seattle: University of Washington Press, 1936).

43. Neil Gilbert, Harry Specht, and Paul Terrell, *Dimensions of Social Welfare Policy* (Englewood Cliffs, NJ: Prentice Hall, 1993).

44. Marc Bendick, *Privatizing the Delivery of Social Welfare Service* (Washington, DC: National Conference on Social Welfare, 1985), p. 1.

45. Charles Peters, "A New Politics," *Public Welfare* 41, no. 2 (Spring 1983), pp. 34, 36.

46. Randall Rothenberg, *The Neoliberals* (New York: Simon & Schuster, 1984), pp. 244–245.

47. David Stoesz, *Small Change* (New York: Longman, 1995).

48. Robert Reich, *The Next American Frontier* (New York: Times Books, 1983).

49. Anthony Giddens, *The Third Way* (Cambridge, MA: Polity Press, 1999), p. 117.

50. Bruce Stokes, *Helping Ourselves: Local Solutions to Global Problems* (New York: W.W. Norton, 1981).

51. Sugata Dasgupta, "Towards a No-Poverty Society," *Social Development Issues* 12 (Winter 1983), pp. 85–93.

52. Some of these economic principles were addressed by E. F. Schumacher in *Small Is Beautiful* (New York: Harper & Row, 1973).

53. Barry M. Goldwater, *The Conscience of a Conservative* (New York: Putnam, 1960), pp. 109–110.

54. See Peter Steinfels, *The Neoconservatives* (New York: Simon & Schuster, 1979).

55. Interview with Stuart Butler, Director of Domestic Policy at the Heritage Foundation, October 4, 1984.

56. Alan Walker, "The Strategy of Inequality: Poverty and Income Distribution in Britain 1979–89," in I. Taylor (ed.), *The Social Effects of Free Market Policies* (Sussex, England: Harvester-Wheatsheaf, 1990), pp. 43–66.

57. Kristen Geiss-Curran, Sha'ari Garfinkle, Fred Knocke, Terri Lively, and Sue McCullough, "The Contract with America and the Budget Battle," unpublished manuscript, University of Houston, Spring 1996.

58. The Libertarian Party, "Statement of Principles," Washington, DC, 1996.

59. Daniel Patrick Moynihan, *Came the Revolution* (New York: Harcourt Brace Jovanovich, 1988), p. 291.

60. See Harold Wilensky and Charles Lebeaux, *Industrial Society and Social Welfare* (New York: Free Press, 1965); and Mimi Abramovitz, "The Privatization of the Welfare State," *Social Work* 31 (July–August 1986), pp. 257–264.

61. R. Erikson, E. Hansen, S. Ringen, and H. Uusitalo, *The Scandinavian Model* (Armonk, NY: M.E. Sharpe, 1987).

62. Richard Titmuss, *Commitment to Welfare* (New York: Pantheon, 1968), p. 127.

63. Wilensky and Lebeaux, *Industrial Society and Social Welfare*, p. 147.

64. Alvin Rabushka, "Tax and Spending Limits," in Peter Duignan and Alvin Rabushka (eds.), *The United States in the 1980s* (Stanford, CA: Hoover Institution, 1980), pp. 104–106.

65. Martin Anderson, "Welfare Reform," in Peter Duignan and Alvin Rabushka (eds.), *The United States in the 1980s*, pp. 171–176.

66. Peter Berger and John Neuhaus, *To Empower People: The Role of Mediating Structures in Public Policy* (Washington, DC: American Enterprise Institute, 1977).

67. Michael Novak, *Toward a Theology of the Corporation* (Washington, DC: American Enterprise Institute, 1981), p. 5.

68. Stuart Butler and Anna Kondratas, *Out of the Poverty Trap: A Conservative Strategy for Welfare Reform* (New York: Free Press, 1987).

69. William Lind and William Marshner, *Cultural Conservatism: Toward a New National Agenda* (Washington, DC: Free Congress Research and Education Foundation, 1987), p. 83.

70. George Gilder, *Wealth and Poverty* (New York: Basic Books, 1981), p. 118.

71. Anderson, "Welfare Reform," p. 145.

72. Jacob. S. Hacker, *The Great Risk Shift: The Assault on American Jobs, Families, Health Care, and Retirement* (New York: Oxford University Press, 2006).

73. Ibid.

74. Lawrence Mischel, Jared Bernstein, and Sylkvia Allegretto, *The State of Working America 2004/2005* (Ithaca, NY: IRL Press, 2005).

75. Julie Appleby, "Bush Unveils Health Plan Tied to Tax Deduction," *USA Today*, January 24, 2007. Retrieved March 17, 2007, from www.usatoday.com

76. John Judis and Michael Lind, "For a New Nationalism," *The New Republic* (March 27, 1995), p. 26.

77. Mitchell Landsberg, "Nation's Social Health Declined in '93," *Houston Chronicle* (October 16, 1995), p. 1C.

78. Domestic Policy Council, Up from Dependency (Washington, DC: White House Domestic Policy Council, December 1986).

79. For a classic description of the assimilation phenomenon, see Nathan Glazer and Daniel Patrick Moynihan, *Beyond the Melting Pot* (Cambridge, MA: MIT Press, 1970).

80. Thomas Muller et al., *The Fourth Wave* (Washington, DC: Urban Institute, 1985).

81. The three auspices of social welfare in the United States have been termed the "mixed economy of welfare." See Sheila Kamerman, "The New Mixed Economy of Welfare," *Social Work* 28 (January–February 1983), pp. 43–50.

82. For further details, see David Stoesz, "The Functional Conception of Social Welfare," *Social Work* 34 (March 1989), pp. 86–91.

83. U.S. Treasury Office of Economic Policy, "The 2008 Annual Report of the Board of Trustees of the Federal Hospital Insurance and Federal Supplementary Medical Insurance Trust Funds," March 25, 2008. Retrieved March 26, 2008, from www.treas.gov/offices/economic-policy/social_security.shtml

84. Paul Samuelson, "The Deficit Chicken Hawks," *Washington Post* (October 10, 2003), p. A27.

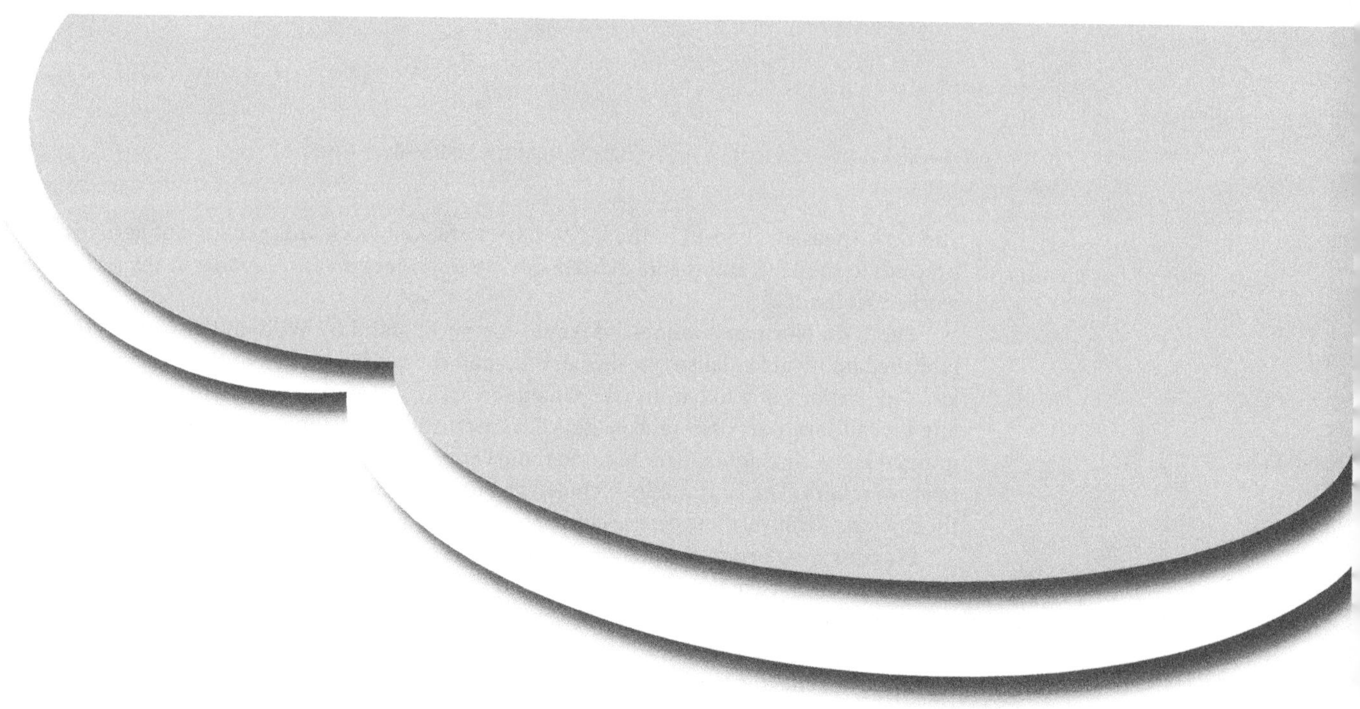

Social Values and Social Welfare

England from the Middle Ages Onward

For the poor shall never cease out of the land; therefore I command thee, saying: "Thou shalt surely open thy hand unto thy poor and needy brother in thy land."

—Deuteronomy 15:11

Overview

In this chapter we examine the chief trends and major social welfare events, primarily in England, from the Middle Ages to the development of the Poor Laws, the Speenhamland system, the workhouses, and the Poor Law of 1834. We undertake this review to demonstrate that attitudes following the Middle Ages represented a significant departure from earlier perceptions of poor people. We also do this because U.S. social welfare has been influenced in so many ways by historical developments in England and English perspectives on the poor.

The Early Middle Ages

The Middle Ages have been divided into three separate phases. The first stage was the feudalization of western European society, roughly from the sixth to the tenth centuries, when barbarian successor states replaced a collapsed Roman Empire. From the king down, a hierarchy was created in which each person knew his or her place and responsibilities. The manorial system of vassalage (vassals were granted feudal land in return for homage and military service) was a system for control of society and included the lord, his vassals, and serfs (peasants bound to the land). The serf owed work and portions of agricultural produce to the lord, and the lord ostensibly owed protection and support to the serfs who worked his land.

The 1066 Norman conquest of Anglo-Saxon England by William the Conqueror established political feudalism on the basis that all the land belonged to this king, who then granted portions of it to barons (the tenants-in-chief) in return for certain services, generally for military purposes such as guard, escort, and provisioning of troops. The barons granted lands to knights, who became their vassals, and, in turn, the knights could grant lands to others. The land grants included the tenants with their obligations to the lords of the manors. Relatively few people controlled most of England's land.

Peasants were tied to the manor and owed work and taxes. They had to mill their grain at the lord's mill; bake their bread in the lord's oven; pay a fine at the marriage of a daughter; give the lord their best beast at their death; and answer in the lord's court for failure to perform any required services.[1]

The serf's life was hard. Housing was poor, food was short, and starvation loomed during famines. The lord owned the land; he controlled the meadow and the woods. The serfs owed rents, gave labor service and gifts, and also paid fines to the lords. Each household was expected to give tithes to the church and charity to the local poor. The lord's rulings were final and the serf's status was servile. The lords, on their side, gave protection. Welfare benefits did exist for the serfs tied to the manors on which they were born. They could be released from the year-round work for up to thirty days if sick. If they died, their wives did not have to serve for the following thirty days. Even so, boon work (additional work at plowing time and harvest) had to be done or a substitute found and paid.[2]

This agrarian economy produced very little surplus; production for market was low. Rents were paid in labor or in-kind because there was little money in circulation. Upper-class incomes were measured in produce rather than cash. There was little effective demand for luxuries. Town populations were small, with the lords and peasants constituting the overwhelming majority of the population.[3] Life was hard for both landlords and tenants, and famines were common. Between the tenth and fifteenth centuries, there were— excluding local outbreaks—49 general famines.[4]

But it was not just famine and wars that threatened stability. Periodically the demands on the peasantry would become increasingly burdensome, including demands for higher farm rents, restrictions on the freedom of the tenants on lords' estates, or labor obligations added to the rent. Naturally this increased existing tensions among landholders, serfs, and tenants.[5]

The poor were not without certain protections. Canon law demanded that each parish, the church subdivision on the local level, provide for the poor. Poverty was not a crime. Brian Tierney contrasted the attitude of the English in the early Middle Ages with their views during the early twentieth century, when as late as 1909 an English royal commission assumed that every poor person was poor because of a "defect in the citizen character."[6]

In thirteenth-century society, an individual whose wealth exceeded his needs consistent with his status was obligated to assist the poor. The following canonical directives confirm this: "Feed the poor. If you do not feed them, you kill them." "Our superfluities belong to the poor." "Whatever you have beyond what suffices for your needs belongs to others." "A man who keeps for himself more than he needs is guilty of theft."[7]

It was the responsibility of the clergy of each parish to provide "hospitality" for travelers and other guests and to take care of the poor. Even Saint Francis of Assisi made a distinction between holy poverty and other kinds of poverty. He wrote in his last testament: "I have worked with my hands and I choose to work, and I firmly wish that all my brothers should work at some honorable trade. And if they do not know how, let them learn."[8]

The only grounds for refusing to provide charity was the belief that it would encourage idleness. The "willfully idle" should not be assisted. Every able-bodied person was expected to earn his keep after a few days. Several centuries later, distinguishing between the *deserving* and *undeserving* poor became crucial in determining aid. In the early Middle Ages, however, such distinctions apparently were not clearly defined.

As prescribed by canon law, parishes and monasteries practiced charitable acts and provided relief. These efforts may have been somewhat haphazard and were clearly insufficient, but they must be viewed within the broader context of scarcity and want. Consider, for example, the general plight of many peasants:

> They all lived in unsanitary conditions; they had no doctors, and at times pestilence swept away whole communities. Few families could store grain; a year of flood or drought created terrible famines. The peasants could not defend themselves against heavy-armed feudal cavalry, and if their lord became involved in a war they were almost sure to see their fields ravaged and their houses burned. It is not surprising that the span of life was short, that a man of forty was considered old.[9]

The Middle Middle Ages

The second phase of the Middle Ages—from the eleventh to the early fourteenth centuries—brought a growth of the population, an expansion of cultivated areas, some technical progress, and market-oriented production. A surplus appeared owing to three factors: (1) increased technical efficiency, (2) improved administration, and (3) increased pressure to transfer more of the surplus from producers to lords.

The quickened pace of economic activity generally benefited the urban areas, which became a focus for the efforts of artisans, retail traders, industrial entrepreneurs, unskilled laborers, servants, and other poor people. The movement into the towns also was the consequence of rural overpopulation, which became acute by the end of the thirteenth century. Despite these positive signs, persistent demands for rents, tithes, and taxes by landowners, the church, and the state continued to produce social upheavals and uncertainty.

For example, a village revolt in 1261 at Mears Ashby, Northamptonshire, was followed by another in 1278 in Harmondsworth, Middlesex. Sometimes these conflicts related to rent collections; at other times they were connected with the collective refusal to provide services for the landlords.[10] Serfdom was degrading, and people were forced into hierarchical relationships. There was confusion regarding individual rights and restraints. But the line between liberty and servitude could never be forgotten. Serfdom meant subordination and arbitrariness, which people feared and resented. At the same time they lacked mobility and freedom.[11]

On a broader scale, the violent and widespread English Peasants' Revolt of 1381 was set off by an attempt to levy a poll tax (per head) with little variation in the burden to substitute for the taxation of the more well-to-do according to their property, which had been the norm. The attempted shift of taxation down to those with less aroused bitter resentment, especially since the change took place during a population shortage. Violence was directed against manorial lords, the government that supported them, and culminated in a brief occupation of London. Among the demands of those revolting were the abolition of serfdom, a reduction of rents, and an increase in wages.[12]

Still, in the context of U.S. social welfare and our ideas about the poor, one must consider Tierney's view about how the poor were treated in the Middle Ages. He concluded that "in this particular matter, I am inclined to think that, taken all in all, the poor were better looked after in England in the thirteenth century than in any subsequent century until the present one. The only reservation we need make is that perhaps that is not saying much."[13]

Thus, the relationships of the lords and the peasantry were complicated, reflecting both their need for each other and the tensions relating to their conflicting needs and status differences.

The Late Middle Ages to Elizabethan Poor Laws

The fourteenth and fifteenth centuries have been characterized as the third or last phase of the Middle Ages. In the late Middle Ages, new towns arose, colonization of new lands began, and the growth of international trade spurred the formation of money economies. The feudal system gave way to wage-based relationships, which severed the allegiances and responsibilities connecting the serf and the lord. There was a loss of what economic security existed. By the thirteenth century, many English peasants had become small landholders. Poverty persisted but there also were indications of prosperity: cathedral building and the production of metal, cloth, and other goods. With the rise of wage labor, serfdom declined and those on the land experienced new freedom and independence. The retreat of feudal society was also accompanied by the appearance of vagrants, transients, and migrants. A rooted society was giving way to one in which mobility was becoming more the norm. From a life defined by *status*—the relationship of lord and serf—a new relationship was evolving determined by *contracts* between parties. Power had become a negotiable commodity.

Those needing a steady and dependable labor supply did not appreciate a state of affairs in which people could escape from the traditional roles and places. Nor were they prepared to deal with marauders. *Begging* became widespread and gained a degree of acceptance, especially because the act of giving charity to care for the poor was a religious obligation and both begging and giving had long been practiced with the blessings of the Church.[14]

Going beyond individual acts of charity, more than 8,000 *parishes* did organized charitable work in medieval England. Religious *monastic orders* served both the local poor and strangers passing through.[15] It is of interest, however, that during the Middle Ages, the percentage of monastic income actually devoted to charity varied widely. Estimates ranged from 1 percent to more than 22 percent; however, the national average did not reach 2.5 percent.[16] Strangers were to be helped without discrimination, as were infidels and excommunicants. Thus, in the thirteenth century, there was little if any discrimination based on eligibility categories or residence.

Other institutions served important roles for the poor. The *guilds*, which were voluntary commercial and social associations of merchants and artisans, functioned as mutual aid societies and charitable organizations for their own members. They built and maintained hospitals,[17] fed the needy on feast days, annually distributed corn and barley, provided free lodgings for poor travelers, and gave other incidental help.[18]

In addition, the guilds provided disaster insurance, specifying assistance for poverty, sickness, old age, blindness, loss of limb, loss of cattle, fall of a house, false imprisonment, and temporary financial problems, as well as losses by fire, flood, robbery, or shipwreck. There were eligibility limitations, and a member could be helped only three times in a lifetime and then only when the crisis was not of his own doing.

Another pillar of social welfare was the *private foundation*, created by the bequests and gifts of individual philanthropists. At the time of the Reformation there were at least 460 charitable foundations in England. As much a part of medieval life as they are today, foundations established almshouses, hospitals, and other institutions; provided money for funerals; and disbursed funds on the anniversaries of the benefactors.[19]

Hospitals of various types were established during the Middle Ages, including leper houses, orphanages, maternity homes, and institutions for the aged and the infirm. In fact, in mid-fourteenth-century England there were 600 hospitals.[20] For the most part, however, peasants would not have had access to hospitals or monasteries for retirement and terminal illness. They formed voluntary organizations on their own that provided some benefits to the aged and the helpless. Of 507 guilds that returned descriptions of their charters in 1389, about one-third (154) provided their members with benefits during disaster or old age.

It is estimated that there were some 500 to 700 hospitals in late medieval England, but only a few specialized in caring for the aged, poor women in childbirth, maimed soldiers, and the "deserving poor." Mostly, they provided temporary shelter, taking persons in for only one night. Furthermore, most were small, serving perhaps a dozen persons. A comment by Henry VII in 1509 suggested concern over this situation:

> There be fewe or non such commune Hospitalls within our Reame, and that for lack of them, infinite nombre of pouer nedie people miserably dailly die, no man putting hand of help or remedie.

Tithing was a feature of life in the Middle Ages, and in England church funds secured from parishioners were divided: one-third for the maintenance of the church, one-third for the poor, and one-third for the priests.[21] Individuals at every level of society were expected to give to the poor. During the thirteenth century, King John—in debt himself—continued to give alms to the poor from his revenues.[22]

Several important factors combined to force on the English of the late Middle Ages changed attitudes toward the poor. The movement from rural to urban settings was stimulated by the introduction of woolen manufacturing. Within a relatively short period of time the manufacture of woolen goods in England became so extensive that an export trade was established. With the growth of cities, trade, money economies, and international relations, the expiring feudal system forced large numbers of people into social chaos. People were displaced from their former positions, physically and psychologically. The old truths were no longer valid. With the necessity for sheep grazing in order to grow wool for the textile industry, land was "enclosed," and peasants were forced from the land, dislocated, unattached, and without means of support.

Population pressures in the late Middle Ages also had a tremendous impact on social changes during this period. Prior to the first part of the fourteenth century, the population of England had grown. Severe cold weather throughout Europe from 1200 to 1400 C.E. contributed to erratic eras of drought and flood, abundance and famine. Commencing with flood and famine from 1315 to 1317, the population began to decline. About the middle of the fourteenth century, ensuing events intensified a rapid diminution of the population.

Much starvation and disease followed the first wave of the Black Death (bubonic plague) in 1348. The plague continued through the fifteenth century, which saw the demise of serfdom. The plague revisited England in 1361, 1368, and 1375 and was not completely eliminated until the seventeenth century. Not only was there population loss in England, but a series of plagues also decimated the European population during this time. Although there is a dispute as to the exact dimensions of the population loss, the estimates range from 20 to 50 percent of the population.[23]

Even before the middle of the fourteenth century there were difficulties finding tenants for numerous landholdings due to poor weather, famines, and continuous wars in northern Europe, among other reasons. Migration to towns exacerbated the pronounced shortage of agricultural workers. It was the plague of 1348, however, that greatly increased the scarcity of labor and greatly increased the value awarded to the available labor.

The loss of population undermined the manorial system by the close of the sixteenth century. In England, more than 1,300 villages were deserted between 1350 and 1500, almost all in marginal farming lands. The emancipation of the serfs ground to a halt, and landlords tried desperately to retain the traditional services of their tenants. Free laborers, of course, used the shortage of labor as leverage to demand higher wages.[24]

There was a general breakdown of law and order as the economic and military power of the landholders, as well as their social prestige, declined. Moreover, wars created a pool of wanderers who were skilled thieves and therefore not eager to stay in one place. Local landholders operated the police and the courts because law enforcement was a local prerogative. This breakdown is reflected by the increased incidence of homicide, which from 1349 to 1369 was about double that of the period from 1320 to 1340.[25]

Because of the shift in power from landholders to workers, the late Middle Ages has been referred to as the "Golden Age of Laborers," and it is believed that real wages were higher in the fifteenth century than at any time in history until the twentieth century. From the beginning of the thirteenth century to the beginning of the fifteenth century, agricultural prices fell by 10 percent, real wages multiplied 2.5 times, and cash wages nearly doubled.[26]

Scarcity enabled laborers to seek higher wages and to make demands where historically demands had all come from lords and landholders. Illustrative of this trend is the pay scale for ploughmen:

> A ploughman who was paid 2 shillings a week in 1347 received 7 shillings in 1349 and 10 shillings 6 pence by 1350. Day laborers not only received higher wages, but asked for and got lunches of meat pies and golden ale.[27]

To deal with the new freedom of the serfs and a scarcity of labor and to ensure a supply of agricultural workers, a series of laws was enacted. In 1351, the *Statute of Labourers* was passed to force those who were able-bodied and without other means of support to work for an employer in their own parish *at rates prevailing before the plague*. This statute is the first example of poor law legislation that evolved over the next four centuries.

A national system of enforcement was established that made it illegal to demand or offer higher wages than had been the standard in 1346. Laborers were expected to contract to stay with an employer for a year or another appropriate period, and there was to be no daily hiring. Laborers had to swear an oath that they would obey the provisions of the statute or be placed in the stocks. Those with sufficient land to keep them occupied were exempt from the obligation to work for wages. In some areas, during the first ten years following the statute's enforcement, laborers paid, through fines, as much as one-third or half of the tax burden that the wealthier formerly had paid. But, ultimately, such measures were not successful and ended in a sense of grievance as all efforts to control the workers failed. The landlords discovered the only way to retain laborers was to pay the going rate.[28]

In 1352, in England, workers demanded, and some employers paid, wages two and three times the pay rate before the plague.

The effects of the bubonic plague not only were problematic in the countryside but also affected urban centers and commercial activity. The wealthy of the cities also tried to retain what they had, and restrictive guild regulations and city ordinances were enacted. In the twelfth century, any industrious young apprentice might become a master after completion of the appropriate training.[29] By the latter part of the fourteenth century, eligibility for becoming apprenticed in many guilds was limited to the sons of masters or to those who married the masters' daughters. A large group of urban laborers lived at the beck and call of their masters and were forbidden to organize to foster their own interests. Not surprisingly, there was much resentment among these laborers and frequent riots among the peasants, including the French Jacquerie (1358), the English Peasants' Revolt (1381), and the town revolts by artisans in Bruges (1302), Ghent (1381), and Rouen (1382)—all of which were quickly crushed. One exception occurred in Florence (1378), where workers held control of the city for three years.[30]

In an effort to maintain the traditional system, the statute provided that all able-bodied persons under 60 years of age without means of subsistence must work, that alms could not be given to able-bodied beggars, and that runaway serfs could be made to work for anyone who claimed them. In medieval society, work was expected of all; idleness was a crime.

During the 1350s and 1360s, fugitive laborers were declared outlaws; if caught they were branded on the forehead with an F, for "fugitive" or "falsity"; stocks were set up for punishment; and imprisonment was often used as a penalty. Those who were wandering and unemployed outside their own parishes were whipped, branded, sent to toil in the royal galleys, or set into stocks for three days.[31]

Begging was permissible for the *impotent* poor, that is, those who could not possibly work. By the last years of the fifteenth century, pregnant women and extremely sick men and women were considered among the impotent. Shortly after, those poor over the age of 60 years were added to the list of the impotent. The categorization of those in need was established, beginning the differentiation between the "*deserving*" and the "*undeserving*" poor. Thus continued a series of punitive laws that culminated in the Elizabethan Poor Laws in the latter part of the sixteenth century.

Work and Religion

Martin Luther in 1517 presaged still other changes with his momentous posting of the 95 Theses on the door of Castle Church in Wittenberg, becoming the initiator and focal point of a religious revolution. The foundations of Roman Catholicism were challenged, especially the notion of papal authority, and the Protestant Reformation followed. This one act lit a theological conflagration and began a political revolution that weakened the Holy Roman Empire and fostered the development of the modern nation-state.

Luther defined *vocation* as a calling to do God's work in all things; a vocation was an

exaltation of the common occupations as the appropriate spheres in which to serve God acceptably. The term vocation was transferred by Luther from the cloister to the workshop. [T]he farmer, the doctor, the school teacher, the minister, the magistrate, the house-mother, the maidservant and the manservant were all of them religious callings, vocations in which one was bound to render no lip service but to work diligently at serving not merely an earthly but also a heavenly master.[32]

Luther's teachings improved the morale of laborers, giving them a sense of duty in doing an honest day's toil; his beliefs also resulted in an elevation of the family, and of individuals as well, in the sense that all callings were important.

During the sixteenth century, Calvinism also began to make its mark. The distinction between the cloister and the marketplace was broken down even more; one could serve God as well in the marketplace as in any other place. Work was a divine vocation and thus a religious activity. Idleness and the temptations of the world distracted people from the pursuit of righteous living; work was for the glory of God. Max Weber describes Calvinism as "not leisure and enjoyment, but only activity [which] serves to increase the glory of God. Waste of time is thus the first and in principle the deadliest of sins." Loss of time through sociability, idle talk, luxury, even more sleep than is necessary for health (six to at most eight hours) is worthy of absolute moral condemnation. Work could be viewed as a chief end for life and, as Saint Paul suggested, "He who will not work shall not eat."[33]

Paradoxically, the "elevation" of the individual enhanced by the "calling" of an occupation was a double-edged sword. According to Calvinist doctrine, a calling reduced uncertainty—the reality of life—by limiting mobility. For the sake of order, each person had an obligation to remain within his or her calling:

> The best way, therefore, to maintain a peaceful life is when each one is intent on the duties of his own calling, carries out the commands that the Lord has given, and devotes himself to these tasks; when the farmer is busy with the work in cultivation, the workman carries on his trade, and in this way each keeps within his proper limits. As soon as men turn aside from this, everything is thrown into confusion and disorder.[34]

The values of Calvinism have very much affected our ideas on social welfare through the centuries. The Calvinism of England in particular stressed personal responsibility and discipline and an intense individualism in social affairs. Pauperism was viewed as a question of character. Calvin himself condemned indiscriminant almsgiving and urged church authorities to visit families regularly to see if they were idle, drunken, or otherwise undesirable. Idleness was a sin against God and a social evil; not to work meant to refuse to listen to God's word. For the glory of God, society must be served. Those who were dependent were somehow "marred."[35] The impulse to work was sacred. Upright character, integrity, and work were the products of faith. If one's economic state was improved as a result of industry, sobriety, honesty, and frugality, this was only a byproduct of doing God's work.[36] Conspicuous consumption was still frowned on, so wealth tended to be reinvested, to become capital.

A new system was being created, both economic and social; people were being separated from the land and moving to the cities. Towns and cities were being enlarged for manufacture and commerce, including international commerce. Poor people were not just the victims of famines and war; new forces came into play that victimized them in new ways. Employment became variable, with cycles influenced not only by local events but also by unseen international occurrences.

Serfdom provided some insurance against sickness and old age; now poverty of a new kind developed. During the Middle Ages people were poor, but those who had the greatest difficulty surviving were those we would now refer to as *case poverty* (widows, orphans, the old, the blind, the mutilated, and those infirm from long illnesses) in the sense that they resulted from *individual* tragedies. But from the fourteenth century, English poverty included the *structural* type that developed from the changed *economic structure* of society. When living on feudal manors, a person disabled by injury could be assisted at the local level. However, when entire industries located in cities were affected by their international markets and people were thrown out of work, the resources available for those affected were far more limited. People could not fall back on the farmland. Previously famine could cause widespread danger, but now industry and commerce could cruelly cause poverty and do so in complex ways beyond the control of individuals. The extent of exemptions from taxation on the grounds of poverty suggests at least one-third of the population lived marginally in most cities, and in some cities the percentage was more than half. Those who migrated into towns were mainly unskilled and found only intermittent work.[37]

The expansion of markets and the creation of new technologies in combination with many other factors gave impetus to the Industrial Revolution. According to one interpreter, many factors contributed to that revolution, including the rise of "factory towns, the emergence of slums, the long working hours of children, the low wages of certain categories of workers, the rise in the rate of population increase [and] the concentration of industries." All these in the view of Polanyi "were merely incidental to one basic change, the establishment of market economy." But the rise of a market economy demanded certain costs. Polanyi continues, "Machine production in a commercial society involves, in effect, no less a transformation than that of the natural and human substance of society into commodities."[38]

When people are needed to strive in the "satanic mills," to produce for markets within industrializing and urbanizing societies, they become essential parts, as labor, of the grinding wheels. When this role is viewed within the context that productivity is a sign of the elect's standing in the world, the burden of poverty falls squarely on the shoulders of individuals, regardless of the complicated causation of their impoverished conditions. The message communicated was that individuals demonstrate their spiritual condition through the signs that God has provided. Poverty, then, means unworthiness, and in fact, poor people can be viewed as undeserving.

In 1531, in an attempt to deal with the phenomenon of beggars and vagabonds, the government of England introduced for the first time the *principle of governmental responsibility* and provision. Evolving out of great concern about the numbers of persons who were idle, or committing thefts and murders, this initial act first provided for those in *genuine need*, such as aged and disabled poor persons. Local authorities were authorized to certify these people by letter indicating they were eligible to beg, the first legal assumption by government of "responsibility" for care of the poor.

The *able-bodied poor*, however, were treated much differently. Fines were imposed on those who would give "any harboring, money, or lodging to any beggars being strong and able in their bodies to work." An idle man was whipped and after the punishment was forced to return to the place of his birth or last dwelling place and there to "put himself to labour like as a true man oweth to do."[39]

In 1536, Henry VIII, under the Dissolution of the Monasteries Act, expropriated all monasteries with an annual income of less than 200 English pounds. The property and wealth of the monasteries were given to the King's followers. By 1540 all monasteries and their wealth were taken with few exceptions. These actions effectively did away with one of the pillars of social welfare and also minimized the ascetic ideal. The people most adversely affected were those monks who had to rely on rather meager pensions, nuns who remained unmarried and were not otherwise employed with still smaller pensions, domestic servants who found it difficult to obtain alternative employment, and an unknown number of poor persons who relied on the monasteries for charity. Those less wealthy persons who donated livestock or other in-kind resources to the monasteries in exchange for permanent food and shelter were protected by the Dissolution Act and paid in cash rather than in-kind.[40]

Also in 1536, a statute was passed creating a comprehensive English system of relief. The statute provided that those returned after punishment to their former places of residence were entitled to food and lodging every ten miles for one night from the parish constable. Further loitering would be punished by whipping, cutting off the right ear, or even death. Children aged 5 to 14 could be apprenticed out. Church collections were to be used to care for "the poor, impotent, lame, feeble, sick, and diseased people, being not able to work." When parishes had a surplus it was to be used to provide support for the poorer parishes. The collectors were to be paid "good and reasonable" wages and thus became the first paid public welfare personnel. In addition to registration of need, licensed begging was replaced by funds derived from contributions stimulated through the force of the state and the clergy. Those who were "strong enough to labor" were given employment. Although this responsibility for providing jobs was not spelled out, the important principle of public responsibility to provide work when work could not be found was laid down for the first time in England. Thus work relief was born in the welfare system.[41]

Idlers were detested in English society and by 1547 a "V" could be marked on their breasts with a hot iron and they could be enslaved for two years. When idlers who ran away were captured, an "S" could be burned on their foreheads or cheeks and they could be enslaved forever. For any repetition of this behavior, the sentence was death. These laws proved to be too severe and were repealed in 1550. Concurrently, licensed begging was revived.

When the nation-state developed as a full-blown institution in society, there was a simultaneous reevaluation of the role of the monolithic church. Where there had been parallel bodies of binding law, the state began to take on many of the responsibilities that previously rested more fully with the church.

As early as 1526 in Spain, Juan Luis Vives set forth a plan for communal care of the poor in his *De Subventione Pauperum* (*On the Supervision of the Poor*). According to his plan, two senators with a secretary were to visit each institution where paupers were housed and investigate the living conditions, meanwhile counting and listing names. Those living in private homes were to be similarly registered. Those who were of a certain age and without a trade were to be taught one. Irksome tasks were to be assigned to those who dissipated their "fortunes in riotous living." Those unable to find work, including the blind, were to be assigned such work. This plan included a communal duty to care for the poor, local-level inquiry into the situations of the poor so as to prioritize them, and the registration and development of different categories of the poor, particularly based on moral grounds. Similar plans were developed in Germany in the early 1520s, in the southern Netherlands in 1524–1525, in Venice in 1528–1529, and in France in the 1530s.

It is instructive to review the Venetian plan for the sake of comparison and to acknowledge the international nature of the problems of poverty and the similar approaches to dealing with those problems. Venice established machinery for discriminating between the worthy and the unworthy poor, developed a system of priorities for giving relief so as to eliminate "social parasites," and distinguished among paupers who were physically handicapped, able-bodied but not employed, and physically whole but ill-equipped by upbringing to do manual labor. The Venetians encouraged the greatest number of applicants to be self-supporting: They gave the able-bodied opportunities to work, and they forced those able-bodied who did not want to work to do so through corporal punishment or threat of expulsion from Venice. Beggar children were educated so as to enable them to work and be absorbed into the economic system. The impotent poor, the aged, the crippled, and others were helped through accommodation in hospitals and through distribution of charity to their homes. As a last resort, they were given licenses to beg, which signified their worthiness to be given charity. Paupers were the responsibility of their native communities. Native paupers had priority over strangers, and there was a municipal organization to supervise and administer poor relief.[42]

The Poor Laws

Beginning with the Ordinance of Laborers (1349) and the Statute of Laborers (1351), as early as 1388, an English statute was enacted to regulate the movement of laborers, thus attempting to control homeless vagabonds and focusing on an issue of concern to the evolution of Poor Laws. The statute distinguished between the impotent and the able-bodied poor and introduced into legislation the concept of settlement, one's legal residence, as a condition for assistance.[43] However, it was during the sixteenth century that a series of laws called the *Poor Laws* were enacted in England. The result of centuries of periodic social unrest—famines, epidemics, wars, enclosures, urbanization, unemployment and labor supply problems, rising prices, and increases in the number of persons seeking poor relief—the laws consisted of experiments with methods of alleviating distress, preventing vagrancy, and maintaining social stability.

In 1572, the aged, poor, and disabled were to be "sought out, registered and assigned for their habitations and abidings." Justices of the peace were to determine weekly charges to maintain them; to tax and assess all inhabitants of every city, town, and village; and to use the proceeds for the relief of the poor. Collectors were appointed as well as overseers of the poor and work relief. Thus was started the first legislation for taxes for poor relief and the institution of overseers of the poor who were to put the able-bodied to work. Those who refused to work were sent to the houses of correction. Severe punishments were to be taken against "idlers, beggars, rogues, and vagabonds." These latter types were to receive funds only after the worthy poor had their needs met, and the able-bodied were to be helped only in return for their labor.[44]

The Poor Law Compilation of 1601

Following a period of near famine beginning around 1594, increased destitution led to periodic small rebellions and greater vagrancy. Legislation was enacted in 1597 (39 Eliz. c3) and in 1601 (43 Eliz. c2; see Box 1) that systematized earlier laws.

These laws provided for the implementation of a national system of Poor Laws, placing greater emphasis on civil power. It became compulsory for every parish to provide for the poor by levying a tax on all occupiers of property within its bounds. Relief was to be locally financed and administered for local residents. An unpaid parish officer—the overseer of the poor—was appointed to collect the tax and see that it was spent on relief, to apprentice the children of paupers to a trade, and to assign work to the able-bodied poor. Piecework

---

BOX 1 THE CHIEF PROVISIONS OF THE 1601 POOR LAWS

1. A central administration was formed to ensure implementation of the laws throughout England.

2. Each parish was responsible to provide for the poor by levying a tax on occupiers of property.

3. Unpaid officers—overseers of the poor and church wardens—were appointed to collect taxes, spend the funds on poor relief, assign work to the able-bodied, and apprentice the children of paupers.

4. Parents were responsible for their children and grandchildren, as were the grandchildren and children for the grandparents.

5. Justices of the peace were to send to jail those who did not pay their poor taxes or refused to work.

6. Parishes could call upon other parishes when they were unable to provide relief for their poor.

was to be arranged for persons in their own homes to repay the charity of the local community. It was the responsibility of the overseers and of the church wardens to take care of the various categories of poor people: able-bodied, disabled, children, aged, blind, or those who for other reasons were impoverished. Direct grants were available for the unemployable and a work policy existed for those who were able-bodied. Parents with means were liable for their children and grandchildren. Children with means were responsible for parents and grandparents who were unable to work for their own sustenance.

Justices of the peace could jail those who refused to work or imprison those who did not pay the poor tax. If a parish was unable to support its own poor, it could levy other parishes for additional funds. Beyond this, a central administration was formed to ensure the execution of the laws in all parts of England. However, financing and administration of poor relief remained local. Repression had not worked, so government reluctantly assumed a responsibility to help people who could not provide for themselves.[45]

In its basic form of 1601, the worthy poor were to be housed and provided with a weekly provision. Poor children and children born out of wedlock were to be apprenticed. The laboring poor were to be given work, and the willfully idle were to be punished and forcefully employed. All these were to be administered by the overseers of the poor.

The importance of charity continued, as did the self-help efforts of the poor. Individual gifts to the poor were organized and disbursed by the church wardens through face-to-face charity, including bread and beer. Even with weekly stipends, the aged poor struggle for survival continued. The weekly pensions were not intended for the total support but only to supplement the efforts of the aged poor through work, informal and organized charity, various relief efforts and proximity to their family members. The poor also worked by delivering messages, babies, nursing the sick, washing the dead, sweeping the church, and if possible continuing to receive poor relief.[46]

Although parishes were responsible for the maintenance of their own indigent persons, there was occasional difficulty in knowing which parish was responsible. Where there was doubt, applicants would be steered to another parish. As a result, one emphatic and important alteration in the basic poor laws was the *Act of Settlement of 1662*. This statute "empowered (two) magistrates to return to his former residence any person, coming to occupy a property renting for less than ten pounds a year, who in the opinion of the overseers might at some future time become in need." The act also applied to anyone who had not been a resident for 40 days.[47] It was expected by the various parishes that they would be protected from the poor who belonged elsewhere—at least back in their own parishes.

The Act of Settlement was passed, in part, to remedy a problem created by masses of disbanded soldiers seeking work. Reportedly, this law was never rigidly enforced because a high degree of labor mobility was needed in an economically expanding society. However, such legislation strengthened the local basis of the Poor Laws, and a strong trend toward residency requirements was united with local responsibility, a theme that has continued to the present. It was only three centuries later, in *Shapiro v. Thompson* (U.S. Supreme Court, April 1969), that residency laws as a factor determining eligibility for public assistance were held to be unconstitutional in the United States. This decision finally recognized the reality that local events, at least in regard to employment, poverty, and rights to freedom of movement, were truly reflective of structural problems on a national and international scale. But, *Shapiro v. Thompson* was not the end of the issue. As late as 1999, states argued that long-term and new residents should be treated differently in relation to public assistance benefits.

During the eighteenth century, there was a growing tendency to deal stringently with able-bodied poor persons, including granting them relief only within an institution (*indoor relief*) in which they would be required to work. After this strategy failed,

Gilbert's Act (1782) required that work be found outside the workhouse for the able-bodied (and subsidized out of the poor tax). The poorhouse became an institution for the aged and infirm.

The poor relief system was a ready means for disciplining potentially disorderly persons and the laboring poor. In the closing decades of the seventeenth century and throughout the eighteenth, it is estimated that one-third of the population, despite work and good health, were unlikely to be able to support themselves on a regular basis without assistance. This led to people trying by whatever means possible to support themselves and their families. The Poor Laws were seen as a more agreeable means of controlling the poor than dealing with frequent criminal charges and executions.[48]

The statute enacted in 1601 was a summary codification of what has come to be called the Elizabethan Poor Laws, incorporating the attitudes and provisions discussed in the preceding pages. The responsibility for poor relief had been shifted from voluntary charities sponsored by the church, monasteries, foundations, guilds, and private citizens to local governments, which provided orphanages, hospitals, and almshouses for the old. These legal responsibilities were defined by national legislation with accompanying punishments for noncompliance. The control the Poor Laws exerted on individuals was related to productivity and the scarcity of manufactured goods.

> To make them available, it was necessary to have not only land and capital but also human labor. If every human being in society could somehow be converted into an operating unit and induced to work, more manufactured goods would become available. It thus became important to emphasize the virtues of work and the evils of idleness.[49]

What began in the fourteenth century as a means of dealing with a shortage of labor for agricultural work developed by the sixteenth and seventeenth centuries into an entire philosophy that demanded that the undeserving poor (the able-bodied) be controlled and dealt with punitively while the deserving poor were treated differently. This system was a result of alterations in the economic, religious, social, and governmental aspects of society. The Poor Laws then stood for almost 300 years as the basis for English and U.S. social welfare.

Speenhamland

The issue of subsidies to individuals and families has often focused on the Speenhamland experiment. The specific context in which the justices at Speenhamland decided to create a subsidy is significant. In 1794 and 1795 (including the severe winter of 1794–1795), there had been short harvests and high prices. Imports were sparse because the Baltic Sea was frozen well into spring, thus delaying food shipments from Poland and southern Prussia. England also was at war with France, which was seizing English vessels, and the armed forces needed grain. These factors led to a steep rise in the price of bread, a staple food, and there were increases in destitution, starvation, discontent, and bread riots.

In 1795, meeting at the Pelican Inn at Speenhamland, Berkshire, England, the justices of the peace decided to pay subsidies to currently employed individuals and families when the cost of bread rose to one shilling. The justices chose to provide the subsidy rather than regulate wages. They urged farmers and others to raise laborers' wages, recommended that a few areas be set aside for the poor to grow potatoes for their own use and sale, and suggested that fuel be collected in the summer for cheap sale in the winter. The subsidy, called the "bread scale," received much publicity. The pension list previously consisted of women, many widows, children, invalids, and old men. Suddenly, with the enactment of the Speenhamland system, the majority of new names were of men. The subsidy supplemented agricultural wages on a scale that varied with the price of bread and the size of the laborer's family.

The supplementation of low and inadequate wages was not a new development at Speenhamland. *Outdoor relief* (relief in one's own home) was widespread from 1760 to 1795, preceding Speenhamland's subsidy. Parishes adopted outdoor relief policies as a response to two major changes in the southern and eastern parts of England: a decline in allotments of land for agricultural laborers and a decline in cottage industries. Parishes responded to the lost income caused by these developments by guaranteeing seasonally unemployed laborers a minimum weekly poor relief income. These subsidies were not intended to cover maintenance needs but were supplementary to low and inadequate wages. There are definite instances in which allowances were provided for men with families too large to be supported by their wages. This practice was well established at the close of the seventeenth century.[50] Farmers were thus subsidized by other parish taxpayers because rural areas were dominated by labor-hiring farmers.

There were objections to the subsidy. According to one view, the subsidy led to ambiguity in the distinction between pauperism and independence. The fear was that the Speenhamland subsidy system was undermining the initiative and independence of agricultural laborers. Critics believed that the expansion of poor relief promoted dependency on the parish and resulted in making laborers paupers, dependent on community funds. Such fears strengthened the idea that no outdoor relief should be given to the able-bodied poor except when they were maintained in a workhouse. Further, their lives should be regulated and made less comfortable than those outside and fending for themselves; that is, they should be "less eligible."

The Speenhamland system transformed the character of poor relief. All those employed or unemployed whose income fell below a minimum subsistence level were now entitled to assistance. This led to soaring costs and led to intensification of a return to Poor Law policies

A prior history and tradition existed for supplementing inadequate wages in the parishes. The poor were put to work on the land where they were needed in a process called "going the rounds" and were given relief at what was considered an appropriate level. Able-bodied persons became regular recipients of relief, and employers took advantage of the system to maintain wages at a low level.[51]

The *roundsman* system provided for the pauper-laborer to go from house to house seeking work. If work was provided, he received food for the day and a small wage, while the parish paid a supplemental sum. In some places the Poor Law administrator contracted with employers who would pay a fixed sum for a certain number of poor laborers; the workers' wages were supplemented by relief funds. Another method used was the labor rate. A parish tax was levied to cover the support of the able-bodied unemployed, and a price was set for their services. Taxpayers could employ a number of paupers at the appropriate wage or pay the tax. In all cases allowances were used to restore order by enforcing work at very low wage levels.[52]

Following the implementation of the Speenhamland system in many parts of England, criticism that has a familiar ring was voiced. It was surmised allowances would undermine individual responsibility, lead people to produce children recklessly, and deplete productivity. Furthermore, such allowances, it was thought, would alter fundamentally the basic psychology of "necessary" goading and encourage freedom of choice in regard to work. Moreover, it would cost too much. Essentially this argument derives from the belief that people must be forced to produce. From another point of view, at times subsidies are needed even by the working poor to prevent starvation and to provide a healthier family life in order to best support productivity and society in general.

After the beginning of the nineteenth century the birthrate did not rise dramatically as predicted, and historians differ as to whether productivity actually fell or rose under the Speenhamland system.[53] One of the lessons of Speenhamland is that such subsidies do not necessarily result in less productive workers or increased birthrates.

Debates on wage supplementation continue today, following the basic arguments established when Speenhamland was in operation. So long as we operate on the theory of the economic being, wage supplementation may demean the labor market, in the sense that employers may lower wages by taking the supplementation into account. The basic problem is that of *less eligibility*: the belief that no person on relief should be paid as much as the lowest wage earner in the community for fear such a wage will impair the labor market. For those who accept the economic view of human beings, such supplements will prove counterproductive by diminishing the motivations of those at the poverty level and those just above it.

The Workhouse

By 1662, urban poverty was an increasing problem. As we saw earlier, destitute individuals were the responsibility of their parish of birth. When sent to their parish of origin, they often took dependent children with them. These children were strangers to the parish, a factor that was even more problematic for those orphaned or abandoned children who were completely unfamiliar to the parish residents. Children whose parents died or disappeared seemed to have no real connection to the parish to which they were removed. This led to great resentment. Sometimes they were apprenticed at the ratepayers' (taxpayers') expense and sometimes placed in a workhouse.

In 1723, the English Parliament authorized any parish to establish a workhouse. The poor were to produce goods that would earn money for the state. Typically, notice would be given to the poor that their weekly pensions were to be discontinued. Those who were unable to support themselves could apply for admission to the workhouse.

By the end of the eighteenth century, about 20 percent of all paupers on permanent relief were in workhouses. Most communities of market-town size had a workhouse. By 1803, there were 3,765 workhouses in England. Those housed included neglected children, able-bodied paupers of both sexes, aged and impotent persons, mothers who bore children out of wedlock, prostitutes, the blind, mentally ill, those who were developmentally disabled, immigrants, vagrants, and criminals. Discipline was loose. Eventually, the workhouses reached a point where they were mainly for the helpless poor and they rarely employed the able-bodied. The elderly and children predominated.[54]

According to one contemporary quotation, "A workhouse is a name that carries along with it an idea of correction and punishment and many of our poor have taken such an aversion to living in it, as all the reason and argument in the world can never overcome."[55] All categories of the poor were housed under one roof, including "fallen" women, the insane, the old, children, paupers, the sick, the disabled, and vagrants. The problems of the workhouses were so bad that in 1762 the Act for Keeping Poor Children Alive was passed. This law required parishes to maintain records of all children admitted to the workhouses so death rates for institutions and their caretakers could be ascertained.

Infant death in the workhouses took place within a particular historical context. The rise of the propertyless within the population stimulated child abandonment and infanticide. During the eighteenth century, many abandoned infants were sent to parish workhouses, where they died from starvation, beatings, and disease. Overseers of the poor sometimes received lump sum payments from the father or putative father for an infant born out of wedlock. Overseers sometimes murdered such children for the profit to be made from the lump sum payment. At London's Foundling Hospital during its first four years of existence (1741–1745), of the 15,000 children placed there, approximately 10,000 died. In Dublin from 1790 to 1796, of 12,600 children placed in a hospital, almost 10,000 died. Although some abandoned children were born out of wedlock, the majority were from couples unable to support them. There are estimates that in eighteenth-century Europe anywhere from 10 percent to 40 percent of urban children were abandoned.[56]

By the nineteenth century, 3,800 workhouses existed in England with approximately 83,500 residents. Despite the widespread use of the workhouse, relief of the poor in their own homes (outdoor relief) was the predominant mode of subsidy, utilizing both in-kind and monetary payments.[57]

Workhouses fell short of their goals. The major aim of the workhouses, which was the profitable employment of the poor, proved to be unsuccessful. Workhouse labor had to be inefficient: The laborers were either incapable or unwilling. Workhouses were not capable of providing work in spinning and weaving, precisely those tasks more and more performed by machines. The training some children received proved to be obsolete. In other cases, the use of the workhouse as a punitive deterrent, as a house of correction, was contradictory to the aim of production. Thus, the principles of deterrence and of profitable employment conflicted.

The evidence suggests that workhouses gave only temporary relief to the tax rates. The harshness of the workhouses encountered growing criticism, while many institutions became "unsupervised asylums for a mixed population of the impotent and the vicious, and (unfortunately) children."[58]

The Poor Law of 1834

At the beginning of the nineteenth century, the tax to be paid for the poor rose rapidly, as did per capita expenditures for the poor in the latter part of the eighteenth century. Following the defeat of Napoleon, unemployment increased, food prices fell, many small farmers faced bankruptcy, and starvation forced people to apply for relief. Parishes drove paupers out of their territories, and the enactment of the Corn Law of 1815 increased the price of bread while wages remained low. The Corn Laws created import tariffs to protect corn prices (grain and cereal crops) against competition from less expensive foreign imports. Doing so enhanced the profits and political power of land owners.

In 1832, a royal commission was established to review the Poor Laws. The commission was biased against the poor from the start and was supported by several ideological strands derived from Adam Smith, Thomas Malthus, and Jeremy Bentham. Adam Smith, a theoretician of laissez-faire capitalism, believed that the private interests of individuals in the market were led by an "invisible hand" toward the interest of the whole society. Government should passively police the market and has only three duties: (1) protect society from invasion and violence by other societies; (2) protect, as far as possible, members of society from injustice and oppression of every other member of it; and (3) develop and maintain public works and institutions that can never be the interest of any individual or small group to create and maintain. He believed in the liberty of the individual and free trade among nations.

Thomas Malthus suggested that the human species would breed itself into starvation and ruin. The geometric increase in population that resulted from each woman's ability to produce multiple children would be greater than the ability to increase food supplies. As a result, Malthus concluded pessimistically that misery and vice would spread. Further, the increase in population would decrease demand for labor and result in lowered wages, which would increase suffering even more. The poor could only achieve prosperity by abstaining from reproduction (an impossible task). The resources given to undeserving and unproductive paupers can only be given at the expense of deserving laborers because to do so raises the price of food and reduces real wages. Relief leads to increased poverty, whereas the more severe the attitude toward the poor, the greater the true benevolence.[59]

Jeremy Bentham was an exponent of utilitarianism. The "good" equals adding to the sum total of pleasures or diminishing the sum total of pain for a community. In social and economic matters, government should have a hands-off policy. It was his belief that the greatest good for the greatest number would be reached when salaries arrived at their true level in a free-market system with no state control. However, this idea is based on the assumption there is a free market and employers would not collude against low earners keeping their pay at low levels, with the workhouse always in the background.

In 1834, the Reform Poor Law (the New Poor Law) was enacted. Outdoor relief would be available for the sick and the aged but not for the able-bodied. No relief would be given to able-bodied persons unless they were residents of the workhouse, a highly stigmatized institution. There would be a three-member central Poor Law commission with the power to group parishes into unions for Poor Law administration and to supervise the work of local authorities. Poor Law guardians elected by local taxpayers would be in charge of the disbursement of local relief. The principle of less eligibility and punitive stigmatization of relief recipients were basic principles of the new law.

However, the 1834 law was a compromise enactment in that strict Malthusians, laissez-faire economists, and others wanted a law that completely put an end to Poor Law relief. In reality, one of the motivations for the revised law was to reduce poor taxes, which did in fact occur following the enactment of the 1834 law, although good harvests and the building of railways undoubtedly had some effect on this drop. The trend soon reversed itself and taxes began to climb once again, although more modestly than in the past. It is likely that voluntary charity played some part in minimizing the need for more rapidly expanding public assistance. However, some fifteen years after the enactment of the New Poor Law of 1834, which was intended primarily to do away with outdoor relief, five times as many people were relieved outside the workhouses as were being given relief inside them.

Still more complex motivations impelled the attempt to abolish outdoor relief. Farming communities were actually in favor of retaining subsidies such as Speenhamland's. However, Parliament was dominated by large landowners who were convinced that outdoor relief was a threat to their rental incomes. On the other hand, grain farmers developed such subsidies as an inexpensive means to provide income for seasonally unemployed workers. So the original abolishment of subsidies was not because it had disastrous effects on the rural economy. Instead it was because landowners who controlled Parliament feared such future consequences.[60]

After 1834, there were two priorities: (1) transfer surplus population from rural to industrial districts where labor was scarce and (2) save the urban rate (tax) payers from the costs of the rural settlers. The workhouse responded to the first priority, and removal of people under the Settlement Laws answered the second priority. The repression of the able-bodied male pauperism and reduction of the taxes coupled with a vigorous development of workhouses was intended to deal with the two major priorities.[61]

The attitudes exemplified by the 1834 law reflected values with long histories. For example, a prevalent idea was that individual moral delinquency resulted in impoverishment. Deterrence was the solution. There was a belief that with the abolishment of outdoor relief, the end of wage subsidies, and forcing the able-bodied off the rolls and into the labor market, poverty would disappear. The point was made sharply by an observer late in the eighteenth century who stated: "Everyone but an idiot knows that the lower classes must be kept poor or they will never be industrious."[62]

Principles of the Poor Laws

As we have seen, the principles by which treatment of the poor was determined changed dramatically after the thirteenth century. The Poor Laws evolved as a result of changing features of society, including the dissolution of the feudal system, the alteration of the churches, the emphasis on individual responsibility, and the growth of international money and trade economies. All these factors combined to ensure a market in which labor was simply another resource to be maintained. The series of Poor Laws was created to maintain a motivated work force available for productive employment as well as to minimize the number of shiftless vagrants who might commit violent acts and the number of those dependent on the community.

The Poor Laws themselves were based on and slowly evolved several principles for dealing with the poor that have remained with us, sometimes in disguised form but often explicitly. Secularism was established as the basic direction of social welfare, despite the existence of a religious social welfare subsystem. Whereas during the Middle Ages there existed both a governmental and a church system, along with other voluntary systems, gradually social welfare became a public responsibility—that is, a secular task for the entire body politic. This development is part of the rise of nation-states, with their need to care for their citizens in order to maintain morale and build the nation. It is also a result of the secularization trend that has evolved over centuries, by which certain church functions and controls have been shifted to public and governmental bodies. The powers of the church system and the demands it could make on people diminished, while the demands of the nation-state on its citizens increased. Although recent U.S. history has seen a shift away from federal responsibility and toward state, local, and voluntary welfare efforts, overall the provision of social welfare for the masses remains the responsibility of the taxing authority: the secular state.

The concept of risk or categories also developed as a principle. For example, not only were the poor divided into categories—aged, children, lame, ill, and so forth—but also these categories were further defined in moral terms: *the worthy and the unworthy poor.* Such definitions led to *means-testing,* or establishing need on the basis of one's income (which has to be below the level required to purchase necessary goods or services). These definitions were congenial to the view that the poor had caused their own poverty, were morally at fault, and could by sufficient motivation and willpower alter their life circumstances. Such views of the poor remain with us, accompanied by the idea that poverty should be punished, a remnant of philosophies centuries old. Whereas in the Middle Ages all poor were given assistance without consideration of the "category" they were in, now one differentiates between those who are worthy or unworthy of receiving assistance.

Another principle was the establishment of the distinction between indoor and outdoor relief. When work was demanded from the poor (a demand present in the early monasteries as well), they would have to take shelter in a public house or hospital (indoor), whereas others "more deserving" would be supported in their own homes (outdoor). The outdoor–indoor controversy, of which the workhouse is the prime example, continues today in terms of community care for those with chronic mental illness, persons with developmental disabilities, juvenile delinquents, and others.

Residency laws, as a principle, required that laborers be tied to their lords and employers and then to their home parishes or place of birth. Binding people to places (a throwback to serfdom) served to minimize their bargaining power through restrictions on their freedom to move and thus set limits on what employers had to pay as wages. Thus, residency laws served important economic purposes and had the intention of maintaining a pool of available labor for production accompanied by control over wages.

The principles of *less eligibility* and *wage supplementation* are hotly debated even today. The question of less eligibility (the poor must not be supported at a level as high as that of the lowest employed person in the community) is one of the most intractable problems in social welfare policy. The establishment of less eligibility recognized this problem and provided a solution based on the assumption that humans are economic beings.

The solution, however, has proved problematic. Although the original intent for less eligibility assumed that the poor could be motivated only by economic deprivation, the results of following such a principle are open to question. As we saw in the case of Speenhamland, the "payoff" was really not for the employees but actually was a use of public means to subsidize employers: The main effect of the allowance system was to depress wages below the subsistence level. Methods need to be found to deal with this problem, especially ways that recognize the structural nature of high unemployment and poverty in a multinational, technological economy.

Finally, the fact that the social problems of the needy were approached by and large on a *case-by-case* basis has supported the assumption that the problem rests with the individual or family. Such views are still subtly expressed in current social work when insufficient attention is paid to the structural determinants of social need and too much emphasis is placed on the responsibility of individuals and families. Such views have far-reaching implications for social welfare.

Summary

In this chapter, we surveyed the major trends and social welfare events from the Middle Ages to the early nineteenth century in England. We also examined some of the moral, religious, philosophical, and economic theories and principles behind the practices, institutions, and laws developed to deal with the poor.

Questions for Consideration

1. What were the benefits and limitations for individuals and families in a *status* relationship, and what are they in a *contract* relationship?
2. What relationships can you identify between the Poor Laws and people's ideas about social welfare today?

3. Have any states or the Congress recently attempted to make residency laws regarding social welfare? Does anything stand in their way? For some groups? For all groups?
4. Did Speenhamland provide a family allowance, a wage supplementation, or a subsidy for employers? Do any of these exist in the United States today?
5. Is there anything in the United States today that is like—in any way—the workhouse earlier in England?

MySearchLab CONNECTIONS

Watch and Review

Watch These Videos

Atlantic Connections: Sugar, Smallpox, and Slavery

Creating Apartheid in South Africa

Read and Review

Read These Cases/Documents

Before the Birth of One of Her Children (c. 1650)

Jane Addams, The Subjective Necessity of Social Settlements, 1892

Explore and Assess

Explore These Assets

Social Work History Station, The - http://www.boisestate.edu/socwork/dhuff/xx.htm

American Sociological Association -http;//www.asanet.org/

Assess Your Knowledge

Assess your knowledge with a variety of topical and chapter assessment.

Conclude your assessment by completing the chapter exam.

* = CSWE Core Competency Asset

Δ = Case Study

Notes

1. Clayton Roberts and David Roberts, *A History of England: Prehistory to 1714*, Vol. 1, 2nd ed., Englewood Cliffs, NJ: Prentice Hall, 1985, pp. 75–81.
2. L. C. B. Seaman, *A New History of England, 410–1975*, Totowa, NJ: Barnes and Noble, 1982, pp. 114–120.
3. Fernand Braudel, *The Structures of Everyday Life*, New York: Harper & Row, 1979, p. 74.
4. Rodney Hilton, Bond Men Made Free: *Medieval Peasant Movements and the English Rising of 1381*, New York: Viking Press, 1973, p. 65.
5. Ibid., p. 86.
6. Brian Tierney, *Medieval Poor Law*, Berkeley, CA: University of California Press, 1959, p. 12.
7. Ibid., p. 37.
8. Ibid., p. 11.
9. Joseph R. Strayer and Dana C. Munro, *The Middle Ages, 395–1500*, New York: Appleton-Century-Crofts, 1970, p. 130.
10. Hilton, op.cit., pp. 15–16, 86, 88.
11. Richard W. Southern, *The Making of the Middle Ages*, New Haven, CT: Yale University Press, 1970, pp. 106–107.
12. George Holmes, *Europe: Hierarchy and Revolt 1320–1450*, Second Edition, Oxford, UK: Blackwell Publishers, 2000, p. 94.
13. Brian Tierney, *Medieval Poor Law*, Berkeley, CA: University of California Press, 1959, p. 109.
14. David Nicholas, *The Evolution of the Medieval World: Government and Thought in Europe, 312–1500*, New York: Longman, 1992, p. 410.
15. Brian Tierney, *Medieval Poor Law*, Berkeley, CA: University of California Press, 1959, p. 61.
16. J. Gilchrist, *The Church and Economic Activity in the Middle Ages*, New York: Macmillan, 1969, p. 79. According to Gilchrist, the income expended on charity never exceeded 5 percent. However, Pound suggests the percentage of monastic income devoted to charity ranged from less than 1 percent to more than 22 percent. But even Pound finds that the generosity of some houses was insufficient to raise the national average to 2.5 percent. See John Pound, *Poverty and Vagrancy in Tudor England*, London: Longman, 1975, pp. 21–22.
17. Roland Bainton, *The Penguin History of Christianity*, Vol. 2, Harmondsworth, UK: Penguin, 1967, p. 9.
18. Karl de Schweinitz, *England's Road to Social Security*, New York: A. S. Barnes & Company, 1975, p. 15.
19. W. K. Jordan, *Philanthropy in England: 1480–1660*, London: Allen & Unwin, 1959, p. 41.
20. Gilchrist, op. cit.
21. de Schweinitz, p. 17.
22. Gilchrist, op. cit.
23. Recent research hypothesizes that the Black Death was not solely the result of bubonic plague but probably also caused by anthrax or some similar disease spread by cattle. See John Kelly, *The Great MortalityAn Intimate History of the Black Death, the Most Devastating Plague of All Time. New York*: Harper and Collins Publishers, 2005, p.113.
24. Robert S. Gottfried, *The Black Death: Natural and Human Disaster in Medieval Europe*, New York: Free Press, 1983, pp. xii, xvi, 86, 135.
25. Ibid., pp. 97–98.
26. Ibid., p. 98.
27. Ibid., p. 94.
28. Hilton, p. 155.
29. Barbara W. Tuchman, *A Distant Mirror: The Calamitous 14th Century*, New York: Knopf, 1978, p. 124. One historian suggests about this period that "if it was a golden age, it was the golden age of bacteria." Sylvia L. Thrupp, "The Problem of Replacement-Rates in Medieval English Population," in *Society and History*, Raymond Grew and Nicholas H. Steneck, eds., Ann Arbor, MI: University of Michigan Press, 1977, p. 186.
30. Brian Tierney and Sidney Painter, *Western Europe in the Middle Ages, 300–1475*, New York: Knopf, 1978, pp. 511–512.
31. Barbara W. Tuchman, *A Distant Mirror: The Calamitous 14th Century*, New York: Knopf, 1978, pp. 125–126.
32. Roland Bainton, *The Reformation of the Sixteenth Century*, Boston, MA: Beacon Press, 1964, p. 246.
33. Max Weber, *The Protestant Ethic and the Spirit of Capitalism*, Los Angeles, CA: Roxbury, 1998, passim.
34. William J. Bouwsma, *John Calvin: A Sixteenth-Century Portrait*, New York: Oxford University Press, 1988, p. 74.
35. See Bainton; Georgia Harkness, *John Calvin: The Man and the Ethics*, New York: Abingdon Press, 1958, pp. 182–183; and R. H. Tawney, *Religion and the Rise of Capitalism*, New York: Mentor Books, 1950, passim.
36. The distinction must be made between the original writings of Calvin and Calvinism as it developed. Weber and Tawney suggest that Calvinism equates amassing wealth with a sign of individual grace and election. Their view is that Calvinism thus contributed to the development of capitalism. Calvin himself, however, did not regard prosperity in this life as associated with election. See John T. McNeill, ed., *Calvin: Institutes of the Christian Religion*, Philadelphia, PA: Westminster Press, 1960, in particular p. 438.

37. David Nicholas, *The Evolution of the Medieval World: Society, Government and Thought in Europe, 312–1500*, New York: Longman, 1992, p. 410.

38. Karl Polanyi, *The Great Transformation*, Boston, MA: Beacon Press, 1960, pp. 40, 42.

39. de Schweinitz, pp. 20–22.

40. John Pound, *Poverty and Vagrancy in Tudor England*, London: Longman, 1975, pp. 16–24; and David Loades, *Revolution in Religion: The English Reformation, 1530–1570*, Cardiff, UK: University of Wales, 1992, p. 90.

41. de Schweinitz, pp. 22–23.

42. Brian Pullan, *Rich and Poor in Renaissance Venice*, Cambridge, MA: Harvard University Press, 1971, pp. 239–240.

43. Jan L. Hagen, "Whatever Happened to 43 Elizabeth I, c2? *Social Service Review*, 56 (1), 1982, pp. 108–119.

44. Anthony Brundage, *The English Poor Laws 1700–1930*, New York: Palgrave, 2002, p. 9; and Sidney and Beatrice Webb, *English Poor Law History, Part 1, The Old Poor Law*, London: Frank Case, 1963, pp. 52–66.

45. Sidney and Beatrice Webb, *English Poor Law History*, Part 1, *The Old Poor Law*, London: Frank Case, 1963, pp. 52–66.

46. L. A. Botelho,The Aged Parish Parishioner, *Old Age and the English Poor Law 1500-1700*, Rochester, NY: The Boydell Press, 2004, pp. 104–152.

47. John R. Poynter, *Society and Pauperism*, London: Routledge & Kegan Paul, 1969, p. 50; and Brundage, op. cit., p. 48.

48. J. A. Sharpe, *Crime in Early Modern England*, London: Longman, 1984, pp. 91, 184.

49. Robert Boguslaw, *The New Utopians*, Englewood Cliffs, NJ: Prentice Hall, 1965, pp. 132, 134.

50. George R. Boyer, *An Economic History of the English Poor Law 1750–1850*, New York: Cambridge University Press, 1990, pp. 265–267; and Dorothy Marshall, "The Old Poor Law, 1662–1795," in *Essays in Economic History*, Eleanora Mary Carus-Wilson, ed., London: Edward Arnold Publishers, 1954, p. 304.

51. Geoffrey W. Oxley, *Poor Relief in England and Wales, 1601–1834*, London: David and Charles, 1974, p. 113; and Michael Rose, *The Relief of Poverty, 1834–1914*, London: Macmillan, 1981, p. 8.

52. Catherina Lis and Hugo Soly, *Poverty and Capitalism in Pre-Industrial Europe*, Atlantic Highlands, NJ: Humanities Press, 1979, p. 199.

53. According to Marcus, a fall in production accompanied a rise in the poor rates (taxes); Steven Marcus, "Their Brothers' Keepers: An Episode from English History," in *Doing Good,* W. Gaylin, Ira Glasser, Steven Marcus, and David J. Rothman, eds., New York: Pantheon, 1978, p. 49. According to Blaug, however, the allowances did not encourage people to "breed recklessly" and did not devitalize the working class; furthermore, after the turn of the century, there was an increase in production. Blaug suggests that the allowance systems were almost entirely a rural problem in particular parts of the country. The device was chosen to deal with surplus labor in a lagging sector of an expanding but underdeveloped economy; it was a method for dealing with problems of structural unemployment and substandard wages. According to this view, the allowance system contributed to economic expansion. Mark Blaug, "The Myth of the Old Poor Law and the Making of the New," *Journal of Economic History,* 23 (2), June 1963, pp. 151–184; and Mark Blaug, "The Poor Law Report Reexamined," *Journal of Economic History,* 24 (2), June 1964, pp. 229–245.

54. Margaret A. Crowther, *The Workhouse System 1834–1929*, Athens, GA; The University of Georgia Press, 1982, pp. 24–25, 28.

55. Frank Crompton, *Workhouse Children*, Phoenix Mill, UK: Sutton Publishing, 1997, p. 3; and Norman Longmate, *The Workhouse*, London: Temple Smith, 1974, p. 24.

56. See Lawrence Stone, *The Family, Sex and Marriage in England 1500–1800*, New York: Harper & Row, 1977, pp. 473–478; and John Boswell, *The Kindness of Strangers: The Abandonment of Children in Western Europe from Late Antiquity to the Renaissance*, New York: Pantheon, 1988, p. 40.

57. John R. Poynter, *Society and Pauperism*, London: Routledge & Kegan Paul, 1969, p. 189.

58. Ibid., pp. 14–17.

59. Robert Pinker, *Social Theory and Social Policy*, London: Heinemann Educational Books, 1973, pp. 55–61.

60. George R. Boyer, *An Economic History of the English Poor Law 1750–1850*, New York: Cambridge University Press, 1990, p. 267.

61. David Englander, *Poverty and Poor Law Reform in Britain 1834–1914*, New York: Longman, 1998, p. 7.

62. David Englander, *Poverty and Poor Law Reform in Britain 1834–1914*, New York: Longman, 1998, pp. 5, 81.

The Colonial Period: 1647–1776

The Historical Society of Pennsylvania

The Colonial Period: 1647–1776

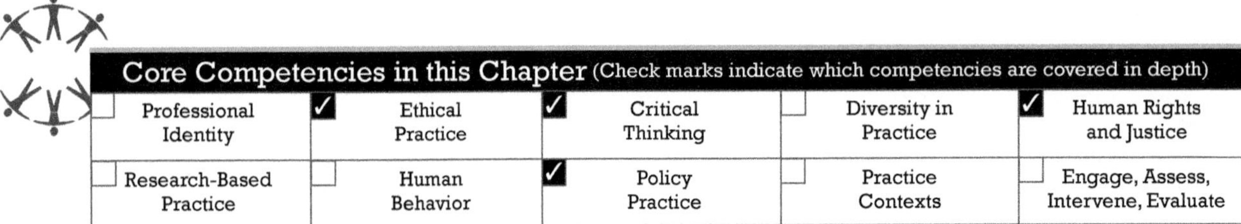

	Professional Identity	✓ Ethical Practice	✓ Critical Thinking	Diversity in Practice	✓ Human Rights and Justice
	Research-Based Practice	Human Behavior	✓ Policy Practice	Practice Contexts	Engage, Assess, Intervene, Evaluate

The earliest white settlers of New England came to North America to establish the ideal religious community, "a city upon a hill," that would provide an example for European reform. Yet, as soon as they arrived, they were confronted with a set of realities that forced them to adapt their ways. A radically different ecology, complex relationships with Native Americans, and different economic and demographic realities forced them to tailor the institutions they had brought from England—including the Poor Laws—to these new realities.

As early as 1647, at the first session of its colonial legislature, Rhode Island announced the Elizabethan Poor Law principles that stressed, most importantly, public responsibility for relief of the poor who could not work, and work for the able-bodied:

> It is agreed and ordered by this present Assembly, that each towne shall provide carefully for the relief of the poor, to maintain the impotent, and to employ the able, and shall appoint an overseer for the same purpose. Sec. 43 Eliz.[1]

Needy widows and their children would receive aid but were expected to help with their own support by working. Those judged able to work and those who had worked in the past were expected to support themselves through work. They were not generally eligible for public aid even though they might be poor, despite working.

Considering the severe economic and physical privations of the early settlers, it is not surprising that public responsibility for relief should have been buttressed by the principles of English Poor Law: local responsibility, family responsibility, and the residency requirement of legal settlement. These principles had been evolving in England and Western Europe for some 200 years and had been codified in 1601 in the Poor Law.

The principle of local responsibility made public aid the domain of towns and cities. Family responsibility originally denoted the legal obligation of support that adults had for their minor children and grandchildren and for their aged parents. Settlement, added in 1662, made a designated period of residence a requirement for the receipt of assistance. Settlement—the fact that only residents of a particular community were entitled to aid—was a response to the new economic realities of early modern Britain. Population growth had combined with new commercial opportunities to push a large share of the rural population off the land. Although the emergence of textile and mining industries offered new opportunities, the supply of labor outstripped the new demand. The ultimate effect was the creation of a large class of mobile labor—vagabonds, beggars, and tramps—who were no longer tied to a particular locality. These sturdy vagabonds, the beggars, and the unemployed poor, whose numbers and potential for civil disorder loomed frighteningly large, were people caught in the middle of forces beyond their control. They were people in need, and the Poor Laws, in providing public relief, were designed to meet—and control—their needs.[2]

The terms upon which relief was offered reflected much more than the interests of the poor. Parliament was subject to conflicting pressures. The owners of large farms wanted to ensure the availability of local, low-cost, seasonal workers; the emerging industrialists needed to encourage the migration of factory labor; town officials wanted to minimize the need to levy taxes to support the homeless. The decision of Parliament to make local settlement an eligibility condition for relief reflected the power of the landed gentry. In supporting this interest, the government provided an incentive for labor to remain on the farms—the risk of leaving was clear. At the same time, they were able to satisfy the towns' concern for minimizing local costs. Furthermore, by limiting the mobility of the poor, government could respond to the interest of landowners and of industrialists in maintaining law and order.

In accordance with the Act of Settlement of 1662, newcomers could be returned to their place of legal residence even though there was no actual application for assistance.

> That it shall and may be lawful upon complaint made by the churchwardens or overseers of the Poor of any Parish . . . for any two Justices of the Peace . . . where any Person or Persons are likely to be chargeable to the Parish shall come to inhabit . . . to remove and convey such Person or Persons to such Parish where he or they were last legally settled.[3]

The policy objectives of the Poor Laws, however, could be shifted to respond to changing conditions. By 1795, as urban centers grew and immigration increased, the Poor Laws were amended to control relief costs. Behavioral restrictions on relief recipients increased, and punishment, including whipping for not working, became more widespread. Residency requirements were made stiffer, but the penalties for vagrancy eased. A passport system was introduced, permitting increased mobility of labor between communities.

THE POOR LAWS IN THE COLONIES

Although the long evolution of the Poor Laws in England served both as a hindrance and as an aid to the process of commercial development, that evolution was always contingent on the availability of masses of workers. The climate of the American colonies was strikingly different. There was no persistent unemployment problem; no mass of employables had been pushed off the land; no industries existed to pull workers into towns; no pool of workers awaited hiring. Initially there was neither an economic reason nor a law-and-order reason to reduce mobility. The rationale for the adoption of the Poor Laws rested on other grounds.

In the main, those colonists who were potential recipients of relief were the poor who were largely incapable of self-support: the ill, the disabled, the elderly, orphans, and widows with young children. Widows and their children made up a large percentage of the poor—as high as half in some towns.[4]

Frequent wars, in part a response by Native Americans to the invasion of their land by the settlers; recurring epidemics of smallpox, dysentery, measles, and yellow fever; major uncontrollable fires; high child mortality rates; the hazards of fishing and the consequent loss of life at sea—all gave rise to economic need. These risks to which the colonists were subject were ones for which all held common concern. The colonists were small bands of individuals joined together in enterprises whose success depended upon the contribution and well-being of each. The smallness of their numbers made it possible to keep friendly, public watch over individual misfortunes. Their isolation made this public watch over community affairs a matter of individual self-interest. The Poor Laws ensured individual and public protection. Those settled colonists known to be in need through no fault of their own could be helped with cash relief in their own homes or in the homes of neighbors. Relief for people in home—that is, family—settings was well regarded because of the order and stability such settings promised for the community as a whole.

In seventeenth-century New England, the modern boundaries between public and private and church and state would have made little sense. Community leaders sought to ensure that sinful behavior was suppressed, including idleness, which in an agricultural society could threaten everyone's well-being. At first, there was no voluntary sector to respond to people's troubles. The Scots Charitable Society was established in Boston in 1657.[5] In 1713, the Friends Almshouse was established in Philadelphia to provide relief for poor Quakers.[6] In 1724, the Boston Episcopal Society was formed, and in 1767, the Society of House Carpenters was organized in New York.[7]

Voluntary responses to need remain an enduring feature of American social welfare. Yet, like later efforts, the resources of colonial charitable societies and churches fell far short of the need they sought to address. Thus, in many respects, the Poor Laws seemed a rational approach to a severe problem. The laws offered some support to the disabled and served as a deterrent to the able-bodied who might consider not working. The specific provisions regarding settlement and family responsibility limited the number of inhabitants for whose relief the town might be called upon to accept responsibility.

The family (and its structure) was a central force for maintaining economic, social, and political stability. The vast majority of the colonists were farmers, and their farms were isolated, small, and poorly equipped. For the most part, these farming families had to supply their own food, clothing, and equipment, as well as their own education, entertainment, and health care. Family governance was hierarchical—generally with the husband in command. Women were not entitled to vote, had little part in governance, and lived in patriarchal families. Indeed, even their clothing was designed to show their sexual subordination.[8] Within this structure, all persons made valued contributions. Men and boys cleared fields, farmed, cut wood, and trapped. Women and girls spun thread, engaged in weaving, turned cloth into clothes, and took responsibility for myriad internal household chores. Men and women together worked to produce and to improve whatever implements, utensils, furniture, and weapons the household needed.

Childbearing was viewed as a productive contribution to the family economy, because young children often took on important chores and older children served as a form of social security for their aging parents. If the husband were killed or disabled, the wife moved naturally into the family and economic role he had held. In English colonies, more than in Spanish or Portuguese colonies, women in the Colonial period could—and did—hold property, run small businesses, and work for wages.[9]

During the eighteenth century, even as the colonies became more firmly established and the colonists benefited from improved technology, expanding commercial activities and shipbuilding, and increased trade with the native population, home manufactures continued to flourish. Improvements in the spinning wheel—particularly after 1765, when the invention of the spinning jenny made it possible for a person to spin eight to ten yarns simultaneously—made possible some home production for market sale. With men continuing to concentrate on farming, the newly oriented home manufacturing fell largely to women. In effect, women—and children—began to expand a function that had long been theirs, and did so in their own homes so that their work was easily integrated into family life.

The increasing centrality of women's work to the colonial economy drove a number of changes. In 1750, Boston opened a group of spinning schools for female children. In 1751, the Society for Encouraging Industry and Employing the Poor was founded to promote the manufacture of woolen cloth and to employ "our own women and children who are now in great measure idle."[10] The Massachusetts Province Laws of 1753–1754 supported the manufacturing of linen, again with the employment of women and children in mind:

> The number of poor is greatly increased . . . and many persons, especially women and children, are destitute of employment and in danger of becoming a public charge.[11]

The colonies welcomed home manufacturing and the employment it provided. Cities and towns could cut the taxes that supported dependents and, instead, offer employment to women and children who might otherwise be "useless, if not burdensome, to society."[12]

The dire language of the Poor Laws and subsequent legislation designed to ensure their rigorous administration rested on cultural as well as economic factors. The popularity of spinning schools and the enthusiastic attendance at and participation in spinning bees sponsored by New England townships in the years preceding the Revolutionary War suggest the extent to which the essential isolation of the colonists had "produced a home-bred, home-living, and a home-loving people—a people who found both their employment and their pleasure in their own and their near neighbor's home."[13]

The importance of home and family was balanced against a commitment to worldly engagement that would later be labeled the "Protestant work ethic." A fuller explanation of the meaning and operation of the Poor Laws must take account of the moral underpinnings provided by Puritan Calvinism.

The New England colonists had emigrated to escape religious persecution and to seek freedom to worship in accordance with their own religious beliefs. The result was a unity of church and government peculiarly suited to New World conditions. The stark need for labor in New England required that the colonists operate with regard for the common store of wealth—that is, for profit in their joint enterprise—but they also operated out of religious necessity with regard for individual, private control of resources. With individual status and economic reward a manifestation of predestined grace, the Puritan work ethic was a conceptually useful tool for minimizing what was publicly, communally available to maximize individual and family wealth and well-being. Although poverty could not be equated with unworthiness, it could suggest—especially if public relief was necessary—a character and moral flaw that dared not be pampered for the common welfare and for the individual's state of grace. Philanthropy was encouraged, but charity reflected a concern for the salvation of the rich—the stewards of God's wealth—more than a concern for the poor. Despite the family's usefulness, the impetus to maximize individual and family well-being did not center on the individual as a family member or on the individual family as a unit. When a family was in trouble, the concern was to save its potentially productive members. Hence, there developed social welfare measures such as farming out, indenture, and apprenticeship, which provided a family structure for governance and a means for productivity.

Poor Law provisions for public aid were inconsistent in their treatment of the family as a social entity to be helped. Indeed, the provisions for relief established categories of individuals—the young, the old, the disabled, and the able-bodied. By implication, the family consisted of a number of individuals living together for the purpose of ensuring self-support and, by extension, avoiding the necessity for support by taxpayers. At the same time, the Poor Laws were quite expansive in their definition of family responsibility for supporting dependents. Not only parents and children but also grandparents and grandchildren could be tapped for support. Such designation was perhaps quite purposeful at a time when financial independence, worthiness, and divine reward were perceived as facets of individually achieved success. In this context, the family that could not maintain financial independence was not simply unsuccessful but actually dangerous, both economically and morally. Such families could not by example, precept, or education be expected to prepare the young for adult, independent living. The colonists, therefore, provided for the binding out of children as apprentices for "better educateing of youth in honest and profitable trades and manufactures, as also to avoyd sloath and idleness wherewith such young children are easily corrupted"[14] and required that in addition to a trade, children learn to "read and understand the principles of religion & the capitall lawes of this country."[15] These were preventive measures designed to protect children from the contagion of parental failures.

Unattached, neglected, or dependent children could be placed with persons willing to take responsibility for their care and who would educate and train them for a useful calling. Persons assuming such responsibility for children were expected to recoup their expenses from the child's work. Thus, indenture and apprenticeship were designed to protect against the danger of pauperism and to ensure that children were immediately profitable to themselves and to the community.

Apprenticeship reflected colonial society's concern with the home life, the work life, and the spiritual life of the child. Ideally, each child would grow up "under some orderly family government"[16] that would provide support and an opportunity for learning both for economic and for religious salvation. When the natural family did not provide these essentials, apprenticeship to a contracted family was an alternative that often eased the burden on the public treasury.

> If after warning and admonition given by any of the Deputies; or Selectmen, unto such Parents or Masters, they shall still remain negligent in their duty, in any the particulars aforementioned, whereby Children or Servants may be in danger to grow Barberous, Rude or Stubborn, and so prove Pests instead of Blessings to the Country; That then a fine of ten shillings shall be levied on the Goods of such negligent Parent or Master, to the Towns use, except extreme poverty call for mitigation of the said fine.
>
> And if in three months after that, there be no due care taken . . . then a fine of twenty shillings to be levied. . . .
>
> And Lastly, if in three months after that, there be no due Reformation of the said neglect, then the said Selectmen with the help of two Magistrates, shall take such children and servants from them, and place them with some Masters for years (boyes till they come to twenty-one, and girls eighteen years of age) which will more strictly educate and govern them according to the rules of this Order.[17]

Apprenticeship was used for economy and for control. New England colonies varied in practice, but all reacted to the economic hardships of the wars with the native population and the increase in the number of poor families by looking toward an expansion in indenture and apprenticeship for job training, religious training, and education. The emphasis for Native American children, apprenticed to the English, was particularly on Christian education and the imposition of European religious beliefs on the native population.[18]

The practice of indenturing the children of the poor did not always occur without protest. When the British government sent a large group of Palatine German refugees to Manhattan in 1710, Governor Robert Hunter issued

Ethical Practice

Critical Thinking Question: Imagine you were a social worker in New York, when Governor Hunter ordered the apprenticing of the German children. What ethical issues would it raise for your practice?

an order to apprentice the children to families in faraway Westchester, Long Island, and Rhode Island, to keep them off public support. The parents, despite illness and destitution, protested the separation and loss.[19]

Children of poor parents—both in and out of the almshouse—were subject to bonding and indenture. Complaints about cruel treatment and lack of appropriate education and job training increased as the eighteenth century progressed.[20]

The counterparts of the systems of indenture and apprenticeship for children were the systems of indenture contracting or farming out for adults. In accordance with colonial welfare legislation, overseers of the poor were empowered "to take effectual care that . . . persons of able body living within the same town or precincts thereof (not having estates otherwise to maintain themselves) do not live idly or misspend their time loitering, but that they be brought up or employed in some honest calling, which may be profitable unto themselves and the public."[21]

Broadside Letter from Four Slaves, Asking to Return to Africa, 1773, Boston

B O S T O N, April 20th, 1773.

S I R,

THE efforts made by the legislative of this province in their last sessions to free themselves from slavery, gave us, who are in that deplorable state, a high degree of satisfaction. We expect great things from men who have made such a noble stand against the designs of their *fellow-men* to enslave them. We cannot but wish and hope Sir, that you will have the same grand object, we mean civil and religious liberty, in view in your next session. The divine spirit of *freedom,* seems to fire every humane breast on this continent, except such as are bribed to assist in executing the execrable plan.

WE are very sensible that it would be highly detrimental to our present masters, if we were allowed to demand all that off *right* belongs to us for past services ; this we disclaim. Even the *Spaniards,* who hawe not those sublime ideas of freedom that English men have, are conscious that they have no right to all the services of their fellow-men, we mean the *Africans,* whom they have purchased with their money ; therefore they allow them one day in a week to work: for themselve, to enable them to earn money to purchase the residue of their time, which they have a right to demand in such portions as they are able to pay for (a due appraizment of their services being first made, which always stands at the purchase money.) We do not pretend to dictate to you Sir, or to the honorable Assembly, of which you are a member : We acknowledge our obligations to you for what you have already done, but as the people of this province seem to be actuated by the principles of equity and justice, we cannot but expect your house will again take our deplorable case into serious consideration, and give us that ample relief which, *as men,* we have a natural right to.

BUT since the wise and righteous governor of the universe, has permitted our fellow men to make us slaves, we bow in submission to him, and determine to behave in such a manner, as that we may have reason to expect the divine approbation of, and assistance in, our peaceable and lawful attempts to gain our freedom.

WE are willing to submit to such regulations and laws, as may be made relative to us, until we leave the province, which we determine to do as soon as we can from our joynt labours procure money to transport ourselves to some part of the coast of *Africa,* where we propose a settlement. We are very desirous that you should have instructions relative to us, from your town, therefore we pray you to communicate this letter to them, and ask this favor for us.

In behalf of our fellow slaves in this province,
And by order of their Committee.

PETER BESTES,
SAMBO FREEMAN,
FELIX HOLBROOK,
CHESTER JOIE.

For the REPRESENTATIVE of the town of *Thompson.*

To the end that individuals be profitable to themselves and to the commonwealth, indenture contracts enforced labor by sentencing potential paupers to servitude, sometimes to a master of their own choosing and sometimes to an assigned master. Under farming out, the adult poor could be turned over to the bidder willing to contract, at the lowest charge to the community, to take on the care of paupers and to put them to work. Such care might permit the individual to remain home. Assistance to the elderly, under this formulation, was quite flexible. It ranged from care in a private home for those who were feeble all the way to assistance in finding employment if the older person were capable of working.[22]

By the middle of the eighteenth century, cities began to build almshouses to replace individual homes for those poor who were very old, disabled, or seriously ill. As demand for help rose, cash relief and noninstitutional help became harder to obtain. Urban poverty and unemployment increasingly meant commitment to a privately owned workhouse, a publicly owned house of correction, a poor farm, or an almshouse where care or proper punishment and hard labor could more easily be administered. The first almshouse was established in Rensselaerswyck, New York, in 1657. Plymouth ordered the construction of an almshouse in 1658, and Boston did the same two years later.

The early development of workhouses and almshouses—welfare mechanisms that were both sophisticated and expensive—was a response to the rapid population growth experienced by the colonies and of the increased financing ability to be found in some colonies. Occasionally, where towns could not afford such institutions, private philanthropists made contributions to the public effort.[23]

The popularity of indenture as a means of dealing with dependency was indicative of the transition to a "free" labor system in which employers were free to hire and fire as they saw fit and workers had to find a buyer for their labor. The new mobility of the population in the late seventeenth and early eighteenth centuries placed strains on all forms of established authority. Community leaders could not regulate people as they moved in and out of town. Even colonial authorities were challenged to cope with a hard-to-follow population of floating laborers. The binding of labor to a particular authority was one means of slowing this mobility and the social disorder it might breed.

Colonial welfare legislation stressed the provision of indoor relief; that is, care offered in homes other than one's own or in institutions. Nevertheless, the seasonally unemployed might benefit from tax remissions, and the overseers of the poor could legally provide outdoor relief—money payments to persons permitted to remain in their own homes because their poverty resulted from physical disability, widowhood, or old age. Taxes were collected for the latter purpose. Frequent wars coupled with postwar recessions created increased demands for help. In crises, private philanthropy supported the practice of outdoor relief by the provision of items such as blankets and stockings. During the severe winter of 1761–1762, the Quakers in Philadelphia distributed fuel stamps—"tickets of recommendation"—to be redeemed for wood.[24]

Even worthiness had its limits. The stigma of poverty was not reserved for the underserving. In 1718, a statute of the Province of Pennsylvania made it obligatory that every person receiving public relief "upon the shoulder of the right sleeve . . . in open and visible manner, wear . . . a large Roman P. together with the first letter of the name of the county, city or place whereof such poor person is an inhabitant, cut either in red or blue cloth, as by the overseers

The stigma of poverty was not reserved for the underserving. In 1718, a statute of the Province of Pennsylvania made it obligatory that every person receiving public relief "upon the shoulder of the right sleeve . . . in open and visible manner, wear . . . a large Roman P."

Human Rights and Justice

Critical Thinking Question: How have definitions of "worthiness" changed through American history and what role have they played in advancing or retarding the search for social justice?

of the poor, it shall be directed and appointed."[25] In New York, relief recipients were required to wear badges inscribed with the large letters "N.Y."[26]

The coercive work features of the Poor Laws and the meagerness of relief provisions deterred many of the eligible from seeking aid. Not only did the laws spell out the kinds of care that might be made available to those who applied, but they also directed the overseers to seek out those whose situations or ways of living portended financial burden for the community. Direct deterrence was enhanced by the Poor Law principle of family responsibility requiring that "the father and grandfather and the mother and grandmother and the children of every poor, old, blind, lame, and impotent person, or other poor person not able to work . . . shall at their own charges relieve and maintain every such poor person as the justices of the peace . . . shall order and direct."[27] The overt demand that relatives support each other in time of need was covertly strengthened by the stigma of resorting to public aid.

The Poor Laws were designed to protect those who held legal claim to settlement in particular localities. They offered protection against strangers who threatened the stability—namely, the morality and physical safety—of a society singularly concerned with order and wary of new ways and different cultures. In regard to strangers, the Poor Laws demonstrated most clearly their law-and-order nature. The requirement of settlement for public assistance—for example, forty days in New York, three months in Massachusetts, a year in North Carolina—clarified the absence of local responsibility for outsiders.

By the end of the eighteenth century, residency requirements had become even stricter. In New York, for example, the time needed to establish settlement rose to a year and the annual rental value required more than doubled, increasing from five pounds to twelve pounds a year.[28] Beyond that, "warning out" the practice of expelling strangers became more common. Strangers were carefully screened. In the 1690s, as in the 1990s, the newcomer was suspect and major efforts were made to reduce the potential costs of support for migrants. Those few who could ensure their financial independence and future contribution to the community were permitted to remain and to acquire settlement. More frequently, they were escorted beyond local geographical jurisdictions.

The low numbers of the reported poor in the early years of the eighteenth century are deceptive. They did not usually include people receiving temporary relief, for example, during the severe winter months. Nor did they include the "near poor" and those needy but ineligible people, displaced Indians, and nonresidents who were poor but excluded from aid. Even with the small number who received help, the cost of aid made up a large part of the total budget and sometimes even exceeded total tax receipts.[29] The colonists were concerned with the threat to economic survival posed by possible drains on the public treasury resulting from the potentially poor and sick outsider. This fear often outweighed the value of labor skills the stranger might bring.

Additional evidence that the protection of society, rather than the care of the poor, dictated the writing of the colonial Poor Laws is offered by the fact that the laws contain no expression of concern for the poor beyond the concise statements of provision for their care. The laws do, however, make explicit the rights and duties of the overseers of the poor and spell out in detail methods for selecting and appointing overseers, their taxing powers, their responsibilities, their accountability—as well as the penalties to which they were subject if they performed improperly. The laws indicate that the tasks of the overseers were considered onerous. In Pennsylvania, for example, the overseers were appointed to a one-year term of office but, on penalty of having to serve a second year or pay a heavy fine, were required to set forth the names of their successors.[30]

CONQUEST, EXPANSION, AND POPULATION GROWTH: NATIVE AMERICANS, IMMIGRATION, AND SLAVERY

In New England, the township became the unit of colonial Poor Law administration, and, as might be expected, the major foci of administrative practice implementing welfare legislation were work and religion. Although they were adapted to local conditions and to variations of religious tenets, colonies outside of New England also adopted the poor-relief system of England.

The colonists, whether Anglican as in Virginia, Puritan as in Massachusetts Bay, or Catholic as in Maryland, were English in their political and social heritage. The English character of these colonial enterprises was enhanced by the fact that they were essentially private enterprises. All were financed through private capital raised by investment organizations such as the London and Massachusetts Bay companies or, as in the case of Maryland, by individual landowners ready to risk their own fortunes. In either instance, royal support was given in the form of charters or land grants. Colonization was a reflection of England's longtime process of democratization, industrialization, and commercialization forged within the military and political struggles of older powers. Along with that came a view of the resident population as uncivilized, barbarous, and consequently without rights to their land or even their lives. Their success derived from a combination of patriotism, profit seeking, religious fervor, and belief in the superiority of English culture.

The newcomers to America were not just settlers; they were conquerors as well. The English and the Europeans attacked and conquered the resident population in many ways, both direct and indirect. Combat played a major role. Guns, armor, horses, ships, and strong forts were all factors in the conquest of the native population. The forced resettlement of Native Americans was common. Native Americans were pushed from their communities. Despite royal decrees of protection and endless promises of security, they were marched westward, leaving the most valuable and useful land to the victors.

The newcomers to America were not just settlers; they were conquerors as well.

The weakening of the native population through the introduction of firearms, alcohol, and new and fatal diseases was another aspect of the story. Europeans—the Spanish in Florida and the Southeast, the English in New England—brought diseases that took a heavy toll on the native population. Smallpox, measles, and mumps arrived with the Europeans and frequently decimated the indigenous population.

Even the introduction of friendly trade played a part. Native hunters and traders were frequently cheated and robbed. More than that, the competition for the goods to be acquired, the lure of alcohol, English tools, cloth, and guns, led to destructive intratribal warfare.

The end result of colonization was to dispossess the Native Americans from their land and from their government. Many were killed; some were enslaved. Those remaining lost sovereignty and ownership of their property through conquest, through trading, and by way of negotiated treaties.[31]

The process of establishing colonies was not, however, an easy task for the newcomers. The colonists shared a common experience of hardship and scarcity in America. The severity of the New England winter, the "horrid snow" described by Cotton Mather,[32] was counterpart to the unexpected, unbearable heat that brought death to one-half of the Virginia settlers during their first summer in America. Captain John Smith, a leader of the Virginia Company, wrote, "Nothing can be expected thence, but by labor."[33] In the South, as in the North, the Poor Laws constituted a reasonable response to a situation in which financial disaster and death seemed imminent and which, in fact, did produce social and physical disabilities.

The intent of the original colonists to settle permanently in the New World was strengthened by the rapid addition of new settlers and new settlements. The English revolution that led to the overthrow of King Charles I in 1649, the establishment of the Puritan Commonwealth, and the restoration of the monarchy in 1660 spurred emigration, especially of those who were seeking freedom and purity of religion. The emigrants to New England were of all classes of English society and consisted of whole families and individuals ready to establish homes and families in the new country.

The Restoration of the British monarchy sparked an increased emigration of Puritans to New England and reinforced the dominance of Puritanism in colonial America. Later, French Huguenots and Scot Calvinists emigrated to Carolina as a result of religious persecution and trade restrictions. The possibilities for religious and political freedom and for economic stability brought additional settlers—Welsh, Jews, Swiss—and the colonial population soared. By 1640, more than 27,000 Englishmen were scattered through Massachusetts, Connecticut, Rhode Island, New Hampshire, Maine, Maryland, and Virginia. In 1690, there were 200,000 inhabitants; by 1710, there were 350,000; and in 1760, 1.5 million people lived in the thirteen colonies, representing many parts of Europe and Africa. The numbers of Africans grew from the original twenty brought in 1619 to 16,700 in 1690; 44,900 in 1710; and 325,000— 22 percent of the population—in 1760.[34]

European population growth in the New England colonies was controlled by the factors that led to their founding. The colonists were bound by a common set of religious and ethical motivations and, for the most part, had underwritten the expenses of their passage and of supplies through the purchase of shares in a joint enterprise. The New England colonies, despite official ties to England, were essentially independent and used their independence to accept and reject immigrants on the basis of religious beliefs and potential for economic self-sufficiency. Although slavery persisted in the North through most of the eighteenth century, African American slavery was not central to the Northern economy.

A different pattern evolved in the South, reflecting the different base for settlement and the economic base that developed. Virginia was settled solely as a commercial enterprise. A large number of its settlers were working-class Englishmen who paid for their passage through indenture contracts, a four- to seven-year commitment to work. In 1625, documents show that 487 people— almost 40 percent of Virginia's population—were indentured servants.[35] The South grew as it developed tobacco and prospered with the establishment of plantations. Some Native Americans were enslaved for service in Florida and Georgia; some were traded in the Caribbean islands. The first blacks to come to Virginia came as indentured workers. As servants and as freemen, they had much in common with their white counterparts in terms of status and problems. However, the chasms of skin color and culture quickly differentiated white servants from black chattel. By the middle of the seventeenth century, much of the Southern economy was based on the use of slave labor to produce crops for export—indigo, low-land cotton, but especially tobacco.

With New England practicing selectivity in the acceptance of immigrants and the South relying increasingly upon the use of slave labor, immigrants were quite naturally funneled into the Middle Atlantic colonies. Large numbers were unable to pay for their passage and came under contracts of indenture. It is estimated that two-thirds of the settlers in Pennsylvania came under such provisions of servitude. German and Scotch–Irish families who arrived during the eighteenth century came as "redemptioners," people who had made a down payment on passage and who used the promise of work as collateral for the balance. Indentured servitude resulted for those who defaulted.

By the close of the Colonial period, British North America had prospered. When Georgia was declared a crown colony in 1752, all thirteen American colonies were formal geographic and political entities. Between 1700 and 1776, a great deal of cultural, social, political, and economic change occurred. Population growth had occurred not only by natural increase but also by way of immigration. The resulting intermingling of various religious, ethnic, and racial groups lent a cosmopolitan air to the busy ports of trade and entry— Boston, New York, Philadelphia, and Baltimore. The regular plying of sailing vessels between North America and the European continent brought not only economic returns to all but also, to the upper classes, the latest turns of fashion in dress, belles lettres, and social amenities. The establishment of active legal and political ties between the separate colonies and London and the frequent exchange of representatives required lent additional encouragement to the maintenance of continental social graces, at the same time that the separation of the American and European continents presented the colonies with opportunity for self-government.

The colonies took an early interest in expanding schooling because their leaders believed that the population should be able to read the Bible. A college—soon to be called Harvard—was established at Cambridge in the Massachusetts Bay Colony as early as 1636. By the mid-eighteenth century, William and Mary, Yale, the University of Pennsylvania, Princeton, Brown, Rutgers, and Dartmouth were all established. The ties of communication among the colonies were fostered by a flood of printed materials and broadsides and the practice of letter writing. Newspapers proliferated, and the instituting of a mail service, carried regularly by 1732 between Massachusetts and Virginia, was additionally encouraging to writings of all kinds.

By the end of the eighteenth century, the many changes that marked colonial life sharpened class differences. By the time of the American Revolution, many residents were already third- and fourth-generation Americans. By the middle of the eighteenth century, a new elite, based on commercial success, had come to dominate both Northern and Southern societies. Beneath this class existed a group, again largely Protestant, of middle-class farmers, artisans, small tradesmen, and laborers in the fledgling manufacturing establishments. Alongside and below this group existed another large group—non-English, frequently non-Protestant, sometimes nonwhite, and almost always without property.

Different bases for prosperity for the North and South resulted in different views of people and of their need for social welfare programs. New England and the Middle Atlantic colonies shifted from sole dependence upon farming

However, the chasms of skin color and culture quickly differentiated white servants from black chattel. By the middle of the seventeenth century, much of the Southern economy was based on the use of slave labor to produce crops for export—indigo, low-land cotton, but especially tobacco.

Policy Practice

Critical Thinking Question: Policy decisions are often modified as economic conditions change. How might the increased needs of the older people and people with disabilities influence the operation of the Poor Laws?

and fishing to home manufacturing, shipbuilding, and trading. These colonies were sufficiently urbanized to add the risks of a market economy to those of colonial frontier life. Problems of dependency increased with the influx of poorly paid immigrants and with the growing numbers of disabled men resulting from the wars of European powers in America and from wars with Indians. Particularly stark were the needs of elderly and disabled blacks, who had been freed as a way of avoiding their care in old age.[36] These factors, combined with an economy of scarcity and with a growing population, made the enforcement of the Poor Laws attractive to town governments.

In the South, the introduction of slavery and the continued reliance on an agricultural economy prevented the development of a large, free, laboring class. If the large plantation holdings of Virginia contrasted sharply with small tenant farmer holdings of Carolina, the two were, nevertheless, joined in a feudal system that created a degree of economic stability. The milder climate, the availability of fertile land, and the mixture of less austere religious sects fostered a warmer, more favorable view of the free man. As early as 1728, William Byrd, a prosperous and educated gentleman who served on a commission set up to run the dividing line between Virginia and North Carolina, may have exaggerated when he observed the way of life in North Carolina:

> Surely there is no place in the World where the inhabitants live with less labour . . . by the great felicity of the Climate, the easiness of raising Provisions. . . . Indian Corn is of so great increase, that a little Pains will Subsist a very large Family with Bread, and then they may have meat without any pains at all, by the Help of the Low Grounds, and the great Variety of Mast that grows on the Highland.[37]

While such ease of living might have led to laziness and an "Aversion to Labor," as Byrd feared, the fact was that it also led to greater tolerance of human misfortune—again for free men. By the middle of the seventeenth century, Virginia had adopted both the Poor Laws and apprenticeship to provide for poor free men: white and black, orphans, illegitimate children, and mulatto children of white women. The original resident population—Native Americans—was excluded from these arrangements. There was no recognition of any social welfare needs that Native Americans, slaves, or indentured servants might have, and it was left to these groups to develop their own informal self-help mechanisms.

CHALLENGE TO THE POOR LAWS

The Poor Laws were a product of a society that used the legal system to constrain a dynamic population during a time of social change. In America, as in England, efforts at control increasingly were at odds with the fluidity of the emerging social order. For many in authority, the response to the Poor Laws' ineffectiveness was to make them more restrictive. Yet, for others, the alternative conclusion was that the entire effort to help the poor was counterproductive. For them, the effort to help the poor would make poverty more attractive. Anticipating later generations of "welfare reformers," Benjamin Franklin argued for the abolition of the Poor Laws. As Franklin saw it, the causes of poverty were of the individual's own making; the social system worked well, the growing wealth of the upper classes was justified, and an assumption of social responsibility would inevitably aggravate the problem by fostering further dependency.

> I have sometimes doubted whether the laws peculiar to England, which *compel the rich to maintain the poor*, have not given the latter a dependence, that very much lessens the care of providing against the wants of old age.
>
> I have heard it remarked that the *poor* in *Protestant* countries, on the continent of Europe, are generally more industrious than those of *Popish* countries. May not the more numerous foundations in the latter for relief of the poor have some effect towards rendering them less provident? To relieve the misfortunes of our fellow creatures is concurring with the Deity; it is godlike; but, if we provide encouragement for laziness, and supports for folly, may we not be fighting against the order of God and Nature, which perhaps has appointed want and misery as the proper punishments for, and cautions against, as well as necessary consequences of, idleness and extravagance?. . .
>
> However, as matters now stand with us, care and industry seem absolutely necessary to our well-being. They should therefore have every encouragement we can invent, and not one motive to diligence be subtracted; and the support of the poor should not be by maintaining them in idleness, but by employing them in some kind of labour suited to their abilities of body, as I am informed begins to be of late the practice in many parts of England, where workhouses are erected for that purpose. If these were general, I should think the poor would be more careful, and work voluntarily to lay up something for themselves against a rainy day, rather than run the risk of being obliged to work at the pleasure of others for a bare subsistence, and that too under confinement.[38] [Italics in original]

Franklin's view highlights a belief in the responsibility of people for their own welfare in an ordered society that rewards industry and thrift. Franklin rationalized poverty and inequality in income distribution:

> Much malignant censure have some writers bestowed upon the rich for their luxury and expensive living, while the poor are starving, & c.; not considering that what the rich expend, the labouring poor receive in payment for their labour. It may seem a paradox if I should assert, that our labouring poor do in every year receive *the whole revenue of the nation*; I mean not only the public revenue, but also the revenue or clear income of all private estates, or a sum equivalent to the whole. . . .
>
> In support of this position I reason thus. The rich do not work for one another. Their habitations, furniture, cloathing, carriages, food, ornaments, and everything in short, that they or their families use and consume, is the work or produce of the labouring poor, who are, and must be continually, paid for their labour in producing the same.[39]

Some went so far as to argue that, for the market economy to function, individual earned income should never be supplemented. This would compel labor force participation and ensure a supply of workers willing to perform menial, difficult, and unpleasant tasks.

> It seems to be a law of nature, that the poor should be to a certain degree improvident, that there may always be some to fulfil the most servile, the most sordid, and the most ignoble offices in the community. The stock of human happiness is thereby much increased, whilst the more delicate are not only relieved from drudgery, and freed from those

Critical Thinking

Critical Thinking Question:
On what assumptions about human nature were Franklin's conclusions about the effects of the Poor Laws? How might a different set of assumptions lead to different conclusions?

occasional employments which would make them miserable, but are left at liberty, without interruption, to pursue those callings which are suited to their various dispositions, and most useful to the state. As for the lowest of the poor, by custom they are reconciled to the meanest occupations, to the most laborious works, and to the most hazardous pursuits; whilst the hope of their reward makes them cheerful in the midst of all their dangers and their toils.[40]

By the end of the Colonial era, the poor and unfortunate were no longer seen as an organic part of the social order. Often they were literally outsiders; addressing their problems was no longer the responsibility of respectable citizens. As Americans began to consider the meaning of "liberty" and "equality" in their political thought, these words meant little for the poor—free and enslaved—whose well-being was increasingly marginalized.

VETERANS: A SPECIAL CLASS

Welfare measures for veterans, however, differed from those applied to the general population. The English "Acte for Reliefes of Souldiours" of 1593 set the tone for colonial legislation. It had recognized both the special services and the special needs of disabled soldiers and sailors and provided relief for this group *as a right* on the basis of disability, with payments scaled to military pay. As early as 1624, the colony of Virginia passed similar legislation. In 1636, Plymouth Colony declared that any soldier injured in defense of the colony was entitled to support.

> That in case necessity require to send forces abroad, and there be not volunteers sufficient offered for the service, then it be lawfull for the Governor and [his] assistants to presse [men into service] in his Majesties name . . . provided that if any that shall goe returne mamed & hurt, he shall be mayntayned completely by the Colony during his life.[41]

Other colonies followed the precedent, and by 1777 all but Connecticut had made special provisions for veterans. The entitlement to these provisions did not carry the onus of pauperism and, equally important for the future, carried no requirement of local settlement. Colonies, not towns, were responsible for financing and administration. The pattern was so well accepted that the Continental Congress in 1776 adopted a report of the Committee on Disabled Soldiers and Sailors recommending to the states pensions for invalid and disabled veterans.[42] This special attention to veterans, and in some instances to other persons identified as the "unsettled poor," broke ground for eventual contributions by the states and by the federal government to social welfare.

Of more immediate interest, however, is the logic by which the colonies selected veterans for preferential treatment—domiciliary care, pensions for elderly and disabled veterans, and outdoor relief for widows and children of veterans. This selection for special treatment was, after all, consistent with the colonial view of humanity. Veterans had participated in an unusual kind of work. In doing so, they had made an extraordinary contribution to the commonwealth at the same time that they had made visible their own individual worth. Certainly such work and such worthiness were not to be deterred in a society where their special services were so badly needed.

Log onto **www.mysocialworklab.com** and answer the following questions. (*If you did not receive an access code to* **MySocialWorkLab** *with this text and wish to purchase access online, please visit* www.mysocialworklab.com.)

1. **Watch the Core Competency video "Recognizing Personal Values."** How would your personal values be challenged if you were providing social services in the 1700s?

2. **Read the MySocialWorkLibrary case study "Foster Care: Crisis and Kinship in Foster Care."** If the Raney family had lived in the eighteenth century, how would they have been treated?

PRACTICE TEST
The following questions will test your knowledge of the content found within this chapter. For additional assessment, including licensing-exam-type questions on applying chapter content to practice, visit **MySocialWorkLab**.

1. In accordance with the Act of Settlement of 1662, newcomers to a parish could
   a. be forced to work for the church.
   b. be returned to their place of legal residence.
   c. homestead any property for five years for free.
   d. apply for assistance after proving need.

2. In the 1700s, social services began to be provided by
   a. the gentry landowners.
   b. state and federal government.
   c. ethnic and religious groups.
   d. no one; there were no services.

3. Care offered to the poor who lived in homes other than their own or in institutions was referred to as
   a. charity.
   b. indoor relief.
   c. outdoor relief.
   d. welfare.

4. In the eighteenth century, when the natural family could not provide learning and religion to its children,
   a. parents would be fined or their children would be apprenticed.
   b. children were placed in foster homes.
   c. children would be sent to reform institutions.
   d. parents would be sterilized and indentured as punishment.

5. Discuss how the stigma of poverty was made public in the early eighteenth century.

ASSESS YOUR COMPETENCE
Use the following scale to rate your current level of achievement on the following concepts or skills associated with each competency presented in the chapter:

1	2	3
I can accurately describe the concept or skill	I can consistently identify the concept or skill when observing and analyzing practice activities	I can competently implement the concept or skill in my own practice

_______ Describe the role that economics plays in the development of social welfare programs.

_______ Differentiate between indoor relief and outdoor relief.

_______ Apply the current state of the economy to current social welfare policies.

_______ Distinguish between personal and professional values in the development of policies.

The Colonial Period

The two documents selected to illustrate the thrust of social welfare during the colonial era are *An Act of Supplement to the Acts Referring to the Poor* (Massachusetts Bay, 1692) and the contract of indenture entitled *The Binding of Moses Love* (1747). The documents illustrate legislative and judicial actions taken to achieve societal stability and individual well-being. For society and the individual, the actions were protective and preventive and called upon a family unit to perform the functions of a social welfare institution. Where no natural family existed to support members in need, a substitute family was found. The number of colonists was very small and the community itself functioned in part as an extended family.

An Act of Supplement expresses governmental concern for all the inhabitants of Massachusetts Bay. The act explicitly states that its provisions extend beyond those who receive public alms; its intent is to ensure that all single persons under the age of twenty-one years live "under some orderly family government." The significance of such an assurance stems from the nature of a society in which government and family mirrored one another in their responsibility to fulfill God's plan that people work and produce. Both were organized in a fixed hierarchical structure to which each individual had been called to an assigned place. Fulfilling one's responsibility within the structure was a duty to oneself, to the community, to God. Family government was protective of the individual who might be tempted to fall away from that responsibility and protective of the community that would bear the cost of such a fall. The family model reinforced the Puritan values of work and frugality as religious observances. In a society of scarcity, such a joining of religious and secular concerns was particularly felicitous.

The Binding of Moses Love demonstrates that the colonists observed the human condition with a certain solicitousness. Moses Love was bound out when only two years and eight months of age. The indenture contract is concerned with avoiding future dependency of the children of the poor. Support, education, and employability are the long-term goals. All in all, the rights and responsibilities bestowed on Moses Love's master are those of a parent. As indicated in *An Act of Supplement,* this discharge of governmental and familial responsibilities toward children generally endeavored "to defend them from any wrongs or injuries" and to prepare them for economic self-sufficiency in adulthood.

The family model reinforced the Puritan values of work and frugality as religious observances. In a society of scarcity, such a joining of religious and secular concerns was particularly felicitous.

THE ACTS AND RESOLVES, Public and Private

of the

PROVINCE OF THE MASSACHUSETTS BAY:

CHAPTER 14.

AN ACT OF SUPPLEMENT TO THE ACTS REFERRING TO THE

POOR,

&c.

1692–3, ch. 28, & 7

Whereas the law for the binding out poor children apprentice is misconstrued by some to extend only to such children whose parents receive almes; for explanation whereof—

Be it declared and enacted by His Excellency the Governour, Council and Representatives in General Court assembled, and by the authority of the same,

[Sect. 1.] That the selectmen or overseers of the poor in any town or district within this province, or the greater part of them, shall take, order and are hereby impowred from time to time, by and with the assent of two justices of the peace, to set to work, or bind out apprentice, as they shall think convenient, all such children whose parents shall, by the selectmen or overseers of the poor, or the greater part of them, be thought unable to maintain them, (whither they receive almes or are chargeable to the place or not), so as that they be not sessed to publick taxes or assessments, for the province or town charges; male children till they come to the age of twenty-one years, and females till they come to the age of eighteen years, or time of marriage: which shall be as good and effectual in law, to all intents and purposes, as if any such child were of full age, and by indenture of covenant had bound him or herself, or that their parents were consenting there [un] to: provision therein to be made for the instructing of children so bound out, to read and write, as they may be capable. And the selectmen or overseers of the poor shall inquire into the usage of children bound out by themselves or their predecessors, and endeavour to defend them from any wrongs or injuries.

And, for the better preventing of idleness, and loose or disorderly living,—
Be it further declared and enacted by the authority aforesaid,

[Sect. 2.] That the selectmen or overseers of the poor, or the greater part of them, be and are further impowred, by and with the assent of two justices of the peace, to set to work all such persons, married or unmarried, able of body, having no means to maintain them, that live idlely and use or exercise no ordinary and daily lawful trade or business to get their living by. And no single person of either sex, under the age of twenty-one years, shall be suffered to live at their own hand, but under some orderly family government; nor shall any woman of ill fame, married or unmarried, be suffered to receive or entertain lodgers in her house. And the selectmen or overseers of the poor, constables and tythingmen, are hereby ordered to see to the due observance of this act, and to complain and inform against any transgressions thereof to one or more justices of the peace, or the court of general sessions of the peace, who are hereby respectively required and impowred, upon due conviction of the offender or offenders for living idely or disorderly, contrary to the true intent of this act, to commit or send such offenders to the house of correction or work-house, there to remain and be kept to labour, until they be discharged by order of the court of general sessions of the peace, unless such person or persons so complained of shall give reasonable caution or assurance, to the satisfaction of the justice or court, that they will reform: provided, this act shall not be construed to extend to hinder any single woman of good repute from the exercise of any lawful trade or imployment, for a livelihood, whereto she shall have the allowance and approbation of the selectmen or overseers of the poor, or the greater part of them, any law, usage or custom to the contrary notwithstanding: *provided,*—

[Sect. 3.] This act shall continue in force for the space of three years next coming, and to the end of the session of the general assembly next after. *[Passed November 27; published December 3.]*

Volume I. Boston: Wright & Potter, Printers to the State, 1869.

* * *

THE BINDING OF MOSES LOVE, 1747

This Indenture made the fourteenth day of September Anno domini 1747 by and between Luke Lincoln, Benja Tuckor, Nathall Goodspeed and John Whittemor all of Leicester in the Covnty of Worcester selectmen of sd Leicester on the one part, Matthew Scott of Leicester aforesaid yeoman on the other part Wittnesseth that the above sd selectmen by virtue of the Law of this province them Impowering & with the assent of two of the Majesties Justices of the Peace for sd Covnty hereto annexed to put and bind out to the sd Matthew Scott & to his heirs Execvtors & Adminrs as an Apprentice Moses Love a Minor aged two years and Eeight Months with him & them to Live and dwell with as an apprentice dureing the term of Eighteen years and fovr months (viz) untill he shall arrive to the age of twenty-one years—he being a poor Child & his parants not being well able to support it. Dureing all which the sd apprentice his sd Master his heirs Execvtors & Adminrs shall faithfully serve at such Lawfull imployment & labovr as he shall from time to time Dureing sd term be Capable of doing and performing & not absent himself from his or their service without Leave & In all things behave himself as a good & faithful apprentice ought to do and the sd Matthew Scott for himself his heirs Execvtors & Adminrs do Couenant promise and grant to & with the above sd selectmen of Leicester aforsaid & with their successors in the office or trust of selectmen of Leicester aforsaid & Inbehalf of sd apprentice that he the sd Matthew Scott his heirs Execvtors & Adminrss shall & will Dureing the term aforsd find and provide for the sd apprentice sufficient Cloathing meet drink Warshing and Lodging both in Sickness & in health & that he will teach him or cavse him to be tavght to read & write & siffer fiting his degree if he be Capable of Learning and at the Expiration of the term to Dismiss him with two suits of apparril one to be fitt for Lords days In Wittness where of the partyes to these present Indentvrs haue Interchangably set their hands & seals the day and year first written. Signed sealed & Delivered in presence of

    Steward Southgate
    John Brown

        Luke Lincoln (seal)
        Benja Tucker (seal)
        John Whittemor (seal)

New England Historical and Genealogical Register, Boston, 1880, Vol. XXXIV, p. 311.

NOTES

1. *Records of the Colony of Rhode Island and Providence Plantations in New England,* Vol. 1, *1636–1663* (Providence: A. Crawford Greene and Brother, State Printers, 1856), pp. 184–185.

2. Danby Pickering, ed., *The Statutes at Large from the Thirty-Ninth Year of Q. Elizabeth to the Twelfth Year of K. Charles II, Inclusive,* Vol. 7 (Cambridge: Bentham & Bathurst, 1763), pp. 30–37.

3. The Act of Settlement of 1662 may be found in "An Acte for the Better Reliefe of the Poor of the Kingdom," in *The Statutes at Large from the First Year of King James the First to the Tenth Year of the Reign of King William the Third,* Vol. 3 (London: Basket, Woodfall and Strahan, 1763), pp. 243–247.

4. William P. Quigley, "Work or Starve: Regulation of the Poor in Colonial America," *University of San Francisco Law Review,* Fall 1996, p. 41.

5. Katherine D. Hardwick, *As Long As Charity Shall Be a Virtue : Boston Private Charities from 1657 to 1800* (Boston: Massachusetts Charitable Society, 1964), p. 5.

6. Thomas J. Scharf and Westcott Thompson, *History of Philadelphia, 1609–1884* (Philadelphia: L. H. Everts, 1884), pp. 1452–1453.

7. Raymond A. Mohl, "Poverty in Early America, a Reappraisal: The Case of Eighteenth-Century New York," *New York History,* Vol. L, January 1969, p. 19.

8. David Hackett Fischer, "Growing Old in America," in Jill Quadagno, ed., *Aging, the Individual and Society: Readings in Social Gerontology* (New York: St. Martin's Press, 1980), pp. 34–45.

9. Carl N. Degler, *At Odds: Women and the Family in America from the Revolution to the Present* (Oxford: Oxford University Press, 1980), p. 194.

10. Edith Abbott, *Women in Industry: A Study in American Economic History* (New York: D. Appleton, 1909), p. 21.

11. *Province Laws* (Mass.), 1753–1754.

12. Quoted in Abbott, op. cit., p. 33.

13. Milton T. Rolla, *Household Manufacturers in the United States, 1640–1860* (Chicago: University of Chicago Press, 1919), p. 6.

14. Act XXVII, October 1646, in William Waller Henning, ed., *The Statutes at Large: Being a Collection of All the Laws of Virginia from the First Session of the Legislature in the Year 1619,* Vol. 1 (New York: Piser and Russell, Printer, 1846), p. 336.

15. *Records of the Governor and Company of the Massachusetts Bay in New England,* Vol. 2, *1624–1629,* p. 6.

16. *Acts and Resolves, an Act of Supplement to the Acts Referring to the Poor,* Province of the Massachusetts Bay, 1703.

17. William Brigham, ed., *The Compact with the Charter and Laws of the Colony of New Plymouth. . . .* This contains *The Book of the General Laws of the Inhabitants of the Jurisdiction of New Plymouth. . . .* To be found in Marcus Wilson Jernegan, *Laboring and Dependent Classes in Colonial America, 1607–1783* (Chicago: University of Chicago Press, 1931), pp. 98–99.

18. Ibid., pp. 102, 233–234.

19. Robert E. Cray Jr., *Paupers and Poor Relief in New York City and Its Rural Environs, 1790–1830* (Philadelphia: Temple University Press, 1988), pp. 42–43.

20. Ibid., pp. 79–81.

21. *Acts and Resolves,* Province of Massachusetts Bay, 1692.

22. For a discussion of the application of the Poor Laws to the elderly in colonial society, see Jill S. Quadagno, "Policies toward the Elderly," in David Van Tassel and Peter N. Stearns, eds., *Old Age in a Bureaucratic Society* (Westport, Conn.: Greenwood Press, 1986), pp. 129–136.

23. Scharf and Thompson, op. cit., p. 1450.

24. Gary B. Nash, "Poverty and Poor Relief in Pre-Revolutionary Philadelphia," *William and Mary Quarterly,* Third Series, Vol. 33, January 1976, pp. 12–13.

25. Raymond A. Mohl, *Poverty in New York: 1783–1825* (New York: Oxford University Press, 1971), p. 57.

26. Ibid., p. 42.

27. *Statutes at Large of Pennsylvania,* 1682–1801, Vol. 2, chap. 154.

28. Mohl, op. cit., p. 57.

29. Ibid., p. 42.

30. *Statutes at Large of Pennsylvania,* op. cit., Vol. 3, pp. 76–77.

31. For an excellent review of this process, see Francis Jennings, *The Invasion of America: Indians, Colonialism, and the Cant of Conquest* (New York: W. W. Norton, 1976), and *500 Nations,* television production by Jack Leustig, Vol. 3, "Clash of Cultures," and Vol. 5, "Cauldrons of War" (Burbank, Calif.: TIG Productions, 1994).

32. Cotton Mather, A Letter [An Horrid Snow], 10d. X m. 1717, in Norman Foerster, ed., *American Poetry and Prose* (New York: Houghton Mifflin, 1934), pp. 79–80.

33. Jeannette P. Nichols and Roy F. Nichols, *The Growth of American Democracy* (New York: Appleton-Century, 1939), p. 16.

34. U.S. Department of Commerce, Bureau of the Census, *Historical Statistics of the United States: Colonial Times to 1957* (Washington, D.C.: Government Printing Office, 1960), p. 756.

35. Merrill Jensen, ed., *English Historical Documents: American Colonial Documents to 1776* (London: Eyre and Spottiswoode, 1955), p. 480.

36. David Schneider, *The History of Public Welfare in New York State, 1609–1866* (Chicago: University of Chicago Press, 1938), p. 87.

37. William Byrd, "The History of the Dividing Line" [Life in North Carolina] [March 25, 1728], in Foerster, *American Poetry and Prose,* pp. 87–92.

38. Letter to Richard Jackson, May 5, 1753, in Albert Henry Smith, ed., *The Writings of Benjamin Franklin,* Vol. 3, *1750–1759* (New York: Macmillan, 1907), pp. 134–135, 137.

39. "Essay on the Labouring Poor," in *The Writings of Benjamin Franklin,* Vol. 5, pp. 124–125.

40. Joseph Townsend, "A Dissertation on the Poor Laws by a Well-Wisher to Mankind," in J. R. McCulloch, ed., *A Select Collection of Scarce and Valuable Economic Tracts* (London: Lord Overstone, 1859), pp. 397–449.

41. U.S. Congress, House Committee Print No. 4, *Medical Care of Veterans,* 90th Cong., 1st sess., April 17, 1967, p. 21.

42. *Ibid.,* p. 28.

Progress and Reform: 1900–1930

The National Archives

Progress and Reform: 1900–1930

Core Competencies in this Chapter (Check marks indicate which competencies are covered in depth)				
✔ Professional Identity	✔ Ethical Practice	☐ Critical Thinking	☐ Diversity in Practice	☐ Human Rights and Justice
✔ Research-Based Practice	☐ Human Behavior	✔ Policy Practice	☐ Practice Contexts	☐ Engage, Assess, Intervene, Evaluate

The rapid social and economic changes of the late nineteenth century had caught many Americans by surprise. As the new century dawned, they felt like strangers in their own land. In the countryside, the creation of a global market for agricultural goods meant that the price of wheat in Kansas was tied to not only the success of the year's harvest, but how well farmers in Canada and Australia did as well. In the cities, a predominantly native-born, white middle class and a foreign-born working class studied one another across barriers of social class, language, and culture. But the striking economic reality of the era was the emergence of economic giants: trusts, monopolies, and corporations.

Over the first thirty years of the twentieth century, Americans from all walks of life tried to come to terms with these changes and their implications for their welfare. It was an era of experimentation and innovation, but ultimately, most of the reform efforts of the era fell short of their goals. Although the motivation for reform was in abundant supply, Progressive reforms lacked two critical ingredients for success: ideas and institutions.

Intellectually, Americans lacked a set of coherent ideas for changing the economic and social structure. Many of their ideas looked to the past, to returning to a society dominated by small-town values. Others, like the creation of a socialist commonwealth that would eliminate capitalism, never received serious consideration by most Americans.

The institutional realities of the early twentieth century, too, could not support serious reform. The forces that were reshaping economic and social life were national and international in scope. Yet, most Americans owed their allegiance to social institutions that were local or sectarian. Fraternal organizations, political parties, and labor unions—even if they were affiliated with national federations—were effective only in addressing local issues.

If reform were to succeed, it would need to reach across the rigid cultural barriers that dominated American society in the early twentieth century: the lines between the countryside and the city, between workers and the middle class, between foreigners and native born, and between men and women.

The Progressives made a start at building the ideas and institutions that could ultimately reform American society, but it was only a start. Ironically, many of its gains occurred after the end of the Progressive Era with America's entry into World War I. After the war, the dominant political climate turned more conservative as the culture sought "100 percent Americanism" and "normalcy."[1] Yet, below the surface, many reform movements would continue to grow, although their eventual success was years away.

By the 1920s, the United States had become the richest country on earth— a world leader in farm and manufacturing output. By 1925, it was producing 55 percent of the world's iron ore, 66 percent of the steel, 62 percent of the petroleum, 52 percent of the timber, 60 percent of the cotton, 80 percent of the sulfur, and 95 percent of the automobiles. Solutions to all economic problems seemed within the reach of rational individuals.[2]

Revolutions in technology and communication began to knit America into a single country. The American frontier had disappeared only in the last decade of the nineteenth century. By the turn of the twentieth century, train lines connected cities and regions. In American cities, trolley lines and commuter trains made it possible for people to live in one section of town and work or shop in another. Before the 1920s had ended, the automobile and the airplane were becoming increasingly common forms of transportation.

The telephone had an equally dramatic impact on communications. In 1890, only about 2 percent of American homes had a telephone. By 1930,

40 percent did. No longer did it take days or hours to get word across town or across the nation. During the first three decades of the twentieth century, motion pictures and radio improved people's access to information and culture from across the world.

Twentieth-century inventions and innovative managerial skills revolutionized industry and agriculture. Between 1899 and 1929, the total output of manufacturing increased 273 percent.[3] Growth occurred throughout the period but was particularly stimulated by the war, when new industries were developed to replace the previously imported German dyes, chemicals, and optical instruments. When European industries were left devastated by World War I, the United States became the leading world supplier of both manufactured and agricultural products.

The period from the turn of the century to the depression of the 1930s saw the development of new power supplies, greater mechanization, and the spread of "scientific management." Whereas in 1913 it had taken fourteen hours to assemble a car, in 1914 the job was done in ninety-three minutes. By 1925, Henry Ford was able to produce an automobile every ten seconds.

In agriculture, too, mechanization and new sources of power joined with improved transportation to increase productivity. The value of agricultural output rose steadily, due almost entirely to the increase in crop yields per acre. As farming became mechanized, labor was freed to move into manufacturing. By the end of the period, although the United States had only 4 percent of the world's farmers and farm laborers, it was producing nearly 70 percent of the world's tobacco, 25 percent of the oats and hay, 20 percent of the wheat, 13 percent of the barley, and 7 percent of the potatoes.[4]

Technological progress and relatively steady employment levels resulted in a climbing gross national product (GNP), despite brief recessions. GNP stood at about $17 billion in 1900 and $104 billion in 1929. Per capita GNP rose by 73 percent in the first thirty years of the century.[5]

The increase in GNP was based on the ability of the agricultural sector to support a growing urban, industrial population. Between 1900 and 1930, the population of the United States increased by 47 million to reach 123 million. During these years, the total number of persons living in urban areas increased by 38 million to a total of 69 million. Forty percent of the population lived in urban areas in 1900; this rose to 51 percent in 1920 and to 56 percent in 1930.[6] Much of the shift from an agricultural to a predominantly urban society was achieved by a steady migration to the cities. This was true for both the black and white populations. For the United States as a whole, 27 percent of the black population and 49 percent of the white population lived in urban areas in 1910; in 1930, 44 percent of the black population and 58 percent of the white population lived in urban areas.[7] Although the Southern African American population remained predominantly rural, in the Northern and Western parts of the country, blacks concentrated in urban areas. After 1915, as changes in Southern agriculture forced many African Americans to abandon their farms, they moved to the cities of the North and South.

A measure of the economy's strength was its ability to absorb the almost 20 million immigrants who entered the country. Most of this immigration occurred during the first fifteen years of the century, when 14.5 million people came, many from southern and eastern Europe. The anti-Chinese legislation of the 1880s was followed by restrictions on Japanese immigration early in the twentieth century and then by anti-Filipino legislation. Eventually, nativist sentiment prevailed completely and general restriction of immigration became the policy of the United States in 1924. The National Origins Act of 1924 set up a system of quotas for immigration, with each country allotted a quota related to the proportion of nationals already present in the United States. Reflecting anti-Catholic and anti-Jewish sentiments of the era, the act was intended to slow the immigration rates of southern and eastern Europeans and to limit the total number of foreigners admitted.

However, despite the constraints of World War I and the legislative restrictions of the 1920s, the number of foreign born as a percentage of the total population stayed at 13 to 14 percent—one of seven people were immigrants. An even larger number of people had at least one foreign-born parent. Immigrants and their children accounted for more than one-third of the population. Most—about 75 percent—lived in cities, where rapid population growth meant a period of booming construction.[8]

Between 1920 and 1930, some 6 million people moved from farms to cities, resulting for the first time in a net loss—of 1.2 million—in farm population. As cities grew, they became commercial and industrial in character. The number of cities with populations of at least 100,000 grew from 38 in 1900 to 83 in 1930.[9] The growth was haphazard, causing crowded, unsanitary, tenement living. Families, both from abroad and from rural areas, were unfamiliar with urban living. Their social and economic vulnerability provided opportunities for political leaders—often organized into citywide "machines"—to gain their allegiance. Although city governments succeeded in addressing many social problems, especially where building infrastructure could also provide jobs, contracts, and kickbacks, the social needs of the urban working class were often ignored.

Growth and change occurred in the organization of industry, as well as in its output. In 1897, about a dozen corporations other than railroads were capitalized at $10 million. By 1903, the number had risen to 300, of which about 50 were capitalized at more than $50 million; 17 were capitalized at more than $100 million; and one, U.S. Steel, became the first billion-dollar corporation. These were the years in which some of the largest trusts in America were formed: Standard Oil, Consolidated Tobacco, and American Smelting, in addition to U.S. Steel. At the same time, many corporations became "vertically integrated," controlling their supply of raw materials as well as networks for distributing and selling their goods. The efforts of the federal government to regulate big business were largely ineffective. By 1914, large corporations dominated anthracite coal, agricultural machinery, sugar, telephone and telegraph, and public utilities in addition to iron and steel, railroads, oil, tobacco, and copper. Control of American industry had shifted from individual owners to a professional managerial class responsible to a board of directors often controlled by a small and powerful group of investment bankers.[10]

Paralleling the concentration of corporate power was a concentration of wealth and income. As the nation prospered, the income and asset growth at the top far exceeded that of either the middle class or the working class. Andrew Carnegie, for example, was said to have had an average annual income of more than $10 million—not subject to any income tax—at the turn of the century. In 1899, the richest 1.6 percent of the population had received 10.8 percent of national income. By 1910, this had jumped to 19 percent. Rising wages and relatively steady employment meant that working-class incomes rose, too, but at a much slower rate. A 1915 report by the Commission on Industrial Relations took the critical question of the era to be, "Have workers received a fair share of the enormous increase in wealth which has taken place in this country during the period, as a result largely of their labor?" Its response, "The answer is emphatically—No!"[11]

POVERTY AND THE WORKING CLASS

The commission's report pointed out that during 1890–1912, personal wealth had increased 188 percent, but the aggregate income of wage earners in manufacturing, mining, and transportation had risen only 95 percent. The wage earner's share of the net product in manufacturing had actually declined. The commission estimated that to achieve a minimum decency level, an average family of 5.6 members required an annual income of $700. Because 79 percent of the country's fathers earned less than $700 a year, earnings from other family members were necessary to sustain a family. Although reformers railed against child labor, many low-income parents were moved more by economic necessity than by moral injunctions. The Census Bureau reported that 1,750,000 children between ten and fifteen years of age were gainfully employed in 1900; by 1910, this number had dropped to 1,600,000. In 1930, however, the figure still stood at 667,000.[12]

The report of the Commission on Industrial Relations concluded that, despite the labor of wives and children, and the widespread practice of taking in boarders and lodgers, 50 to 66 percent of working-class families were poor and that a third lived in "abject poverty." Other estimates confirmed the judgment of poverty and risk. Robert Hunter, a social worker, writing in 1904, estimated the poverty population at 10 million.[13] Father John A. Ryan, ethical theorist and economist, writing in 1906, found that the average family needed an annual income of at least $600 and that 60 percent of all wage earners received less.[14] Within the ranks of the working class, as the American Federation of Labor (AFL) succeeded in unionizing some crafts, dissatisfaction was further aggravated by the notable difference in payments to skilled and unskilled workers. Each recession (1910–1911, 1914–1915, 1920–1921) meant increased unemployment and wage cuts, especially for unskilled workers—largely ex-farmhands, African Americans, and immigrants. Indeed, by 1928–1929 social welfare agencies were reporting increased caseloads. Between the newly rich, with their extreme wealth, and the working class, with their extreme poverty, lay the large middle class—a group with adequate income but little to spare, a group that was dissatisfied because it could not keep pace with the rapidly rising standard of living of those at the top.

The pre–World War I period was one of prosperity marked by rising farm income. The closing of the frontier, however, meant rising land prices. This, combined with rising costs of mechanization, made easy access to low-cost credit to buy land and machinery a major issue for most farmers. For the marginal farmer, land became more and more difficult to acquire. As the average size of farms started to grow, farm tenancy, already prevalent in the South, began to spread to the Midwest. In 1900, 35 percent of the nation's farms were tenant operated; by 1930, this had risen to 42 percent. For black farmers in the South, the figure reached 79 percent in 1930. The demands of World War I had led to an overextension of agriculture. The debt burden, cutthroat competition, and declining profits pushed the farm sector into depression before the slowdown hit industry. Between 1919 and 1929, the number of farms actually declined.[15]

The well-being of African Americans in the early twentieth century was worse than at any time since the end of slavery. With the end of Reconstruction, the African Americans had lost any real political power; they had been abandoned to the "oppression of those who had formerly exercised unlimited domination" over them. They still retained some of the political and civil rights they had won after the Civil War.[16]

The Populist revolt of the 1890s created fear among the white elite, however, that an alliance of poor whites and blacks might challenge their power. In the early years of the twentieth century, Southern states moved to pass Jim Crow laws that excluded African Americans from voting or serving on juries, segregated schools and public accommodations, and provided economic elites with even more power with which to control black workers.[17]

The segregation and suppression of Jim Crow was given judicial respectability by the Supreme Court's approval in 1896 of the "separate but equal" doctrine.[18] Rationalization of the necessity for segregation was epitomized by the widespread acceptance of D. W. Griffith's 1915 film *The Birth of a Nation,* in which freed blacks were stereotyped as cruel, vengeful rulers over starving, helpless whites and as "racially incapable of understanding, sharing, or contributing to Americanism."[19] In this atmosphere, Booker T. Washington's belief that African Americans should focus on acquiring skills and better work habits found support among whites, who gained comfort and conviction from the seeming acquiescence of the country's outstanding Negro leader—the founder of Tuskegee Institute—in policies of social segregation and political cooperation. Washington wrote:

> The wisest among my race understand that the agitation of questions of social equality is the extremest folly, and that progress in the enjoyment of all the privileges that will come to us must be the result of severe and constant struggle rather than of artificial forcing. No race that has anything to contribute to the markets of the world is long in any degree ostracized. It is important and right that all privileges of the law be ours, but it is vastly more important that we be prepared for the exercise of these privileges.[20]

Thus, the Progressive Era was not one of progress for African Americans. Sunk in the tenancy-mortgage morass of the sharecropper and crop-lien systems and subjected to lynching and harassment, the black population began to migrate to urban areas. In 1900, there were only 2 million blacks living in cities. The largest single group was in Washington, D.C. Baltimore, New Orleans, Philadelphia, and New York each had more than 60,000 black residents.[21] Net migration of blacks to Northern states amounted to 426,000 between 1910 and 1920 and jumped to 713,000 during the next decade.[22]

The beginning of the flight from the South coincided with a period of dramatically increased labor productivity, as mass production techniques and assembly lines were introduced. From 1919 to 1929, manufacturing output increased by 53 percent, while the number of wage earners in manufacturing remained stable.[23] Annual real earnings rose and the length of the workweek fell, so that for the employed it was a prosperous period. But for blacks forced off the farms and trying to gain entry into the labor market, times were always hard. Although there were not enough black migrants in the cities for them to have political or economic clout, their numbers were sufficient to foster white hostility, both because of competition with whites for jobs and because of their use, along with immigrants, as strikebreakers in labor disputes. Discrimination dominated white–black relations, and blacks were successfully excluded from the ranks of organized labor. Indeed, African Americans were even excluded from unskilled factory jobs in most cities, even though these jobs were near the bottom of the occupational ladder (Figure 1).

A new feature of African American life in Northern cities was residential segregation. In the South, African Americans typically lived in small towns

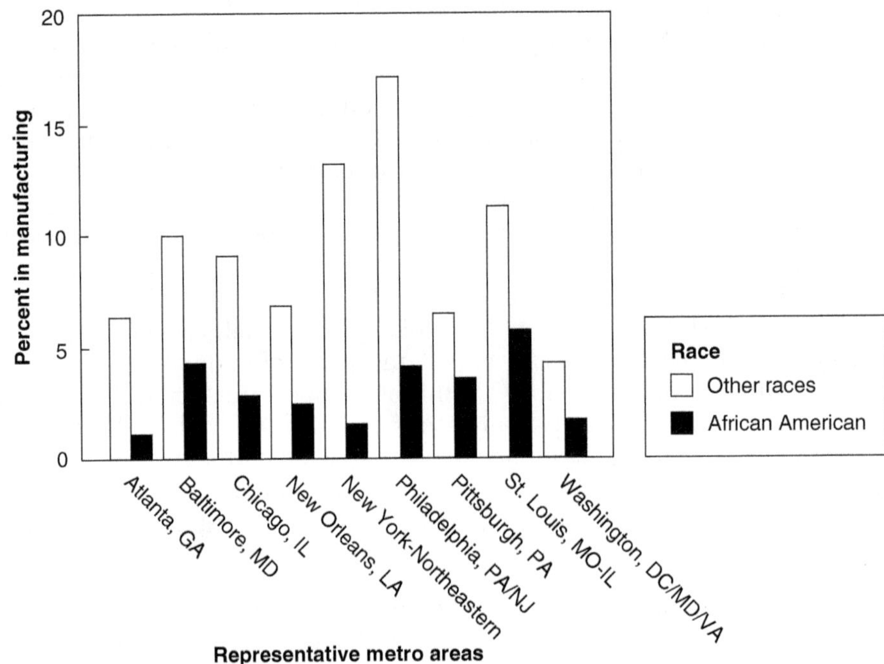

Figure 1

Racial discrimination in manufacturing jobs. African Americans migrated from rural to urban areas during the early years of the twentieth century; yet, they continued to face severe discrimination. In most cities, even factory employment was closed to them.

Source: U.S. Census 1910, author's calculation

Ethical Practice

Critical Thinking Question: Settlement houses and other charity institutions segregated services for African Americans during the Progressive Era. How did this violate the ethical principles of the profession?

on isolated farms. In the North, white residents and landlords conspired to push most black residents into small, overcrowded enclaves. Yet, the growth of the black population in many cities pushed black families to seek housing outside their neighborhoods. Clashes between whites and blacks over maintaining the *color line* resulted in frequent riots, the most notorious of which took place in Chicago in 1919.

The black population was generally unaffected by reform activities and the social welfare benefits that resulted from them. In an era marked by economic progress and social mobility, this group remained poor and powerless. More social legislation aiding and protecting the working class was passed during the Progressive Era than had been passed in any previous century. For the most part, however, legislation affecting the labor of women and children, workmen's compensation, regulation of hours and wages, and industrial safety all applied to industries in which black participation was minimal. This fact eluded social welfare reformers who tended to view the problems of all minorities as coextensive with the problems of immigrants. Despite periodic race riots, the relatively small number of blacks in the cities of the North (where most agitation for social reform was concentrated) and their segregation from the mainstream of economic, political, and social life made it possible to ignore their special problems. When reformers did focus on the needs of African Americans, they often provided help on a segregated basis. For example, in Chicago, philanthropists funded social services in the black ghetto so African Americans would not create white reprisals by seeking help at settlement houses in white neighborhoods.[24]

For Native Americans, too, conditions improved very slowly. They were poor, largely uneducated, and deprived of citizenship and suffrage. Of those living on reservations, almost three-quarters of the children received no schooling. Much of the education that occurred was in boarding schools, which alienated the children and left them prepared for very little. Not until 1928 were federal funds increased, and it was to be the mid-1930s before states received special funds to provide public education for Native Americans.[25] Only in 1924 were Native Americans recognized as citizens of the United States of America.[26]

COALITIONS FOR REFORM

Progressivism grew out of middle-class concerns that the battle between big business and labor would engulf American society. It was the first attempt to fashion a political ideology between unregulated capitalism and a more radical alternative. Reformers, however, found themselves pulled in two directions. Culturally, they had much in common with the social and economic elite whose actions they feared. Although many reformers had sympathy for the plight of workers, they were suspicious of the political and labor leaders who were their representatives. Although many Progressives worked hard to forge new coalitions for reform, their contradictory impulses often undermined their effectiveness.

Progressivism grew out of middle-class concerns that the battle between big business and labor would engulf American society. It was the first attempt to fashion a political ideology between unregulated capitalism and a more radical alternative.

The industrial collapse of 1893 produced hardships for 4 million unemployed and for small businessmen, farmers, and investors. Many demanded a change in power relationships and the development of a more equitable system of distribution of wealth and income. The march of "General" Jacob Coxey's army of the unemployed on Washington, D.C. in 1894, the increased prevalence of strikes and industrial violence, the growth of union membership (particularly in the Western Federation of Miners and the United Mine Workers), and the strength of the Populist movement were part of an agrarian/working-class coalition for reform.

In the early years of the twentieth century, the reform movement shifted toward the center. The AFL, representing more highly paid craft workers than the older, industrial unions, became the dominant force in the labor movement. Writers and educators undertook an exposé of big business; new political leadership took on the task of city and state reforms; and social workers worked on behalf of the poor segregated into urban slums. Social protest became the property of intellectuals and professionals.

It became clear to more and more Americans that laissez-faire and small business no longer characterized their economy. The era of small business firms engaged in competition had supported a model of individual achievement, but the emergence of large corporations or trusts engaged in monopolistic market control made this model appear irrelevant. In a competitive, individualistic society, the dominant social theorists had argued for social reform based on individual change; the corporate universe of the twentieth century seemed to require a reform of institutions.

During most of the nineteenth century, it had been liberal dogma that the limited government action was good for the economy and society. In the early twentieth century, more Americans were willing to ask if government had a role in creating a more just social order. A "new liberalism" based on a belief in positive government action provided the ideological basis for many Progressives.

Research would provide knowledge of social and political problems, and the extension of democratic institutions in government would lead to enactment of the appropriate legislation. In retrospect, it was a romantic and an optimistic belief in rational, peaceful, and democratic social change.

Key to the Progressive vision was a belief that immigrants would eventually adopt the language, tastes, and culture of white Protestants. In settlement houses, southern and eastern Europeans were encouraged to eschew olive oil and garlic in their cooking in favor of butter and bland ingredients.[27] Efforts to Americanize immigrants extended to the growing Latino population of the Southwest, where children were encouraged to abandon their native language and culture.[28] Progressives wanted to maintain the cultural values of an earlier time—individuals, opportunity, "lifting one's self by one's bootstraps"—even as the social order that supported those values disappeared. This contradiction limited the effectiveness of many reform efforts.

The reform activities of the Progressive Era were spearheaded by many groups, some working independently, some working cooperatively as particular issues warranted cooperation, some working for individual aggrandizement, and some working altruistically for the larger society. One group was composed of small businessmen who were anxious to control and stop the domination of trusts and banking establishments. They were joined by writers, social workers, lawyers, and clergymen, as well as other professionals who were suspicious of big business. Farmers, in search of easy credit, also became a part of the struggle against the domination of "organized money."

The growth of the Socialist Party in the early years of the century strengthened the hand of reformers by raising the specter of more radical alternatives to Progressive reform. Starting with a membership of less than 5,000 in 1900,

Scenes from "The Twig of Thorn" given by a club of working girls in King Philip Settlement, Fall River, Massachusetts, 1916. Settlement houses worked to improve living conditions, inter-group relations, and the cultural lives of the residents of working-class neighborhoods

it enrolled 118,000 members by 1912, including many of the nation's leading intellectuals—John Dewey, Stuart Chase, Paul Douglas, Jack London, Walter Lippmann, and Alexander Meikeljohn. Eugene Debs, running for president as the Socialist candidate, polled 6 percent of the popular vote in 1912. More important perhaps was the Socialists' success that same year in electing more than 1,000 members to various public offices. Socialist doctrines were widely reviewed, discussed, and quoted. Socialists were sometimes allied in specific causes with other reform groups. The growth of the Socialist Party and its increased visibility served as a threat and catalyst for more moderate reform groups seeking regulation of industry. The Socialist Party's opposition to American entry into World War I in 1917 led to government suppression and the jailing of many leaders, including Debs.[29]

During the Progressive Era, the federal government took some halting steps to regulate business in the public interest. In 1902, President Theodore Roosevelt instructed the attorney general to bring suit under the Sherman Antitrust Act against the Northern Securities Company, a consolidation of railways including the Northern Pacific, the Great Northern, and the Chicago, Burlington, and Quincy systems. The Supreme Court sustained the government's appeal and effectively frustrated the plan of E. H. Harriman to bring all the important railways in the country under his control. In 1906, Congress passed the Hepburn Act, which permitted the Interstate Commerce Commission (ICC) to fix the rates of railroads, of storage, refrigeration, and terminal facilities, and of sleeping car, express, and pipeline companies. In 1910, authority was extended to the ICC to regulate telephone and telegraph companies.

Economic and regulatory reforms took various shapes. As a result of Upton Sinclair's *The Jungle* and of other exposés of the food and pharmaceutical industries, editors of popular journals and the American Medical Association, among others, formed a coalition to secure passage of the Food and Drug Act in 1906. In 1909, the Sixteenth Amendment, which established a federal income tax, was introduced in Congress by Cordell Hull. By 1913, it had been ratified by the states and became law. During this same year, Congress created the Federal Reserve System, a first step by the federal government to regulate banking.

Through much of the nineteenth century, federal and state courts had restricted the ability of workers to organize unions. A new wave of organizing gained greater public attention during these years. The passage of the Clayton Antitrust Act in 1914 represented the success of small business and labor unions to unite behind efforts to control the power of big business. The act also provided some safeguards for organizers, by restricting the use of injunctions against unions. Although these provisions were ultimately watered down by the Supreme Court, the Clayton Act represented an important step in acknowledging working people's right to organize. The Federal Trade Commission Act established a commission whose purpose was to bring to bear the knowledge and advice of a group of economic experts on "unfair" methods of competition and infractions of antitrust laws.

The democratic thrust of the Progressive Era made political reform a partner of economic reform. Just as muckraking publications had reported lurid instances of fraud and graft and of monopolistic control in industry, in railroading, and in public utilities, they detailed corruption in state and local governments, in the courts, and in the U.S. Senate.[30] A veritable avalanche of widely read, eagerly awaited exposés of *The Shame of the Cities* or "*The Treason of the Senate*" led the way to political change. The effort was twofold: to expand citizen participation in political affairs and to increase governmental responsiveness and honesty. Progressives worked for women's suffrage, the secret ballot, direct primaries, direct election of senators, initiative, referendum, recall, and municipal home rule. In addition, they demanded civil service reform, the short ballot, the regulation of campaign expenditures, accountability and leadership on the part of elected officials, and the commission and city manager plans of municipal government.

Middle- and upper-class white women, including the founders of social work, exercised unprecedented political influence during these years. Although the search for gender equality motivated many of them, their broadest influence was tied to their traditional roles as mothers and wives. *Maternalism*—an ideology based on the moral authority associated with women's traditional role—provided a means of uniting women whatever their position on equality. A variety of reforms, including mother's pensions, the creation of the Children's Bureau, child and women labor legislation, and efforts to improve maternal and child health, were tied to the rise of maternalism.[31]

On the federal level, Congress, in 1907, banned political contributions by corporations. In 1913, the Seventeenth Amendment to the Constitution provided for direct election of senators. In 1919, the Nineteenth Amendment, providing for women's suffrage, was passed. It was ratified by the required thirty-six states just one year later, bringing victory to this cause after almost seventy-five years of campaigning.

On a state and local level, twenty states introduced the initiative (making it possible for the citizenry to propose legislation) and the referendum (making it possible for voters to pass on measures introduced in legislative bodies). By 1915, direct primary and presidential preference laws were on the books of two-thirds of the states, challenging the power of political bosses.

Efforts to reform local politics highlighted a value conflict among Progressives between efficiency and democratic control. Although local governments and political machines were often corrupt, they also were responsive to lower-middle- and working-class voters. In many cases, upper-class professionals led efforts to reduce the power of these voters by increasing the role of professionals and experts in running city government. The drive for efficiency, economy, and honesty in the administration of local governments began in Galveston, Texas, in 1900, when the entire political machinery of mayor, council, and bureaus was abolished and replaced by a board of commissioners. Thereafter, the commission form of government spread rapidly, especially in smaller cities, where its structure—generally five commissioners elected at large and each responsible for a particular department—was most appropriate. Starting with Dayton, Ohio, in 1914, the city manager type of government—a government run by an appointed expert in city administration—also found widespread acceptance.

In public welfare administration, change resulted in an initial shift of responsibility from local overseers of the poor to local or county departments of welfare. Kansas City, Missouri, established a city department of welfare in 1910, with authority to provide for the relief of the poor and the care of delinquents, the unemployed, and other needy groups. St. Joseph, Missouri, established a county–city department of public welfare, and Chicago set up the Cook County Bureau of Public Welfare, both in 1913.

The rise of public welfare marked a dramatic break with late-nineteenth-century thought about poverty. In place of a voluntary movement to limit "excessive almsgiving," philanthropic leaders called for government action to reduce the distress of the poor. Increasingly, Progressives came to see that poverty was primarily an economic, not a moral, condition.

Professional Identity

Critical Thinking Question: How has the predominance of women in social work influenced its professional identity? How did feminism and maternalism influence its development?

Efforts to reform local politics highlighted a value conflict among Progressives between efficiency and democratic control.

Nor did the country's entry into World War I completely stop local governmental restructuring. Westchester County, New York, established a department of welfare in 1916. In 1917, an important reorganization of the Illinois state government occurred with the passage of the Civil Administrative Code, which provided for the grouping of all state functions and activities into nine departments, each with its own director. Among the nine was a Department of Welfare with its director of public welfare responsible for administering the state's assistance, services, and institutional programs. The Illinois code was emulated by other states and was the start of a new era in public administration. In many states, for example, public welfare services were consolidated into statewide systems administered by appointed heads of state departments of welfare. Both in the statewide scope of the organizations and in the removal of department executives "from current political responsibility, except through [the ultimate political responsibility of] the governor,"[32] the trend foreshadowed the requirements of the Social Security Act of 1935.

No reform activities were more representative of the Progressive Era than those that occurred in the arena of social welfare. The reform movement responded to and fostered the new profession of social work. Individual social workers, through research, persistence, and expertise, moved to the forefront of advocacy for social legislation. Theodore Roosevelt himself, acting on the commonly held conviction that all were personally responsible for the current state of affairs depicted so graphically in muckraking literature, called upon each citizen to contribute to "reform through social work."[33] Social work, acting on society's will for social change, carried that projection in two sometimes converging but basically different operations—the Charity Organization and Settlement House movements.

Those who labored for social reform were primarily concerned, as a matter of social justice, "to bring the power of the state and national governments into the economic struggle on the side of women, children, and other unprotected groups."[34] Whether prompted by the Charity Organization hope to sustain and strengthen individuals in their own efforts to cope, or by the Settlement House conviction that any intervention short of intrinsic societal restructuring must be considered only "a down payment toward justice,"[35] social workers could find common ground for the work that needed doing.

At the height of the reform movement, between 1905 and the beginning of World War I, leaders of the Charity Organization and Settlement House movements came together in behalf of social reform activity. Changing views of the family prompted the participation of organized charity in reform. In 1900, Charles Faulkner's presidential address at the National Conference of Charities and Corrections had labeled the family "the unit of social order" and laid out a program of education in the home and in the school for the moral improvement of individuals. His Darwinian bent took him from a concern for the maintenance of "the blessings and protection of society through its family life" to call for avoiding "unrestrained comingling of . . . defectives with the people."[36] By 1908, however, Mary Richmond was arguing for the protection of family life against the onslaughts of a hostile environment.

Richmond, whose *Social Diagnosis* was an important milestone in the evolution of casework, referred to the family as "the great social unit, the fundamental social fact." She demanded changes in agency practices, action in regard to child labor laws, industrial safety regulations, and protection of working women, as well as administrative changes in industrial operations to strengthen family life. She challenged the members of her social work audience to ask themselves, "Have we at least set plans in motion that will make the children better heads of families than their parents have been?"[37] Richmond's challenge was based on a new recognition of "the overwhelming force of heredity *plus* the environment that we inherit." Social workers and their allies advocated for legislation to regulate tenement and factory construction; to prevent and compensate for industrial accidents and diseases; to prohibit child labor and provide for compulsory education; to improve sanitary and health conditions; to provide social insurance as security against unemployment, retirement, or death of the breadwinner; and to protect workers—especially women—in regard to minimum wages and working hours.

Improvement in housing conditions had been a concern of social workers at least since 1882, when the Boston Associated Charities appointed a Committee on Dwellings of the Poor. In the same year, the New York and Buffalo Charity Organization Societies combined to get a tenement housing bill through the state legislature. During the next decade, they allied themselves with settlement residents and others to investigate and publicize the housing conditions of the poor. The New York City Tenement House Law was passed in 1901. Aimed at preventing the construction of lightless, airless tenements, the law became a model to follow. Similar legislation was passed for Chicago in 1902; by 1910, most large cities had inaugurated some housing reform.

SOCIAL REFORM: WORKING CONDITIONS

No reform crusade better illustrates Progressives' belief in *maternalism* than their advocacy of child and women's labor legislation. In 1900, nearly 2 million children aged ten to fifteen and almost 5 million women over fifteen were in a labor force totaling about 29 million.[38] Twenty-eight states had already adopted some legal protections for children. By 1914, as a result of the continued assault by the National Child Labor Committee, the National Consumer's League, the General Federation of Women's Clubs, and others, almost all the states had laws covering hours and conditions of child labor in factories, mills, and workshops and setting minimum ages for leaving school.[39]

But the laws were weak and inadequate. Owen R. Lovejoy, secretary of the National Child Labor Committee and chairman of the Committee on Standards of Living and Labor of the National Conference of Charities and Corrections, reported the following:

> No state has made any adequate plan to protect its children to sixteen years from bare-handed contact with the red hot tools of our industrial competition. Nearly half the states have no effective way of protecting children even to the fourteenth birthday. Several permit their employment at twelve or even younger.[40]

Much of the problem occurred in industries engaged in interstate commerce, and, therefore, federal intervention seemed necessary. The first formal attempts to bring child labor under federal control were made in 1906, when bills were introduced in Congress to prohibit the interstate shipment of articles produced in factories or mines employing children. The bills were not passed. A few years later, President Theodore Roosevelt directed the secretary of labor to investigate the situation. In 1912, the Children's Bureau was created to report, among other things, on "dangerous occupations, accidents and diseases of children, employment legislation affecting children."[41] The bureau's investigations bolstered the report of the secretary of labor as to the need for child protections, and further efforts to obtain federal regulation of child welfare followed. The Keating–Owen bill was passed by Congress in 1916, but it was found unconstitutional two years later on the grounds that it transcended "the authority delegated to Congress over commerce."[42] Subsequent improvements in child labor legislation remained with the states; by 1930, all of the states and the District of Columbia had taken legal measures to safeguard the employment and working conditions of children. In many instances, old provisions had been strengthened.[43]

In the country as a whole, child labor had steadily declined so that by 1930 less than 5 percent of the children between ten and fifteen years of age were employed, compared to 18 percent in 1900. Even in the South, which had lagged in regulatory legislation, the ratio of children employed in its newly developing textile industry was no higher than that in its Northern counterpart. These advances were chronicled in the census of 1930. Despite within-industry equivalency, however, there were large industrial and geographic differences. For example, only 3 percent of children between ten and fifteen years were at work in industrial Rhode Island, whereas 24 percent were at work in Mississippi, a state in which child welfare laws were loosely enforced and the all-white legislature cared little about the well-being of black children. Nor did the census takers secure information concerning the paid employment of children under ten.[44]

Efforts to effect child labor legislation were paralleled by efforts to regulate conditions and hours of work for female workers, who constituted 20 percent of the labor force. Maternalists argued that, like children, women needed to be protected from the physical harm of long work hours.

The National Consumer's League, under the leadership of its executive, Florence Kelley, was particularly active in regard to legal protections for working women. Under the aegis of the league, Kelley and Josephine Goldmark, a social worker, completed research that was successfully used by Louis Brandeis in arguing the constitutionality of Oregon's law limiting working hours for women to ten hours per day. Brandeis marshaled data from around the world to support his case, that women's physical well-being was threatened by an excessively long workday. Ironically, when the Supreme Court sided with Brandeis in upholding the Oregon law in 1908, a Progressive victory was built on the assumption of women's inherent weakness.

By 1912, the year in which the Committee on Standards of Living and Labor of the National Conference of Charities and Corrections made its report, the battle had shifted to the eight-hour day and the six-day workweek. The committee predicted, "The day will come—come tripping on the heels of social regulation— when our manufacturers and merchants will be able to distribute ... [their products] without compelling the sacrifice of the health of our mothers or burning out the eyes of our little children who now bend over their work ... at all hours of the night."[45]

Progressive women, many of them social workers, were able to use women's traditional roles as wife and mother to win successes in regulating women's and children's labor. However, by basing their arguments on the special vulnerability of women and children, they faced difficulties in extending labor law to the adult male population. It also prevented women's groups from finding common cause with organized labor.

The average workday at the close of the Civil War remained at eleven hours.[46] A movement to limit the workday to eight hours collapsed in 1886, when the violence and aftermath of Chicago's Haymarket Square riot proved disastrous to the Knights of Labor. In 1900, according to an estimate based on information of the Bureau of Labor Statistics, the average standard workweek was still more than fifty-seven hours, having declined very little during the previous decade.[47] For industry as a whole, there was wide variation, so that unorganized workers, such as those in the blast furnaces of steel mills, ordinarily worked a twelve-hour day and eighty-four-hour week, whereas organized workers in the building trades had achieved a forty-eight-hour week, working eight hours a day, six days a week.[48]

During the early years of the twentieth century, workers struggled to develop responses to the threat of unemployment. Workers viewed the eight-hour movement as a way to increase the number of jobs, by reducing the hours worked by each worker. Unionized workers, who remained a small share of the total workforce, also experimented with work-sharing systems, in which workers would reduce their weekly hours of work so that fewer workers would be laid off, and voluntary unemployment funds, in which union members would make weekly contributions and then draw benefits if they were laid off. However, these efforts rarely were sufficient to cope with sharp increases in joblessness during depressions.

Differentials in work hours between unionized and nonunionized industries indicate the significance of unionization for reduced work hours. Average weekly hours in 1900 for unionized manufacturing industries were fifty-three, compared to sixty-two for nonunion manufacturing. By 1920, unionized manufacturing hours had declined to forty-six per week and nonunion manufacturing to fifty-four. Unionized manufacturing had achieved the eight-hour day and nonunion manufacturing had made significant gains. The gap between organized and unorganized labor narrowed.[49]

In response to the increased militancy of labor following World War I, major corporations pursued the "American plan" during the 1920s. This combined "welfare capitalism"—the expansion of programs to employees, including unemployment and pension benefits—with an aggressive antiunion campaign. Companies like the Ford Motor Company employed "social secretaries" to provide social services to workers. Yet, without a fully developed set of professional ethics, these social workers often reported "undesirable" behavior to employers, including labor union membership and drinking. Although welfare capitalism died during the Great Depression, the idea that employers would provide significant social welfare benefits to their employees became one of the defining features of American social welfare.

SOCIAL REFORM: WOMEN, WORK, AND SUFFRAGE

In 1900, the National American Women's Suffrage Association (NAWSA), representing the joining of the two earlier rivals in the women's suffrage movement, was still unclear as to directions for achieving votes for women. The association's flirtation with "educated suffrage," offering to counter the votes of lower-class blacks and immigrants with those of middle-class women, contributed to a separation of white women from black women, middle-class women from lower-class women, nonworking women from working women, and native-born women from immigrant women. There were seemingly irreparable divisions.

In the Progressive Era, racism and nativism, as integral parts of the suffrage movement, began to subside. Josephine Shaw Lowell's statement of 1888, pointing up the discrepancy between middle-class rhetoric and lower-class reality in the matter of working mothers, signified a beginning shift in her own stance toward people in need.[50] The NAWSA moved away from a position that not only failed but was generally untenable in the climate of the times. In addition, the limiting nature of a single-issue organization became apparent as other women's groups moved to the fore. These new organizations—for example, the National Consumer's League, the National Women's Trade Union League, and the Young Women's Christian Association—were concerned both with matters affecting women as women and with the potential of the vote for addressing social injustice that affected women and others. For example, the NAWSA publication, *The Woman's Journal,* supported the garment workers' strike of 1909 and 1910 and reported the tragic Triangle Shirt-Waist Company fire of 1911, which led to the death of 146 workers, as demonstrating the need for women's votes to ensure "more effective factory legislation and a larger number of [factory] inspectors."[51] This broadened view resulted in increased membership. By 1910, the official numbers in NAWSA had risen to 100,000; in 1917, the membership stood at 2 million.

Part of the reality of the Progressive Era was the increasing participation of women in the labor force. In 1900, there were more than 5 million gainfully employed female workers. Most worked as unskilled factory hands or as domestics; most were foreign born or black; some were married. The number of female workers increased rapidly to meet the demands of this generally prosperous era—later, the added demands of a Europe at war, and finally, in 1917, the demands of the United States itself as its own male workers, drafted for wartime service, had to be replaced. By 1910, the number of gainfully employed women had risen to 8 million. Although the end of World War I brought a return to traditional gender roles for many men and women, by 1920, the number of women in the paid labor force had risen to more than 8.5 million.[52] The formation of the National Women's Trade Union League and its activities in supporting existing unions of women wage earners testifies to the increase in the numbers of women workers, their beginning entrance in skilled positions, and their increasing political consciousness.

Progress toward the unionization of women was nevertheless slow and fraught with difficulty. Much of the history was characterized by spontaneous work stoppage and strikes against low wages and torturous working conditions. These strikes resulted in efforts to organize, but even when success in gaining demands followed, unionization tended to fall apart. In skilled industry, the responsibility for this can be traced to the overall antagonism of male workers, who accused women of scabbing during strike actions on the part of male-dominated unions, of taking men's jobs, and of lowering wage rates. These antagonisms carried over in the halfhearted attempts by the AFL, an organization of craft unions made up of skilled workers, to organize women's unions or to admit women into existing organizations. The AFL, like its constituents, was suspicious of women's commitment to work, of their staying power during strikes, and of their effect upon wages. The AFL's lack of interest was encouraged by the fact that by far the largest number of women continued to work in unskilled jobs—in textiles, shirt and waist making, laundries, and domestic service. Among these unskilled workers, foreign-born and black women predominated. Black women particularly suffered exclusion from unionizing efforts, even from the efforts of other unskilled workers.

The task of bringing together the work-related and suffrage-related concerns of women was not easy. Concern for their physical, moral, and emotional well-being sprang from the conviction that "the prime function of woman must ever be the perpetuating of the race. . . . The woman is worth more to society . . . as the mother of healthy children than as the swiftest labeler of cans."[53] The result was a great deal of effort to estimate "a living wage" for women and to clarify the special needs of women in regard to working hours and working conditions. Although similar concerns were being explored in connection with all workers, very special legislative protection was sought for the unique circumstances of women. The culmination of these concerns for women, reflecting the additional burdens they had assumed during World War I, came with the establishment by Congress in 1920 of the Women's Bureau within the Department of Labor.

By the time of the armistice in 1918, women's groups had become accustomed to cooperation. This unity of action comprised a powerful political force. Under the direction of Carrie Chapman Catt, who had been reelected its president in 1915, the NAWSA was revitalized and led the final march toward victory. Catt was able to gain President Wilson's support. Not the least of that support derived from the contribution of women and of women's organizations to the war effort. The Nineteenth Amendment to the Constitution was approved by Congress on June 4, 1919, and ratified by the required number of states on August 26, 1920. The NAWSA went out of existence but was revived as the League of Women Voters.

The end of World War I also brought success to another women-led movement, the drive for Prohibition. The battle against alcoholic beverages was long and complicated. It combined a Progressive concern for the workers' health and family stability with a reaction by Protestant and rural people against the diversity and growth of urban populations. In fact, the strength of the National Women's Christian Temperance Union combined with the government's wartime conservation efforts—that is, the need to limit the use of grain for the production of liquors—to win congressional approval for Prohibition sooner than women's suffrage. The Eighteenth Amendment to the Constitution prohibiting the manufacture, sale, and import or export of liquor was ratified in 1919. Ironically, within a year, the U.S. census would report that a majority of Americans lived in cities. Urban resistance to Prohibition ultimately led to its repeal by the Twenty-First Amendment to the Constitution in 1933.

Organized women were successful on a host of issues during the Progressive Era. Certainly, achieving suffrage and passing Prohibition were two significant victories. Women would go on to serve important roles in other reform movements over the next half century, but political feminism would not revive as a separate movement until the late 1960s.

SOCIAL REFORM: INCOME SECURITY

Progressive reformers struggled to find strategies to address the major hazards of an industrial society—accident, illness, death of the breadwinner, old age and retirement, and unemployment. Industrialization and urbanization required enormous change on the part of the family. Economic survival required mobility, freedom to move from farms to industrial sites where jobs existed. The mobile family was almost by definition a small family. Having moved to the cities, the families were then trapped by low wages and a lack of resources and industrial skills. Most family members had to stand ready to work to meet the costs of urban living. The family became increasingly dependent for income on factory owners, who themselves felt no responsibility for their workers' welfare, and on nonfamily members for services previously performed internally—child care for working mothers, for example. The family of the Progressive Era was a unit caught in the stress of a period of social change, a unit socially and economically insecure in its day-to-day living and vulnerable to anxieties about an unknown future.

Reformers proposed two strategies to cope with families' increased economic vulnerability. Some suggested that *social insurance*—contributory plans that would provide aid to workers—was the best model, while others focused on modernizing *public assistance* programs—targeted to low-income families. During the Progressive Era, each won a victory with the adoption of workmen's compensation and mother's pensions.

Workmen's compensation for injuries resulting from industrial accidents was first discussed at the American Sociological Conference of 1902. During this same year, when the National Conference of Charities and Corrections appointed a committee to investigate the topic, Maryland's Workmen's Compensation Act was declared illegal. The fact that no one could be found to appeal this decision of the lower court did not impede growing national enthusiasm for such a measure. Action was spurred by the realization that "the industries of our country every year claim an army of 15,000 men killed, and some half a million injured."[54] President Theodore Roosevelt's enthusiastic support of Senate action resulted in the Federal Employee's Act of 1906.

Commissions in Massachusetts and Illinois recommended industrial insurance in 1904 and 1907, respectively, but failed to lead to legislative action. Discussion of workmen's compensation occurred again at the annual meetings of the National Conference of Charities and Corrections in 1905 and 1906; a National Conference on Workmen's Compensation was held in 1909. By 1910, the year of the second National Conference on Workmen's Compensation, a groundswell of support had developed. Many industrial employers were attracted to workmen's compensation as a means of reducing lawsuits and bringing predictability to the cost of industrial accidents. In 1911, the year regarded "as the beginning of an intelligent grappling with the problem," ten states enacted workmen's compensation laws.[55]

Yet, other efforts to enact social insurance were less successful. The issue of old age security was raised for discussion in the United States in the decade before World War I. The number of older people in the population had risen as birth rates fell, and, at the same time, industrialization increased the likelihood of dependency in old age. The more advanced European industrial nations, France, Germany, and England, had already instituted old age support systems. Both the National Conference of Charities and Corrections and the Progressive party endorsed the principles of social insurance as a response to economic need from unemployment, illness, and old age in 1912. Case studies documented the inability of individuals to save for their own old age, the inadequacy of private charity, and the inability or unwillingness of industry to provide private pensions. Nonetheless, attempts to provide income in old age either through public or private pensions failed. At the outbreak of World War I, only Arizona and Alaska had even limited pension plans, and less than 1 percent of American workers were covered by private insurance. The economic status of the elderly declined and their dependence on public welfare rose steadily.

In the years immediately following World War I, reform groups, especially the National Consumer's League, the American Association for Labor Legislation, and the National Women's Trade Union League, gave health insurance their first priority, and the impetus toward old age pensions came to a standstill.

Only with the coming of the Great Depression at the end of the 1920s did the old age pension movement begin to gather support. Then the research and leadership of social reformers, economists, and social scientists had a new grassroots base of support. The Fraternal Order of Eagles, a broad-based popular group, began to organize community pension clubs and lobby for state pension bills. Three states—Montana, Nevada, and Pennsylvania—passed voluntary, limited pension bills in 1923. Most other states followed suit in the next few years. By 1927, the American Association for Old Age Security, headed by Abraham Epstein, was created to work for an income support program for the elderly. Together with the American Association for Labor Legislation, they lobbied for old age assistance pensions and laid the groundwork for the enactment of social security.

By 1929, however, they had achieved little success. In all, eleven states had pensions for the aging and reached 1,000 people with total benefits of $222,000. The first mandatory system was legislated in California where the percentage of people over sixty-five was twice the national average and unemployment among the aged, high. In every state that had pensions, the payments were far too low and the coverage was woefully inadequate, but a precedent of state responsibility for old age security had been set.

SOCIAL REFORM: FAMILY WELFARE

Although the drive for social insurance stalled during the 1920s, maternalist efforts to link reform to the protection of women and children succeeded. Legislation to regulate the working conditions of women and children and to insure against loss of income due to industrially caused illness and accident was one part of a package that might loosely be identified with family welfare. The development of juvenile courts and federal efforts to improve maternal and child health and widows' pensions completed this agenda. Social workers and other women professionals worked as researchers and advocates in moving these proposals forward.

As professional services developed, social research became a tool for advancing social legislation. Social work's contribution to social reform during the Progressive Era was in large measure derived from its introduction of systematic surveys to the study of social problems. This was best illustrated by the Pittsburgh Survey of 1907–1908, directed by Paul Kellogg, a social worker and assistant editor of *Charities and the Commons*, the national journal published under the auspices of the New York Charity Organization Society. An article in the March 1906 issue of *Charities and the Commons*, "Neglected Neighborhoods in the Alleys, Shacks and Tenements of the National Capitol," led to the suggestion by the chief probation officer of the Allegheny County (Pennsylvania) Juvenile Court that a similar investigation be made in the Pittsburgh area. The suggestion was favorably received by the Publications Committee of the Charity Organization Society and an advisory committee was formed. Among the members of the committee, in addition to Kellogg, were William H. Matthews, head worker at Kingsley House in Pittsburgh; Robert A. Woods, another leading settlement house worker and former Pittsburgh resident; Florence Kelley, director of the National Consumer's League; and John R. Commons, a well-known economist. Funding was secured from a number of sources but primarily from the Russell Sage Foundation, which used the survey as its initial large investment in social research.

The Pittsburgh Survey was "the first major attempt to survey in depth the entire life of a single community,"[56] and for this purpose, Kellogg pulled together a study team of workers and students of social welfare and the social sciences. The findings, published serially in *Charities and the Commons* and later in book form, covered "wages, hours, conditions of labor, housing, schooling, health, taxation, fire and police protection, recreation [and] land values."[57] They became widely known not only through their publication in professional literature but also through their being brought to the public's attention in popular periodicals such as *Collier's Weekly*. The result was a factual base for use in social action.

Similarly, social research was a major weapon of the National Child Labor Committee, whose primary interest was child labor legislation. The officers of the National Child Labor Committee included persons who were active on the many fronts of the social reform movement. Edgar Gardner Murphy had seen to the formation of the committee. Also on the committee were Jane Addams, founder of Hull House; Florence Kelley; Felix Adler of Columbia University and longtime crusader for tenement housing reform; Lillian Wald, founder of the Henry Street Settlement House; and Edward T. Devine and Robert W. DeForest, executive and president, respectively, of the New York Charity Organization Society. An awareness of the value of coalitions for achieving social welfare goals was demonstrated when the committee set up headquarters in Chicago's United Charities Building, which also sheltered the Association for the Improvement of the Conditions of the Poor, the Charity Organization Society, the Children's Aid Society, and the National Consumer's League.

As early as 1906, the National Child Labor Committee was able to have introduced in Congress a bill for the establishment of a children's bureau. As part of a campaign to have the bill passed, the committee was successful in influencing President Roosevelt to call the 1909 White House Conference on Child Dependency. The president established the theme of the conference by extolling the virtues of home life and by urging that children "not be deprived of it except for urgent and compelling reasons."[58] The conference went on record as favoring home care for children—care in their own home as well as foster home care—and recommended the creation of a publicly financed bureau to collect and disseminate information affecting the welfare of children and a national voluntary organization to establish and publicize standards of child care. The first, the Children's Bureau, was created in 1912; the Child Welfare League of America followed in 1921. Equally important was the establishment of the principle of federal interest in child welfare, a principle that has resulted in the reconvening of the conference at ten-year intervals.

The juvenile court movement was an expression of a growing consensus as to the importance of differentiating the needs of children. The first juvenile court law, An Act to Regulate the Treatment and Control of Dependent, Neglected, and Delinquent Children, had been enacted in 1899 by Illinois, where the Illinois State Conference of Charities had taken responsibility for having the act drafted. The law applied to children under sixteen years of age and provided for a special juvenile courtroom and record-keeping system and for probation officers "to take charge of any child before and after trial as may be directed by the court."[59] Within ten years, similar laws had been passed in twenty-two states. By 1919, all the states except Connecticut, Maine, and Wyoming had enacted juvenile court laws emphasizing the "principle of separate treatment of juvenile delinquents

Research-Based Practice

Critical Thinking Question: How can "fact-finding" efforts like the Pittsburgh Survey influence the development of policy and practice?

and . . . cure rather than punishment."[60] Once again Illinois set the character of juvenile probation services, when several agencies assigned social workers to the court in the hope of making the state's new juvenile court law operate effectively by providing casework services.

A group of social workers associated with Hull House and Chicago's School of Social Service Administration, including Edith and Grace Abbott and Julia Lathrop, were instrumental in the establishment of the Children's Bureau in 1912, and Lathrop became its first director. The Children's Bureau documented the threats to maternal and child health that was crucial to the passage of the Act for the Promotion of the Welfare and Hygiene of Maternity and Infancy, better known as the Sheppard–Towner Act, in 1921.

The Sheppard–Towner Act approved appropriations for five years to states designating a child hygiene or child welfare division to carry responsibility for the local administration of the act's provisions. The general purpose of the act was educational. Instruction in maternal and infant care was offered by nurses and physicians through itinerant conferences held either in homes or at established health centers. Instruction in maternal and infant care was also offered to professionals involved in teaching or caring for mothers and young children. The life of the Sheppard–Towner Act was extended for two years in 1927, with the understanding that the act would lapse after June 30, 1929. At the time of its expiration, forty-five states and Hawaii were cooperating. Although organized opposition by physicians led to the demise of the Sheppard–Towner Act, the programs it established were ultimately incorporated into the Social Security Act in 1935.

The recommendation of the White House conference that children not be deprived of home care except for "urgent and compelling reasons" stimulated controversy. On one side were those social workers who supported the conference's position that private—not public—funds be used to prevent the removal of children from their own homes. On the other were prominent juvenile court judges such as Ben Lindsey and Merritt Pinckney, whose daily practice required the institutionalization of children of poor (though competent) mothers. There was an underlying conflict, too, posed by the question of whether mothers should work at all. Before the enactment of the first mother's pension in 1911, while the possibility of such pensions was still being explored, the question of balance between pension and earnings was major. A speaker at the National Conference of Charities and Corrections in 1910 stated the problem:

> The first question to consider, after regular relief on a pension basis has been decided upon, is whether it should be a full pension or whether the widow should be encouraged to earn. At a recent meeting of the Secretaries of the Boston Associated Charities . . . most . . . felt that a day or two of work a week outside was really better for the mother than to keep her always at home, for life can be too dull some times.[61]

The emergence of mother's pensions represented changes in the ideas and institutions that guided social welfare in the early twentieth century. Although leaders in the Charity Organization Movement still held to their belief in strict investigation and limited aid, frontline social workers had come to learn that the inadequacy of aid to widows with children had caused irreversible harm to these families. The old tenets of voluntary charity were supplanted by a maternalist belief that women's role as mothers provided the surest compass to guide social welfare policy. Although often advocated by women who had chosen to remain unmarried and childless, maternalism provided a means for broadening public support for reform, because it did not threaten traditional ideas about a woman's sphere. As a result, mother's pensions were embraced by the General Federation of Women's Clubs and the National Congress of Mothers (predecessor to the Parent–Teachers Associations), support that was critical to their passage.[62]

The first mother's pension law was passed by Missouri in April 1911. The law had been enacted at the behest of a single county and its provisions left the decision to provide assistance to the individual counties. The first statewide mandatory law, the Funds to Parents Act, was passed by the General Assembly of Illinois in June 1911. Many social work leaders were shocked by the sudden adoption of laws providing public funds for the aid of dependent children in their own homes. Richmond's objection that the Funds to Parents Act had been "drafted and passed without consulting a single social worker" expressed the view of an older generation of charity workers for which the expansion of *public* welfare was anathema. Yet, a younger generation of social workers—the first products of professional social work schools and training programs—embraced the idea that public welfare was critical to improving the condition of the poor.[63]

After the passage of the act, social workers did rally to help establish the program and to survey its operation. But Richmond, for all her concern with the burdens that society placed on family life, maintained that the supervision of social workers was necessary to ensure that "the children of the widow are in school, that they are morally protected, that their health is safeguarded, that they have a good chance to grow up right."[64] Frederic Almy, secretary of the Buffalo Charity Organization Society, was more willing to permit experiments in public relief giving. Nevertheless, he viewed private charity as safer. He warned that "to the imagination of the poor the public treasury is inexhaustible and their right, and that they drop upon it without thrift, as they dare not do on private charity."[65] Almy stressed the importance of professional casework in investigating the need for relief and for redeeming recipient families. And since such help was not characteristic of public relief giving, he favored having public relief funds administered by voluntary agencies. He objected to relief being dispensed without professional help, for "like undoctored drugs, untrained relief is poisonous to the poor. . . . Poor charity is worse than none."[66]

The number of states with Mother's Assistance programs increased rapidly. Within two years of the passage of the Illinois Funds to Parents Act, twenty states had provided cash relief programs for widows with children, and within ten years, forty states had done the same.[67] The Children's Bureau's study of Mother's Assistance, conducted in ten representative localities during October 1923 to April 1924, reported that "the principle of home care for dependent children as a public function is generally accepted in this country."[68] The bureau also reported generally good relationships between the voluntary agencies and the public agencies studied and, of most importance, that families were functioning with the help of Mother's Assistance "on a par with . . . self-supporting families."[69] By the 1920s, then, both the ideas and institutions of "scientific philanthropy" had come to a dead end. Even before the Great Depression caused political upheaval, the public sector had established itself as the innovator in addressing poverty and need.

The policy intent that widowed mothers were not to be expected to work was clear, but this intent was undermined by inadequate funding. Emma O. Lundberg, director of the Children's Bureau, and C. C. Carstens, executive of the Child Welfare League of America, made this clear when they addressed the national conference in 1921. Carstens noted:

> The granting of this aid [mother's pensions] was intended to meet the needs of the budget. . . . In theory this was a clearly established policy . . . but in practice . . . in many of the states the mother is expected to earn a very large share of the budget and much more than it is best that she should earn in view of her own needs and those of her children.[70]

A Children's Bureau report of a study of the administration of mother's pensions suggests the latent intent of inadequate budgets.

> It was the testimony of the workers in the field and of the executives that the aid did not tend to develop a spirit of dependency but on the contrary developed self-confidence, initiative, and generally a desire for economic independence as at early a date as possible.[71]

The example of someone in the family working was important. To be expected then was the failure of another intent of the various state mother's and widow's pensions—that is, the education of women, particularly immigrant women, for American motherhood:

> The degree to which mothers receiving aid were encouraged to join clubs and classes of an educational character varied greatly. . . . In some communities the grants were too small to permit the mothers to give their time to anything more than housekeeping and gainful employment.[72]

These implementation problems, however, need not detract from mother's pensions' contribution to redefining the plight of women in the American economic structure. Until the 1930s, this remained a state responsibility. After World War I, federal programs were restricted to insuring federal employees against a loss of income due to retirement or disability and to insuring the families of veterans against the loss of the breadwinner's life. Insurance programs operated or required by the states were few, scattered, and inadequate. In the private sector—notably in the railroad industry—pension systems were started and then collapsed. For the most part, then, the responsibility for resolving family economic problems continued to fall on local public welfare departments or on private agencies. The sparseness of the public effort is shown in the data on public welfare expenditures at federal, state, and local levels. In 1913, they totaled only $57 million—1 percent of total government expenditures and only 0.1 percent of the GNP.[73]

SOCIAL WORK AND THE BLACK POPULATION

Neither the public nor the private sector was responsive to the needs of black families. The overall indifference of white social welfare workers to black problems was demonstrated by the thrust of interests of the Charity Organization and Settlement House movements, those movements that had taken the lead in social welfare. In 1905, the year in which W. E. B. Du Bois and his followers met at Niagara Falls to consider legal solutions to Negro problems, an entire issue of *Charities and the Commons* was devoted to "The Negroes in the Cities of the North."[74] In 1909 and 1910, *The Survey* gave the news of the first and second national Negro conferences, respectively, at which the National Association for the Advancement of Colored People was organized.[75] In 1913, *The Survey*, in recognition of the fiftieth anniversary of the Emancipation Proclamation, carried a special collection of articles on the status of Negroes.[76]

The primary interest of Charity Organization Societies, however, was not in African Americans, nor in their deprivation or segregation as factors requiring broad social reform. Nonetheless, their emphasis on character reform might have helped fuel public discussions of blacks' ability to function in a civilized society. In the 1905 examination of blacks in the cities of the North, for example, the famous anthropologist Franz Boas said:

> There is every reason to believe that the Negro when given facility and opportunity will be perfectly able to fill the duties of citizenship as well as his white neighbor. It may be that he will not produce as many great men as the white race and that his average achievement will not quite reach the level of the average achievement of the white race, but there will be endless numbers who will be able to outrun their white competitors, and who will do better than the defectives whom we permit to drag down and to retard the healthy children of our public schools.[77]

Such interest in the plight of blacks as might have developed from direct contact was constrained by the relatively few blacks in the caseloads of Charity Organization Societies. Many agencies enforced a color line and refused to serve African Americans, a reflection of discrimination and the small number of African Americans living in cities. In Chicago in 1900, for example, blacks numbered 108,000 in a total population of 1,698,000. They ranked tenth among the city's ethnic groups.[78] The black population did, of course, have major social welfare problems, and in 1910, the National Urban League was established to help with those problems, as well as to promote interracial cooperation.

Settlement House workers were more geared to social change, but they, too, tended to lump the problems of blacks with those of immigrant groups and then to expend their energies on the latter. Among the leaders and allies of the Settlement House Movement, however, were those who gave greater prominence to the race problem. Louise de Koven Bowen, Sophonisba Breckenridge, and others spoke out in opposition to discrimination and prejudice that held minorities responsible for the economic and social inferiority to which they had been condemned. Kelley and Wald were among those who gathered for the first meeting of the National Committee on the Negro held in New York on May 31, 1909. Addams was among a group of distinguished white reformers who joined Du Bois and the Niagara group in founding the National Association for the Advancement of Colored People. When antiblack discrimination surfaced at the Progressive party's presidential convention of 1912, Addams debated leaving. Her decision to remain suggests again the tenor of the times. The party's nominee, Theodore Roosevelt, eventually lost the election, partly because his having entertained Booker T. Washington at the White House dashed any hope of gaining votes in the solid South.

The limited government programs for blacks and for whites and the overall absence of a sense of responsibility for helping families meet the risks of industrial life demonstrate the strength of conservative resistance in these years. Indeed, many nineteenth-century beliefs about poverty and dependency still retained their power. Family problems were indicative of the deviant family, the family that was unable and unwilling to make use of its own potential

Many agencies enforced a color line and refused to serve African Americans, a reflection of discrimination and the small number of African Americans living in cities.

Policy Practice

Critical Thinking Question: Advocates, like Addams, often must choose between standing by their principles or compromising to build coalitions. What are the arguments in favor and against Addams's decision to remain inside the Progressive party despite its racial bias?

and the abundant opportunities provided by American society. Unquestionably, a great deal had been accomplished as America's attention shifted to the war in Europe. Nevertheless, the amount of reform activity should not obscure the fact that basic inequities remained intact and basic needs unmet.

THE END OF REFORM

The end of World War I did not see a return to reform activity. The years between the close of the war and the Depression of the 1930s were a time of peace during which many Americans achieved individual prosperity. They found it through credit and installment buying and through participation in the glittering promises of speculation. They did not concern themselves with the problems of those brushed aside by society's advances or with the obvious abuse of power and influence by those who led the way in speculative activity. Despite the recession of 1921, urban standards of living improved. Booming profits, high levels of employment, and rising real wages meant that Americans felt able to purchase and enjoy a flood of new products—cars, radios, home electricity, motion pictures, silk stockings. There was new life in the doctrine of laissez-faire and a renewed belief that what was good for business was good for the nation. The solution to poverty did not lie in corporate regulation, minimum wages, social insurance, or public welfare, but rather in providing an atmosphere that was encouraging to business.

Americans were determined to believe assurances offered by President Herbert Hoover in his inaugural address:

> We in America today are nearer to the final triumph over poverty than ever before in the history of any land. The poorhouse is vanishing among us. We have not yet reached the goal, but given a chance . . . we shall soon with the help of God be in sight of the day when poverty will be banished from this nation.[79]

At the close of the war, the era of the reform coalition had come to an end, and a new era of professionalization of social work had begun. The change seems attributable to a number of factors. The war itself had wrought havoc among social work leaders who, prior to the events leading to the country's involvement, had in the main counted themselves pacifists. Addams was a leader in pacifist causes. Her membership on the Platform Committee of the Progressive party in 1912 was an effort to further specific social goals despite her disagreement with the party's stand in regard to war and defense.[80] World War I split those who could not abandon a lifetime's philosophical stance from those who supported the war and saw this support as serving their country in a time of crisis. The Russian Revolution further split the reform spirit of social workers. Some moved closer to revolutionary positions; some moved further away from an interest in social action.

Government suppression played a role in quieting voices of dissent. During World War I, antiwar activists were accused of disloyalty. The post office banned their literature and the most vocal leaders were jailed. The Russian Revolution and labor unrest after the war sparked a "Red Scare" orchestrated by the U.S. Attorney General Mitchell Palmer. The wartime and postwar fear of subversive activity, sparking a demand for law and order, led to severe political repression, to expulsion of radical aliens, and, in turn, to hostility toward expressions of need for political change or political redress. Even modest efforts at community revitalization, like the pioneering Social Unit Plan in Cincinnati, were labeled *"socialistic"* and saw their funding cut off.[81] Emphasis shifted to personality reform, as psychoanalysis—the work of Sigmund Freud—offered a new professional direction for social workers and social work education.

The push for social reform was further dissipated by the stemming of the flow of immigrants. The increase in immigration during the early years of the twentieth century, with masses of immigrants coming from eastern Europe at a time of anarchy and revolution there and of labor unrest and wartime preparation here, had stimulated efforts for social reform and socialization. Severe legal restrictions caused the numbers to drop dramatically and almost disappear during the late 1920s. As immigration declined, ethnic communities were increasingly dominated by a second generation more oriented to life in the United States.

While the impetus toward social reform had waned, the Progressive Era was one of major and lasting importance. The first Mother's Pension law was enacted in 1911 and established the principle that single mothers of young children should receive support to stay at home as parents. It was the beginning of a safety net that was to prevail for eighty-five years.

The prosperity of the 1920s—with its surge of economic growth and affluence accompanied by the hope for the imminent disappearance of poverty—came on top of the seeming achievement of many of the goals of the reform movement and decreased the pressure for further social legislation. In actuality, the reform spirit of the agencies regulating business was often reversed by administrative practices; new political bosses arose to negotiate the ballot reforms, and much of the social legislation passed by the states was thrown out by the courts. The moral fervor that pervaded the Progressive movement shifted to the drive against alcoholic beverages. The success of Prohibition became a crowning moral victory.

With social reform abandoned, character reform was revived as an orientation toward people in need. Emil Frankel's *Poor Relief in Pennsylvania,* a statewide survey published in 1925, demonstrated the persistent suspicion of public relief and of relief recipients. In a report that generally attacked historic fears of public welfare, Frankel supported the significance of professional social work service, if only to allay the fear that public aid would be considered a right. Frankel wrote:

> Outdoor relief without constructive service can lead only to increasing dependency because while a certain portion of the families receiving relief may pull themselves out of a rut with the aid of the grants, a good many will not. . . .
>
> A good many have the feeling that inasmuch as the poor fund is raised through public taxation they have a right to demand relief and are entitled to it as a matter of course. And a good many families feel that although they may not be in need of relief they can see no reason why they should not get it when other families do.[82]

Public and voluntary orientations toward relief giving—especially toward public relief—seemed to have changed little since the inception of the Charity Organization in 1877. The views and foreboding of Frankel, a public official, were not unlike those of Lowell, who had argued in 1890 that public relief should be given only in cases of extreme distress, "when starvation is imminent." The refuge from pauperism, according to Lowell, was self-support or help provided by private sources. The similarity in their views is probably not surprising when one considers the 1918 appeal of Francis McLean, director of the American Association for Organizing Charities, that member agencies aid "in the socialization [i.e., professionalization] of both staff and methods of work of . . . public family social work agencies."[83] Not until 1921 was membership in the association extended to public agencies.

THE SOCIAL WELFARE OF VETERANS

Social welfare in the early twentieth century was strongly influenced by the veterans of two wars. Most men who had fought in the Civil War had reached retirement age by the early years of the century, and their economic needs were a major domestic policy issue during these years. As the Civil War generation aged, America's entry into World War I created a new generation of veterans. The entitlements of World War I veterans influenced politics during the 1920s and dramatized the nation's problems during the early years of the Great Depression.

In the late nineteenth century, the federal government had enacted generous pensions for Union veterans with disabilities and the dependents of soldiers who died in the Civil War. These pensions had become important in competition between Republicans and Democrats during many elections. Yet, in the first decade of the twentieth century, a much larger number of veterans reached old age. As their ability to support themselves declined, they too turned to the federal government for support.

As in other periods of American history, poor veterans avoided the strict use of eligibility rules used to deny aid to the needy. Indeed, in the early years of the century, eligibility for pensions was liberalized by classifying old age alone as qualifying a veteran for pension and by easing the length of service and the supporting documentation that were necessary to qualify for a pension.

As a result, the number of veterans receiving pensions and their cost increased during the first twenty years of the twentieth century. By some estimates, nearly half of all native-born elderly men living in the North at the turn of the century received pensions. The number of pensioners peaked at around a million in the first decade of the century, but disbursements for pensions increased until 1912 when it reached $170 million. Armed forces participants in World War I numbered 4,744,000.[84] The war brought about an enormous expansion of benefits and services, first to attract enlistees, later to compensate veterans and their families for services rendered.

On September 2, 1914, only one month after the declaration of war in Europe, Congress passed the War Risk Insurance Act, insuring enlistees in the merchant marines against the hazards of submarine warfare. In 1917, President Wilson appointed a Council of National Defense to review and make recommendations in regard to veterans' benefits. The council's report, incorporated shortly after into law, introduced a new concept: the offer of readjustment and rehabilitation services, along with monetary benefits. The new package of benefits and services included the following:

1. Compulsory allotments and allowances to families of soldiers, paid for by the soldiers themselves and by the government
2. A system of voluntary insurance against death and total disability

3. Medical and surgical hospital treatment, as well as prosthetic appliances for those injured in the line of duty

4. Vocational rehabilitation services for injured veterans who could not resume prewar occupations

The close of the war on November 11, 1918, created further consideration of veterans' benefits. Not only had an enormous number of Americans served in the armed forces, but a large number—116,000—had died and an even greater number—204,000—had been wounded. By mid-1920, the Public Health Service had increased its total available beds to 11,639 in fifty-two hospitals. A year later, the use of available beds in army and navy hospitals and in National Homes for Disabled Volunteer Soldiers was also authorized. The necessarily rapid expansion of in-hospital services to meet the needs of wounded veterans helped clarify the returning veterans' need for outpatient and nonmedical services. The urgency of the need also pointed up the extent to which veterans' benefits were fragmented by the historical delegation of responsibility for benefits among the Bureau of War Risk Insurance, the Rehabilitation Division of the Federal Board for Vocational Education, the Public Health Service, and the armed services themselves.

Early in 1921, President Warren G. Harding appointed the Dawes Commission to devise a program for the immediate and future needs of ex-servicemen "to the end that the intention of Congress to give the full measure of justice to ex-servicemen may be adequately, promptly, and generously met." The commission's report concluded that "no emergency of war itself is greater than is the emergency which confronts the Nation in its duty to care for those disabled in its service and now neglected."

The new Congress, which convened on April 11, 1921, took up consideration of the commission's report and incorporated most of its recommendations in Public Law No. 47, passed on August 9, 1921. The commission's most important recommendation, the creation of a single entity to administer veterans' affairs, resulted in the establishment of the Veterans' Bureau. The bureau brought together most veterans' benefits, including medical care, insurance payments, and vocational rehabilitation services.

A still further expansion of benefits for veterans occurred in 1924, when Congress made hospital services available for honorably discharged veterans with nonservice-connected disabilities. The recommendation for this particular benefit had been submitted jointly by the director of the Veterans' Bureau, the American Legion, the Disabled American Veterans, and the Veterans of Foreign Wars to the House Committee on World War Veterans' Legislation. The enactment of this law highlighted the continuing, enlarging interest that Congress had in providing special consideration for the needs of veterans. Additionally, the 1924 enactment demonstrated the strength of the constituencies organized to advance and to protect the social welfare rights of this particularly "worthy" group of Americans.

THE PROFESSIONALIZATION OF SOCIAL WORK

The professionalization of social work had begun with the formation of voluntary charitable associations after the Civil War. It expanded with the growth of reform organizations. For a time during the Progressive Era, charity organizations and settlements worked together for social reform, but eventually their different ideologies drove them away from each other and toward their separate professionalization, rather than social change.

No such constituencies as supported veterans' rights—neither the Charity Organization nor the Settlement House Movement—stood ready to support public relief giving as a major requirement for the maintenance of family welfare. In voluntary social welfare as well as in corporate management, the 1920s were years of bureaucratization and professionalization. For Charity Organization Societies and for settlements, scientific philanthropy had led to internal organizational changes paralleling the managerial changes of corporate enterprise. The developing of supervision, of supervisors accountable for the successful operation of professional workers, was a further example of internal adherence to structural authority. Beyond that, Charity Organization Societies were largely responsible for the formation of Councils of Social Agencies accountable for social welfare planning and of Federated Funds that undertook "effective economy" in funding the social welfare establishment.[85]

The definition of scientific philanthropy was broadened to encompass developments in helping methodology. The failure of friendly visiting, the hiring of paid agents, and, finally, the emergence of social workers were sequential steps in the search for techniques to deal with the variety of situations uncovered by individualized investigations of families. The body of techniques that were codified in Richmond's *Social Diagnosis* (1917) and *What Is Social Casework?* (1922) established casework as a major methodology of social work. Casework represented a therapeutic model of professional service. In addition, the development of casework from friendly visiting, at a time when these Charity Organization Societies were relinquishing responsibility for social reform, not only reawakened an old image of the rich helping the poor but also strengthened the view of individual and family responsibility for social and economic problems. In later years, the psychological theories of Freud and others were incorporated into models of casework.

The overriding interest of Charity Organization Societies in relief, their longtime charity organizing purposes, and their slowness in moving toward a focus on *family* welfare are reflected in the successive names given the societies' national association. Not until 1919, when the era of professionalization had begun to take hold, did the association's name include the word *family*: American Association for Organizing Family Social Work. Not until 1930, with the adoption of Family Welfare Association of America as its name, did the title suggest an aggressive force for the welfare of families. This slow evolution of purpose from charity organization to social work organization to family welfare can be traced through a review of the *Proceedings of the National Conference of Charities and Corrections* (1880–1929) for the contributions of Charity Organization leaders. Particularly striking is the extreme fragmentation of topics discussed at the conference and the limited focus on the family as a unit or with the interaction between family life and social institutions.

The settlement movement shifted to its own brand of professionalism. Social reform activity diminished as an area of functional responsibility, and "social group work," a methodological approach to helping through recreational and educational activities, became the core of Settlement House programming. The extent of the shift was indicated by George Bellamy of Cleveland's Hiram House in 1914, when he addressed the National Conference on the use of recreational programs by neighborhood centers to help neighborhood residents maintain community control and strengthen family life. "It is far better," he said, "for the city to throw the responsibility of self-support and self-improvement upon the people themselves than to hire at great expense . . . others to entertain the community. We need a recreation by the people, not, for the people."[86] In 1926, Mary K. Simkhovitch addressed the National Federation of Settlements on settlement goals for the "next third of a century." She argued that settlements had "turned the social welfare corner" and were "launched on the larger task of social education" in an effort to democratize and civilize industrial society by popularizing art and developing the creative instinct.[87]

The definitive statement on the professionalization of social work was made by Porter R. Lee in his presidential address at the National Conference in 1929. Lee traced the development of social work as "a movement directed toward the elimination of an entrenched evil" and its culmination as a profession with a professional responsibility for operating "a methodical, organized effort . . . to make enduring the achievement of the cause."

> In the last analysis I am not sure that the greatest service of social work as a cause is contributed through those whose genius it is to light and hand on the torch. I am inclined to think that in the capacity of the social worker, whatever his rank, to administer a routine functional responsibility in the spirit of the servant in a cause is the explanation of the great service of social work.[88]

Amazingly rapid development occurred in social work during 1900–1929. The organization and professionalization of social work was carried out by the Charity Organization and Settlement House movements. Both movements claimed a concern with the family as the core unit of society, and each, to its own lights, developed its program so as to try to bring stability and fulfillment to family living. While the economy appeared to prosper, social work turned to family dynamics and individual personality development. Therapy had become the door to social well-being.[89]

Log onto **www.mysocialworklab.com** and answer the following questions. (*If you did not receive an access code to* **MySocialWorkLab** *with this text and wish to purchase access online, please visit* www.mysocialworklab.com.)

1. **Watch the Career Explorations video "Deborah Vingle—Program Director, Battered Women's Program."** Considering the role that feminism and maternalism played in the development of social work, how does this agency reflect change?

2. **Watch the Core Competency video "Participating in Policy Changes."** If you had lived in 1925, what policies would you have tried to change and why?

PRACTICE TEST

The following questions will test your knowledge of the content found within this chapter. For additional assessment, including licensing-exam-type questions on applying chapter content to practice, visit **MySocialWorkLab**.

1. The White House Conference on Children in 1909 proclaimed the twentieth century as the Century of the Child. As a result,
   a. the government was deemed responsible for the support of single mothers.
   b. home and family life were declared to be society's goal for children.
   c. public education was established as a right for all children.
   d. children were invited to the White House for the event.

2. Unionization led to increased unemployment for
   a. women.
   b. children.
   c. immigrants.
   d. skilled workers.

3. The push for further reform in the 1920s slowed down due to
   a. an increase in immigration.
   b. the success of Prohibition.
   c. the professionalization of social work.
   d. a shift to the war in Europe.

4. A belief in positive government action provided the basis for Progressives as well as a belief that
   a. immigrants would adopt the culture and language of white Protestants.
   b. America would continue to welcome immigrants into its melting pot.
   c. democratic change would be embraced by legislators.
   d. the economy would be stimulated by a stronger workforce.

5. Discuss how the Socialist Party affected reform in the early 1900s.

ASSESS YOUR COMPETENCE

Use the following scale to rate your current level of achievement on the following concepts or skills associated with each competency presented in the chapter:

1	2	3
I can accurately describe the concept or skill	I can consistently identify the concept or skill when observing and analyzing practice activities	I can competently implement the concept or skill in my own practice

______ Describe how unions have been instrumental in the development of social policy.

______ Discuss how women and African Americans have been both enemies and partners in the fight for rights.

______ Apply past discriminatory policies to current views toward immigrants.

______ Understand the role of economics in social reform.

Progress and Reform

The three documents that follow, Florence Kelley's statement on *The Family and the Woman's Wage* (1909), the text of the first *Funds to Parents Act* (1911), and the National Conference of Charities and Corrections discussions of *Public Pensions to Widows* (1912), highlight major conflicts in social welfare during the Progressive Era.

Kelley, both as an individual and as secretary of the National Consumer's League, was in the forefront of social welfare reform activity during the Progressive Era. Her close personal connections with leaders in the Settlement House Movement and the coalitions they formed with other groups on behalf of an array of social welfare measures make her utterances a reflection of the settlement view. She pictured the family and family members as needing economic and legal protections against industrial and political hindrances that prevented their full democratic participation in society. Kelley's special interest was in wages and working hours and their meaning for family welfare. In *The Family and the Woman's Wage*, she challenges the depth of the value placed on the home as "the fundamental thing in our national life." Her point is that truly valuing the home and the family would require legislation to regulate the conditions and places of employment of children—in this instance, girls—and the working hours and wages of women. She is convinced of the importance of home life for children and, therefore, of the necessity for making it financially possible for mothers and children to remain in the home. Her outcry against the economic exploitation of women and children is, therefore, not only a demand for higher wages but also a condemnation of conditions that make it necessary for them to work at all. The necessity to work, she believed, distracted the mother from the care of children: "if one really thought about the family and the home . . . one should have none of that work today."

One result of the kind of agitation for reform encouraged by Kelley was the Funds to Parents Act, passed by the state of Illinois in June 1911. The act provided public funds for the care of dependent and neglected children, making it unnecessary to remove them from their own homes when parents were otherwise adequate. The significance of the act resides in its being the first demonstration of public responsibility for supporting the care of children at home. The act is, therefore, the predecessor of the Aid to Dependent Children program included in the Social Security Act in 1935.

The discussions of Frederic Almy, Mary Richmond, Homer Folks, and Merritt Pinckney of "public pensions to widows" indicate the controversy resulting from the passage of the Funds to Parents Act. Supporting widows and dependent children in their own homes was still a controversial issue for workers in charities and corrections, despite the recommendation of the first White House Conference on Children. By 1912, however, the discussants of public pensions no longer addressed themselves to this particular question. Their arguments centered on the use of public, rather than private, funds and on the necessity for social work professionals to oversee the use of funds.

Almy, secretary of the Buffalo Charity Organization Society, wavers in his opinion. He is not entirely afraid of public funds—"neglect is the great pauperizer, not relief"—but he is afraid of relief that is not professionally dispensed: "untrained relief is poisonous to the poor." Richmond, a most eminent figure in social work, is also fearful of the possible lack of supervision over the use of funds by recipients. For her, the question is twofold. First, there is the issue of money versus service as a key to helping. Second, there is the fear that increases in public funding will dry up sources of private funding—that bad money will drive out good money—and that private agencies might themselves become pauperized through dependence on government grants. Folks, secretary of New York's State Charities Aid Association, also argues for private funds and private agency control. He concludes, however, "If we do not secure from private sources sufficient funds, then, without hesitation we ought to have a system of public relief for widows." As might be expected, Judge Pinckney, who spearheaded the drive to make public funds available for the care of dependent children, disagrees with opponents of public funding. Speaking from experience, he insists that his court is "doing something toward administering this law efficiently, intelligently, and honestly, too, and through public channels."

PROCEEDINGS OF THE
NATIONAL CONFERENCE OF CHARITIES
AND CORRECTIONS

1909

THE FAMILY AND THE WOMAN'S WAGE
BY MRS. FLORENCE KELLEY, SECRETARY OF THE NATIONAL
CONSUMER'S LEAGUE

There is no subject concerning which we more persistently live in a fool's paradise than this of woman's wage. We say on all occasions that we consider the home the fundamental thing in our national life. If we really valued the home, such things could not happen as I saw last Thursday in the night court in the city of New York. A girl, seventeen years of age, was taken away by a policeman from her two-year-old, fatherless boy to spend three years in a prison which, with the bitterest irony, we call a house of mercy. No charge has been proved against her. As a little cash girl, at fourteen years, in the enlightened city of New York, she went out from her home and worked under the temptations of a great department store. Before her fifteenth birthday her little fatherless boy was born, because of the conditions under which our laws allowed her to work. Her mother thought that the home needed the little girl's wages more than the little girl needed protection. When she was seventeen years old she had been working nearly a year, every night, in a telephone exchange, and she could bear it no longer. She was so weary that she could not even endure being with her little boy during the day. Finally she left her work, which meant taking six dollars a week out of her mother's family budget. She took her child and went away to look for other work, for her mother refused to keep the child unless the six dollars a week were paid. After a week she confessed herself beaten and sent the little boy back through a neighbor to his grandmother, with word that she believed she would have work in a few days and could take care of him. This mother sent her daughter to prison for three years under no other charge than that, for less than a week, the girl had not been able to maintain herself and her little boy and was therefore "a wayward girl."

That girl, after she comes out of prison, will never make a home for her little boy. Her heart is effectively broken; three years hence it will be effectively hardened. There are thousands of little cash girls working in our stores, and thousands of young girls never before did in the history of the world, because there never were telephone exchanges to be served in the dead of night.

If we valued home life as we hypocritically say that we do, there would not be one of these young girls away from the family home in the dead of night serving the public, not because they serve it better than men would do, but because they are cheaper and because the interest of the stockholders and the bondholders of the corporation is of greater importance than the sacrifice of these young girls. Now every man and woman of us who passively consent, as we do, to be served by telephone exchanges which employ these young victims in the night, everyone of us who is not striving to get legislation, and protesting as only subscribers can protest, is *particeps criminis* with these employers and stockholders. If there be a telephone exchange in this country which is served at night exclusively by men over twenty-one years of age, I beg that its patrons stand up now. I have never been able to hear of one in any city.

Lest anyone should believe that the young girls in New York City are less cherished in this service than those of other cities, I know of a city not far from Buffalo, where, within a month, a factory inspector took out of a leading hotel a girl under sixteen years of age who worked regularly until three o'clock in the morning serving a telephone exchange in that lobby, subject to the insults of passing travelers. But on her sixteenth birthday there will be no legal offense if her cruel father sends her back insisting, like the mother of the telephone girl, upon having six dollars a week.

The telephone exchange commands girls chiefly because there they are paid fifty-two weeks in the year, while the rest of our industries are so ill-organized that very few of them offer steady work throughout the year.

It may be said that I have spoken unjustly of the store where the first little girl was working. It is true that many young girls go as cash girls into stores and advance until they become clerks, and come out unhurt, so far as one can see, from that experience. It is also true that some of our boys came home sound in mind and limb from the Cuban war. Some children do not take scarlet fever, although exposed to it. Some unvaccinated people never take smallpox. But the risk is not greater which the families took who sent their sons to the Cuban war, than the risk these parents take who send their little girls into department stores. The protest cannot be made too strong, to those who believe that they value the home, against sending future mothers and makers of homes out of the schools knowing nothing of that which they should know when they shall have homes of their own, into institutions, commercial and otherwise, which, as Mr. Lee has said, "diseducate" the children and unfit them for life in the home.

It is not only the earnings which the future mothers bring into the homes that are earned at a frightful social price. The widows of working men, cleaning the filthy floors of railway stations, and hotels, and stores, and offices on their knees, after inhaling first the dust from the dry broom—is there any greater exposure to tuberculosis conceivable than that of the weary mother of little children doing such work at night? A friend of mine has conceived the monstrous idea of having a night nursery to which women so employed might send their children. And this idea was seriously described in so modern a publication as Charities and the Commons "before it changed its name" without a word of editorial denunciation. The mothers of young children cannot be sent away from their homes to do such work without the gravest social injury, any more than daughters can be sent away so young and untrained as they are sent in this country today. The proper place for a workingman's widow who has young children is in her home taking care of those children, unless she is a bad woman or a drunkard, or so ill that her proximity is a menace to the health of her children. But assuming that the mother is bad or ill, there is nothing gained by sending the children away for a few hours a day to a nursery. If she is infectious she would infect the children in their close sleeping quarters.

There is no subject concerning which we are more foolish than this of the wages of women in their homes, this idea of establishing institutions to take little children away from good mothers during their working hours, insisting that widowed mothers shall perform the tasks of fathers while some hired person pretends to be mother to their little ones.

There are conditions under which the day nursery is acceptable. For instance, where the mother is temporarily in the hospital for treatment from which her convalescence may be reasonably prompt; or, if there is illness in a home and the mother ought to be relieved temporarily of the care of the children. But when Americans boast of a national, or state, or city society of day nurseries (instead of humbly apologizing that we need more than one in Greater New York) we show how little we value the presence of the mother in her home. The day nursery which encourages the mother to go out to work, leaving the larger children to spend their day on the street and to buy penny lunches, is an argument for school luncheons for the larger children. No money earned in the United States costs so dear, dollar for dollar, as the money earned by the mothers of young children.

When we permit mothers to work in the homes industrially, on a large scale, as is the case in New York, we have the degradation of the home by industry, and the mother distracted from the care of the children through the invasion of the home. If we really thought about the family and the home as we say we do, we should have none of that work today.

***

LAWS
of the
STATE of ILLINOIS

Enacted by the
FORTY-SEVENTH GENERAL ASSEMBLY
at the
REGULAR BIENNIAL SESSION

BEGUN AND HELD AT THE CAPITOL, IN THE CITY OF
SPRINGFIELD, ON THE FOURTH DAY OF JANUARY
A.D. 1911, AND ADJOURNED SINE DIE ON THE
FIRST DAY OF JUNE, A.D. 1911.

Printed by authority of the General Assembly
of the State of Illinois.

Juvenile Courts—Funds to Parents

1. Amends section 7, Act of 1907. 7. As amended, provides for
funds to parent or parents.

(Senate Bill No. 403. Approved June 5, 1911.)

AN Act to amend an Act entitled, "An Act relating to children who are now or may hereafter become dependent, neglected or delinquent, to define these terms, and to provide for the treatment, control, maintenance, adoption and guardianship of the person of such children," approved June 4, 1907.

Section 1. Be it enacted by the People of the State of Illinois, represented in the General Assembly: That section 7 of the Act entitled "An Act relating to children who are now or may hereafter become dependent, neglected or delinquent, to define these terms and to provide for the treatment, control, maintenance, adoption and guardianship of the person of such children," approved June 4, 1907, be and the same is hereby amended so as to read as follows:

7. If the court shall find any male child under the age of seventeen years or any female child under the age of eighteen years to be dependent or neglected within the meaning of this Act, the court may allow such child to remain at its own home subject to the friendly visitation of a probation officer, and if the parent, parents, guardian or custodian consent thereto, or if the court shall further find that the parent, parents, guardian or custodian of such child are unfit or improper guardians or are unable or unwilling to care for, protect, train, educate or discipline such child, and that it is for the interest of such child and the people of this State that such child be taken from the custody of its parents, custodian or guardian, the court may make an order appointing as guardian of the person of such child, some reputable citizen of good moral character and order such guardian to place such child in some suitable family home or other suitable place, which such guardian may provide for such child or the court may enter an order committing such child to some suitable State institution, organized for the care of dependent or neglected children, or to some training school or industrial school or to some association embracing in its objects the purpose of caring for or obtaining homes for neglected or dependent children, which association shall have been accredited as hereinafter provided.

If the parent or parents of such dependent or neglected child are poor and unable to properly care for the said child, but are otherwise proper guardians and it is for the welfare of such child to remain at home, the court may enter an order finding such facts and fixing the amount of money necessary to enable the parent or parents to properly care for such child, and thereupon it shall be the duty of the county board, through its county agent or otherwise, to pay to such parent or parents, at such times as said order may designate the amount so specified for the care of such dependent or neglected child until the further order of the court.

APPROVED June 5, 1911.

***

PROCEEDINGS OF THE
NATIONAL CONFERENCE OF CHARITIES
AND CORRECTIONS

1912

PUBLIC PENSIONS TO WIDOWS
EXPERIENCES AND OBSERVATIONS WHICH LEAD ME TO
OPPOSE SUCH A LAW.

By Frederic Almy, Secretary Buffalo Charity Organization Society.

This paper will not discuss the recent laws giving pensions to widows in Illinois, Missouri, California, Michigan and Oklahoma, or the bills now pending in New York and Ohio, or the State Commission studying this subject in

Massachusetts, or the efforts in Colorado, but will discuss general principles. I find I am scheduled to oppose such laws, though for over a year in the SURVEY and elsewhere I am on record as well disposed towards them, though of the opinion that private charity is, for the present, safer.

Widowhood is a most innocent cause of poverty, especially pitiful because of its pain and waste, and very costly to society because the poverty is apt to increase in geometrical progression, two-fold, four-fold, or even more in each generation, as the neglected children mature. Sickness is also usually an innocent cause of poverty, though there are sexual diseases of appetite. The poverty of a family is still greater when the husband is not dead but is a living cost and danger. In such cases, the children have a father's counsel but less food than if they had none.

Neglected childhood is, in all the world, the very most innocent, appealing and frequent cause of poverty and crime. Poverty is often chosen, but the pauper child never chooses his poverty and his curses punish the society which has so foolishly neglected him. The cry of the children has been heard; street children are gone, factory children are going and the institution child must go. Home made children give the best results and even the foster home must go, unless the parents of the child are unfit.

A stupid fear of spending on the part of the Philistines of charity, who do not comprehend it, and a fear of pauperizing on the part of the Pharisees of charity, who have made a creed of it has made us penny wise and pound foolish. Neglect is the great pauperizer, not relief. The devil of pauperizing has been made a bogy of. That devil has his claws cut long ago by organized charity; but organized charity hates to give, and in some cities gives only in secret. When organized charity learns to be generous, without blushing, it will come into its own, and the widowhood of poverty will then get as liberal indemnity as the widowhood of industrial disaster. Such widowhood is just as innocent; and it is just as dangerous to society if not relieved.

I should like to see in every city a survey of all the children who are in institutions and in foster homes, and then a statement of the cost of maintenance of those children among them whose own homes are more fit except for poverty. I have always favored private out-door relief, but it is inadequate, and to-day all over the country, except in a few cities, families of widows are being ruthlessly scattered for lack of charity. Will public out-door relief be more adequate or better? Students of public out-door relief know well how it increases pauperism, but does not neglected childhood increase pauperism even more?

For nearly twenty years I have been a charity organization secretary and a special student and opponent of public out-door relief. In Charities for 1899, I had elaborate articles on the public and private out-door relief of forty cities. I know the dangers of relief, but last year at Boston I said, with Devine, "Our resources for relief are woefully inadequate. Our use of relief has been most sparing and timid. I am inclined to believe that we have caused more pauperism by our failure to provide for the necessities of life, for the education and training of children, and for the care and convalescence of the sick, than we have by excessive relief, even if we include indiscriminate alms." Can we harness public relief as we have harnessed steam and electricity through skillful engineers, so that we can have its power without its danger?

Why am I opposed to this plan of public pensions for widows? My opposition is not academic. I do not care whether the relief is a public or a private function, or whether it is given by the poor master, or by the Juvenile Court as in Chicago, or by children's guardians, or by a board of home assistance as proposed in New York. I think much, very much, of Thomas Mackay's classic argument that to the imagination of the poor the public treasury is inexhaustible and their right, and that they drop upon it without thrift, as they dare not do on private charity, and this argument is one that cannot be met by any excellence of administration; but I remember too that pauperizing by alms is no worse than pauperizing by neglect. Moreover, Mackay's argument applies mainly to indolence and improvidence, which are voluntary. The poverty of widowhood is not usually due to lack of thrift, and what widow ever became a widow because aid was public rather than private?

The crux of my opposition to public pensions today is that the public does not stand for fit salaries for relief. I am an advocate of more adequate relief, but I am an advocate first of more adequate brains and work for the poor. Relief without brains is as bad as medicine without doctors. I would much rather see doctors without medicine, or salaries without relief, as is the practice of some of the best of our charity organization societies. Like undoctored drugs, untrained relief is poisonous to the poor. Good charity is expensive, and poor charity is worse than none, yet what city would support adequate case work for its public aid?

In Buffalo where we have had organized charity for thirty-five years and for five years much talk and less practice of adequate relief, public opinion supports adequate salaries for a large staff in the charity organization society. Nevertheless, the city poor office has but five investigators, while we have fourteen, of better ability. Moreover, the city investigators merely investigate, while we make plans, find friends and find money from natural sources. Last month the money found by our paid visitors from relatives, employers and friends nearly equalled the total of their salaries, and if we add the wages for work found by them it would have exceeded their salaries. Of course these visitors gave the poor also a service which is worth ten times more than the money they get for them; but I find that the monthly statement of this money got by them for their poor, does much to justify the salaries in the eyes of the public.

Will the voters stand in any city for the salaries without which charity is a pest and curse? Even in Chicago where a bad law in a good cause is redeemed by a good judge, I do not find any indication of adequate case work. Judge Pinckney has voluntarily associated with himself a salaries case committee, paid for by private charities and not from the public treasury; but the record stories, which I have glanced at in the few days since I undertook this paper, would not pass muster for case work in some cities. They show good diagnosis and study of temperament, but I have not noticed in them search for relatives who can give, or attempts to find work or to find better paid work, or official records of the school attendance of children as a condition of aid, or constructive plans for removing poverty. A pension committee needs all of these things for its action. Even under Judge Pinckney, the Chicago relief looks like mere relief, which keeps the family from deteriorating after the bread-winner has gone. Indemnity relief may have no higher function than to prevent deterioration, but charity relief aims to redeem the family. It is not too much to ask that the tax payers' money should be educational and constructive.

How does the adequacy of Judge Pinckney's relief compare with private charity relief? I have only Buffalo to compare with. Judge Pinckney has pretty nearly carte blanche; his work has been splendidly guarded and intelligent and is the high-water mark of what can be expected today of public charity. In eleven months (to June 1, 1912) 316 families had an average of $262.00 each per year. In Buffalo, which is above the average in private relief, 707 widows applied last year, of whom 230 had money aid, averaging $35.00 a year each. This means nothing, however, for the figures include old widows without children, widows who had one month's casual aid, etc., twenty-four widows, who had our aid for twelve consecutive months, averaged $152.00 per annum from us or with city aid included, $180.00 per annum, which is 70 per cent of the Chicago aid. The Buffalo families have earnings, however, and aid from relatives, as the Chicago families must have had also. The only fair comparison would be the budgets rather than the pensions, and these I have not on tap for Buffalo, though I have been given the Chicago figures. The maximum C. O. S. pensions in Buffalo were $301.00 and $307.00 per year. An adequate family budget for the poor is not less than $700.00 a year.

A fact of the very first importance in this connection was stated last year in my Boston paper at this Conference that out of 2,240 families treated in that year by the Buffalo Society only seven were found to be absolutely dependent for as much as even six months with no income at all from earnings, relatives, lodgers, or any source except charity. This shows clearly both the danger of exaggeration and the need of investigation.

Salaries are usually far more adequate with private charity than with public. Money relief is inadequate with either, but bad, very bad, as the relief given by private charity has been in many cities it has not been so bad or so niggardly with individual families as public outdoor relief. We still find doles with either public or private charity, though $2.00 a week orders to widows every one, two, or three weeks (with $2.00 weekly or $104.00 a year as a maximum for the family) is still typical with public charity, but the rare exception with private. The private charity which has not the energy to find adequate relief will not be likely to have the wisdom to use it wisely when found. The valuable pension system of private charity is not half developed as a money raiser. It is my belief that modern organized charity is the most liberal as well as the most tender, personal and effective charity that the world has ever known. Politics exist with either public or private charity, but more with public charity. Fit men are more often found by private charity than by public where the tail of a long ticket is often designated by party managers with little public attention. The valuable co-operation of volunteers through case committees is a splendid part of the Chicago plan and exists with Boston out-door relief but is as exceptional with public charity as it is universal with private charity.

Will public relief check the giving of private relief as suggested in Chalmers "seven fountains" so that nothing will be gained because private givers will leave it all to the public treasury? My elaborate study in Charities, in 1899 seemed to show that just this happened, and that private giving was trifling in cities where public aid was given. Dr. Devine thinks this and said at the last New York State Conference of Charities at Watertown that public out-door relief would require at least a million dollars a year in New York City and that he firmly believed from ample experience in Berlin, Paris, and this country, that with it there would be more neglected poverty and distress than without it. Dr. Devine thinks private relief most inadequate, however, and so do Alexander Johnson, Folks, Hebberd, Tucker, Kingsley and many others who differ as to public pensions.

The question is active in New York State where the report of the congestion commission February 28, 1911, which was reviewed at length in the Survey for March 11, 18, and 25, 1911, was followed by the report to the New York City Conference of Charities and Correction rendered last May after a year's consideration. This report advocated public pensions to widows. Both this report and the New York bill recognize the danger of public administration as inadequate and provide that the public money shall go through private charities. If this is a return to public subsidies to private charities it seems to me indescribably bad, for such subsidies lead to sectarian appeals, to lobbying and to a scrambling at the public trough for patronage.

I have the detail of many of the state bills and laws, but they cannot be described in a paper so short as this must be if there is to be time for discussion.

It is no light thing to reverse a policy of many years in regard to public out-door relief. It was abolished in New York and Brooklyn thirty years ago, and in many of our chief cities and it was thought to be a dead issue in this Conference. Times change, however, and I am not willing to believe that in this day public out-door relief cannot be successful. It weighs with me that the equally delicate work of child placing is successfully done by public charity, though the arguments against it would be similar. Over and over private charity has blazed the way for what became public safety after standards had been developed and established, and this process I believe in. The curse of the old name of city out-door relief is something and the new and better associations will make it easier to keep up the new and better standards.

I am myself still opposed to public pensions, though with their aims I am so much in sympathy that I shall welcome experiments, in states not my own which may demonstrate whether they will succeed. Even if in the beginning such public relief does not reach the best standards of private relief I shall be willing to wait before judging if it improves steadily. Universal suffrage does not give immediate good government.

This paper has been prepared under extreme pressure as a basis for discussion. It is not a straddle, but voices the doubts which I have been expressing publicly for some time. I am here to learn.

DISCUSSION

MR. HOMER FOLKS—It seemed to me I could best make my thoughts on this matter clear by asking a few questions in serial order and then answering them as best I could. So far as I deal with facts I have in mind entirely the facts in New York City.

The first question is this: Is it desirable that children of widows of good character and efficiency be kept with their mothers? Is poverty alone a sufficient cause for breaking up families?

I think that all of us here probably without exception would answer this first question in the affirmative. There are those who would answer it in the negative, but they don't come to conferences, and we have to deal with them when we get home. I think we can assume that substantially all those present would agree with the conclusion of the White House Conference in that regard. I, at least, stand without qualification on the answer as stated in those conclusions.

Again, if such families should be kept together, should the relief come preferably from private sources?

I take it that there is difference of opinion. A very considerable, and perhaps an increasing number, probably, would say that they would have no special preference, or even prefer public relief. Personally, I take the other side. Under present circumstances I decidedly prefer the relief of such families from private sources for these three reasons:

First, it is desirable to develop and maintain private relief giving, and that this offers a clear and easy division of the field—the public authorities to maintain the public institutions and the private societies to give the family relief.

Second, the administration of public family relief is perhaps admitted by all to be decidedly difficult. I do not agree with Mr. Almy that the difficulty lies in getting adequate salaries for relief officers. I think it is the rule that public work pays better salaries than private work. Charity may be the one exception, but if it is, I believe we can change that particular exception, and that adequate money for adequate salaries for an adequate number of officers, could be had.

But the more difficult point is the clumsiness of the machinery by which public employees are selected. It is still difficult, to be sure, by any process that we now know of to get competent people at a given time for a given job in the public service.

But the most serious objection of the three is, that I think there is a subtle psychological, but very important difference between the feeling of reliance upon private relief and the feeling of reliance upon public charity claimed as a matter of right. I am not so sure, in the case of widows, that it is not a matter of right. A feeling of reliance upon a steady and regular income wisely adapted to the family needs and the family budget, ought to be a good thing. I am not so sure that it is not a desirable thing in the home of the widow or where the totally disabled wage earner is concerned, but certainly it is a very dangerous thing in other households where there is a wage earner, able-bodied, but disposed to shirk his responsibility.

If it is preferable that relief come from private sources, is sufficient relief now given from private sources to such families? Speaking as to New York: I doubt if any person would have the hardihood to say that such is the case at the present time and for one, I have to state most emphatically, that it is not sufficient, and that families of that character are not kept together and that considerable numbers of children of widows who should be kept at home are committed, and that the process which Judge Pinckney described of the tearing apart of children from their mothers for poverty alone, occurs from time to time in every borough of the City of New York.

Third. If it is desirable that such families should be kept together and if the relief should come preferably from private sources, and if sufficient relief does not come now, is it, after all, a very serious thing to break up such families and send the children to institutions? I doubt whether any person present would answer that question thus put, in the negative, and yet some of our best friends do by their actions, answer it in the negative, because, while this breaking up of families goes on admittedly and openly, they do not actually do anything in a large way to stop it.

It is suggested sometimes that the proper course is to relieve in the best and finest and most constructive and up-to-date method such families as can be aided by existing resources. As to what is to happen to the other families not so aided, no particular reply is made.

What should we think of a city which had a thousand destitute aged persons and which was about to construct a new almshouse, and which proposed plans for an entirely modern building to accommodate two hundred persons, and pointed with pride to its sanitary arrangements, its bath rooms and cottage plan, and spoke of this as a model provision for the aged poor, but refused to answer the question as to what is to happen to the other eight hundred? What would the people of the city think of that sort of a municipal policy? But in my judgment that would be far more defensive, far less serious than to provide adequately for a few families leaving others to the tender resources of nothing.

Now, if it is desirable that these families be kept together, and if the relief should come preferably from private sources, and if it is really a very serious matter, is it possible to find from private sources sufficient relief? Some say yes and some say no, and I say that I do not think any of us know, for the reason that in New York it has never been intelligently tried.

We have possibly between six and seven thousand children of widows in institutions in New York City. Not all of them should be at home. Is it possible to secure from private sources sufficient additional funds to provide for them? I am not sure, and I hope the relief societies will make one more combined serious, final effort to secure such funds. But I think they should distinctly realize that this is the last call for dinner, and if they don't get together and secure such funds they will be provided from some other source in some other way.

Now, just one question more: If it develops that sufficient private resources are not to be had, is the evil of breaking up families as we are now doing, a lesser evil than public relief to widows? A good many say yes. My opinion is distinctly not; and that if we do not secure from private sources sufficient funds, then, without hesitation we ought to have a system of public relief for widows.

HON. MERRITT W. PINCKNEY—I am not convinced, notwithstanding what I have heard, against the "Funds to Parents" law—no, I am not convinced. I have listened with great interest to a very able and intelligent paper read by Mr. Almy. Anybody who knows him, knows of his ability to grasp this subject, must treat what he says with the highest consideration, and I do. If I had known him as well and liked him as well as I do now, before I came to Cleveland, I don't know whether I would have taken the opposite side of any question that he was to discuss. He certainly looks to me as though he was by experience authorized to speak, and I want to thank him personally, too, for the way he treated the subject. He didn't shut the door in our faces and say, "Stay outside." He didn't say to us, "The honest and judicious administration of the law of the Funds to Parents Act is impossible, go away and don't bother me." He left the door open, as I always believe he has left his mind open, for honest, intelligent thought, regardless of what his years of experience have been, and regardless of what his thought was on any particular subject, and I want to thank him for that consideration.

It comes to me now that someone of the speakers said it will cost a million dollars to try this out in the City of New York. I have read with interest the report of the State Board of Charities for the State of New York for the year 1911, and I recognize Mr. Hebberd as the Secretary of that Board. I assume that those gentlemen in their experience and grasp of this subject, and in their study of it, in their service to the State of New York, have made investigation and inquiry and have consulted with the various organizations, private and otherwise, through the State of New York, and therefore, when I read in their report that it is confessedly admitted by the private charities in the City of New York that they have not the adequate means to meet the needs of the dependents in that city, that it stands for something; and when I see in that report that thirty-four thousand five hundred and thirty children were in dependent institutions at the close of the fiscal year ending September 30, 1910, that it must take three hundred and fifty thousand dollars of New York's money to take care of those children for one month and that it must take for the year something over four million of dollars. I say, when these gentlemen, after their investigation, tell us these things and report that many of the children could have been taken care of at home in the normal condition of family life, that it means something, and I say it would pay the City of New York, as an experiment, to keep some of those children at home with their mothers instead of sending them away to institutions, even if it did cost one million dollars.

I want to say to Judge Baker from Boston, when you say that the administration of this relief ought not to be left to the Juvenile Court of Chicago, or to any Juvenile Court, I say, Amen! but I do say it is possible to so frame a law that public officials will be able to administer this relief.

Now, Mr. Persons, I want to say to you that it is probably due to the short time allowed me that I did not explain about these eight hundred and fifty families who were refused relief. I have the figures here on those families and I think there must be three hundred and fifty of them who were, through undisclosed property interests, money or funds of some kind, amply able to take care of themselves. That shows, if it shows anything, that we have a committee that is doing its work of investigation and inquiry well.

So, out of eight hundred and fifty families, three hundred and fifty were able to take care of themselves, and naturally, under the law, we couldn't give them relief. And of the other five hundred there are various reasons set down for refusing them relief. They were turned over to other agencies to be taken care of. Under the law, we say that these families, for reasons set down by the conference group after consultation with the Court, are not entitled to relief, but they are taken care of wherever it is necessary to take care of them.

Now, with reference to supervision, I wish to say to Miss Richmond that she is mistaken when she says that there is no supervision in Chicago. I will admit, ladies and gentlemen, after eleven months, under a law that is too brief, and into which we have had to read certain essentials before we undertook to administer it—I will admit that the law is not complete. I will admit that we are in the beginning of the dawn, but I say we are doing something toward administering this law efficiently, intelligently and honestly, too, and through public channels.

Don't let us be satisfied with what is partial, but let us ask for all. Why, we have been working for years now, for what? For compulsory insurance against accident, sickness, old age and invalidity.

Let us nail our colors to the mast and insist on what we have been asking for these many years, the full program; insurance against industrial accident, insurance against sickness, insurance against old age, insurance against invalidity, and compulsory insurance against all these four items in every State of the Union.

MISS M. E. RICHMOND—Mr. Senior has struck the keynote, I think. We must not attempt to meet our present difficulties, serious though they be, in such a bungling way as to put up permanent barriers against their solution. So far from being a forward step, "funds to parents" is a backward one—public funds not to widows only, mark you, but to private families, funds to the families of those who have deserted and are going to desert!

The breaking up of homes through poverty alone is, as I have said, a serious evil, but its prevention demands elements that this Chicago experiment, so carefully watched and safeguarded by some of the best known social workers in the country, conspicuously lacks. Even here, with their hearty good will and earnest co-operation, and with a judge willing to aid them, there has been practically no competent supervision of the pensioned families; there has been, in some cases, less adequate relief than private charity was giving, and far less supervision. If this has been the case in Chicago, what may we expect, at this stage of social service development, from experiments less co-operative and under administrations less able to withstand undue influence?

Another point in my too brief four minutes: This Illinois bill was drafted and passed without consulting a single social worker, and then they had to ask the social workers to come to their rescue in order that the worst might not happen. Watch your Legislatures carefully, when you go back to your several states, and see that the social workers are consulted in time.

Miss Lathrop has said that the private charities have been "pauperized" in Chicago by the new law, and are turning their cases over to the court. There is another aspect of that. No private fund for relief can successfully compete very long with a public fund, whether the latter is adequate or not. Inevitably the sources of private charitable relief dry up. A greater danger threatens in the state of New York, where it is actually proposed publicly to pay private charities for the relief of widows one hundred cents for every fifty that they spend in relief from their own funds—a two for a cent plan that will be an admirable way of hammering down our standards of adequate treatment in such cases. If we spend any of the fifty cents in seeing that the children of the widow are in school, that they are morally protected, that their health is safeguarded, that they have a good chance to grow up right, we are to get less than a dollar for the family; but if we, or our colleagues, spend all of the fifty cents on material relief, we get a dollar. The methods of public pensioning so far proposed are full of such incongruities as I have pointed out.

When a widow is granted relief under the law, the last thing that is said to her in court by myself, is to explain to her the necessity of accounting to a regular probation officer as to how she spends her money. And she is cautioned to keep her receipts, and that probation officer's duty is to visit that family regularly, and report on that family, giving it such supervision as it is possible for him or her to give. I don't say that this is enough, but I say that somewhere along the line, when we have had the experience and we get right down to what is possible to do under public administration, that we can rightly supervise and investigate and control this situation.

Now, I noticed in Mr. Almy's paper, the argument which he read, that to the imagination of the poor the public treasury is inexhaustible, and they drop on it without thrift—that is a forceful statement, that is true, but which is the worse, the pauperizing by alms or by neglect? For my part, I would rather have a pauper with a well-filled stomach than a pauper who is starving to death.

NOTES

1. Herbert Hoover, *The New Day* (Stanford, Calif.: Stanford University Press, 1928), p. 16.
2. S. E. Forman, *The Rise of American Commerce and Industry* (New York: Century, 1927), p. 369.
3. U.S. Department of Commerce, Bureau of the Census, *Historical Statistics of the United States: Colonial Times to 1957* (Washington, D.C.: Government Printing Office, 1960), p. 414 (hereafter cited as *Historical Statistics*).
4. Forman, op. cit., p. 442.
5. *Historical Statistics*, p. 139.
6. Ibid., p. 14.
7. U.S. Bureau of the Census, *Fourteenth Census of the United States: 1920*, Vol. 3, p. 15, and *Fifteenth Census of the United States: 1930*, Vol. 2, p. 27.
8. Roger Daniels, *Coming to America: A History of Immigration and Ethnicity in American Life* (New York: Harper Collins, 1990).
9. *Historical Statistics*, p. 14.
10. Alfred D. Chandler, *The Visible Hand: The Managerial Revolution in American Business* (Cambridge, Mass.: Belknap Press of Harvard University Press, 2002); Arthur R. Burns, *The Decline of Competition* (New York: McGraw-Hill, 1936).
11. U.S. Commission on Industrial Relations, *Final Report* (Washington, D.C.: Government Printing Office, 1915), p. 8.
12. U.S. Bureau of the Census, *Sixteenth Census of the United States: 1940, Comparative Occupation Statistics for the United States, 1870 to 1940*, p. 93.
13. Robert Hunter, *Poverty* (New York: Grosset & Dunlap, 1904), pp. 2–7, 56–65, 76–88, 96–97, 350–351. Reprinted in Roy Lubove, ed., *Poverty and Social Welfare in the United States* (New York: Holt, Rinehart & Winston, 1972), pp. 7–18.
14. John A. Ryan, *A Living Wage: Its Ethical and Economic Aspects* (New York: Macmillan, 1910), pp. 123–177. Ryan estimated the minimum "living wage" at more than $900 for the large eastern cities.
15. *Historical Statistics*, p. 278.
16. Slaughterhouse Cases, 16 Wallace 36, 1873. Opinion of Justice Samuel Miller, U.S. Supreme Court; Steven Hahn, *A Nation Under Our Feet: Black Political Struggles in the Rural South from Slavery to the Great Migration* (Cambridge, Mass.: Belknap Press of Harvard University Press, 2003).
17. C. Vann Woodward, *The Strange Career of Jim Crow* (New York: Oxford University Press, 1957).
18. *Plessy v. Ferguson*, 163 U.S. 537 (1896).
19. Hiram W. Evans, "The Klan of Tomorrow." Quoted in William Miller, *A New History of the United States* (New York: Braziller, 1958), pp. 355–356.
20. Booker T. Washington, "The Atlanta Cotton Exposition Address of 1895." Quoted in *"Up from Slavery,"* in Louis R. Harlan, ed., *The Booker T. Washington Papers*, Vol. 1 (Urbana: University of Illinois Press, 1972), p. 333.
21. Lillian Brandt, "The Make-up of Negro City Groups," *Charities and the Commons*, Vol. 15, October 7, 1905, p. 7.
22. *Historical Statistics*, p. 46. New York, Pennsylvania, Ohio, Illinois, and Michigan accounted for 78 percent of this.
23. Ibid., pp. 73, 409.
24. Thomas L. Philpott, *The Slum and the Ghetto: Immigrants, Blacks, and Reformers in Chicago, 1880–1930* (Belmont, Calif.: Wadsworth Publishing, 1991).
25. Phyllis J. Day, *A New History of Social Welfare* (Englewood Cliffs, N.J.: Prentice Hall, 1989), p. 247.
26. Daniels, op. cit., p. 114.
27. Gwendolyn Mink, *The Wage of Motherhood: Inequality in the Welfare State, 1917–1942* (Ithaca: Cornell University Press, 1995).
28. George J. Sanchez, *Becoming Mexican American: Ethnicity, Culture, and Identity in Chicano Los Angeles, 1900–1945* (Oxford and New York: Oxford University Press, 1993).
29. Sidney Lens, *Poverty: America's Enduring Paradox* (New York: Thomas Y. Crowell, 1969), pp. 209–210; Nick Salvatore, *Eugene V. Debs: Citizen and Socialist* (Urbana: University of Illinois Press, 1982).
30. Lincoln Steffens, *The Shame of the Cities* (New York: McClure, Phillips, 1904); David Graham Phillips, "The Treason of the Senate," *Cosmopolitan*, Vol. 40, March 1906, pp. 603–610.
31. Theda Skocpol, *Protecting Soldiers and Mothers: The Political Origins of Social Policy in the United States* (Cambridge, Mass.: Harvard University Press, 1992).
32. Arthur P. Miles, *An Introduction to Public Welfare* (Washington, D.C.: Heath, 1947), p. 124.
33. Theodore Roosevelt, "Reform Through Social Work," *McClure's Magazine*, Vol. 26, March 1901, pp. 448–454.
34. Arthur S. Link, *American Epoch: A History of the United States Since the 1890's* (New York: Knopf, 1955), p. 68.
35. Lens, op. cit., p. 212.
36. Charles Faulkner, "Twentieth Century Alignments for the Promotion of Social Order," *Proceedings, NCCC: 1900*, pp. 2–6.
37. Mary E. Richmond, "The Family and the Social Worker," *Proceedings, NCCC: 1908*, pp. 76–79.
38. U.S. Census Bureau, *Sixteenth Census: 1940*, pp. 93, 100.
39. *The Child Labor Bulletin*, Vol. 3, No. 1, May 1914 (New York: National Child Labor Committee).
40. Owen R. Lovejoy, "Report of the Committee on Standards of Living and Labor," *Proceedings, NCCC: 1912*, p. 386.
41. U.S. 37 stat. 79, the act establishing the Children's Bureau, approved April 7, 1912.
42. *Hammer v. Dagenhart* 247 U.S. Reports 251, 268 (June 1918). To be found in Grace Abbott, *The Child and the State* (Chicago: University of Chicago Press, 1938), pp. 495–506.
43. "State Child-Labor Standards, January 1, 1930," a chart prepared by the U.S. Department of Labor, Children's Bureau, and reprinted by permission of the Federal Board for Vocational Education (Washington, D.C.: Government Printing Office, 1930), chart no. 2.
44. *Fifteenth Census: 1930*, Vol. 2, pp. 1180–1196.
45. Lovejoy, op. cit., p. 383.
46. Edward C. Kirkland, *A History of American Economic Life* (New York: Appleton-Century-Crofts, 1969), p. 409.
47. Paul H. Douglas, *Real Wages in the United States, 1890–1926* (Boston: Houghton Mifflin, 1930), p. 208.
48. George Soule, *American Economic History* (New York: Dryden Press, 1957), p. 277.
49. Douglas, op. cit., pp. 112–114.

50. "Discussion on Charity Organization," *Proceedings, NCCC: 1888*, p. 420.

51. Alice Stone Blackwell, "Editorial," *The Woman's Journal*, April 11, 1911.

52. U.S. Department of Labor, Women's Bureau, *Handbook on Women Workers*, Bulletin No. 294 (Washington, D.C.: Government Printing Office, 1969); *Historical Statistics*, pp. 132–133.

53. Annie Marion MacLean, *Wage-Earning Women* (New York: Macmillan, 1919), p. 178.

54. Douglas, op. cit., p. 384.

55. An excellent review of this history may be found in Clarke A. Chambers, *Seedtime of Reform* (Minneapolis: University of Minnesota Press, 1963), pp. 151–182.

56. Clarke A. Chambers, *Paul U. Kellogg and the Survey* (Minneapolis: University of Minnesota Press, 1971), p. 36.

57. Ibid.

58. Special message by the president of the United States to the Senate and House of Representatives at the conclusion of the White House Conference Meeting of 1909. Reprinted in *Dependent and Neglected Children*, Report of the Committee on Socially Handicapped—Dependency and Neglect—of the White House Conference on Child Health and Protection (New York: Appleton-Century, 1933), p. 56.

59. Abbott, op. cit., Vol. 2, p. 395.

60. Ibid., p. 332.

61. Alice Higgins, "Helping Widows to Bring Up Citizens," *Proceedings, NCCC: 1910*, p. 140.

62. Skocpol, op. cit., pp. 424–479.

63. Mary E. Richmond, "Public Pensions to Widows— Discussion," *Proceedings, NCCC: 1912*, pp. 492–493.

64. Ibid.

65. Frederic Almy, "Public Pensions to Widows: Experiences and Observations Which Lead Me to Oppose Such a Law," *Proceedings, NCCC: 1912*, p. 482.

66. Ibid.

67. Abbott, op. cit., Vol. 2, p. 229.

68. U.S. Department of Labor, Children's Bureau, *Administration of Mother's Aid in Ten Localities*, prepared by Mary F. Bogue in Children's Bureau Publication No. 184 (Washington, D.C.: Government Printing Office, 1928), p. 4.

69. Ibid., pp. 25–26.

70. C. C. Carstens, "Discussion" of Emma O. Lundberg's "The Present Status of Mother's Pension Administration," *Proceedings, NCSW: 1921*, pp. 230–240. Carsten's remarks are to be found on p. 240.

71. Mary F. Bogue, *Administration of Mother's Aid in Ten Localities: With Special Reference to Health, Housing, Education and Recreation*. Children's Bureau Publication No. 184 (Washington, D.C.: Government Printing Office, 1928), p. 5.

72. J. S. Parker, *Social Security Reserves* (Washington, D.C.: American Council on Public Affairs, 1942).

73. *Historical Statistics*, pp. 139, 723.

74. "The Negroes in the Cities of the North," *Charities and the Commons*, Vol. 15, October 7, 1905.

75. W. E. Burghardt Du Bois, "National Committee on the Negro," *The Survey*, Vol. 22, June 12, 1909, pp. 407–408, and "National Negro Conference," *The Survey*, Vol. 24, April 23, 1910, p. 124.

76. George Burman Foster, "The Status and Vocation of Our Colored People"; George Edmund Haynes, "The Basis of Race Adjustment"; W. E. B. DuBois, "Social Effects of Emancipation"; Ida B. Wells-Barnett, "Our Country's Lynching Record"; Sophonisba P. Breckinridge, "The Color Line in the Housing Problem"; George Packard, "A Civic Problem and a Social Duty," *The Survey*, Vol. 29, February 1, 1913, pp. 567–581.

77. Franz Boas, "The Negro and the Demands of Modern Life: Ethnic and Anatomical Considerations," *Charities and the Commons*, Vol. 15, October 7, 1905, p. 2.

78. Steven Diner, "Chicago Social Workers and Blacks in the Progressive Era," *Social Service Review*, Vol. 44, December 1970, pp. 393–410.

79. Hoover, op. cit.

80. Jane Addams, *The Second Twenty Years at Hull House* (New York: Macmillan, 1930), pp. 10–48.

81. Robert Fisher, *Let the People Decide: Neighborhood Organizing in America* (New York: Twayne Publishing, 1994), pp. 1–31.

82. Emil Frankel, *Poor Relief in Pennsylvania: A State-Wide Survey of Pennsylvania* (Commonwealth of Pennsylvania: By the Public Board of Welfare, 1925), pp. 65–66.

83. Margaret E. Rich, *A Belief in People: A History of Family Social Work* (New York: Family Service Association of America, 1956), p. 74.

84. All material dealing with the expansion of benefits to veterans in the Progressive and pre-Depression eras is based on information to be found in U.S. Congress, House Committee Print No. 4, *Medical Care of Veterans*, 90th Cong., 1st sess., April 17, 1967. Printed for the use of the Committee on Veterans' Affairs.

85. Roy Lubove, *The Professional Altruist: The Emergence of Social Work as a Career, 1880–1930* (New York: Atheneum, 1969).

86. George A. Bellamy, "The Culture of the Family from the Standpoint of Recreation," *Proceedings, NCCC: 1914*, pp. 104–105.

87. Arthur Kennedy, ed., *Settlement Goals for the Next Third of a Century: A Symposium* (Boston: National Federation of Settlements, 1926), p. 45.

88. Porter R. Lee, "Social Work: Cause and Function," *Proceedings, NCSW: 1929*, p. 20.

89. An interesting analysis of the development of social work may be found in Stanley Wenocur and Michael Reisch, *From Charity to Enterprise* (Urbana and Chicago: University of Illinois Press, 1989).

The Depression and
the New Deal: 1930–1940

National Archives

The Depression and
the New Deal: 1930–1940

CHAPTER OUTLINE

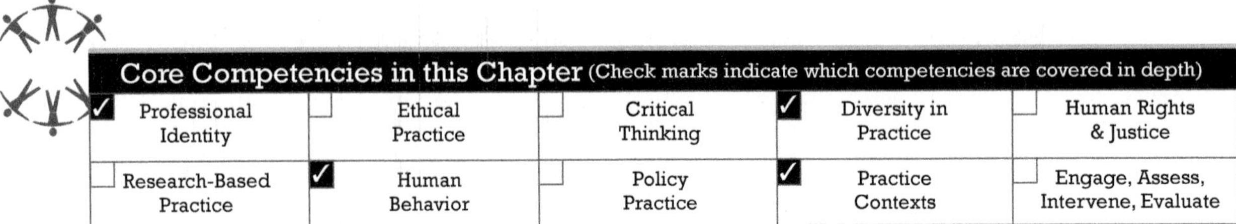

Core Competencies in this Chapter (Check marks indicate which competencies are covered in depth)				
✓ Professional Identity	☐ Ethical Practice	☐ Critical Thinking	✓ Diversity in Practice	☐ Human Rights & Justice
☐ Research-Based Practice	✓ Human Behavior	☐ Policy Practice	✓ Practice Contexts	☐ Engage, Assess, Intervene, Evaluate

The economic prosperity of the 1920s was both real and imaginary. Factory workers and second-generation ethnics experienced better economic times than during any previous era of American history. Like the subprime mortgage "bubble" of the early 2000s, however, much of the economic growth of the 1920s was fueled by speculation and plain fraud. Thanks to the availability of consumer credit, working families no longer had to save patiently for years to purchase an icebox or a radio; for a few dollars down and a few more every month, they could bring these new consumer products home. Like the 1990s, some economists and politicians believed that depression was a thing of the past.

The crisis that descended upon the country had not come without forewarning. In addition to the large-scale stock speculation, several other factors indicated the precariousness of the prosperity of the 1920s. A study by the Brookings Institution analyzed the income and savings of families in the richest pre-Depression year, 1929, and found that almost 6 million families, 21 percent of the population, had annual incomes of less than $1,000. These families of necessity spent more than they earned—$2.1 billion more. The next income group, the 5.8 million families with incomes between $1,000 and $1,500, had very slight savings—less than $200 million. Thus, 40 percent of the population had no reserves to fall back on when the Depression set in. The fact was that 30 percent of American families had incomes under $3,100 and had saved only 2 percent of all that families had saved during 1929. And could it have been any different? The Brookings study had declared that $2,000 in 1929 prices was sufficient to supply a family with only basic necessities. An annual income of $2,500 was a very moderate one. Nevertheless, 60 percent of all families had incomes below $2,000, and 71 percent of all families had incomes below $2,500.[1] Despite the talk of prosperity, low incomes were the reality for the vast majority of American families before the Depression hit.

Equally clear is the reason for the collapse of consumption once the unsoundness of the economic situation became evident and the fear of its consequences took hold. Families reduced their consumption, provoking a new second round of increased unemployment, from "overproduction of capital; overambitious expansion of business concerns; overproduction of commodities . . . the maintenance of an artificial price level for many commodities."[2] The gross national product (GNP) dropped yearly from an all-time high of $103.1 billion in 1929 to reach $55.6 billion in 1933. GNP started upward in 1934, reached $90.4 billion in 1937 but fell back to $84.7 billion the following year. Not until 1941 did national income reach precrisis levels.[3]

Other economic indicators followed the same pattern. Unemployment, which had averaged about 4 percent of the civilian labor force in the 1920s, rose by 4 million, or about 9 percent during 1930. In 1933, the year that marked the depth of the Depression, an average of 13 million persons, some 25 percent of the civilian labor force, were unemployed, and many more could find only part-time employment. Despite recovery programs, 14 percent of the American workforce was still jobless in 1937, and by 1938, that figure was up again to 19 percent.[4] The crash of 1929 was the start of a twelve-year period of deprivation.

In a situation in which earnings for most workers were near poverty level, security was necessarily measured in terms of steady employment. Unemployment of a breadwinner was obviously disastrous for a family. The finding of the Relief Census conducted by the Federal Emergency Relief Administration (FERA) during October 1933 that 3 million families, consisting of more than 12.5 million persons (about 10 percent of the population), were dependent upon unemployment relief suggests the scope of the disaster that had befallen the country. A new view of poverty and of the poor was in order.

The clear barrier between the deserving and undeserving poor that had guided social welfare policy for a century weakened as a result of mass unemployment. Despite earlier economic crises, Americans had remained convinced that the United States was the land of opportunity and that anyone who really wanted to work could find a job. That some people could not manage—that some apparently able-bodied individuals could be classed as permanently poor—had been observed, of course. In 1924, a century after the Yates report had provided a rationale for using the almshouse as a means of motivating the poor to work harder and become self-reliant, the New York Association for Improving the Conditions of the Poor released a study that argued that assistance levels were too low and that raising them might enable recipients to break the "vicious circle of poverty."[5] The Depression demonstrated that one could be poor and unemployed because of social—not individual—dysfunction. Both the temporary relief programs developed to meet the exigencies of the Depression, and later permanent programs of the Social Security Act recognized the possibility that the economy could fail.

There was, of course, dissent from the dominant view of poverty as a self-induced condition. The emergence of a distinctive subculture among professional social workers was one contributor to this alternative view of need and deprivation. Illustrative and factual support for such dissent began to appear in the publications of the Family Welfare Association of America (FWAA) and of the National Federation of Settlements. The FWAA journal, *The Family*, reported a study of breakdown in family income during 1928. One thousand cases, including 3,996 individuals known to three Boston family-relief agencies, were analyzed for factors associated with dependency. Of the total 1,000 cases, 41 percent showed that "some form of physical incapacity made charitable aid necessary," while 30 percent of the families were dependent as a result of joblessness.[6]

Still, this new recognition that unemployment was a structural risk of an industrial society sat uncomfortably with older characterizations of the poor. Thus, the Boston agencies still concluded that 7 percent of their clients were dependent because they had "bad character." This was in sharp contrast with the results of Amos Warner's classic study, *American Charities*, of 1892, which found intemperance to be the cause of dependency in one-fifth of the cases studied. The principal researcher of the later study hoped that the analysis would contribute to an understanding of "the inevitable economic maladjustments in a society which distributes its wealth to individuals capable of earning it . . . and assumes that the family system of consumption surviving from an earlier economic organization will have its needs supplied."[7]

In 1931, the Unemployment Committee of the National Federation of Settlements sponsored *Case Studies of Unemployment*, an account of 150 cases offering "cross-sections of human experience where unemployment is due to industrial rather than individual causes."[8] In the mid-1930s, E. Wight Bakke's studies of family life and unemployment documented the painful process of readjustment that loss of work initiated. In some cases, unemployment led to strengthen family ties as members worked together to get through the crisis, whereas in other cases, it led to a disintegration of both family relations and connections to neighbors and kin.[9] The volume was distributed widely and the impact of its illustrations from life contributed not only to the eventual acceptance of federal participation in emergency relief measures but also to the

Practice Contexts

Critical Thinking Question: How did the changing economic circumstances of American families during the Great Depression change the social context within which social work practitioners operate?

recognition of the need for permanent insurance against the risks of the industrial society. Looking beyond the immediate crisis, the National Federation declared:

> Experience has taught us to recognize broken work not merely as a symptom of financial crises, but as a recurring fault of modern production. We are confronted by unemployment, not as a single episode in the history of a household, but as something that may come again and again, impeding and stopping the normal development of the family.[10]

THE HOOVER RESPONSE TO CRISIS

The years that elapsed between the early recognition by social workers of rising unemployment and the beginning of federal involvement in the financing and administration of direct relief underlined the unwillingness of the federal government to recognize the depth of the crisis. President Herbert Hoover had been seen as a Progressive during the 1920s because of his leadership of the effort to feed a hungry Europe after World War I, but had retreated to an advocacy of "rugged individualism" during his 1928 campaign. He believed that government's proper role was to encourage voluntary action, a conviction that was woefully inadequate to cope with the magnitude of the economic dislocation of the Great Depression. In 1930, President Hoover engaged in a major campaign of optimistic rhetoric and a minor campaign of public works that failed to stop the precipitous economic decline. This refusal to depart from traditional political and ideological thinking imposed serious restraints on responses considered appropriate to deal with the event. Trapped by the hope of his own prediction of an early return to economic normalcy and by his belief in balanced budgets, laissez-faire, and states' rights, Hoover was reluctant to have the federal government assume new responsibilities and powers.[11] This was especially true in matters of social welfare, long considered a province for state and local activities as well as the special domain of private voluntary activity. Not until 1932 did Congress charter the Reconstruction Finance Corporation (RFC) "to provide emergency financing facilities for financial institutions to aid in financing agriculture, commerce and industry, and for other purposes."[12]

During the Hoover administration, the RFC's ability to stimulate economic recovery was stymied by its being restricted largely to making loans to help maintain the stability of financial, industrial, and agricultural institutions. In effect, the RFC became federally mandated aid for businessmen, while individuals and families were left to the mercy of inadequate state and local treasuries. Later, in 1932, the powers of the RFC were extended to permit federal loans to states "for relief and work relief to needy and distressed people and in relieving the hardship resulting from unemployment."[13] But even then the need for direct relief, as indicated by the findings of the National Federation of Settlements' case studies of unemployed families, generally went unheeded:

> Neither savings in cash, nor in homes, furniture, or personal keepsakes, neither charity nor getting into debt to butcher and baker, neither moving to cheaper quarters nor scrimping on food, nor the enforced labor of mothers and children gave adequate assurance of livelihood. . . . All combined, these makeshifts did not offer a reasonable solution of their predicament nor one which we should tolerate as part of our going life.[14]

Human Behavior

Critical Thinking Question: What changes in the family system are linked to loss of employment? How might the reaction of families during the 1930s differ from what might occur today?

Trapped by the hope of his own prediction of an early return to economic normalcy and by his belief in balanced budgets, laissez-faire, and states' rights, Hoover was reluctant to have the federal government assume new responsibilities and powers.

The platform statements of the Republican and Democratic parties demonstrated the essential conservatism of both parties as they entered the presidential campaign of 1932. Ironically, the Republican platform gave more explicit recognition to the human suffering occasioned by the Depression and to the need "to bring encouragement and relief to the thousands of American families that are sorely afflicted."[15] The Democratic platform did not use the word *depression* at all, and although it did mention the "unprecedented economic and social distress of the times," it did not refer to the personal consequences of this distress. Nevertheless, the Democratic platform called for public works and unemployment and old age insurance. The Republican platform "true to American traditions and principles of government . . . [confirmed] the relief problem as one of State and local responsibility"—and voluntary action.

FDR AND THE NEW DEAL

During the 1932 presidential campaign, the Democratic nominee, Franklin D. Roosevelt, moved somewhat unevenly toward a more innovative position as he pledged a New Deal for the American people. On the one hand, he advocated increased spending for the unemployed and more public works; on the other hand, he advocated a 25 percent cut in federal expenditures.[16] Roosevelt's original program did not see social welfare programs as central to economic recovery. He hoped that restricting competition through programs like the National Recovery Act and the Agricultural Adjustment Act (AAA) would increase corporate profits and revive the economy. Welfare payments were a short-term emergency measure that Roosevelt hoped to end as soon as possible. During his first term, however, political and economic dynamics served to make social welfare measures more central to New Deal economic policy. It slowly dawned on government officials that increasing the purchasing power of the ordinary people was more important than business profits in stimulating economic growth.

Roosevelt was no radical. In his 1932 speech accepting the presidential nomination, Roosevelt had stated:

> The great social phenomenon of this depression, unlike others before it, is that it has produced but a few of the disorderly manifestations that too often attend upon such times.
>
> Wild radicalism has made few converts, and the greatest tribute that I can pay to my countrymen is that in these days of crushing want there persists an orderly and hopeful spirit on the part of the millions of our people who have suffered so much.[17]

The eloquence of the speech and the breaking of tradition that brought a presidential nominee to his party's convention for the first time could not mask the traditionalism of the proposed program for recovery: economy in government, shorter working hours, public works financed and self-sustained by the issuance of government bonds, protective tariffs for industry and agriculture, and increased prices for industrial and farm products. The pledge of assistance with "distress relief" seemed almost an afterthought.

The effects of the crisis were visible for all to see. In addition to the inability of the stock market to sustain a rally, banks were closing, industries were failing, and farms were going into bankruptcy. Corporate profits, farm income, and wage earnings all fell, and the need for money brought the meaning of economic collapse into every home. By the time that Roosevelt came into office in

March 1933, governmental intervention in social and economic affairs was expected and accepted—particularly on the federal level. As one contemporary commentator noted:

> There is a country-wide dumping of responsibility on the Federal Government. If Mr. Roosevelt goes on collecting mandates, one after another, until their sum is startling, it is because all the other powers—industry, commerce, finance, labor, farmer and householder, state and city—virtually abdicate in his favor. America today literally asks for orders. . . .
>
> Among all the phenomena on the landscape, viewed from any angle, none is more striking than the reversal of the traditional relation between the country and the capital; for once Washington is the center of activity and the states beyond are passive, waiting for direction. Here is the stage, scene of a performance partly rehearsed, partly prompted by events; the nation is like a vast audience, hanging on to their seats to see what happens.[18]

New Deal policy contained a combination of three contradictory strategies in economic policy. First, there was a basic belief in the efficacy of the market system as a tool of economic "control," if only prices could be pushed upward. Second, there was the traditional view of the importance of a balanced budget; whenever possible, the Roosevelt administration moved to cut expenditures and reduce deficits. Finally, and often in conflict with what was seen as sound fiscal policy, there was the Keynesian theory of "effective demand," which saw the key to recovery in increased spending—government programs to increase purchasing power and direct spending for public works to increase employment. The regulated economy and the free market economy, compensatory finance and debt reduction, all played their parts in New Deal programs.

The early responses of the New Deal were, despite the rhetoric of change, conservative. Roosevelt's initial emphasis was to try generally to instill confidence and specifically to induce inflation in the expectation that a price rise would increase profits and thus stimulate output. A variety of measures were instituted to this end.

The banking crisis required immediate attention. There were 4,400 bank failures between 1930 and 1932, and by January 1933 panic was widespread. Runs and heavy withdrawals led one state after another to declare "bank holidays." When Roosevelt took office on March 4, 1933, banks were either closed or severely curtailed in forty-seven states. Within two days, on March 6, FDR had declared a national bank holiday, forbidden all gold payments and exports, and instituted new penalties for hoarding gold. Three days later Congress met in special session, the start of the "Congress of the Hundred Days," and passed an emergency Banking Bill. The emergency legislation that supervised the reopening of the banks and the more permanent banking reforms instituted within the next few years demonstrated the determination of the Roosevelt administration to maintain and restore the free enterprise system. Banking was not nationalized. Instead, the federal government, through the Federal Reserve banks, the RFC, and the Treasury Department, was to aid and regulate the banking industry so as to permit the emergence of a strengthened system of private financial institutions. In order to extend the system of control and to offer increased security to investors as well as to depositors, the Glass–Steagall Act regulated stock exchanges and the financial operations of holding companies.

In housing, too, the New Deal moved to preserve the concept of private property. The 1,000 homeowners threatened with foreclosure each month in

1933 were helped to refinance their mortgages through the Home Owners Loan Corporation, established in June 1933. The home construction industry, almost at a standstill in 1933, was revived through the National Housing Act of 1934, which insured loans for home repairs and mortgages for new houses.

Roosevelt hoped to induce inflation through experimental monetary policy measures. There was a retreat from the gold standard, a forced devaluation of the dollar, and a program of gold and silver purchases. He expected currency manipulation, support, and regulation of credit institutions, along with rising prices, to increase business investment.

Despite the talk and promise of inflation, prices did not rise. In part this was due to the reluctance of the Federal Reserve to expand the money supply and in part due to the deflationary impact of fiscal policy. The Economy Act of March 11, 1933, called for major cuts in government spending in an effort to balance the budget. Although Congress restored the cuts, political leaders were slow to understand that government spending was the key to stimulating the economy. Budget deficits were kept small, seen as a problem more than a solution, and, in fact, when production started to show real signs of recovery in 1937, government spending was cut and taxes increased. As a result, production, which in 1937 finally reached 1929 levels for the first time since the stock market crash, dropped precipitously in 1938 and unemployment rose again.[19]

The conflicting thrusts of New Deal policies were particularly dramatic in the development of agricultural and land policy. Native Americans saw some relief from their difficulties in land ownership during the period. The Dawes Act of 1887 had divided their land. But, in too many cases, Native American land was allotted to white people. In 1934, the Indian Reorganization Act helped end this practice. Additionally, Congress gave the tribes more than a million acres of new land, permitted more autonomy in local government, improved health services and education, and supplied credit for agricultural development and industrial projects. Native Americans were given preferential hiring in the Bureau of Indian Affairs, and the development of native crafts was encouraged. The secretary of the interior still exercised political control, regulated land management, and supervised expenditures. Nevertheless, New Deal policy provided a new beginning for the relationship of the federal government and Native Americans, one that acknowledged the government's past mistakes and the importance of indigenous culture and autonomy.[20]

For farmers, generally, the Depression of the 1930s seemed an extension and deepening of a crisis that had descended during the 1920s with the collapse of domestic and European demand for farm commodities. At first the problem seemed part of the general economic recession that plagued the country during 1920 and 1921, but subsequent improvements, during the 1920s, in the overall situation did not bring full recovery to farmers. Thus, whereas the share of agriculture in the national product had been 13 percent in 1919, its share was only 10 percent in 1929.[21] The situation became desperate during the 1930s. The ratio of prices for commodities sold by farmers to prices paid for purchases—using 1909–1914 as the base period—fell from 92 percent in 1929 to 58 percent in 1932.[22] Total farm income dropped to $2.5 billion in 1932, less than one-half of total farm income in 1919. Individual farm income dropped from $945 per farm in 1929 to $379 per farm in 1933.[23] Ironically, farm production fell by less than 5 percent, dashing hopes for an increase in prices of farm commodities. Farm debt soared as the value of farm property declined sharply. Farmers organized, demonstrated, and threatened a nationwide strike.

Despite agricultural difficulties, the Depression brought about a brief reversal of the long-term trend in the decline in the farm population. In 1929, 30.6 million persons—25 percent of the total population—lived on farms; by 1933, the farm population had risen to 32.4 million—26 percent of the total population. After 1933, the number of persons living on farms resumed its downward trend.[24] Disenchantment with the realities of farm living had set in, industrial production had started a slow recovery, and, perhaps most important, relief, when needed, was more readily available in the cities. As with farm population, the number of farms rose during the early Depression years and then began to fall.

The Roosevelt administration's New Deal package responded to the farmers' plight and unrest with legislation and administrative regulations designed to ease credit and to raise commodity prices through restricting output. In particular, the AAA, approved by Congress on May 10, 1933, authorized the imposition of production controls to achieve a balance between production and consumption of farm commodities at the index parity level of farm income enjoyed during 1909–1914.

The restriction of output contributed to a decline in the number of farms during the Depression years. By 1940, the number of farms stood at 6,097,000, representing a ten-year loss of almost 200,000 farms.[25] Since the number of farms owned or operated by whites remained essentially unchanged, the loss was almost entirely among black farms—down from 15 percent of the total number of farms in 1930 to 12 percent in 1940.[26] This rapid decline testifies to the precarious position of black farmers in the Southern agricultural economy. As farm prices fell, black tenant farmers were more likely to face eviction. At the same time, many African Americans were evicted because of their involvement with the Southern Tenant Farm Union that attempted to negotiate fairer conditions for poor black and white farms. These efforts to push poor African Americans off rural farms contributed to the rapid black migration to Northern cities over the next three decades.

As the Depression progressed, the percentage of fully owned farms increased as the total number of farms fell. This was true for black-owned as well as white-owned farms. The percentage of fully owned farms rose from 46 in 1930 to 51 in 1940; the percentage of black farms that were fully owned rose from 17 to 23 in the same period.[27] Farm ownership was accompanied by a steady increase in farm size—from an average of 150.7 acres in 1930 to an average of 167.1 acres in 1940.[28] Growth in farm ownership and in the average size of farms was stimulated directly and indirectly by New Deal policies.

Following his inauguration, President Roosevelt consolidated all federal agricultural credit agencies into the Farm Credit Administration. Congress authorized loans to save farmers from the immediate danger of foreclosures, to underwrite production costs, and to regain lost property on easy credit terms. The result of this package of New Deal farm legislation, including the AAA, was to raise net farm income from $2.5 billion in 1932 to more than $5.9 billion in 1935.[29] Additionally, the $9.6 billion farm mortgage debt load of 1930 was reduced to $7.6 billion in 1935 and to $6.6 billion in 1940.[30]

The success of early New Deal legislation, designed to help farmers through easy credit, supported not only farm ownership but also the introduction of farm machinery, which, in turn, encouraged the development of larger farms. The Farm Security Administration had authority to lend money to make it possible, among other things, for farmers to become landowners and to refinance and rehabilitate their lands. The withdrawal of submarginal land was encouraged.

Diversity in Practice

Critical Thinking Question: How might have social workers located in rural America of the 1930s adapted their practice to work with farm families?

In its early years, New Deal legislation spelled disaster for the most marginal group of farmers—tenants. In general, government support was for large farmers, with little assistance going to the small farmer. Not until 1935 was a tenant clause added to the AAA requiring farmers to keep the same number of tenants they had when they joined the program. Thus, between 1930 and 1940, while the number of full-farm owners increased by 172,000, the number of tenants decreased by 303,000. All of the decrease was accounted for by changes occurring in the South where the number of white tenant farmers dropped by 149,289 and the number of black tenants by 192,291. Blacks accounted for 56 percent of the total decrease in the number of tenant farmers. In terms of total numbers of tenant farmers, the loss represented a 28 percent decrease in the total number of black tenant farmers and a 14 percent decrease in the total number of white tenant farmers.[31] As the most marginal part of the farm population, tenant farmers and sharecroppers bore the heaviest burden of the agricultural depression. Homeless, they joined the other jobless and dispossessed who wandered the country.

The reduction in farm tenancy sparked two important migrations. Many African American and white Southerners found their way to the industrial centers of the Midwest and the East where they played an important role in the social and political crises of those cities during the postwar years. More immediately, tens of thousands of dispossessed farmers streamed westward where they joined Mexicans and Asian Americans in the labor force for California's expanding agricultural region. This migration was accelerated by a period of extreme drought during the early 1930s, which combined with poor land-use practices to create the "Dust Bowl." As immortalized in John Steinbeck's *The Grapes of Wrath*, low wages, inadequate housing and sanitation, and discrimination against the "Okies" created hardship. The Roosevelt administration stepped in both to improve conditions in California and, through the Civilian Conservation Corps (CCC), to reduce wind erosion on the Great Plains.

In industry, as in agriculture, New Deal policy sought to regulate prices and output. Large firms tended to dominate policy. The major legislation aimed at bringing about a manufacturing revival was the National Industrial Recovery Act (NIRA) presented to Congress on May 15, 1933. The NIRA was designed to meet labor's demand for limited hours of work in order to spread employment and business's demand for the relaxation of antitrust laws in order to stabilize output and raise prices.

Title I of the NIRA established a set of industry codes that would end cut-throat competition, raise prices, limit output, and provide for workers a reasonable workweek at a reasonable wage. Each industry was, in theory, to be regulated by a tripartite committee representing management, labor, and the public. FDR signed the bill on June 16, 1933. An interim, blanket code was established with the Blue Eagle, as posted by business, as its symbol of acceptance. Within a few weeks, almost 2.5 million employers, with 16 million workers, had signed codes. By September, within three months of the inception of the codes, the ten largest industries were brought under the National Recovery Administration (NRA). All the codes contained minimum wage and maximum hour scales; all contained provisions for collective bargaining. In practice, however, the industry codes reflected the price and output policies of the dominant firms in each industry, and competition restraint operated to the serious disadvantage of small businessmen. When the NRA was declared unconstitutional by the Supreme Court in May 1935, it was already under severe attack.

Application for funds for Rural Rehabilitation camps for
migratory laborers in California.

Introduction

"...we found filth, squalor, an entire absence of
sanitation, and a crowding of human beings into
totally inadequate tents or crude structures built
of boards, weeds, and anything that was found at
hand to give a pitiful semblance of a home at its
worst. Words cannot describe some of the conditions
we saw." (Federal report on Imperial Valley, California).

· · · · ·

"No provision is made for sanitation, water supply, or
even general camp cleanliness... A sorry picture is presented of a condition that threatens to be a serious
menace to those communities where squatter camps exist.
Moving the occupants away simply spreads the condition..."
(California Department of Industrial Relations report on
squatters camps).

· · · · ·

It may be true that alien Mexicans... live better in
Imperial Valley than they do in their own country, but
this cannot constitute an excuse for countenancing
poverty and squalor in the United States." (General
Pelham D. Glassford, Federal Conciliator in Imperial
Valley, California).

Decent camp facilities for seasonal workers in agriculture
are an urgent need in California. Every month more thousands of
migratory families are being set in motion to serve the 1935
harvests which are already under way. Camp conditions remain
about as they were in 1933 and 1934. The incessant labor strife
which marked those years is not stilled; 1935, too, is already
building its own strike record. Living conditions remain a basic
aggravating factor in these disturbances.

The present application is the first request by the
California Division of Rural Rehabilitation for FERA funds in
the name of elevation of the living standards of depressed
laborers. Therefore, a somewhat fuller presentation is made of
the unique role of labor in agricultural California than might
otherwise seem necessary to a simple proposal for decent camps.
But California labor deviates from the national rural labor
pattern in many essential respects. Inevitably, the problem of
its rehabilitation is so uniquely affected thereby that the more
salient features of its background have been set forth in the
following outline.

Application for federal emergency funding to construct migrant worker housing in California, 1935

The application for migrant worker housing funds was accompanied by photographs by Dorthea Lange of existing conditions. Kern County, California February 1935

How successful was this organization of industry for recovery? During its two years of operation, employment rose by 2 million, industrial production rose from 62 percent to 79 percent of the 1929 level of output, and GNP increased from $55.6 billion to $72.2 billion.[32] But 20 percent of the labor force was still unemployed, industrial output was 21 percentage points less than before the crash, and GNP was still far below the level of prosperity. Paralleling the irony of the AAA's curtailment of food production and destruction of livestock when people were starving, the NRA limited competition and output when what was needed for prosperity was an expansion of industry.

Title II of the NIRA provided for a Public Works Administration (PWA) and allocated $3.3 billion for this program. Had this money been used speedily to increase employment and purchasing power, it might have been an extremely helpful stimulant. PWA was intended, however, for capital investment and pump priming. Under the cautious direction of Harold Ickes, its immediate expansionary potential was never realized.

LABOR AND SOCIAL WELFARE

Perhaps the most significant and long-lasting result of the experiment in industrial control was its impact on organized labor and the precedent for social legislation it established. As the United States entered the 1930s and economic depression, labor was largely unorganized. Union gains made during World War I were lost in a postwar environment of generally steady employment, increasing real wages, and political repression. Furthermore, the American Federation of Labor (AFL), representing skilled labor, tended to cooperate with management in a "welfare capitalism" effort. Ignored by that effort was the great mass of unskilled workers in the basic manufacturing industries. Trade union membership declined from 5 million in 1920 to 3.4 million in 1930; membership in the AFL declined from 4.1 million in 1920 to 3 million in 1930.[33] The violent and largely unsuccessful strikes led by the United Mine Workers in 1921 and 1922 and by the United Textile Workers in 1929 further weakened organized labor as the Depression settled in.

The fortunes of labor began to turn in 1932 with the passage of the Norris–LaGuardia Act, which restricted the right of the federal courts to issue injunctions against unions engaged in peaceful strikes and to enforce "yellow dog" contracts. In 1933, the newly formulated codes of the NRA reaffirmed the right of collective bargaining in covered industries, established the forty-four-hour week, outlawed child labor, and set minimum wages ranging from thirty to forty cents an hour. The underlying motive was to maintain wages at the same time that the elimination of child labor and the reduction in working hours spread jobs among a larger number of adult workers. Falling wages stimulated workers to organize and unions to recruit membership. By 1935, union membership had grown to 3.7 million.[34]

The labor movement was only one of many efforts at social reform during the period that eventually pushed the Roosevelt administration to a more aggressive set of policies. During the early years of the Depression, Unemployment councils in many large cities organized protests to demand the expansion of relief. The colorful governor and U.S. senator from Louisiana, Huey Long, promoted a "share our wealth" plan that would have taxed corporate and individual wealth and used the proceeds to reduce poverty. Third parties, like the Farm-Labor Party, also enjoyed significant support, especially in Minnesota where the party elected three governors and two senators during the 1930s. One of the Farm-Labor senators, Ernest Lundeen, sponsored a more-radical social insurance bill that competed with the Roosevelt's Economic Security Act (that would eventually become law as the Social Security Act).[35]

Labor's success was not easily attained. Its efforts to organize and to force concessions were matched by management's determination to prevent unionization and to preserve the open shop. In August 1933, President Roosevelt established the National Labor Board to mediate labor disputes. When it failed for lack of authority to enforce decisions, it was replaced by the National Labor Relations Board. The new board, authorized to hold elections to determine the right of unions to conduct collective bargaining, but lacking authority to prevent unfair management practices, was equally unsuccessful in preventing and settling labor disputes. By May 1935, when the NRA was declared unconstitutional, business had generally revolted against the labor provisions of the codes.

The National Labor Relations Act—the Wagner Act—was signed into law on July 5, 1935. The new law contained all that had been foreshadowed in the

The labor movement was only one of many efforts at social reform during the period that eventually pushed the Roosevelt administration to a more aggressive set of policies.

Norris–LaGuardia Act and NIRA. In addition, it outlawed company-dominated unions and gave the new National Labor Relations Board authority to supervise elections and determine the appropriate bargaining unit, to hear complaints of unfair labor practices, and, when necessary, to petition the courts to enforce its orders. The legal authorization of collective bargaining led to the unionization of large numbers of unskilled workers in basic industries.

The AFL's reliance on *craft* unions hamstrung its efforts to organize the manufacturing sector. Rather than form an *industrial* union that would include all autoworkers or steelworkers, the AFL sought to divide workers into a number of distinct crafts and have each craft organized separately. Advocates of industrial unions split with the AFL in 1937 to form the Congress of Industrial Organizations (CIO). Through an aggressive organizing campaign, the CIO and its member unions achieved major victories in the automobile and steel industries.[36]

A report of the La Follette Civil Liberties Committee, the first part of which was made public in December 1937, strengthened the hand of the National Labor Relations Board and ultimately ensured the passage of the Fair Labor Standards Act of June 1938. The report publicized in detail industry's disregard for labor's legal rights. Not the least of its revelations was the fact that a selected list of companies had spent a total of $9.4 million for labor spies, strikebreakers, and munitions between 1933 and 1936.[37] The disclosures were important in moving management toward collective bargaining. As the 1930s ended, organized labor could boast a total membership of 10.6 million. Of the total, 5 million workers belonged to the CIO and 4.6 million belonged to the AFL.[38]

The Fair Labor Standards Act legislatively retrieved those provisions of the NRA that had dealt with work hours, minimum wages, and child labor. The act established a minimum wage of twenty-five cents an hour (rising to forty cents an hour in seven years), a forty-four-hour week to be reduced to forty hours in three years, and sixteen years as the age below which a child could not work in industries whose products entered interstate commerce. The act's provisions were, for the most part, already a reality for much of organized labor, so those largely affected were nonunionized, unprotected workers—women, minors, and minority group members, the rank and file of the unskilled. As a result, the hourly pay of 300,000 workers was immediately raised and the workweek was shortened for 2,382,000 people.[39]

The success of the CIO in its efforts to organize the mass industries was enormously significant for unskilled workers. Such workers were frequently members of minority groups, women, and children, and their status was easily exploited in times of labor strife or economic recession. In the strikes of 1921 and 1922, unorganized blacks had been extensively used as strikebreakers. Blacks were often the first to feel the crush of the Depression of the 1930s as social discrimination played its role in decisions to release workers. A National Urban League survey of 106 cities disclosed that 20 to 30 percent of the black population was unemployed in 1931.[40] As the economic situation worsened, many industries replaced men with women at cheaper rates; many replaced men and women with children. In other situations, "desperate heads of families took women's jobs at women's wages, Negro jobs at Negro wages, leaving the minority groups without means of support."[41]

The size of the labor force increased between 1930 and 1940. This was true for both male and female workers.[42] As with blacks, the severity of the unemployment situation aggravated long-established patterns of prejudice and discrimination against women. The notion of women's "proper place" was enhanced by the urgency of a drive to "get the men back to work." The country as a whole was convinced that employment for men was the priority, and this was the view of many social workers and social scientists, as well as the official position of unions and government. Congresswoman Florence Kahn said, "Woman's place is not out in the business world competing with men who have families to support."[43] In 1932, Congress established a "married persons' clause" for all federal and service employees, whereby the first employees to be considered redundant when reductions in personnel were necessary were those whose spouses were also federal employees.[44] For the most part, this meant that women were dismissed.

Actually, the get-the-men-back-to-work slogan was aimed at all women, and single women seem to have suffered even greater discrimination than married women. Nevertheless, the percentage of married female workers rose. In 1920, married women comprised 23 percent of female workers; by 1930, one of the earlier years of the Depression, the percentage had risen to 28.9; and in 1940, married women represented 36.7 percent of women in the labor force.[45] Married or single, the fact was that employers found in women a pool of workers suitable for employment at low wages.

VETERANS AND THE BONUS

The Depression years were years of distress for veterans as for others, but the difference was that their visibility as veterans and as a strongly organized constituency meant a continuing ability to elicit special consideration. Almost immediately after World War I, veterans began pushing for a bonus that would provide an economic redress to balance the wartime earnings of workers in industry. A bill making such provisions in the form of "adjustment compensation certificates" was passed over President Calvin Coolidge's veto in 1924. Payments were to come due in 1945. By 1930, with unemployment mounting, demands for immediate payment began to be made. The demand culminated in June 1932 in the "bonus march" on Washington, D.C., of some 15,000 to 20,000 veterans, many accompanied by their families. The march ended a month later when, on the order of President Hoover, army troops were dispatched to clear the veterans from their Washington campsites. Despite Hoover's objections, however, and over his veto, Congress passed a bill allowing veterans to obtain, in cash, half the value of the certificates.

Smaller bonus marches were attempted in 1933 and 1934, but with little immediate success. Payment of the bonus was made in 1937, the year of a disastrous reversal of the long climb out of the Depression. The bonus succeeded in putting almost $3.5 billion into the hands of veterans and, eventually, into the nation's economy.

Veterans' social welfare policy led to confrontations between Congress and the Roosevelt administration. The bonus marches of 1933 and 1934 were triggered by the Economy Act of March 1933, the same act that had cut congressional salaries and reduced federal expenditures. The act also cut the amount of veteran's benefits and the number of eligible recipients. Especially hard-hit were thousands of veterans who needed care for nonservice-connected conditions and who were unemployed because of the Depression. The resulting outcry was such that in 1934, Congress passed new legislation in effect rescinding the Economy Act. The expansion of veterans' cash, medical, and hospital benefits led President Roosevelt to veto the bill, but it became law when both houses of Congress voted to override the veto. In connection with the provisions for money payments, the new legislation stressed the word *compensation* to define the uniqueness of such payments to veterans.

Veterans were given special attention in the matter of job opportunities, too. From the bonus armies of 1933 and 1934, more than 10,000 veterans—transients stranded in Washington—were enrolled in the CCC and assigned to work camps. Additional camps were established by the FERA for veterans whose physical condition made them ineligible for CCC camps. Still other veterans were assigned to Works Progress Administration (WPA) projects. In all, some 17,000 veterans were certified by the Veterans Administration for CCC, FERA, or WPA employment between 1933 and 1935.[46] The bonus payment of 1937 was, of course, of much greater significance because of the number of individuals reached and the dollar amount of benefits received. The bonus concept, joined to the benefit structure of the veterans' legislation of 1934, set a pattern that would influence veterans' legislation during and after World War II.

PUBLIC MONEY FOR RELIEF

One of the most urgent and immediate problems of Roosevelt's first year in office was certainly the problem of relief. In response, he proposed three types of remedial legislation: (1) grants to states for direct relief, (2) public works programs to stimulate investment, and (3) immediate public employment programs.

A commonly held belief had been that anyone who really wanted to work could find a job. This particular myth had been shattered by every household's firsthand experience, by newly developed systems of statistical fact-finding in regard to unemployment, and by social agency revelations of the causes and effects of dependency. More difficult to dispel were the myths that the chief burden of relief was being carried by privately supported agencies and that, in any case, relief was a local responsibility. The development of a powerful, voluntary family welfare movement and the existence of local public welfare departments that were "stereotyped, inarticulate, politics-ridden, and generally of lower standards"[47] had obscured the shift to public relief that had already occurred in 1929.

The larger part of relief was being paid with public funds, although it was generally administered by voluntary family agencies directly or by family agency workers on loan to public agencies. This realization stimulated a reconsideration of alignments between voluntary family and public welfare agencies. In effect, the Depression had created a functional crisis for family agencies. These agencies had historically opposed the giving of public relief and the development of public welfare agencies, arguing that they themselves were best equipped to handle relief problems. Now, with the coming of the Depression, they could not meet the financial demands no matter how much they wanted to help. Furthermore, mushrooming caseloads of "new poor" families whose only need was money distracted attention from families requiring professional casework services. Necessity was forcing the separation of professional service from the provision of financial help.

Noting that the four large family agencies of Manhattan had had, during November 1930, 5,739 applications for "material need" and only 669 other types of applications, social worker Gordon Hamilton admitted that voluntary agencies had "attempted to carry . . . many types of problems which should be carried under public auspices."[48] She suggested the appropriateness of a public family agency geared primarily to offering financial help but also offering casework help when requested by the family. In such a realignment of public–private welfare relationships, "the contribution of private social work to welfare administration is chiefly through urging a professional rather than political considerations in the selection of personnel, the idea of budgeted rather than fixed relief, and the attempt to offer trained casework service to those who desired it."[49]

Hamilton's presentation of the situation in New York was borne out by information derived from fifty-one agencies reporting to the Russell Sage Foundation between March 1929 and March 1931. As might be expected, all the agencies had dealt with enormously increased numbers of families. They had met the emergency by classifying the unemployment cases as a separate and distinct group, by using volunteers and "junior" workers for routine duties, and by protecting the intensive treatment of "regular run" cases from being swamped.[50] Overall, the fifty-one reporting agencies had emphasized "the urgent need for giving individualized treatments so far as possible, and . . . stood out against such mass methods of treatment as bread lines and soup kitchens, with the result that these primitive, inadequate, and demoralizing devices for giving large scale relief . . . [had] been used but very little"[51] with families.

Despite the ideology of voluntary charity, even before the Great Depression, relief efforts were dominated by public funds. A compilation of the Department of Statistics of the Russell Sage Foundation of relief expenditures of eighty-one American cities showed that 74 percent of such expenditures ($31 million) had come from public funds during the last year before the Depression, 1929. Expenditures in 1930 for relief were about double those of 1929. Seventy-five percent of relief expenditures ($51 million) had come from public funds. An emergency appeal for private funds reduced the share of public relief expenditures to 66 percent during 1931, but public relief expenditures had, nevertheless, increased to $54 million.[52] Obviously, voluntary giving could not meet the demand.

By 1931, it was clear, too, that local units of government could not keep pace with the need for public funding. Municipal welfare payments, where they existed, were painfully small. As the Depression deepened, the need for relief increased, and it became less and less possible for cities to meet that need.

New York—with its Temporary Relief Administration set up in 1931—was the first state to appropriate funds to be disbursed to cities and counties for home-relief and work-relief programs. Other states followed suit so that by the close of 1931, New Jersey, Rhode Island, Illinois, Wisconsin, Ohio, and Pennsylvania had joined New York in making relief funds available to localities. Efforts to obtain federal participation in relief funding also occurred during 1931 but were defeated by presidential veto. Be that as it may, New York, in setting up its Temporary Relief Administration to administer that state's relief appropriations, provided the prototype for the federal program to come.

FEDERAL EMERGENCY RELIEF ADMINISTRATION

On May 12, 1933, acting on the overwhelming need of states for money for relief, Congress established the FERA to channel a half billion dollars in relief money through state and local welfare agencies. That same month, the PWA was established as a stimulant to business investment. In November 1933, recognizing the urgent need for jobs, and interpreting flexibly the provisions of the NIRA, President Roosevelt established the Civil Works Administration (CWA) and made $400 million of PWA money available to finance programs of "civil works." Both FERA and CWA came under the direction of Harry Hopkins. When CWA proved too expensive a means of job creation, the Emergency Work Relief Program was established within FERA. Subsequent temporary measures to deal directly with unemployment and the needs of the unemployed led to the creation of the Federal Surplus Commodities Corporation, the CCC, and finally, when direct federal relief was phased out, the WPA. From the beginning of the New Deal, a threefold approach to income maintenance was envisioned: cash relief, short-term work relief, and the expansion of employment through the pump-priming effects of public works.

The major direct relief effort of the federal government was FERA. It was established "to provide for cooperation by the Federal government with the several States and Territories and the District of Columbia in relieving the hardship and suffering caused by unemployment and for other purposes." Half of the appropriation was to be made available to the states on a matching basis—$1 of federal money for every $3 of state and local expenditures; the other $250 million was to be distributed to the states on the basis of need without matching funds.[53] In authorizing direct grants to states for relief, the legislation set a major precedent for a new fiscal relationship between the federal government and the states and for a new interpretation of the responsibility of the federal government for social welfare.

Of more immediate importance, however, was the speedy flow of cash to the needy. Grants for seven states were approved one day after Hopkins took office in May 1933, and by the end of the next month, $51 million had been paid out to forty-five states, the District of Columbia, and the territory of Hawaii. During the last half of 1933, about 3.5 million people were supported, and by the end of December 1933, $324.5 million had been distributed—with all states and territories participating. In the three years of its existence, FERA spent more than $3 billion. Despite some tendency of state and local governments to substitute federal money for local effort, the states also increased their relief expenditures during this period. In all, something over $4 billion was distributed in cash and work relief by federal and state governments.[54]

Relief money was not always distributed fairly. Racial discrimination in the administration of funds was a major problem. As with other New Deal programs, particularly in Southern rural areas, the black population found it difficult to get on relief rolls. For example, the CCC had racial quotas, the AAA distributed funds based in part on race, and the codes for pay rates of the National Labor Administration discriminated against people of color. Blacks were more apt to receive relief in Northern cities. Overall, they suffered much higher rates of unemployment and poverty, and this was reflected in the relief rolls. In 1933, nearly 18 percent of all black family heads were certified for relief and about 15 percent in 1935—about twice the rate for white breadwinners.[55] For all, black and white grants were pitifully low throughout the period.

In part, the shortfalls of the relief effort reflect the speed with which the federal government tried to establish a federal–state public welfare program. The need was widespread and immediate, and the administrators of FERA tried to provide cash to meet that need as quickly as possible. The difficulties arose, too, from a conflict between ideology and necessity. The philosophy of the New Deal was relief for the unemployed through the provision of jobs. Direct relief was to be a temporary, necessary expedient until those who were

Relief money was not always distributed fairly. Racial discrimination in the administration of funds was a major problem. As with other New Deal programs, particularly in Southern rural areas, the black population found it difficult to get on relief rolls.

employable could be employed. For the moment, in the emergency, "employables" and "unemployables" were brought together in one program, but direct relief for the able-bodied was only a stopgap measure.

Hopkins, the president's mentor on welfare matters, had indicated as much in his clarification of the purpose of the Federal Emergency Relief Act. Addressing the National Conference of Social Workers, Hopkins had said:

> The intent of this act is that relief should be given to the heads of families who are out of work and whose dependency arises from the fact that they are out of work, and to transient families, as well as the transient men and women roaming about the country. . . .
>
> Our job is to see that the unemployed get relief, not to develop a great social work organization throughout the United States.[56]

FDR's distaste for relief can be measured by his statement two years after assuming office:

> The Federal Government must and shall quit this business of relief.
>
> I am not willing that the vitality of our people be further sapped. . . . We must preserve not only the bodies of the unemployed from destitution but also their self-respect, their self-reliance and courage and determination.[57]

However, Roosevelt's condemnation of relief as the "subtle destroyer of the human spirit" did not lead him to ignore government's important role in social welfare.[58] To the contrary, he contrasted cash relief with the positive role that work relief and social insurance should play for Americans. Roosevelt had a Committee on Economic Security to develop a plan of income security for individuals and families. The committee's recommendations were to echo the president's concern that the productivity of American workers be secured at the same time that their loyalty to the American "free" market system be assured.

In his congressional message of January 4, 1935, President Roosevelt had separated the productive from the nonproductive poor, accepting primary responsibility for the former, the group that was "the victim of a nation-wide depression caused by conditions which were not local but national."[59] Approximately 5 million families and single people were then on the relief rolls. FERA estimated that 3.5 million of these recipients were employable, and FDR was determined to give them employment "pending their absorption in a rising tide of private employment." Although not abandoning the additional 1.5 million people remaining on the relief rolls, he nevertheless stated his intention that those who in the past had been "dependent upon local efforts" be maintained again "by State, by counties, by towns, by cities, by churches, and by private welfare agencies."[60]

The fact that excessive unemployment continued year after year and gave rise to the specter of a huge demoralized and unproductive class dependent upon a public dole required not only insurance against future industrial hazards but also an immediate new approach to unemployment relief. With a program of work-related social insurance already in the making by the Committee on Economic Security, the president's interim solution was the establishment of the WPA to "supersede the Federal Emergency Relief Administration with a coordinated authority . . . charged with the orderly liquidation of our present relief activities and the substitution of a national chart for the giving of work." As for those who could not work, said the president, "I stand ready through my personal efforts, and through the public influence of the office that I hold, to help these local agencies to get the means necessary to assume this burden."

The WPA, funded in 1935 at $4.9 billion, actually spent more than twice that amount in its lifetime. Eventually, it provided jobs for 8 million Americans in a wide range of activities, from heavy construction to the painting of murals in local libraries and orchestral performances in schools. For those for whom jobs were provided, life was much improved. Wages were higher than relief payments, and there was no deterrent income eligibility test. But work projects got under way slowly and many employables never found work at all.

The federal government did not immediately substitute work relief for all cash relief. Congress did not pass the Emergency Appropriation Act until April 1935 and included requested funds to cover a period of transition from home relief to work relief. The work was constituted by executive order in May, and Hopkins was appointed its administrator. Actual liquidation of FERA was not begun until the closing months of the year, and the final emergency relief grants went out to the states in December 1935.

By the end of 1935, with the phasing out of federal participation in direct relief under way, with the inability or unwillingness of many states to replace the lost funds, and with the transfer of employables to WPA projects slower than had been contemplated, the transition period became a "bitter one for families on relief in many parts of the country."[61] The problem was exacerbated by the slowness with which the public assistance programs of the Social Security Act—programs designed to help some categories of unemployables—were implemented by the states.

Social workers were wary of the phasing out of federal funding for direct relief. Some had been catalysts for the organization of client groups of which they were themselves members. Many had a personal and professional intimacy with problems resulting from unemployment and a new understanding of poverty and the poor.[62]

Private agencies were not able to pick up the slack even as much as they had prior to 1933 because the events of the Depression had begun to define a new role for them. Hopkins's administration of FERA had formalized the changed relationship between public and voluntary family agencies. Regulation No. 1 of the *Rules and Regulations* promulgated by FERA required that public relief funds be administered by public agencies. Recognition was given to the thousands of private family and child welfare agency workers who had helped with the administration of public funds, but Regulation No. 1 required that they be designated as public officials working under the control of public authority.[63] The process by which private family agencies had already begun to delineate the uniqueness of their service was now accelerated and suddenly required consideration of alignments not only with public agencies but also with private child welfare agencies.

FERA's Regulation No. 3 clarified further the separation of public and private agencies in regard to administering public relief funds. At the same time, the regulation revealed the extent to which public officials were influenced by private agency experience. Regulation No. 3 required the investigation and the demonstration of need on the part of the individual family. Means testing and budgeting to ensure that "no relief is given to persons unless they are actually in need and that such relief . . . is adjusted to . . . actual needs"[64] was the outcome. The use of trained and experienced investigators, at least in supervisory positions, regular home visiting, and attention to state relative responsibility laws were required.

FERA's *Rules and Regulations* represented an advance in standard-setting over pre-Depression approaches to public giving. They also established certain operating principles that were to have negative consequences in later years: administrative discretion, rather than legal definitions, for establishing eligibility for aid; a professional casework service orientation toward relief giving; and a subtly pervading, if unnoted, reservation that relief was somehow a necessary evil. For the moment, however, people were helped and their need was of primary importance. Hopkins stated:

> We are now dealing with people of all classes. It is no longer a matter of unemployables and chronic dependents, but of your friends and mine who are involved in this. Everyone of us knows some family of our friends which is or should be getting relief.[65]

Hopkins's statement, his administration of FERA, and his realization that "however well this thing is administered, this enormous relief business can never be anything more than a makeshift"[66] set the stage for a major shift in the federal approach to income maintenance. The change had several facets. For the short run, there had been a switch in the allocation of federal funds to employment—work relief—programs and a return to the states of responsibility for the direct relief of unemployables. For the long run, there were to be permanent social security programs.

THE SOCIAL SECURITY ACT

The Social Security Act, signed into law by President Roosevelt on August 15, 1935, was the major legislative achievement of the New Deal. It was a landmark in American political and social history, reflecting a public commitment to the economic rights of people and, consequently, extending federal responsibility for social welfare. The act, from the point of view of program provisions, administrative structuring, and federal–state fiscal arrangements, represented a watershed for the mingling of old and new orientations toward people as social and economic beings.

During the early decades of the twentieth century, Congress considered, but did not accept, plans to provide old age and unemployment insurance. By 1935, however, demographic, economic, and political pressures for federal action were overwhelming.

The aged as a percentage of the population were increasing at twice the rate of general population growth as life expectancy rose and birthrates fell. They suffered severe unemployment and for the most part had little in the way of savings to fall back upon. Existing state pensions reached only 5 percent of the aged and in any case were unable to provide anywhere near adequate support. Private pensions were virtually nonexistent. The elderly and their adult children were faced with an unbearable burden. Roosevelt's Advisory Council on Economic Security noted that:

> Many children who previously supported their parents have been compelled to cease doing so, and the great majority will probably never resume this load. . . . The Depression has deprived millions of workers past middle life of their jobs. . . . Regardless of what may be done to improve their condition, this cost of supporting the aged will continue to increase. In another generation it will be at least double the present total.[67]

There was strong political pressure for the federal government to act to provide old age insurance. In California, the Townsend movement, a major lobby for aged pensions under the direction of Francis E. Townsend, gained enormous support with its demand for a $200-a-month pension for all over the age of sixty, provided they left the labor market and spent the money. There were many other popular schemes. The Old Folks Picnic Association, End Poverty in California (EPIC), the Ham and Eggs movement, and many others suggested a variety of plans for helping the aging that ranged from free fishing licenses to monthly payments of $400. The proposal of Senator Huey Long of Louisiana to "share our wealth" and provide a minimum income of $5,000 a year for all was receiving enthusiastic support around the nation. Overall, popular pressure pushed the Roosevelt administration to adopt a moderate pension plan for the aged.[68]

The Social Security Act evolved from the work of the Committee on Economic Security, which submitted its report to the president on January 15, 1935. The report was accompanied by drafts of bills representing an expedient "piecemeal approach" whose primary aim was "the assurance of an adequate income to each human being in childhood, youth, middle age, or old age in sickness or in health."[69] Within an overall recommendation that the federal government assume responsibility for employment assurance, the committee made specific recommendations in regard to security against the risks of unemployment, retirement in old age, and ill health. Additional recommendations provided for the current security of old people and children through the provision of federally aided, state-administered pensions. Finally, the committee recommended an array of employment, health, educational, and rehabilitative services. Many of these were to be administered by the states, with standard setting to be stimulated by the federal government through the offer of financial and other types of assistance.

Having made sweeping recommendations in regard to federal involvement in a program of assurances against the hazards of life, the committee recognized the need for residual relief for "genuine unemployables—or near unemployables." The committee commended the care and guidance of this group to the states—and to social workers:

> With the Federal Government carrying so much burden for pure unemployment, the State and local governments . . . should resume responsibility for relief. The families that have always been partially or wholly dependent on others for support can best be assisted through the tried procedures of social casework, with its individualized treatment.[70]

President Roosevelt recommended the committee's report to Congress in January 1935 as the basis for legislation. His message emphasized the soundness of the committee's proposals and the caution with which they should be considered.

> The detailed report of the Committee sets forth a series of proposals that will appeal to the sound sense of the American people. It has not attempted the impossible nor has it failed to exercise sound caution and consideration of all the factors concerned: the national credit, the rights and responsibilities of States, the capacity of industry to assume financial responsibilities and the fundamental necessity of proceeding in a manner that will merit enthusiastic support of citizens of all sorts.[71]

The president's sense of fiscal and political realities led him to specifying legislative principles that necessarily ordained a modest beginning program of social assurances: no health insurance, no federal administration of relief programs and only fiscal administration of unemployment insurance, and no use of the general revenues for old age insurance. Not unexpectedly, then, the

Social Security laws, when enacted, were more conservative than the recommendations of the Committee on Economic Security.

The policy of the United States in regard to permanent programs of income maintenance was stated in the preamble to Public Law No. 271:

> An Act to provide for the general welfare by establishing a system of Federal old-age benefits, and by enabling the several States to make more adequate provision for aged persons, blind persons, dependent and crippled children, maternal and child welfare, public health, and the administration of their unemployment compensation laws.[72]

The law's program provisions covered loss of income due to temporary loss of job (Unemployment Compensation), inability to participate in the labor force due to age or disability (Federal Old Age Insurance, Old Age Assistance, Aid to the Blind, Aid to Dependent Children [ADC]), the promotion of the welfare of mothers and children (Maternal and Child Health Services, Services for Crippled Children, Child Welfare Services), and the encouragement of adequate state and local public health services. Provisions for the extension and improvement of maternal and child health services offered by local health authorities restored programs that had languished or collapsed when the Sheppard–Towner Act had been permitted to expire in 1929. Nonetheless, the decision against legislating health insurance at that time effectively stopped the movement toward the development of a health insurance mechanism. Not until thirty years later did the movement again become viable. The decision was especially constraining because the overall thrust of the Social Security Act toward cash payments as opposed to in-kind services simultaneously limited federal contributions toward the development of a comprehensive health care delivery system.

Social Insurance

The enactment of Federal Old Age Insurance and Grants to States for Unemployment Compensation recognized flaws in the country's private enterprise market system and the need for institutional change to mitigate unavoidable economic and social distress. Insurance against the hazards of unemployment and of retirement in old age bolstered the security of beneficiaries and of the private enterprise system itself because these institutional reforms, aimed at meeting universal needs, guaranteed permanent economic stabilizers for both. Thus, social insurance benefits, based on a joint employee–employer contributory scheme, ensured an income for individuals who had worked steadily but could not necessarily be expected to maintain the burden of self-support in retirement or unemployment. The structure of social security was meant to fit the demographic and market structure of most families: one wage earner, working full-time for a full year with just a few employers during a working life. It was a model for an industrial economy. The social insurance approach assumed the essential viability of the market system while acknowledging the need to support the public's purchasing power. This assumption by the federal government of responsibility for the worker's income security suggested that the flaws in society were, after all, correctable.

Social insurance started out closely modeled on private insurance, with benefits tightly tied to contributions. The insurance emphasis on individual equity was one thrust. Concern for the poverty of the aged was another. The intent was to have characteristics of both insurance and social welfare. An insurance model would make benefits closely dependent on contributions. A social model would show concern for the poorest of the aged and feature redistribution from the wealthy to lower income groups so that lower income workers would receive more in return for their contributions than would high-income workers. The emphasis in 1935 on equity—an insurance approach—outweighed concerns for adequacy—a social welfare approach.

Although the 1935 law was conservative, the 1939 amendments added benefits for the spouses and children of deceased workers and expanded the number of workers covered by old age insurance. The formula for calculating benefits was adjusted to become more redistributive in its structure. Benefits were expanded between 1939 and 1974, which retained the connection between contributions and benefits, but loosened it to permit large families to receive more than small families, and low-wage earners to receive a higher proportion of their contributions than highly paid earners. Workers who earned low wages would still receive pensions that were smaller than those of better-off workers, but the difference in pensions was smaller than that in their wages. As a result, the income distribution of older Americans became more equal over the next five decades. Many of the controversies during these years flowed from efforts to maintain the delicate balance between adequate benefits for all recipients and the link between wage history and benefits.

The desire to model social insurance after private insurance programs was reflected in the concept of a reserve fund to hold the assets of the program. A trust fund is essentially a bookkeeping mechanism for specifying that particular revenues be related to specific programs. The original concept in 1935 was to establish a fund in accordance with accepted actuarial principles: at any time, the fund should be large enough to pay off all future obligations. But by 1939, Congress began to worry that the assets might grow too large. The law required Social Security assets to be invested exclusively in special issues of U.S. government bonds. The fear was that there would not be enough government debt for appropriate investment. The Social Security Board was required to report to Congress whenever the assets of the trusts reached three times the size of benefit payments and thus became so large that they would absorb too much of the government debt. After 1939, the trustees abandoned a full actuarial reserve to a partial or contingency reserve fund that would build assets to meet needs for a limited period of time.

The 1935 Social Security Act and its 1939 amendments had many flaws. Many workers, including domestic workers and farm laborers, were excluded from coverage. In addition, other common sources of poverty, including disability and the desertion of one's spouse, were ignored by its insurance provisions. In addition, for those groups it did cover, the programs needed time to build up funds from which benefits might be dispensed. These factors meant that programs of temporary assistance were required. Categorical programs that made federal grants-in-aid available to the states were designed to assist the destitute aged, the blind, and dependent children.

Although it was hard to see at the time, the greatest flaw of the Social Security Act was its construction of a two-class social welfare system. Workers who were regularly employed in established industries were protected against the major risks of an industrial society—old age, unemployment, and (eventually) disability. Workers with less stable industries would continue to rely on the old poor law system for aid. The decisions of Congress to exclude the major industries that employed African Americans—domestic and farm labor— quickly imposed a racial division on this class structure.[73]

Public Assistance

Although the Depression had obscured the line between the worthy and unworthy poor, the New Deal often revived this division. The Social Security Act established a dual system for federally supported income maintenance. The result for the country was a three-part approach to public relief. The act provided for federally administered insurance programs and federally aided, state-administered assistance programs for selected groups. The grant-in-aid, state-administered financial assistance programs served to separate again the old poor from the new. The new poor, the unemployed, were covered by social insurance; the old "worthy" poor, by categorical public assistance. Left to the states was the third group, the "unworthy" poor, for whom states and localities were to develop programs without federal aid.

The creation of federally aided categories of assistance evolved from long-time state efforts to help certain classes of the poor whose circumstances could not readily be attributed to personal inadequacy and who, therefore, were not to be stigmatized as recipients of the dole. State provisions of aid for the aged, the blind, and the widowed were generally viewed as pensions without stigma. By 1935, aid to the blind was available in twenty-four states; aid to the aged, in thirty-four states; and aid to mothers, in all states and jurisdictions except Alabama, Georgia, and South Carolina. The decision of Congress to lend federal support for the beneficiaries of these programs acknowledged the legitimacy of their claim. Besides, many policymakers believed that public assistance would eventually wither away as federal measures for social insurance, maternal and child welfare, and public health work took hold.[74]

The contrast between the act's social insurance and public assistance programs was striking. While old age insurance became a federal responsibility, Congress chose to allow states to continue to define their own welfare policies, albeit with increased federal funding and oversight. By focusing federal aid on specific categories of the needy—the elderly, the blind, and dependent children—the Social Security Act reinforced earlier policy decisions for differentiating these groups from the able-bodied poor. Indeed, until 1950, mothers of dependent children did not qualify for their own grant.

Still, the public assistance titles of the Social Security Act were not simply a return to older policy traditions. The federal public assistance categories were community oriented, in that they required that recipients be living in their own homes. Furthermore, the Social Security Act defined assistance as "money payments," requiring that grants be made in cash. Finally, the act mandated the opportunity for a fair hearing for any individual whose claim for assistance was denied. These particular provisions, plus the fact that they legislatively joined insurance and assistance programs, gave some support to the concept of the "right to assistance" for eligible recipients.

Federal oversight of public assistance pushed recalcitrant states—especially in the South—to bring greater transparency and professionalism to their assistance programs. The act required states to submit plans making assistance programs mandatory in all political subdivisions, appointing a single state agency responsible for administering or supervising the state's assistance program, ensuring the efficiency of state program administration, and guaranteeing compliance with the Social Security Board's regulations and reporting requirements. Of equal significance was that the federal government pushed states to reduce or eliminate burdensome residency requirements, a break with public assistance's Poor Law legacy. For all the differences still possible under its essentially permissive requirements, the act did succeed in bringing the federally funded public assistance programs to all the states and in giving the various programs an identifiable common base.

The Social Security Act had profound significance for family welfare generally, and for the roles of family members in particular. For women, the addition to Old Age Insurance of dependents' benefits in 1939 reinforced their roles as wives and homemakers. Despite the increase in the labor-force participation of women, the act did not cover many traditionally female jobs. It penalized heavily for interrupted employment, and compensated inadequately for pay discrimination. Thus, over the years, many women workers discovered that their contributions to Social Security counted for nothing, because their spousal benefits were higher than those they had earned through work.

For the larger society, Old Age Insurance and Old Age Assistance meant that a major portion of the financial burden of caring for aged parents was lifted from adult children. The money thus freed could be shifted to the care of minor children. The adequacy of ADC benefits was questionable from the start.

The Committee on Economic Security had described mothers' pensions as "defensive measures for children."

> They are designed to release from the wage-earning role the person whose natural function is to give her children the physical and affectionate guardianship necessary not alone to keep them from falling into social misfortune, but more affirmatively to rear them into citizens capable of contributing to society.[75]

Despite the committee's encouragement and the seeming popularity of Mothers' Aid among the states, limited professional social work attention was given to ADC during congressional hearings. Katherine Lenroot, chief of the Children's Bureau,[76] and Jacob Kepecs, president of the Child Welfare League (CWL) of America,[77] were the only social workers to testify in favor the new program. Edwin Witte, executive for the committee, stated after the passage of the Social Security Act that the poor outcome of provisions for dependent children, as compared to provisions for other needy groups, was mainly due to this lack of interest.[78]

The inattention to provisions for dependent children resulted, first, in the administration of ADC along with the adult categories of assistance. The original intent that the program be under the jurisdiction of the Children's Bureau was thus ignored. Second, as the title "aid to dependent children" suggested, caretakers did not receive their own grant until 1950. Third, the grant-in-aid formula limited federal payments to one-third of a total of $18 per month per family provided for one dependent and to one-third of $12 per month provided for additional dependent children. The formula contrasted sharply with that used for Old Age Assistance. In the latter instance, the federal government offered payment monthly of one-half of $30 for each eligible person. ADC obviously provided less than the "defense measures" envisioned by the Committee on Economic Security. The contrast between the provisions for dependent children and for the aged and the blind foreshadowed future development of the programs. Aid for the elderly and blind (later expanded to include people with disabilities) would eventually become full federal programs with more generous benefits, while ADC—equated with welfare—experienced repeated attacks at the federal and state levels for the next six decades and was eventually scrapped.

One basis perhaps for the suspicion and distrust of the new ADC program was uncertainty about who was to be helped by it. The older, states' Mothers'

Aid programs, for the most part, did not provide for payments for children born out of wedlock; they were widows' pensions. Many social workers felt either unprepared to accept these clients or unprepared to fight for them. By June 1938, 604,142 children in forty states were being helped by ADC. It is estimated that less than 4 percent of these were children who lived with unmarried mothers. Sixteen percent of the reporting states had not accepted any children of unwed mothers.

The low coverage rate reflects the unwillingness to move from the old Mothers' Aid to the less restrictive coverage. While neither the Social Security Act nor the Social Security Board regulations restrict coverage to children of unmarried mothers, scarcity often left distribution of funds to the interpretation of local boards and workers. What is a suitable home? In a 1939 article, Mary S. Labaree noted the variation in local policies:

> There is surprising little of a censorious attitude towards girls with limited opportunities in our mountain counties. . . . Give aid to dependent children . . . to an unmarried mother from an undesirable home but . . . consider . . . the unmarried from a good family with good background has committed an inexcusable act.
>
> Any mother is considered fit to care for her child unless she is so unfit that a petition for neglect should be filed.
>
> If all the children in a family were illegitimate the commission would decide this was not a fit mother. If only one or two were illegitimate it might be overlooked or forgiven.
>
> It is a matter of state policy that the parent must not have had an out-of-wedlock child within a year.[79]

There was even more variation in the treatment of children of color than of white children, and in most communities it was difficult for black mothers to receive help. As one field supervisor put it, "Communities . . . see no reason why the employable Negro mother should not continue her usually sketchy seasonal labor or indefinite domestic service rather than receive a public-assistance grant."[80] From its start, the economics of the marketplace, concepts of morality and appropriate sexual behavior, and racism combined to limit the scope and the effectiveness of this program. The Social Security Act of 1935 put federal social welfare policy on its trajectory for the remainder of the twentieth century. The division between insurance programs that were "earned" and assistance programs that were not grew stronger during the next fifty years. The groups that received insurance coverage, including people with disabilities who were added to the program in 1956, saw their poverty rates decline steadily between 1940 and 2000. Over the same years, poor mothers and their children were left behind; their proportion of all poor people increased steadily in subsequent decades.

THE ECLIPSE OF REFORM

The expansion of federal social welfare legislation during the Roosevelt administration was largely confined to the years between 1935 and 1938. In 1937, the administration decided to cut spending on social welfare in an effort to balance the government's budget. Within a few months, the economy had descended into recession, and unemployment, which had never fallen below 10 percent, spiked. Roosevelt's and the Democratic Party's popularity suffered a setback.

The 75th Congress that convened in 1939 still boasted a large majority in support of New Deal legislation, although conservative Southern Democrats were able to use their voting strength to tailor legislation to their liking. In particular, they steadfastly blocked policy that would interfere with their states' rights to discriminate against African Americans.[81]

Federal public housing policy as it was defined by the Housing Act of 1937 (Wagner–Steagall Act) demonstrated the political constraints on the New Deal, even when it enjoyed large Congressional majorities. Efforts to provide decent housing for poor and working-class families dated from the late nineteenth century. Typically initiated by charitable organizations, a variety of "social housing" developments advanced the idea that shelter could not be left simply to the laws of supply and demand. During World War I, the federal government had created the United States Housing Corporation and the Emergency Fleet Corporation to help the war effort by building housing in shipbuilding centers, but at the end of the war, these efforts were terminated.[82]

During its early years, the Roosevelt administration initiated a variety of experiments in housing and community development. The Resettlement Administration, under the leadership of Rexford Tugwell, constructed three model towns, including Greenbelt, Maryland; Greendale, Wisconsin; and Greenhills, Ohio, before its efforts were declared unconstitutional by the Supreme Court. A collaboration of the hosiery-workers union and the PWA led to the construction of a model housing project, the Carl Mackley Houses, in Philadelphia in 1934.[83]

Yet, the path from experimentation to a permanent public housing program was a difficult one. Developers, construction companies, and their allies—the strength of the private housing industry—opposed public intervention in their sector, while conservative politicians railed against the centralization of power in Washington. In the end, the Wagner–Steagall Act included significant limits on the success of public housing. First, public housing projects were initiated by local housing authorities, not by the federal government. As a result, most public housing was limited to central cities; suburban communities often did not even establish housing authorities. Second, stringent limits were placed on the amount that could be spent to construct a unit of public housing. This requirement was included in the legislation to assure that public housing would never compete with the private sector for any but the lowest-quality shelter. Finally, Southern politicians were able to block any attempts to include antidiscrimination language in the bill. As a result, throughout the nation, public housing was constructed on a segregated basis.[84]

Public housing was an early example of how court, private-industry, and Southern opposition could limit the reform impulse of the New Deal. The start of World War II in Europe in 1939 ended the Roosevelt administration's focus on social reform.

FAMILY LIFE AND SOCIAL WORKERS

A summary of staff reports prepared for the Committee on Economic Security declared that "the chief aim of social security is protection of the family life of wage earners, and the prime factor in family life is the protection and development of children."[85] As the Depression deepened, social workers insisted that the economic base of the family be strengthened and that the federal government share in the cost.

Changes in the family were particularly evident in the move of women to occupations outside the home. The number of wage-earning women sixteen years of age and over increased from 1,701,000 in 1870, when the Bureau of the Census first collected such data, to 10,546,000 in 1930.[86] During the 1920s, the increase in female employment was 29 percent, while the increase of the female population was 22 percent. The number of employed married women had reached 3,071,000 in 1930, a nearly 300 percent increase over the 769,000 employed at the beginning of the century. Were it not "for the retardation of business activity which was well under way at the time of the 1930 census, probably even more women would have reported themselves as occupied." As it was, 33 percent of those who worked were in domestic and personal services, 18 percent were in manufacturing and mechanical industries, 19 percent were in clerical occupations, and 12 percent were in trade and transportation. The vast majority were in semiskilled or unskilled positions.

The unemployment crisis of the 1930s of necessity affected family life. The formation of new families—getting married and having children—was delayed. The marriage rate per 1,000 unmarried women declined from 92 percent in 1920 to 68 percent in 1930.[87] In 1933, the birthrate was 18.4 per 1,000 of population, down from 27.7 per 1,000 of population in 1920 and from 21.3 in 1930.[88] The psychological climate, as well as economic reality, was one of depression for families already formed. Unemployment struck women as well as men, with discrimination falling heavily upon the former as jobs became scarcer and men displaced women. At the same time, the well-paid industrial and construction work performed by most men was more liable to layoffs than the lower-paid, unskilled work performed by most women. One result was role reversal, wherein wives worked and supported families while husbands were confined to the home. Although the divorce rate showed no appreciable change between 1920 and 1940—actually the rate for 1930 (7.5 per 1,000) married women was slightly lower than the 1920 rate (8.0 per 1,000)—family instability was evidenced by a sharp increase in suicide and desertions.[89] And the plight of older people forced permanently out of the labor force by the Depression was frightening to contemplate.

Thus the attitude of the social work and social welfare community toward the Social Security Act as a family welfare measure is noteworthy. The act itself had been approved on August 15, 1935, but federal funds did not become available until February 1936. Beyond that, the process of having states submit plans for the administration of public assistance and of having those plans approved by the newly created Public Assistance Board proved slow. By mid-November 1936, forty-two states had finally received grants for Old Age Assistance. Only twenty-six states had received grants for ADC, bearing out the lack of concern for this group of recipients. The states, in their reluctance to move into this category of assistance, reflected the attitude of the federal government in its differential treatment of children.

All in all, social workers were alarmed by the course of events, and the delegate conference of the American Association of Social Workers, held in Washington, D.C., February 14–16, 1936, considered carefully "this business of relief." The delegates gave public hearing to a number of convictions and concerns.[90]

1. That the factors that made relief necessary were demoralizing, not the act of receiving relief itself

2. That the work provided by WPA should be productive in itself and not just a technique for avoiding idleness

3. That need should be the criterion for federal assistance and that separating employables from unemployables left the matter to the uncertain mercies of states and localities

4. That there was a residual relief problem caused by the fact that WPA work relief payments were inadequate to cover the needs of large families and by the fact that some groups were not covered by the federally aided public assistance categories at all

5. That permissive requirements for state participation in federally aided public assistance programs threatened irresponsibility

The dissatisfaction expressed at the delegate conference did not alter the course of events. The collapse of social work's pressure for a return to a federal program geared primarily to direct relief seems first of all due to the political odds against such a return but also to a conflict among social workers as to their professional view of the poor and of the needs of the poor.

Aubrey Williams, deputy administrator for the WPA, expressed his bewilderment and concern at the "growing disposition on the part of social workers to advocate the return of the federal government to direct relief." He implied that this pressure resulted from the tendency on their part to see caseworkers as necessary to the poor and casework as a necessary adjunct to poor relief. "To put caseworkers into the old poor relief system," Williams argued, "is to put new wine into old bottles that will crack." He warned that the demolition of the WPA would give social workers "3.5 million people on direct relief and nothing else" and, in a final thrust, said that "the sooner social work as a profession can turn its back on direct relief as a valid form of social treatment, the better off will be the nation and the higher the standing of social work."[91] Like Hopkins back in 1933, Williams seemed to be saying that federal programs should not be used "to develop a great social work organization throughout the United States." Those who led the attack against the WPA could not easily dismiss the accusation.

Having been admonished by Williams to think of new approaches to unemployment and income security, the delegates were also treated to Ewan Clague's description of the potentialities of the provisions of the Social Security Act.[92] Perhaps because it did join, no matter how uneasily, new social insurance and old public relief measures, the act offered some satisfaction to those social workers who had urged social reform through social insurance and to those who urged reform through the professionalization of relief giving.

Many social workers—especially those working for public agencies—demanded more sweeping action to address the Depression that put them to the left of the New Deal and their professional organizations. The Rank-and-File movement and its publication *Social Work Today* became the voice of this concern. At its peak, the Rank-and-File movement claimed 15,000 members. The Rank-and-File movement represented an attempt to redefine social workers as *both* professionals and as workers, workers with the right and need to organize into labor unions. The idea of social workers' unions outlived the demise of the movement in 1942.[93]

The early years of the Depression were ones during which social workers clarified their own views about relief and about people who needed financial help. The professional literature between 1930 and 1935 abounds with discussion and controversy. One issue, federal versus state and local responsibility for relief, was settled quite easily. State and local coffers were empty. The issue of public versus private responsibility for relief was similarly resolved. A third issue was that of cash versus in kind. In 1933, Dorothy Kahn, director of the Philadelphia County Relief Board and soon to become chairman of the American Association of Social Workers, made "an ardent appeal for one form [of relief giving], namely, cash."[94] As demonstrated by the categorical programs of the Social Security Act, the proponents of cash payments won the day. The literature would suggest that social workers believed the issue of right versus privilege as a basis for financial aid to have been settled in favor of the right to assistance. Certainly, this was true for the social insurances whose benefits were related to worker contributions. As for the categorical programs, the Social Security Act's use of the word *claim* in connection with the receipt of benefits distributed in cash and the right to a fair hearing both indicated an entitlement to public assistance, no matter how conditioned that entitlement might be. Hopkins thought the federal administering agency, along with state and local boards, would pass benefits on "as a pension without stigma."[95]

Perhaps most important to an understanding of the fate of ADC was the issue of social insurance versus public assistance. Although both types of programs were included in the Social Security Act, the reality was that the social insurance mechanism was favored as an approach to income security. The strengthening of the work ethic by relating premiums and benefits to earnings and the attempted simulation of actuarial, private insurance soundness (with almost no contribution from the general revenue) was designed to ensure the political attractiveness of social insurance.

Of course, the current unemployment crisis required public relief programs, but whatever fears remained about supporting public, nonwork-related programs could be allayed with the belief that such programs would wither away. The need for Old Age Assistance would disappear as Old Age Insurance matured and covered an increasing number of workers. Of importance, too, was the fact that survivors of workers, although not sufficiently provided for, had not been entirely forgotten. The Committee on Economic Security had recommended that a death benefit be paid to a worker's surviving dependents should the worker die before the age of sixty-five or before the amount of his own contributions had been paid to him as an annuity.[96] The committee had also given consideration to the future when "families and widows would be given primary consideration in broad plans for survivors' insurance or insurance for widows and orphans."[97] The Social Security Act did in fact provide for a lump sum benefit to survivors as recommended by the Committee on Economic Security. There was reason to believe that insurance coverage eventually would be extended to widows and orphans and that ADC, like Old Age Assistance, would fade in significance. Perhaps that is one reason why the Senate and House committees heard only perfunctory social work support for ADC and little social work criticism of its deficiencies as a program.

NEW ALIGNMENTS IN SOCIAL WELFARE

An exploration of social work's attitude toward ADC must take into account that the Depression required social workers to clarify not only their views about relief and relief recipients but also alignments between public and private social welfare. Inevitably this meant a reconsideration of the functions of professional social work. Regulation No. 1 had begun the reversal of a tradition whereby voluntary agencies shaped the contribution of public agencies to social welfare. The enactment of the Social Security Act furthered the process and established the dominance of public welfare. The impact on voluntary agencies—on voluntary family agencies, in particular—was enormous. Voluntary family agencies and family agency personnel had impeded the development of public welfare prior to the Depression. And despite their beginning development of casework as a professional methodology and of family counseling as a professional function, they had remained absorbed with problems of relief giving. With the onset of the Depression, they became involved in cooperative efforts to help families needing relief because of the unemployment crisis, and their day-to-day practice consisted chiefly of relief-related activities. The FWAA described the extent of its member agencies' involvement:

> Every good public program owes something to the pioneer work of private agencies. . . . Private agencies have readily loaned or released trained persons for service in public agencies, often at a great cost to their own programs. Supervisory and advisory aid have been accorded continuously by many private agencies to public agencies. In addition . . . private agencies have also engaged actively in obtaining general support of public welfare programs.[98]

Now, with the passage of the Social Security Act, family agencies seemed devoid of a viable social welfare function. Family agency workers, who in large measure carried the professional status for social work, seemed similarly affected. Both agencies and workers needed to find a raison d'être, and it was perhaps the knowledge of this, as much as anything else, that underlay the heated discussions of public welfare at the February 1936 delegate conference of the American Association of Social Workers. The apparent collapse of organized social work support for unemployment relief suggests a perception that professional social work practice and relief giving were separate entities, however overlapping their concerns.

This recognition was confirmed in March 1936, when the FWAA published a report of responses by member agencies to questions related to "the crisis in community programs." Of the total of ninety-three agencies responding, eighty-nine agreed that "it would be folly for private agencies . . . to attempt to meet any appreciable part of the unemployment relief burden . . . being abandoned by the Federal Government." They agreed that it was essential "to hold firmly to the principle that intensive casework treatment is the primary function of a family service organization." Nevertheless, when asked to list developments of new or more clearly defined channels of services to the community, the agencies gave "a great variety of answers which constitute[d] a confusing picture." Many listed their emphasis on "intensive casework" as a new development.

The extent to which voluntary agencies were threatened by the Social Security Act's establishment of a permanent public welfare structure and by the vacuum created by the loss of a primary relief-giving responsibility can also be discerned from FWAA's report of responses to its questionnaire. When asked what they were doing to rally community support for public welfare, one-third of the respondents expressed interest in helping but were inactive; another one-third were indifferent. Perhaps they felt all the more upset by the fact that the problem was again largely of their own making. If earlier they had impeded the development of an adequate public sector of social welfare, now they must share responsibility for the existence of a permanent, powerful establishment they could not control. Furthermore, the existence of such an establishment required change at the core of the voluntary agency.

Professional Identity

Critical Thinking Question: The Great Depression represented a critical juncture in the professional identity of social workers. How did the Rank-and-File movement and family agencies represent two different views of the role of the profession?

Despite the frequent reference in the social work literature to a "right to assistance," this view was inconsistent with the philosophy that guided the development of voluntary social welfare. The latter had begun with an assumption of a character flaw for which—as with man's original fall—man was himself responsible. This view of human nature as essentially evil and of society as the blameless victim of human frailty led to religious, eventually voluntary, social welfare efforts to change the human being. The Protestant ethic was particularly concerned with work, thrift, and financial independence. When voluntary social welfare secularized this ethic, the family agency tied social work practice and relief giving into a single package. Public welfare was to be avoided at all costs.

The Depression of the 1930s revolutionized conventional thinking about social need. The discovery that people could be unemployed and in need through no fault of their own led, first, to an admission of fault in the economic and social system and, second, to a conception of the individual-at-risk in the system. Society, therefore, had an obligation to help. In such a circumstance, financial need was truly secularized—one might say, publicized—and the need for public welfare was inherent. Furthermore, the acceptance of social responsibility for financial need led quite naturally to the depersonalization of relief giving. Relief recipients needed money, not service. They did not require the skill of professional service and could best be helped by government aid administered objectively. Federal and state aid represented a decision to separate financial assistance and service provision.

Voluntary social agencies renewed efforts to define a unique professional service function. The widespread dissemination of Freudian theory demonstrating the significance of parent–child relationships brought home the psychological underpinnings of family survival. Having moved away from providing relief for families, voluntary family agencies moved to the further development of highly skilled "casework treatment to assist individuals in removing their own handicaps." The Freudian symbiotic tie of parent to child suggested family, rather than individual, treatment, and attention was focused on the relationship between voluntary family and children's agencies and on the possibility of their merging.

In November 1937, the FWAA distributed an outline of points discussed in meetings of its Committee on Relationship between Family and Children's Work in a meeting of that committee with a similar committee of the CWL of America.

> In considering the relationship between family and children's case work . . . it is evident that they have the same roots in social case work, as far as the basic knowledge and equipment of the case worker are concerned. . . .
>
> Any family case work agency is also a children's case work agency, in the sense that it has the same obligation for skilled treatment of the problems of children in families as it does for meeting the needs of adults. Any children's case work agency, dealing with children in their own homes or in foster homes, is or should be a family case work agency, in so far as it attempts to treat children's needs in relation to the family setting, or to deal with those difficulties in family relationships that affect the child.[99]

Relationships between voluntary family and children's agencies were to be the subject of controversy throughout the 1940s and 1950s, but already in 1937, mergers between family and children's agencies were considered because of similarities in method and overlaps in their clients. As casework with individuals eclipsed social work with groups and communities, differences between family and children's agencies seemed less important. In the *Social Work Year Book, 1951*, Frank J. Hertel reported:

> Figures available to FSAA [Family Service Association of America] over the past eight years show that the number of its member agencies engaging in this multiple service [family and child welfare services] increased from 46 in 1942 to 82 (33 percent of the member agencies) by the close of 1949. Of these, 42 had expanded their services to include child placement, whereas 40 represented the merging of two or more agencies . . . to provide the services formerly considered special to each.[100]

By 1960, the number of merged family and children's agencies holding common membership in FSAA and CWL had risen to sixty. In 1974, FSAA and CWL were themselves considering a merger, which they finally rejected.

At the same time that there was a strong trend toward the merging of concerns of family and child welfare agencies, specialized services for each appeared in response to the strains the Depression put on family life. Marital counseling emerged as a particular concern and the first marriage clinic opened in 1930. A variety of family support programs—visiting housekeepers and parent education programs to name just two—developed and the number of child guidance clinics increased.

CONCLUSION

The Depression of the 1930s left an indelible mark on the United States and on a generation of Americans. Despite the effort expended in the attempt to wrest the country out of the crisis, neither Franklin Roosevelt nor the New Deal programs achieved success until World War II boosted the economy to full employment. Nevertheless, the president had been able to invest the people with psychological endurance and, in the face of severe challenges from the political right and the left, to preserve the basic economic system of private property.

The essential conservatism of the New Deal, however, does not negate the fact that the federal government had emerged as the prime promoter of social welfare. Voluntary welfare as well as state and local governments had been tried and found wanting. The extent to which a new realism had taken hold was exhibited in the Supreme Court opinion delivered by Justice Benjamin Cardozo upholding the constitutionality of the Social Security Act:

> The concept of the general welfare is not static. Needs that were narrow or parochial a century ago may be interwoven in our day with the welfare of the nation. What is critical or urgent changes with the times.[101]

The United States emerged from the Depression aware of the hazards of the industrial society and having accomplished a major structural change in its income transfer system. The provision of social insurance—and, for the moment, public assistance too—represented aggressive federal responsibility for guaranteeing minimum financial security as a matter of right.

Unquestionably, the Social Security Act was the major legislative accomplishment of the New Deal. The act declared the birth of the welfare state and established a direction for its growth and development. As a start, the necessity for opening up jobs for young adults (which required that the elderly be retired from the labor market) and the political clout of older people meant that the welfare measures of the act were geared primarily to persons over age sixty-five. The risks suffered by children and young adults were given short shrift, a situation not really repaired by the minimum wage and hour or child labor provisions of the Fair Labor Standards Act of 1938. For the most part, the Fair Labor Standards Act did little more than give federal sanction to provisions that already existed in many of the states. Nevertheless, precedent for societal protection for all had been established and would serve as a base for substantial expansion of old programs and the creation of new ones.

For social work, the return to prosperity meant a return to a period of further introspection and professionalization. In the early years of the New Deal, many social workers had been active social reformers and community organizers. In 1934, the general sessions and section meetings of the National Conference of Social Work strongly emphasized unemployment, health, and justice as social welfare policy concerns and social legislation as the route to social change. By 1936, the meetings emphasized social work methodology, social agency administration, and social work education.[102]

Succeed with PEARSON **mysocialworklab**

Log onto **www.mysocialworklab.com** and answer the following questions. (*If you did not receive an access code to* **MySocialWorkLab** *with this text and wish to purchase access online, please visit* www.mysocialworklab.com .)

1. **Watch the Core Competency video "The Ecological Model Using the Friere Method."** How could this model have been used to help citizens understand the New Deal in the 1930s?

2. **Read the MySocialWorkLibrary case study "Community Practice: Golem, Albania."** Compare and contrast the efforts made by the social worker in this case to those made by Harry Hopkins in the FDR administration.

PRACTICE TEST The following questions will test your knowledge of the content found within this chapter. For additional assessment, including licensing-exam-type questions on applying chapter content to practice, visit **MySocialWorkLab**.

1. The event in which thousands of veterans pushed for promised monies to balance wartime earnings was known as
   a. Civil Rights March.
   b. Vietnam Veterans March.
   c. Bonus Army March.
   d. Hoover Town March.

2. Hoover's response to the Depression was
   a. a belief that government's role was to encourage voluntary action.
   b. a major campaign of the federal government developing public works.
   c. to provide emergency financing for financial institutions.
   d. to further regulate banking and commerce.

3. The Secretary of Labor in the FDR administration who was also a professional social worker was
   a. Jane Addams.
   b. Dorothea Dix.
   c. Harry Hopkins.
   d. Frances Perkins.

4. Which of the following were strategies in the New Deal?
   a. a basic belief in the importance of states' rights.
   b. the traditional view of the importance of a balanced budget.
   c. government programs will have no effect in increasing purchasing power.
   d. families must be the primary focus for economic reform.

5. How did the New Deal assist farmers in surviving the Depression?

ASSESS YOUR COMPETENCE Use the following scale to rate your current level of achievement on the following concepts or skills associated with each competency presented in the chapter:

1	2	3
I can accurately describe the concept or skill	I can consistently identify the concept or skill when observing and analyzing practice activities	I can competently implement the concept or skill in my own practice

_______ Discuss the impact that the Depression had on families.

_______ Compare and contrast the Depression to the current recession.

_______ Apply economic theory to understanding current economic policies.

_______ Differentiate between states' rights and the role of the federal government in social welfare policy.

The Depression and the New Deal

The documents used to demonstrate social welfare issues during the Depression of the 1930s are excerpts from the *Monthly Reports of the Federal Emergency Relief Administration* (1933) and from the *Social Security Act* (1935) as originally passed by Congress. The two documents illustrate continuity and change in social policy.

The monthly reports of the FERA set forth the famous *Rules and Regulations*, which not only governed the administration of developing public welfare programs but also revolutionized the relationship between the public and private sectors of social welfare. The most famous of these regulations, Regulation No. 1, ordered that relief funds be administered by public agencies. This new principle—"public funds in public hands"—removed voluntary agencies from the business of relief. Taking into account the enormous significance of cash relief for social welfare during the Depression, the dominance of the public sector was immediately established.

Nevertheless, the influence of voluntary agency experience and tradition can be detected. Regulation No. 3 requires that need be determined on the basis of individual budgeting and that a variety of individual and family resources be taken into account in establishing the final amount of the relief grant. The requirements for individualized budgeting and resource determination led directly to the investigations of applications and the use of trained investigators at least in supervisory positions.

The Social Security Act was the most important piece of social welfare legislation of the Depression era. It substituted a group of permanent programs for the temporary programs of FERA and, in so doing, acknowledged long-term federal responsibility for social welfare. This new thrust did not, however, make a total break with the past. In fact, a major characteristic of the act is its dual nature, its putting together of old and new orientations.

On the one hand, the Social Security Act establishes a number of social insurance programs to meet the hazards of old age and unemployment. The insurance programs are meant to cover those with former or current workforce connections. They are financed through payroll-tax deductions. Simultaneously, the act provides for a group of categorical nonwork-related programs of assistance for the elderly, the blind, and dependent children. These programs are funded through a grant-in-aid formula providing a joint federal–state funding device. They are to be administered by states and provide an income safety net for this population.

The social insurance and public assistance programs differ markedly in their orientation to people in need. The former, perhaps because of the direct taxation involved, makes carefully spelled-out benefits available to claimants as a matter of right. The public assistance categories, because they are based on a "demonstrated need" approach, continue the practice of investigation and individualized budgeting.

The delineation of categories of public assistance recipients indicates the extent to which need per se as a determinant for helping was compromised. Nevertheless, the new public assistance programs were also a break with the past. The Social Security Act requires that each participating state develop a state plan for public assistance and that the plan meet certain requirements. In this regard, the act is standard setting. In addition, the act requires that grants be made in cash and to people living in their own homes, marking the end of institutional almshouse care for the poor. Finally, the act provides for a fair hearing for those applicants who believe they have been unfairly treated. The changes are such that social welfare workers began to talk of a "right to assistance."

MONTHLY REPORT

OF

THE FEDERAL EMERGENCY RELIEF ADMINISTRATION

LETTER OF TRANSMITTAL

JULY 1, 1933

Sir: Pursuant to subsection (d) of section 3 of the Federal Emergency Relief Act of 1933, the Federal Emergency Relief Administration has the honor to submit this report of its activities from May 22, 1933, to June 30, 1933, inclusive. . . .

RULES AND REGULATIONS

Rules and Regulations Nos. 1, 2, and 3 were promulgated by the Federal Emergency Relief Administrator, and were printed and distributed to the governors and State Emergency Relief Administrators. They read as follows:

No. 1

(a) Grants of Federal emergency relief funds are to be administered by public agencies after August 1, 1933.

Just as all State commissions responsible for the distribution of Federal and State funds to local communities are public bodies, so in turn should those local units be public agencies responsible for the expenditure of public funds in the same manner as any other municipal or county department.

This policy obviously must be interpreted on a realistic basis in various parts of the United States. Hundreds of private agencies scattered throughout the land have freely and generously offered their services in the administration of public funds. It would be a serious handicap to relief work if the abilities and interests of these individuals were lost. But these individuals should be made public officials, working under the control of public authority. Thousands of these workers are serving and will continue to serve without pay, but if paid, they should be compensated in the same manner as any other public servant.

It is not the intention of this regulation to instruct the several States to make hasty changes in agreements which the State administration may have made with the private agencies. Adjustment, however, to this policy is to be made no later than August 1, 1933.

This ruling prohibits the turning over of Federal emergency-relief funds to a private agency. The unemployed must apply to a public agency for relief, and this relief must be furnished direct to the applicant by a public agent.

(b) Grants made to the States from Federal funds under the Federal Emergency Relief Act of 1933 may be used for the payment of medical attendance and medical supplies for those families that are receiving relief.

(c) These funds may also be used to pay the cost of shelter for the needy unemployed.

(d) These funds may not be used for the payment of hospital bills or for the boarding out of children, either in institutions or in private homes, or for providing general institutional care. These necessary services to the destitute should be made available through State or local funds.

(e) The personnel employed on work relief projects by the States or their subdivisions are not Federal employees and must not be considered as such; therefore, premiums for accident insurance in connection with work relief programs may not be paid from Federal funds, but should be paid out of State or local moneys.

No. 2

Grants of Federal relief funds cannot be made on the basis of expenditures for rental of buildings used for relief operation; salaries of regularly employed public employees other than those employed full time in connection with emergency unemployment relief and under the supervision of the unemployment relief authority; salaries of relief workers not working directly under the supervision of the unemployment relief authority; and the purchase of automobiles and other equipment used in connection with relief administration.

No. 3

SUPPLEMENT TO RULES AND REGULATIONS NO. 1

Rule No. 1 stated: "Grants of Federal emergency relief funds are to be administered by public agencies after August 1, 1933." The rule further stated, "This ruling prohibits the turning over of Federal Emergency Relief funds to a private agency. The unemployed must apply to a public agency for relief and this relief must be furnished directly to the applicant by a public agent."

Three points need to be clarified:

(a) Public agency.

(b) Public agent or public official.

(c) Use of private agency personnel.

(a) Public agency.—A public welfare department, supported by tax funds and controlled by local government, if approved by the State emergency relief administration to administer unemployment relief, is a "public agency." Where a public welfare department does not exist and a local unemployment relief administration is responsible for unemployment relief this local unemployment relief administration, in order to be recognized as a "public agency" in the meaning of that term as used in Rules and Regulations No. 1, must have the following factors:

(1) It must have the full sanction and recognition of the State emergency relief administration.

(2) It must be vested with full authority and control in the expenditure of State and Federal public funds appropriated for local relief purposes.

(3) It must conform to the rulings of the State emergency relief administration.

(4) It must keep such records and forms as are required by the State emergency relief administration.

Note.—This interpretation recognizes as a "public agency," an agency created and sustained by Executive action in the absence of creative local legislation.

(b) Public official or public agent.—"Public official" or "public agent" in the meaning of the term as used in Rules and Regulations No. 1, includes every person who is engaged in carrying out the purposes of the public agency, and so must be:

(1) A member of the official staff of the public agency responsible to the chief executive employed by the public agency to administer the entire organization

of unemployment relief. This relationship must be made official by definite appointment and acceptance of such appointment.

(2) The compensation of the "public official" or "public agent" may or may not be paid from public funds. Such official may be loaned by a private agency, but when so loaned must become a member of the official staff of the public agency.

(c) Use of personnel loaned by private agency.—The public agency may make use of personnel of private agencies provided—

(1) Where such personnel is used for the giving of unemployment relief it becomes for the time being an integral part of the public agency. The public agency must assume full responsibility over personnel loaned by the private agency.

(2) That visible evidence of the integration into the public agency is provided as follows:

a. The name of the public agency clearly set out on the office door so that clients may know that they are applying to a public agency for relief.

b. All order forms must be those of the public agency; receipts must be made out to the public agency; identification cards of relief workers must be as staff members of the public agency and relief workers at all times in handling unemployment relief clients must report themselves as public agents or officials.

c. All bills for direct relief, wages for work relief, service or administration costs must be paid directly by the public agency; e.g., when grocery orders are issued by the relief worker the bills must be paid by the public agency directly to the grocer and not through a private agency.

d. It is expected that on other matters than the determination of relief there will be cooperative relationships established between public agencies and private agencies, but the public agency shall not pay for supplemental services so rendered by private agencies.

ADEQUACY OF RELIEF

(Either work relief or direct relief)

Relief shall be given as provided in this act to all needy unemployed persons and/or their dependents. Those whose employment or available resources are inadequate to provide the necessities of life for themselves and/or their dependents are included.

This imposes an obligation on the State emergency relief administration and on all the political subdivisions of the States administering relief, insofar as lies in their power, to see to it that all such needy unemployed persons and/or their dependents shall receive sufficient relief to prevent physical suffering and to maintain minimum living standards.

It also imposes an obligation on the part of the State emergency relief administration and the local relief administration to see that no relief is given to persons unless they are actually in need, and that such relief as is allowed is adjusted to the actual needs of each individual or family.

At the same time the obligation exists to develop maximum efficiency and economy in the furnishing of relief, with a minimum of delay in providing relief to those in distress.

The amount of relief to be given must be based on the following:

(1) An estimate of the weekly needs of the individual or family including an allowance for food sufficient to maintain physical well-being, for shelter,

the provision of fuel for cooking and for warmth when necessary, medical care and other necessities. Taxes may be allowed in lieu of allowances for shelter, and not to exceed the normal rent allowance providing such tax allowance is necessary in order to maintain the shelter or home of the relief recipient.

(2) An estimate of the weekly income of the family, including wages or other cash income, produce of farm or garden, and all other resources.

(3) The relief granted should be sufficient to provide the estimated weekly needs to the extent that the family is unable to do so from its own resources.

Any or all of the following types of relief may be allowed under direct relief or under work relief:

(1) Food, and/or food orders or allowance, determined by the number, ages, and needs of the individual members of the family in general accordance with standard food schedules.

(2) Orders or allowances for the provision of shelter, or its equivalent, where necessary.

(3) Orders or allowances for light, gas, fuel, and water for current needs.

(4) Orders or allowances for necessary household supplies.

(5) Clothing or orders or allowances for clothing sufficient for emergency needs.

(6) Orders or allowances for medicine, medical supplies, and/or medical attendance to be furnished in the home.

See further interpretation under *"Direct relief."*

INVESTIGATION AND SERVICE

(Work relief and direct relief)

To carry out the purposes of the Federal Emergency Relief Act of 1933 the investigation of all applications for direct and/or work relief is required. The following rules are hereby established:

(1) Each local relief administration should have at least one trained and experienced investigator on its staff; if additional investigators are to be employed to meet this emergency, the first one employed should have had training and experience. In the larger public welfare districts, where there are a number of investigators, there should be not less than 1 supervisor, trained and experienced in the essential elements of family case work and relief administration, to supervise the work of not more than 20 investigating staff workers.

(2) Registration records of all local applications for relief should be kept at a central office. Where no such central registration index now exists, one should be established by the local relief administration. This is absolutely necessary if duplication is to be avoided where there is more than one agency, either public or private, administering relief.

(3) The minimum investigation shall include a prompt visit to the home; inquiry as to real property, bank accounts, and other financial resources of the family; an interview with at least one recent employer; and determination of the ability and agreement of family, relatives, friends, and churches and other organizations to assist; also the liability under public welfare laws of the several States, of members of a family, or relatives, to assume such support in order to prevent such member becoming a public charge.

(4) Investigation shall be made, not only of persons applying directly to the office but also of those reported to it. In this emergency, it is the duty of those responsible for the administration of unemployment relief to seek out persons

in need, and to secure the cooperation of clergymen, school teachers, nurses, and organizations that might assist.

(5) There must be contact with each family through visits at least once a month, or oftener if necessary. The local field worker should be in sufficiently close touch with the family situation to avoid the necessity of applicants reapplying to the office for each individual order.

(6) Investigators should not be overloaded with cases. While no exact standard is being set as to the number of cases per worker, State emergency relief administrators should see to it that a sufficient number of workers are utilized in each local relief district to insure reasonable investigation procedure.

(7) Relief should be given only to persons in need of relief, and on the basis of budgetary deficiency established after careful investigation.

(8) Duplication of relief must be avoided, and every precaution should be taken to prevent overlapping of relief agencies, both public and private.

(9) Frequent and careful reinvestigation should be undertaken at regular intervals in order to establish the continued need of those who are receiving relief in order to determine whether or not some member of the family may have obtained part or full-time work, which would indicate the necessity for cutting down or cutting off on relief. Where adequate staff for investigation is provided, under able direction and supervision, these reinvestigations may be carried out automatically and the relief rolls kept clear of those who do not qualify.

DIRECT RELIEF

Such relief shall be in the form of food, shelter, clothing, light, fuel, necessary household supplies, medicine, medical supplies, and medical attendance, or the cash equivalent of these to the person in his own home.

Direct relief does not include relief—where provision is already made under existing laws—for widows or their dependents, and/or aged persons. There is further disallowed the payment of hospital bills or institutional care, and the costs of the boarding out of children.

Any or all of the following types of relief may be granted:

(1) Food, in the form of food orders, determined by the number, ages, and needs of the individual members of the family in general accordance with standard food schedules.

(2) Orders for the payment of current rent, or its equivalent, where necessary.

(3) Orders for light, gas, fuel, and water for current needs.

(4) Necessary household supplies.

(5) Clothing or orders for clothing sufficient for emergency needs.

(6) Orders for medicine, medical supplies, and/or medical attendance to be furnished in the home.

A broad interpretation of direct relief may be followed by the State relief administration where such is called for in meeting the immediate needs of individuals or families, or in aiding such needy persons in providing the necessities of life for themselves and/or their dependents.

Feed for livestock cannot be allowed as a relief expenditure except feed for domestic livestock may be allowed as a relief expenditure where such allowance makes it possible for the distressed family to produce additional food for the immediate family need.

Seed for gardens under the same reasoning may likewise be allowed as a relief measure.

Tax or mortgage interest payments on real property (home and land) may be allowed in lieu of rent as a relief measure where such allowance is no greater than the normal minimum relief rent allowance and when such payment of tax or mortgage interest is vitally necessary in preventing the loss of the home and the eviction of the owner.

A liberal interpretation of direct relief as above indicated must be controlled by the rule of reason and public policy. Under no circumstances shall an allowance be made which makes provision for other than the emergency needs of the immediate family. State relief administrations are not authorized to make allowances for feed or seed to such an extent that provision is made possible for more than the individual family requirements. Likewise, tax or mortgage interest payments in lieu of rent shall be allowed only on properties occupied and held title to by relief recipients. In no event shall a relief grant be made which directly or indirectly makes possible an increased capital investment in private properties.

WORK RELIEF

(Work relief wages and projects)

Work relief wages in cash or in kind are to be interpreted as follows:

(1) All work relief wages shall be based upon the relief need of the individual and/or his dependents.[1]

(2) The rate of wages should be a fair rate of pay for the work performed. Total compensation should meet the budgetary requirement of the relief recipient.

(3) Payment shall be by check, in cash, or in kind.

(4) Allowance should be on the basis of days' wages, or the equivalent, for the hours worked.

(5) Work relief should be allowed only to those who are employable.

(6) There shall be no discrimination because of race, religion, color, noncitizenship, political affiliation, or because of membership in any special or selected group.

(7) Where skilled personnel is required, skilled wages for skilled work must be paid. Such personnel taken from the work relief lists should be staggered. Where such skilled personnel is required full time, it should be provided otherwise than on a work relief basis.

(8) Work relief projects must be projects undertaken on Federal, State, or local public properties. Work projects for private institutions or agencies, nonprofit or otherwise, are therefore prohibited except as such projects, undertaken by governmental units, may benefit the public health or welfare as, for example, the prosecution of a drainage project which may benefit private interests but is withal of definite benefit to the public health of the community.

It therefore follows that work relief may not be used in the improvement of hospitals, libraries, churches, parks, cemeteries, etc., which are privately owned or incorporated, except that if State or local public moneys are regularly contributed to the support of such institutions, and such public support creates a quasi-public institution which may receive the benefit of work relief.

(9) Work relief projects under this act must be for work undertaken by a State or local relief administration independent of work under a contract or for

---

[1]See further interpretation under "Direct relief" and "Adequacy." Allowances on work relief may be made to cover food, shelter, clothing, light, fuel, necessary household supplies, medicine, supplies, and medical attendance.

which an annual appropriation has been made. It must be, in general, apart from normal governmental enterprises and not such as would have been carried out in due course regardless of an emergency.

The construction, as a work relief project, of public buildings, such as schools, firehouses, garages, etc., would in general not be acceptable as a proper work relief project, such construction falling within the usual contract work which would provide labor for those unemployed at large.

(10) Persons employed on work relief projects are not Federal employees and the premiums for their compensation or accident insurance may not be paid from Federal funds. If such insurance is provided, it therefore must be carried by State or local moneys.

Persons employed on work-relief projects by the States and their subdivisions ought to be covered by compensation or accident insurance.

(11) All local work relief projects must be submitted for approval to the State emergency relief administration.

* * *

THE SOCIAL SECURITY ACT

Approved, August 14, 1935

[PUBLIC—NO. 271—74TH CONGRESS]

[II. R. 7260]

AN ACT

To provide for the general welfare by establishing a system of Federal old-age benefits, and by enabling the several States to make more adequate provision for aged persons, blind persons, dependent and crippled children, maternal and child welfare, public health, and the administration of their unemployment compensation laws; to establish a Social Security Board; to raise revenue; and for other purposes.

Be it enacted by the Senate and House of Representatives of the United States of America in Congress assembled,

TITLE I—GRANTS TO STATES FOR OLD-AGE ASSISTANCE

APPROPRIATION

SECTION 1. For the purpose of enabling each State to furnish financial assistance, as far as practicable under the conditions in such State, to aged needy individuals, there is hereby authorized to be appropriated for the fiscal year ending June 30, 1936, the sum of $49,750,000, and there is hereby authorized to be appropriated for each fiscal year thereafter a sum sufficient to carry out the purposes of this title. The sums made available under this section shall be used for making payments to States which have submitted, and had approved by the Social Security Board established by Title VII (hereinafter referred to as the "Board"), State plans for old-age assistance.

STATE OLD-AGE ASSISTANCE PLANS

SEC. 2 (a) A State plan for old-age assistance must (1) provide that it shall be in effect in all political subdivisions of the State, and, if administered by them, be mandatory upon them; (2) provide for financial participation by the State; (3) either provide for the establishment or designation of a single State agency to administer the plan, or provide for the establishment or designation of a single State agency to supervise the administration of the plan; (4) provide for granting to any individual, whose claim for old-age assistance is denied, an opportunity for a fair hearing before such State agency; (5) provide such methods of administration (other than those relating to selection, tenure of office, and compensation of personnel) as are found by the Board to be necessary for the efficient operation of the plan; (6) provide that the State agency will make such reports, in such form and containing such information, as the Board may from time to time find necessary to assure the correctness and verification of such reports; and (7) provide that, if the State or any of its political subdivisions collects from the estate of any recipient of old-age assistance any amount with respect to old-age assistance furnished him under the plan, one-half of the net amount so collected shall be promptly paid to the United States. Any payment so made shall be deposited in the Treasury to the credit of the appropriation for the purposes of this title.

(b) The Board shall approve any plan which fulfills the conditions specified in subsection (a), except that it shall not approve any plan which imposes, as a condition of eligibility for old-age assistance under the plan—

(1) An age requirement of more than sixty-five years, except that the plan may impose, effective until January 1, 1940, an age requirement of as much as seventy years; or

(2) Any residence requirement which excludes any resident of the State who has resided therein five years during the nine years immediately preceding the application for old-age assistance and has resided therein continuously for one year immediately preceding the application; or

(3) Any citizenship requirement which excludes any citizen of the United States.

PAYMENT TO STATES

Sec. 3. (a) From the sums appropriated therefore, the Secretary of the Treasury shall pay to each State which has an approved plan for old-age assistance, for each quarter, beginning with the quarter commencing July 1, 1935, (1) an amount, which shall be used exclusively as old-age assistance, equal to one-half of the total of the sums expended during such quarter as old-age assistance under the State plan with respect to each individual who at the time of such expenditure is sixty-five years of age or older and is not an inmate of a public institution, not counting so much of such expenditure with respect to any individual for any month as exceeds $30 and (2) 5 per centum of such amount, which shall be used for paying the costs of administering the State plan or for old-age assistance, or both, and for no other purpose: Provided, That the State plan, in order to be approved by the Board, need not provide for financial participation before July 1, 1937 by the State, in the case of any State which the Board, upon application by the State and after reasonable notice and opportunity for hearing to the State, finds is prevented by its constitution from providing such financial participation. . . .

DEFINITIONS

Sec. 6. When used in this title the term "old-age assistance" means money payments to aged individuals.

TITLE II—FEDERAL OLD-AGE BENEFITS

OLD-AGE RESERVE ACCOUNT

SECTION 201. (a) There is hereby created an account in the Treasury of the United States to be known as the "Old-Age Reserve Account" hereinafter in this title called the "Account." There is hereby authorized to be appropriated to the Account for each fiscal year, beginning with the fiscal year ending June 30, 1937, an amount sufficient as an annual premium to provide for the payments required under this title, such amount to be determined on a reserve basis in accordance with accepted actuarial principles, and based upon such tables of mortality as the Secretary of the Treasury shall from time to time adopt, and upon an interest rate of 3 per centum per annum compounded annually. The Secretary of the Treasury shall submit annually to the Bureau of the Budget an estimate of the appropriations to be made to the Account. . . .

OLD-AGE BENEFIT PAYMENTS

SEC. 202. (a) Every qualified individual (as defined in section 210) shall be entitled to receive, with respect to the period beginning on the date he attains the age of sixty-five, or on January 1, 1942, whichever is the later, and ending on the date of his death, an old-age benefit (payable as nearly as practicable in equal monthly installments) as follows:

(1) If the total wages (as defined in section 210) determined by the Board to have been paid to him, with respect to employment (as defined in section 210) after December 31, 1936, and before he attained the age of sixty-five, were not more than $3,000, the old-age benefit shall be at a monthly rate of one-half of 1 per centum of such total wages;

(2) If such total wages were more than $3,000, the old-age benefit shall be at a monthly rate equal to the sum of the following:

(A) One-half of 1 per centum of $3,000; plus

(B) One-twelfth of 1 per centum of the amount by which such total wages exceeded $3,000 and did not exceed $45,000; plus

(C) One-twenty-fourth of 1 per centum of the amount by which such total wages exceeded $45,000.

(b) In no case shall the monthly rate computed under subsection (a) exceed $85.

(c) If the Board finds at any time that more or less than the correct amount has theretofore been paid to any individual under this section, then, under regulations made by the Board, proper adjustments shall be made in connection with subsequent payments under this section to the same individual.

(d) Whenever the Board finds that any qualified individual has received wages with respect to regular employment after he attained the age of sixty-five, the old-age benefit payable to such individual shall be reduced, for each calendar month in any part of which such regular employment occurred, by an amount equal to one month's benefit. Such reduction shall be made, under regulations prescribed by the Board, by deductions from one or more payments of old-age benefit to such individual.

PAYMENTS UPON DEATH

SEC. 203. (a) If any individual dies before attaining the age of sixty-five, there shall be paid to his estate an amount equal to 3 1/2 per centum of the total wages determined by the Board to have been paid to him, with respect to employment after December 31, 1936.

(b) If the Board finds that the correct amount of the old-age benefit payable to a qualified individual during his life under section 202 was less than 3 1/2 per centum of the total wages by which such old-age benefit was measurable, then there shall be paid to his estate a sum equal to the amount, if any, by which such 3 1/2 per centum exceeds the amount (whether more or less than the correct amount) paid to him during his life as old-age benefit.

(c) If the Board finds that the total amount paid to a qualified individual under an old-age benefit during his life was less than the correct amount to which he was entitled under section 202, and that the correct amount of such old-age benefit was 3 1/2 per centum or more of the total wages by which such old-age benefit was measurable, then there shall be paid to his estate a sum equal to the amount, if any, by which the correct amount of the old-age benefit exceeds the amount which was so paid to him during his life.

PAYMENTS TO AGED INDIVIDUALS NOT QUALIFIED FOR BENEFITS

SEC. 204. (a) There shall be paid in a lump sum to any individual who, upon attaining the age of sixty-five, is not a qualified individual, an amount equal to 3 1/2 per centum of the total wages determined by the Board to have been paid to him, with respect to employment after December 31, 1936, and before he attained the age of sixty-five.

(b) After any individual becomes entitled to any payment under subsection (a), no other payment shall be made under this title in any manner measured by wages paid to him, except that any part of any payment under subsection (a) which is not paid to him before his death shall be paid to his estate. . . .

OVERPAYMENTS DURING LIFE

SEC. 206. If the Board finds that the total amount paid to a qualified individual under an old-age benefit during his life was more than the correct amount to which he was entitled under section 202, and was 3 1/2 per centum or more of the total wages by which such old-age benefit was measurable, then upon his death there shall be repaid to the United States by his estate the amount, if any, by which such total amount paid to him during his life exceeds whichever of the following is the greater: (1) Such 3 1/2 per centum, or (2) the correct amount to which he was entitled under section 202. . . .

DEFINITIONS

SEC. 210. When used in this title—

(a) The term "wages" means all remuneration for employment, including the cash value of all remuneration paid in any medium other than cash; except that such term shall not include that part of the remuneration which, after remuneration equal to $3,000 has been paid to an individual by an employer with respect to employment during any calendar year, is paid to such individual by such employer with respect to employment during such calendar year.

(b) The term "employment" means any service, of whatever nature, performed within the United States by an employee for his employer, except—

(1) Agricultural labor;

(2) Domestic service in a private home;

(3) Casual labor not in the course of the employer's trade or business;

(4) Service performed as an officer or member of the crew of a vessel documented under the laws of the United States or of any foreign country;

(5) Service performed in the employ of the United States Government or of an instrumentality of the United States;

(6) Service performed in the employ of a State, a political subdivision thereof, or an instrumentality of one or more States or political subdivisions;

(7) Services performed in the employ of a corporation, community chest, fund, or foundation, organized and operated exclusively for religious, charitable, scientific, literary, or educational purposes, or for the prevention of cruelty to children or animals, no part of the net earnings of which inures to the benefit of any private shareholder or individual.

(c) The term "qualified individual" means any individual with respect to whom it appears to the satisfaction of the Board that—

(1) He is at least sixty-five years of age; and

(2) The total amount of wages paid to him, with respect to employment after December 31, 1936, and before he attained the age of sixty-five, was not less than $2,000; and

(3) Wages were paid to him, with respect to employment on some five days after December 31, 1936, and before he attained the age of sixty-five, each day being in a different calendar year.

TITLE III—GRANTS TO STATES FOR UNEMPLOYMENT COMPENSATION ADMINISTRATION

APPROPRIATION

SECTION 301. For the purpose of assisting the States in the administration of their unemployment compensation laws, there is hereby authorized to be appropriated, for the fiscal year ending June 30, 1936, the sum of $4,000,000, and for each fiscal year thereafter the sum of $49,000,000, to be used as hereinafter provided.

PAYMENTS TO STATES

SEC. 302. (a) The Board shall from time to time certify to the Secretary of the Treasury for payment to each State which has an unemployment compensation law approved by the Board under Title IX, such amounts as the Board determines to be necessary for the proper administration of such law during the fiscal year in which such payment is to be made. The board's determination shall be based on (1) the population of the State; (2) an estimate of the number of persons covered by the State law and of the cost of proper administration of such law; and (3) such other factors as the Board finds relevant. The Board shall not certify for payment under this section in any fiscal year a total amount in excess of the amount appropriated therefor for such fiscal year.

(b) Out of the sums appropriated therefor, the Secretary of the Treasury shall, upon receiving a certification under subsection (a), pay, through the Division of Disbursement of the Treasury Department and prior to audit or settlement by the General Accounting Office, to the State agency charged with the administration of such law the amount so certified.

PROVISIONS OF STATE LAWS

SEC. 303. (a) The Board shall make no certification for payment to any State unless it finds that the law of such State, approved by the Board under Title IX, includes provisions for—

(1) Such methods of administration (other than those relating to selection, tenure of office, and compensation of personnel) as are found by the Board to be reasonably calculated to insure full payment of unemployment compensation when due; and

(2) Payment of unemployment compensation solely through public employment offices in the State or such other agencies as the Board may approve; and

(3) Opportunity for a fair hearing, before an impartial tribunal, for all individuals whose claims for unemployment compensation are denied; and

(4) The payment of all money received in the unemployment fund of such State, immediately upon such receipt, to the Secretary of the Treasury to the credit of the Unemployment Trust Fund established by section 904; and

(5) Expenditure of all money requisitioned by the State agency from the Unemployment Trust Fund, in the payment of unemployment compensation, exclusive of expenses of administration; and

(6) The making of such reports, in such form and containing such information, as the Board may from time to time require, and compliance with such provisions as the Board may from time to time find necessary to assure the correctness and verification of such reports; and

(7) Making available upon request to any agency of the United States charged with the administration of public works or assistance through public employment, the name, address, ordinary occupation and employment status of each recipient of unemployment compensation, and a statement of such recipient's rights to further compensation under such law.

(b) Whenever the Board, after reasonable notice and opportunity for hearing to the State agency charged with the administration of the State law, finds that in the administration of the law there is—

(1) a denial, in a substantial number of cases, of unemployment compensation to individuals entitled thereto under such law; or

(2) a failure to comply substantially with any provision specified in subsection (a); the Board shall notify such State agency that further payments will not be made to the State until the Board is satisfied that there is no longer any such denial or failure to comply. Until it is so satisfied, it shall make no further certification to the Secretary of the Treasury with respect to such State.

TITLE IV—GRANTS TO STATES FOR AID TO DEPENDENT CHILDREN

APPROPRIATION

SECTION 401. For the purpose of enabling each State to furnish financial assistance, as far as practicable under the conditions in such State, to needy dependent children, there is hereby authorized to be appropriated for the fiscal year ending June 30, 1936, the sum of $24,750,000, and there is hereby authorized to be appropriated for each fiscal year thereafter a sum sufficient to carry out the purposes of this title. The sums made available under this section shall be used for making payments to States which have submitted, and had approved by the Board, State plans for aid to dependent children.

STATE PLANS FOR AID TO DEPENDENT CHILDREN

SEC. 402. (a) A State plan for aid to dependent children must (1) provide that it shall be in effect in all political subdivisions of the State, and, if administered by them, be mandatory upon them; (2) provide for financial participation by the State; (3) either provide for the establishment or designation of a single State agency to administer the plan, or provide for the establishment or designation of a single State agency to supervise the administration of the plan; (4) provide for granting to any individual, whose claim with respect to aid to a dependent child is denied, an opportunity for a fair hearing before such State agency; (5) provide such methods of administration (other than those relating to selection, tenure of office, and compensation of personnel) as are found by the Board to be necessary for the efficient operation of the plan; and (6) provide that the State agency will make such reports, in such form and containing such information, as the Board may from time to time require, and comply with such provisions as the Board may from time to time find necessary to assure the correctness and verification of such reports.

(b) The Board shall approve any plan which fulfills the conditions specified in subsection (a), except that it shall not approve any plan which imposes as a condition of eligibility for aid to dependent children, a residence requirement which denies aid with respect to any child residing in the State (1) who has resided in the State for one year immediately preceding the application for such aid, or (2) who was born within the State within one year immediately preceding the application, if its mother has resided in the State for one year immediately preceding the birth.

PAYMENT TO STATES

SEC. 403. (a) From the sums appropriated therefor, the Secretary of the Treasury shall pay to each State which has an approved plan for aid to dependent children, for each quarter, beginning with the quarter commencing July 1, 1935, an amount, which shall be used exclusively for carrying out the State plan, equal to one-third of the total of the sums expended during such quarter under such plan, not counting so much of such expenditure with respect to any dependent child for any month as exceeds $18, or if there is more than one dependent child in the same home, as exceeds $18 for any month with respect to one such dependent child and $12 for such month with respect to each of the other dependent children. . . .

DEFINITIONS

SEC. 406. When used in this title—
(a) The term "dependent child" means a child under the age of sixteen who has been deprived of parental support or care by reason of the death, continued absence from the home, or physical or mental incapacity of a parent, and who is living with his father, mother, grandfather, grandmother, brother, sister, stepfather, stepmother, stepbrother, stepsister, uncle, or aunt, in a place of residence maintained by one or more of such relatives as his or their own home;
(b) The term "aid to dependent children" means money payments with respect to a dependent child or dependent children.

TITLE V—GRANTS TO STATES FOR MATERNAL AND CHILD WELFARE

PART 1—MATERNAL AND CHILD HEALTH SERVICES

APPROPRIATION

SECTION 501. For the purpose of enabling each State to extend and improve, as far as practicable under the conditions in such State, services for promoting the health of mothers and children, especially in rural areas and in areas suffering from severe economic distress, there is hereby authorized to be appropriated for each fiscal year, beginning with the fiscal year ending June 30, 1936, the sum of $3,800,000. The sums made available under this section shall be used for making payments to States which have submitted, and had approved by the Chief of the Children's Bureau, State plans for such services.

ALLOTMENTS TO STATES

SEC. 502. (a) Out of the sums appropriated pursuant to section 501 for each fiscal year the Secretary of Labor shall allot to each State $20,000, and such part of $1,800,000 as he finds that the number of live births in such State bore to the total number of live births in the United States, in the latest calendar year for which the Bureau of the Census has available statistics.

(b) Out of the sums appropriated pursuant to section 501 for each fiscal year the Secretary of Labor shall allot to the States $980,000 in addition to the allotments made under subsection (a), according to the financial need of each State for assistance in carrying out its State plan, as determined by him after taking into consideration the number of live births in such State.

(c) The amount of any allotment to a State under subsection (a) for any fiscal year remaining unpaid to such State at the end of such fiscal year shall be available for payment to such State under section 504 until the end of the second succeeding fiscal year. No payment to a State under section 504 shall be made out of its allotment for any fiscal year until its allotment for the preceding fiscal year has been exhausted or has ceased to be available.

APPROVAL OF STATE PLANS

SEC. 503. (a) A State plan for maternal and child-health services must (1) provide for financial participation by the State; (2) provide for the administration of the plan by the State health agency or the supervision of the administration of the plan by the State health agency; (3) provide such methods of administration (other than those relating to selection, tenure of office, and compensation of personnel) as are necessary for the efficient operation of the plan; (4) provide that the State health agency will make such reports, in such form and containing such information, as the Secretary of Labor may from time to time find necessary to assure the correctness and verification of such reports; (5) provide for the extension and improvement of local maternal and child-health services administered by local child-health units; (6) provide for cooperation with medical, nursing, and welfare groups and organization; and (7) provide for the development of demonstration services in needy areas and among groups in special need.

(b) The Chief of the Children's Bureau shall approve any plan which fulfills the conditions specified in subsection (a) and shall thereupon notify the Secretary of Labor and the State health agency of his approval. . . .

PART 2—SERVICES FOR CRIPPLED CHILDREN

APPROPRIATION

SEC. 511. For the purpose of enabling each State to extend and improve (especially in rural areas and in areas suffering from severe economic distress), as far as practicable under the conditions in such State, services for locating crippled children, and for providing medical, surgical, corrective, and other services and care, and facilities for diagnosis, hospitalization, and aftercare, for children who are crippled or who are suffering from conditions which lead to crippling, there is hereby authorized to be appropriated for each fiscal year, beginning with the fiscal year ending June 30, 1936, the sum of $2,850,000. The sums made available under this section shall be used for making payments to States which have submitted, and had approved by the Chief of the Children's Bureau, State plans for such services.

ALLOTMENTS TO STATES

SEC. 512. (a) Out of the sums appropriated pursuant to section 511 for each fiscal year the Secretary of Labor shall allot to each State $20,000, and the remainder to the States according to the need of each State as determined by him after taking into consideration the number of crippled children in such State in need of the services referred to in section 511 and the cost of furnishing such services to them.

(b) The amount of any allotment to a State under subsection (a) for any fiscal year remaining unpaid to such State at the end of such fiscal year shall be available for payment to such State under section 514 until the end of the second succeeding fiscal year. No payment to a State under section 514 shall be made out of its allotment for any fiscal year until its allotment for the preceding fiscal year has been exhausted or has ceased to be available.

APPROVAL OF STATE PLANS

SEC. 513. (a) A State plan for services for crippled children must (1) provide for financial participation by the State; (2) provide for the administration of the plan by a State agency or the supervision of the administration of the plan by a State agency; (3) provide such methods of administration (other than those relating to selection, tenure of office, and compensation of personnel) as are necessary for the efficient operation of the plan; (4) provide that the State agency will make such reports, in such form and containing such information, as the Secretary of Labor may from time to time require, and comply with such provisions as he may from time to time find necessary to assure the correctness and verification of such reports; (5) provide for carrying out the purposes specified in section 511; and (6) provide for cooperation with medical, health, nursing, and welfare groups and organizations and with any agency in such State charged with administering State laws providing for vocational rehabilitation of physically handicapped children.

(b) The Chief of the Children's Bureau shall approve any plan which fulfills the conditions specified in subsection (a) and shall thereupon notify the Secretary of Labor and the State health agency of his approval. . . .

PART 3—CHILD-WELFARE SERVICES

SEC. 521. (a) For the purpose of enabling the United States, through the Children's Bureau, to cooperate with State public-welfare agencies in establishing, extending, and strengthening, especially in predominantly rural areas, public-welfare services (hereinafter in this section referred to as "child-welfare services") for the protection and care of homeless, dependent, and neglected children, and children in danger of becoming delinquent, there is hereby authorized to be appropriated for each fiscal year, beginning with the fiscal year ending June 30, 1936, the sum of $1,500,000. Such amount shall be allotted by the Secretary of Labor for use by cooperating State public-welfare agencies on the basis of plans developed jointly by the State agency and the Children's Bureau, to each State, $10,000, and the remainder to each State on the basis of such plans, not to exceed such part of the remainder as the rural population of such State bears to the total rural population of the United States. The amount so allotted shall be expended for payment of part of the cost of district, county or other local child-welfare services in areas predominantly rural, and for developing State services for the encouragement and assistance of adequate methods of community child-welfare organization in areas predominantly rural and other areas of special need. The amount of any allotment to a State under this section for any fiscal year remaining unpaid to such State at the end of such fiscal year shall be available for payment to such State under this section until the end of the second succeeding fiscal year. No payment to a State under this section shall be made out of its allotment for any fiscal year until its allotment for the preceding fiscal year has been exhausted or has ceased to be available. . . .

Part 4—Vocational Rehabilitation

Sec. 531. (a) In order to enable the United States to cooperate with the States and Hawaii in extending and strengthening their programs of vocational rehabilitation of the physically disabled, and to continue to carry out the provisions and purposes of the Act entitled "An Act to provide for the promotion of vocational rehabilitation of persons disabled in industry or otherwise and their return to civil employment," approved June 2, 1920, as amended (U.S.C., title 29, ch. 4; U.S.C., Supp. VII, title 29, secs. 31, 32, 34, 35, 37, 39, and 40), there is hereby authorized to be appropriated for the fiscal years ending June 30, 1936, and June 30, 1937, the sum of $841,000 for each fiscal year in addition to the amount of the existing authorization, and for each fiscal year thereafter the sum of $1,938,000. Of the sums appropriated pursuant to such authorization for each fiscal year, $5,000 shall be apportioned to the Territory of Hawaii and the remainder shall be apportioned among the several States in the manner provided in such Act of June 2, 1920, unamended. . . .

Part 5—Administration

Sec. 541. (a) There is hereby authorized to be appropriated for the fiscal year ending June 30, 1936, the sum of $425,000, for all necessary expenses of the Children's Bureau in administering the provisions of this title, except section 531.

(b) The Children's Bureau shall make such studies and investigations as will promote the efficient administration of this title, except section 531.

(c) The Secretary of Labor shall include in his annual report to Congress a full account of the administration of this title, except section 531. . . .

TITLE X—GRANTS TO STATES FOR AID TO THE BLIND

APPROPRIATION

Section 1001. For the purpose of enabling each State to furnish financial assistance, as far as practicable under the conditions in such State, to needy individuals who are blind, there is hereby authorized to be appropriated for the fiscal year ending June 30, 1936, the sum of $3,000,000, and there is hereby authorized to be appropriated for each fiscal year thereafter a sum sufficient to carry out the purposes of this title. The sums made available under this section shall be used for making payments to States which have submitted, and had approved by the Social Security Board, State plans for aid to the blind.

STATE PLANS FOR AID TO THE BLIND

SEC. 1002. (a) A State plan for aid to the blind must (1) provide that it shall be in effect in all political subdivisions of the State, and if administered by them, be mandatory upon them; (2) provide for financial participation by the State; (3) either provide for the establishment or designation of a single State agency to administer the plan, or provide for the establishment or designation of a single State agency to supervise the administration of the plan; (4) provide for granting to any individual, whose claim for aid is denied, an opportunity for a fair hearing before such State agency; (5) provide such methods of administration (other than those relating to selection, tenure of office, and compensation of personnel) as are found by the Board to be necessary for the efficient operation of the plan; (6) provide that the State agency will make such reports, in such form and containing such information, as the Board may from time to time require, and comply with such provisions as the Board may from time to time find necessary to assure the correctness and verification of such reports; and (7) provide that no aid will be furnished any individual under the plan with respect to which he is receiving old-age assistance under the State plan approved under section 2 of this Act.

(b) The Board shall approve any plan which fulfills the conditions specified in subsection (a), except that it shall not approve any plan which imposes, as a condition of eligibility for aid to the blind under the plan—

(1) Any residence requirement which excludes any resident of the State who has resided therein five years during the nine years immediately preceding the application for aid and has resided therein continuously for one year immediately preceding the application; or

(2) Any citizenship requirement which excludes any citizen of the United States.

PAYMENT TO STATES

SEC. 1003. (a) From the sums appropriated therefor, the Secretary of the Treasury shall pay to each State which has an approved plan for aid to the blind, for each quarter, beginning with the quarter commencing July 1, 1935, (1) an amount, which shall be used exclusively as aid to the blind, equal to one-half of the total of the sums expended during such quarter as aid to the blind under the State plan with respect to each individual who is blind and is not an inmate of a public institution, not counting so much of such expenditure with respect to any individual for any month as exceeds $30, and (2) 5 per centum of such amount, which shall be used for paying the costs of administering the State plan or for aid to the blind, or both, and for no other purpose. . . .

SHORT TITLE

SEC. 1105. This Act may be cited as the "Social Security Act."
Approved, August 14, 1935.

NOTES

1. Maurice Leven, Harold G. Moulton, and Clark Warburton, *America's Capacity to Consume* (Washington, D.C.: The Brookings Institution, 1934).

2. Frederick Lewis Allen, *Only Yesterday* (New York: Bantam, 1959), p. 241.

3. U.S. Department of Commerce, Office of Business Economics, *The National Income and Product Accounts of the United States, 1929–1965—Statistical Tables* (Washington, D.C.: Government Printing Office, 1966).

4. U.S. Department of Commerce, Bureau of the Census, *Historical Statistics of the United States: Colonial Times to 1957* (Washington, D.C.: Government Printing Office, 1960), p. 73 (hereafter cited as *Historical Statistics*).

5. William H. Matthews, "Breaking the Poverty Circle," *Survey*, Vol. 52, April 15, 1924, pp. 96–98.

6. Lucille Eaves, "Studies of Breakdowns in Family Income," *The Family*, Vol. 10, December 1929, p. 228.

7. Ibid., p. 227.

8. Marion Elderton, ed., *Case Studies of Unemployment* (Philadelphia: University of Pennsylvania Press, 1931), p. xxiv.

9. E. Wright Bakke, *The Unemployed Man: A Social Study* (New York: E.P. Dutton and Company, 1934).

10. Ibid., pp. xxiii–xxiv.

11. Joan Hoff Wilson, *Herbert Hoover: Forgotten Progressive* (Boston: Little Brown, 1975).

12. U.S. 72nd Cong., 1st sess., Public Law No. 2, January 22, 1932.

13. 47 Stat. 1932, p. 709.

14. Elderton, op. cit., p. xlix.

15. U.S. Congress, House, *Platforms of the Two Great Political Parties, 1932* (Washington, D.C.: Government Printing Office, 1945), pp. 335, 340, 343.

16. Franklin D. Roosevelt, speeches at Sioux City, Iowa, September 1932, and Pittsburgh, Pennsylvania, October 1932. Quoted in William Leuchtenberg, *Franklin D. Roosevelt & the New Deal* (New York: Harper & Row, 1963), p. 11.

17. President Franklin D. Roosevelt, "Acceptance of the Nomination for the Presidency," Chicago, Illinois, July 2, 1932, in S. I. Rosenan, ed., *The Pubic Papers and Addresses of Franklin D. Roosevelt*, Vol. 2 (New York: Russell and Russel, 1969), pp. 647–659.

18. Anne O'Hare McCormick, "Vast Tides That Stir the Capital," *New York Times Magazine*, May 7, 1933. Also to be found in Frank Freidel, ed., *The New Deal and the American People* (Englewood Cliffs, N.J.: Prentice Hall, 1964), p. 5.

19. *Historical Statistics*, pp. 409, 473.

20. Phyllis J. Day, *A New History of Social Welfare* (Englewood Cliffs, N.J.: Prentice Hall, 1989), p. 300.

21. *Historical Statistics*, p. 141.

22. Ibid., p. 283.

23. U.S. Department of Agriculture, Economic Research Service, *The Farm Income Situation*, July 1958.

24. *Historical Statistics*, pp. 7, 47.

25. Ibid., p. 278.

26. Ibid.

27. Ibid.

28. U.S. Department of Commerce, Bureau of the Census, *Statistical Abstract of the United States* (Washington, D.C.: Government Printing Office, 1969), Table 892, p. 590.

29. *Historical Statistics*, p. 283.

30. Ibid., p. 286

31. Ibid., p. 278.

32. Ibid., pp. 73, 409; U.S. Department of Commerce, *National Income and Product Accounts*.

33. Arthur S. Link, *American Epoch: A History of the United States Since the 1890s* (New York: Knopf, 1935), p. 347.

34. Ibid., p. 395.

35. Frances Fox Piven and Richard A. Cloward, *Poor People's Movements: Why They Succeed, How They Fail* (New York: Random House, 1977), pp. 41–95.

36. Ibid., pp. 96–180; David Montgomery, *Workers' Control in America: Studies in the History of Work, Technology, and Labor Struggles* (Cambridge and New York: Cambridge University Press, 1980), pp. 153–180.

37. U.S. Congress, Senate, Committee on Education and Labor, 74th Cong., 1st sess., Hearings on Senate Resolution 266, and 75th Cong., 1st sess., Hearings on Senate Resolution 60.

38. Link, op. cit., pp. 431–432.

39. Dixon Wecter, *The Age of the Great Depression: 1929–1941*, Vol. 13 of Arthur M. Schlesinger and Dixon Ryan Fox, eds., *A History of American Life* (New York: Macmillan, 1948), pp. 119–120.

40. National Urban League, "The Negro in the Industrial Depression: Negroes Out of Work," *Nation*, April 22, 1931, pp. 441–442.

41. Bruce Minton and John Stuart, *Men Who Lead Labor* (New York: Modern Age, 1937), p. 167.

42. *Historical Statistics*, p. 71.

43. Quoted in William H. Chafe, *The American Woman* (New York: Oxford University Press, 1972), p. 107.

44. The National Economy Act, 1932, Sec. 213. For extensive documentation in regard to federal and state restrictions on the employment of married women, see ibid., p. 283.

45. *Historical Statistics*, p. 72.

46. U.S. Congress, House Committee Print No. 4, Medical Care of Veterans, 90th Cong., 1st sess., April 17, 1967, pp. 154–155. Printed for use of the Committee on Veterans' Affairs.

47. Joanna C. Colcord, "The Challenge of the Continuing Depression," *The Annals*, Vol. 176, November 1934, p. 17.

48. Gordon Hamilton, "Refocusing Family Casework," *Proceedings: NCSW*, 1931, p. 176.

49. Ibid., p. 178.

50. Wendell F. Johnson, "How Caseworking Agencies Have Met Unemployment," *Proceedings: NCSW*, 1931, pp. 189–200.

51. Ibid., p. 197.

52. Joanna C. Colcord, "Unemployment Relief, 1929–32," *The Family*, Vol. 13, December 1932, pp. 270–274.

53. U.S. Federal Emergency Relief Administration, Monthly Report, May 22–June 30, 1933, pp. 1–2.

54. U.S. Federal Emergency Relief Administration, *Final Statistical Report* (Washington, D.C.: Government Printing Office, 1942).

55. A. F. Kifer, "The Negro Under the New Deal: 1933–1941" (Ph.D. diss., University of Wisconsin, 1961).

56. Harry L. Hopkins, "The Developing National Program of Relief," *Proceedings: NCSW*, 1933, pp. 65–67, 71.

57. President Franklin D. Roosevelt, "Annual Message to Congress," January 4, 1935. *Public Papers and Addresses*

of *Franklin D. Roosevelt*, Vol. 4 (New York: Random House, 1938), pp. 15–25.

58. Ibid., pp. 43–46.

59. Ibid., pp. 15–25.

60. Ibid.

61. William Hodson, "Unemployment Relief," in *Social Work Year Book: 1937* (New York: Russell Sage Foundation, 1937), p. 522.

62. Helen Seymour, *When Clients Organize* (Chicago: American Public Welfare Association, 1937), pp. 16–17.

63. U.S. Federal Emergency Relief Administration, Monthly Report, May 22–June 30, 1933, *Rules and Regulations*, p. 7.

64. Ibid., p. 10.

65. Hopkins, op. cit., p. 68.

66. Ibid., p. 69.

67. *Report of the Committee on Economic Security* (Washington, D.C.: Government Printing Office, 1935), p. 3.

68. D. H. Fischer, *Growing Old in America* (New York: Oxford University Press, 1978).

69. *Report of the Committee on Economic Security*, p. 25.

70. Ibid., p. 44.

71. President Franklin D. Roosevelt, "Message of the President Recommending Legislation on Economic Security," pp. 43–46.

72. U.S. 74th Cong., 1st sess., Public Law No. 271.

73. Michael K. Brown, *Race, Money, and the American Welfare State* (New York: Cornell University Press, 1999).

74. James T. Patterson, *America's Struggle Against Poverty in the Twentieth Century* (Cambridge, Mass.: Harvard University Press, 2000).

75. *Report of the Committee on Economic Security*, p. 36.

76. U.S. Congress, Senate, Committee on Finance, *Statement of Miss Katherine F. Lenroot, Hearings on S. 1130, The Economic Security Act*, January 22 to February 20, 1935, revised, pp. 337–341.

77. U.S. Congress, Senate, Committee on Finance, *Statement of Mr. Jacob Kepecs, Hearings on H.R. 4120, The Economic Security Act*, January 1935, pp. 500–503.

78. Edwin Witte, *The Development of the Social Security Act, a Memorandum on the History of the Committee on Economic Security and Drafting and Legislative History of the Social Security Act* (Madison: University of Wisconsin Press, 1962), p. 164.

79. Mary S. Labaree, "Unmarried Parenthood under the Social Security Act," *Proceedings: NCSW*, June 1939, pp. 470–454. Reprinted in *Journal of Progressive Human Services*, Vol. 6, No. 2, November 2, 1995, pp. 73–76.

80. Ibid., p. 78.

81. Ira Katznelson, *When Affirmative Action Was White: An Untold Story of Racial Inequality in Twentieth-Century America* (New York: W. W. Norton, 2005).

82. Gail Radford, *Modern Housing for America: Policy Struggles in the New Deal Era* (Chicago: University of Chicago Press, 1996), pp. 7–28.

83. Ibid., pp. 111–145.

84. Katznelson, *When Affirmative Action Was White*.

85. Committee on Economic Security, Social Security in America, *The Factual Background of the Social Act as Summarized from Staff Reports for the Committee* (Washington, D.C.: Government Printing Office, 1937), p. 229.

86. S. P. Breckinridge, "The Activities of Women Outside the Home," in *Recent Social Trends in the United States: Report of the President's Research Committee on Social Trends*, Vol. 1 (New York: McGraw-Hill, 1933), pp. 711–717.

87. *Historical Statistics*, p. 23.

88. Ibid., p. 30.

89. Caroline Bird, *The Invisible Scar* (New York: David McKay, 1966), pp. 41–70.

90. American Association of Social Workers, "This Business of Relief," in *Proceedings of the Delegate Conference, Washington, D.C.*, February 14–16, 1936 (New York: AASW, 1936).

91. Aubrey Williams, "The Works Progress Administration," *AASW Proceedings*, 1936, pp. 128, 137.

92. Ewan Clague, "The Social Security Act as a Relief Measure," *AASW Proceedings*, 1936, pp. 78–82.

93. Stanley Wenocur and Michael Reisch, *From Charity to Enterprise: The Development of American Social Work in a Market Economy* (Urbana: University of Illinois Press, 1989), pp. 182–207.

94. Dorothy C. Kahn, "The Use of Cash, Orders for Goods, or Relief in Kind, in a Mass Program," *Proceedings: NCSW*, 1933, p. 273.

95. Harry L. Hopkins, *Spending to Save* (New York: W. W. Norton, 1936), p. 81.

96. *Report of the Committee on Economic Security*, p. 30.

97. Ibid., p. 239.

98. Family Welfare Association of America, The Crisis in Community Programs, March 1936. Multigraph.

99. Family Welfare Association of America, Committee on Relationship between Family and Children's Work, Preliminary Report, November 1937. Multigraph.

100. Frank J. Hertel, "Family Social Work," *Social Work Year Book, 1951* (New York: American Association of Social Workers, 1951), p. 187.

101. *Helvering v. Davis*, 301 U.S. 619 (1937).

102. National Conference on Social Welfare, *Proceedings, 1934*, and *Proceedings, 1936* (Chicago: University of Chicago Press, 1934 and 1936, respectively), tables of contents.

Library of Congress

Social Welfare and the Information Society: 1992–2011

Core Competencies in this Chapter (Check marks indicate which competencies are covered in depth)				
Professional Identity	✔ Ethical Practice	✔ Critical Thinking	✔ Diversity in Practice	Human Rights and Justice
Research-Based Practice	Human Behavior	✔ Policy Practice	Practice Contexts	Engage, Assess, Intervene, Evaluate

The 1990s and 2000s were a period of wild swings for the economic and social well-being of Americans. The nation endured two recessions, the second of which caused economic dislocation comparable only to that of the Great Depression, but it also included a period of rapid economic growth that lifted the incomes of low-wage workers for the first time in a generation. Politically, too, the breakdown of reliable coalitions led to erratic outcomes. One of the most conservative administrations in generations—that of George W. Bush—was sandwiched between those of two Democrats—Bill Clinton and Barack Obama—while Congress went from overwhelmingly Democratic in 1992 to strongly Republican in 1994 to strongly Democratic in 2006 and 2008. The 2010 elections resulted in a Republican House of Representatives and a Democratic Senate.

The erratic character of economic and political life had an impact on social welfare policy. The conservative rise of the early 1990s led to a fundamental restructuring of public assistance in 1996, ending families' entitlement to aid from states and the federal government. The Democrats return to power after 2006 allowed liberals to achieve a goal they had sought for two generations—a national health insurance plan that would go a long way toward reducing the number of uninsured in the population. Yet, the return of Republicans to power in Congress during the 2010 elections raised questions about whether the new health insurance law and other policy initiatives of the Obama administration would survive.

The 1990s began in the shadow of a recession. After falling to 5.3 percent of the labor force in 1989, the unemployment rate rose to 7.5 percent in 1992. Yet, the economic gloom of the early 1990s rapidly dissolved. By 1996, the unemployment rate had fallen to under 5.5 percent, the figure that many economists had claimed was the lowest unemployment could go without sparking inflation. In the years that followed, it fell even lower, reaching just over 4 percent by the end of the 1990s, even though inflation remained relatively low.

In spite of the remarkable economic growth of the 1990s, however, the business cycle still existed. Beginning in 2000, the American economy began to falter. Within three years, unemployment had increased to over 6.4 percent of the civilian labor force; the federal government—which had experienced its first years of budget surpluses in two generations—was forecasting record deficits; and the economy could do no better than anemic growth.

Yet, the recession of the early 2000s was simply a prelude to a much more significant recession between 2007 and 2009. Sparked by the near crash of the world financial system brought about by speculation in the American mortgage industry and international sovereign debt, that recession pushed unemployment over 10 percent for the first time since the 1980s. What is more, in contrast to the 1980s, unemployment remained at above 9 percent for more than two years, causing millions of families to face downward mobility as they lost their jobs and homes. Although unemployment insurance provided some protection for families, cutbacks in that program since the 1980s made it less effective than it had been formerly.

The American public's confidence was shaken by other events. In 2001, the worst terrorist attack on American soil destroyed the World Trade Center in New York and heavily damaged the Pentagon. In the next several years, America launched wars in Afghanistan and Iraq that the Bush administration viewed as battles in the "war against terrorism." At home, a set of unpopular tax cuts was enacted by Congress, raising the prospect that the old Reagan gambit—using high deficits as a way of cutting social programs—would again be used by a conservative president.

After two decades of sluggish economic growth, the robust economy of the 1990s puzzled policymakers and scholars. Although many reasons for the turnaround were suggested, the most compelling explanation linked economic growth to the transition of the United States (and much of the world) to an information-based economy. By the middle of the 1990s, technological discoveries in biotechnology, communications, and computers had pushed the world economy in a new direction. New products, new markets, and higher efficiency led to increases in productivity and the standard of living that had not been seen since the early 1970s.

Yet, social policy ideas failed to keep up with economic growth. The new economic and social realities of the 1990s undermined some of the old ways of addressing social problems. Social welfare programs between the 1930s and 1980s had sought to promote stability in the workplace and in family life. Although workers and families still found stability attractive, American business and domestic life failed to deliver. Increasingly, the American workplace was organized along *flexible* lines; there was more turnover, more part-time workers, and more temporary employees. At the same time, the decline of the traditional family—spurred by increases in divorce rates, single motherhood, and the increased visibility of gay and lesbian populations—made many assumptions of twentieth-century social welfare programs obsolete.

Powerful interests blocked many attempts to address the new realities at work and at home. Attempts to reform the health care system foundered because of opposition from the insurance and pharmaceutical industries. Although a Family and Medical Leave Act was passed and signed into law in 1993, more ambitious plans to provide support to families failed. In their everyday life, more and more Americans were living new realities, but social policy failed to keep pace with these changes.

Americans did unite, however, around one "reform," a restructuring of the federal public assistance program that ended the *entitlement* to aid, required recipients to seek work, and set a five-year time limit on the receipt of aid. Although the real impact of welfare reform on the lives of poor people remained controversial, it marked a major change in the way the federal government articulated its responsibility for addressing poverty and dependency.

THE ECONOMY: PRODUCTIVITY, GROWTH, AND EMPLOYMENT

Since 1970, the federal government had struggled to use monetary and fiscal policy to ensure sustained economic growth. During the 1970s, the economy swung between periods of rapid growth and recession. After the economic slowdown of 1981–1982, the economy grew, but unemployment remained stubbornly high.

During the 1990s, it appeared that the economy finally got it right. After the recession of 1991, the economy expanded for the remainder of the decade. Gross domestic product grew every quarter between 1992 and 2000, increasingly by 31 percent in real terms between 1993 and 2000. Productivity moved ahead as well. Although output per hour for all persons had increased only by 1 percent between 1992 and 1995, productivity accelerated during the last half of the decade. Output per hour in the business sector rose by 17 percent between 1993 and 2000.[1]

Much of the robust economic expansion could be linked to the technological revolutions of the 1980s and 1990s. After many years of investment, the application of computers and communications innovations began to make the economy more efficient and productive. In manufacturing, computers assumed a greater role in production and the management of inventories. In the burgeoning service sector, the expansion of the Internet created new industries and made existing services more efficient. Even as unemployment declined as low as 4 percent at the end of the decade, the threat that inflation would short-circuit the expansion seemed distant. Yet, at the same time, a *digital divide* opened, as low-income groups were unable to gain the computer literacy, Internet access, and computers that would allow them to link to these new resources.

But the new economy carried new costs. The success of the restructuring of the American economy was based on a newly "flexible" labor force. More workers found themselves working without fringe benefits. The risks of displacement were higher. More workers found themselves permanently working in "temporary" jobs. Thus, even as incomes went up and unemployment declined, workers faced a new world of insecurity that neither the private sector nor the government was prepared to address.

At the bottom of the economic ladder, an old phenomenon gained greater prominence. An "informal economy" composed of businesses and workers who operated in a twilight zone between the established economy and the world of crime became a more important part of all productive activities. The informal economy was particularly important for low-income workers. Many jobs in the personal and domestic service sector—house and office cleaners, childcare workers—operated in the informal economy, avoiding Social Security and other taxes.[2]

Welfare provided one motivation for workers to enter the informal economy. Because a large share of earnings was subtracted from one's benefits under Aid to Families with Dependent Children (AFDC) and other public assistance programs, welfare mothers often constructed survival strategies that included "off the books" work. At the same time, the growth of the informal economy provided a safety valve for welfare reform. Poor women on welfare often had more sources of income than official statistics suggested. As states moved to restrict welfare payments, poor women were likely to expand their efforts in other areas.[3]

Unemployment fell, but it remained unequally distributed. Among whites, unemployment fell from 4.8 to 3.6 percent between 1990 and 1999, but the unemployment rate of African Americans fell from 11.4 to 8.3 percent over the same period. Teenagers who were in the labor force in 1999 still had an unemployment rate of 15 percent.

In the previous two decades, government policymakers had used unemployment to keep inflation down. As a result, even as the economy improved, low-wage workers hardly benefited. Finally in the late 1990s, a sustained period of low unemployment improved the economic position of low-wage workers. Low-wage workers—whose incomes had hardly increased at all during the 1980s—enjoyed the first real increase in their wages as the century came to a close. Only in 1997 did the upper limit for the bottom 20 percent of the income distribution reach its 1990 level.[4]

The drive for greater economic flexibility was also responsible for the recession of 2007–2009. The immediate cause of the recession was the near collapse of large parts of the home mortgage market. Yet, the seeds of the crisis were sown during the Clinton administration when Clinton and the Republican leadership in Congress collaborated on the deregulation of the securities industry and the elimination of the barrier between commercial and investment banking that had been constructed during the New Deal. The "securitization" of home mortgages—their combination into pools and then slicing into tranches (the French word for *slice*)—allowed American mortgage securities to flow into the international financial system. When home prices stopped rising in 2006, it became clear that many of the mortgages and the securities that were backed by those mortgages were not as secure or valuable as investors had believed. A crisis of confidence and liquidity spread through the world economy in September 2008. After one major investment bank, Lehman Brothers, was allowed to fail, world credit markets ground to a halt. The Federal Reserve system and the federal government quickly changed course and sponsored a major bailout of other financial institutions that were judged to be "too big to fail."[5]

Although the bailout was judged a success in rescuing the financial sector, the longer-term effects of the crisis proved to be more difficult to address. The unemployment rate rose from 4.6 percent in 2006 to 10.1 percent in October 2009 and did not fall below 9.5 percent through the fall of 2010. The impact of the credit crisis and the decline in home prices led to an explosion in home foreclosures as millions of families could no longer afford their mortgages. The first wave of foreclosures in 2007 and 2008 affected many homeowners who bought homes that they never could have afforded, but by 2009 and 2010, the bulk of foreclosures were the result of families facing unemployment and declining economic fortunes.

Income inequality, which had begun to increase during the 1970s and 1980s, accelerated in the first decade of the twenty-first century. Although families with the lowest wages saw some improvement during the 1990s, these gains were lost during the recession of the early 2000s and the 2007–2009 recession left average families' income at the same level it had been thirty years earlier. Meanwhile, the large share of the expanding economic pie continued to go to the most affluent. In 1990, the income cutoff for the top 5 percent of the population ($118,163) was just over 7.5 times as large as the cutoff for the bottom 20 percent ($15,589). This ratio increased sharply during the decade, reaching a peak of 8.22 in 1997 before declining slightly. Only the top 5 percent showed substantial gains (see Figure 1). Whereas in 1947 the poorest 20 percent of households had received 5.1 percent of the income, by 1998 they had only 3.6 percent. In contrast, the top 20 percent in 1998 received 49.1 percent; almost half of that, 21.2 percent, went to the top 5 percent of households.[6]

During the first decade of the twenty-first century, the distribution of economic gains became even less equal. In 2001, the top 1 percent of tax units received 17 percent of national income. In six short years, this proportion increased to 23 percent. Cumulatively, since the late 1970s, the bottom fifth of the income distribution had seen their after-tax income rise by 11 percent, while those between the 80th and 98th percentile's average had increase by 55 percent. But even the rich did poorly compared to the very rich. The top 1 percent of householders' after-tax income increased by 256 percent between 1979 and 2006. Looked at another way, between 2002 and 2007, the income of the bottom 99 percent increased by 1.3 percent per year while that of the top 1 percent rose by 65 percent. Perhaps the most outrageous pattern, however, occurred *during* the recession. While most Americans' income fell by nearly 7 percent a year between 2007 and 2008, that of the top 1 percent grew by 47 percent.[7]

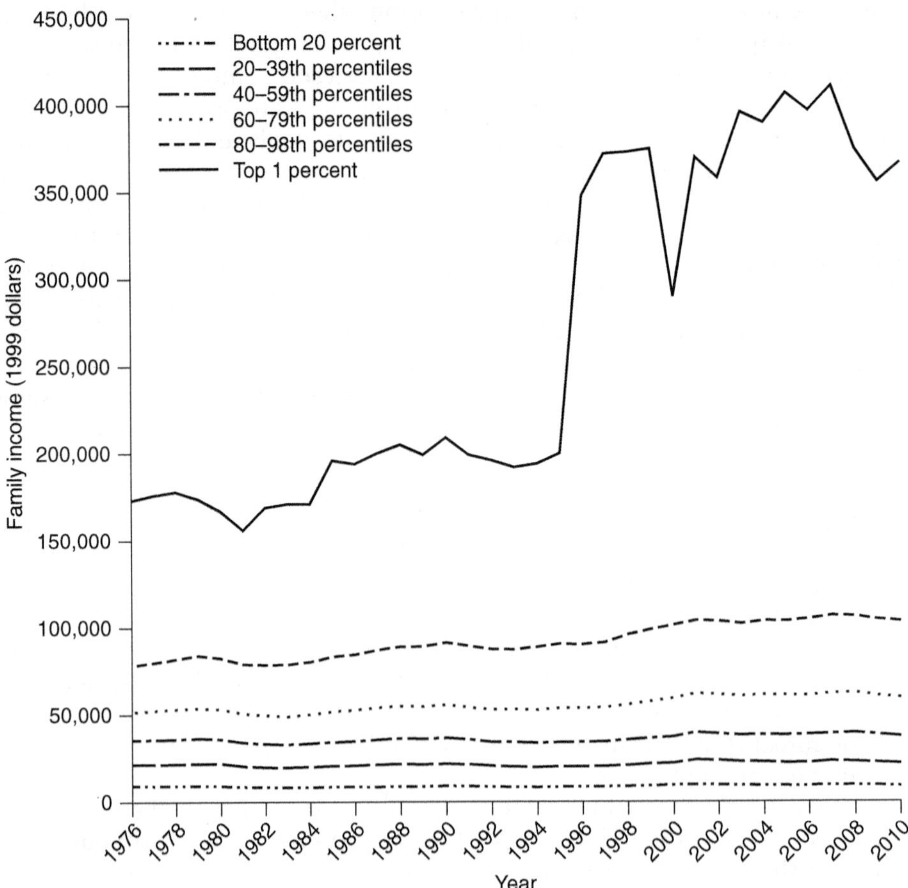

Figure 1

For most American families, incomes have not changed much over the past thirty-five years. However, for the wealthiest 1 percent of the population, it was a different story

Source: Author's calculation using Integrated Public Use Microdata Series, U.S. Census Bureau, *Current Population Survey, 1976–2010*

POVERTY

After rising from 12.8 to 15.1 percent between 1989 and 1993, poverty fell steadily, reaching 11.3 percent in 2000, its lowest level since 1979. However, the recession of 2007–2009 led poverty to rise rapidly, reaching 14.3 percent in 2009.

The good economic conditions of the 1990s reduced poverty, but it still remained higher than it had been twenty years earlier, then the recession of 2007–2009 pushed the largest number of Americans into poverty—43.6 million in 2009—since the official poverty rate was first calculated in the 1960s. Although the national income grew rapidly during the 1990s, the proportion of the population below the poverty line declined slowly. After rising from 12.8 to 15.1 percent between 1989 and 1993, poverty fell steadily, reaching 11.3 percent in 2000, its lowest level since 1979. However, the recession of 2007–2009 led poverty to rise rapidly, reaching 14.3 percent in 2009. Children, African Americans, Hispanics, and female-headed households continued to have significantly greater risks of poverty than the population as a whole.

African Americans enjoyed a rapid decline in poverty, between 1990 and 2001, falling from 32 to 23 percent; by 2009 it had risen to 26 percent. Although the white poverty rate in 1998—10.5 percent—was significantly lower than the black rate, white poverty was far more common than it had been in the early 1970s. Hispanic poverty rates also dropped at the end of the 1990s, but stood at 25 percent in 2009.[8]

Although President Clinton had been elected on a promise to "make work pay," the number of Americans whose work did not pay enough to get them out of poverty increased during his administration. The expansion of low-wage employment and the informal economy combined with welfare reform to increase the importance of the working poor. In 1990, 2 million persons worked full-time for the full year, but remained in poverty. By 1998, 2.8 million Americans were in this unenviable condition.

Children, however, continued to bear the real cost of social change and public neglect. Although their poverty rate fell from 20.6 to 16.3 percent between 1990 and 2001, they still remained more likely to be poor than either the working-age population or the aged. The expansion of female-headed households was one contributor to children's difficulties. In 2001, 24 percent of female-headed households still lived in poverty. Although the risk of child poverty remained high for black children, it fell from 44.8 to 30.2 percent between 1990 and 2001. The two recessions of the 2000s reversed any improvement in the poverty status of children. By 2009, the child poverty rate stood at 20.7 percent, roughly where it had been twenty years earlier. More ominously, most observers agreed that poverty would continue to rise in the new decade.

CHANGES IN FAMILY COMPOSITION

After the rapid changes of the previous two decades, the structure of family life was relatively stable during the 1990s. As the baby-boom generation entered middle age, the number of two-parent households with children increased by 700,000 from 1990 to 1995. This came after a twenty-year decline. The divorce rate decreased from 23 divorces per 1,000 married women in 1980 to 20.5 in 1995. But the median age of marriage continued to rise, as did the number of people who never marry. Births to unmarried mothers were still going up, albeit at a slower rate.[9]

Women's labor-force participation—irrespective of race, ethnicity, marital status, or the presence of children—continued to rise. In 1992, 66 percent of all single women and 60 percent of all married women were in the labor force. Two-earner families as well as single-parent working households were typical.[10]

Rising life expectancy and falling fertility rates meant that the U.S. population continued to age. Median age went from 32.8 years in 1990 to 35.8 years in 2000. As the population aged, more two-earner families were finding themselves caught in a time bind. By 1996, some 10 to 12 percent of the workforce had responsibility for the care of an aging parent. Demographers estimated that by 2020, 33 percent of working-age adults would have this responsibility.

One of the first pieces of legislation signed by President Clinton was the Family and Medical Leave Act of 1993. The act requires employers to grant workers up to twelve weeks of unpaid leave annually for the birth or adoption of a child, to care for an ill family member, or to recover from serious illness. Although the leave is unpaid, health benefits remain intact throughout the period. When workers return to their jobs, they are guaranteed an equivalent position with seniority maintained. The legislation applies to private and public employers with fifty or more workers.

Regulations issued in early 1995 defined family members for whose care a worker might take leave as a spouse, a child, or a parent. Leave is not granted to care for the parent of a spouse, nor is it to be applicable for the care of a partner. The definition of covered illness has been extended so that it is clear that problems connected with pregnancy are included and that the leave need not be for consecutive days. Substance abuse and stress were covered if they constitute mental illness.[11]

That the leave is unpaid clearly limits its usefulness in meeting the needs of most workers. In general, women with higher incomes have received more family benefits. A 1990 national childcare survey found, for example, that 39 percent of women in professional occupations but only 15 percent of women in production, 11 percent of women in services, and none in agriculture were offered at least one childcare benefit by their employers. Two-career families were most likely to make use of the offered benefit, while single parents were the least likely.[12] The Family Leave Act was a small step forward in meeting the needs of working families.

POPULATION SHIFTS

Immigration led to a marked shift in the ethnic composition of the American population during the 1990s and 2000s. In the middle of the twentieth century, the United States was typically defined as black or white. By the first decade of the new century, the influx of Asian Americans and Latin Americans created a more complex mosaic. In 1980, 80 percent of Americans were non-Hispanic whites; in 1995, it was 74 percent. Overall, changing immigration patterns as well as differential birthrates created one of the largest racial and ethnic shifts in U.S. history.[13]

The Census Bureau estimates that the proportion of people of color would continue to rise. In 2000, the American population was 12 percent African American, 3.6 percent Asian, and 0.9 percent Native American. The 2000 census, for the first time, allowed individuals to identify themselves as multiracial, a choice taken by 2.4 percent of the population. By 2050, the estimates indicate that the proportion of African Americans will increase from 13 to 15 percent of the population. Those of Asian extraction will increase from 5 to 8 percent of the population, and Hispanics will increase from 16 to 24 percent of the population. By 2050, non-Hispanic whites share of the population will fall from 65 to 50 percent. These dramatic shifts have had major implications for social welfare in the United States. Immigration policy, affirmative action, public welfare, social services, education, health care, and social security are just some of the areas affected as the color, the culture, and the age mix of the population changes.

THE FALL AND RISE OF HEALTH CARE REFORM

At least since the Truman administration, presidents had proposed schemes to achieve comprehensive health care coverage for all Americans. During the 1970s, both political parties had advanced proposals to achieve the goal, but could not agree on a final plan. As the Republican Party drifted to the right during the 1970s and 1980s, it was inclined to trust market-based solutions rather than support comprehensive reform. As health care became a partisan, rather than a national, goal, it became more difficult to achieve the right political environment in which it could be achieved. During the Clinton administration, a possible opportunity to achieve health care reform was missed. The Democratic victories in the 2006 and 2008 elections finally led to its enactment, although the virulence of Republican opposition during 2010 left the ultimate fate of the plan uncertain.

For more than four decades, increases in health care costs had absorbed an increasing share of national income. The steady stream of new technologies has made health care more expensive as well as more effective. Additionally, demand for health care has risen as the population has aged and as public and private insurance provide a ready market for health and medical services. In 1965, before Medicare and Medicaid, health expenditures absorbed just under 6 percent of our gross national product; in the mid-2000s, they absorbed 17 percent.[14]

The number of individuals without any health insurance had risen, as well. In 1987, about 31 million people were uninsured throughout the year; by 1994, this was up to 40 million people. The 2007–2009 recession boosted the number of uninsured to 50 million persons, 17 percent of the population. This increase in the health insurance gap occurred despite the large expansion of Medicaid coverage and the increasing proportion of the population eligible for and covered by Medicare. In 1987, 76 percent of the population had employment-related coverage for health; in 1994, only 70 percent were so insured. Changes in our labor market—the downsizing of large manufacturing and the expansion of temporary and part-time work—were largely responsible.[15] Having insurance does not guarantee adequate health care. The lack of coverage of preventive services in most health plans combined with a ceiling on lifetime benefits increases the risk of bankruptcy in the event of major illness. The government safety net constructed during the 1960s—Medicare, Medicaid, and the Veterans' Administration health system—met many of the health care needs of the aging, the poor, and veterans with service-connected problems. Medicaid covered long-term care for the poor, who make up about half of all people in nursing homes. But less than half of poor people received it, and for those it did cover, availability of care was a major problem. Hospital emergency rooms often substituted for doctors' offices. Remarkably, President George W. Bush suggested at one point that access to care was not really a national problem because the uninsured could always go to the emergency room.[16]

Overall, the United States has lagged behind other developed countries in the provision of health care to all residents. We spend more per capita and have less satisfactory results. Infant mortality is higher, life expectancy lower. This is particularly true for people of color—African Americans, nonwhite Hispanics, and Native Americans—whose poverty is accompanied by poor health and shorter lives. Public health, environmental programs, and medical research take up a small percentage of health care expenditures as compared to personal health care expenses.

The Failure of Comprehensive Reform in the 1990s

Debates about our health care system, or, more precisely, about the financing and the availability of health care, occupied center stage during the early years of Clinton's presidency. The thirty-five working groups that made up the Hillary Rodham Clinton Task Force on Health Care Reform produced a detailed health plan more than 1,300 pages long. The bill, the Health Security Act (S1757), was introduced in Congress in the fall of 1993. It provided for universal access to a comprehensive package of benefits, using managed care to control utilization and costs. The plan involved many regional health alliances, each of which would have three different plans to offer consumers. It was a highly complex bill with an enormous amount of detail on eligibility, coverage, premiums, and benefits. During much of 1993 and 1994, it was explained, debated, ridiculed, defended, and finally defeated. Clinton had hoped that the prospect of containing health care costs would build business support for his plan, but the strong opposition of the lobbyists for small businesses—many of which did not offer health care to any employees—and the fear of increased government regulation eventually convinced larger businesses to oppose it, as well. Without business support, the plan never came to a vote in Congress.[17]

A piecemeal approach, in the Congress and at the state level, replaced the effort to achieve a major overhaul of health care financing in the United States. Congress began to consider a number of proposals for smaller expansions of Medicare and Medicaid, and for the regulation of private health insurance plans to keep insurance companies from dropping people.[18]

In the face of congressional inaction, the private sector undertook its own form of "health care reform." Although opponents of government reform had raised the specter of bureaucratic controls of the patient–doctor relationship to defeat the Health Security Act, the rise of managed care did just that, but without the protections that the Clinton bill had included. Exclusion of pre-existing conditions, routine denial of expensive treatment, and the frantic effort to get people out of hospitals faster and faster reignited the demands for reform as the decade came to a close. "Patients' Bill of Rights" legislation that protected consumers from some of the more overt abuses of the managed care industry gained the support of a majority of Americans and was passed by the Senate in 2001, but was again frustrated by special interests.[19]

Health care for the poor followed a similar pattern. Although Republican proposals to turn Medicaid funding into a block grant failed, more Medicaid recipients found themselves unwillingly pushed into managed care plans. Because poor people often lacked the knowledge and skill to negotiate the complex regulations that governed these plans, they were likely to find themselves denied needed services and frustrated when they were sick. The costs and benefits of managed care remained difficult to assess. Did managed care encourage companies to offer preventative care to keep the cost of treating more serious illnesses down or did they simply use administrative hurdles to make it more difficult for recipients to receive the care they needed? It was clear that one group—corporate executives—benefited handsomely when winning public contracts boosted private managed care companies' stock prices.

The decline in the welfare rolls after welfare reform reduced the number of working-age Americans on Medicaid. Those who left the welfare rolls were supposed to have access to transitional medical coverage, but many states failed to inform former recipients of this right. In Pennsylvania, for example, the state was forced to sign a consent decree in 1999 in which it promised to preserve the medical coverage of all welfare recipients who had left the rolls, a reversal of the routine cutoff that had been implemented in 1997. The passage of a national children's health insurance program (CHIP) in 1997 added many new children to the rolls, but much of this increase was canceled out by the number of children losing Medicaid coverage as a result of welfare reform.[20]

The elderly were vulnerable to changes in health policy. Older Americans already pay much more for their own health care than they did prior to the passage of Medicare. Further increasing costs and reducing coverage would be a serious drain on the incomes of many. The elderly are worried, too, about the availability and ease of access to doctors and health care providers, and they feel threatened by health maintenance organizations (HMOs) and managed care. A more extreme proposal would offer a privatization alternative. Recipients could elect to have the government set up individual medical savings accounts and have private health insurance with high deductibles.

Even when Congress appeared to make progress on health care, the results were often confusing. In 1997, a bill was signed into law to require insurers to provide parity between coverage for physical and behavioral health. Although the intent of the bill was to expand the coverage of individuals and families for behavior health services, insurers were able to use managed care as a means of restricting patients' access to these services.[21]

The failure of the Clinton health care plan set the stage for Republicans to capture both houses of Congress in 1994. Although they would lose the Senate briefly in 2001 and 2002, Republicans retained control of at least one house until the 2006 elections. At the behest of President Bush, in 2003, Congress passed legislation to add prescription drug coverage to Medicare (Part D). Consistent with the ideological foundation of the Republican Congress, the legislation gave a major role to private insurance companies in offering coverage to older Americans and people with disabilities. While the legislation offered *choice* to recipients, it was less clear that Medicare Part D provided the optimal protection. Most notably, the structure of the program required recipients to make substantial out-of-pocket co-payments when their annual drug cost exceeded $2,250. Only when their annual costs exceed $6,000, did Part D again pay most of the cost. In addition, the legislation explicitly forbade Medicare from attempting to negotiate cheaper price for drugs, again adding to the cost of the plan. Although the president heralded prescription drug coverage as this administration's major domestic legislative achievement, it raised as many doubts as it addressed about the Republican's market-based approach to health care.[22]

The same legislation established the Medicare Advantage program that provided subsidies to private insurance companies to offer an alternative to the standard Medicare coverage. Medicare Advantage was widely seen as providing overly generous support for the insurance companies and undermining political support for standard Medicare. Indeed, curtailing these subsidies became a significant element of Barack Obama's health care plan, and opponents of these changes portrayed the proposals as attacks on Medicare itself. A significant decline in older Americans' support of Democrats in the 2010 election may have been a result of this confusion.

Achieving Comprehensive Reform in 2010

With the exception of the Medicare Part D, the two parties remained far apart in their approach to health care reform through the 1990s and 2000s. Republicans argued that individual health savings accounts were the best answer to the soaring costs of health care, although more sober analysis suggested that there was little evidence to support that position. Democrats, meanwhile, groped toward a strategy that would address the uninsured and soaring costs but that would avoid the label of government-run health care that had doomed the Clinton plan.

Democratic successes in the 2006 and 2008 elections provided them with the opportunity to move forward with a new effort at comprehensive reform. The basic outlines of reform were set in place early in 2009. Individuals would be required to have health insurance. If they were not covered by an employer or existing government plan, Americans would be able to purchase insurance through health care *exchanges* organized at the state level. These exchanges would negotiate with private insurance companies to provide similar coverage and rates to those received through employer-based plans. A system of subsidies would assure that low-income households could afford insurance. Employers who did not offer coverage for their employees would be required to pay taxes that partially covered the cost of those subsidies and to eliminate their "free ride" for not insuring their workers.[23]

The major bone of contention among those considering reform was the so-called public option. This proposal would require the government to offer plans through the exchanges that would compete with the private insurance plan. The goal of the public option was to provide leverage that the government could use to impose cost containment of private plans. Yet, although it would have covered only a small percentage of the population, the public option raised the specter of "government-run" health care again. Ultimately, because of resistance by more conservative Democrats—and in what was ultimately a vain effort to attract any Republican support—the public option was dropped from the final legislation.

Legislative strategy also played a role in the passage of reform. During the fall and early winter of 2009, both houses of Congress passed versions of health care reform. In the Senate, however, the bill had to be weakened to attract all sixty Democrats and avoid a Republican filibuster. The Democrats' strategy, however, was thrown into disarray by a special election. Ted Kennedy, who had been a senator since 1963 and had been the foremost advocate of health care reform for more than four decades, died in August 2009. The election to replace him in January 2010 led to a Republican victory, which destroyed the Democrats "veto-proof" majority. After several months of uncertainty, Congress and the president moved forward using the *budget reconciliation* process (which could not be filibustered) to enact the final bill. Because of this change of strategy, the final bill, passed in March 2010, was somewhat more liberal than that passed by the Senate the previous year.

The signing of the health care reform law by President Obama, however, was hardly the end of the process, and the prospects for fully implementing the law remained cloudy. Almost immediately, the law was challenged in federal court. The suit brought by a number of Republican state attorneys general argued that the requirement that individuals purchase insurance violated the interstate commerce clause of the Constitution. Although dominant legal opinion belittled this argument, a federal district judge ruled in favor of the law's opponents. Ultimately, the litigation would find its way to the Supreme Court. At a more basic level, the law required states to proceed with a variety of reforms to implement the new law. Many states—usually those dominated by Republicans—resisted these requirements. Most threatening to the law, however, was the long period of time it would take to implement it fully. Republican victories in the 2010 elections gave support to the party's efforts to repeal the law. While Republicans could not do so as long as Democrats controlled the Senate and the presidency, they could use a variety of tactics to undermine public support for the plan, and whoever won the presidency in 2012 would have significant influence over the law's final implementation.

The final reconciliation bill also allowed Congress to enact reform to student loan programs. Since the 1960s, the majority of loans to college students had flowed through private banks that received subsidies and guarantees for handling the business. Yet, during the 1990s and early 2000s, two problems gained visibility. First, a number of scandals surfaced in which SLM Corporation (better known as Sallie Mae)—the major servicer of student loans—and a number of banks used kickbacks and other shady business practices to gain student loan business. In the face of lax federal oversight, New York state took the lead in forcing lenders and universities to change their practices to reduce students' debt. Second, proprietary or for-profit educational institutions used government-guaranteed student loans and grants for low-income students to enroll students in programs without concern for whether the program benefited the student financially or if they were able to repay their loans. It was not unusual for programs in car mechanics or culinary arts to leave students with tens of thousand dollars of debt, but without increased earning power.[24]

In response to these problems, the Obama administration proposed and Congress passed legislation to substitute direct government loans for the subsidies to private lenders. This allowed the government to reduce the incentive for corruption and increased its regulatory authority over proprietary schools. As with health care, the passage of legislation was hardly the end of the battle. Private universities and trade schools mounted a giant lobbying effort, accusing the government of a "takeover" of student loans. The effort was successful at delaying implementation of parts of the reform law.

Policy Practice

Critical Thinking Question: What roles might professional social workers play in influencing the fate of health care reform in the coming years?

ADDRESSING POVERTY AND DEPENDENCY: THE SCOPE OF WELFARE REFORM

The most lasting change in American social welfare during the 1990s was the reform of programs for low-income Americans. As in previous decades, middle-class Americans had a distorted view of the size of the welfare population, how long recipients stayed on the rolls, and the cost of public programs. The massive entry of women into the labor force in the previous three decades had undermined a major assumption of public assistance: that mothers should stay home with their children. Finally, new research results suggested that long-term dependency was a much more significant problem than had previously been believed.

The welfare population of the 1990s was sharply divided into two strata. The vast majority of women who *ever* collected welfare did so for less than two years. Yet, a significant minority stayed on welfare for more than eight years. Thus, depending on how one phrased it, welfare could be seen as a temporary program or a permanent trap. During the early 1990s, the second image of the welfare population—that it was dominated by a permanent dependent population—drove the welfare debate.

The new alarm with long-term dependency was supported as well with a healthy dose of self-interest and ideology. The driving force behind welfare reform during the early 1990s was cost, not so much for the federal government, but for the states. In reality, the federal government spent $20 billion on AFDC in its peak year, less than 2 percent of the federal budget of over $1 trillion in the early 1990s.[25]

For the states, however, the rise in welfare rolls had a more severe fiscal impact. In 1992, more than 20 percent of expenditures by the states went to public welfare—including AFDC and Medicaid. Increased welfare rolls, declining state revenues (because of the recession), and the requirement that states balance their budgets combined to focus attention on reducing the cost of the program.

The first indicator of the fiscal problem was the fate of the Family Support Act (FSA), which had been enacted in 1988. Although the FSA refocused AFDC on the goal of self-sufficiency, much of the federal financing for the job-training program (Jobs Opportunities and Basic Skills [JOBS]) went unused because it required state matching funds. In the stringent budget years of the early 1990s, state legislatures were unwilling to spend their own dollars to promote self-sufficiency, even if the federal government offered to match their effort.

The Changing Dynamics of the Welfare Debate

Concerns about cost combined with worries about morality. During the late 1980s and early 1990s, the proportion of children born out of wedlock rose. Part of this rise was a statistical artifact—the fall of the marital fertility rate meant that a larger share of births occurred out of wedlock. Although the out-of-wedlock birthrate rose by 37 percent between 1985 and 1992, the percent of all births that occurred outside of marriage increased from 22 to 30. Moreover, illegitimacy became more visible in the white community. As late as 1980, African Americans had accounted for more out-of-wedlock births than whites. By 1992, however, 59 percent of out-of-wedlock births were to whites and only 38 percent were to blacks.[26]

The increased strength of the New Right within the Republican Party put pressure on legislators to focus on the problem of illegitimacy. Yet, instead of asking complex questions about the opportunity structure for poor teenagers, the availability of sex education, and the adequacy of reproductive services, conservatives dwelt on the supposed incentive that AFDC provided for young women to have children out of wedlock. Whatever the merits of their arguments, the battle against illegitimacy had a major impact on the politics of welfare.

As conservatives focused on the role of costs and morality in welfare reform, many liberals and moderates—many of whom called themselves New Democrats—were rethinking their position on public assistance. Mainstream academic thought had become more skeptical about the effects of welfare on the poor. First, David Ellwood and Mary Jo Bane concluded that previous research had understated the importance of long-term dependency. The nineteenth-century belief that welfare was a trap that fostered dependency and undermined efforts at self-sufficiency took on a new shine in light of their findings.[27] Ellwood and Bane also suggested that welfare bureaucracies at the state and local levels had become a barrier to the reduction of dependency. Second, William J. Wilson, the eminent African American sociologist, gave new credence to the belief that poor neighborhoods had become seedbeds for dependency and other "pathologies." Again, a nineteenth-century image—that the poor lived in a different social and moral universe than the mainstream— found intellectual support.[28]

This line of academic research found a responsive chord among many liberal politicians. For three decades, liberals had been pilloried by conservatives because of their "permissiveness," their unwillingness to stand up for traditional moral positions on family, work, and gender. A new position on welfare—one that stressed responsibility, work, and self-sufficiency—provided a way for liberals and moderates to defend themselves against charges of permissiveness.

Ellwood again provided the crucial synthesis. In his book *Poor Support*, Ellwood was able to articulate an analysis of poverty that merged traditional liberalism with the New Democratic concern with responsibility. Ellwood argued that changes in welfare had to be teamed with efforts to improve the status of low-wage workers. By "making work pay," through the expansion of tax credits and increases in the minimum wage, Ellwood's plan would increase the incentives of welfare recipients to enter the workforce. Time limits and work requirements would give them additional incentives to get off welfare.[29]

Ellwood's proposals became the core of Bill Clinton's welfare reform agenda during the 1992 presidential election. During the first year of his presidency, Clinton was able to get Congress to agree to a critical part of his plan, the expansion of the earned income tax credit (EITC) as part of the Omnibus Budget Reconciliation Act. The EITC had first been enacted in the 1970s to provide a small wage subsidy for low-income workers with children. The 1993 legislation increased both the size of the tax credit and the number of families who were eligible for it.

The Clinton administration moved more slowly on the reform of public assistance. In the meantime, many states had received *waivers* from the federal government to adopt experimental schemes for welfare. A few of these actually expanded cash assistance. For example, a number of states increased the earnings disregard, so that welfare recipients could earn more without having their welfare benefits reduced. For the most part, however, the waiver programs tested a set of initiatives to reduce benefits. These included more aggressive efforts to require welfare recipients to work or face sanctions, and a set of *behavioral* reforms focusing on the supposed immoral behavior of welfare recipients. Welfare recipients in some states were faced with cuts in their benefits if their children missed school too often, if they failed to document their children's vaccination records, or if they missed a rent payment.

The most widely debated of these behavioral reforms was the "family cap." Until 1996, welfare benefits were tied to family size. If a welfare recipient had an additional child while on welfare, her check would rise to reflect the increase in family size. The family cap froze the family's payment at its level before the new baby was born. To many Americans, the image of a welfare recipient having additional children brought together all of the negative stereotypes of the poor—irresponsibility, promiscuity, dependency, and rising costs. The family cap became the shorthand for an increased focus on "personal responsibility" in the welfare debate.

By the time President Clinton released his plan for welfare reform in the summer of 1994, events had largely overtaken the administration. Clinton's efforts to reform health care were in the last stage of their slow death. Efforts at the state level had moved the welfare debate in a more conservative and harsh direction. Finally, that fall, the Republicans achieved a resounding electoral victory in congressional elections, capturing majorities in both the Senate and the House of Representatives. If welfare reform were to occur during the 1990s, it would take the ideas of congressional Republicans as its starting point.

Welfare reform was a key tenet of the "Contract with America," which many Republicans credited with their electoral victory in 1994. The Personal Responsibility Act (H.R. 4) introduced in 1995 outlined a radical shift in welfare policy.[30] The entitlement to welfare would be ended and a host of welfare programs, including AFDC, food stamps, federal child welfare spending, and Medicaid, would be transformed into a block grant to the states. Welfare recipients would be required to work and limits would be set on the time one could collect welfare. In addition, a number of groups of mothers and children would be defined as undeserving and ineligible of aid: teen mothers, those who refused to work, immigrants, and convicted drug felons.

The New Consensus over Welfare Reform

Although the debate over welfare reform during 1995 and 1996 was acrimonious, there was much that the two sides held in common. Both the Clinton administration and Congress wanted stronger work requirements and supported the idea of time limits. In addition, although they squabbled over the nature of federal–state cooperation, both sides anticipated that welfare reform would give the states more discretion in charting welfare policy. In addition, adopting time limits implied that the "entitlement" to cash assistance would be weakened.

The Clinton administration and Congress used the popularity of welfare reform as a cover for policy changes that could not be enacted on their own. For example, the Supreme Court decision of 1990 had extended Supplemental Security Income (SSI) to children who suffered from a set of behavioral disabilities. Both the administration and Congress were willing to include a reversal of this decision in the welfare reform legislation.

The battle over welfare waxed and waned during 1995 and 1996 as the president and congressional Republicans played an elaborate game of chicken. The public backlash over the budget deadlock of 1995–1996 and the resulting shutdown of the federal government gave the president and congressional Democrats the upper hand through most of 1996. As a result, they were able to make significant changes in the Republicans' original plan. Food stamps, Medicaid, and child welfare services were removed from the block grant. The amount of money available for childcare increased substantially. Many of the behavioral reforms—such as the family cap—changed from a national mandate to a state option. In addition, Congress agreed to "maintenance of effort" stipulations that required states to continue their welfare spending.

Yet, as the 1996 elections approached, it was clear that President Clinton and many Democrats feared that they would be blamed if no welfare reform was enacted. As a result, after President Clinton vetoed several versions of the bill, the Personal Responsibility and Work Opportunity Reconciliation Act (PRWORA) of 1996 was passed and signed into law in August.

The welfare reform debate ended where it had started: with a preoccupation with reducing the cost of welfare. The new legislation ended the entitlement to cash assistance. Temporary Assistance for Needy Families (TANF) was substituted for AFDC. Combined with the adoption of time limits and work requirements, the states were able to use their new authority to discourage families from applying for welfare and to raise barriers to their receiving benefits. The major "liberal" element in the law was a dramatic expansion in the size of the childcare and development block grant that provided a large increase in subsidized childcare for low-income families.[31]

The most glaring omission of the welfare reform law was its failure to require states to offer educational and training opportunities to welfare recipients. Pennsylvania was representative of many states in its adoption of a "rapid attachment" strategy, which put an incentive on getting welfare recipients into low-wage jobs and off welfare as quickly as possible. Although congressional supporters might claim that they wished to break the cycle of dependency, the lack of substantial job training opportunities ensured the cycle of poverty would continue.

In 2005, Congress reauthorized TANF. The new legislation included two major changes. First, in line with the Bush administration's efforts to politicize the debate over family life, the new bill included funding for "marriage promotion" efforts. Second, the bill tightened the work requirements governing state plans to compel states to place more welfare recipients into work programs.

The Impact of Welfare Reform

If the purpose of welfare reform was primarily to reduce the cost of public assistance, it was a stunning success in its first several years. When PRWORA was signed in 1996, the average AFDC caseload nationally was about 12.5 million individuals. By March 1999, the TANF caseload had fallen to 7.3 million recipients. By 2004, fewer than 5 million Americans were served by TANF. Yet, the wide variations of declines from state to state suggested that these data were not the result of the overall improvement in the economic status of the poor, but rather testimony to the states' increased ability to use welfare rules to push poor families off the rolls or to discourage them from entering. Thus, while Minnesota recorded a 13 percent decline between January 1997 and March 1999, Wisconsin—with the most publicized efforts to reduce their rolls—recorded a 78 percent decline.[32]

In some states, like general assistance before it, public assistance for needy families began to disappear, in spite of "maintenance of efforts" requirements. Idaho, which had provided aid to 24,000 individuals in 1996, had only 2,461 on its TANF rolls in March 2002. In the South, Florida and Georgia had a million people on welfare in 1996, but only a quarter of that number in 2002.[33]

In spite of the devastating recession of the late 2000s, TANF caseloads remained fairly stagnant. While the number of Americans receiving food stamps (which had been renamed the Supplemental Nutritional Assistance Program [SNAP]) increased to more than 36 million during the recession, the number of individuals receiving TANF benefits actually fell from 4.4 million in October 2005 to 4.3 million in March 2010.[34]

The evidence on the well-being of former recipients, however, hardly provided a cause for celebration. Most of those who left welfare, although earning more than they would have collected from welfare, continued to live in poverty. The failure of welfare reform to provide much incentive to the state to train and educate recipients meant that as recipients left the rolls, they found themselves in low-wage jobs that could not lift them out of poverty.

Female heads of household and their children were especially hard-hit. Between 1993 and 1995, they had benefited as a group by the improving economic conditions, their average earning rising from $14,668 to just under $17,000. But as welfare reform pushed millions of poorly educated women into the labor force, it exerted a downward pressure on their wages. Between 1995 and 1997, as the economy soared and unemployment dropped below 5 percent, the wages of female heads of household stalled, increasing by only a few hundred dollars per year. After 1998, even these gains ceased.[35]

Careful analyses of evidence on low-wage, female-headed families suggested that as public assistance became a smaller share of family income, women scrambled to make ends meet. Old survival strategies—accepting "off the books" employment, obtaining resources from friends and families, doubling up to reduce housing costs—had again become permanent parts of the family economy of the poor. During the 1960s, it had been said that welfare policy should provide "floors and doors"—a safety net and opportunities to escape poverty. By 2011, the welfare system, serving an ever-smaller share of families in need, seemed to offer neither.

The new welfare regime required public assistance workers to use considerable discretion in the use of *sanctions*. The new behavioral and work requirements incorporated into state TANF programs meant that clients who did not meet these standards could have their benefits either partially or fully cut off. In some states, policy worked to differentiate clients to provide greater latitude in the imposition of sanctions, while in other places, all clients faced welfare cutoffs regardless of their mental or physical ability.[36]

The impact of welfare reform on children's well-being is still unknown. Although the welfare reform law had expanded funding for child care, the Department of Health and Human Services estimated that the childcare and development block grant provided funding for only 1.25 million children out of the 10 million who were income eligible for childcare subsidies. The experience of states that made a real effort to provide adequate child care provides one indication of the gap between the demand for child care and the available resources. In Illinois, for example, the use of subsidized child care expanded by 80 percent between 1997 and 1999.[37]

Diversity in Practice

Critical Thinking Question: Ideally, how might differences in clients' physical and mental abilities influence how they are treated by TANF?

WELFARE REFORM AND "IMMIGRATION CONTROL"

The welfare reform law targeted the cutoff of aid to immigrants as a major policy focus. Despite voluminous data demonstrating that the availability of public assistance and social services had little to do with the dynamics of migration, lawmakers viewed welfare reform as an easy way to promote a popular cause. In 1994, California Proposition 187 demonstrated the popular appeal of limiting the availability of educational and social services for immigrants and undocumented migrants. The initiative barred undocumented migrants from using schools, hospitals, and public assistance and sought to give teachers, social workers, and hospital personnel responsibility for identifying ineligible individuals. Although the major provisions of the initiative were blocked by the courts, "Prop 187" became a model for congressional action. Some of the harshest changes in the welfare law were directed at preventing noncitizens from receiving means-tested programs. In 1996, Congress also passed legislation that raised the income threshold required to sponsor new immigrants, enacted new penalties against those who overstayed temporary visas, limited the due process rights of migrants who could not demonstrate they were in the United States legally, and put new money into the militarization of the border between the United States and Mexico.[38]

By 1997, congressional Republicans—many chastened by their electoral defeats in the 1996 election—moved to restore some of the benefits denied to immigrants. Yet, the true irony of the immigrant bashing of the 1990s was that it accelerated the pace at which immigrants attained citizenship. With even legal immigrants finding themselves denied benefits and at risk for harassment, many Americans who had been born in other countries decided that their futures were more secure as citizens.

The punitive approach to immigration provoked a backlash. During 2006, the Republican-controlled Congress debated legislation to criminalize undocumented workers and build 700 miles of walls along the Rio Grande to keep

Latin American, undocumented workers out, a proposal opposed even by the president. In the heat of the 2006 midterm elections, the president abandoned the search for a more comprehensive approach to immigration reform and ultimately signed a bill authorizing the construction of the wall. In the face of Republican hostility, Latin American voters, many of whom supported George W. Bush for re-election, voted in greater numbers for Democrats in 2006, a major reason why they retook both houses of Congress.

Still, immigration remained a contested issue as the second decade of the twenty-first century began. Efforts to reach a comprehensive approach that would increase border security and provide a path toward citizenship for the estimated 14 million undocumented people living in the United States failed. Instead, many cities, towns, and states experimented with their own form of immigration reform. For example, in 2010, Arizona passed a law that required local law enforcement officials to check the immigration status of persons they deemed suspicious, a policy that many saw as *racial profiling*. Although this and similar approaches were judged to be unconstitutional by federal courts, politicians continued to be rewarded for supporting these efforts.[39]

THE RETURN TO VOLUNTARISM AND THE RISE OF PRIVATIZATION

Since the 1980s, many conservatives had argued that one consequence of the expansion of social welfare programs had been to discourage voluntarism. Thus, as the federal government began to limit social programs, advocates tried to demonstrate the vitality of the voluntary sector and its capacity to take up the slack created by a shrinking government role. During the 1980s, these efforts had often appeared as little more than window dressing designed to deflect criticism of program cuts.

Certainly, the fate of homelessness policy during the 1980s and 1990s suggested that the claims of voluntarists rarely were consistent with realities. As the homeless became a more visible part of the social landscape during the 1980s, public attention focused on the role of voluntary organizations, including churches and other religious organizations, in responding to the needs of this population. Yet, it was only with the passage of federal legislation that adequate funding for homeless programs became available.

Inconvenient realities did not weaken the enthusiasm of budget-cutters for the possibilities of voluntary activity. The welfare reform law provided new opportunities for voluntary organizations to become involved in the routine provision of services to the poor. In addition, PRWORA opened up the opportunities for religious congregations to become eligible for welfare funding. Supported by a body of research on the importance of churches in aiding the poor, federal and state policies encouraged religious congregations to take a more active role in poverty policy.[40] The expanding role of religion in public policy affected educational policy as well. In contrast to the 1960s, when Congress took special care in defining a role for religious schools in funding for elementary and secondary education, by the 1990s, many federal and state policymakers were willing to move aggressively to make public funding available for church schools. A number of states and localities adopted "voucher" plans that made certificates available to low-income parents that they could use for either public or private education.

The cause of faith-based social welfare received a big boost from the inauguration of George W. Bush in 2001. The president claimed that his "compassionate conservatism" could be implemented by expanding the role of religious institutions in providing social services. Although Congress resisted his proposals, the Bush administration used a number of executive orders to expand religion's role in public social welfare in spite of the constitutional concerns raised by these policies.

The September 11 tragedy highlighted both the strengths and weaknesses of voluntary social welfare. There was a huge outpouring of concern for the victims of terrorism with more than $2.4 billion being donated to private charities. Yet, the coordination of aid was poor with help not always reaching those most in need. The Red Cross drew particular criticism because it was slow to distribute aid and used September 11 funds for purposes not directly connected to the disaster. As a result, an August 2002 poll reported that 42 percent of respondents had lost confidence in private charities as a result of September 11, while only 19 percent had gained confidence.[41]

The efficacy of voluntary charity was dealt a blow in August 2005 when Hurricane Katrina blasted through the Gulf Coast and New Orleans, leaving that city almost entirely submerged for three days. The Bush administration's approach to social welfare was cast in dramatic relief as actually helping victims of the tragedy took a back seat to a public-relations effort to show that the president "cared" about what had happened. Yet, as government failed in its most basic responsibilities—providing food and water, searching for survivors, caring for the sick, and burying the dead—the administration's claims ran headlong into a monstrous reality. The fact that a large number of the victims of the hurricane were poor and black only served to underline the limits of voluntarism and the failure of conservative governance.

Yet, Hurricane Katrina did benefit many. In an age of privatization and outsourcing, private contractors who provided the food, housing, social services, and transportation for the hurricane's victims often were handsomely rewarded for their work, even when it was shoddy or failed to reach victims. Although personal responsibility was the hallmark of conservative social policy, this principle did not extend to private contractors, or for that matter, to the president.

Private, for-profit businesses had a larger role in social welfare by the late 1990s. The availability of third-party reimbursements under private health insurance, Medicare, and Medicaid had greatly expanded the role of for-profit enterprises in some fields of social welfare during the 1970s and 1980s. Child care, nursing homes, hospitals, and residential treatment facilities all expanded. Between 1977 and 1987, the for-profit share of establishments increased by 80 percent in child care, 22 percent in individual and family services, and 45 percent in residential care.[42]

This trend accelerated during the next twenty years. PRWORA, for example, enabled for-profits to enter the child welfare field in greater numbers. In addition, businesses discovered a new set of "profit centers" in certain areas of social welfare, for example, in data processing and research and evaluation.

The entry of for-profit enterprises into child welfare took on particular urgency because of other changes in policy. After a decade of supporting *family preservation* as the chief approach to child welfare, Congress in 1997 passed the Adoption and Safe Families Act (ASFA), which placed additional pressure on child welfare agencies to find permanent homes for children removed from homes because of abuse or neglect. After three decades of increased effort to preserve the link between children and their parents, ASFA was a shift back to an older tradition of *child rescue*, harking back to the approach of nineteenth-century "child savers."[43]

Welfare reform meant more than changes in a handful of means-tested programs. It was a symbol of a whole set of changes affecting social welfare during the 1990s. From the New Deal until the 1970s, government had moved steadily to expand the right of ordinary citizens to protection against the risks of poverty and discrimination. Yet, the cost of providing these rights set off a strong backlash. As the public sector sought to reduce taxes and the programs supported by them, policy was increasingly farmed out to nonpublic institutions. The expanded role of nonprofits, religious institutions, and for-profit businesses was as much a part of welfare reform as the death of AFDC and the birth of TANF.

Ethical Practice

Critical Thinking Question: Losing one's welfare benefits can contribute to child neglect. What ethical dilemmas might welfare reform pose for child protective service workers? How might they respond to these dilemmas?

Although welfare reform offered new opportunities to for-profit business, Old Age, Survivors, and Disability Insurance (OASDI), the core of the Social Security program, offered the most lucrative target. The trust funds for the program ran persistent deficits during the 1970s and early 1980s. After the Social Security reform of 1983, however, the program had been put on a path toward surpluses for the remainder of the twentieth century and into the first decades of the next.

Yet, the specter of a "Social Security crisis" remained. In many respects, the politics of Social Security policy were the reverse of the health care reform experience. In health care reform, a popular reform proposal was sidetracked because it would threaten the power and profits of insurance companies, hospitals, and other health care providers. With Social Security, the potential profits of privatization kept "reform" alive even though the public embraced the existing system.

During the 1990s, however, Social Security faced a new challenge: the interests of the financial services industry. The major conservative proposal for privatizing Social Security was to allow individuals to create their own retirement account in lieu of paying Social Security taxes. If such a proposal were enacted, literally billions of dollars that are currently collected in payroll taxes would instead filter through banks, stockbrokers, and other financial institutions. The financial services industry spent much of the decade spreading a message that workers could not count on Social Security when they retired. Over time, these coordinated attacks increased public concern about the system.[44]

In spite of these efforts, however, support of the existing system continued to frustrate those who wished to undermine it. President Clinton's proposal to commit a large share of future budget surpluses to Social Security was warmly received by the public. The future of Social Security, however, was put in jeopardy by the actions of the second Bush administration and Congress between 2001 and 2003. With the support of the president, Congress passed a series of tax cuts heavily tilted toward the richest Americans. As a result, the federal budget—excluding Social Security taxes—went from a surplus of $236 billion in 2000 to a projected deficit of $455 billion in 2003, before the impact of the 2003 tax cuts had been felt.

Where the Clinton administration had proposed that the budget surplus of his administration be used to insure Social Security's economic well-being, President Bush chose the exact opposite strategy; he planned to use ballooning deficits in the budget to force a restructuring of the system in the coming years.

At least in the short term, however, President Bush again miscalculated. His 2005 proposal to shift Social Security to private accounts met with such a chilly reception from the public and Congress that it never came for a vote.

Yet, the first decade of the twenty-first century continued the pattern of the previous thirty years with tax-subsidized private pensions accounting for a larger share of retirement income.

In some ways, those backing private pensions had already won the battle. Since the resolution of the Social Security crisis in 1983, most public policy around the income security of the aged had been directed to private plans. The expansion of individual retirement accounts (IRAs), 401(k) accounts, and other "defined-contribution" plans had far exceeded increases in public pensions.[45]

During the 1990s, the proportion of the population that depended on these private plans increased dramatically, reaching more than half of the elderly by 2000. Yet, this growth was spread unequally across the population; two-thirds of the richest fifth of the population had pensions, but less than 20 percent of the bottom fifth did. As a result, of the $88 billion of pensions distributed in 1990, 57 percent went to the richest fifth of the population.

The rise of publicly subsidized private pensions had both economic and political implications. Thanks to the Social Security system, the distribution of income among the elderly had become more equal between 1960 and 1990. During the 1990s and 2000s, however, inequality among the elderly increased because of the rapid rise in pensions.

More significantly, the increased role of private pensions puts the political support for Social Security in jeopardy. When the next Social Security "crisis" comes, it will be easier to convince the affluent elderly to support proposals that hurt older people of more modest means.

THE CONTINUING CIVIL RIGHTS BATTLE

Americans continued to struggle with the definition of rights and responsibilities during the 1990s. Welfare reform had been justified as a means of righting this balance by requiring poor people to be more responsible; at the same time, many of them lost any right to assistance from the federal government. Although policies that were meant to correct social inequality were under attack, those tied to the right of privacy gained more support from the political and legal systems.

Education

Educational programs have been the target of a great deal of backlash against people of color and of different ethnic groups. The drive to require all teaching to be done in English targeted Hispanic-speaking children, a growing group in the United States. For immigrants, legal and illegal, there are now many challenges to their right to public education.

The elimination of remedial courses, in the name of economy, at colleges and universities hurt black, Hispanic, and Native American students particularly hard. In the 1992–1993 school year, 11 percent of white but 15 percent of Native American and 19 percent of black, Hispanic, and Asian American undergraduates took remedial courses. Changing college admission standards and cutting the number of remedial courses, or offering them only at junior colleges, blocked the efforts of students to correct inadequate education at the elementary and secondary school levels.[46]

The Supreme Court ruled against a school desegregation program in Kansas City where magnet city schools were used to bring white students from the suburbs into the inner city, one of many court decisions limiting the

AP/World Wide Photo

As the twentieth century drew to a close, new pressing social issues—such as the AIDS epidemic—stimulated new social movements. Although many of these movements borrowed methods from past social movements, including the civil rights movement, they also created new ways of dramatizing their concerns and influencing public policy

responsibilities of schools to promote desegregation. The black community appeared split on the issue. Some saw the retreat from integrated schooling as a retreat from equality, while others urged a return to neighborhood schools with an equalization of facilities and opportunities.

Large cuts in the budget for the Bureau of Indian Affairs have led to what the Office of Indian Education Programs called "a major, major problem," putting children in physical danger in buildings with inadequate ventilation, plumbing, and fire-escape routes. The quality of education provided is reflected in the level of spending. Although the Bureau of Indian Affairs is required to finance tribal schools at the per student average for their state, the rule was ignored because insufficient funding was provided by Congress. Congress had, in effect, opted to continue separate and unequal education for Native Americans.[47]

In our colleges and universities, consideration of race, ethnicity, and gender as part of admission decisions has been attacked vigorously. Objections have been particularly vociferous in California and in Texas. In California, Governor Pete Wilson urged that there be no preferential admission. Shortly thereafter, a suit was filed against the medical and law schools of the University of California attacking preferential consideration. The University of California banned admissions that used race or gender as a criterion. Other state legislatures, governors, and university boards were considering and acting to eliminate preferential admissions on the basis of race or ethnicity. A major decision banning preferential admissions came in a 1996 University of Texas case in the Fifth Circuit Court of Appeals that clearly banned race-based admissions. In 2003, however, the Supreme Court—in *Gratz* v. *Bollinger* and *Grutter* v. *Bollinger*—ruled that promoting racial diversity in education settings was a legitimate criterion for college admissions. Although the decisions restricted the practices that could be used to promote diversity and called for a time limit on the use of affirmative action, proponents of affirmative action saw these decisions as significant victories.

Affirmative Action in the Labor Market

The courts, which in the past had supported the drive of vulnerable groups, particularly blacks and women, to seek a redress of the opportunity structure they faced in the market, have now moved against preferential hiring and contracting.

Almost any set of data that is examined shows the subordinate position of women and of people of color in our economy. Wages, incomes, promotion rates, middle management, top management, number of contractors, number of independent manufacturing firms—the numbers all tell the same story. Women and minorities suffer severely because of their gender and their race. And yet there is a growing series of objections from white men who claim to have suffered because of affirmative action programs. A National Opinion Research Center survey in 1990 found that only 7 percent of white Americans had personally experienced reverse discrimination and 16 percent knew of someone who had. On the other hand, 70 percent thought that whites were being hurt by affirmative action programs.[48]

Efforts to eliminate affirmative action programs are gaining ground at the state and the federal levels. In California, an initiative to outlaw affirmative action received strong support in the fall of 1996. Other states were attempting similar actions, with varying results. The Supreme Court ruled in 1995 in a 5–4 decision that the federal government was highly restricted in its use of affirmative action programs applied to contractors with the federal government. Federal "set-aside" provisions were not ruled out completely, but they were ordered to meet the more stringent requirements already set for the states. The Pentagon, rather than providing a set-aside provision for minority contractors in long-distance telephone services, gave them a pricing advantage in their bids. The program appeared to be successful, but now officials are backing away from it.

President Clinton ordered a review of the federal government's affirmative action programs. A report, released in May 1995, concluded that race or sex could be acceptable as one of several factors in such programs, and that programs involving "goals" rather than quotas should be used.[49] The president supported reform, but not abolition, of affirmative action programs.

Abortion and the Right to Privacy

In the early 1990s, the right to abortion that the Supreme Court had established in 1973 seemed to be at risk. The appointment of conservative justices to the Court during the 1980s and early 1990s had decisively changed its ideological complexion. In spite of strong support for abortion rights in public opinion polls, state legislators became increasingly willing to enact restrictions on reproductive services.

The Webster decision, announced by the Court in 1989, provided an equivocal reassertion of *Roe* v. *Wade*. The Court agreed that the right to abortion was constitutionally guaranteed, but the decision expanded the ability of states to limit that right through notification procedures, waiting periods, and the regulation of providers. Although abortion rights advocates were relieved that the Court did not overturn *Roe*, the decision made that "right" seem less real. In fact, it became more and more difficult for a majority of women to gain access to abortion services, as clinics closed their doors and few hospitals offered abortions. In addition, an underground network of terrorists targeted abortion clinics and physicians for violence at the same time that civil disobedience campaigns like "Operation Rescue" impeded women's ability to exercise reproductive choice safely and peaceably.[50]

At the same time, the foundation of *Roe* v. *Wade* in the "right to privacy" first articulated in the Supreme Court's *Griswold* decision in 1965 made steady progress. In 2003, to the surprise of many, the Supreme Court took the unusual step of claiming that an earlier Court decision on the rights of adults to engage in consensual sex—whatever their gender—had been incorrect. The decision in *Lawrence* v. *Texas* was notable because it used evolving thought in Europe and recent scholarship in gay and lesbian history to support the decision. (See the end of this chapter for excerpts from this decision.)

The *Lawrence* decision was notable as well because the rights of sexual minorities had become a major flashpoint in the culture wars. By the early twenty-first century, virtually no Americans defended the morality of racial and gender discrimination; the struggles were primarily about how much needed to be done to remedy them. In contrast, a significant minority of Americans continued to view gay, lesbian, bisexual, and transgender people as sinful. The legitimacy of discrimination against sexual minorities affected many social policies from the debate over civil unions or gay marriage to the rights of domestic partners to work-related benefits to the funding of HIV/AIDS drugs and services. As the twenty-first century began, activists were developing new strategies for mobilizing public sentiment about these issues.

In 2004, the debate over gay civil rights took a public turn when the supreme court of Massachusetts found that the commonwealth's constitution provided the legal basis for same-sex marriage. Congress had already acted in the 1990s to "defend marriage" against the progress of civil unions. Now, conservatives demanded a constitutional amendment to prevent same-sex marriage (and perhaps recognized civil unions as well). Although many states passed bans on same-sex marriage, over time it was hard for most Americans to reconcile their dislike of discrimination with the advocacy of a same-sex marriage ban. Even the political benefits of opposition to gay marriage declined over time. Where in 1996, 68 percent of Americans opposed gay marriage, by 2010, the proportion had declined to 53 percent. Because opposition to gay marriage was highest among older Americans and lowest among younger people, it seemed that gay marriage supporters would likely see their numbers grow in the coming years.[51]

THE GREAT LOCKUP

The biggest retreat on human rights occurred largely out of the public's view. During the 1990s, a larger share of Americans found themselves under the control of the criminal justice system. As prison construction boomed, imprisonment became the most common American response to behavior that was out of the mainstream. By the end of the century, the United States had locked up a larger share of its population than any democracy ever had.

In many ways, the imprisonment boom was curious. Victimization rates—the number of Americans who had actually suffered from a criminal act—declined steadily during the 1990s. In 1993, 5.2 percent of Americans over the age of twelve had experienced some personal crime and 31 percent had experienced a crime against property. By 2003, both of these rates had declined significantly, to 2.3 percent for personal crimes and to 16.1 percent for property crimes.[52]

Yet, this decline in real criminal behavior had little impact on the number of arrests. In 1990, there were 12 arrests for every 1,000 Americans. By 1997, this rate had only declined to 10.4. The disparity between victimization and arrests was even greater for personal crimes. Although the victimization rate for violent crimes had declined from 4.9 to 3.7 percent between 1993 and 1998, the number of arrests for violent crimes only fell from 2.9 to 2.7 per 1,000 during the 1990s.

While actual crime plummeted and arrests remained stable, the number of Americans under correctional supervision—in prison, on probation, or on parole—exploded. In 1990, 4.3 million adults were under correctional supervision. In 2006, the number had reached 7.2 million.

The real focus of the great lockup, however, was racial minorities. By 1996, 2 percent of all whites in the United States were under correctional supervision, but 9 percent of African Americans were. At every stage of the criminal justice system, African Americans found themselves likely to suffer more harsh punishments than whites.

The great lockup of the 1990s carried huge implications for the future of social welfare in the United States. As the amount of prison construction expanded, the amount of school construction languished. The cost of incarcerating such a large share of the population restricted funding for programs that might reduce crime further. Truly frightening was the fact that the costs paled in comparison to what would happen in the future. The popularity of "three strikes" laws, which required life sentences without parole for repeat offenders, made it likely that the prison system of the twenty-first century would be home to a large, aging population.

But the implications of criminal justice policy went beyond prison walls. A criminal record made it more difficult for former inmates to reintegrate in American society. As a result, the great lockup added incentives for former inmates to enter the informal economy, in either criminal or quasi-criminal activities. At the same time, the lockup of so many men meant that the chances of poor women to find stable partners declined. Even as conservatives called for reinforcing the traditional family, their advocacy of harsh criminal justice policy worked to remove men from poor neighborhoods.

Critical Thinking

Critical Thinking Question: What conclusions could one draw about criminal justice policy from these facts about trends in victimization, arrests, and incarceration?

CONCLUSION

American society during the 1990s and early twenty-first century was buffeted by crosscurrents. As revolutions in technology and economic restructuring pushed individuals and families into a brave, new world of computers, genetic engineering, and instantaneous global communications, the fear of change provided a large audience for those who appealed to tradition. The solutions that Americans had developed earlier in the century for the problems of industrial society were less effective at addressing the problems of an information society. As a result, Americans experimented with new ideas at the same time that they hoped the old ones could get them through.

Most important, the implications of the new social and economic realities had yet to penetrate government and the political system. Much like the late nineteenth century, public policy could not keep up with the rapid changes that Americans were experiencing. The public looked to government for solutions to the new realities it faced: less stable jobs, more frequent need for retraining, the challenges of dual-earner families, and acceptance that "life without father" was now the common experience for many children. Yet, the political system seemed intent on rehashing a set of ideological disputes from the previous twenty years. At a time when business seemed interested in managing the realities of a new, diverse workforce, the political system used affirmative action as a wedge issue to divide the public. Where most Americans had come to accept new sexual mores and wanted policy that would prevent these behaviors from leading to illness and death, politicians wanted to discuss the need for "abstinence" and to block the distribution of condoms and family planning information.

The first decade of the new century posed a great challenge to American democracy. Buffeted by many new problems—globalization, international terrorism, the wars in Iraq and Afghanistan, a new wave of immigration, and Hurricane Katrina—many asked if the American people could disenthrall themselves from the comfortable, simplistic view of the world marketed by conservative politicians and develop new answers for a new century. As they staggered forward, the answer to that question remained very much up in the air. Americans seemed torn between a pessimistic, defensive posture toward change and an optimistic openness to its new possibilities. Only time would tell which side of their character would prevail.

Succeed with **PEARSON** **mysocialworklab**

Log onto **www.mysocialworklab.com** and answer the following questions. (*If you did not receive an access code to* **MySocialWorkLab** *with this text and wish to purchase access online, please visit* www.mysocialworklab.com.)

1. **Read the MySocialWorkLibrary case study "Medical Social Work: Stephanie and Rose Doer."** Given the resistance to universal health care in America, what would be society's response to the needs of this family today?

2. **Watch the Core Competency video "Engaging the Client to Share Their Experiences of Alienation, Marginalization."** How are these concepts present in today's views toward social welfare policies?

PRACTICE TEST The following questions will test your knowledge of the content found within this chapter. For additional assessment, including licensing-exam-type questions on applying chapter content to practice, visit **MySocialWorkLab**.

1. The robust economy of the 1990s was due to
   a. new restrictions limiting immigration of persons with low skills.
   b. increased benefits in both social insurance and public assistance.
   c. the United States moving to an information-based economy.
   d. the war in the Middle East.

2. The informal economy was important for low-income workers because
   a. it allowed them to work more than two jobs without penalties.
   b. it allowed them to avoid Social Security and other taxes.
   c. they could make more money in illegal crime activities.
   d. more family members could work without legal papers.

3. Which of the following groups suffered the greatest cost from poverty in the 2000s?
   a. children
   b. elderly
   c. working families
   d. female-headed households

4. The Family and Medical Leave Act has been more useful for
   a. female-headed households.
   b. low-income families.
   c. extended families.
   d. two-career families.

5. Why has there been so much resistance to health care reform?

ASSESS YOUR COMPETENCE Use the following scale to rate your current level of achievement on the following concepts or skills associated with each competency presented in the chapter:

1	2	3
I can accurately describe the concept or skill	I can consistently identify the concept or skill when observing and analyzing practice activities	I can competently implement the concept or skill in my own practice

______ Describe the role that conservatism has played in recent policy decisions.

______ Differentiate between the conservative and liberal view of social welfare policies today.

______ Demonstrate how social workers can play an active role in shaping social welfare policies.

______ Apply the Ecological Model to understanding current social welfare practices.

Social Welfare and the Information Society

The single most important policy innovation of the 1990s was the reform of the public assistance system brought about by PRWORA of 1996. This act changed federal funding for cash assistance to poor families from an open-ended entitlement to a block grant. The act focused the new cash assistance program—TANF—on the short-term relief of need; assistance was limited to five years and states were allowed to impose stricter time limits if they wished. In addition to pushing the states to require welfare recipients to work, the act identified a set of groups—unmarried teen mothers, drug felons, and immigrants—for even greater restrictions on their ability to qualify for assistance.

In order to justify this new departure, the 104th Congress began the act with a set of "Findings" that sought to connect welfare dependency, illegitimacy, and the "crisis" of the American family. As often occurs, advocates of welfare reform drew selectively on a large and complex body of data to support their position. The findings reproduced here are as notable for what they leave out as for what they include. For example, no mention is made of the increasingly unequal distribution of income, worker displacement, or high unemployment that sparked the increase in the welfare rolls during the early 1990s.

Undocumented foreign workers, or "illegal aliens" as many conservatives chose to call them, were also a focus of the supporters of California Proposition 187. This citizen initiative was proposed by Governor Pete Wilson in August 1995 and passed into law on November 4 of that year. The proposal was a response to the fear of Californians that a large number of immigrants—legal and illegal—would threaten wage rates, increase the costs of public welfare, and lead to overcrowding in the schools. The legislation barred all undocumented workers and their families from using public social services, publicly funded health care services, public elementary or secondary schools, or public postsecondary educational institutions. The institutions involved were required to notify the attorney general of California and the U.S. Immigration and Naturalization Service of the presence of any "illegal alien."

Emergency health care, the Supplemental Food Program for Women, Infants, and Children (WIC), school lunches and breakfasts, and public education are the only federally mandated benefits available to undocumented workers. Thus, this act effectively would have removed any safety net. In response to a suit brought by the American Civil Liberties Union, the Mexican American Legal Defense and Education Fund, and other immigrant rights groups, most of Proposition 187 was declared unconstitutional in California just one year after it was enacted. It will be years before the case reaches the Supreme Court. Meanwhile, however, the intent to discourage Mexican immigration is clear.

Changes in Americans' ideas about gender and sexuality were at the heart of social transformations of the 1990s and early twenty-first century. The Supreme Court entered this debate in its 2003 decision overruling Texas's antisodomy law. The Court had to reverse its 1986 decision that upheld a similar law in Georgia. Justice Kennedy did so by drawing on recent work by scholars who found that legal discrimination against gays and lesbians is a relatively recent development. He also cited the findings of European courts to rebut the belief that "Western civilization" had a long-standing antipathy to gays and lesbians.

The legal strategy used by the Court majority, however, could come to haunt pro-choice forces in the future. Justice Scalia, in a characteristically forceful dissent, noted that the Court had chosen not to overrule *Roe* v. *Wade* in 1992 because of its respect for precedents, *stare decisis*. If the Court were willing to overturn precedents in this case, Scalia suggested, it might eventually revisit whether *stare decisis* needed to be respected in the case of abortion.

UNITED STATES PUBLIC LAWS

104TH CONGRESS—SECOND SESSION

PUBLIC LAW 104-193 [H.R. 3734]

AUGUST 21, 1996

PERSONAL RESPONSIBILITY AND WORK

OPPORTUNITY RECONCILIATION ACT

OF 1996

104 P.L. 193; 110 STAT. 2105;

1996 ENACTED H.R. 3734;

104 ENACTED H.R. 3734

An Act

To provide for reconciliation pursuant to section 201(a)(1) of the concurrent resolution on the budget for fiscal year 1997.

Be it enacted by the Senate and House of Representatives of the United States of America in Congress assembled,

SECTION 1. SHORT TITLE

This Act may be cited as the "Personal Responsibility and Work Opportunity Reconciliation Act of 1996."

TITLE I—BLOCK GRANTS FOR TEMPORARY ASSISTANCE FOR NEEDY FAMILIES

Sec. 101. FINDINGS.
The Congress makes the following findings:

(1) Marriage is the foundation of a successful society.

(2) Marriage is an essential institution of a successful society which promotes the interests of children.

(3) Promotion of responsible fatherhood and motherhood is integral to successful child rearing and the well-being of children.

(4) In 1992, only 54 percent of single-parent families with children had a child support order established and, of that 54 percent, only about one-half received the full amount due. Of the cases enforced through the public child support enforcement system, only 18 percent of the case-load has a collection.

(5) The number of individuals receiving aid to families with dependent children (in this section referred to as "AFDC") has more than tripled since 1965. More than two-thirds of these recipients are children. Eighty-nine

percent of children receiving AFDC benefits now live in homes in which no father is present.

(A) (i) The average monthly number of children receiving AFDC benefits—

(I) was 3,300,000 in 1965;

(II) was 6,200,000 in 1970;

(III) was 7,400,000 in 1980; and

(IV) was 9,300,000 in 1992.

(ii) While the number of children receiving AFDC benefits increased nearly threefold between 1965 and 1992, the total number of children in the United States aged 0 to 18 has declined by 5.5 percent.

(B) The Department of Health and Human Services has estimated that 12,000,000 children will receive AFDC benefits within 10 years.

(C) The increase in the number of children receiving public assistance is closely related to the increase in births to unmarried women. Between 1970 and 1991, the percentage of live births to unmarried women increased nearly threefold, from 10.7 percent to 29.5 percent.

(6) The increase of out-of-wedlock pregnancies and births is well documented as follows:

(A) It is estimated that the rate of nonmarital teen pregnancy rose 23 percent from 54 pregnancies per 1,000 unmarried teenagers in 1976 to 66.7 pregnancies in 1991. The overall rate of nonmarital pregnancy rose 14 percent from 90.8 pregnancies per 1,000 unmarried women in 1980 to 103 in both 1991 and 1992. In contrast, the overall pregnancy rate for married couples decreased 7.3 percent between 1980 and 1991, from 126.9 pregnancies per 1,000 married women in 1980 to 117.6 pregnancies in 1991.

(B) The total of all out-of-wedlock births between 1970 and 1991 has risen from 10.7 percent to 29.5 percent and if the current trend continues, 50 percent of all births by the year 2015 will be out-of-wedlock.

(7) An effective strategy to combat teenage pregnancy must address the issue of male responsibility, including statutory rape culpability and prevention. The increase of teenage pregnancies among the youngest girls is particularly severe and is linked to predatory sexual practices by men who are significantly older.

(A) It is estimated that in the late 1980's, the rate for girls age 14 and under giving birth increased 26 percent.

(B) Data indicates that at least half of the children born to teenage mothers are fathered by adult men. Available data suggests that almost 70 percent of births to teenage girls are fathered by men over age 20.

(C) Surveys of teen mothers have revealed that a majority of such mothers have histories of sexual and physical abuse, primarily with older adult men.

(8) The negative consequences of an out-of-wedlock birth on the mother, the child, the family, and society are well documented as follows:

(A) Young women 17 and under who give birth outside of marriage are more likely to go on public assistance and to spend more years on welfare once enrolled. These combined effects of "younger and longer" increase total AFDC costs per household by 25 percent to 30 percent for 17-year-olds.

(B) Children born out-of-wedlock have a substantially higher risk of being born at a very low or moderately low birth weight.

(C) Children born out-of-wedlock are more likely to experience low verbal cognitive attainment, as well as more child abuse, and neglect.

(D) Children born out-of-wedlock were more likely to have lower cognitive scores, lower educational aspirations, and a greater likelihood of becoming teenage parents themselves.

(E) Being born out-of-wedlock significantly reduces the chances of the child growing up to have an intact marriage.

(F) Children born out-of-wedlock are 3 times more likely to be on welfare when they grow up.

(9) Currently 35 percent of children in single-parent homes were born out-of-wedlock, nearly the same percentage as that of children in single-parent homes whose parents are divorced (37 percent). While many parents find themselves, through divorce or tragic circumstances beyond their control, facing the difficult task of raising children alone, nevertheless, the negative consequences of raising children in single-parent homes are well documented as follows:

(A) Only 9 percent of married-couple families with children under 18 years of age have income below the national poverty level. In contrast, 46 percent of female-headed households with children under 18 years of age are below the national poverty level.

(B) Among single-parent families, nearly 1/2 of the mothers who never married received AFDC while only 1/5 of divorced mothers received AFDC.

(C) Children born into families receiving welfare assistance are 3 times more likely to be on welfare when they reach adulthood than children not born into families receiving welfare.

(D) Mothers under 20 years of age are at the greatest risk of bearing low birth weight babies.

(E) The younger the single-parent mother, the less likely she is to finish high school.

(F) Young women who have children before finishing high school are more likely to receive welfare assistance for a longer period of time.

(G) Between 1985 and 1990, the public cost of births to teenage mothers under the aid to families with dependent children program, the food stamp program, and the medicaid program has been estimated at $120,000,000,000.

(H) The absence of a father in the life a child has a negative effect on school performance and peer adjustment.

(I) Children of teenage single parents have lower cognitive scores, lower educational aspirations, and a greater likelihood of becoming teenage parents themselves.

(J) Children of single-parent homes are 3 times more likely to fail and repeat a year in grade school than are children from intact 2-parent families.

(K) Children from single-parent homes are almost 4 times more likely to be expelled or suspended from school.

(L) Neighborhoods with larger percentages of youth aged 12 through 20 and areas with higher percentages of single-parent households have higher rates of violent crime.

(M) Of those youth held for criminal offenses within the State juvenile justice system, only 29.8 percent lived primarily in a home with both parents. In contrast to these incarcerated youth, 73.9 percent of the 62,800,000 children in the Nation's resident population were living with both parents.

(10) Therefore, in light of this demonstration of the crisis in our Nation, it is the sense of the Congress that prevention of out-of-wedlock pregnancy and reduction in out-of-wedlock birth are very important Government interests and the policy contained in part A of title IV of the Social Security Act (as amended by section 103(a) of this Act) is intended to address the crisis. . . .

PART A—BLOCK GRANTS TO STATES
FOR TEMPORARY ASSISTANCE FOR NEEDY FAMILIES

401 Sec. 401. Purpose.

(a) In General.—The purpose of this part is to increase the flexibility of States in operating a program designed to—

(1) provide assistance to needy families so that children may be cared for in their own homes or in the homes of relatives;

(2) end the dependence of needy parents on government benefits by promoting job preparation, work, and marriage;

(3) prevent and reduce the incidence of out-of-wedlock pregnancies and establish annual numerical goals for preventing and reducing the incidence of these pregnancies; and

(4) encourage the formation and maintenance of two-parent families.

(b) No Individual Entitlement.—This part shall not be interpreted to entitle any individual or family to assistance under any State program funded under this part. . . .

***

Prop. 187   NOVEMBER ELECTION PROPOSITIONS

INITIATIVE STATUTE—ILLEGAL ALIENS—PUBLIC SERVICES, VERIFICATION, AND REPORTING

PROPOSITION 187

PROPOSED LAW

The People of California find and declare as follows:

SECTION 1. Findings and Declaration.

That they have suffered and are suffering economic hardship caused by the presence of illegal aliens in this state.

That they have suffered and are suffering personal injury and damage caused by the criminal conduct of illegal aliens in this state.

That they have a right to the protection of their government from any person or persons entering this country unlawfully.

Therefore, the People of California declare their intention to provide for cooperation between their agencies of state and local government with the federal government, and to establish a system of required notification by and between such agencies to prevent illegal aliens in the United States from receiving benefits or public services in the State of California.

SECTION 2. Manufacture, Distribution or Sale of False Citizenship or Resident Alien Documents: Crime and Punishment.

Section 113 is added to the Penal Code, to read:

113. Any person who manufactures, distributes or sells false documents to conceal the true citizenship or resident alien status of another person is guilty of a felony, and shall be punished by imprisonment in the state prison for five years or by a fine of seventy-five thousand dollars ($75,000).

SECTION 3. Use of False Citizenship or Resident Alien Documents: Crime and Punishment.

Section 114 is added to the Penal Code, to read:

114. Any person who uses false documents to conceal his or her true citizenship or resident alien status is guilty of a felony, and shall be punished by imprisonment in the state prison for five years or by a fine of twenty-five thousand dollars ($25,000).

SECTION 4. Law Enforcement Cooperation with INS.

Section 834b is added to the Penal Code, to read:

834b. (a) Every law enforcement agency in California shall fully cooperate with the United States Immigration and Naturalization Service regarding any person who is arrested if he or she is suspected of being present in the United States in violation of federal immigration laws.

(b) With respect to any such person who is arrested, and suspected of being present in the United States in violation of federal immigration laws, every law enforcement agency shall do the following:

(1) Attempt to verify the legal status of such person as a citizen of the United States, an alien lawfully admitted as a permanent resident, an alien lawfully admitted for a temporary period of time or as an alien who is present in the United States in violation of immigration laws. The verification process may include, but shall not be limited to, questioning the person regarding his or her date and place of birth, and entry into the United States, and demanding documentation to indicate his or her legal status.

(2) Notify the person of his or her apparent status as an alien who is present in the United States in violation of federal immigration laws and inform him or her that, apart from any criminal justice proceedings, he or she must either obtain legal status or leave the United States.

(3) Notify the Attorney General of California and the United States Immigration and Naturalization Service of the apparent illegal status and provide any additional information that may be requested by any other public entity.

(c) Any legislative, administrative, or other action by a city, county, or other legally authorized local governmental entity with jurisdictional boundaries, or by a law enforcement agency, to prevent or limit the cooperation required by subdivision (a) is expressly prohibited.

SECTION 5. Exclusion of Illegal Aliens from Public Social Services.

Section 10001.5 is added to the Welfare and Institutions Code, to read:

10001.5. (a) In order to carry out the intention of the People of California that only citizens of the United States and aliens lawfully admitted to the United States may receive the benefits of public social services and to ensure that all persons employed in the providing of those services shall diligently protect public funds from misuse, the provisions of this section are adopted.

(b) A person shall not receive any public social services to which he or she may be otherwise entitled until the legal status of that person has been verified as one of the following:

(1) A citizen of the United States.

(2) An alien lawfully admitted as a permanent resident.

(3) An alien lawfully admitted for a temporary period of time.

(c) If any public entity in this state to whom a person has applied for public social services determines or reasonably suspects, based upon the information provided to it, that the person is an alien in the United States in violation of federal law, the following procedures shall be followed by the public entity:

(1) The entity shall not provide the person with benefits or services.

(2) The entity shall, in writing, notify the person of his or her apparent illegal immigration status, and that the person must either obtain legal status or leave the United States.

(3) The entity shall also notify the State Director of Social Services, the Attorney General of California, and the United States Immigration and Naturalization Service of the apparent illegal status, and shall provide any additional information that may be requested by any other public entity.

SECTION 6. Exclusion of Illegal Aliens from Publicly Funded Health Care.

Chapter 1.3 (commencing with Section 130) is added to Part 1 of Division 1 of the Health and Safety Code, to read:

CHAPTER 1.3. PUBLICLY-FUNDED HEALTH CARE SERVICES

130. (a) In order to carry out the intention of the People of California that, excepting emergency medical care as required by federal law, only citizens of the United States and aliens lawfully admitted to the United States may receive the benefits of publicly-funded health care, and to ensure that all persons employed in the providing of those services shall diligently protect public funds from misuse, the provisions of this section are adopted.

(b) A person shall not receive any health care services from a publicly-funded health care facility, to which he or she is otherwise entitled until the legal status of that person has been verified as one of the following:

(1) A citizen of the United States.

(2) An alien lawfully admitted as a permanent resident.

(3) An alien lawfully admitted for a temporary period of time.

(c) If any publicly-funded health care facility in this state from whom a person seeks health care services, other than emergency medical care as required by federal law, determines or reasonably suspects, based upon the information provided to it, that the person is an alien in the United States in violation of federal law, the following procedures shall be followed by the facility:

(1) The facility shall not provide the person with services.

(2) The facility shall, in writing, notify the person of his or her apparent illegal immigration status, and that the person must either obtain legal status or leave the United States.

(3) The facility shall also notify the State Director of Health Services, the Attorney General of California, and the United States Immigration and Naturalization Service of the apparent illegal status, and shall provide any additional information that may be requested by any other public entity.

(d) For purposes of this section "publicly-funded health care facility" shall be defined as specified in Sections 1200 and 1250 of this code as of January 1, 1993.

SECTION 7. Exclusion of Illegal Aliens from Public Elementary and Secondary Schools.

Section 48215 is added to the Education Code, to read:

48215. (a) No public elementary or secondary school shall admit, or permit the attendance of, any child who is not a citizen of the United States, an alien lawfully admitted as a permanent resident, or a person who is otherwise authorized under federal law to be present in the United States.

(b) Commencing January 1, 1995, each school district shall verify the legal status of each child enrolling in the school district for the first time in order to ensure the enrollment or attendance only of citizens, aliens lawfully admitted as permanent residents, or persons who are otherwise authorized to be present in the United States.

(c) By January 1, 1996, each school district shall have verified the legal status of each child already enrolled and in attendance in the school district in order to ensure the enrollment or attendance only of citizens, aliens lawfully admitted as permanent residents, or persons who are otherwise authorized under federal law to be present in the United States.

(d) By January 1, 1996, each school district shall also have verified the legal status of each parent or guardian of each child referred to in subdivisions (b) and (c), to determine whether such parent or guardian is one of the following:

(1) A citizen of the United States.

(2) An alien lawfully admitted as a permanent resident.

(3) An alien admitted lawfully for a temporary period of time.

(e) Each school district shall provide information to the State Superintendent of Public Instruction, the Attorney General of California, and the United States Immigration and Naturalization Service regarding any enrollee or pupil, or parent or guardian, attending a public elementary or secondary school in the school district determined or reasonably suspected to be in violation of federal immigration laws within forty-five days after becoming aware of an apparent violation. The notice shall also be provided to the parent or legal guardian of the enrollee or pupil, and shall state that an existing pupil may not continue to attend the school after ninety calendar days from the date of the notice, unless legal status is established.

(f) For each child who cannot establish legal status in the United States, each school district shall continue to provide education for a period of ninety days from the date of the notice. Such ninety day period shall be utilized to accomplish an orderly transition to a school in the child's country of origin. Each school district shall fully cooperate in this transition effort to ensure that the educational needs of the child are best served for that period of time.

SECTION 8. Exclusion of Illegal Aliens from Public Postsecondary Educational Institutions.

Section 66010.8 is added to the Education Code, to read:

66010.8 (a) No public institution of postsecondary education shall admit, enroll, or permit the attendance of any person who is not a citizen of the United States, an alien lawfully admitted as a permanent resident in the United States, or a person who is otherwise authorized under federal law to be present in the United States.

(b) Commencing with the first term or semester that begins after January 1, 1995, and at the commencement of each term or semester thereafter, each public postsecondary educational institution shall verify the status of each person enrolled or in attendance at that institution in order to ensure the enrollment or attendance only of United States citizens, aliens lawfully admitted as permanent residents in the United States, and persons who are otherwise authorized under federal law to be present in the United States.

(c) No later than 45 days after the admissions officer of a public postsecondary educational institution becomes aware of the application, enrollment, or attendance of a person determined to be, or who is under reasonable suspicion of being, in the United States in violation of federal immigration laws, that officer shall provide that information to the State Superintendent of Public

Instruction, the Attorney General of California, and the United States Immigration and Naturalization Service. The information shall also be provided to the applicant, enrollee, or person admitted.

SECTION 9. Attorney General Cooperation with the INS.

Section 53069.65 is added to the Government Code, to read:

53069.65. Whenever the state or a city, or a county, or any other legally authorized local governmental entity with jurisdictional boundaries reports the presence of a person who is suspected of being present in the United States in violation of federal immigration laws to the Attorney General of California, that report shall be transmitted to the United States Immigration and Naturalization Service. The Attorney General shall be responsible for maintaining on-going and accurate records of such reports, and shall provide any additional information that may be requested by any other government entity.

SECTION 10. Amendment and Severability.

The statutory provisions contained in this measure may not be amended by the Legislature except to further its purposes by statute passed in each house by rollcall vote entered in the journal, two-thirds of the membership concurring, or by a statute that becomes effective only when approved by the voters.

In the event that any portion of this act or the application thereof to any person or circumstance is held invalid, that invalidity shall not affect any other provision or application of the act, which can be given effect without the invalid provision or application, and to that end the provisions of this act are severable.

SUPREME COURT OF THE UNITED STATES

No. 02-102

JOHN GEDDES LAWRENCE AND TYRON GARNER, PETITIONERS

v.

TEXAS

ON WRIT OF CERTIORARI TO THE COURT OF APPEALS OF TEXAS,

FOURTEENTH DISTRICT
[June 26, 2003]

JUSTICE KENNEDY delivered the opinion of the Court.

Liberty protects the person from unwarranted government intrusions into a dwelling or other private places. In our tradition the State is not omnipresent in the home. And there are other spheres of our lives and existence, outside the home, where the State should not be a dominant presence. Freedom extends beyond spatial bounds. Liberty presumes an autonomy of self that includes freedom of thought, belief, expression, and certain intimate conduct. The instant case involves liberty of the person both in its spatial and more transcendent dimensions.

I

The question before the Court is the validity of a Texas statute making it a crime for two persons of the same sex to engage in certain intimate sexual conduct. In Houston, Texas, officers of the Harris County Police Department were dispatched to a private residence in response to a reported weapons disturbance. They entered an apartment where one of the petitioners, John Geddes Lawrence, resided. The right of the police to enter does not seem to have been questioned. The officers observed Lawrence and another man, Tyron Garner, engaging in a sexual act. The two petitioners were arrested, held in custody over night, and charged and convicted before a Justice of the Peace.

The complaints described their crime as "deviate sexual intercourse, namely anal sex, with a member of the same sex (man)." App. to Pet. for Cert. 127a, 139a. The applicable state law is Tex. Penal Code Ann. §21.06(a) (2003). It provides: "A person commits an offense if he engages in deviate sexual intercourse with another individual of the same sex." . . .

The petitioners exercised their right to a trial *de novo* in Harris County Criminal Court. They challenged the statute as a violation of the Equal Protection Clause of the Fourteenth Amendment and of a like provision of the Texas Constitution. Tex. Const., Art. 1, § 3a. Those contentions were rejected. The petitioners, having entered a plea of *nolo contendere*, were each fined $200 and assessed court costs of $141.25. App. to Pet. for Cert. 107a-110a.

The Court of Appeals for the Texas Fourteenth District considered the petitioners' federal constitutional arguments under both the Equal Protection and Due Process Clauses of the Fourteenth Amendment. After hearing the case en banc the court, in a divided opinion, rejected the constitutional arguments and affirmed the convictions. 41 S. W. 3d 349 (Tex. App. 2001). The majority opinion indicates that the Court of Appeals considered our decision in *Bowers v. Hardwick*, 478 U. S. 186 (1986), to be controlling on the federal due process aspect of the case. *Bowers* then being authoritative, this was proper.

We granted certiorari, 537 U. S. 1044 (2002), to consider three questions:

> (1) Whether Petitioners' criminal convictions under the Texas "Homosexual Conduct" law—which criminalizes sexual intimacy by same-sex couples, but not identical behavior by different-sex couples—violate the Fourteenth Amendment guarantee of equal protection of laws?
>
> (2) Whether Petitioners' criminal convictions for adult consensual sexual intimacy in the home violate their vital interests in liberty and privacy protected by the Due Process Clause of the Fourteenth Amendment?
>
> (3) Whether *Bowers v. Hardwick*, 478 U. S. 186 (1986), should be overruled? Pet. for Cert. i.

The petitioners were adults at the time of the alleged offense. Their conduct was in private and consensual.

II

We conclude the case should be resolved by determining whether the petitioners were free as adults to engage in the private conduct in the exercise of their liberty under the Due Process Clause of the Fourteenth Amendment to the Constitution. For this inquiry we deem it necessary to reconsider the Court's holding in *Bowers*.

There are broad statements of the substantive reach of liberty under the Due Process Clause in earlier cases, including *Pierce v. Society of Sisters*, 268 U. S. 510 (1925), and *Meyer v. Nebraska*, 262 U. S. 390 (1923); but the most pertinent beginning point is our decision in *Griswold v. Connecticut*, 381 U. S. 479 (1965).

In *Griswold* the Court invalidated a state law prohibiting the use of drugs or devices of contraception and counseling or aiding and abetting the use of contraceptives. The Court described the protected interest as a right to privacy and placed emphasis on the marriage relation and the protected space of the marital bedroom. *Id.*, at 485.

After *Griswold* it was established that the right to make certain decisions regarding sexual conduct extends beyond the marital relationship. In *Eisenstadt v. Baird*, 405 U. S. 438 (1972), the Court invalidated a law prohibiting the distribution of contraceptives to unmarried persons. The case was decided under the Equal Protection Clause, *id.*, at 454; but with respect to unmarried persons, the Court went on to state the fundamental proposition that the law impaired the exercise of their personal rights, *ibid*. It quoted from the statement of the Court of Appeals finding the law to be in conflict with fundamental human rights, and it followed with this statement of its own:

> "It is true that in *Griswold* the right of privacy in question inhered in the marital relationship. . . . If the right of privacy means anything, it is the right of the *individual*, married or single, to be free from unwarranted governmental intrusion into matters so fundamentally affecting a person as the decision whether to bear or beget a child. *Id.*, at 453.

The opinions in *Griswold* and *Eisenstadt* were part of the background for the decision in *Roe v. Wade*, 410 U. S. 113 (1973). As is well known, the case involved a challenge to the Texas law prohibiting abortions, but the laws of other States were affected as well. Although the Court held the woman's rights were not absolute, her right to elect an abortion did have real and substantial protection as an exercise of her liberty under the Due Process Clause. The Court cited cases that protect spatial freedom and cases that go well beyond it. *Roe* recognized the right of a woman to make certain fundamental decisions affecting her destiny and confirmed once more that the protection of liberty under the Due Process Clause has a substantive dimension of fundamental significance in defining the rights of the person.

In *Carey v. Population Services Int'l*, 431 U. S. 678 (1977), the Court confronted a New York law forbidding sale or distribution of contraceptive devices to persons under 16 years of age. Although there was no single opinion for the Court, the law was invalidated. Both *Eisenstadt* and *Carey*, as well as the holding and rationale in *Roe*, confirmed that the reasoning of *Griswold* could not be confined to the protection of rights of married adults. This was the state of the law with respect to some of the most relevant cases when the Court considered *Bowers v. Hardwick*.

The facts in *Bowers* had some similarities to the instant case. A police officer, whose right to enter seems not to have been in question, observed Hardwick, in his own bedroom, engaging in intimate sexual conduct with another adult male. The conduct was in violation of a Georgia statute making it a criminal offense to engage in sodomy. One difference between the two cases is that the Georgia statute prohibited the conduct whether or not the participants were of the same sex, while the Texas statute, as we have seen, applies only to participants of the same sex. Hardwick was not prosecuted, but he brought an action in federal court to declare the state statute invalid. He alleged he was a practicing homosexual and that the criminal prohibition violated rights guaranteed to him by the Constitution. The Court, in an opinion by Justice White, sustained the Georgia law. Chief Justice Burger and Justice Powell joined the opinion of the Court and filed separate, concurring opinions. Four Justices dissented.

. . .

In academic writings, and in many of the scholarly *amicus* briefs filed to assist the Court in this case, there are fundamental criticisms of the historical premises relied upon by the majority and concurring opinions in *Bowers*. . . . We need not enter this debate in the attempt to reach a definitive historical judgment, but the following considerations counsel against adopting the definitive conclusions upon which *Bowers* placed such reliance.

At the outset it should be noted that there is no longstanding history in this country of laws directed at homosexual conduct as a distinct matter. Beginning in colonial times there were prohibitions of sodomy derived from the English criminal laws passed in the first instance by the Reformation Parliament of 1533. The English prohibition was understood to include relations between men and women as well as relations between men and men. See, *e.g., King v. Wiseman*, 92 Eng. Rep. 774, 775 (K. B. 1718) (interpreting "mankind" in Act of 1533 as including women and girls). Nineteenth-century commentators similarly read American sodomy, buggery, and crime-against-nature statutes as criminalizing certain relations between men and women and between men and men. . . . The absence of legal prohibitions focusing on homosexual conduct may be explained in part by noting that according to some scholars the concept of the homosexual as a distinct category of person did not emerge until the late 19th century. See, *e.g.,* J. Katz, The Invention of Heterosexuality 10 (1995); J. D'Emilio & E. Freedman, Intimate Matters: A History of Sexuality in America 121 (2d ed. 1997) ("The modern terms *homosexuality* and *heterosexuality* do not apply to an era that had not yet articulated these distinctions"). Thus early American sodomy laws were not directed at homosexuals as such but instead sought to prohibit nonprocreative sexual activity more generally. This does not suggest approval of homosexual conduct. It does tend to show that this particular form of conduct was not thought of as a separate category from like conduct between heterosexual persons.

Laws prohibiting sodomy do not seem to have been enforced against consenting adults acting in private. A substantial number of sodomy prosecutions and convictions for which there are surviving records were for predatory acts against those who could not or did not consent, as in the case of a minor or the victim of an assault. As to these, one purpose for the prohibitions was to ensure there would be no lack of coverage if a predator committed a sexual assault that did not constitute rape as defined by the criminal law.

. . .

In summary, the historical grounds relied upon in *Bowers* are more complex than the majority opinion and the concurring opinion by Chief Justice Burger indicate. Their historical premises are not without doubt and, at the very least, are overstated.

. . .

Of even more importance, almost five years before *Bowers* was decided the European Court of Human Rights considered a case with parallels to *Bowers* and to today's case. An adult male resident in Northern Ireland alleged he was a practicing homosexual who desired to engage in consensual homosexual conduct. The laws of Northern Ireland forbade him that right. He alleged that he had been questioned, his home had been searched, and he feared criminal prosecution. The court held that the laws proscribing the conduct were invalid under the European Convention on Human Rights. *Dudgeon v. United Kingdom*, 45 Eur. Ct. H. R. (1981) ¶52.

Authoritative in all countries that are members of the Council of Europe (21 nations then, 45 nations now), the decision is at odds with the premise in *Bowers* that the claim put forward was insubstantial in our Western civilization.

In our own constitutional system the deficiencies in *Bowers* became even more apparent in the years following its announcement. The 25 States with laws prohibiting the relevant conduct referenced in the *Bowers* decision are reduced now to 13, of which 4 enforce their laws only against homosexual conduct. In those States where sodomy is still proscribed, whether for same-sex or heterosexual conduct, there is a pattern of nonenforcement with respect to consenting adults acting in private. The State of Texas admitted in 1994 that as of that date it had not prosecuted anyone under those circumstances.

. . .

In explaining the respect the Constitution demands for the autonomy of the person in making these choices, we stated as follows: "These matters, involving the most intimate and personal choices a person may make in a lifetime, choices central to personal dignity and autonomy, are central to the liberty protected by the Fourteenth Amendment. At the heart of liberty is the right to define one's own concept of existence, of meaning, of the universe, and of the mystery of human life. Beliefs about these matters could not define the attributes of personhood were they formed under compulsion of the State." Persons in a homosexual relationship may seek autonomy for these purposes, just as heterosexual persons do. The decision in *Bowers* would deny them this right.

. . .

To the extent *Bowers* relied on values we share with a wider civilization, it should be noted that the reasoning and holding in *Bowers* have been rejected elsewhere. The European Court of Human Rights has followed not *Bowers* but its own decision in *Dudgeon v. United Kingdom*. See *P. G. & J. H. v. United Kingdom*, App. No. 00044787/98, ¶56 (Eur. Ct. H. R., Sept. 25, 2001); *Modinos v. Cyprus*, 259 Eur. Ct. H. R. (1993); *Norris v. Ireland*, 142 Eur. Ct. H. R. (1988). Other nations, too, have taken action consistent with an affirmation of the protected right of homosexual adults to engage in intimate, consensual conduct. See Brief for Mary Robinson et al. as *Amici Curiae* 11-12. The right the petitioners seek in this case has been accepted as an integral part of human freedom in many other countries. There has been no showing that in this country the governmental interest in circumscribing personal choice is somehow more legitimate or urgent.

. . .

Bowers was not correct when it was decided, and it is not correct today. It ought not to remain binding precedent. *Bowers v. Hardwick* should be and now is overruled.

The present case does not involve minors. It does not involve persons who might be injured or coerced or who are situated in relationships where consent might not easily be refused. It does not involve public conduct or prostitution. It does not involve whether the government must give formal recognition to any relationship that homosexual persons seek to enter. The case does involve two adults who, with full and mutual consent from each other, engaged in sexual practices common to a homosexual lifestyle. The petitioners are entitled to respect for their private lives. The State cannot demean their existence or control their destiny by making their private sexual conduct a crime. Their right to liberty under the Due Process Clause gives them the full right to engage in their conduct without intervention of the government. "It is a promise of the Constitution that there is a realm of personal liberty which the government may not enter." *Casey*, supra, at 847. The Texas statute furthers no legitimate state interest which can justify its intrusion into the personal and private life of the individual.

Had those who drew and ratified the Due Process Clauses of the Fifth Amendment or the Fourteenth Amendment known the components of liberty in its manifold possibilities, they might have been more specific. They did not presume to have this insight. They knew times can blind us to certain truths and later generations can see that laws once thought necessary and proper in fact serve only to oppress. As the Constitution endures, persons in every generation can invoke its principles in their own search for greater freedom.

The judgment of the Court of Appeals for the Texas Fourteenth District is reversed, and the case is remanded for further proceedings not inconsistent with this opinion. It is so ordered.

. . .

JUSTICE SCALIA, with whom THE CHIEF JUSTICE and JUSTICE THOMAS join, dissenting.

"Liberty finds no refuge in a jurisprudence of doubt." *Planned Parenthood of Southeastern Pa. v. Casey*, 505 U. S. 833, 844 (1992). That was the Court's sententious response, barely more than a decade ago, to those seeking to overrule *Roe v. Wade*, 410 U. S. 113 (1973). The Court's response today, to those who have engaged in a 17-year crusade to overrule *Bowers v. Hardwick*, 478 U. S. 186 (1986), is very different. The need for stability and certainty presents no barrier.

Most of the rest of today's opinion has no relevance to its actual holding—that the Texas statute "furthers no legitimate state interest which can justify" its application to petitioners under rational-basis review. *Ante*, at 18 (overruling *Bowers* to the extent it sustained Georgia's anti-sodomy statute under the rational-basis test). Though there is discussion of "fundamental proposition[s]," *ante*, at 4, and "fundamental decisions," *ibid.* nowhere does the Court's opinion declare that homosexual sodomy is a "fundamental right" under the Due Process Clause; nor does it subject the Texas law to the standard of review that would be appropriate (strict scrutiny) if homosexual sodomy *were* a "fundamental right." Thus, while overruling the *outcome* of *Bowers*, the Court leaves strangely untouched its central legal conclusion: "[R]espondent would have us announce . . . a fundamental right to engage in homosexual sodomy. This we are quite unwilling to do." 478 U. S., at 191. Instead the Court simply describes petitioners' conduct as "an exercise of their liberty"—which it undoubtedly is—and proceeds to apply an unheard-of form of rational-basis review that will have far-reaching implications beyond this case. *Ante*, at 3.

I

I begin with the Court's surprising readiness to reconsider a decision rendered a mere 17 years ago in *Bowers v. Hardwick*. I do not myself believe in rigid adherence to *stare decisis* in constitutional cases; but I do believe that we should be consistent rather than manipulative in invoking the doctrine. Today's opinions in support of reversal do not bother to distinguish—or indeed, even bother to mention—the paean to *stare decisis* coauthored by three Members of today's majority in *Planned Parenthood v. Casey*. There, when *stare decisis* meant preservation of judicially invented abortion rights, the widespread criticism of *Roe* was strong reason to *reaffirm* it:

> "Where, in the performance of its judicial duties, the Court decides a case in such a way as to resolve the sort of intensely divisive controversy reflected in *Roe*[,] . . . its decision has a dimension that the resolution of

the normal case does not carry. . . . [T]o overrule under fire in the absence of the most compelling reason . . . would subvert the Court's legitimacy beyond any serious question." 505 U. S., at 866–867.

Today, however, the widespread opposition to *Bowers*, a decision resolving an issue as "intensely divisive" as the issue in *Roe*, is offered as a reason in favor of *overruling* it. See *ante*, at 15–16. Gone, too, is any "enquiry" (of the sort conducted in *Casey*) into whether the decision sought to be overruled has "proven 'unworkable,' " *Casey, supra*, at 855.

Today's approach to *stare decisis* invites us to overrule an erroneously decided precedent (including an "intensely divisive" decision) *if*: (1) its foundations have been "eroded" by subsequent decisions, *ante*, at 15; (2) it has been subject to "substantial and continuing" criticism, *ibid*.; and (3) it has not induced "individual or societal reliance" that counsels against overturning, *ante*, at 16. The problem is that *Roe* itself—which today's majority surely has no disposition to overrule—satisfies these conditions to at least the same degree as *Bowers*.

. . .

It seems to me that the "societal reliance" on the principles confirmed in *Bowers* and discarded today has been overwhelming. Countless judicial decisions and legislative enactments have relied on the ancient proposition that a governing majority's belief that certain sexual behavior is "immoral and unacceptable" constitutes a rational basis for regulation. See, *e.g., Williams v. Pryor*, 240 F. 3d 944, 949 (CA11 2001) (citing *Bowers* in upholding Alabama's prohibition on the sale of sex toys on the ground that "[t]he crafting and safeguarding of public morality . . . indisputably is a legitimate government interest under rational basis scrutiny"); *Milner v. Apfel*, 148 F. 3d 812, 814 (CA7 1998) (citing *Bowers* for the proposition that "[l]egislatures are permitted to legislate with regard to morality . . . rather than confined to preventing demonstrable harms"); *Holmes v. California Army National Guard* 124 F. 3d 1126, 1136 (CA9 1997) (relying on *Bowers* in upholding the federal statute and regulations banning from military service those who engage in homosexual conduct); *Owens v. State*, 352 Md. 663, 683, 724 A. 2d 43, 53 (1999) (relying on *Bowers* in holding that "a person has no constitutional right to engage in sexual intercourse, at least outside of marriage"); *Sherman v. Henry*, 928 S. W. 2d 464, 469–473 (Tex. 1996) (relying on *Bowers* in rejecting a claimed constitutional right to commit adultery). We ourselves relied extensively on *Bowers* when we concluded, in *Barnes v. Glen Theatre, Inc.*, 501 U. S. 560, 569 (1991), that Indiana's public indecency statute furthered "a substantial government interest in protecting order and morality," *ibid.*, (plurality opinion);

. . .

State laws against bigamy, same-sex marriage, adult incest, prostitution, masturbation, adultery, fornication, bestiality, and obscenity are likewise sustainable only in light of *Bowers*' validation of laws based on moral choices. Every single one of these laws is called into question by today's decision; the Court makes no effort to cabin the scope of its decision to exclude them from its holding. . . . The impossibility of distinguishing homosexuality from other traditional "morals" offenses is precisely why *Bowers* rejected the rational-basis challenge. "The law," it said, "is constantly based on notions of morality, and if all laws representing essentially moral choices are to be invalidated under the Due Process Clause, the courts will be very busy indeed."

JUSTICE THOMAS dissenting. I join JUSTICE SCALIA'S dissenting opinion.

I write separately to note that the law before the Court today "is . . . uncommonly silly." *Griswold v. Connecticut*, 381 U. S. 479, 527 (1965) (Stewart, J., dissenting). If I were a member of the Texas Legislature, I would vote to repeal it. Punishing someone for expressing his sexual preference through noncommercial consensual conduct with another adult does not appear to be a worthy way to expend valuable law enforcement resources.

Notwithstanding this, I recognize that as a member of this Court I am not empowered to help petitioners and others similarly situated. My duty, rather, is to "decide cases 'agreeably to the Constitution and laws of the United States.' " *Id.*, at 530. And, just like Justice Stewart, I "can find [neither in the Bill of Rights nor any other part of the Constitution a] general right of privacy," *ibid.*, or as the Court terms it today, the "liberty of the person both in its spatial and more transcendent dimensions," *ante*, at 1.

NOTES

1. "Economic Indicators," June 2003. Prepared for the Joint Economic Committee by the Council of Economic Advisors (Washington, D.C.: Government Printing Office, 1999).

2. Saskia Sassen, "The Informal Economy," in John H. Mollenkopf and Manuel Castells, eds., *Dual City: Restructuring New York* (New York: Russell Sage Foundation, 1991), pp. 79–102.

3. Kathryn Edin and Laura Lein, *Making Ends Meet: How Single Mothers Survive Welfare and Low-Wage Work* (New York: Russell Sage Foundation, 1997).

4. U.S. Census Bureau, "Money Income in the United States, 2001," *Current Population Report 60–206* (Washington, D.C.: Government Printing Office, 2002).

5. *New York Times*, "Credit Crisis—The Essentials," updated July 12, 2010. http://topics.nytimes.com/top/reference/timestopics/subjects/c/credit_crisis/index.html. Accessed November 9, 2010.

6. Authors' calculations based on Miriam King, Steven Ruggles, J. Trent Alexander, Sarah Flood, Katie Genadek, Matthew B. Schroeder, Brandon Trampe, and Rebecca Vick, *Integrated Public Use Microdata Series, Current Population Survey: Version 3.0* [machine-readable database] (Minneapolis: University of Minnesota, 2010).

7. Emmanuel Saez, "Striking It Richer: The Evolution of Top Incomes in the United States." http://elsa.berkeley.edu/~saez/saez-UStopincomes-2008.pdf. Accessed November 9, 2010.

8. U.S. Census Bureau, *Income, Poverty, and Health Insurance Coverage in the United States: 2009* (Washington, D.C.: Government Printing Office, 2010). www.census.gov/prod/2010pubs/p60-238.pdf. Accessed November 9, 2010.

9. Carol J. De Vita, *The United States at Mid-Decade* (Washington, D.C.: Population Reference Bureau, Inc., 1996).

10. Bureau of Labor Statistics, "Labor Force Statistics Derived from the Population Survey, 1948–1987," August 1988, Bulletin 2307.

11. Mary Rowland, "A Clearer Picture of Unpaid Leave," *New York Times*, "Money" section, January 29, 1995, p. 13.

12. Carol Kleiman, "Study Shows Job Status Skews Family Benefits," *Chicago Tribune*, February 8, 1993.

13. U.S. Census Bureau, "U.S. Interim Projections by Age, Sex, Race, and Hispanic Origin." http://www.census.gov/ipc/www/usinterimproj/. Accessed November 9, 2010.

14. Unless otherwise specified, data on health care are from U.S. Centers for Medicare and Medicaid Statistics. http://www.cms.gov. Accessed November 9, 2010.

15. Center on Budget and Policy Priorities, Number without Health Insurance Remains at Record Level, October 6, 1995, pp. 1–2.

16. Dan Froomkin, "Mock the Press," *Washington Post*, July 11, 2007. http://www.washingtonpost.com/wp-dyn/content/blog/2007/07/11/BL2007071101146_pf.html. Accessed November 9, 2010.

17. Paul Starr, *The Social Transformation of American Medicine* (New York: Basic Books, 1982), provides an excellent review of this history.

18. Abigail Trafford and Spencer Rich, "Health Care Reform in Congress?" *Washington Post*, September 20, 1994, pp. 12–14; Robert P. Hey, "Reform Drive Fights for Life," *AARP Bulletin*, Vol. 35, No. 8, September 1994, pp. 1–10.

19. U.S. Congress, "Patients' Bill of Rights Act of 1999," H.R. 358.

20. Families USA, "One Step Forward, One Step Back: Children's Health Coverage after CHIP and Welfare Reform," October 1999.

21. U.S. Congress, 105 Public Law 34, 111 Stat. 788; 1997 Enacted H.R. 2014; 105 Enacted H.R. 2014. "Mental Health Parity Act of 1996," August 5, 1997.

22. Medicare Prescription Drug, Improvement, and Modernization Act of 2003, Public Law 108-173.

23. "Health Care Reform." http://topics.nytimes.com/top/news/health/diseasesconditionsandhealthtopics/health_insurance_and_managed_care/health_care_reform/index.html. Accessed November 9, 2010.

24. Peter S. Goodman, "The New Poor: In Hard Times, Lured into Trade School and Debt," *New York Times*, March 14, 2010.

25. U.S. Census Bureau, *Statistical Abstract of the United States 1998* (Washington, D.C.: Government Printing Office, 1998), p. 312.

26. Ibid., p. 76.

27. Mary Jo Bane and David T. Ellwood, *Welfare Realities: From Rhetoric to Reform* (Cambridge, Mass.: Harvard University Press, 1994), pp. 28–66.

28. William J. Wilson, *The Truly Disadvantaged: The Inner City, the Underclass, and Public Policy* (Chicago: University of Chicago Press, 1987), pp. 20–62.

29. David T. Ellwood, *Poor Support: Poverty in the American Family* (New York: Basic Books, 1988), pp. 231–244.

30. U.S. Congress, 104th Congress, "Personal Responsibility Act of 1995," H.R. 4.

31. U.S. Congress, 104th Congress, "The Personal Responsibility and Work Opportunity Reconciliation Act of 1996," Public Law 104–193 [H.R. 3734].

32. U.S. Department of Health and Human Services, Temporary Assistance for Needy Families (TANF) Program, *Fifth Annual Report to Congress*, August 2002, pp. 20–21.

33. Ibid.

34. U.S. Department of Health and Human Services, Administration for Children and Families, "TANF—Data and Reports." http://www.acf.hhs.gov/programs/ofa/data-reports/index.htm. Accessed November 9, 2010.

35. U.S. Department of Health and Human Services, *Fifth Annual Report to Congress*, pp. 132–133.

36. Richard C. Fording, Joe Sosss, and Sanford F. Schram, "Devolution, Discretion, and the Effect of Local Political Values on TANF Sanctioning," *Social Service Review*, Vol. 81, No. 2, June 2007, pp. 285–316.

37. U.S. Department of Health and Human Services, *Fifth Annual Report to Congress*, pp. 132–133.

38. Douglas S. Massey, "March of Folly: U.S. Immigration Policy after NAFTA," *The American Prospect*, Vol. 37, March–April 1998, pp. 22–33.

39. Randal C. Archibold, "Arizona Enacts Stringent Law on Immigration," *New York Times*, April 23, 2010.

40. Ram Cnaan, "Our Hidden Safety Net," *Brookings Review*, Vol. 17, No. 2, Spring 1999, p. 50.

41. Paul C. Light, "Rebuilding Trust in Charity." http://www. brookings.edu/opinions/2002/0516nonprofits_light.aspx. Accessed November 22, 2010.

42. Lester M. Salamon, "The Marketization of Welfare: Changing Nonprofit and For-Profit Roles in the American Welfare State," *Social Service Review*, March 1993, p. 32.

43. Amy D'Andrade and Jill Duerr Berrick, "When Policy Meets Practice: The Untested Effects of Permanency Reforms in Child Welfare," *Journal of Sociology and Social Welfare*, Vol. 33, No. 1, March 2006, pp. 31–52; Jane Waldfogel, *The Future of Child Protection: How to Break the Cycle of Abuse and Neglect* (Cambridge, Mass.: Harvard University Press, 1998), pp. 65–93.

44. Robert J. Shiller, *The New Financial Order: Risk in the 21st Century* (Princeton: Princeton University Press, 2003).

45. Jacob S. Hacker, *The Divided Welfare State: The Battle over Public and Private Social Benefits in the United States* (Cambridge and New York: Cambridge University Press, 2002).

46. "Report Warns against Reducing Remedial Classes in Colleges," *New York Times*, February 13, 1996.

47. "Schools on Reservation Crumbling for Lack of Repair Money," *New York Times*, September 3, 1995.

48. Orlando Patterson, "Affirmative Action on the Merit System," *New York Times*, August 9, 1995.

49. Robert Pear, "Report to Clinton Faults Programs to Aid Minorities," *New York Times*, May 31.

50. "Abortion: The Rate vs. the Debate," *New York Times*, February 25, 1996.

51. Jeffrey M. Jones, "Americans' Opposition to Gay Marriage Eases Slightly." http://www.gallup.com/poll/128291/Americans-Opposition-Gay-Marriage-Eases-Slightly.aspx. Accessed November 9, 2010.

52. U.S. Department of Justice, Bureau of Justice Statistics, "Federal Justice Statistics, 2008-Statistical Tables." http://bjs.ojp.usdoj.gov/index.cfm?ty=pbdetail&iid=1745. Accessed November 9, 2010.

Poverty: The Central Concept

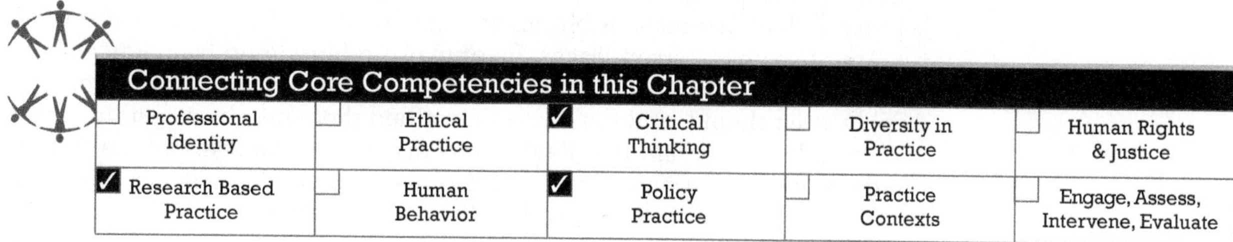

The alarm wakes Patty with its obnoxious buzz. She groans as she slaps the bedside table in an attempt to shut it off before it wakes the kids. Lying in bed, trying to wake up but wishing she did not have to, Patty thinks about her day—it is going to be a killer. Whoever said life on welfare is easy has never been there.

Patty Sanchez is a twenty-three-year-old divorced mother of two children, four-year-old Tina and two-year-old Ray. She has been receiving welfare—Temporary Assistance to Needy Families (TANF)—for fourteen months, ever since her husband Ernesto deserted her. Ernie lost his job as a truck driver just about the time Patty discovered that she was pregnant with Ray. For a while, they lived on unemployment benefits; then they scraped by on what Patty's mother could spare (not much) and on what Ernie made from the few odd jobs he could get (also not much). After Ernie overcame his pride, they applied for and received food stamps. After he lost his job as a trucker, Ernie never did get another "real job." It was a horrible time. Patty was pregnant and sick, Tina was demanding and whiny, and they were evicted from their apartment. They were able to move into the dump where Patty still lives only because a local church helped them out. Finally, Ernie became depressed and began to abuse Tina; then he moved out.

After Ernie left, Patty and the kids began receiving TANF and Medicaid in addition to their food stamps. Their name is at the top of the waiting list for a rent-subsidized apartment, and Patty has calculated that with low-cost housing she will finally be able to balance her budget. The prospect of going through a day without fear of the power being turned off or of creditors at the door seems almost too good to be true.

Patty and Ernie's relationship had been unstable since before Tina's birth. Ernie's unemployment was the last straw. After Ernie left, Patty saw him around the neighborhood occasionally for a few months, but then he dropped out of sight. One of his friends told Patty that Ernie had gone to California because he had heard they were hiring truckers, but Patty felt that he had left because he couldn't stand the embarrassment of seeing his family supported by welfare while he just sat around and did nothing.

Before waking the kids, Patty sits down with a cup of coffee and thinks about her day. At 9:00 in the morning Chuck Patterson, a social worker with the child welfare office, will be coming by for the last time. In the months before Ernie left, he had begun to drink and to take out his frustration on his family, mainly on Tina. After one particularly bad incident, Patty took Tina to the emergency room to see if she had any broken bones. Tina did not, but the physician called the hospital social worker, who in turn called the child welfare office. Chuck Patterson was the social worker assigned to the case. At first Patty was scared, thinking that her children would be taken away from her. It turned out that Mr. Patterson was helpful, and he spent a lot of time with Ernie helping him to develop better ways of dealing with anger and frustration. But now that Ernie is gone, there is really no reason for the child welfare people to be involved, so this will be the last visit. Patty feels both happy and sad that she will no longer be seeing Chuck—happy because she feels that there are too many people involved in her life, but sad because with all her responsibilities she can use all the friends she can get.

After Chuck Patterson leaves, Patty plans to bundle up baby Ray and take him to the public health clinic for an evaluation. He has not been developing as quickly as he should, and the doctors are afraid there may be something wrong with him. Patty is afraid that Ray's problems may be the result of the fact that she did not eat right and did not get any medical care during her pregnancy. Because they had so little money, her diet consisted mainly of bread, rice, potatoes, and other cheap, starchy food. She had heard of a program called WIC

(Women, Infants, and Children) that would have given her coupons to buy supplementary food during her pregnancy and Ray's infancy, but Ernie was in his macho proud phase and refused even to consider it. Now it looks as though little Ray is going to pay the price for his father's pride. At two, he is not yet walking, talking, or even responding well when someone plays with him.

At noon Patty has a group meeting at the community mental health center. After Ernie left, she felt so bad that she spent most of each day in bed crying. Chuck Patterson helped her join a support group at the center. The group is composed of eight other women who are undergoing life crises of various sorts, and they spend an hour each week just talking and comparing notes on how they cope. The group is led by a clinical social worker named Carol Crenshaw, who gets the group going, occasionally makes a suggestion or interpretation of what is being said, and sums up at the end of the meeting. Patty thinks about how much better she is doing now than when she first joined the group, and the thought of quitting enters her mind, as it has frequently in the past few weeks. She decides that she will continue to go for a little longer because she enjoys the fellowship of the group and feels that the other women need her.

After the meeting at the community mental health center, Patty will rush home, feed the kids, and put them down for a short nap while she does her laundry and housework. At 2:30 she will wake up the kids and walk two blocks to the Learning Center, a local child-care facility. At the Learning Center, Patty drives the van that picks up kids after school; then she supervises their play group until 6:00, when the last parents will pick up their children. Patty is paid only minimum wage for this job, but it includes child care for her own children as a benefit. She looked at other jobs, including full-time ones, after Ernie left, but when she deducted child care-expenses, she would be left with almost nothing. Patty's TANF grant allows her to make a small amount of income with no reduction in her grant or other benefits, so this job improves her life a little bit and strengthens her self-image a whole lot.

After work at the child-care center, Patty will rush home, feed her kids, and take them to her mother's house for the evening. While her mother cares for the kids, Patty will go to the local high school, where she is enrolled in night classes. Patty quit school when she was sixteen, shortly after she met Ernesto. She thought she had it made. He had a good job and seemed to have lots of money, and Patty was sure he would take care of her forever. With a setup like that, why did she need an education? "Well," she thinks, "once again I learn the hard way." The course she is pursuing at the high school not only will lead to a high school diploma but also will get her a certificate in drafting with emphasis on computer-assisted design (CAD). Patty has always been good in art, and the counselor at the school told her the salary and job prospects of drafters with computer skills are very good. She likes school and plans to continue after she gets a job. Her dream is to eventually become a civil engineer.

With her coffee finished, Patty gets the kids up. Ray, who is sluggish at the best of times, is positively inert in the morning, and it will take the better part of an hour to feed him. Tina will want some attention, and the apartment needs to be straightened up before Chuck Patterson arrives. Facing two cranky kids, a messy apartment, and a schedule that is full until 10:00 P.M., Patty thinks, "Boy, being a welfare mother sure isn't all it's cracked up to be!"

The case of Patty Sanchez illustrates a number of key points discussed in this chapter and the two that follow. The first point, and probably the most important, is that nearly all the social welfare problems discussed in this book are closely related to poverty. The Sanchez family has experienced unemployment and underemployment, marital breakdown, health problems, alcohol abuse, mental health problems, educational deficits, and child abuse. Some of these have contributed to their poverty, and some have resulted from it; in most cases the relation has been circular—lack of education has led to poverty, and poverty, in turn, has led to a lack of educational opportunity. That is why we are devoting three chapters to poverty and only one chapter to each of the other major social welfare problems. Scratch any social welfare problem, and underneath it you will find poverty.

The Sanchez family, following Ernesto's abandonment, consists of a woman and her children. This is typical and is becoming even more common. As discussed later in this chapter, two of three poor adults are women, 50 percent of poor families are headed by females, and one-half the children in female-headed families are poor. This trend has come to be identified by a phrase coined by Diana Pearce in 1978: "the feminization of poverty."

The next notable fact about the Sanchez family is that they belong to a minority group, in this case Hispanic. This fact may seem to fit a popular stereotype about poor people in the United States—that they are mainly members of minority groups. This stereotype is not true—more than half the poor people in this country are white. However, it is true that minority groups are greatly overrepresented among the poor. One of three African Americans in the United States lives in poverty, one of four Hispanic people is poor, but only one of ten non-Hispanic whites falls below the poverty line. It is only because whites make up such a large majority of the population that they are numerically the largest group in poverty.

Another popular stereotype about poor people and welfare recipients is that they remain in this condition for an extended time and that most likely their kids will inherit their poverty. Social workers and social scientists have been as guilty as laypeople of perpetuating this belief. Recent data provide a strong basis for refuting this idea and indicate that the case of Patty Sanchez may be fairly typical. A study discussed in this chapter, the Michigan Panel Study of Income Dynamics, has found that only about one-half of people who are classified as poor during one year will be so classified the next, and only one-tenth of poor people will remain so for an extended period. Far more common are people like Patty Sanchez, who use welfare for a short time while they deal with problems in their lives and then go on to more prosperous futures.

In this chapter we discuss basic factors about poverty—what it is, how we define it, how we measure it, and whom it affects.

POVERTY: MAJOR ISSUES
AND COMMON TERMS

The question and the answer are familiar. You will hear them during almost any political campaign.

> *Reporter:* "Ms. Porkbarrel, the figures recently released by the Census Bureau indicate that over the past ten years, the share of income of the richest people in this country has gotten significantly larger, while the share of the poorest has become smaller. In fact, there are still more than 37 million Americans living below the poverty line. So what we have is a situation with a small number of people spending money on second homes, European vacations, jewelry, and the like, while an increasingly larger number can't

afford even the necessities of life. My question is, do you consider this to be a problem? And, if so, what will you do about it if you are elected?"

Candidate Porkbarrel: "Well, John, I'm glad you asked that question. Let me say this. First, I want to say that I firmly believe that the problem is the size of the pie, not how we cut it. I have an economic development program that will increase the size of the pie, and thereby deal with the people below the poverty level without cutting into the good life earned by hard-working people. Second, I'm not sure that I agree with the figures released by the Census Bureau. I think that our poverty line is set at an unrealistically high level. Do you realize that a middle-income person in England has an income that would place him or her below our poverty line? Also, our poverty figures do not include all of the in-kind benefits we give poor people. We may have more people below the poverty line than we had in the 1960s, but these people have many benefits their 1960s counterparts did not have—benefits like food stamps and Medicaid, to name just two."

When listening to an exchange like this, we say, "Wait a minute. What does she mean that she would make the pie bigger rather than cutting it differently? What does she mean that the poverty line is too high? And what's all this business about in-kind benefits?" These are some of the major issues and common terms that come up in discussions of the problem of poverty. The size-of-the-pie question refers to the distribution of income in our country. Some people believe that the rich are too rich, and they propose a kind of Robin Hood solution to poverty—you simply take from the rich and give to the poor. Others feel this is not a good idea and that to reduce poverty, we must have economic growth. The other questions have to do with defining and measuring poverty. Discussion of these issues can, we realize, be somewhat tedious. To discuss poverty intelligently, however, you must understand these issues. Even though on the surface the issues may seem rather dry, we hope that by the end of this chapter you will realize they have a very human face.

RICH COUNTRY, POOR COUNTRY

Poverty in developing nations such as Haiti or Bangladesh is explainable in terms of the total wealth of the nation. If you were to take the total income of these nations and divide it up evenly among the population, everyone in the country would be poor. This is not the case in the United States. In 2005, the total personal income of the United States was $12,233.5 billion, and the number of household units was 117,181,000.[1] By dividing the number of households into the total personal income, you can see that if income were distributed evenly, every household would have received $104,398, an adequate amount of money by almost anyone's standards. However, income in the United States is not divided evenly. A few people have incomes greatly in excess of $104,398, and a larger number of people have incomes below this figure, with many far, far below it. Columnist Molly Ivins has given a particularly graphic description of the income distribution in the United States: "If we visualize the class structure at all in this country, we tend to think it looks like a fat jar with a small base (poor folks). Actually, what it looks like is the profile of a fireplace with an immensely tall chimney. There's this big huddle of folks at the bottom and along the ledge of the fireplace; then it slopes back into this chimney that goes up, up, up, so that as a chart on your wall, the chimney hits your ceiling long before it even gets near the truly rich."[2]

To understand poverty in the United States, first we must understand economic inequality. In this section we look at how inequality is measured, how income is distributed in this country, whether the income distribution is becoming more or less equal, and how the distribution of income is viewed from liberal and conservative perspectives.

The Measurement of Economic Inequality

The U.S. Bureau of the Census is one of the most highly regarded data collection agencies in the world. On a regular basis, the Census Bureau collects a wide range of information regarding the population in the United States. Among these data is information on income and wealth. For purposes of summary and comparison, the Census Bureau aggregates the data on income and wealth into quintiles (fifths) of the population. In this form we can see how much income and wealth is earned or held by the poorest fifth of the population, the next poorest fifth, and so on up to the wealthiest fifth. In addition, the bureau also figures the income of the richest 5 percent and the wealth held by the top 1 percent and $^1/_2$ percent of the population. These data are also broken down by racial and ethnic group and geographic region, and they are gathered and reported in a consistent manner so that comparisons over time can be made. An example of Census Bureau data on income is presented in Table 1. The data in this table are discussed later in this section.

Table 1 **Money Income of Families: Income of Selected Positions and Percentage of Income Received by Each Fifth and Top 5 Percent of Families, 2005**

Item	All Families	
Income at selected positions (dollars)	Upper Limit of Each Fifth	Average Income of People in Each Fifth
Lowest	20,712	11,656
Second	39,000	29,517
Third	62,725	50,132
Fourth	100,240	79,760
Highest	No limit	171,056
Lower limit of top 5 percent	180,000	294,709
Percent distribution of aggregate income:		
Lowest fifth	3.4	
Second fifth	8.6	
Third Fifth	14.7	
Fourth Fifth	23.3	
Highest Fifth	50	
Top 5 percent	21.5	

Source: U.S Bureau of the Census, Historical Income Inequality Tables (Washington, DC: U.S. Government Printing Office, 2009). Available online at www.census.gov.

Data such as that presented in Table 1 are useful, and they tell us a few things, but the information is not really clear, particularly for the purposes of comparison. Imagine, for example, trying to compare two or three such tables that presented data for several points in time or for different geographic regions. To make better sense of these types of data, economists have developed two techniques, the Lorenz curve and the Gini coefficient. The *Lorenz curve* is a curve that "shows the percentage of total household incomes received by successively larger fractions of the population, starting with the poorest group."[3] It traces out the share of total income held by different subgroups in the population. In the case of Census Bureau figures, it shows the income held by the lowest 20, 40, 60, 80, and 100 percent of the population. If income were distributed evenly—that is, if 20 percent of the population had 20 percent of the income, 40 percent of the population had 40 percent of the income, and so on—the Lorenz curve would be a straight line, as shown in Figure 1. If, on the other hand, one person held all the income, the Lorenz curve would form a right angle, as shown in Figure 2. It is obvious that neither situation actually occurs; the curve always falls somewhere between the 45-degree slope representing perfect equality and the vertical line representing perfect inequality. Examples of two Lorenz curves, one for a very equal distribution of income and one for a very unequal distribution, are presented in Figure 3.

The Lorenz curve gives a nice graphic depiction of income structure, but it is still difficult to make comparisons over time and between countries. For these purposes, a summary statistic called the *Gini coefficient* is necessary. Using the situations depicted in Figure 3 (on next page) as examples, the Gini coefficient is the area between the Lorenz curve and line OE, divided by the area of OEZ. As you can see, as the Lorenz curve approaches equality (curve a), the Gini coefficient approaches zero. As the Lorenz curve approaches inequality (curve b), the Gini coefficient approaches one. Thus the Gini coefficient has possible values ranging from zero (perfect equality) to one (perfect inequality). The Gini coefficient makes comparisons clear and easy. If country A has a Gini coefficient of .423 and country B has a Gini coefficient of .297, we can see clearly that country B has a more equal income distribution. Likewise, if the

Critical Thinking Question

How do the Lorenz curve and the Gini coefficient help social workers understand poverty in the United States.

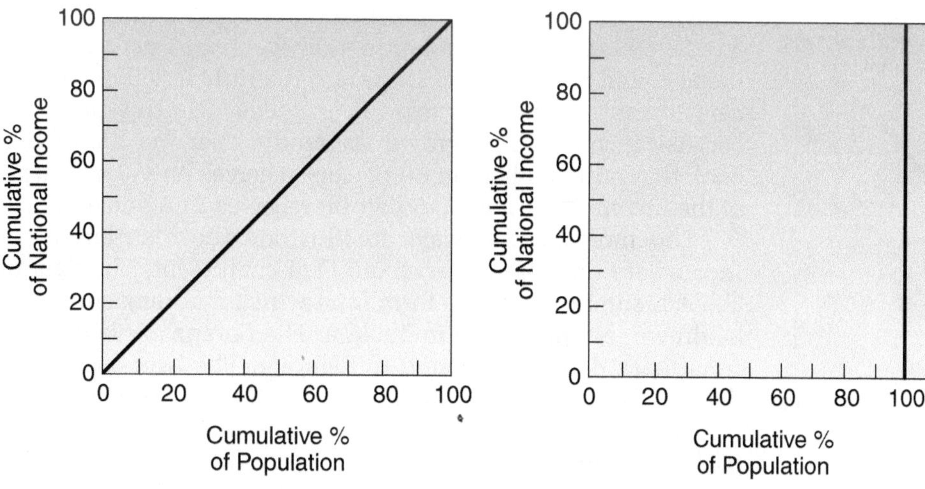

Figure 1
Lorenz Curve for Absolute Income Equality

Figure 2
Lorenz Curve for Absolute Income Inequality

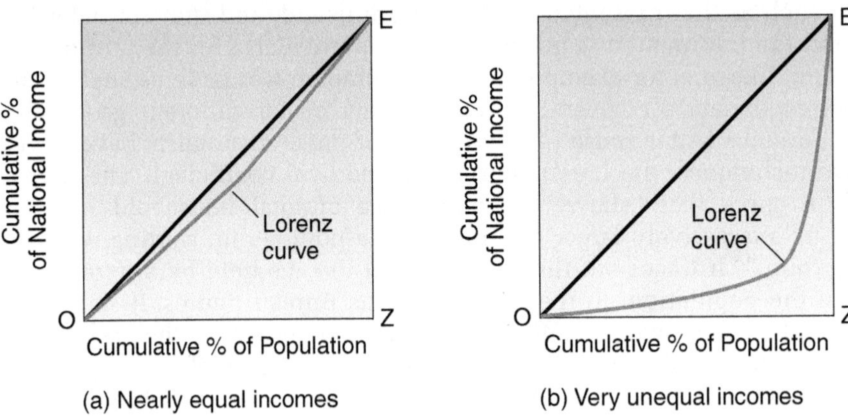

Figure 3

Extreme Cases of the Lorenz Curve

Source: John Craven, *Introduction to Economics: An Integrated Approach to Fundamental Principles* (Oxford, England: Blackwell Publishers, 1984), 100. Reprinted by permission.

Gini coefficient for country A was .324 in 1960 and .423 in 1998, we can conclude that the distribution of income is becoming even more unequal.

Now that you are familiar with some of the major sources of data and some of the tools used to study income and wealth, let's look at the situation in the United States.

The Distribution of Income and Wealth in the United States

If you spend an hour driving around any city in the United States, it will be readily apparent that income and wealth are unequally divided. Within the space of a few miles, you can see neighborhoods with houses valued at half a million dollars or more and neighborhoods with houses that most people would judge to be unfit for human habitation. You will see BMW dealerships next to Fast Freddie's Used Cars ("no credit, no problem—we tote the note"). You will see an Ethan Allen Furniture Gallery and a Salvation Army Thrift Store. We could go on and on, but there is no point in belaboring the obvious. What is not obvious, however, is just how unequal the distribution of income and wealth is.

In 2009, the Census Bureau reported the data presented in Table 1. In 1990, when we wrote the first edition of this book, we suggested that a convenient and illustrative way to summarize these types of data was what we called the *20/5 principle*. This principle stated that in the United States the bottom 20 percent of the population received about 5 percent of the income, and the top 5 percent received a little less than 20 percent of the income. But we can no longer use this principle because inequality has grown so rapidly over the life of this book that now the bottom 20 percent receives only 3.4 percent of the income, and the top 5 percent receives 21.5 percent.

The most precise ways to illustrate the distribution of income are the Lorenz curve and Gini coefficient. The data in Table 1, summarized in a form from which a Lorenz curve can be drawn, are presented in Table 2. The Lorenz curve derived from these data is presented in Figure 4. The Gini coefficient derived from the data is .463. We will return to this coefficient later when we look at trends in inequality in the United States over time and as compared with other countries.

We can see from the preceding data that the distribution of income in this country is very unequal. This is not the entire

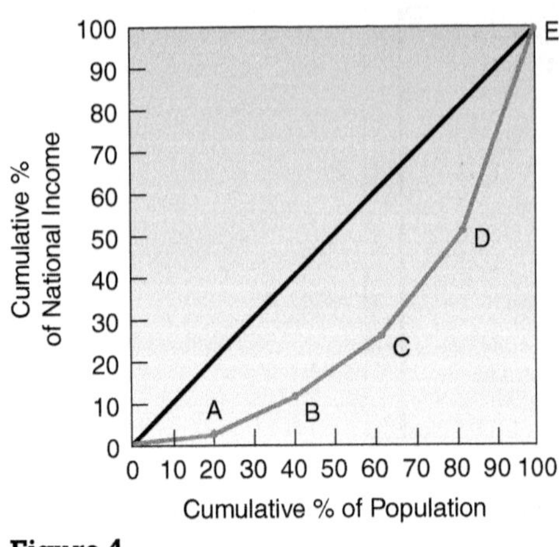

Figure 4

Lorenz Curve Showing Income Distribution for the United States in 2005

Table 2 — Income Data from Table 1 Prepared for Presentation on a Lorenz Curve

Point	Group	Percentage of Population	Cumulative Percentage of Population	Upper Limit of Group Income	Percentage of National Income	Cumulative Percentage of National Income
A	Poorest	20	20	20,712	3.4	3.4
B	Next Poorest	20	40	39,000	8.6	12.0
C	Next	20	60	62,725	14.7	26.7
D	Next	20	80	100,240	23.3	50
E	Richest	20	100	No limit	50	100

story, however. Annual income refers only to the amount of money coming in during a one-year period; it does not say much about wealth. Income is the flow of money into a household; wealth consists of accumulated assets and includes things such as houses, real estate, cars, jewelry, savings accounts, stocks, and bonds. Wealth is much harder to measure than income. Income must be reported each year on federal income tax returns, and although it is acknowledged that tax reporting is not precise, it is at least a fairly close estimate. People are not required to report their wealth. However, data on wealth is estimated by the Federal Reserve Board by means of a statistical sample collected every three years by the Survey of Consumer Finances (SCF). The most recent SCF was conducted in 2007.

The distribution of wealth is even more unequal than the distribution of income. Data reported from the 2007 Survey of Consumer Finances by Kennickell, summarized in Table 3, indicate that the majority of the total wealth in the United States, 71.5 percent, is owned by one-tenth of the families. Even more astounding is the finding that as of 2007 the top 1 percent of families owned 33.8 percent of all privately held wealth. Think about that—one one-hundredth of the population owns more than one-third of everything in the country.[4]

Even more astounding is the finding that as of 2007 the top 1 percent of families owned 33.8 percent of all privately held wealth.

Table 3 — Survey Estimates of Wealth Distribution in the United States (Percent of Total Wealth Owned by Each Group)

Wealth Percent Group	1989	1992	1995	1998	2001	2004	2007	Changes 1989–2007
Lowest 50%	3.0	3.3	3.6	3.0	2.8	2.5	2.5	−0.5
50%–90%	29.9	29.6	28.6	28.4	27.4	27.9	26	−3.9
90%–95%	13.0	12.5	11.9	11.4	12.1	12.0	11.1	−1.9
95%–99%	24.1	24.4	21.3	23.3	25.0	24.1	26.6	2.5
Richest 1%	30.1	30.2	34.6	33.9	32.7	33.4	33.8	3.7

Source: Adapted from Arthur B. Kennickell, "Ponds and Streams: Wealth and Income in the U.S., 1989 to 2007," Staff working paper, Finance and Economics Discussion Series, Division of Research & Statistics and Monetary Affairs, Federal Reserve Board, Washington, D.C., 2009

The fact that some people are very rich is not in and of itself a problem. The popularity of TV shows that portray the lives of rich people is testimony to our society's fascination with the rich. The problem is that while some people are very rich, others are very poor. Wolff reports that the bottom 17 percent of the population own absolutely nothing of value. In fact, these people have negative net worth—they owe more than they own. The middle three-fifths of the population collectively own only 15.1 percent of all privately held wealth.[5] James Smith of the University of Michigan's Institute for Social Research has pointed out that even this low figure overstates the assets of many of these people. The wealth of the lower end of this group is likely made up of money in checking accounts that will be spent for monthly living expenses and perhaps a car. Toward the upper end of this group, the wealth consists primarily of a house. Smith says, "For many Americans, owning a home is the *only* way to have net worth at all." Due to the recent decline in home values, it is a good guess that the wealth of all but the richest Americans has declined. And finally, of course, we get back to the upper 20 percent who own 84.6 percent of everything, including more than 90 percent of corporate stocks and business assets and 95 percent of bonds.[6]

Trends in the Distribution of Wealth and Income

Information that can be used to compare the concentration of wealth is available for the past eighty-eight years. These data indicate that between 1922 and 1953 wealth distribution was fairly stable, with the top 1 percent of wealth holders owning an average of 30 percent of total household sector wealth. During the 1950s and early 1960s, wealth inequality began to increase, until 1962, when the top 1 percent owned 33.5 percent of household sector wealth. Keister observes, "Most striking is evidence of the decline in the wealth of the poorest 80 percent of households. The wealth of this group decreased by almost 3 percent, from 18.7 percent of total wealth in 1983 to 16.4 percent in 1989."[7] By 2004 this had further shrunk to 15.3 percent. Reflecting on these developments, Richard Freeman observes that "the United States has now cemented its traditional position as the leader in inequality among advanced countries."[8]

Numerous analysts using different methods have all concluded that the distribution of income has become more unequal in recent years and that income inequality is increasing at an even more rapid rate than that of wealth. Daniel Weinberg, who monitors income trends for the Census Bureau, recently looked at the historical data and observed that "the Gini index (also known as the index of concentration) indicated a decline in family income inequality of 4 percent from 1947 to 1968." In other words, for that period of twenty-one years, the distribution of income was becoming significantly more equal in this country. But in 1968 this trend reversed sharply. The Census Bureau recorded an increase in the Gini of 17.1 percent from 1968 to 1992 and 22.4 percent from 1968 to 1994.[9] An updated version of the Census Bureau data on which Weinberg bases his analysis is presented in Table 4.

Sociologist Stanley Eitzen, adding a value dimension to the data, has stated that "the U.S. has the most unfair distribution of wealth and income in the industrialized world. Moreover, the rate of growth in inequality is faster than

Research Based Practice

Critical Thinking Question

How does the evidence of the growing inequality in the United States affect social work practice?

Table 4 **United States Gini Index for Income 1951–2005**

Year	Gini Index	Year	Gini Index
2007	0.463	1976	0.398
2001	0.466	1971	0.396
1996	0.455	1966	0.349
1991	0.428	1961	0.374
1986	0.425	1956	0.358
1981	0.406	1951	0.363

Source: U.S Bureau of the Census, Income, Poverty, and Health Insurance Coverage in the United States, 2005; U.S. Bureau of the Census, *Income, Poverty, and Health Insurance Coverage in the United States, 2007*, Table A-3.

in any other industrialized country." He supports his position with the following facts:

- The richest 1 percent in the United States own more wealth ($3.6 trillion in 1992) than the bottom 90 percent ($3.4 trillion).
- Between 1983 and 1991 (the Reagan years), the nation's net worth increased from $13.5 trillion to $20.2 trillion, and 58 percent of that $6.7 trillion increase went to the fortunate top one-half of 1 percent. That works out to a $3.9 million bonanza per wealthy household.
- In 1960, the average cheif executive officer (CEO) earned about as much as 41 factory workers. In 1992, that chief executive officer (CEO) made as much as 157 factory workers. In 1995, the average compensation of CEOs (salary, bonus, and stock options) increased by 26.9 percent compared with the 2.8 percent increase in wages for the average worker.
- In a fifteen-year period ending in 1993, the richest 1 percent almost doubled their income and had their tax rates cut by 23 percent. In sharp contrast, the poorest one-fifth saw their tax rates go up and their incomes go down.
- The real value (adjusted for inflation) of a standard welfare benefit package has declined by some 26 percent since 1972.
- From 1967 to 1979, a full-time, year-round minimum-wage worker earned at a level above the official poverty line for a family of three. In 2003, a worker earning the minimum wage of $5.15 earned $10,712 annually, $3,636 below the poverty line for a family of three.[10]

Another way of looking at trends in inequality is to compare the average pay of CEO with that of average factory workers. *Business Week* magazine and the Associated Press have collected this data for many years. The ratio of CEO pay to factory worker pay was 42 to 1 in 1960 and 344 to 1 in 2007. By way of comparison, the ratio in Europe is currently about 25 to 1. In terms of income growth, between 1990 and 2005 the pay of an average factory worker grew, adjusted for inflation, by 4.3 percent; during the same period, average CEO pay grew by 298.2 percent.

Focus on Diversity

Race, Ethnicity, and Increasing Inequality

Ever since the civil rights movement of the 1960s, a major goal of social and economic policy has been to correct historical injustices and make the American dream a reality for all groups in our society. But the data on trends in income inequality paint a depressing picture that indicates we are moving in the opposite direction. In a study of twenty-five years of data, the period between 1967 and 1992, Lynn Karoly found that inequality had increased for all groups in our country, but that the increase has been larger for minority groups. White families fared the best over this period with a 24.8 percent growth in median adjusted family income between 1970 and 1987. Over the same period, adjusted family income increased by 20.1 percent for African American families and by only 8.6 percent for Latino families. White families experienced positive income growth at all points in the income distribution. However, white families with incomes at the 90th percentile experienced more growth than those at the 10th percentile; thus, inequality became greater even for whites. African American and Latino families at the 10th and 25th percentiles actually experienced declines in adjusted family income after 1973. Combined with the growth of adjusted family income for families at the 75th and 90th percentiles, the data indicate that inequality has increased for minority groups at a rate greater than for whites.

Source: Lynn A. Karoly, "The Trend in Inequality among Families, Individuals, and Workers in the United States: A Twenty-Five-Year Perspective," in Sheldon Danzinger and Peter Gottschalk, eds., *Uneven Tides: Rising Inequality in America* (New York: Russell Sage Foundation, 1993), 19–100.

As is clear from Table 3 and from other data presented here, inequality has increased in recent years and may well continue to increase. What this means is not clear, however; it is the subject of much debate between those with liberal and those with conservative perspectives.

Perspectives on Inequality

Liberals, conservatives, and radicals agree that equality is a basic part of the American creed and that greater equality is, at least theoretically, desirable. Liberals and conservatives also agree that economic inequality is an inevitable fact of life. Even some radicals (although not all) will agree that some inequality is tolerable, for example, that a nuclear physicist may earn more than the person who sweeps out the physicist's laboratory. There is disagreement, however, about the degree and trend of inequality, the positive and negative effects of inequality, and how much inequality is desirable in our society.

First, let's look at the degree and trend of inequality. All the social scientists cited in the preceding section would be classified as political liberals. They measure the growth of inequality and conclude that it is a fact, that it is getting worse, and that this is a result of unjust social and economic pressures. Hout and Lucas, for example, say that

> not only is the inequality in income between the richest and the poorest in the United States greater now than in the past, but it is also greater than that of any other populous, industrialized country. Workers in such countries also have had to deal with the globalization of trade and the disruptions caused by new technology; yet only workers in the United States have lost so much ground. . . . Inequality surged between 1991 and 1993 as the most recent recession lowered incomes for all but the richest Americans. Executives killed jobs in ways that would be illegal in Germany and France—for example, shutting down plants in some

regions and relocating them in jurisdictions with right-to-work laws. Wall Street rewarded the executives with a mid-recession rally that boosted the value of their stock options."[11]

The conservative interpretation of the data on inequality is, predictably, quite different. Using the Gini index presented earlier, Novak and Green argue that inequality in the United States is similar to that in other Western democracies. The heart of their argument is that inequality is caused less by unfairness than by the age structure of the labor force. Persons in the early years of their careers and those in retirement will have lower incomes than persons in their peak earning years. Thus the same person will be at different positions along the Lorenz curve during different periods of his or her life. In 1986, Novak and Green used this argument to explain why statistical measures of inequality had been increasing in the 1980s. According to their argument, a greater number of people were living in retirement because of increased life span, and the baby boom generation had been entering careers and setting up households in large numbers. For these reasons, income figures included more people at low earning points in their careers. As the baby boom generation continued "its long trek through its lifetime positions along the Lorenz curve," presumably the Gini would decrease.[12]

Lynn Karoly has debunked this argument by dividing income data into two components, one that addressed inequality related to the changing age structure of the population and one related to the changes in within-group inequality. She found that almost all the increase in inequality over the previous twenty years was attributable to inequality within age cohorts, not to changes in the relative size of the cohorts.[13] Additionally, if Novak and Green's 1986 argument were correct, inequality should have declined beginning in the late 1980s as baby boomers entered their peak earning years. As we have seen, quite the opposite has occurred.

Conservatives and liberals also differ on whether high inequality is a bad thing. Liberals believe that high, and especially increasing, inequality is a cause for great concern. They fear that if inequality is too great, social disruption will likely occur. Harrison and his colleagues note "the fear— expressed by a growing number of journalists and political analysts—that the frustrated expectations of significant numbers of younger workers unable to attain the living standards of their own parents could lead to potentially serious social unrest."[14] Similarly, economist Lester Thurow asks, "How much inequality can a democracy take? The income gap in America is eroding the social contract. If the promise of a higher standard of living is limited to a few at the top, the rest of the citizenry, as history shows, is likely to grow disaffected, or worse."[15] Henry Reuss has said, "From a social standpoint, when whole classes feel themselves endangered, bloodshed and revolution have been the outcome, as in France in the 1790s and Germany in the 1930s."[16]

Conservatives argue that wage inequality is no particular cause for concern but in fact is actually desirable. George Gilder summarizes this argument:

> Under capitalism, when it is working, the rich have the anti-Midas touch, transforming timorous liquidity and unused savings into factories and office towers, farms and laboratories, orchestras and museums— turning gold into goods and jobs and art. That is the function of the rich: fostering opportunities for the classes below them in the continuing drama of the creation of wealth and progress.[17]

Gilder argues that rich people (entrepreneurs, to be more exact) serve a critical social function by being willing to risk their money on the hope that they will win great profits. When their risks pay off, they create new wealth for everyone in the form of jobs and economic growth. Therefore, rich people are entitled to hundreds of times the income of regular people for two reasons: (1) They take great risks, often losing everything, and therefore, they deserve great profits when their risks pay off, and (2) rich people use their money not for conspicuous consumption but to create more wealth for us all. Gilder says that this moral dynamic at the heart of the system drives entrepreneurs constantly to reinvest their profits. Entrepreneurs do not consume their wealth; they recycle it by giving it to other people in productive ways. This means that the very people who have proved their ability to create wealth control the process of future wealth creation. In the form of investments, they endow other entrepreneurs who are judged best able to prevail in the competitions in service that impel the progress of the capitalist economy.[18]

It should be noted that Gilder provides virtually no empirical evidence to support his contentions. Nobel Prize–winning economist Robert M. Solow, in his review of Gilder's *The Spirit of Enterprise,* a sequel to *Wealth and Poverty,* remarked, "Only someone with a sense of humor could survive reading this book. And no one with any trace of a sense of humor could have written it."[19]

Finally, although liberals and conservatives agree that some inequality is necessary, they disagree on how much inequality is desirable. Conservatives, as can be inferred from the quotes from Gilder, are not really concerned with the amount of inequality. They agree that poverty is a bad thing, but they contend that poverty is not a result of inequality. They argue that the situation is really quite the opposite—when people make a lot of money, we all benefit, so why should we care how rich some people are? They argue that if the average income of the wealthiest people in the country increased from, say, $5 million a year to $10 million a year, and if as a result of their profit seeking your income went up by $5,000, you would probably think it a good thing.

Liberals question this trickle-down theory and argue that it does not follow that increased income for the rich necessarily results in increased income for other groups in society. They point out that as inequality in income has increased during recent years, the number of people below the poverty line also has increased. They believe that social efficiency (that is, providing enough reward to motivate the most highly qualified people to pursue the most difficult jobs) could be achieved with a much smaller amount of inequality than currently exists. William Ryan, one of the most articulate spokespersons of this "fair shares" approach, says

> I don't think many of us have strong objections to inequality of monetary income as such. A modest range, even as much as three or four to one, would, I suspect, be tolerable to almost everybody. . . . The current range in annual incomes—from perhaps $3,000 to some unknown number of *millions*—is, however, intolerable, impossible to justify rationally, and plain inhuman.[20]

Most radicals would strongly agree.

No agreement about the effects, positive or negative, of increasing inequality has been reached, and our society has seemingly become willing to live with a high level of inequality. Paul Krugman makes the rather discouraging observation that

> income distribution, like productivity growth, is a policy issue with no real policy debate. The growing gap between rich and poor was arguably the central fact about economic life in America in the 1980's. But no policy changes now under discussion seem likely to narrow this gap significantly.[21]

POVERTY—THE DARK SIDE OF INEQUALITY

Most people would not consider inequality to be a problem if those on the low end of the distribution had at least enough income to live in a minimally adequate fashion. However, a large number of people do not have this amount of income. We refer to the living condition of these people as *poverty*. In this section we look at several aspects of poverty: We examine how it is defined, how the official poverty line is set, and some unresolved issues in measuring and defining poverty; and we look at liberal and conservative perspectives on poverty. We do not refer to a radical perspective in this section because radicals are interested more in the larger question of inequality than in how the poverty line is set.

The Definition of Poverty

We see the items in the newspaper frequently: "Poverty Rate up by 2%" or "More Children Growing Up in Poverty Now Than Any Year since 1961." From these articles we assume that it is possible to measure poverty in a manner similar to measuring the annual rainfall—that there is some objective standard against which to measure poverty. But we also see headlines that say things like "Administration Questions Poverty Statistics" and "Aide Claims That If All Benefits Are Counted, Poverty Level Has Declined by 3%." The question we are left with is, can we measure poverty? And if so, how accurately? The answer, as you will see, is that yes, we can measure poverty with a fairly high degree of accuracy, but there is widespread disagreement on what poverty is, what the best measure is, and what the immense quantity of data we have on poverty means.

The way we measure and define poverty depends on which of two classes of definitions we use. The first class of definitions is referred to as *economic definitions;* it basically defines poverty as a lack of money and other resources. The second class of definitions is known as *cultural definitions;* it defines poverty not only as a lack of money but also as a lifestyle composed of values, attitudes, and behaviors that are related to being poor. According to cultural definitions, important attributes of poverty include feelings of hopelessness and alienation and a matriarchal (mother-dominated) family structure.[22] In this chapter we are dealing with poverty as an economic phenomenon and do not concern ourselves with the cultural aspects. We will look at two broad categories of economic definitions of poverty—absolute definitions and relative definitions.

Absolute Definitions

An absolute definition of poverty is a relatively fixed level of income below which a person cannot function in a productive and efficient manner in a given society. It is based on calculations derived from minimum costs of food, housing, clothing, and transportation in that society. The emphasis is on *minimum* cost; no allowance is made for luxuries such as travel (even if it is for a purpose generally thought to be essential, such as visiting a sick relative) or entertainment. An absolute poverty line will increase along with the cost of living and as conditions in society change certain expenditures from nonessential to essential. For example, in the 1920s, indoor plumbing was not considered essential, so the cost of sewer service was not included in poverty-line calculations. Today, an outdoor toilet is illegal within city limits in this country, so the cost of sewer service has become essential and is therefore a part of poverty-line calculations.

Today in the United States we consider a person poor if that person rarely can afford to eat meat and fresh fruit, even if his or her nutritional intake is adequate and he or she is getting needed protein and vitamins from other sources. In developing nations, this diet would not result in a person being classified as poor. Therefore, even an absolute definition is relative because it is only absolute in relation to the social, economic, and historical environment in which it occurs.

Mollie Orshansky, one of the people responsible for conceptualizing the official poverty line in the United States, has commented that there is no reason to count the poor, and hence no reason for defining poverty, unless you intend to do something about it.[23] It was not until the late nineteenth century that anyone even began to think that something could be done about poverty on a societal level, and this is when interest was first shown in setting a poverty line so that the poor could be counted. The earliest attempts were made in England. In the 1890s, Liverpool businessman Charles Booth defined poverty in the following way:

> [B]y the word "poor" I mean to describe those who have a sufficiently regular though bare income, such as 18s to 21s per week for a moderate family, and by "very poor" those who from any cause fall much below this standard. The "poor" are those whose means may be sufficient, but are barely sufficient, for decent independent life; the "very poor" those whose means are insufficient for this according to the usual standard of life in this country. My "poor" may be described as living under a struggle to obtain the necessaries of life and make both ends meet, while the "very poor" live in a state of chronic want.[24]

Booth arrived at these figures by observing thirty families who struck him as "poor" or "very poor" and using their expenditures as the basis for his poverty line.

Booth's definition was improved on a few years later in a study by another Englishman, Seebohm Rowntree. Booth defined poverty using a subjective idea of the "necessaries of life." Rowntree wanted to be more scientific and to calculate the income necessary for "physical efficiency" as the dividing line between poverty and nonpoverty. To arrive at this figure, he turned to the work of nutritionists who had conducted rigorous studies to determine how many calories were necessary for men to carry out "moderate muscular work." They had concluded that 3,500 calories a day was the minimum intake required for physical efficiency. Using this as a standard, Rowntree developed a 3,560-calorie menu that would supply 137 grams of protein at the lowest possible cost. He then priced the menu items at the cheapest shops he could locate and calculated the lowest cost possible to feed a man at a level that would enable that man to work efficiently. Rowntree then added in the cost for the cheapest housing he could locate and an amount he considered adequate for "household sundries." By adding these figures, Rowntree arrived at his poverty line.

There have been attempts to develop better absolute poverty lines than those of Booth and Rowntree. Rowntree himself revised his calculations and methods in 1936 and again in 1950. The official U.S. government poverty line, discussed later in this section, is based on a methodology similar to that of Rowntree. According to Holman, all of these absolute definitions share three elements. First, the poverty line is set at a level that will enable people to be physically efficient. No allowance is made for enjoyment of life or for personal development of any sort. Of his poverty line, Rowntree said, "It was a standard of bare subsistence rather than living." Second, the poverty line is based on calculations of utmost stringency. The only people considered poor are those whose lives, in Booth's words, entail "a struggle to obtain the necessaries of life." Finally, absolute definitions of poverty are not related to the incomes of society as a whole. These definitions do not compare people with people; they attempt to compare people with an objective yardstick that changes only with the cost of living or when certain things, such as sewer service, become necessary expenditures.[25]

The major advantage of absolute definitions and measures of poverty is that they provide a constant standard against which one dimension of the economic progress of a country can be measured. Using an absolute standard, we can look at the percentages of people living below the subsistence level at various points in history and draw conclusions about whether things are getting better or worse for the most disadvantaged segment of the population. We also can look at statistics over a shorter period of time and see if policies designed to help the poor are really having any effect.

There are some major problems with absolute definitions of poverty, however. The first and major problem is that absolute definitions are based only on physical needs and assume that people will spend their money with absolute efficiency. These definitions ignore social and psychological needs and the fact that most people do not spend money with absolute rationality. Rowntree, for example, assumed that a family

> must never purchase a halfpenny newspaper or spend a penny to buy a ticket for a popular concert. They must write no letters to absent children for they cannot afford to pay the postage. They must never contribute anything to their church or chapel, or give any help to a neighbor which costs them money. . . . [T]he children must have no pocket money for dolls, marbles or sweets. The father must smoke no tobacco and must drink no beer.[26]

We all realize that this is not the way people actually spend their money. No one is so coldly efficient that he or she will refuse to call or write relatives, send a few holiday cards, or occasionally go to a movie. Also, absolute definitions assume that people go to the cheapest stores and buy items at the lowest possible price. Not only do most poor people, like people in general, lack the knowledge to get the best bargains, but the stores in their neighborhoods generally charge higher prices than those in more affluent areas.[27] Thus the calculations used to set absolute definitions of poverty are based on assumptions that are false.

The second problem is a result of the first problem: Because the assumptions on which absolute poverty lines are based are false, the lines are set at too low a level. Studies in both England and the United States that ask the general

What Americans Believe

There are two ways of setting a relative poverty line. One is to take an arbitrary percentage of the median income of a country and define anything below that as poverty. The other, and probably more sensible, means is to ask people where they think the poverty line should be set and define poverty as anything falling below the average of their answers. The General Social Survey in 1993 asked people to indicate what they thought should be the poverty line for two types of families, one a husband and wife and two children and the other a single woman and two children. The responses are summarized in Table 5.

In the case of the couple with two children, 29.6 percent of respondents selected the interval in which the official poverty line was located ($10,401 to $15,600; the actual line for a family of this size and composition was $14,654). A little over 27 percent selected a lower figure, and 42.8 percent placed the poverty line at a higher level. In the case of the single woman and her two children, 29.5 percent of respondents selected the interval containing the actual official poverty line ($10,401 to $15,600; the actual line for this family was $11,642), nearly the exact percentage as in the previous example. However, when considering the single woman, the percentages selecting a higher and a lower line were nearly reversed from the case with the two-parent family, with 40 percent selecting a lower line and only 30.8 percent selecting a higher line.

These data, collected during only one survey and reflecting a sample of not quite 1,400 people, does not, of course, furnish proof of anything. It does, however, provide fuel for some interesting speculation. One interesting point is that it does not appear that a relative poverty line in the United States, selected on the basis of public opinion, would be drastically different from the line set using the current official method. In both the examples used in this survey, the vast majority of respondents selected the category containing the official line or else the one directly above or below.

Another interesting aspect of these data is that people seem to be considerably more generous toward the two-parent family than toward the single-parent family. This is probably, at least partially, a result of the resentment felt by people in this country toward welfare because they believe that it has encouraged illegitimacy. This is a major factor behind the most recent round of welfare reform.

Table 5 Where Would Americans Set the Poverty Line (1993)?

What Amount of Weekly Income Would You Use as a Poverty Line for a Family of Four (Husband, Wife, and Two Children) in This Community?*

	Number	Percent
Less than $5,200	54	3.9
$5,201 to $10,400	322	23.2
$10,401 to $15,600	411	29.6
$15,601 to $20,800	282	20.3
$20,801 to $26,000	212	15.3
$26,001 to $52,200	100	7.2
More than $52,000	6	.04

1993 poverty line for a family of four with two adults and two children = $14,654

What Amount of Weekly Income Would You Use as a Poverty Line for a Family of Three, Made Up of a Woman and Two Children, in This Community?

	Number	Percent
Less than $5,200	93	6.7
$5,201 to $10,400	452	32.7
$10,401 to $15,600	408	29.5
$15,601 to $20,800	250	18.0
$20,801 to $26,000	122	8.8
$26,001 to $52,000	56	4.0
More than $52,000	2	.001

1993 poverty line for a family of three with one adult and two children = $11,642

*Answers to these questions were given in weekly income. These have been converted to yearly income.

population to set an absolute poverty line always result in figures much higher than the actual line. A study in England commissioned by London Weekend Television found that the general public set the poverty line 33 percent higher than the actual line.[28] As can be seen in Table 5, a significant proportion of Americans also would select a higher poverty line.

The final problem with absolute definitions of poverty is that they consider the wealth of the rest of society only as it influences the kinds of expenses a family incurs in order to get by at a subsistence level. We previously used sewer service as an example: Because everyone living in a city must pay for sewer service, the poverty line will be higher in wealthy societies than in poor societies. However, beyond this, the wealth of the rest of society is not considered. That is, if the average income in a society triples over a period of years but the cost of living stays the same, the poverty line will not increase. The reason that this is a problem with absolute definitions has to do with the concept of *relative deprivation,* which asserts that people feel rich or poor not in relation to some absolute yardstick but rather in relation to the wealth of other people. Thus, even though people living at the poverty line may be no poorer when the wealth of the rest of society increases, the fact is they feel poorer. This phenomenon is the reason some people argue that poverty should be defined not in absolute but in relative terms.

Relative Definitions

Absolute definitions attempt to set an objective line that separates the poor from the nonpoor. Relative definitions see poverty as subjective; that is, it is a matter of opinion on the part of both the poor and the nonpoor as to what constitutes poverty. Poverty is viewed as relative to the wealth of the rest of society. According to relative definitions, a family with an income of $12,000 a year will consider itself, and be considered by others, as poor in a society such as the United States, where the median annual income in 2005 was over $46,000. This family would not be considered poor in a country such as Mexico, however, where the median family income is much lower.

Thus, even though people living at the poverty line may be no poorer when the wealth of the rest of society increases, the fact is they feel poorer.

There are two main methods of setting relative poverty levels. One is to take an arbitrary percentage of the median family income and define this as the poverty level. The line in most countries is set at the 50–66 percent level. The European Union generally uses 60 percent of median income as its poverty line. In the United States, the relative poverty line is set at 44 percent of the median income, resulting in a figure of $20,240, only $249 more than the official poverty threshold set at $19,991 for a family of four. The other method, exemplified by the Townsend study in England, is to survey the general population to find out their opinion about where the poverty level should be.[29]

The major problem with relative definitions and measures of poverty is related to the fact that they are subjective. The question is, what criteria do you use in setting the line? In setting an absolute line, you have the criterion of physical efficiency, which can be ascertained by things such as caloric needs and the cost of a menu sufficient to obtain these calories. But when you attempt to set a relative line, there is no similar criterion. Desai proposes two principles to be used in setting a relative poverty line:

1. . . . economic entitlement to an adequate living standard should be such that citizens can take full part in the political community.

2. . . . the level of the poverty threshold, i.e., the specific contents of the level of living flowing from a citizen's economic entitlement, must be determined by the community.[30]

These principles fit with the current trend of defining poverty as social exclusion as opposed to simply economic deprivation.[31]

The authors agree with Desai, but we would broaden the first principle by eliminating the word *political*. Thus, when considering whether to include an item in a poverty line budget, we would ask the question, "Is this item necessary for full participation in the community?" rather than asking the absolute definition question, "Is this item necessary for physical efficiency?" For example, if you were considering whether to include the cost of a bicycle for a family with a ten-year-old child, using an absolute definition, you would not include any money for this because the family can function with physical efficiency without a bicycle. Using a relative definition, however, you would include it because there is little doubt that a ten-year-old needs a bike in order to not be excluded from full participation in the life of the community.

As you might expect, using a relative definition can result in a much higher poverty line than using an absolute definition—and consequently, a much higher poverty rate. The London Weekend Television study in England and the Gallup poll in the United States cited earlier resulted in figures that are 33 and 55 percent above the official poverty line. The Townsend study in England resulted in a figure that was 50 percent above the official level. On average, the poverty line set by these groups was 90 percent greater than the official U.S. government level. Even when the very low relative poverty line figure of 44 percent of median income is used in the United States, the relative line comes out to be slightly higher than the official line.

Relative poverty measures have several advantages over absolute measures. The first and probably greatest advantage is that they are much more realistic than absolute measures. People do not live their lives according to the assumptions used for absolute poverty lines. They purchase toys for their children; they visit relatives; they celebrate occasions such as anniversaries and birthdays. And they generally do not manage their affairs with absolute efficiency. A second major advantage is that relative definitions recognize that poverty is subjective. Poverty is a matter of feeling and opinion among both the poor and the nonpoor, and relative definitions take opinions into account.

The major drawback of relative definitions is that they present a moving target, so to speak, for poverty policy and programs. One of the major reasons for defining poverty to begin with is so that we can measure progress in our attempts to do something about it. Using absolute definitions, we can see over time what progress has, or has not, been made. Using relative definitions, any change that occurs is likely to be as much a result of changing perceptions as it is a change in the level of well-being of the poorest section of the population.

It is easy, and a common practice, to dismiss arguments for relative definitions of poverty as a reflection of bleeding heart liberalism and to say, in effect, "So what if a person feels that he or she is poor; as long as his or her basic needs are taken care of, what difference does it make?" Cassidy has summarized research on the subject of relative deprivation and concludes that it makes quite a lot of difference. For example, Sir Michael Marmot, of the University College of London, followed the health status of a group of British civil servants and found that those who had not succeeded in rising past lower-level positions were significantly more likely than their superiors in the hierarchy to develop a range of health problems including heart disease, high blood

---

A Closer Look

Poverty Definition Quiz

Do you think the following things are essential or nonessential?

1. For a ten-year-old child to have a bicycle
2. For a family to have a car, even though it may be a junker
3. For a sixteen-year-old girl to have a formal dress or a sixteen-year-old boy to rent a tuxedo to attend the junior prom
4. For a family to have enough food to be able to serve coffee and cookies, or beer and chips, when friends drop in
5. For a family to have a television set in good working order
6. For a family to have a personal computer with an internet connection

If you answered that all, or most, of these things are nonessential, you are operating from an absolute definition of poverty. It is true that none of these things is necessary for life or for efficiency (although it could be argued that in 2010 a personal computer with an internet connection is essential for social efficiency). If you answered that all, or most, of these are essential, you are operating from a relative definition. There is little doubt that a family that does not have these things, as well as many others not listed here, is not able to participate fully in the life of our society.

---

pressure, lung cancer, and gastrointestinal problems. Amartya Sen, winner of the 1998 Nobel Prize in economics, has found that African Americans, who are poor relative to American society, have a shorter life span than Indians born in the impoverished state of Kerala, where they are much poorer than the Americans in absolute terms but much better off in relative terms. In addition to health consequences, relative deprivation is also reflected in the fact that lower-income (although above the poverty line) people have limited access to things such as computers, cell phones, and the Internet, all things that are essential for a person to have an equal chance of success in twenty-first-century America. Cassidy concludes, "Since relative deprivation confers many of the disadvantages of absolute deprivation, it should be reflected in the poverty statistics."[32]

The Official Poverty Line in the United States

Various government agencies in the United States have formulated definitions of poverty since the late nineteenth century. In 1907, the Bureau of Labor Statistics devised two budgets, one to meet "minimum standards" (an absolute measure) and one that was called a "fair standard" (a relative measure).[33] However, there was no "official" poverty line until the 1960s, when the U.S. government became serious for the first time in its history about reducing poverty. The official poverty line is defined as an attempt to "specify the minimum amount required to support an average family of given composition at the lowest level consistent with standards of living prevailing in this country."[34]

The first official poverty line in the United States was a crude measure developed in 1964 by the Council of Economic Advisors (CEA). This line used the same methodology that Rowntree had devised half a century earlier, which was based on the cost of food. The line was formulated using the *Engle's coefficient,* a technique that resulted in the conclusion that the average poor family spent one-third of its income on food. The Department of Agriculture

(USDA) had developed menus to show what it cost families to eat at various levels, ranging from an economy budget to three higher-cost budgets. Initially the line was set using the "low cost" menu and multiplying it by three (because food is supposed to take up one-third of a family's budget), which resulted in a poverty level of $3,995. This amount was deemed too high, so the CEA reformulated the line using the "economy budget," which resulted in a poverty level of $3,000. The main problem with this poverty line was that it had only two categories: families and single individuals. The poverty line was $1,500 for an individual and $3,000 for a family—regardless of size, age of family members, or type of residence. Thus a couple with no dependents and an income of $2,900 was considered poor, whereas a family of eight with an income of $3,100 was not.

Because of the problems with the CEA poverty measure, the Social Security Administration (SSA) decided to revise it in 1965. A panel was appointed to accomplish this task; Mollie Orshansky, an SSA statistician, was designated as the chairperson. The SSA panel decided to continue to use the Engle's coefficient and the USDA economy food plan as the base for its calculations because this method was thought to have resulted in a realistic poverty line for a nonfarm family of four. Beyond this, however, the panel felt that the method developed by the CEA was too crude to differentiate among different family types, places of residence, and other factors. The result of this panel's work was a poverty table known as the "Orshansky Index."[35] The new index was based on two major changes in the method of computation. The first was that the Engle's coefficient was reformulated to reflect the fact that smaller families spend a smaller percentage of their incomes on food. For single individuals, the food budget was multiplied by a factor of 5.92; for couples, the factor was 3.88; and for all larger families, the factor was 3.0. The second change was that the budget was reduced by 30 percent for farm families because it was presumed that they would grow a portion of their food. The resulting index differentiated among 124 different kinds of families based on the sex of the head of household, the number of children under eighteen, the number of adults, and whether the family lived on a farm.

The poverty table developed by the Orshansky panel was updated each year based on changes in the price of food in the USDA economy food budget. In 1969, the Census Bureau adopted the index as its official measure of poverty and began to issue a statistical series on poverty. Over the years, the Census Bureau has made several changes in the index. The first is that they ceased updating it based on the cost of food and instead began to update it based on changes in the consumer price index (CPI). The second major change is that the differential between farm and nonfarm families was gradually reduced until it was entirely eliminated in 1982. These changes, along with some other minor ones, have caused the current table to be simplified considerably. The official poverty table for 2009 is presented in Table 6. Because of the need for trend data, the Census Bureau extrapolated the poverty line back to 1959. The poverty trend data for 1959–2007 are summarized in Figure 5.

The official U.S. government poverty line has been criticized for the same shortcomings as all absolute measures of poverty: It does not reflect how people actually spend their money, it ignores the fact that people have emotional needs that may be even more important to them than physical needs (parents may buy a child a birthday present even if it means they do not have enough money left to pay the rent), and it is set at a level that is much lower than

Policy Practice

Critical Thinking Question

How is the official poverty line set in the United States? What are the limitations to using this approach?

Table 6 **2009 HHS Poverty Guidelines (Extended until at least March 1, 2010)**

Persons in Family or Household	48 Contiguous States and D.C.	Alaska	Hawaii
1	$10,830	$13,530	$12,460
2	14,570	18,210	16,760
3	18,310	22,890	21,060
4	22,050	27,570	25,360
5	25,790	32,250	29,660
6	29,530	36,930	33,960
7	33,270	41,610	38,260
8	37,010	46,290	42,560
For each additional person, add	3,740	4,680	4,300

Source: The poverty guidelines are updated periodically in the *Federal Register* by the U.S. Department of Health and Human Services under the authority of 42 U.S.C. 9902 (2).

many people in our society would personally set it. These are shortcomings of all absolute poverty measures, not just of the specific line used in this country. There is, however, a hot debate between liberals and conservatives about how useful and accurate the line is and just what it means. It is to this debate that we now turn.

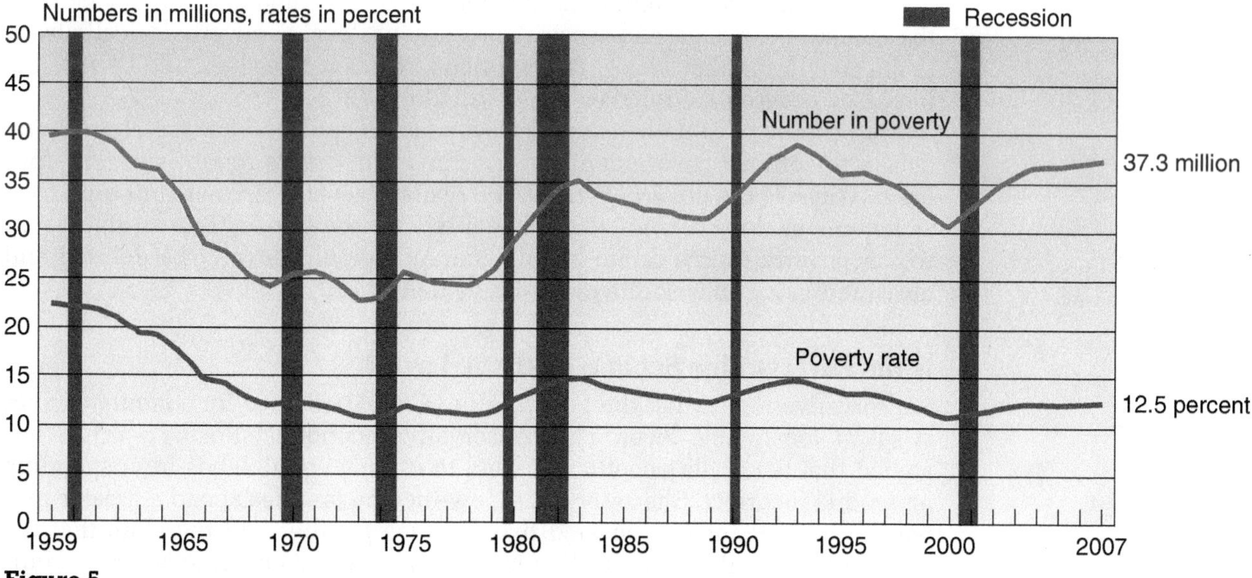

Figure 5

Number in Poverty and Poverty Rate: 1959 to 2007
Source: U.S. Census Bureau, Current Population Survey, 1960 to 2008 Annual Social and Economic Supplements.

Issues and Perspectives in Measuring and Defining Poverty

At first it sounds strange to speak of clashing perspectives and heated disagreements about something so seemingly dry and technical as the definition and measurement of poverty. However, as we shall see, these disagreements do occur, and although the matter may be dry and technical, it is certainly not unimportant. The definition of poverty is an inherently political act and one that has grave implications. The power to define poverty is the power to control statistics—and, as Harrington has noted, "the control of statistics is one of the critical functions of power in a democratic society. The numbers define the limits of the possible; they confer the awesome mathematical legitimacy of 'fact' upon some parts of reality and deny it to others."[36] Orshansky, the primary author of the official poverty line, is quite candid about the political nature of the line. She comments, "In the Social Security Administration poverty was first defined in terms of the public or policy issue: To how many people, and to which ones, did we wish to direct policy concern."[37] Orshansky and her committee wished to create a line that was politically credible. To be credible, they felt that they had to select a figure that identified a group that was not so small that people would be tempted not to worry about it or so large that a solution would appear impossible.

Conservatives support the status quo and are generally opposed to government programs. Because of these views, they tend to favor definitions that minimize the amount of poverty in America. If the level of poverty is shown to be low, this logically leads to the conclusion that society is working well (which supports the status quo) and that there is little need for more government programs. Nicholas Eberstadt of the conservative American Enterprise Institute wrote in 2002, "The poverty rate misleads the public and our representatives, and it thereby degrades the quality of our social policies. . . . It should be discarded for the broken tool that it is."[38] Liberals support change and are generally in favor of government programs that they believe will lead to an improvement in society. They favor definitions that maximize the amount of poverty because the existence of a large, and especially a growing, level of poverty logically leads to the conclusion that society is not functioning as well as it should be and that increased government intervention is called for.

In keeping with their respective agendas, liberals and conservatives hotly debate the official government poverty line. The debate revolves around four basic issues: Is the poverty line set at a realistic level? Do you count only cash as income or do you count other benefits? Are the Census Bureau figures on which poverty estimates are based accurate? Should poverty be defined and measured using an absolute or a relative definition?

Is the Poverty Line Set at a Realistic Level?

Conservatives argue that the poverty line, $20,650 in 2007 for a family of four, is set at too high a level. The conservative economist Rose Friedman has argued that the Engle's coefficient used to estimate total needs from spending on food is incorrect. She asserts that low-income families spend a greater proportion of their income on food than average families and therefore that the food budget should be multiplied by a number less than the three that is currently used. Friedman argues that the use of this incorrect coefficient has resulted in an overestimation of poverty by as much as 100 percent.[39]

Conservatives also argue that tying the poverty line to the consumer price index has further increased the already too high poverty line. The CPI measures increases in the cost of living by figuring the cost of a specific "market basket" of goods. Butler and Kondratas say that this method ignores substitution of one commodity for another by households in order to keep the cost down.[40] For example, if the price of soft drinks increased by 30 percent and the price of fruit juice did not increase at all, most consumers would substitute fruit juice for at least part of their soft drink consumption. As a result of this substitution, the actual cost of their "market basket" of goods would increase at a rate lower than the CPI. This is only one of several flaws in the CPI that conservatives believe have artificially inflated the poverty line.

Liberals, to no one's surprise, take the opposite position and argue that the poverty line is too low. They point out that the U.S. Department of Agriculture, whose budgets are used as the basis of the poverty calculations, admits that the budgets are set at an unrealistically low level. USDA analysts have estimated that only about 10 percent of persons spending the amount allowed in the economy food budget are able to get a nutritionally adequate diet.[41] The USDA has also revised the Engle's coefficient. In 1965, an analysis by the department concluded that for poor families the coefficient should be 3.45 rather than 3.0. This increase would raise the poverty line by 15 percent and result in a large increase in the number of families defined as poor. Even the originator of the official poverty line, Mollie Orshansky, eventually came to believe that the methodology had, over time, broken down, resulting in a figure that was too low. She updated the methodology and, applying the new methodology to Census Bureau data, concluded that the official figures underestimated the amount of poverty by between 38 and 54 percent, depending on which Census survey was used.[42]

How Should Noncash Benefits Be Counted?

A good deal of assistance to poor families is given in forms other than cash. Poor people may receive food stamps, medical care, low-cost public housing, legal services, social services, and other items and services; these are referred to as *in-kind benefits*. Although these items do not constitute income as such, it does cost money to provide them, and they are of tangible benefit in improving the lives of the recipients. Most of these benefits were not available when the current methodology for defining and measuring poverty was adopted. The current method of computing the poverty line counts only cash as income; no value whatsoever is given to in-kind benefits.

Conservatives argue that in-kind benefits should be counted as income. Butler and Kondratas point to the irony of not counting these benefits; they observe that "the federal government could give every poor person in America a free car, free housing and education, and free food for life, but as far as the official poverty definition is concerned, that would have no impact whatsoever on poverty."[43] They observe that the majority of the increases in benefits provided to the poor since the early 1960s have been in the form of goods and services rather than cash and that if these benefits were counted, the poverty rate would greatly decrease. Martin Anderson, a leading conservative analyst on the subject of social welfare, has gone so far as to say, "The 'War on Poverty' that began in 1964 has been won. . . . Any Americans who truly cannot care for themselves are now eligible for generous government aid in the form of cash, medical benefits, food stamps, housing, and other services."[44] Anderson, using data from the Census Bureau and from a Congressional Budget Office study, estimates that largely because of the value of in-kind benefits, the number of people in poverty in 1978 was only one-quarter of the official figure.

Liberals agree that in-kind benefits have value and should be considered when we define and measure poverty. Their argument is that excluding all benefits other than cash from poverty-line calculations obscures the successes of social programs, especially Medicaid and food stamps. They point out that this is why conservative critics such as Charles Murray have been able to argue that liberal social programs have largely failed. It has been estimated by liberal policy analysts that if all government benefits were included, the number of people living below the poverty line would be about one-third lower.[45] However, liberals have some ambivalence about this issue owing to what they see as the difficulty of accurately assessing the value of noncash benefits. Harrington gives the following example of the problems involved:

> How does one evaluate the value of medical care that goes mainly to the aging poor? The Bureau of the Census gives an excellent case in point. In 1979, the market value of Medicaid coverage for an elderly person in New York State was estimated at $4,430. But this was almost $1,000 more than the poverty line for that person ($3,472). Clearly this $4,430 is "income" in a very special sense, since it cannot be spent on food, housing, or any other need (and it is indeed most unwelcome "income" since one has to be ill to get it). If one were to take that $4,430 at face value, then a person could enter the middle class, by virtue of having a long, expensive, subsidized terminal illness.[46]

Should Poverty Be Defined in Absolute or Relative Terms?

This question is closely related to our earlier discussion of inequality. If you think for a few moments, you will realize that if you use a relative definition of poverty, the only way poverty will show a reduction is for the Gini coefficient to show a reduction. By way of example, let's use two rather improbable economic scenarios. In the first scenario, the economy enters a tremendous boom period with the result that the income of everyone in the country doubles while prices remain the same. This means that a family of four that was living on $10,000 a year, a little below the poverty line, now is earning $20,000 a year, well above the poverty line. It also means that the family whose income was $250,000 a year, many times more than it needs, now has even more. If you apply an absolute definition of poverty to this scenario, poverty would almost disappear. However, if you apply a relative definition, the poverty level would be exactly the same because at the same time the median income doubled, the relative poverty line also would have doubled. Therefore, inequality would be the same, the Gini coefficient would be the same, and the poverty level would be the same—even though people would be twice as well off in absolute terms.

The second scenario is the opposite. In this scenario, the country enters a tremendous depression. Everyone's income takes a nosedive; however, let's suppose that the richer you are, the harder you are hit. People in the bottom 20 percent (quintile) of the income distribution suffer a 30 percent reduction in income; people in the next quintile suffer a 40 percent reduction; the next quintile is reduced by 50 percent; the fourth quintile is reduced by 70 percent; and the richest quintile see their income go down by 90 percent. This means that the family in the first scenario, whose income was $10,000 per year, now has an income of $7,000. The family whose income was $250,000 now has an income of only $25,000 per year. If an absolute definition of poverty were applied to this scenario, the poverty rate would skyrocket. However, if a relative definition were applied, the poverty rate would drop dramatically. Before the crash, the income of the low-income family was only 4 percent of that of the high-income family. After the crash, it "improved" to 28 percent. This example is far-fetched, but the point it illustrates is not: When one uses a relative definition, the only way to show a reduction in poverty is to reduce inequality.

As you know from the previous discussion of inequality, conservatives see no particular reason to reduce inequality and so do not generally favor relative definitions. They believe that absolute definitions such as the official poverty line, while not perfect, are satisfactory for the purposes they serve. Murray, for example, says

> The poverty definition has been attacked from all sides but continues to be used because, finally, it has a good deal of merit. The poverty line does not truly divide the "poverty-stricken" from the rest of us—the transition consists of a continuum, not a dividing line—but it gives us a common yardstick for talking about the issue. It is widely accepted, takes family size and inflation into account, and provides a consistent definition for examining income over time. Also, no one has proposed an alternative definition that has attracted widespread support.[47]

Liberals believe that the reduction of inequality would be a good thing and so are more favorable toward relative definitions of poverty and more critical of absolute definitions. Rodgers, for example, criticizes the official poverty line on the grounds that it has not kept up with the growth in personal income. He notes that in 1959 the poverty line was 53 percent of median income; by 1984, it had declined to only 38 percent. Rodgers believes that a relative definition is the only meaningful way of describing poverty and that the United States does not use this method because the amount of poverty revealed would be embarrassing to the government.[48]

Should the Poverty Line Be Based on Net Disposable Income?

When the initial poverty measure was developed, it was based on the mostly accurate belief that the majority of people with incomes below the poverty line were not employed. Thus the simplest means of calculating the poverty line was that of basing it on gross income. As we have seen, in the years since the original poverty measure was developed, the poverty population has changed significantly; currently, most are employed. The growth of the working poor creates two major inaccuracies in the poverty measure. The first is that a working person's gross income is significantly reduced by taxes and other deductions before it ever reaches the recipient. The second is that even after taxes, the income is further reduced by work-related expenses, primarily child care. Thus a nonworking mother of three whose income is $20,000 a year is considered to be poor by the current measure, but a working mother whose gross income is $21,000 a year, but whose net income after deductions and work-related expenses is only $14,000, is not considered to be poor. Both liberals and conservatives agree that something should be done to base the poverty line on actual disposable income rather than gross income.

Conservatives have long argued that if in-kind benefits such as food stamps were counted, the number of people classified as being below the poverty line would greatly decrease. The new poverty measure recommended by the National Science Foundation counts in-kind benefits as a kind of income.

Experimental Poverty Measures

Because of the problems in the current poverty measure discussed in previous sections, plus additional problems resulting from social and economic changes that have occurred since the current measure was developed, the Census Bureau has been considering revising the method used to define and measure poverty. A National Academy of Sciences (NAS) panel that is advising the Census Bureau has identified six weaknesses in the current poverty measure:

1. Because of the increased participation of mothers in the labor force, there are more working families who must pay for child care, but the current measure does not distinguish between the needs of families in which the parents do or do not work outside the home. More generally, the current measure does not distinguish between the needs of workers and nonworkers.

2. Because of differences in health status and insurance coverage, different population groups face significant differences in medical care costs, but the current measure does not take account of them.

3. The thresholds are the same across the nation, although significant price variations across geographic areas exist for needs such as housing.

4. The family-size adjustments in the thresholds are anomalous in many respects, and changing demographic and family characteristics (such as the reduction in average family size) underscore the need to reassess the adjustments.

5. Changes in the standard of living call into question the merits of continuing to use the values of the original thresholds updated only for inflation. Historical evidence suggests that poverty thresholds—including those developed according to "expert" notions of minimum needs—follow trends in overall consumption levels. Because of rising living standards in the United States, most approaches for developing poverty thresholds (including the original one) would produce higher thresholds today than the current ones.

6. Finally, because the current measure defines family resources as gross money income, it does not reflect the effects of important government policy initiatives that have significantly altered families' disposable income and, hence, their poverty status. Examples are the increase in the Social Security payroll tax, which reduces disposable income for workers, and the growth in the Food Stamp Program, which raises disposable income for beneficiaries.

The NSF panel has recommended a new poverty measure that, like the current measure, is based on the three basic budget categories of food, clothing, and shelter, with a small additional amount added for personal needs.[49] Since 1996 when this panel first made its recommendations, there have been 30 alternative poverty measures developed and over 50 research papers written evaluating these measures. Facing this mass of data, the Committee on National Statistics (CNSTAT) convened a workshop in June 2004 of leading researchers and statisticians to evaluate progress that had been made toward developing a new way of defining and measuring poverty. The workshop report concluded that some recommendations were so widely accepted that they needed no discussion. These areas of agreement were that "the measure of family income should consist not only of gross cash income (the current official definition), but it should also

- Account for taxes (subtract taxes, add the Earned Income Tax Credit and realized capital gains/losses).
- Add the value of food stamps and other near-cash benefits, including child-care subsidies, school lunch subsidies, home energy assistance, and, if the data are available, benefits received under the Women, Infants, and Children nutrition program and the school breakfast program.
- Subtract from income any child support payments made by the payer, if data are available."

There was less agreement about a number of other issues, such as how to annually update the poverty line, how to adjust for family size and composition, whether to include geographic adjustments, how to account for medical and child-care expenses, and how to incorporate the value of housing.[50]

The Census Bureau is currently evaluating alternative poverty measures. No time frame has been established for deciding on and implementing a new measure.

CONCLUSION

It has been said that statistics are problems with the tears wiped away. It is important that we keep this in mind when discussing somewhat dry, technical subjects such as inequality and the definition and measurement of poverty. How we define and measure poverty has very real consequences for a large number of people. The eligibility requirements for many assistance programs are computed by means of formulas derived from the poverty line. Some housing assistance programs, for example, are open to people whose income does not exceed 125 percent of the poverty line. A revision of a few hundred dollars up or down in the poverty line will result in thousands of people becoming eligible or ineligible for a decent place to live. What the correct Engle's coefficient is may be puzzling to a student and fascinating to a professor, but it has very real consequences for a child who does not want to sleep with rats.

Log onto **MySocialWorkLab** to access a wealth of case studies, videos, and assessment. (*If you did not receive an access code to* **MySocialWorkLab** *with this text and wish to purchase access online, please visit* www.mysocialworklab.com.)

1. **Read the case:** *Community Practice: Organizing Social Work in the Republic of Armenia,* Part I. What are the advantages and disadvantages of applying a relative definition of poverty in the Republic of Armenia?

2. **Read the case:** *Foster Care: The Leon Family.* Which definitions of poverty best explain what is occurring in the Leon Family?

PRACTICE TEST The following questions will test your knowledge of the content found within this chapter. For additional assessment, including licensing-exam type questions on applying chapter content to practice, visit **MySocialWorkLab**.

Policy Practice

1. The *Lorenz curve* is a technique of measuring income data that:
   a. describes the degree of equality in income distribution.
   b. traces out the share of total income held by different subgroups.
   c. illustrates the size-of-the-pie theory.
   d. breaks it down by racial and ethnic group.

2. The *Gini coefficient* is a technique of measuring income data that:
   a. describes the degree of equality in income distribution.
   b. traces out the share of total income held by different subgroups.
   c. illustrates the size-of-the-pie theory.
   d. breaks it down by racial and ethnic group.

3. What percentage of the national income do the poorest 20% of the population receive?
   a. 5.1%
   b. 4.8%
   c. 3.4%
   d. 5.9%

4. In recent years, the distribution of wealth has:
   a. stayed roughly the same.
   b. become more equal.
   c. become more unequal.
   d. become less relevant.

5. Lynn Karoly's findings that the increase in inequality over the previous twenty years was attributable to inequality within age cohorts rather than changes in the relative size of age cohorts debunks the argument that:
   a. inequality is caused less by unfairness than by the age structure of the labor force.
   b. inequality is the result of the personal failings of the poorest cohort.
   c. inequality declined beginning in the late 1980s as the baby boomers entered their peak earning years.
   d. inequality can lead to social disruption.

Human Behavior

6. An absolute definition of poverty is:
   a. a subjective opinion based on an analysis of wealth relative to the rest of society.
   b. a lifestyle composed of values, attitudes, and behaviors related to being poor.
   c. an inaccurate measure of actual income.
   d. a relatively fixed level of income below which a person cannot function in a productive and efficient manner in a given society.

7. Which element is not taken into consideration when developing an absolute definition of the poverty line?
   a. The minimum level that enables a person to be physically efficient
   b. The degree to which a person must struggle to obtain this minimum level
   c. The relative wealth of society as a whole
   d. Objective yardsticks that change only with the cost of living or when certain things become necessary expenditures

8. The concept of *relative deprivation* asserts that:
   a. the poverty line will be higher in wealthy societies than in poor societies.
   b. the assumptions on which absolute poverty lines are based are false.
   c. the wealth of society influences the costs that a family incurs in order to get by at a subsistence level.
   d. people feel rich or poor not in relation to an absolute measure but in relation to the wealth of other people.

Log onto **MySocialWorkLab** once you have completed the Practice Test above to access additional study tools and assessment.

Answers:

Key: 1) b 2) a 3) c 4) c 5) a 6) d 7) c 8) d

NOTES

1. U.S. Census Bureau, *Income, Poverty, and Health Insurance Coverage in the United States: 2008,* Table 1, "Income and Earnings Summary Measures by Selected Characteristics: 2007 and 2008, (September 2009); U.S. Department of Commerce, *National Economic Accounts,* Table 2.1, "Personal Income and Its Disposition" (January 29, 2010).
2. Molly Ivins, "GOP Says Some Topics Off Limits," *Kalamazoo Gazette* (January 12, 1995).
3. John Craven, *Introduction to Economics: An Integrated Approach to Fundamental Principles* (Oxford, UK: Basil Blackwell, 1984), 99.
4. Arthur Kennickell, "Currents and Undercurrents: Changes in the Distribution of Wealth, 1989–2004," www.federalreserve.gov/pubs/oss/oss2/method.html.
5. Edward N. Wolff. "Household Wealth in the United States: Rising Debt and the Middle-Class Squeeze," Working Paper No. 53, The Levy Economics Institute at Bard College, New York University (June 2007).
6. Quoted in University of Michigan Institute for Social Research, "Wealth in America," 3.
7. Lisa A. Keister, *Wealth in America* (Cambridge, UK: Cambridge UP, 2000), 65.
8. Richard B. Freeman, "Solving the New Inequality," in Richard B. Freeman, *The New Inequality; Creating Solutions for Poor America* (Boston: Beacon Press, 1999), 3; Richard Wolff, "Recent Trends" (2007), 11.
9. Daniel H. Weinberg, "Income Inequality," U.S. Bureau of the Census, "The Official Statistics," www.census.gov/hhes/income/incineq/p60asc.
10. D. Stanley Eitzen, "Dismantling the Welfare State," *Vital Speeches of the Day* 62 (June 15, 1996): 532–36, updated by author.
11. Michael Hout and Samuel R. Lucas, "Narrowing the Income Gap between Rich and Poor," *Chronicle of Higher Education* (August 16, 1996).
12. Michael Novak and Gordon Green, "Poverty Down, Inequality Up?" *The Public Interest* (Spring 1986): 49–57.
13. Sheldon Danzinger and Peter Gottshalk, "Introduction," in Sheldon Danziger and Peter Gottshalk, eds.,*Uneven Tides: Rising Inequality in America* (New York: Russell Sage Foundation, 1993), 13.
14. Bennett Harrison, Chris Tilly, and Berry Bluestone, "Wage Inequity Takes a Great U-Turn," *Challenge* (March–April 1986): 27.
15. Lester Thurow, quoted in D. Stanley Eitzen, "Dismantling the Welfare State," 4.
16. Henry Reuss, "Inequality, Here We Come," *Challenge* (September–October 1981): 52.
17. George Gilder, *Wealth and Poverty* (New York: Basic Books, 1981), 63.
18. George Gilder, "Wealth and Poverty Revisited," *American Spectator* 26 (July 1993): 37.
19. Robert M. Solow, "The Entrepreneur as Hero," review of George Gilder, *The Spirit of Enterprise,* in *The New Republic* (October 22, 1984): 37–39.
20. William Ryan, *Equality* (New York: Pantheon, 1981), 30.
21. Paul Krugman, "The Income Disparity," *Challenge* (July–August 1990): 6.
22. L. F. Hayes, "Non-Economic Aspects of Poverty," *Australian Journal of Social Issues* 5 (February 1970): 41–54.
23. Mollie Orshansky, "How Poverty Is Measured," *Monthly Labor Review* 92 (February 1969): 37.
24. Quoted in Albert Fried and Richard M. Elman, eds., *Charles Booth's London: A Portrait of the Poor at the Turn of the Century, Drawn from His "Life and Labour of the People in London"* (New York: Pantheon, 1968), 10.
25. Robert Holman, *Poverty: Explanations of Social Deprivation* (New York: St. Martin's, 1978), 7–8.
26. Quoted in Holman, *Poverty,* 11–12.
27. Howard J. Karger, *Shortchanged: Life and Debt in the Fringe Economy* (San Francisco: Berrett-Koehler, 2005).
28. Joanna Mack and Stewart Lansley, *Poor Britain* (London: Allen and Unwin, 1985).
29. Peter Townsend, P. Corrigan, and U. Kowarski, *Poverty and the London Labor Market: The Third London Survey, Interim Report* (London: The Low Pay Unit, 1987).
30. Meghnad Desai, "Drawing the Line: On Defining the Poverty Threshold," in Peter Golding, ed., *Excluding the Poor* (London: Child Poverty Action Group, 1986), 3–4.
31. A. J. Berghman, "Social Exclusion in Europe: Policy Context and Analytical Framework," in G. Room, ed., *Beyond the Threshold: The Measurement and Analysis of Social Exclusion* (Bristol, UK: Policy Press, 1995).
32. John Cassidy, "Relatively Deprived," *New Yorker* (April 3, 2006): 42–47.

33. Sharon M. Oster, Elizabeth E. Lake, and Conchita Gene Oksman, *The Definition and Measurement of Poverty, Volume 1: A Review* (Boulder, CO: Westview Press, 1978), 6.

34. Mollie Orshansky, "Measuring Poverty," *The Social Welfare Forum: Proceedings of the 92nd Annual Forum of the National Conference on Social Welfare* (New York: Columbia UP, 1965), 214.

35. Orshansky, "How Poverty Is Measured," 37–41.

36. Michael Harrington, *The New American Poverty* (New York: Holt, Rinehart & Winston, 1984), 71.

37. Orshansky, "How Poverty Is Measured," 37.

38. Quoted in John Cassidy, "Relatively Deprived," 45.

39. Rose Friedman, *Poverty: Definition and Perspective* (Washington, DC: American Enterprise Institute, 1965), 36.

40. Stuart Butler and Anna Kondratas, *Out of the Poverty Trap* (New York: Free Press, 1987), 46.

41. Orshansky, "How Poverty Is Measured," 38.

42. Mollie Orshansky, "Measuring Poverty," *Public Welfare* 51 (Winter 1993): 27.

43. Butler and Kondratas, *Out of the Poverty Trap,* 46.

44. Martin Anderson, *Welfare* (Stanford, CA: Hoover Institution, 1978), 15.

45. Gary Burtless and Timothy Smeeding, "The Level, Trend, and Composition of Poverty," in Sheldon H. Danziger and Robert H. Haverman, eds., *Understanding Poverty* (New York: Russell Sage, 2003), 173.

46. Harrington, *The New American Poverty,* 86.

47. Charles Murray, *Losing Ground* (New York: Basic Books, 1984), 271.

48. Harrell R. Rodgers, Jr., "Limiting Poverty by Design," in Richard Goldstein and Stephen Sachs, eds., *Applied Poverty Research* (Lanham, MD: Rowman & Littlefield, 1984), 54.

49. National Research Council, *Measuring Poverty, A New Approach* (Washington, DC: National Academy Press, 1996), 2–5.

50. John Iceland, "The CNSTAT Workshop on Experimental Poverty Measures, June 2004," University of Wisconsin–Madison, Institute for Research on Poverty. *Focus* 23 (Spring 2005): 26–30; John Iceland. *Experimental Poverty Measures: Summary of a Workshop* (Washington, DC: National Academies Press, 2005).

Poverty in America

© PhotoEdit Inc.

255

*T*his chapter examines the characteristics of poverty in the United States, focusing particular attention on the wide range of theories that attempt to explain why some people become poor and why many remain poor. Also examined are demographic aspects and ways of measuring poverty; family constitution and poverty; child poverty and elderly poverty; the urban and rural poor; and the connections between poverty and work-related issues such as the minimum wage, structural unemployment, dual labor markets, job training programs, and the alternative financial sector or the fringe economy. Last, key strategies developed to combat poverty will be surveyed.

Some Theoretical Formulations about Poverty

The word "poverty" can be defined as deprivation—either absolute or relative. Absolute poverty refers to an unequivocal standard necessary for survival (e.g., the calories necessary for physical survival, adequate shelter for protection against the elements, and proper clothing). Those who fall below that absolute standard of poverty are considered poor. Relative poverty refers to deprivation that is relative to the standard of living enjoyed by other members of society. Although basic needs are met, members of a seg-

ment of the population may be considered poor if they possess fewer resources, opportunities, or goods than other citizens. Relative poverty (or deprivation) can be understood as inequality in the distribution of income, goods, or opportunities.

The Culture of Poverty

Culture of poverty (COP) theorists maintain that poverty and, more specifically, poverty traits are transmitted intergenerationally in a self-perpetuating cycle. According to this theory, the COP transcends regional, rural/urban, and national differences and everywhere shows striking similarities in family structure, interpersonal relations, time orientation, value systems, and patterns of spending.[1]

Oscar Lewis maintained that the COP flourishes in certain types of societies where there is a cash economy based on wage labor and production for profit; there is a high rate of underemployment and unemployment for unskilled workers; low wages are common; there is a failure to provide low-income groups with social, political, and economic organization, either on a voluntary basis or by governmental imposition; and there is a set of values held by the dominant class that stress the accumulation of wealth and property, the possibility of upward mobility, thrift, and the idea that low economic status results from personal inadequacy.

According to Lewis, the culture of poverty is characterized by hopelessness, indifference,

spotlight 1

Poverty

People living in poverty fall into three general categories:

1. Those making only minimum wage (the working poor)
2. The unemployed
3. Those who have poor health or an occupational disability (e.g., a deficit in human capital such as poor education or a low quality and quantity of training and skills)

RESULTS is a nonprofit grassroots advocacy organization committed to creating the political will to end hunger and the worst aspects of poverty. RESULTS members lobby elected officials for effective solutions and key policies that affect hunger and poverty. To learn more about RESULTS, go to the organization's website at **www.results.org**.

alienation, apathy, and a lack of effective participation in or integration into the social and economic fabric of society. Key COP elements are a present-tense time orientation; cynicism toward and mistrust of those in authority; strong feelings of marginality, helplessness, dependence, and inferiority; a high incidence of maternal deprivation and a weak ego structure; lack of impulse control and the inability to defer gratification; a sense of resignation and fatalism; a widespread belief in male superiority; a high tolerance for psychological pathology of all kinds; the absence of childhood as a specially protected and prolonged state; early initiation into sexual unions or nonlegal marriages; a high incidence of abandonment of wives and children; a matriarchal family structure with an emphasis on family solidarity; a proclivity toward authoritarianism; and a minimal level of community organization combined with a strong sense of territoriality.

Opponents argue that COP theories divert attention away from the real factors causing poverty and that supposed characteristics of the COP are also evident in the middle and upper classes. For example, the inability to defer gratification underlies many credit card purchases. Sexual unions and informal marriages are a common occurrence among the middle classes and celebrities. The lack of community is an earmark of the modern suburb; the inability to achieve family solidarity is widespread in the United States; and feelings of indifference, helplessness, alienation, and dependence also afflict much of the middle class.

Eugenics and Poverty

Theories based on eugenics and genetic inferiority have periodically surfaced as explanations for poverty, crime, and disease. In 1877, Richard Dugdale reported on a study of the New York penal system that found crime, pauperism, and disease were transmitted intergenerationally.[2] Henry Goddard's *The Kallikak Family* was an account of a Revolutionary War soldier who had an affair with a feebleminded servant girl before marrying a "respectable" woman.[3] Goddard meticulously listed the disreputable descendants of the servant girl and compared them with the respectable achievers of the wife's descendants. Generations of students were taught the dogma of eugenics.

The eugenics movement lost favor when the racial and genetic theories that were used by Hitler to justify genocidal policies. However, the movement

reemerged with the publication of Arthur Jensen's 1969 article "How Much Can We Boost IQ and Scholastic Achievement?"[4] Jensen concluded that compensatory education was doomed to failure because 80 percent of intelligence (measured by IQ tests) was inherited; hence, money spent on compensatory education was badly spent.[5]

William Shockley, a Nobel laureate in physics who became interested in genetics, advocated paying the "unfit poor" (those who paid no income taxes) $1,000 for each point they fell below an IQ of 100, if they agreed to be sterilized.[6] Richard Herrnstein, a Harvard psychologist and a colleague of Shockley and Jensen, claimed that income and wealth are distributed among Americans based on their abilities which, in turn, are related to their IQ score. Herrnstein argued that the United States should become a "hereditary meritocracy," where the most capable citizens receive the greatest rewards as an incentive for assuming leadership.[7]

The eugenics argument was rekindled by Richard Herrnstein and Charles Murray's *The Bell Curve*, published in 1994, in which the authors argued that socioeconomic inequality in the United States was due to the lack of genetic intelligence.[8] Armed with statistics, tables, and charts, Herrnstein and Murray tried to demonstrate that those in the lower socioeconomic classes have lower IQ scores, which explains why white males (who test higher) control so many of society's institutions.[9] They argue that affirmative action programs overlook intellectual meritocracy. Moreover, spending money to educate the poor is wasteful given their innate deficiencies.

The scholarship in *The Bell Curve* has been attacked by a wide range of critics in the scientific and educational communities.[10] Critics argue that Herrnstein and Murray exaggerate IQ as a predictor of job performance, attribute inaccurate validities to IQ scores, and substitute hypotheticals for reality.[11] Assertions about genetic inferiority fail to hold up under scrutiny, and the theories of Shockley, Jensen, Herrnstein, and Murray have been repudiated by scores of educators, psychologists, sociologists, and anthropologists.[12]

The Radical School and Poverty

Radicals define poverty as resulting from exploitation by the ruling capitalist or dominant class. According to socialists, poverty provides capitalists with an army of surplus laborers who will depress the wages of similar workers. For example, employers can use an oversupply of workers to drive down wages knowing that there will be an abundance of job seekers. In an oversupply of labor, employers can more easily threaten recalcitrant workers with dismissal given the intense competition for jobs. Surplus labor is linked to poverty by using the *threat* of poverty (through unemployment) to discipline the labor force and demand concessions.

According to David Gil, poverty can be understood in terms of status, resource allocation, and the division of labor.[13] Most developed societies manipulate these factors. For instance, societies must develop resources—symbolic, material, life-sustaining, and life-enhancing goods and services. They must also develop a division of labor and must assign individuals or groups to specific tasks related to developing, producing, or distributing the resources of the society. This division of labor is used as the basis for assigning status to individuals and groups; that is, the more highly a society prizes the function an individual or group performs, the higher is the status reward. By manipulating the division of labor, a society is able to assign individuals to specific statuses within the total array of statuses and functions available.

The assignment of status roles is complemented by the distribution of rights. Higher-status roles implicitly demand greater compensation than lower-status roles, and such rewards come by way of the distribution of rights. Higher-status groups are rewarded by a substantial and liberal distribution of general entitlements and rights to material and symbolic resources, goods, and services. Conversely, lower-status groups are denied these resources through formal and informal constraints. Societies rationalize this form of status and goods allocation by an expressed belief in the omniscience of the marketplace. In other words, rewards are based on the value of contribution. This ideology is well masked and rarely questioned. Socialists argue that poverty will be omnipresent so long as society reproduces itself on the basis of the private ownership of the means of production. They believe that poverty cannot be altered without fundamentally rearranging the economic fabric of U.S. society.

Who Makes Up the Poor?

Poverty is a fluid rather than static process for most Americans. The University of Michigan's Panel Study of Income Dynamics (PSID) followed 5,000 U.S. families for almost 10 years (1969–1978) and found that only 2 percent of families were persistently poor throughout the entire period.[14] In fact, about one-third of the individuals poor in any given year escaped from poverty the following year, and only about one-third of the poor families in any given year had been poor for at least eight of the preceding years. The data showed that as people gained (or lost) jobs, as marriages were created (or dissolved), or as offspring were born (or left home), people were either pushed into poverty or escaped from it.[15] Changes in family composition, especially divorce or separation, were the leading causes of poverty. Conversely, **spells of poverty** were most often ended by family reconstitution (e.g., remarriage).

"Mobility in the United States is substantial, according to the evidence," concluded researchers from the Urban Institute. "Large portions of the population move into a new income quintile with estimates ranging from about 25 to 40 percent in a single year. The mobility rate is even higher over longer periods—about 45 percent over a 5-year period and about 60 percent over both 9-year and 17-year periods."[16] Bradley Schiller found that upward mobility is also experienced by the poor. According to Schiller, one-third of minimum wage workers had received a raise within a year, and 60 percent were beyond the minimum wage within two years. "The longitudinal experiences of minimum-wage youth . . . refute the notion of a 'minimum-wage trap,'" he concluded. "Youth who started at the minimum wage in 1980 recorded impressive wage gains over the subsequent seven years both in absolute and relative terms."[17] W. Michael Cox and Richard Alm confirmed significant upward movement of the poor:

> Only 5 percent of those in the bottom fifth in 1975 were still there in 1991. Where did they end up? A majority made it to the top three fifths of the income distribution—middle class or better. Most amazing of all, almost 3 out of 10 of the low-income earners from 1975 had risen to the uppermost 20 percent by 1991. More than three-quarters found their way into the two highest tiers of income earners for at least one year by 1991.[18]

Delving deeper into the labor market, David Howell and Elizabeth Howell constructed a matrix of "job contours" consisting essentially of self-employed, white-collar, blue-collar, and low-wage jobs, then analyzed the mobility of workers according to race, gender, and immigrant status. During a period of enormous compression in job opportunities due to an influx of immigrants, the researchers found that among workers who had worked at least 20 weeks in the previous year, "male and female African American and female new immigrant workers show[ed] substantial improvements in their employment distribution, shifting from the two 'worst' (secondary) job contours toward the two 'best' (independent primary) contours."[19] Income data show that poverty is not a permanent status for many, if not the majority, of the poor.

The following statistics from 2006 suggest some important trends in poverty in the United States:

- The poverty rate was 12.3 percent (36.4 million people), up from 11.8 percent in 1999.
- The poverty rate for children under 18 was 17.4 percent, up from 16.7 percent in 2002. The poverty rate for people over 65 was 9.4 percent.
- Beginning in 2001, the poverty rates also grew for nearly every racial and ethnic group. The poverty rate for blacks was 24.2 percent in 2006, more than twice the poverty rate for whites (10.3 percent). For Hispanics the poverty rate was 20.6 percent, but for children under age five it was 29.9 percent. The poverty rate for Asians and Pacific Islanders was 10.3 percent. These numbers represent an important shift because poverty rates had edged downward throughout the 1990s; by 2001 the cycle was reversing and poverty rates began to climb.
- Poverty rates were 11.5 percent in the Northeast, 11.2 percent in the Midwest, 13.8 percent in the South, and 11.6 percent in the West.
- Poverty rates were the lowest outside principal cities; they were high in inner cities (16.1 percent) and rural areas (15.2 percent).[20]

Table 1 describes the characteristics and numbers of poor over a 50-year period.

Measuring Poverty

There are two versions of the federal poverty measure: (1) the poverty threshold and (2) the poverty guideline. The poverty threshold, also called the **poverty line,** is the official federal poverty measure and is used primarily for statistical purposes, such as estimating the number of Americans in poverty each

year. All official population figures are calculated using the poverty threshold. The poverty guideline uses a slightly lower poverty level than the weighted poverty threshold; for example, for a family of four in 2007 the poverty guideline was $20,650 versus $21,386. The poverty guideline is used for determining eligibility requirements for federal programs such as Head Start, food stamps, the National School Lunch Program, and Low-Income Home Energy Assistance Program. Other federal programs, including Temporary Assistance for Needy Families (TANF) and Supplemental Security Income, use the poverty threshold. As noted earlier, in 2007 the federal poverty index for a family of four was $21,386, up from $8,414 in 1980. (See Table 2) These increases do not reflect more liberal standards but are due solely to the effects of inflation.

Set by the Social Security Administration (SSA), absolute poverty is defined by a poverty line drawn at a given income. The poverty threshold used by the federal government was developed by taking the cost of the least expensive food plan (the Thrifty Food Plan developed by the Department of Agriculture) and multiplying that number by 3. This formula was based on 1955 survey data showing that the average family spent about one-third of its budget on food. Formally adopted by the SSA in 1969, the official poverty measure provides a set of income cutoffs adjusted for household size, the number of children under age 18, and the age of the household head. To ensure constant purchasing power, the SSA adjusts the poverty line yearly, using the consumer price index (CPI).

The poverty index is plagued by a variety of structural problems. A 1995 National Academy of Sciences (NAS) report noted the following problems in calculating the current poverty threshold[21]:

- It excludes in-kind benefits when counting family income.
- It ignores the cost of earning income when calculating the net income of working families. For example, $5,000 in wage income does not include work-related costs such as clothing, transportation, and so on.
- It disregards regional variation in the cost of living, especially the cost of housing and food.
- It ignores the impact of tax payments, such as income, sales, payroll, and property taxes in states where those taxes are high.
- It ignores the effects of Earned Income Tax Credits (EITC).

Table 1

Persons Below the Poverty Line, Selected Years and Characteristics, 1959–2006 (number and percentage below poverty, in thousands)

Year	Overall	Aged	Children[a]	Individuals in Female Headed Families[b]	African Americans	Hispanic Origin[c]	White
2006*	36,460	3,394	12,827	13,199	9,048	9,243	24,416
	12.3%	9.4	17.4	30.5	24.3	20.6	10.3
2002	34,570	3,578	12,133	11,667	8,884	8,556	24,074
	12.1%	10.4	16.7	26.5	24.1	21.8	10.3
1999	32,258	3,167	12,109	12,687	9,091	7,439	21,922
	11.8%	9.7	18.9	27.8	22.7	22.8	9.8
1995	36,425	3,318	13,999	12,315	9,872	8,574	24,423
	13.8%	10.5	20.2	32.4	29.3	30.3	11.2
1990	33,585	3,658	14,431	12,578	9,837	6,006	22,326
	13.5%	12.2	20.6	37.2	31.9	28.1	10.7
1986	32,370	3,477	12,876	11,944	8,983	5,117	22,183
	13.6%	12.4	20.5	38.3	31.3	27.3	11.0
1980	29,272	3,871	11,543	10,120	8,579	3,491	19,699
	13.0%	15.7	18.3	36.7	32.5	25.7	10.2
1978	24,497	3,233	9,931	9,269	7,626	2,607	16,259
	11.4%	14.0	15.9	35.6	30.6	21.6	8.7
1969	21,147	4,787	9,961	6,879	7,095	NA	16,659
	12.1%	25.3	14.0	38.2	32.2	NA	9.5
1959	39,490	5,481	17,552	7,014	9,927	NA	28,484
	22.4%	35.2	27.3	49.4	55.1	NA	18.1

*These numbers may appear inconsistent because the U.S. Census Bureau changed the classification of races in the 2000 census to include the designation of more than one race. In addition, the statistics were calculated slightly differently in different years.

[a]All children, including unrelated children.

[b]Does not include females living alone.

[c]People of Hispanic origin may be of any race; it is an overlapping category.

Sources: Compiled from Committee on Ways and Means, U.S. House of Representatives, "Overview of Entitlement Programs",: *1992 Green Book* (Washington, DC: U.S. Government Printing Office, 1992), Tables 5.2 and 5.3, pp. 1274–1275; Joseph Dalaker and Bernadette D. Proctor, U.S. Census Bureau, "Poverty in the United States: 1999," Current Population Reports, Ser. P60-210 (Washington, DC: U.S. Government Printing Office, 2000); and Bernadette D. Proctor and Joseph Dalaker, U.S. Census Bureau, "Poverty in the United States: 2002, Demographic Programs," Current Population Reports: Consumer Income, U.S. Department of Commerce, Economics and Statistics Administration (Washington, DC: U.S. Government Printing Office, September 2003). Carmen DeNavas-Walt, Bernadette D. Proctor, and Jessica Smith, "Income, Poverty, and Health Insurance Coverage in the United States: 2006." Economics and Statistics Administration, U.S. Census Bureau, issued August 2007. Retrieved June 2008, from www.census.gov/prod/2007pubs/p60-233.pdf

Table 2

Changes in the Poverty Line Based on Income and Family Size, 1975–2007

Family Size	Income, Selected Years						
	1975	1980	1985	1990	1995	2003	2007
1	$2,724	$ 4,190	$ 5,250	$ 6,652	$ 7,763	$ 9,393	$10,787
2	3,506	5,363	7,050	8,509	9,933	12,015	13,884
3	4,293	6,565	8,850	10,419	12,158	14,680	16,218
4	5,500	8,414	10,650	13,359	15,569	18,810	21,386
5	6,499	9,966	12,450	15,572	18,408	22,245	25,791
6	7,316	11,269	14,250	17,839	20,804	25,122	29,664
7	9,022	13,955	16,050	20,241	23,552	28,544	34,132

Sources: Compiled from U.S. Census Bureau, *Technical Paper 56,* ser. P-60, nos. 134 and 149 (Washington, DC: U.S. Government Printing Office, 1992); Carmen DeNavas-Walt, Bernadette D. Proctor, and Robert J. Mills, U.S. Census Bureau, "Income, Poverty and Health Insurance Coverage in the United States: 2003," *Current Population Reports,* ser. p. 60–226. Retrieved October 2004, from www.census.gov/prod/2004pubs/p60-226.pdf; U.S. Census Bureau, "Poverty Thresholds 2007." Retrieved June 2008, from www.census.gov/hhes/www/poverty/threshld/thresh07.html

- It ignores the value of health coverage in determining family income, and ignores medical care costs both in terms of health insurance costs and out-of-pocket medical costs for those without health insurance.
- The index was never updated to account for changing consumption patterns and expenses. For example, although food accounted for one-third of all family expenditures in the 1950s, it now accounts for about one-seventh.[22]

The NAS panel made three important recommendations:

1. Change the measure of income by adding non-cash benefits and by subtracting taxes and work-related expenses, child support payments, and out-of-pocket medical expenses.
2. Create a new poverty threshold that is based on clothing, food, shelter, and "a little bit more." The panel also suggested new ways of estimating the poverty threshold for families of different sizes and composition, allowing for geographic variation. They further suggested that annual updates of the threshold be based not simply on inflation but on the growth of median expenditures on basic goods (food, clothing, and shelter).
3. Replace the current use of the *March Current Population Survey* with data from the *Survey of Income and Program Participation,* a measure that would change the percentage and distribution of the poor.

Legitimizing the NAS panel recommendations, former Democratic senator Daniel Patrick Moynihan introduced the *Poverty Data Correction Act of 1999* that would have required that any data relating to poverty be adjusted for geographic differences in the cost of living. Moynihan argued that because the current poverty calculations do not allow for geographical differences, they distort the true incidence of poverty.[23] Indeed, one would be hard-pressed to argue that the cost of living in Houma, Louisiana, is equivalent to that in Los Angeles or New York.

Families and Poverty

Family composition is strongly correlated to poverty, and families at greatest risk of poverty in the United States are those headed by single females. In 2007 the poverty rate for male-present families was 5.7 percent; for female-headed households it was 30.5 percent. These figures become even starker when disaggregated: Families headed by non-Hispanic white women had a poverty rate of 26.5 percent; families headed by African American and Hispanic women had poverty rates of 39.0 and 36.9 percent, respectively.[24]

More than 1 million American children see their parents divorce or separate each year, and more than half will spend some time in a single-parent family. Using six nationally representative data sets tracking more than 25,000 children, Sara McLanahan and Gary Sandefur found that children raised with only one biological parent are disadvantaged in myriad ways. Compared to children who grow up in two-parent families, they are (1) twice as likely to drop out of school; (2) 2.5 times as likely to become teen mothers; (3) 1.4 times as likely to be idle—out of work and out of school; and are (4) likely to have lower grade point averages, lower college aspirations, poorer academic attendance records, and higher rates of divorce in adulthood. These patterns persist even after adjustments for differences in race, the education of parents, the number of siblings, and the child's geographic location.[25]

© Dorothy Littell Greco/The Image Works

The families at greatest risk of poverty in the United States are those headed by single females. This poverty is compounded when child support payments are withheld.

Child Support Enforcement

A 1995 Census Bureau study reported that slightly more than half of families with an absent parent have child support orders in place. Of those with orders, half received full payment and half received partial or no payment.[26] In 1975 Congress enacted Title IV-D, which was later amended by the Child Support Enforcement Amendments of 1984, the Family Support Act of 1988, and the Personal Responsibility and Work Opportunity Reconciliation Act of 1996. Title IV-D of the federal Social Security Act funds state programs designed to recover child support payments. A case is considered IV-D if the family has received public assistance benefits, or if an application for services was filed with a public welfare agency. The attention focused on "deadbeat dads" has important political overtones. Some argue that focusing on deadbeat dads has allowed policymakers to blame a variety of social ills, from poverty to high welfare costs to social pathology, squarely on fathers.[27]

Nevertheless, child support is important for families with only one custodial parent. According to the Census Bureau, 77 percent (5.26 million)

custodial parents received some child support in 2005. The proportion of custodial parents receiving every payment they were due increased from 37 percent in 1993 to 47 percent in 2005.[28] Of the 13.6 million custodial parents in 2006, 7.8 million (57.3 percent) had some type of agreement or court award allowing them to receive financial support from the noncustodial parent for their children. Most of these (7.2 million) were formal legal agreements (established by a court or other government entity). When custodial parents without any agreements and those with informal agreements were asked why a formal legal agreement was not established, the reasons most often cited were that they did not feel the need to go to court or get legal agreements (33.7 percent), the other parent provided what he or she could for support (27.9 percent), and they felt the other parent could not afford to pay child support (24.1 percent).[29] Arguably, child support is very important for low-income families:

- Child support constitutes 26 to 29 percent of the income of divorced families and reduces their poverty rate by 7 to 11 percent.

- Child support is an important income source for poverty-level families. About 66 percent of custodial parents with incomes below the poverty line that were due child support receive at least some payment. The average amount was $3,000 and constituted 40 percent of their total family income.
- Child support lifts about 500,000 children out of poverty and reduces the poverty rate by 8 percent.
- Child support is an important income source for families leaving welfare. About 42 percent of families leaving welfare receive child support, which makes up 30 percent ($2,562) of their income.
- Child support is important for families affected by welfare time limits. The percentage of these families receiving child support and the amounts they receive increase after public assistance is terminated.
- Child support is important for families leaving the TANF program for work. Between 25 and 33 percent of those leaving welfare for work receive between $250 and $400 a month in child support.
- One study of families leaving welfare with regular child support payments found that they had a slower rate of welfare reentry, a faster rate of finding work, and a slower rate of job loss compared to families without steady child support income.[30]

In 1996, President Clinton signed the Personal Responsibility and Work Opportunity Reconciliation Act (PRWORA) into law. The PRWORA was intended to broadly reform the public assistance system, but it also addressed child support enforcement. Specifically, failure to meet child support obligations could result in revocation of driver's and professional licenses; expanded wage garnishment; liens; and denial, revocation, or limitation of passports. Delinquent support obligations could also be collected through unemployment and disability insurance benefits.

Children in Poverty

There were 12.3 million poor children under the age of 18 in the United States in 2007. The poverty rate for children is higher than for any other age group: 17 percent in 2007 compared to an overall poverty rate of 12.5 percent. For children under age five, the poverty rate was even higher, at 20.4 percent (4 million children). While high, this rate is eclipsed by the almost 53.7 percent poverty rate for children five and under living in female-headed households. More than 7 percent of U.S. children live in extreme poverty (family incomes below 50 percent of the poverty line), and 38.5 percent of children live in or near poverty (family incomes below 200 percent of the poverty line).[31] Compared to poverty in later childhood, research indicates that extreme poverty during a child's first five years has especially deleterious effects on their future life chances.[32]

The probability of children growing up poor is strongly correlated with family composition. In 1987, for example, the Census Bureau estimated that 61 percent of the children born in that year would spend some part of their childhood in single-parent families, which are five times more likely to be poor than two-parent families.[33] This prediction turned out to be correct.

Poverty and the Elderly

On the surface, the poverty picture for the elderly (once the poorest group in the country) seems to be growing less bleak. In 1959 the poverty rate for those over 65 was 35.2 percent; the poverty rate and the number of people 65 and older in poverty decreased to 9.4 percent in 2006 from 10.1 percent in 2005. Despite the downward trend, more than 3.4 million elderly citizens live in poverty.[34]

Senior poverty is disproportionately experienced by minority groups. Almost 23 percent of African Americans over age 65 were poor in 2007. For African American women, those numbers were 26.7 percent. About 19.5 percent of elderly Hispanics were poor.[35] The federal government's estimate of the elderly poor is questionable. Specifically, the poverty line is calculated using two classifications: (1) families headed by persons under age 65, and (2) families headed by persons 65 or older, for whom the poverty line is set lower. For example, the poverty line in 2007 for an unrelated individual 65 or older was $9,944 compared to $10,782 for those under 65—a difference of $843 or 8 percent. This differential is based on the assumption that the elderly spend less on food because they require less food to absorb the same amount of nutrients. It does not take into account the higher drug bills for the aged.

The Urban and Rural Poor

About 7.2 million rural Americans live in poverty. This segment of the population is generally overlooked because of the national attention traditionally directed toward urban poverty. Although rural poverty lacks significant media attention, many rural areas have poverty rates equal to those of central cities. In 2007, the rural poverty rate of 15.2 percent almost paralleled the urban poverty rate of 16.1 percent.[36]

In 2007 more than half of the rural poor lived in the South (almost 4 out of 7.1 million), 24 percent in the Midwest, 13 percent in the West, and 8 percent in the Northeast. The farming population accounts for only 10 percent of the rural population, so, therefore, the rural poor are mostly nonfarmers.[37] The number of poor rural communities has dropped since 1960, when 2,083 counties had a poverty rate of 20 percent or more. By 2004 the number of persistently poor counties designated by the United States Department of Agriculture (USDA) as having poverty rates of 20 percent or more had dropped to 386. Traditionally poor rural areas include the Colonias of the Southwest, the Mississippi Delta, Appalachia, and Indian reservations.[38]

Rural minority members experience considerable poverty with figures as follows:

- More than 25 percent of nonmetro Hispanics, African Americans, and American Indians are poor.
- The nonmetro poverty rate in 2003 for African Americans was 30.5 percent. The rate for Hispanics was 25.4 percent.
- Sixty-eight percent of poor nonmetro Hispanics have less than a high school education, compared with 40 percent of nonmetro poor whites. Fifty-two percent of poor nonmetro American Indians have incomes less than half of the poverty line.
- Poverty rates for African Americans and American Indians are more than 10 percentage points higher in nonmetro areas than in metro areas, the largest gap among minority population groups.[39]

The rural poor are more likely than the urban poor to live in chronic long-term poverty. Despite higher unemployment in rural areas, the rural poor rely less on public assistance than the urban poor. Lack of information and access to services, fear of stigma, and reliance on informal employment may help explain some of this difference.[40] Family structure also has a significant bearing on poverty:

- The highest poverty rate by type of family is for female-headed, nonmetro families. More than one out of every three persons living in nonmetro families that are headed by a female is poor. This rate is much higher than the poverty rates for nonmetro families headed by a husband and wife, where only one out of every 14 persons is poor.
- Those persons living in families with a husband and wife present have the lowest rates of poverty with 7.1 percent poor in nonmetro areas and 6 percent poor in metro areas.
- The poverty rate for nonmetro female-headed families is more than 7 percent higher than for metro families.
- In 2003, the child poverty rate in nonmetro areas was 20.1 percent.[41]

Several factors contribute to chronic rural poverty, including high levels of illiteracy, low levels of education, a dearth of highly trained workers, high numbers of low-skill and low-paying jobs, high levels of underemployment and unemployment, and a deficient physical infrastructure. Rural county and city managers also find it difficult to attract major industries. Not surprisingly, the absence of economic opportunity has resulted in the net outmigration of many rural families, especially when the primary wage earner possesses higher-level skills and education.[42]

Work and Poverty

Almost one in four U.S. workers live in or around the edges of poverty. Thirty-five million Americans work full time but fail to make an adequate living. They are the nursing home aides, poultry processors, pharmacy assistants, child care workers, data entry keyers, janitors, and other employees of the secondary and tertiary labor markets.

A Profile of the Working Poor

As a group, the working poor represent a growing sector of the poverty population. The working poor are defined as individuals who spend at least 27 weeks in the labor force (working or looking for work) but whose family or personal incomes fall below the poverty line. About 7.7 million persons were classified as the working poor in 2005, nearly 400,000 more than in 2002. The following represents some of the demographics of the working poor in 2005[43]:

- 11.6 percent of the 23 million part-time workers were classified working poor.
- As workers achieve higher levels of education, their likelihood of being classified as working poor decreases. In 2005, the number of college graduates who were in the labor force for at least 27 weeks counted among the working poor was 1.7 percent, compared with 14.1 percent of those with less than a high school diploma.
- Among families with at least one member in the labor force for 27 weeks or more, those families including children under 18 years old were about four times more likely than those without children to live in poverty or to be among the working poor.
- The proportion of persons in the labor force for at least 27 weeks who lived below the poverty level was higher for women (6.1 percent) than for men (4.8 percent).
- Whites accounted for about 7 in 10 of the working poor in 2005. African Americans and Hispanics had the highest working-poor rates, 10.5 percent each. The rates for whites and Asians, at 4.7 percent each, were less than half as high. [44]

Why Are There Working Poor?

The large numbers of working poor are related to other factors, including the replacement of high-paying industrial jobs with low-paying service jobs. Millions of Americans who were working full time, year-round earned less than the official poverty level. In 2005, 118.7 million full-time workers (3.9 percent) were classified as working poor.[45]

This employment trend reflects a clear movement away from higher-paying manufacturing jobs to low-wage service employment. By the 1980s corporations had eliminated 300,000 manufacturing jobs. Continuing this trend, a million more manufacturing jobs were eliminated during the 1990s. In the 1950s, 33 percent of all workers were employed in primary manufacturing industries (e.g., cars, radios, refrigerators, and clothing). By 1992 only 17 percent were employed in those industries. While manufacturing jobs have declined, service jobs have increased. According to the Bureau of Labor Statistics, service-providing industries are expected to account for approximately 20.8 million of the 21.6 million new wage and salary jobs generated from 2002 to 2012.[46]

Underemployment and Unemployment

The failure of the labor market to meet the economic needs of the population has been the source of important distinctions in employment policy. For example, those over 16 who are looking for work are counted by the Department of Labor as unemployed. But the **unemployment** rate does not assess the adequacy of employment. For example, part-time workers who wish to work full time are counted as employed; and workers holding jobs below their skill levels are not identified, even though such workers are **underemployed.** Finally, **discouraged workers** who simply give up and stop looking for work, relying on other methods to support themselves, do not appear in the unemployment statistics because they are not actively seeking work.

A second set of distinctions relates to economic performance. In a robust economy, businesses start up and close down in significant numbers, leaving workers temporarily out of work until they find other jobs. Such **frictional unemployment** is considered to be unavoidable, the cost of a constantly changing economy. **Structural unemployment,** in contrast, refers to "deeper and longer-lasting maladjustments in the labor market," such as changes in the technical skills required for new forms of production.[47] Because of swings in economic performance, some unemployment may be cyclical, as when recessions pitch the rate upward; but because certain groups of workers in certain regions have persistent difficulty finding work owing to an absence of jobs, some unemployment may be chronic. Michael Sherraden has examined how these components vary in the composition of the unemployment rate and concluded that structural and frictional factors account for about one-third, **cyclical unemployment** for about one-fourth, and **chronic unemployment** for about one-half.[48]

These distinctions are important because social welfare is directly connected to the employment experience of Americans. When people are out of work, they frequently rely on welfare benefits to tide them over. Thus, welfare programs are often designed to complement the labor market. This has led some observers to refer to welfare as a **social wage;** in other words, the amount the government pays to workers through welfare programs when they are not able to participate in the labor market. Logically, much of welfare could be eliminated if well-paying jobs were plentiful, but such has not been the case in the United States. Policymakers have tacitly accepted an unemployment rate of between 4 and 5 percent as normative, which means that at any given time, 5 to 8 million workers are unemployed.[49] Yet in 1978 Congress enacted the Humphrey–Hawkins Full Employment Act, which set an unemployment rate of 3 percent—equivalent to frictional unemployment—as a national goal. Since then, many government programs to aid unemployed, underemployed, and discouraged workers have been reduced or eliminated, leaving many Americans dependent on welfare programs for support.

The outsourcing of U.S. jobs to low-wage countries, such as India and China, may also exacerbate unemployment. A report by the U.S. Department of Labor on mass layoffs found that in the first quarter of 2004, 4,633 workers were laid off because their jobs were moved overseas. However, other economists argue that the report undercounted the total number of jobs lost offshore, with the real number being between 250,000 and 350,000 jobs a year. (This is still a relatively small number in a labor force of more than 130 million people.) The report also did not account for jobs created by U.S. companies overseas that did not involve direct layoffs in the United States. Nonetheless, the trend of outsourcing work overseas raises concerns about the potential loss of the high-wage white-collar jobs (especially in information technology) that were once considered safe from global competition. It also raises the specter that competition from less-expensive overseas workers will slow the wage growth of U.S. workers.[50]

The absence of employment opportunities contributes to other social problems. Research by M. Harvey Brenner shows that a seemingly small increase in the unemployment rate is associated with an increase in several social problems. During the 1973–1974 recession, for example, the unemployment rate increased by 14.3 percent, a change associated with the pathologies shown in Table 3. Brenner calculated that the combination of the 1973–1974 increase in the unemployment rate, the decrease in real per capita income, and the increase in the business failure rate was related to "an overall

Table 3

Consequences of Increases in Unemployment

Pathological Indicator	Percentage Increase due to Rise in Unemployment Increase	Rise in Incidence of Pathology
Total mortality	2.3	45,936
Cardiovascular mortality	2.8	28,510
Cirrhosis mortality	1.4	430
Suicide	1.0	270
Population in mental hospitals	6.0	8,416
Total arrests	6.0	577,477
Arrests for fraud and embezzlement	4.0	11,552
Assaults reported to police	1.1	7,035
Homicide	1.7	403

Source: Reprinted from M. Harvey Brenner, *Estimating the Effects of Economic Change on National Health and Social Well-Being* (Washington, DC: U.S. Government Printing Office, 1984), p. 2.

increase of more than 165,000 deaths [from cardiovascular disease] over a ten-year period (the greatest proportion of which occurs within three years)."[51] Overall, the total economic, social, and health care costs of this seemingly slight increase in unemployment cost $24 billion.[52]

As noted earlier, underemployment and unemployment constitute a major factor in determining poverty. In 2006, employers laid off about 936,000 workers in 4,885 private (nonfarm) extended mass layoff events, similar to the previous year. The reasons for these included employers moving to other U.S. locations or to locations outside of the United States and permanent worksite closures. Extended mass layoffs refer to layoffs of at least 31 days duration that involve the filing of initial claims for unemployment insurance by 50 or more individuals from a single establishment during a consecutive five-week period. In 2006, there were 950,157 claimants for unemployment insurance associated with this type of layoff. Of these, 40 percent were women; 16 percent were African American; 14 percent were Hispanic; and 19 percent were 55 years of age or older. Benefit exhaustion rates were highest for claimants involved in worksite closures (24 percent), and claimants associated with layoffs from employers that did not expect a recall (18 percent) experienced a higher benefit exhaustion rate than workers in events from which a recall was expected (9 percent).[53] These types of events can result in former workers experiencing significant economic losses for a lengthy time after their jobs are lost.

Dual Labor Markets

According to Piore, the labor market can be divided into two segments, or "dual labor markets"—a **primary labor market** and a **secondary labor market:**

> The primary market offers jobs which possess several of the following traits: high wages, good working conditions, employment stability and job security, equity and due process in the administration of work rules, and chances for advancement. The other, secondary sector, has jobs which, relative to those in the primary sector, are decidedly less attractive. They tend to involve low wages, poor working conditions, considerable variability in employment, harsh and often arbitrary discipline, and little opportunity to advance. The poor are confined to the secondary labor market.[54]

Researchers calculated that in 1970, 36.2 percent of workers fell into the secondary labor market, a modest increase over 1950's 35 percent.[55] By the 2000s, however, two factors increased the proportion of workers in the secondary labor market. First, membership in labor unions—the best security for nonprofessional workers—fell from 30.8 percent of nonagricultural workers in 1970 to 12.1 percent in 2007, leaving millions of workers vulnerable to the vicissitudes of the secondary labor market. Second, a higher proportion of the new jobs created were in the service sector, which consists largely of secondary labor market jobs.[56]

Wages and Poverty

The Minimum Wage The low minimum wage is another factor that explains the growth of the working poor. Before the 2006 midterm elections, Democrats promised they would raise the minimum wage within 24 hours if given control of the House.[57] They did not meet that deadline, but Congress did pass the Fair Minimum Wage Act of 2007 that, on July 24, 2007, raised the minimum wage to $5.85 an hour. The bill called for two more phased-in raises, going up to $6.55 an hour on July 24, 2008, and then again to $7.24 an hour on July 24, 2009.

Even with the recent increases, it is difficult for minimum wage employment to provide an adequate household income. Under the 2008 minimum wage of $6.55 an hour, a single parent working full time with two children would earn $12,576 a year and be at 71 percent of the poverty line. A four-person, two-parent family where both adults are working full time and earning the minimum wage would gross $25,152 a year, or only $3,952 above the poverty line. The Economic Policy Institute claims that 13 million workers are likely to be affected by an increase in the minimum wage to $7.24. This includes more than 1.2 million single parents. This legislation will positively impact African American and Hispanic workers. Almost 80 percent of the beneficiaries of the increased minimum wage are adults.[58]

Traditional labor economics assumes that minimum wage increases result in inflation and significant job losses among low-wage workers.[59] Empirical analysis is beginning to challenge this conclusion. The Economic Policy Institute did not find an increase in unemployment following the last federal minimum wage increase in 1996–1997.[60] The Fiscal Policy Institute concluded that states that have enacted minimum wage increases higher than the federal standard have experienced stronger small business and retail sector growth as a result.[61] Of course, these conclusions are not without challenge,[62] but the mere presence of an empirical argument against the standard economist's rejection of higher minimum wages is welcome news to progressives. Moreover, although a higher minimum wage will not eliminate the challenges faced by the working poor, it is a step in the correct direction. The following employment sectors have the highest proportion of minimum wage jobs:

Food service workers (26.6 percent)
Sales occupations (18.7 percent)
Office and administration support workers (13.1 percent)
Transportation and material moving workers (8.2 percent)
Cleaning and building service workers (8.2 percent)
Personal care workers (7.5 percent)[63]

The minimum wage is not adjusted annually to the cost of living. Congress must pass a bill and the president must sign it into law for the minimum wage to rise. Minimum wage increases have been signed into law by Presidents Truman, Eisenhower, Kennedy, Johnson, Nixon, Carter, George H. W. Bush, and Clinton. The minimum wage has risen only slightly during the past 18 years, increasing to $4.25 an hour by 1991 and then remaining at that level for more than five years. By 1996 approximately 10 million American workers were earning between $4.25 and $5.14 per hour. In 1997 the federal minimum wage was again raised, this time to $5.15 an hour. The minimum wage was frozen from 1997 to 2007.

In 1950 the minimum wage brought a worker to 56 percent of the median wage. Throughout the 1950s and 1960s (see Table 4.), the minimum wage hovered between 44 and 56 percent of the average wage. By 1980, however, the minimum wage had fallen to 46.5 percent of the average wage, and in 1988 it dropped even farther to 35.7 percent. Overall, from 1979 to 1996 the minimum wage

The minimum wage has been criticized by both conservatives and liberals.

dropped 29 percent. Even the increase to $5.15 an hour in 1997 raised the minimum wage to only 42 percent of the average wage, bringing a family of three to 83 percent of the poverty line[64] (considerably lower than the 120 percent of the poverty level reached by the minimum wage in 1968).[65] Moreover, the minimum wage increase in 1997 needed to be $6.07 (almost $1.00 higher) to have the same purchasing power as in the 1970s.[66] Even the higher minimum wage of $7.24 projected for 2009 would bring a family of three to only 79 percent of the 2008 poverty line.

Companies in metropolitan areas experiencing labor shortages use a "real" minimum wage that is often $1 to $2 above the federal level. Jared Bernstein maintains that a rise in the minimum wage would affect workers making just above the minimum wage through a "spillover effect." Workers in this group are more likely to be older (87 percent are adults) and to work more hours (69 percent work full time) than minimum wage workers.

The Living Wage Movement An alliance between labor and religious leaders in Baltimore in 1994 led to a campaign for a local law requiring city service contractors to pay a living wage. These

Table 4

Value of the Minimum Wage, Selected Years

Year	Percent of Poverty Line for a Family of Three	Percent of Average Wage	Value of the Minimum Wage, 1995 Dollars	Minimum Wage, Nominal Dollars
1955	73	44	$3.94	$0.75
1960	88	48	4.75	1.00
1965	103	51	5.59	1.25
1968	120	56	6.49	1.60
1970	107	50	5.92	1.60
1975	101	46	5.71	2.10
1980	98	47	5.76	3.10
1985	81	39	4.76	3.35
1988	73	36	4.33	3.35
1989	71	35	4.13	3.35
1990	79	38	4.44	3.80
1993	75	39	4.50	4.25
1995	72	37	4.25	4.25
1997	83	42	4.89	5.15
2007	73	30	4.30	5.85

Sources: Based on data from Isaac Shapiro, *The Minimum Wage and Job Loss* (Washington, DC: Center on Budget and Policy Priorities, 1988), p. 3; U.S. Census Bureau, "Income 1995" (Washington, DC: U.S. Government Printing Office, September 26, 1996); Bureau of Labor Statistics, "May 2007 National Occupation Employment and Wage Estimates." Retrieved July 2008, from www.bls.gov/oes/current/oes_nat.htm#b00-0000; Carmen DeNavas-Walt, Bernadette D. Proctor, and Robert J. Mills, "Income, Poverty, and Health Insurance Coverage in the United States: 2003," August 2004. Retrieved October 2008, from www.census.gov/prod/2004pubs/p60-226.pdf

kinds of campaigns seek to pass local ordinances requiring private businesses that benefit from public money to pay their workers a living wage. Commonly, these ordinances cover employers who hold large city or county service contracts or receive substantial financial assistance from the city in the form of grants, loans, bond financing, tax abatements, or other economic development subsidies. Since the Baltimore campaign in 1994, community, labor, and religious coalitions have fought for and won similar ordinances in St. Louis, Boston, Los Angeles, Tucson, San Jose, Portland, Milwaukee, Detroit, Minneapolis, and Oakland. By 2000, there were more than 75 living wage campaigns under way in cities, counties, and states.

The justification for these campaigns is that when subsidized employers pay workers less than a living wage, taxpayers pay a double bill: the initial subsidy plus increased taxes to pay for food stamps and other social services that low-wage workers require to support themselves and their families. Many citywide campaigns have defined the living wage as equivalent to the poverty line for a family of four, although ordinances that have passed stipulate wages ranging from $6.25 to $11.42 an hour, with some campaigns pushing for even higher wages. Increasingly, living wage coalitions are proposing other community standards in addition to a wage requirement, such as health benefits, vacation days, community hiring goals, public disclosure, community advisory boards, environmental standards, and language that supports union organizing.[67]

In addition to the federal minimum wage, states can institute their own higher minimum wage. (See Table 5) By 2008, 29 states and the District of Columbia had a higher minimum wage, with Washington, Oregon, Arizona, Connecticut, Missouri, Montana, and Vermont linking it automatically to the cost of living.[68]

Table 5

States with Minimum Wages Above the Federal Rate, 2008

State	Minimum Wage	State	Minimum Wage	State	Minimum Wage
Alaska	$7.15	Hawaii	7.25	New Mexico	7.50 (2009)
Arizona	6.90	Illinois	7.75	New York	7.15
Arkansas	6.25	Iowa	7.25	North Carolina	6.15
California	8.00	Maine	7.00	Ohio	7.00
Colorado	7.02	Massachusetts	8.00	Oregon	7.95
Connecticut	7.65	Michigan	7.15	Pennsylvania	7.15
Delaware	7.15	Minnesota	6.15	Rhode Island	7.40
District of		Missouri	6.65	Vermont	7.68
Columbia	7.55	New Hampshire	7.25	Washington	8.07
Florida	6.79	New Jersey	7.15	Wisconsin	6.50

Source: U.S. Department of Labor, Employment Standards Administration Wage and Hour Division, Minimum Wage Laws in the States—January 1, 2008. Retrieved May 12, 2008, from www.dol.gov/esa/minwage/america.htm

Strategies Developed to Combat Poverty

Former Senator Bob Kerrey stated that "In a global economy, your economic health and security is measured by what you own in addition to what you earn."[69] Michael Sherraden concurs: "Despite the prominence of asset ownership in American values and American history, social policy in the modern welfare state—and especially means-tested policy for the poor—has been focused almost exclusively on the distribution of income for consumption. Indeed, means-tested policy usually prohibits savings and the accumulation of assets. . . . After more than 50 years of income maintenance policy, we have confirmed that it is correctly named—it provides only maintenance, not development."[70] Sherraden goes on to suggest that "We should consider a different approach. Social policy, including welfare policy, should promote asset accumulation. In addition to the income and consumption policy of the current welfare state, asset-based policy would focus on savings and investment."[71] For the vast majority of households, the road to ending poverty involves savings, accumulation and assets. These are important prerequisites for purchasing a home, sending a child to college, starting a small business, and for reaching other economic goals. Moreover, when people begin to accumulate assets, their thinking and behavior changes, leading to important psychological and social effects that are not achieved when simply receiving and spending regular income.[72]

Until recently, the importance of asset accumulation for the poor has been virtually ignored in welfare state policies. Nevertheless, the tax system supports asset accumulation for the nonpoor in two primary areas: tax benefits for home equity and for retirement pension accounts. In these two areas alone, the federal government spends well over $100 billion each year and the total is rising rapidly.[73] Unfortunately, poor people fail to benefit from asset accumulation tax policies because they have marginal tax rates that are either zero or too low to receive significant tax benefits. Even worse, means-tested welfare programs count assets and savings as income in calculating eligibility. As such, the poor who have accumulated assets or savings must spend these down in order to qualify for assistance.

IDAs

The concept of individual development accounts (IDAs) was introduced in 1991 by Michael Sherraden in *Assets and the Poor*.[74] IDAs are part of an asset-building policy strategy designed to reduce wealth inequality by enabling asset-poor individuals to accumulate assets. Low-income individuals establish savings accounts matched by public and private resources, which are then used for home purchases, business capitalization, and postsecondary education.[75]

In Sherraden's framework, IDA accounts would be established for all low-income individuals and would be tax benefitted to foster asset accumulation. Depending on the financial circumstances of the depositor, individual savings would be matched by federal, state, or private contributions at varying rates. For instance, a very low–income family might have a match as high as 90 percent while a working family with a relatively good income would receive no match but might receive tax benefits. The matching system would be flexible and permit the government to supplement savings as the economic circumstances of individuals change. IDA accounts would be managed by individuals so that they become familiar with investment options. Despite the flexibility, IDA withdrawals would be restricted to approved purposes such as home purchases, education, retirement, or the creation of a business. IDA assets could be transferred to children at death or prior to death.[76]

Three Approaches to Combat Poverty

Policy analysts identified three basic strategies for combating poverty. The first strategy, used by Lyndon Johnson in the War on Poverty and Great Society programs, was to apply a curative strategy to the problems of the poor. The **curative approach to poverty** aims to end chronic and persistent poverty by helping the poor to become self-supporting through changes in their personal lives and in their environment. By breaking the self-perpetuating cycle of poverty, the curative approach strives to initiate the poor into employment and, later, the middle class. The goal of the curative approach is rehabilitation, and its target is the causes of poverty.

The second strategy is the **alleviative approach to poverty,** which is exemplified by public assistance programs that attempt to ease the suffering of the poor rather than ameliorate the causes of poverty. The third strategy is the **preventive approach to poverty,** exemplified by social insurance programs such as Social Security. In this approach, people are required to utilize social insurance to insure against

the costs of accidents, sickness, death, old age, unemployment, and disability. The preventive strategy sees the state as a large insurance company whose umbrella shelters its members against the vicissitudes of life.

John Kenneth Galbraith's *The Affluent Society* identified two kinds of poverty: **case poverty** and **area poverty.** According to Galbraith, case poverty was the outgrowth of personal deficiencies (i.e., deficits in human capital). Area poverty was related to economic problems endemic to a region. "Pockets of poverty" or "depressed areas" resulted from a lack of industrialization in a region or the inability of an area to adjust to technological change. This kind of poverty was a function of the changing nature of the marketplace.[77]

One example of a case poverty approach is the federal government's attempt to promote education as a means to increase human capital. Poverty is highly correlated with educational deficits, and adolescent parenthood is strongly associated with low levels of basic skills and high school dropout rates.[78] To help address these educational deficits, the federal government initiated the Head Start program, targeted at poor children age three to five and their families.[79]

Area poverty is illustrated by reviewing poverty rates on a state-by-state basis (see Table 6). The overall national poverty rate in 2006 was 12.3 percent, but some states that were poverty pockets had much higher poverty rates, including New Mexico (16.9 percent), Mississippi (20.6 percent), Alabama (14.3 percent), Louisiana (17 percent), Kentucky (16.8 percent), District of Columbia (18.3 percent), Arkansas (17.7 percent), West Virginia (15.3 percent), and Texas (16.4 percent). By contrast, other states like New Hampshire (5.4 percent), Alaska (8.9 percent), Connecticut (8 percent), New Jersey (8.8 percent), Delaware (9.3 percent), Maryland (8.4 percent), Minnesota (8.2 percent), Vermont (7.8 percent), and Washington (8 percent) had poverty rates below the national average.[80]

The various approaches to poverty are not merely hypothetical formulations; they formed the basis for social welfare policy throughout much of the 1960s and beyond. Between 1965 and 1980, social welfare policies were grounded in the view that public expenditures should be used to stimulate opportunities for the poor. As a result, major social welfare legislation was enacted and billions of dollars were earmarked for the remediation of poverty. However, beginning with the Reagan

Table 6

Strategies Developed to Combat Poverty: Percent of Persons in Poverty by State, 2006

State	Average Percentage in Poverty 2006	State	Average Percentage in Poverty 2006
United States	12.3	Missouri	11.4
Alabama	14.3	Montana	13.5
Alaska	8.9	Nebraska	10.2
Arizona	14.4	Nevada	9.5
Arkansas	17.7	New Hampshire	5.4
California	12.2	New Jersey	8.8
Colorado	9.7	New Mexico	16.9
Connecticut	8.0	New York	14.0
Delaware	9.3	North Carolina	13.8
District of Columbia	18.3	North Dakota	11.4
Florida	11.5	Ohio	12.1
Georgia	12.6	Oklahoma	15.2
Hawaii	9.2	Oregon	11.8
Idaho	9.5	Pennsylvania	11.3
Illinois	10.6	Rhode Island	10.5
Indiana	10.6	South Carolina	11.2
Iowa	10.3	South Dakota	10.7
Kansas	12.8	Tennessee	14.9
Kentucky	16.8	Texas	16.4
Louisiana	17.0	Utah	9.3
Maine	10.2	Vermont	7.8
Maryland	8.4	Virginia	8.6
Massachusetts	12.0	Washington	8.0
Michigan	13.3	West Virginia	15.3
Minnesota	8.2	Wisconsin	10.1
Mississippi	20.6	Wyoming	10.0

Source: U.S. Census Bureau, "POV46: Poverty Status by State: 2006." U.S. Census Bureau, *Current Population Survey,* 2007 Annual Social and Economic Supplement. Retrieved July 2008, from http://pubdb3.census.gov/macro/032007/pov/new46_100125_01.htm

administration in 1980, there was a move away from reliance on social welfare expenditures and toward an emphasis on ending poverty through overall economic growth.

Consequently, public expenditures for poverty programs decreased and tax cuts—intended to give people incentives to work and save money—increased. The Reagan approach belied the belief that the poor should wait for gains through increased economic activity rather than rely on welfare programs. This perspective assumed that the trickle-down effect of economic growth would benefit the poor more than direct economic subsidies. According to analyst Kevin Phillips, "Low-income families, especially the working poor, lost appreciably more by cuts in government services than they gained in tax reductions."[81] Despite the nation's long-standing belief in eradicating poverty through market incomes, the major factors influencing the general decrease in poverty from the 1960s to the late 1970s were governmental cash and in-kind transfers.[82]

Employment opportunities are increasingly being based on the proficiency of technological skills, something directly impacted by the relationship between poverty and the digital divide.

The Digital Divide

The Internet and related information technologies represent a major technological breakthrough. However, there are also important policy concerns arising from the use of new technologies, including the balance between social well-being and the free flow of information in a democracy. For those with access, the Internet has become a marketplace of ideas and a marketplace for a wide range of goods and services. But this technology is also leaving some people behind, especially some of the poor.

The term *digital divide* refers to the information "haves" and "have-nots"—the differential access to technology that exists along income, class, and racial lines. The digital divide in the United States is an important social equity issue. For example, those with telecommunications services, such as a home telephone and a computer with Internet access, can effectively engage the global economy, participate in political debates, and interact within the "global village." People bereft of this access risk being left behind, disconnected from the global community, the political system, and the information-driven market economy.

People use the Internet and related technologies for many different purposes: e-mail, information searches, and job searches. Pursuing online courses and school research is also popular. Despite the Internet's utility, certain groups still cannot access it and are unable to benefit from its growing list of uses.[83]

The digital divide cuts across income levels, race and ethnicity, and location. For example, in 2007, of all households with income over $150,000 only 2 percent did not use the Internet at all, while for those households earning between $5,000 and $10,000 per year it was 64 percent. Similarly, there are also significant differences in Internet access across racial and ethnic lines. Of those reporting they had access to the Internet *anywhere*, Asians had 82 percent access followed by whites (75 percent), African Americans (59 percent), and Hispanics (55 percent). Of those who had access *in the home*, the differences were similar with Asians (76 percent) and whites (67 percent) having the highest access and African Americans (45 percent) and Hispanics (43 percent) having much less access. Internet use in rural homes is less than in urban homes. For example, urban households with incomes of $20,000 to $25,000 had 42 percent access while for rural households this was 37 percent.[84] America's digital divide is fast becoming a racial and class divide.

Digital access has occupied policy discussions in national legislative bodies, state capitals, industry boardrooms, and grassroots community organizations since 1998. These discussions, and the media attention surrounding them, are causing society to become increasingly aware of the detrimental effects of the lack of Internet access for e-commerce, civic engagement, political organization, and the like. Several organizations such as Jesse Jackson's Rainbow/PUSH, the Benton Foundation, and notably the National Telecommunications and Information Administration (NTIA) of the U.S. Department of Commerce have identified the digital divide as a major social problem.

To narrow the digital gap, the former Clinton administration initiated the E-Rate program, which was designed to provide schools and libraries with lower-cost Internet access and other telecommunication services. By 1999 E-Rate had funded more than 45,000 schools with more than $2.5 billion in telecommunications subsidies.[85] Despite these efforts, the digital divide between low-poverty schools and high-poverty schools still exists. Welfare retrenchment, deep federal and state budget cuts, the growth of the working poor, under- and unemployment, dual labor markets, and a frozen minimum wage have all conspired to create an alternative financial services sector, or a fringe economy.

America's Fringe Economy[86]

According to the U.S. Department of Commerce's Bureau of Economic Analysis, the personal savings rate of Americans went negative in the first quarter of 2005 and has continued to be negative ever since.[87] The Federal Reserve Bank of San Francisco reports that a negative savings rate means that Americans are spending more than they earn. The declining savings rate that began in the 1980s is partly explained by formerly rising home prices and a robust stock market.[88] In other words, why save when gains can be realized by disposing of an asset?

The problem is more than a failure to save. Since 1960, the ratio of household debt to personal disposable income has more than doubled as Americans have gone on the longest sustained spending spree in history.[89] For example, from 2001 to 2004, home equity loans funneled $425 billion a year into consumption. Inflation-adjusted aggregate household debt during this period increased by more than 26 percent, and measures of the ability of households to repay their debt suggest that it is getting harder for many to repay. Over 83 percent of all consumer debt is now secured by residential property that has been declining in value.[90]

What does all this mean? Basically, the average U.S. middle-class household has become accustomed to a lifestyle that cannot be sustained by their income alone. Instead of saving part of their income to accumulate wealth, the average U.S. family is borrowing to acquire a house and relying on its appreciation to substitute for savings. This means that the financial future for most Americans will depend on the vicissitudes of the housing market which has been on a downward spiral since 2007. Unlike investments in stocks and bonds that can be diversified to protect the investor against downturns, reliance on home appreciation cannot be protected. Converting the house to spendable cash is not a feasible solution if the value of the home has depreciated and is worth less than the mortgage. Relief from impossible debt in the form of personal bankruptcy has become more difficult due to the Bankruptcy Abuse Prevention and Consumer Act of 2005.[91]

Headlines have recently exploded with the phrase "housing bust." Indeed, new home starts have fallen[92] while repossessions have escalated to unparalleled heights.[93] The decline in the housing markets, the strongest non-military–related sector in the U.S. economy for the past few years, is threatening an economic recession.[94] When rent-to-own stores, pawn shops, cash exchanges, and payday lenders are advertising on television for middle-class customers, it is a clear sign that something is afoot and the anachronistic poverty line that focuses exclusively on household income fails to tell the full poverty story.

While much of the economic life of the middle class is rooted in credit,[95] many poor people encounter obstacles to basic credit and are vulnerable to exploitation by fringe businesses. The often shoddy storefronts of fringe economy hide the true scope of this economic sector. Ninety percent of payday lending revenues are based on fees from trapped borrowers. The typical payday borrower pays back $793 for a $325 loan. Predatory payday lending now costs U.S. families $4.2 billion per year in excessive fees.[96]

The past decade has been a good one for check cashers, payday lenders, pawnshops, rent-to-own stores, and the like. Their loans are now legal in 38 states. The number of payday loan outlets increased significantly from just 2,000 in 1995 to 24,000 in 2007. Funded largely by mainstream financial institutions, the total loan volume in 2005 was $40 billion, over 10 times that in 1998. Ten large companies, including listed companies, own or operate about 40 percent of payday loan stores in the United States. Among the industry leaders is QC Holdings Inc., which operates more than 600 Quick Cash and other payday loan stores in 25 states, backed by U.S. Bancorp, the nation's sixth largest commercial bank that provides QC with a $45 million line of credit.[97] The fringe economy is also robust in the housing sector. Subprime (loans to marginal borrowers that carry a higher interest rate) mortgages rose significantly throughout the 1990s, by 880 percent from 1993 to 1998.[98] For subprime mortgages originated from 1998 through to 2006, it has been projected that 2.2 million U.S. households will lose their homes to foreclosure, costing these households as much as $164 billion, and that one out of every five (19.4 percent) subprime loans made will fail.[99] By 2007 the number of subprime loans, many of them shaky at best, had threatened to bring down the international banking sector.

In short, the U.S. fringe economy is not a mom-and-pop operation composed of small storefronts that generate moderate family incomes; instead, it is a multibillion parallel economy that provides low-income consumers with a full range of cash, commodities, and credit lines. Pawnshops, check cashers, and payday lenders are a major part of the fringe economy, but they are only the tip of the iceberg. This subeconomy also includes mainstream banks issuing high-interest credit cards and expensive check overdraft protection, high-interest subprime home financing and refinancing loans, and deferred interest retail payments. Fringe economic services exist in every sector where people borrow or spend money.

The insularity of this sector means that the prices of commodities and financial services in the fringe economy are virtually removed from the real value of these goods and services in the mainstream marketplace. As such, prices in the fringe economy are based on the supposedly higher risk of serving a poor or credit-challenged population. In this economic bubble, used cars can cost twice their book value, housing prices are determined by the financial desperation of home buyers rather than the home's value, a 14-day $200 payday loan can cost $40 in interest/fees, and credit cards come with yearly and monthly service fees plus annual percentage rates (APR) of 30 percent or more. In the fringe economy, economic distress and low credit scores translate into high corporate profits.

The Unbanked and the Functionally Poor

Important clients in the fringe economy are the unbanked (e.g., individuals and families without accounts at deposit institutions). About 12 million U.S. households (one-fourth of all low-income families) have no relationship with a mainstream financial service provider, such as a bank, savings institution, or credit union.[100] The unbanked report they do not have checking accounts because (1) they do not write enough checks to warrant one, (2) they have almost no month-to-month financial savings to deposit, (3) they cannot afford high bank fees, (4) they cannot meet minimum bank balance requirements, (5) they want to keep their financial records private, and (6) they experience discomfort dealing with banks. Almost 85 percent of the unbanked have yearly incomes below $25,000.[101]

One industry-funded study found that the average payday-loan customer was female with children living at home, was between 24 and 44 years old, earned less than $40,000 a year, was a high school graduate, was a renter, was transient (most had lived in the same home for less than five years), and had little job tenure.[102] This group represents the lower- and moderate-income working class rather than the poorest of the poor.

The misconception that only the poor use the fringe economy overlooks the convergence of the traditional poor with growing segments of the middle class that can be categorized as the functionally poor. For instance, the functionally poor can include homeowners who use their houses like ATM machines, regularly drawing out equity to finance credit card debts or other purchases. It also includes the middle class with tarnished credit who carry high-interest-rate credit cards or finance their purchases through tricky time-deferred payments. In

that sense, a burgeoning sector of the middle class is economically closer to the traditional poor than to the traditional middle class.

Total U.S. household debt (including vehicles and mortgages) was $13.3 trillion in 2007 (the equivalent of $44,000 per person), a 500 plus percent increase since 1957. Personal savings rates and home equity were the lowest in recent history. In the 1980s, consumers saved roughly 10 percent of their disposable income; by 2003 it was only 2.5 percent, and by 2007 it was negative or close to it. In 2002, home owners initiated $97 billion in home equity loans, nearly five times the amount in 1993.[103] Consumers spent almost all of it, and about 500,000 home owners are in the foreclosure process.[104] Credit card debt is another factor in the new poverty. Consumers who did not pay off monthly balances in 2002 owed a median average of $2,200 in credit card debt and those who carried over balances owed close to $9,000. Overall, credit card holders carried more than $915 billion in debt in 2007.[105]

Credit and the Poor

Credit is a bridge between real household earnings and consumption decisions, offering relief during periods of economic distress and uncertainty.[106] Payment options are flexible for those with good credit, and collateral is not required. Hence, the middle class can purchase goods and services or borrow cash without losing their possessions. On the other hand, neither trust nor the presumption of goodwill exists in the fringe economy. A borrower with compromised credit typically must provide collateral such as a secured bank account, a postdated check, household goods, or a car title. Those who manage to find unsecured credit are often charged high interest rates combined with onerous loan terms.

Credit card use has become almost mandatory in the United States. Renting a car or reserving a hotel room or flight is almost impossible without a credit card. The average U.S. credit card holder has ten cards—four retail cards, three bank cards, one phone card, one gasoline card, and one travel and entertainment card. Not surprisingly, bank write-offs for uncollectible credit card debt were 5.25 percent in 2007 ($1.2 billion could potentially be written off).[107]

There are two basic types of credit cards: unsecured and secured. The cornerstones of unsecured credit are the cardholder's creditworthiness, past use of credit, and ability to repay debt. Conversely, secured credit cards require cardholders to guarantee their credit line by providing cash collateral which makes it difficult for the borrower to default.

Unsecured Credit Cards Widespread credit card use by consumers with poor credit is a relatively recent phenomenon. Until the 1990s, banks limited their exposure on credit cards by refusing poor credit risks. However, as the credit card market became saturated and more competitive, banks were forced to examine ways to make money from riskier customers. Because bankruptcy laws prevent refiling for six years, banks began to promote "special offers" to newly bankrupted consumers with an income source.[108] Although the default rate for these individuals is high, the cards carry such low credit lines—coupled with high interest rates and fees—that banks can still make money. Terms are strict, and only one late payment results in a cardholder being moved into the default rate category, which carries a 23 to 35 percent or higher APR.

Some credit cards require no security deposit but credit limits are low (in the $100 to $500 range) and cardholders must earn at least $12,000 a year. Fees on these unsecured cards can cost hundreds of dollars, and interest rates are close to 30 percent. For example, Centennial MasterCard/Visa advertised a low 9.9 percent APR. However, two late payments in six months results in the rate jumping to almost 24 percent. Fees for this credit card were $178, including a $48 annual fee and a $6 monthly participation fee. The maximum credit limit was only $250. The Plains Commerce Bank Visa charged $281 for a credit card with a limit of $300, leaving only $19 when the card arrived.[109] This is predatory lending, especially when compared to mainstream credit cards that charge no setup or monthly fees, charge nothing to increase credit limits, and have free electronic access for account management.

Secured Credit Cards Responding to consumers with problematic credit, the industry created a class of credit cards securitized by a cardholder's collateral. Like their unsecured cousins, secured cards are emblazoned with Visa and MasterCard logos. Although these cards require a credit check, they are really quasi-credit cards, because no line of credit is actually extended. The major advantage of secured cards for credit card issuers (CCIs) is that they can easily liquidate a cardholder's collateral and apply it to the outstanding balance.

To receive a secured credit card, the customer must open an interest-bearing savings account for the amount of the credit line, usually a minimum of $200 to $5,000. (Some banks only allow customers a credit line equal to 50 percent of their collateral.) Funds in the savings account are jointly owned by the bank and cannot be accessed by the cardholder. In turn, cardholders are given a Visa or MasterCard with a credit line equal to the collateral. Credit card balances are not subtracted from the savings account; instead, cardholders pay those charges as they would any other credit card. Despite the collateral, fees and interest rates are high: Cross Country Bank charged a $50 origination fee, a 24 percent APR, and a hefty late fee. There was also a 50 cent minimum finance charge and a $10 monthly fee. Because this credit card had no grace period, interest began with each purchase. Wells Fargo's secured credit card had an $18 annual fee, a $300 security deposit, a late and over-the-limit fee of $30, and a 17 percent APR for purchases and 21.8 percent for cash advances.[110]

Preloaded or Stored Value Debit Cards A variation of the secured credit card is the preloaded debit card, sometimes called a stored value card (SVC). Using a Visa or MasterCard logo, SVCs are similar to prepaid phone cards in that they are preloaded with funds. When the funds are exhausted, the card must be reloaded or it becomes inactive. Unlike secured credit cards, prepaid cards are not dependent on credit or banking history because they are not linked to a bank account. (Customers can use the entire amount loaded onto the card.) There is also no debt to repay. Like any fringe economy transaction, there is a downside. For example, WiredPlastic charged an initial $50 fee, a one-time activation fee of $30, a monthly maintenance fee of $7, and $2 for each cash withdrawal (plus any other fees charged by ATM owner/operators). Money could be loaded directly through payroll transfers and government checks, such as Social Security.[111]

Secured and preloaded debit cards reflect the inherent inequities in the fringe economy. For instance, if banks demanded that the middle class securitize their $10,000 Visa or MasterCard credit lines, most would return to cash or checks. Secured credit cards are exploitive in other ways. For instance, customers are compelled to deposit money in a low-interest-bearing savings account. Simultaneously, they are charged a 24 percent APR for purchases, plus other fees to essentially borrow against their own money. Because the credit line is guaranteed by collateral, banks cannot argue that high costs reflect an exceptional risk. The most viable explanation for the high costs is simple avarice. Moreover, secured credit cards are often marketed as a way to build or rebuild credit histories. However, if the CCI does not report the transaction to a credit bureau—which many do not—a cardholder cannot build or rebuild their credit history. In effect, stored value debit cards are often just like expensive gift cards.

Telecommunications and the Alternative Services Market The effects of poor credit are evident in the telecommunication services industry. Consumer telecommunications are divided into two groups: post- and pre-paid services. For post-paid (i.e., paying *after* a charge is accrued) telephone services, customers are required to undergo credit checks, and those without an acceptable credit score are denied local and long-distance service. Denied mainstream telecommunications services, consumers are forced into the more expensive prepaid sector.

Consumers can opt for alternative prepaid local phone service from Competitive Local Exchange Carriers (CLECs), which are small companies that compete with regional carriers such as the Bell companies and GTE. DPI, a CLEC, charged $39 a month for basic local phone service with no option for long distance or directory assistance. Others, such as Direct Telephone, charged $50 a month for local service bundled with some options.[112] In comparison, Southwest Bell charged about $19 a month for full-service local phone service.

Postpaid cell phone service is also dependent on good credit scores, and clients with problematic credit are a lucrative part of the wireless industry. For example, wireless consumers with good credit could get Sprint's $35 postpaid cell phone service, which included 300 daytime minutes and unlimited night and evening minutes. AT&T's $30 plan included 200 daytime and unlimited nighttime minutes.[113] On the other hand, Verizon charged prepaid customers 10 cents a minute and 25 cents for each call (35 cents for the first minute). Cingular (owned by AT&T) charged prepaid customers 35 cents a minute and 10 cents a minute on weekends or 10 cents a minute and $1 a day. AT&T bases its prepaid pricing on the amount of refills a customer bought. For example, customers who could only afford a $10 refill paid from 50 to 85 cents a minute while

the costs for those who could afford a $100 refill ranged from 12 to 22 cents a minute.[114]

Because prepaying customers cannot default, the high costs of these services are based on the customer's economic vulnerability. Prepayment schemes are also unfair because they allow corporations to use a customer's money without paying interest. A single $100 prepayment to AT&T will not generate much interest, but multiplied by tens of thousands of prepaid cell phone customers, the float (i.e., the lag time between when money is received or requested and when the financial institution actually releases it) is sizable. Prepaid customers are therefore penalized twice—once by paying higher prices and then again when the company uses their money without paying interest. Consumers trying to build or rebuild their credit history derive little benefit from prepaying because no credit is extended and therefore there is nothing to report to a credit agency. Lacking cash and mainstream credit, many low-income and credit-impaired consumers also turn to the furniture and appliance rental industry.

The Furniture and Appliance Rental Industry The rent-to-own (RTO) sector targets low- and moderate-income consumers. RTOs advertise no credit checks, weekly or monthly payments, and a choice of appliances, furniture, and jewelry that would otherwise be unaffordable if low-income consumers bought them outright.[115] The $6.8 billion a year RTO industry served over 3 million customers in 2007 and is a major player in the fringe economy.[116] Rent-A-Center (the largest RTO) began with eight stores in 1986; by 2008 Rent-A-Center was the largest rent-to-own operator in the United States with over 3,000 stores nationwide, annual revenues of $2.9 billion, and approximately 37 percent market share.[117] Aaron Rents started in 1955 by renting folding chairs to auction houses for 10 cents a day. By 2008, it had 1,563 owned and franchised stores. Revenue for the first quarter of 2008 alone increased 13 percent to $437.3 million compared to $387.9 million for the first quarter of 2007.[118]

The RTO industry employs two approaches to transactions: (1) customers rent goods and pay weekly or monthly fees, or (2) they rent-to-own with payments extending from 12 to 24 months. In either case, customers can usually cancel the agreement without further cost or obligation. Customers take ownership of the property if the contract is renewed a prescribed number of times (usually 12 to 24 months) or if they complete the lease agreement. No credit bureau reports are obtained or filed because RTO customers make advanced payments.[119]

Renting or leasing is an expensive option. Rainbow Rentals, leased/rented a Frigidaire washer and dryer for $19 a week or $69 a month for 21 months. The total cost was between $1,450 and $1,600 for a washer and dryer that could be purchased for $700 to $800 at a local discount store. A Compaq Presario notebook rented for $38 a week or $144 a month for 24 months, raising the total cost to about $3,500. The same computer could have been bought for one-third of the price—about $1,200 to $1,300—at major discount stores. A 32-inch Toshiba flat screen television cost $1,800 to rent for 24 months while Best Buy sold the same set for $650. The list goes on and on. RTO customers generally pay at least two to three times more than the retail price for furniture or appliances.[120] The RTO industry argues that high prices reflect two variables: The cost of free repairs and the risk of doing business with customers who have poor credit histories and unstable incomes.

RTOs make money in other ways. For one, RTOs retailers offer merchandise at a "cash price and carry" price. According to a 1997 PIRG study, the typical RTO cash price on an item was $389 compared with the average department store price of $217.[121] For example, one Aaron Rents store in Houston, Texas, was selling a used GE refrigerator for $1,134—about the same price as a new one in a discount appliance store. RTOs also make money by repossessions and re-rents. For instance, a 32-inch Toshiba television may cost the RTO store $500. If the set is rented for $69 a month, they will make up the $500 in only seven months and realize a gross profit of $1,173 at the end of the two-year lease term. If the set is repossessed after seven months, the retailer can re-rent it for another two years at a slightly lower rental price. In this way, merchandise can be frequently recycled. One Rent-A-Center store had a $119 VCR that brought in more than $5,000 over a five-year period.[122] Typical RTO stores have revenues of almost $500,000 a year.[123]

The RTO industry is hounded by a controversy over whether transactions are credit sales or purchase option leases. As a credit sale, RTO transactions would carry a 100 to 200 percent APR and would therefore clash with many state anti-usury laws. In addition, federal truth-in-lending laws would apply in a credit sale, triggering interest rate disclosures and other consumer information. Forty-six states currently have laws regulating RTO transactions as leases, mandating a variety of disclosures and other requirements. Consumer groups argue that RTO transactions should be treated as credit sales.[124]

Many fringe businesses long ago realized the importance of treating low-income customers well. Good customer service is important to low-income consumers, especially those who have been subjected to humiliation by mainstream merchants after bad credit checks. Some consumers are so sensitive to poor treatment that they will pay more, sometimes much more, to feel they are being respected. As one former Rent-A-Center manager stated, "If you treat the customer like royalty, you can bleed them through the nose."[125]

Cash Loans Cash loans serve the same purpose for the poor as credit card cash advances for the middle class in that they provide crisis cash for a medical or familial emergency, or when income is insufficient to make ends meet on a short-term basis. Cash loans can be divided into two categories: collateral-based loans and nonsecured or promissory loans. In the former, the borrower provides collateral (either property or guaranteed anticipated income) to the lender that is worth as much or more than the loan. Even though many in the middle class receive unsecured loans, this type of loan is often denied to the poor or those with bad credit. As such, loans available to the poor are generally collateral-based loans such as pawnshop transactions.

Pawnshops Pawnshops are high-growth industries and at least five chains are publicly traded (i.e., EZ Pawn, Cash America Pawn, Express Cash, Famous Pawn, and First Cash Pawn). According to the National Pawnbrokers Association, the number of pawnshops in the United States has nearly doubled in the past ten years from 6,900 in 1988 to 13,000 in 2008, a reflection of the present tough economic times.[126]

A pawnshop loan is a relatively simple transaction. A pawnbroker makes a fixed-term loan that is guaranteed by collateral. The customer is given a pawn ticket that includes his or her name and address, a description of the pledged good, the amount lent, the maturity date, and the amount that must be repaid to reclaim the property. The property is returned when the customer presents the ticket and pays the loan and the fees within the agreed-on time. If the loan is not repaid, the collateral becomes the property of the pawnbroker and the customer's debt is extinguished. Customers can repay a loan at any time during the loan term and redeem the collateral. Pawnshops are typically regulated by state and sometimes local governments, and interest rates can range from 1.5 percent to 25 percent a month, depending on the regulations of the state. The average pawn shop loan is about $75 but can go as low as $15.[127]

In Houston, Texas, a pawnshop transaction works in the following way. A customer brings in an item that is then appraised by the broker. This appraisal is typically very low, with jewelry appraised at wholesale prices, guns appraised at less than 60 percent of their Blue Book value, and appliances at a fraction of their original cost. Many pawnshops have a maximum loan limit on items (usually $500 to $1,000) regardless of the value of the property. Hence, even if an item is worth $2,000, the pawnshop may only lend up to a maximum of $500 or $1,000 (although on higher priced items some pawnshops exercise flexibility).

Pawnshops allow customers to borrow all or part of the appraised value of an item for 30 days, at which time the loan is renewable for up to 90 days. However, many pawnshops have an open-ended policy whereby the customer can extend the pawn indefinitely by paying only the interest on the loan. In most Houston pawnshops, the interest on a $500 loan is $75 for the first month and $75 a month for the fixed term of the three-month loan. At the end of the first 30 days it would cost $575 to redeem the item; after 60 days the price would rise to $650; and at the end of 90 days it would cost $725, or 45 percent of the value of the collateral. One pawnshop manager stated that some people renew their loans for a year or more, which translates into $1,800 in interest charges on a $1,000 loan. Although some state laws cap interest rates, loopholes often allow "lease back" agreements to add fees, sometimes effectively doubling interest rates.[128]

Car Title Pawns Car title pawns (vehicle title lenders) operate similarly to pawnshops. A customer needs a short-term loan, but instead of using his or her television or stereo as collateral, they use their vehicle title. In most cases, this will substantially increase the amount that can be borrowed because vehicles generally have more value than televisions, stereos, or microwaves. Unlike pawnshop transactions, the borrower does not forego the use

of his or her property during the course of the loan, even though the vehicle is technically owned by the lender until the loan is repaid.

Car title pawns operate in the following way. A borrower provides the lender with a free and paid-up vehicle title and an extra set of keys. In return for the loan, the borrower allows the title lender to keep the title or to put a lien on the vehicle.

The vehicle is appraised based on the lowest possible value, which is the wholesale price in poor condition. For example, a 1993 Oldsmobile Cutlass Ciera would have a retail value of $2,217 if bought from a dealer in June 2002. The resale value of the car to a private party would have been $1,530, and the dealer trade-in would have been $1,118.[129] Because car title pawn companies generally lend up to 50 percent of the value of a vehicle, the maximum loan would have been $559. A loan default would therefore provide the lender with a car worth $2,217 for $559 plus the interest payments already made by the borrower. Moreover, if a vehicle is repossessed, the borrower does not receive any proceeds from the sale, even if the resale amount exceeds the loan amount.

Vehicle title loans are usually for one month and often involve an APR of 300 percent or more. Although loan terms vary slightly between companies, one large title loan company operates in the following way. A vehicle is appraised at $2,000 (the wholesale price in poor condition) and a 30-day loan is given for 50 percent of the car's value or $1,000. After 30 days the loan payoff is $1,246.57 (almost 25 percent in interest and fees). If the loan is not repaid, the car is repossessed on the 31st day. The borrower may ask for a 30-day extension after paying the interest and fees. After only 60 days the interest and fees will total almost 50 percent of the original $1,000 loan. The borrower may then ask for a third extension after paying the interest charges of $493 for the first two loan periods. This extension is for a maximum of one year. At that point, the monthly payment rises to $346.57 because the borrower is now expected to pay down $100 a month toward the loan principal as well as pay the interest. By the fourth month, the principal will be only $900 and so on until the loan is paid off or the car is repossessed.[130] If the borrower keeps the loan for 12 months, he or she will have paid almost $3,000 in interest charges/fees for a $1,000 loan. Borrowers will have also paid more than the value of the vehicle.

Payday Loans Although pawnshops are profitable, the payday loan market (sometimes called deferred deposit services) is even more robust. For example, while the average pawnshop loan is $75, the average payday loan ranges from $100 to $500 or more.[131] As stated earlier, the number of payday loan outlets increased significantly from just 2,000 in 1995 to 24,000 in 2007 with a total loan volume of $40 billion, over ten times of what it was in 1998.

To qualify for a payday loan, the customer must have a valid checking account from which a check is issued (or electronically debited) to cover the interest and principal for the loan. On a $300 payday loan, the lender may ask for a $300 check and then deduct the interest from the amount received by the borrower. Borrowers must also provide recent pay stubs and valid identification. Many payday lenders consider benefits as income and will give loans to those on public assistance, recipients of child support or alimony, and Social Security beneficiaries.[132]

Payday loans are typically issued for a maximum of $300 ($500 to $1,000 for established customers) and are usually given for 14 or 18 days. The average fees are almost $20 per $100 borrowed (fees can be as high as $37 per hundred), or 20 percent for the two-week loan period. Since the borrower repays $360 on a $300 loan, this translates into a 500 percent APR. (Nationally, the average APR for payday loans is 474 percent.[133]) Because the lender may extend the loan (called a rollover) for additional 14- or 18-day periods (after the interest is paid), a $300 payday loan extended to 42 days or three loan periods will accrue $180 in interest charges alone, elevating the full loan repayment to $480 in less than two months. Unlike pawnshop transactions where a customer loses his or her collateral if he or she defaults, payday loans can inflict potentially greater damage on borrowers. For instance, defaulting on a payday loan will mar the creditworthiness of the borrower, if not destroy it. It may also result in criminal prosecution for writing a hot check.[134]

Collection tactics for payday loans can be aggressive. If a borrower cannot repay the loan, it may be turned over to a collection agency and result in the loss of a house, car, or the garnishing of wages. In some cases, the collection agency can add additional interest to the original debt.[135] The payday lender may prosecute the customer for writing a "hot check," even though they knew the customer did not have sufficient funds in his or her checking account when he or she wrote it. Some payday loan companies require borrowers to agree beforehand to pay all fees related to the collection of their account, including attorney fees, collection fees, and court costs.[136] A default on a payday loan involves a worthless check, and some state credit laws allow for triple damages when a bad check is used in a retail transaction. Lenders may also require that customers sign statements authorizing them to go directly to the borrower's employer and ask for the amount owed to be deducted from their paychecks.

Tax Refund Anticipation Loans Refund anticipation loans (RALs) are short-term loans secured by an expected tax refund. RALs are expensive and similar to other forms of fringe credit with an APR ranging from 67 to 774 percent.[137] Every year tax preparation services earn about $1 billion dollars in fees from these loans.[138]

RALs are common in low-income neighborhoods where there are a large number of tax refunds associated with the federal earned income tax credit (EITC) program. Under EITC, the working poor receive refunds that exceed what they paid in taxes. In addition to EITC, low- and moderate-income families with children are also eligible for the federal child tax credit (CTC), worth up to $1,000 a child. The EITC and CTC tax refunds created a powerful incentive for mainstream tax preparers to enter the poverty services market.

Sixty-eight percent of EITC- and CTC-eligible families use tax preparers and electronic return originators (EROs) that are authorized by the IRS to electronically transmit federal income tax returns. Low-income tax filers use EROs for several reasons: (1) the EITC and the CTC filing process is complicated;[139] (2) low-income working families can receive large tax refunds and many are eager to claim them quickly, sometimes the day they file; (3) tax preparers are ubiquitous in lower-income neighborhoods (there are 50 percent more EROs in zip codes with high numbers of EITC recipients than zip codes with fewer recipients);[140] (4) free tax assistance is scarce; and (5) the poor cannot afford to pay upfront the $100 plus in tax-preparation fees.

Commercial tax preparers earn high profits by providing financial services to some of the poorest of the poor. According to one study, RAL customers tend to have annual incomes between $10,000 and $15,000, are unemployed or employed in service occupations, and possess less than a high school education.[141] About 40 percent of taxpayers who use RALs are EITC recipients.[142] Moreover, many of the poor are unaware that RALs are actually loans because they are often advertised as "Quick Cash,"

"Super Fast Refunds," or "Instant Money." In April 2001, H&R Block received 2,230 citations from the New York City Department of Consumer Affairs for misrepresenting RALs and luring customers into accepting loans they did not fully understand. The company settled for $4 million and paid $2.4 million in restitution to 61,700 customers. Block also settled a RAL-related class-action suit in Texas for $41.7 million.[143]

RALs are expensive. For example, a tax filer eligible for a $1,900 EITC refund who takes out a RAL will pay $248 (see Table 7), thereby reducing the original $1,900 to $1,652.[144] Most of these costs are incurred simply to get an EITC refund a few days earlier compared to filing electronically and having the IRS directly deposit the refund into a checking account. RALs are also risky for low-income tax filers. Because a RAL is a loan from a bank in partnership with a tax preparer, it must be repaid even if the IRS denies or delays the refund, or if the refund is smaller than expected. Moreover, when tax filers apply for RALs, they give the lender the right to use the tax refund to pay for old tax-preparation debts that may be owed.

If low-income consumers are fleeced when they enter a tax-preparation office, they are ripped off again on their way out. About 45 percent of RAL customers use commercial check cashing outlets (CCOs) to cash their refund checks, paying fees that range from 3 to 10 percent of the face value of the check. Responding to this captive market, ACE Cash Express installed check-cashing machines in some

H&R Block lobbies and charged roughly 3 percent to cash a secure check, thereby further lowering the $1,900 refund to $1,602.[145] All told, EITC-eligible families using EROs and check cashers can lose more than 16 percent of the value of their tax refund.

Tax-preparation fees can take other forms. For example, a consumer is charged a tax-preparation fee of $100 to $118, which they are expected to pay out-of-pocket.[146] Because some families cannot pay the fee or do not have a checking account, tax preparers offer a "refund transfer." Although not a loan, per se, the filer pays about $28 to establish a dummy bank account into which the IRS directly deposits a tax refund check. After the deposit, the tax preparer subtracts their fees, issues a paper check, and closes the account. The $28 fee is high for a 10-day bank account designed for a single lump sum, especially because for a few dollars more the consumer can maintain a checking account for a full year. The advantage to low-income consumers is that tax-preparation fees can be deducted directly from the dummy account, thereby relieving them from paying those fees upfront. In effect, dummy accounts are actually disguised loans because they defer tax-preparation fees. Another variation is an assisted refund transfer or, as Jackson Hewitt calls it, "IRS Direct." With this product, a consumer pays the tax preparer to be an intermediary in processing a tax refund into the tax filer's *own* bank account.[147]

High tax-preparation and RAL fees hurt poor working families and substantially diminish the economic impact of the EITC and CTC. In 2001, tax

Table 7

Draining EITC: 2002 Tax Preparation, RAL Fees, and Check Cashing

Type of Fee	Cost to Tax Filer	Drain on EITC Program (in millions)
RAL loan fee	$75	$363
Electronic filing fee	40	194
Document preparation/application/handling fee	33	160
Tax preparation fee	100	484
Check cashing fee	57	110*
Total	305	1,311

*This was based on 40 percent of low-income tax filers using a check cashing service.

Source: Based on Chi Chi Wu and Jean Ann Fox, "The High Cost of Quick Tax Money: Tax Preparation, 'Instant Refund' Loans, and Check Cashing Fees Target the Working Poor." (Washington, DC: National Consumer Law Center, Consumer Federation of America, January 2003). Reprinted with permission of the National Consumer Law Center, www.consumerlaw.org, 617-542-9595.

filers paid almost $1.8 billion in RAL and other fees,[148] which took a substantial chunk out of the $31 billion EITC program that Congress had targeted for the poor.[149] Table 7 illustrates the impact of tax-preparation fees and RALs on tax filers and the EITC program.

Check Cashing Outlets (CCOs) In large urban areas, from 20 to 40 percent of the unbanked pay fees to cash their paychecks through CCOs.[150] Many larger CCOs are one-stop financial service centers in that they offer a wide range of services in one location: (1) check cashing; (2) utility and other bill pay services; (3) money transfers; (4) payday loans; (5) money orders; (6) telecommunications products (e.g., prepaid long-distance calling cards, prepaid local phone service, cell phones and beepers); and (7) other services such as fax transmissions, copy services, stamps and envelopes, notary services, mailboxes, and lottery tickets.[151]

CCOs with names like ACE Cash Express, Check 'N Go, Mr. Payroll, Dollar, and Money Mart are common sights in inner-city neighborhoods. Behind these 11,000 plus storefronts lies an industry that cashes upwards of 180 million checks a year with a face value of more than $55 billion. The CCO industry generates nearly $1.5 billion a year in revenues.[152]

CCOs are an expensive way to cash checks. Most check-cashing fees range from 1 to 10 percent (plus a service fee in some states) of the face value of a check.[153] Check-cashing charges are often based on a sliding scale, and Dollar—the second largest CCO—charges 3.5 percent, or $35, to cash a $1,000 payroll check.[154] Fees for cashing personal checks can run as high as 10 to 12 percent of the value of the check. If a customer cashes twenty $800 paychecks a year through Dollar, they will pay $560—far more than the costs of even a deluxe checking account. The price list at one ACE Cash Express in Houston, Texas, is typical of the industry:

Cashier's check	5.0%
Government check	2.7%
Handwritten payroll check	2.7%
Insurance drafts/checks	5.0%
Money orders	5.0%
Tax refund checks	3.9%
No I.D. checks	5.0%
Special risk	5.0%
Bank-processing fee	$0.49
Minimum charge per item	$1.99
Returned check charge	$25.00

High check-cashing fees do not correspond to high risk since about 70 to 90 percent of all checks cashed at CCOs are relatively secure payroll checks with an average value of $500 to $600.[155] Losses are also extremely low. For example, ACE uses a system for verifying and assessing the risk of each check-cashing transaction and reports losses of less than one quarter of 1 percent.[156] The profitability of the check cashing business is stunning. In 2002, 797 ACE company-owned stores posted average revenues of $237,000, or a store profit of almost 43 percent.[157] This profitability is leading even non-finance-related industries into the fray. For example, the Eastern Division of the Safeway supermarket chain was once the largest CCO in Maryland. Supermarket chains such as H.E.B. and Kroger's have also established check-cashing operations, although often charging slightly less than commercial CCOs.

Transportation in the Fringe Economy

For the poor who can afford a used vehicle, the path to car ownership is mined with high down payments, dead-end financing, extortionate interest rates, and overpriced insurance. Understanding the used-car industry is necessary to appreciate the obstacles faced by the poor. About 40 million used vehicles are sold annually in the United States—11 million by franchised new-car dealers and the remaining 29 million by independent used-car lots.[158] Used-car lots fall into two categories: independent lots and franchised dealerships. Independent or non-franchised dealers frequently sell older and less expensive vehicles. Franchised used-car lots are part of new-car dealerships and their cars tend to be newer, cleaner, and more expensive. Because of this market segmentation, most poor buyers end up in independent car lots, many of which are "here today and gone tomorrow."

A major obstacle faced by the poor is based on how mainstream financial institutions make loans in the $370 billion used-car industry. Most mainstream lenders like Bank of America, Wells Fargo Bank, and Chase refuse to lend money on vehicles four to six years or older, and those with more than 100,000 miles on them. Some lenders only finance vehicles purchased through dealerships, and some further restrict that to dealerships that also sell new cars. These restrictions limit the choices for the poor, because used cars sold by a dealer are more expensive than private-party sales. According to the Kelly Blue Book, a 1996 Chevrolet Lumina with 76,000 miles bought from an auto dealer in New York City in 2005 would have cost 30 percent more than one purchased privately.

Three tiers of financing exist for used-car buyers. The first is prime lending, which is offered to borrowers with a higher income and a good credit history. Interest rates are low because they are tied to the prime rate. The second tier is subprime lending, which is geared toward buyers with credit problems but who still have sufficient creditworthiness to secure a loan. Subprime loans carry higher interest rates, involve a substantial down payment, and often require that a vehicle be purchased from a franchised dealership. The third tier is nonprime lending or dealer financing, whereby vehicles are financed in-house. This type of financing often carries the highest interest rates and often requires weekly payments.

Buy-Here, Pay-Here used-car lots provide in-house financing, and they do not require buyers to undergo a credit check because the payment history is not reported to a credit bureau. Dealer-financed cars require a hefty down payment (typically $1,000 on a $5,000 vehicle) and late payments can result in immediate repossession.

Buy-Here, Pay-Here used-car lots are more profitable than franchised car dealerships. In 2002, the average retail price of used cars sold by franchised car lots was $11,793 with a gross profit of $1,741. In that same year, the average retail price of a used car in a Buy-Here, Pay-Here lot was $7,810, with a gross profit of $3,772—more than double that of franchised dealers. Lest one believe these dealerships are just small mom-and-pop operations, the National Association of Buy-Here, Pay-Here dealers held an annual convention in 2001 with over 800 attendees and 60 sponsors, including Bank of America, Bank One, SeaWest, and Wells Fargo. The Buy-Here, Pay-Here sector will likely grow as more subprime lenders—some of whom have lost money in recent years—further tighten their credit standards.

Auto insurance is another area where the poor are hard hit. For example, many people with older cars insure them only for state-mandated liability rather than for collision (damage to their vehicle) coverage. It makes little sense to pay $600 a year for collision coverage on a car worth $1,000, especially with a $500 deductible. Unfortunately, consumers who finance through Buy-Here, Pay-Here dealerships or subprime lenders must insure their vehicles for liability *and* collision, regardless of whether it is cost effective.

The poor are hard hit by high auto-insurance rates. According to one study, 92 percent of large insurance companies run credit checks on potential customers, which translate into insurance scores.[159] These insurance scores determine whether the carrier will insure an applicant and for how much. Those with poor or no credit will be denied coverage, while those with limited credit will pay high premiums. Although there is no evidence that residents in low-income or high minority zip codes are involved in more accidents, they pay more for basic auto insurance, even if they have been accident-free and ticket-free for years.[160] Mounting consumer complaints have aroused the suspicion of some state insurance regulators that this may be a new form of redlining—a practice outlawed by the Fair Housing Act of 1968—because it discriminates against low-income, single-parent, young, and minority consumers whose credit histories may be less than perfect.[161]

While mainstream auto insurers calculate premiums based on a six-month or one-year period, fringe auto insurers usually provide only monthly quotations. Many also require a sizable down payment and a service fee. The premiums charged by fringe insurers are exorbitant compared with mainstream auto insurers. For example, in 2005 GEICO charged $700 a year for full coverage on a 1991 Chrysler minivan for a Houston driver with an excellent driving record. In comparison, minimally regulated, high-rate local insurance agencies like Houston's Alamo Insurance charged $2,100 a year for the same vehicle, or three times the $700 quoted by GEICO.

Fringe auto insurers get away with charging high premiums for several reasons. For one, they have captive consumers who are rejected by large insurance carriers. Second, the insurance demands of Buy-Here, Pay-Here dealers and subprime lenders create a steady stream of car buyers desperate for insurance. Third, many fringe auto insurers are minimally regulated and state insurance agencies are lax in rooting out predatory insurers, especially those serving the poor. Not coincidentally, fringe auto insurers take the pressure off mainstream carriers to provide coverage for the poor. Last, many state vehicle inspections require a proof-of-insurance card before a vehicle can pass inspection. Some car owners will pay the high monthly premium only to get the card and pass inspection, after which they drop the coverage. This may explain why fringe auto insurance rates are quoted monthly rather than biannually.

The low-income population pays more than the middle class for financial services in both absolute dollars and relative to their income.[162] These costs are exacerbated by the bifurcation of financial services that results in one system for the poor and another for the middle and upper classes. This bifurcated system leads to even greater inequality: Banks for the middle class and check cashers for the poor; access to savings tools for the middle class and barriers to savings for the poor; low-cost financial services for the middle class and high fee–based services for the poor. The fringe economy represents the financial exploitation of the poor by a predatory market designed to deplete rather than enhance the resources of poor families and communities. To better understand the poor, policy analysts must be aware of the myriad ways in which they are economically exploited. The regulation of the fringe economy is an economic justice issue that should be a central focus of any progressive social welfare agenda.

Conclusion

Poverty is one of the most intractable problems in U.S. society. Because poverty is both a political and a social issue, the policies surrounding it are often less than objective. For example, one can halve the poverty rate simply by redefining the poverty index. One can also cut poverty rates by placing a high dollar value on in-kind benefits such as food stamps and Medicaid. Conversely, one can swell the ranks of the poor by moving the poverty line upward; that is, by increasing the income level at which people are defined as poor. Like all social policies, poverty-related policies exist in a context marked by political exigencies, public opinion, the economic health of a society, and the complex mask of ideology.

Although various kinds of poverty-related data are available, policymakers remain uncertain as to the precise causes of poverty. What is known is that they are complex and involve, among other things, the effects of discrimination; the composition of family life, including the rise in single, female-headed families and teenage pregnancies; geographical location; and age. In large measure, the determination of whether a child is poor depends on chance; that is, on the family the child is born into. Policymakers also know that the skewed distribution of income in society and governmental tax and investment policies have major impacts on the numbers of people in poverty and on the extent of their poverty.

Most policymakers agree that employment is the best antipoverty program. Thus, work-related factors such as the value of the minimum wage (especially its relationship to mean incomes), the level of under- and unemployment, the rise or decrease in family incomes, and the general state of the economy all have a major impact on the level and extent of poverty. The availability of job training programs and the regulation of the dual labor market help determine the salaries workers will make. Taken together, these factors have caused poverty rates to remain higher in the United States than in many other industrialized nations. They have also helped make poverty seem like an intractable problem with few viable solutions.

Discussion Questions

Questions of poverty have long plagued social scientists. Specifically, these questions revolve around why some groups are able to rise out of poverty but others appear only to fall deeper into the poverty trap. Although several theorists have offered explanations for poverty, none hold up to empirical testing. This is because there is no simple or single answer to poverty. The causes of poverty involve a wide range of social, economic, political, and cultural factors. Poverty is one of the most elusive—if not the most elusive—problems facing U.S. social policy. Theories and strategies that address single explanations or single causes of poverty are doomed to failure, only aggravating a public that is already suspect of most antipoverty measures.

1. The measurement of poverty is both complex and controversial. Nevertheless, the way that poverty is measured has important consequences for the development of social policy in the United States. Describe some of the potential pitfalls in measuring poverty rates and discuss how the calculation of poverty rates affects the creation of social policy.

2. Working families make up an important and growing segment of the poor. What is causing the increase in the numbers of working poor? What specific policies should be implemented to reduce the number of working poor families?

3. Several theories have been advanced to explain why some individuals and groups of people are persistently poor while others are not. Theorists who have tried to tackle this problem include Daniel Patrick Moynihan, Oscar Lewis, and Edward Banfield. Although all theories of poverty have intrinsic flaws, which theory or combination of theories described in this book (or elsewhere) do you think best explains the dynamics of poverty?

4. Many strategies have been developed to fight poverty, including the curative approach, the alleviative approach, and the preventive approach. Of these strategies, which is the most effective in fighting poverty and why? What alternative strategies, if any, could be developed that would be more effective in combating poverty?

5. Policy analysts have traditionally argued that jobs are preferable to welfare and that the lack of employment opportunities results in increasing needs for social welfare. Is this relationship apparent in your community? What is the evidence?

6. A commonly held belief is that government make-work jobs are inferior to private sector employment. Yet many New Deal jobs programs have made important contributions to the infrastructure of the nation's cities. What New Deal projects are evident in your community? If a new governmental jobs program were initiated, what community needs might it address?

7. The fringe economy is a high-growth sector that is adversely affecting the economic lives of the poor. What policies or programs would you propose that could regulate, constrain, or abolish the fringe economic sector? What legislative or policy reforms are needed?

Notes

1. See Edward C. Banfield, *The Unheavenly City* (Boston: Little, Brown, 1966) and Oscar Lewis, La Vida (New York: Harper & Row, 1965).

2. Richard Dugdale, *The Jukes* (New York: G. P. Putnam's Sons, 1910).

3. Henry Goddard, *The Kallikak Family* (New York: Arno Publishers, 1911).

4. Arthur R. Jensen, "How Much Can We Boost IQ and Scholastic Achievement?" *Harvard Educational Review* 39 (Winter 1969), pp. 1–23.

5. Winifred Bell, *Contemporary Social Welfare* (New York: Macmillan, 1983), p. 261.

6. William Shockley, "Sterilization: A Thinking Exercise," in Carl Bahema (ed.), *Eugenics: Then and Now* (Stroudsburg, PA: Doidon, Hutchinson & Ross, 1976); see also Bell, *Contemporary Social Welfare*, p. 263.

7. Richard Herrnstein, *IQ and the Meritocracy* (Boston: Little, Brown, 1973).

8. Richard Herrnstein and Charles Murray, *The Bell Curve* (New York: Free Press, 1994).

9. Winnie Chen, Vilma Hernandez, Erin Townsend, and Carol Wyatt, "Affirmative Action," unpublished paper, University of Houston Graduate School of Social Work, Houston, TX, May 1, 1996.

10. T. Beardsley, "For Whom the Bell Curve Really Tolls," *Scientific American* 272, no. 1 (1995), pp. 14–17; Stephen Gould, "Ghosts of Bell Curves Past," *Natural History* 104, no. 2 (1995), pp. 12–19; and C. Lane, "The Tainted Sources of the Bell Curve," *The New York Review of Books* 41, no. 20 (1994), pp. 14–19.

11. Gould, "Ghosts of Bell Curves Past," p. 14.

12. Bell, *Contemporary Social Welfare*, p. 264.

13. David Gil, *Unraveling Social Policy* (Boston: Shenkman, 1981).

14. Blanche Bernstein, "Welfare Dependency," in Lee D. Bawden (ed.), *The Social Contract Revisited* (Washington, DC: Urban Institute Press, 1984), p. 129.

15. Greg J. Duncan et al., *Years of Poverty, Years of Plenty* (Ann Arbor, MI: Institute for Social Research, 1984).

16. Daniel McMurer and Isabel Sawhill, *Getting Ahead* (Washington, DC: Urban Institute, 1998), p. 33.

17. Bradley Schiller, "Relative Earnings Redux." Review of Income and Wealth 40, no. 4 (1994), p. 629.

18. W. Michael Cox and Richard Alm, *Myths of Rich & Poor* (New York: Basic Books, 1999), p. 73.

19. David Howell and Elizabeth Howell, *The Effects of Immigrants on African American Earnings* (New York: New School for Social Research, 1997), p. 23.

20. Carmen DeNavas-Walt, Bernadette D. Proctor, and Jessica Smith, "Income, Poverty, and Health Insurance Coverage in the United States: 2006," Economics and Statistics Administration U.S. Census Bureau, issued August 2007. Retrieved May 2008, from www .census.gov/prod/2007pubs/p60-233.pdf

21. Institute for Research on Poverty, "Improving the Measurement of American Poverty," Focus 19, no. 2 (Spring 1998), p. 2.

22. Ibid.

23. U.S. Senate, "Introduction of the Poverty Data Correction Act of 1999," p. 1. Retrieved 2008, from www.govtrack.us/congress/bill.xpd?bill=s106-204

24. DeNavas-Walt, Proctor, and Smith, "Income, Poverty, and Health Insurance Coverage in the United States: 2006."

25. Sara McLanahan and Gary Sandefur, *Growing Up with a Single Parent* (Cambridge, MA: Harvard University Press, 1997).

26. U.S. Department of Health and Human Services, Support Collections Up 40 Percent Since 1992: $24 Billion More Can Still Be Collected, Shalala Says," December 5, 1995. Retrieved 2008, from www.hhs.gov/news/press/1995pres/951205a.html

27. Ron Dean, "Myths, Legends and the American Way: Deadbeat Dads," August 15, 1995. Retrieved 2008, from www.vix.com/pub/men/child-support/commentar

28. Timothy S. Grall, "Custodial Mothers and Fathers and Their Child Support: 2005," U.S. Census Bureau, August 2007. Retrieved June 2008, from www.census.gov/prod/2007pubs/p60-234.pdf

29. Ibid.

30. Center for Law and Social Policy, "Child Support Substantially Increases Economic Well-Being of Low- and Moderate-Income Families," Washington, DC, 2004.

31. DeNavas-Walt, Proctor, and Smith, "Income, Poverty, and Health Insurance Coverage in the United States: 2006."

32. Neil G. Bennett Jiali Li, Younghwan Song, and Keming Yang, "Young Children in Poverty: A Statistical Update," New York: National Center for Children in Poverty, Columbia University, Mailman School of Health, June 17, 1999.

33. See Congressional Record, Senate, vol. 133, no. 120 (Washington, DC: U.S. Government Printing Office, July 21, 1987), pp. S10400–S10404; and Sheldon Danziger and Marcia Carlson, "Cohabitation and the Measurement of Child Poverty," Poverty Measurement Working Papers, U.S. Bureau of the Census, February 1998. Retrieved 2008, from www.census.gov/hhes/www/ povmeas/papers/cohabit.html

34. DeNavas-Walt, Proctor, and Smith, "Income, Poverty, and Health Insurance Coverage in the United States: 2006."

35. Ibid.

36. Ibid.

37. Ibid.

38. See Ibid. Economic Research Center, "Measuring Rurality: 2004 County Typology Codes," U.S. Department of Agriculture, 2004; Kathryn Porter, *Poverty in Rural America* (Washington, DC: Center on Budget and Policy Priorities, 1989), pp. 7–11; and Scott Barancik, *The Rural Disadvantage: Growing Income Disparities between Rural and Urban Areas* (Washington, DC: Center on Budget and Policy Priorities, April 1990), pp. ix–x.

39. Economic Research Center, "Rural Poverty at a Glance." U.S. Department of Agriculture, 2003. Retrieved October 2004, from www.ers.usda.gov/publications/rdrr100/rdrr100.pdf

40. Porter, *Poverty. in Rural America.*

41. United States Department of Agriculture, "Rural Income, Poverty and Welfare: Rural Poverty." Retrieved July 2008, from www.ers.usda.gov/ Briefing/incomepovertywelfare/RuralPoverty/

42. See Economic Research Service, "Rural America at a Glance," USDA, Rural Development Briefing Room. Retrieved 2008, from www.ers.usda.gov/publications/rdrr97-1/highres_rdrr97-1.pdf

43. U.S. Bureau of Labor Statistics, "A Profile of the Working Poor, 2005," September 2007. Retrieved July 2008, from www.bls.gov/cps/cpswp2005.pdf

44. Ibid.

45. Ibid.

46. Bureau of Labor Statistics, "Tomorrow's Jobs," U.S. Department of Labor, June 2, 2004. Retrieved October 2004, from http://stats.bls.gov/oco/oco2003.htm

47. Michael Sherraden, "Chronic Unemployment: A Social Work Perspective," *Social Work* (September–October 1985), p. 403.

48. Ibid., pp. 404–406.

49. As Sherraden notes, the common understanding that an unemployment rate of 5 percent is "normal" is not supported by economists, who calculate that structural and frictional unemployment can be reduced to 3 percent through astute social policies.

50. "Not Many Jobs Are Sent Abroad, U.S. Report Says," *New York Times* (June 11, 2004).

51. M. Harvey Brenner, *Estimating the Effects of Economic Change on National Health and Social Well-Being* (Washington, DC: U.S. Government Printing Office, 1984), pp. 2–4.

52. Ibid.

53. U.S. Bureau of Labor Statistics, "Extended Mass Layoffs in 2006," April 2008. Retrieved July 2008, from www.bls.gov/mls/mlsreport1004.pdf

54. Michael Piore, "The Dual Labor Market," in David Gordon (ed.), *Problems in Political Economy* (Lexington, MA: D.C. Heath, 1977), p. 94.

55. David Gordon, Richard Edwards, and Michael Reich, *Segmented Work, Divided Workers* (New York: Cambridge University Press, 1982), p. 211.

56. Michael Harrington, Robert Greenstein, and Eleanor Holmes Norton, Who Are the Poor?: A Profile of the Changing Faces of Poverty in the United States in 1987 (Washington, DC: Justice for All, 1987), p. 10.

57. James Parks, "Kennedy, Pelosi Promise Quick Action on Minimum Wage if Democrats Win Congress," October 24, 2006. Retrieved March 20, 2007, from http://blog.aflcio.org/2006/10/24/kennedy-pelosi-promise-quick-action-on-minimum-wage-if-democrats-win-congress/

58. "Minimum Wage: Facts at a Glance," Economic Policy Institute, March 2007. Retrieved March 20, 2007, from www.epi.org/content.cfm/ issueguides_minwage_minwagefacts

59. George. J. Borjas, *Labor Economics* (Boston: McGraw-Hill, 2005).

60. "Minimum Wage: Facts at a Glance."

61. "Sates with Minimum Wages above the Federal Level Have Had Faster Small Business and Retail Job Growth," Fiscal Policy Institute, March 30, 2006. Retrieved March 20, 2007, from http://fiscalpolicy.org/FPISmallBusinessMinWage.pdf

62. David Neumark and William Wascher, "Minimum Wages and Employment: A Review of the Evidence from the New Minimum Wage Research," National Bureau of Economic Research, Working Paper no. 12663, 2006.

63. The Bureau of Labor Statistics, "Characteristics of Minimum Wage Workers: 2007," Tables 4. Retrieved July 2008, from www.bls.gov/cps/minwage2007tbls.htm#5

64. Jared Bernstein and Isaac Shapiro, "Nine Years of Neglect: Federal Minimum Wage Remains Unchanged for Ninth Straight Year, Falls to Lowest Level in More than Half a Century," Center on Budget and Policy Priorities, August 31, 2006. Retrieved 2008, from www.cbpp.org/8-31-06mw.htm

65. Isaac Shapiro, *The Minimum Wage and Job Loss* (Washington, DC: Center on Budget and Policy Priorities, 1988).

66. Center on Budget and Policy Priorities, "Assessing the $5.15 an Hour Minimum Wage."

67. Acorn, National Living Wage Resource Center, "Introduction to ACORN's Living Wage Web Site." Retrieved 2000, from www.livingwagecampaign.org

68. U.S. Department of Labor, Employment Standards Administration Wage and Hour Division, Minimum Wage Laws in the States—January 1, 2008. Retrieved May 12, 2008, from www.dol.gov/esa/minwage/america.htm

69. Cited in Michal Grinstein-Weiss and Jami Curley, "Individual Development Accounts in Rural Communities: Implications for Research." Working Paper no. 03-21, Washington University, Center for Social Development, George Warren Brown School of Social Work, Washington University, St. Louis, MO, 2003.

70. Michael Sherraden, "Can Asset-Based Welfare Policy Really Help the Poor?" in Howard Jacob Karger, James Midgley, and Brene Brown, *Controversial Issues in Social Policy*, 2nd ed. (Boston: Allyn & Bacon, 2003), p. 50.

71. Ibid., p. 51.

72. Ibid.

73. Ibid.

74. Michael Sherraden, *Assets and the Poor: A New American Welfare Policy* (Armonk, NY: M.E. Sharpe, 1991).

75. Ibid.

76. Ibid.

77. John Kenneth Galbraith, *The Affluent Society* (Boston: Houghton Mifflin, 1958).

78. Harrington, Greenstein, and Norton, *Who Are the Poor?* p. 17.

79. Ibid., p. 22.

80. U.S. Census Bureau, "Poverty Status by State: 2006." U.S. Census Bureau, Current Population Survey, 2007 Annual Social and Economic Supplement. Retrieved July 2008, from http://pubdb3.census.gov/macro/032007/pov/new46_100125_01.htm

81. Kevin Phillips, *The Politics of Rich and Poor* (New York: Random House, 1990), p. 87.

82. Sheldon Danziger, "Poverty," *Encyclopedia of Social Work*, 18th ed. (Silver Spring, MD: NASW Press, 1987), pp. 301–302.

83. National Telecommunications and Information Agency, *A Nation Online: How Americans Are Expanding Their Use of the Internet*, U.S. Department of Commerce, February 2002. Retrieved August 2004, from www.ntia.doc.gov/ntiahome/dn/index.html

84. National Telecommunications and Information Agency, "Households Using the Internet In and Outside the Home, by Selected Characteristics: Total, Urban, Rural, Principal City, 2007." Retrieved July 2008, from www.ntia.doc.gov/reports/2008/Table_HouseholdInternet2007.pdf

85. Ekaterina Walsh, Shelley Morrisette, and Nicky Maraganore, "The Digital Melting Pot," *The Forrester Report*. Forrester Research Inc., Jupiter Communications, June 15, 2000.

86. For a fuller examination of the fringe economy see Howard Karger, *Shortchanged: Life and Debt in the Fringe Economy* (San Francisco: Berrett-Koehler, 2005).

87. "Personal Savings Rate," Bureau of Economic Analysis, U.S. Department of Commerce. Retrieved March 22, 2007, from www.bea.gov/briefrm/saving.htm

88. Kenneth J. Lansing, "Spendthrift Nation," *FRBSF Economic Letter,* November 10, 2005. Retrieved March 22, 2007, from www.frbsf.org/publications/economics/letter/2005/el2005-30.html

89. Ibid.

90. Brian K. Bucks, Arthur B. Kennickell, Kevin B. Moore, Gerhard Fries, and A. Michael Neal, "Recent Changes in U.S. Farmly Finances: Evidence from the 2001 and 2004 Survey of Consumer Finances," *Federal Reserve Bulletin,* 2006. Retrieved March 22, 2007, from www.federalreserve.gov/pubs/oss/oss2/2004/bull0206.pdf

91. "President Signs Bankruptcy Abuse Prevention, Consumer Protection Act," April 20, 2005. Retrieved March 22, 2007, from www.whitehouse.gov/news/releases/2005/04/20050420-5.html

92. Brian Louis, "KB Homes First Quarter Net Income Plunges in Slump (Update 3)," *Bloomberg,* March 22, 2007. Retrieved March 22, 2007, from www.bloomberg.com/apps/news?pid=20601087&sid=a13dV_1LQ1cI&refer=home

93. Bob Ivry, "Foreclosures May Hit 1.5 Million in U.S. Housing Bust," *Bloomberg,* March 12, 2007. Retrieved March 22, 2007, from www.bloomberg.com/apps/news?pid=20601109&sid=aoxvdkPVfUNo&refer=home

94. Gerard Jackson, "U.S. Economy: Will a Housing Bust Cause a Recession?" *Free Market News Network,* March 20, 2007. Retrieved March 22, 2007, from www.freemarketnews.com/Analysis/50/7152/gerard.asp?wid=50&nid=7152

95. Robert D. Manning, *Credit Card Nation* (New York: Basic Books, 2000).

96. Center for Responsible Lending, "Financial Quicksand: Payday Lending Sinks Borrowers in Debt with $4.2 Billion in Predatory Fees Every Year," November 30, 2006. Retrieved July 2008, from www.responsiblelending.org/pdfs/rr012-Financial_Quicksand-1106.pdf

97. National Consumer Law Center, "Utilities and Payday Lenders: Convenient Payments, Killer Loans." Retrieved July 2008, from www.consumerlaw.org/reports/content/payday_utility.pdf

98. Ibid.

99. Center for Responsible Lending, "Losing Ground: Foreclosures in the Sub-prime Market and Their Cost to Homeowners," December 2006. Retrieved July 2008, from www.responsiblelending.org/pdfs/foreclosure-paper-report-2-17.pdf

100. Fannie Mae Foundation, 2001.

101. Federal Reserve Board, 2002; IO Data Corporation, Payday Advance Customer Research: Cumulative State Research Report, September 2002. IO Data Corporation, Salt Lake City, UT.

102. IO Data Corporation, 2002.

103. Joint Center for Housing Studies of Harvard University, The State of the Nation's Housing (Cambridge, MA: Harvard University, 2003); Theresa Murray, "Experts Warn Against Milking Home Equity to Extend Debt," *Minneapolis St. Paul Star Tribune* (November 4, 2000), p. B-5.

104. See Noel Paul, "Culture of Consumption," *Christian Science Monitor* (June 12, 2003), 18; and Joint Center for Housing Studies of Harvard University, 2003.

105. Peter Gumbel, "The $915 Billion Bomb in Consumers' Wallets." Retrieved July 2008, from http://money.cnn.com/2007/10/29/magazines/fortune/consumer_debt.fortune/index.htm?postversion=2007103007

106. Manning, *Credit Card Nation.*

107. Murray Coleman, "Mortgage Meltdown Seen Spreading to Credit Cards," *MarketWatch,* November 19, 2007.

108. Joanna Stavins, "Credit Card Borrowing, Delinquency and Personal Bankruptcy," *Questia* (2000). Retrieved 2003, from www.questia.com

109. Ibid.

110. Cardweb.com. Retrieved 2003, from www.cardweb.com

111. Wired Plastic. Retrieved 2003, from www.wiredplastic.com

112. Direct Telephone Company, Inc., Houston, TX.

113. See Sprint PCS. Retrieved 2004, from www.sprintpcs.com; and AT&T Wireless. Retrieved 2004, from www.attwireless.com

114. Ibid.

115. See APRO, "RTO Industry Stats, 2003." Retrieved 2004, from www.aprovision.org/industrystats.html and James M. Lacko, Signe-Mary McKernan, and Manoj Hastak, *Survey of Rent-to-Own Customers, Federal Trade Commission* (Bureau of Economics, Washington, DC, 1999).

116. APRO, "About Rent-to-Own: Rent-to-Own Industry Overview." Retrieved July 2008, from www.rtohq.org/apro-rto-industry-overview.html

117. Rent-a-Center "Investor Relations." Retrieved July 2008, from http://investor.rentacenter.com/phoenix.zhtml?c=90764&p=irol-irhome

118. Aaron Rents, Inc., "2008 First Quarter Report." Retrieved July 2008, from http://media.corporate-ir.net/media_files/irol/10/104698/Chairman_letter_1Q08.pdf

119. Rent-A-Center. Retrieved January 2, 2004, from www.rentacenter.com; ColorTyme. Retrieved January 2, 2004, from www.colortyme.com; Aaron Rents. Retrieved 2004, from www.aaronrents.com; RentWay. Retrieved 2004, from www.rentway.com; Rent Rite. Retrieved 2003, from www.rentrite.com

120. Public Interest Research Group (PIRG), "Don't Rent to Own: The 1997 PIRG Rent-to-Own Survey," U.S. Public Interest Research Group, Washington, DC, June 11, 1997.

121. Ibid.
122. Alix M. Freedman, "Peddling Dreams: A Market Giant Uses Its Sales Prowess to Profit on Poverty," *Wall Street Journal* (September 22, 1993), p. D15.
123. APRO, 2003.
124. John Seward, "Tales of the Tape: Rent-to-Owns Seek Definition in Law," *Wall Street Journal* (October 22, 2003), p. D15.
125. Quoted in Freedman, 1993, p. D16.
126. UPI.com, "Tough Times Send Many to Pawnshops," June 16, 2008. Retrieved July 2008, from www.upi.com/Business_News/2008/06/16/Tough_times_send_many_to_pawn_shops/UPI-47261213629989/
127. American Financial Services Association, "Pawnshops Struggle, 2002." Retrieved 2002, from www.spotlightonfinance.org/issues/August/Stories/story13.htm/
128. John Caskey, Fringe Banking (New York: Russell Sage Foundation, 1994).
129. *Edmund's Used Cars & Trucks Prices: 1992–2001, American & Import,* Spring/Summer, 2002 (Chicago, IL: Edmunds, 2002).
130. Personal communication with Car Title Loans of America, Inc., Missouri office, Columbia, MO, June 5, 2002.
131. American Financial Services Association, 2002.
132. Ibid.
133. Consumer Federation of America, "Predatory Lending, 2002," Retrieved 2002, from www.consumerfed.org/backpage/predatory.html.
134. AARP, "Payday Loans Don't Pay." Retrieved 2008, from www.aarp.org/money/wise_consumer/smartshopping/a2002-10-02-FraudsPaydayLoans.html
135. See Howard Karger, *Shortchanged: Life and Debt in the Fringe Economy* (San Francisco: Berrett-Koehler, 2005), p. 156.
136. Quik Payday, "APR Disclosure, 2002." Retrieved 2002, from www.quikpayday.com/apr-disclosure.html
137. Consumer Federation of America, 2002.
138. Daniel P. McKernan, *The Monitor,* "The Real Cost of Tax Refund Anticipation Loans," December 20, 2007. Retrieved July 2008, from www.fbmonitor.com/2007/12december/122007/pdf/122007part5.pdf
139. Consumer Federation of America, 2002.
140. Ibid.
141. Alan Berube, Anne Kim, Benjamin Forman, and Megan Burns, *The Price of Paying Taxes: How Tax Preparation and Refund Loan Fees Erode the Benefits of the EITC.* Center on Urban & Metropolitan Policy, The Brookings Institution and The Progressive Policy Institute, Washington, DC: The Brookings Institution, May 2002.
142. Consumer Federation of America, 2002.
143. See Karger, *Shortchanged,* p. 93.
144. See Karger, *Shortchanged,* p. 98.
145. Ibid.
146. This is based on national averages.
147. Chichi Wu and Jean Ann Fox, "The High Cost of Quick Tax Money: Tax Preparation, 'Instant Refund' Loans, and Check Cashing Fees Target the Working Poor," National Consumer Law Center, Consumer Federation of America, January 2003. Washington, DC.
148. Ibid.
149. Ibid.
150. John Caskey, "Bringing Unbanked Households into the Banking System," *Capitol Xchange,* The Brookings Institution, January 2002. Retrieved 2002, from www.brookings.edu/articles/2002/01metropolitanpolicy_caskey.aspx
151. ACE Cash Express, "ACE Store Services, 2002." Retrieved 2002, from www.acecashexpress.com/general/services.html
152. See Anne Kim, "The Unbanked and the Alternative Financial Sector. Discussion Comments to the Changing Financial Markets and Community Development Conference." Federal Reserve Bank of Chicago, transcript, April 5, 2001. Retrieved 2002, from www.ppionline.org/ppi_ci.cfm?cp=3&knlgAreaID=114&subsecid=236&contentid=3843; and Financial Service Centers of America, 2003.
153. Sougata MuKherjee, "Consumer Group Pushes for Regulation of Check Cashing Industry," *Houston Business Journal* (August 29, 1997), p. 25.
154. Kim, 2001, op cit.
155. Financial Service Centers of America (FiSCA), 2003.
156. See ACE Cash Express Inc., *Annual Report on Form 10-K for the Fiscal Year Ended June 30, 2000.* Filed with the Securities and Exchange Commission; and Dollar Financial Group, Inc., *Annual Report on Form 10-K for the Fiscal Year Ended June 30, 2000,* filed with the Securities and Exchange Commission.
157. ACE Cash Express, "ACE Cash Express Extends Money Order Relationship with Travelers Express, ACE to Receive $3.4 Million in Signing and Annual Bonuses," October 20, 2003. Retrieved 2008 from http://goliath.ecnext.com/coms2/gi_0199-4021692/ACE- Cash-Express-Extends-Money. html
158. See Karger, *Shortchanged,* p. 145.
159. "Conning & Co. Study Says Auto Insurers Are Paying Closer Attention to Credit Scores," *Insurance Journal* (August 2, 2001).
160. Consumers Union, "Reducing the Number of Uninsured Motorists," *Consumers Union SWRO Issue Pages for the 77th Texas Legislature* (January 2001).
161. A.M. Best Company, Inc., "Insurers Expect Battle on Use of Credit Scores in About Half the United States," *BestWire* (January 30, 2002).
162. John Caskey, Lower Income Americans, Higher Cost Financial Services (Madison, WI: Filene Research Institute, 1997).

The Nature and Causes of Poverty

<table>
<tr><td colspan="6">✓ Connecting Core Competencies in this Chapter</td></tr>
<tr><td>Professional Identity</td><td>Ethical Practice</td><td>✓ Critical Thinking</td><td>✓ Diversity in Practice</td><td>Human Rights & Justice</td></tr>
<tr><td>Research Based Practice</td><td>Human Behavior</td><td>Policy Practice</td><td>Practice Contexts</td><td>Engage, Assess, Intervene, Evaluate</td></tr>
</table>

When I was a child, I lived with my family in Minneapolis. We lived on the south side of town, and our relatives lived on the north side, where my father had grown up. We visited often. One Sunday afternoon in March we set off across town in our car and took a different route than usual. I think it had something to do with the construction of a new freeway, which caused streets to be closed. Our new route took us through the middle of the area that would now be called the ghetto; it was then called the slums. This was new and foreign territory; I had never seen anything like it. I stared out of the window fascinated, horrified, and repulsed all at the same time. There were houses that had burned down and apparently been abandoned, broken glass seemed to be everywhere; and the streets and yards were littered with paper and junk. Even more puzzling were the housing projects, which I could see were relatively new and modern structures, not unlike apartment houses in my neighborhood, but which looked little better than the old dilapidated buildings surrounding them. Their walls were covered with graffiti, there were cars up on blocks, and the yards were lakes of mud separated by scraggly patches of grass.

Groups of children ran around and played; they did not look too different from the children I played with. They were a little ragged—some were wearing torn tennis shoes even though it was still cold—but otherwise they looked familiar. The groups of adults did not seem typical, however. They were standing around in small groups, looking tired and bored, and they lacked the appearance of purpose and command that I expected from the adults in my life.

"Who are these people?" I asked my parents. "Why are they here?" "What is this place?" "Do they like it?" "Why don't they leave?" My parents explained that these were poor people; they were here because they did not have enough money to go anywhere else; and most of them did not like it, but they probably did not know anything else. It was an unfortunate situation, but it was simply a fact of life. This explanation didn't really satisfy me. I knew poor people. My friend Mike was poor. Mike's father had died while serving in the military before Mike was born, and his mother had some sort of chronic illness; people referred to her as frail. She was able to work only part time, answering the phone at the Lutheran church, and her salary from this, plus her small government check, provided very little income. Mike and his mother lived in a tiny two-room cottage in the backyard of a house two blocks down from where my family lived. The cottage had been built for the mother of the owner of the house, and when she died, the owner rented it to Mike's mother for a small sum. Mike slept in the bedroom and his mother slept in a hide-a-bed in the living room. They did not have a car. Mike's mother had a basket that rolled on two wheels and could be folded up for easy carrying. She would carry this to the store, load her groceries in, and roll them home. They didn't have a TV set, even though the last holdout in the neighborhood (my father) had purchased one two years before. Like all of us, Mike worked, mowing lawns in the summer and shoveling snow in the winter. However, unlike us, he could not use his money for anything he wanted. Whatever he earned he gave to his mother, who put it in the bank to be used for school clothes, Boy Scouts, and summer camp. Any money left over went into that mysterious black hole of youthful finance, the college fund.

As we drove out of the ghetto, I thought about Mike. Mike was poor, but he was not like this. The only difference between Mike's family and mine was that we had more money. This neighborhood appeared to be in another country, if not on another planet. Who were these people? Why were these people like this? It had to be more than simply money.

As an adult, I am still asking the questions I asked as a child. Those questions are the subject of this chapter. Who are the poor? Are they all the same? Why are they poor? Regarding the first two questions, as you will see, we know a good deal. We have massive amounts of statistical data to describe the poor. My youthful observation about the difference between my friend Mike and the people I observed in that Minneapolis ghetto was valid—poor people are not all the same, and there is more to poverty than money, although obviously money is the most important part. The answer to the last question is not so clear. We have many theories about the causes of poverty but no certain answers. The answers we do have are greatly clouded by our old friend—political perspectives.

WHO ARE THE POOR?

In this section we present a statistical picture of the population in the United States who live below the poverty line. Two types of pictures are presented. The first is the traditional means of describing this population based on statistical data gathered mainly by the Census Bureau as part of its series of Current Population Reports. This is the source of most of the figures you see on the evening news and that are referred to in statements by lawmakers and interest groups. This type of information has been referred to as *cross-section* or *snapshot* data: It provides a series of statistical pictures at certain points in time, but it does not tell us much beyond a general description of the situation at that time. Poverty statistics show, for example, that the level of poverty in this country is fairly stable, running between 11 and 15 percent each year. However, these statistics do not tell us anything about the individual makeup of those figures at each point in time. Is the 11 to 15 percent composed of the same people this year as last year, or are different people poor each year? If the statistics describe a different population each year, how different is it? Are some people more likely to be part of the statistics for a short time, whereas others are part of them for many years? To answer questions such as these, a different type of data collection is needed. This type of information comes from *longitudinal data*—data collected from the same persons at many successive points in time, which can begin to answer some of these questions. We have only recently begun collecting longitudinal data, the best source currently being the Panel Study of Income Dynamics conducted by the Survey Research Center at the University of Michigan. The first topic in this section, the statistical description of poverty, relies mostly on snapshot data collected by the Census Bureau. The next section, types of poverty, relies more on longitudinal data, mainly from the Panel Study of Income Dynamics.

STATISTICAL DESCRIPTION OF THE POVERTY POPULATION

The Bureau of the Census maintains an Internet web site and periodically publishes a book that presents nearly one hundred pages of statistics on the poverty population.[1] A few of the most interesting of these statistics for 2008 are summarized in Table 1. As can be seen, almost 40 million Americans,

 Characteristics of the Population below the Poverty Line, 2008

Group	Number below Poverty Line (in Thousands)	Rate (% below Poverty Line)
All Persons	39,829	13.2
Race		
Non-Hispanic white	17,024	8.6
Black	9,379	24.7
Hispanic*	10,987	23.2
Asian	1,596	11.8
Age (years)		
Under 18	14,068	19.0
18–24	5,283	18.4
25–34	5,351	13.2
35–44	4,277	10.4
45–54	4,047	9.1
55–59	1,642	8.8
60–64	1,504	9.7
65+	3,656	9.7
Region		
Northeast	6,295	11.6
Midwest	8,120	12.4
South	15,862	14.3
West	9,552	13.5
Nativity		
Native	33,293	12.6
Foreign born	6,536	17.8
Naturalized citizen	1,577	10.2
Not a citizen	4,959	23.3
Family Type		
All Families	8,147	10.3
Married couple	3,261	5.5
Female head, no husband	4,163	28.7
Male head, no Wife	793	13.8
Single Individuals		
All	10,710	20.8
Male	4,759	18.1
Female	5,951	22.6

*Persons of Hispanic origin may be of any race.

Source: Carman DeNavas-Walt, Bernadette D. Proctor, and Jessica C. Smith, U.S. Census Bureau, Current Population Reports, P60-236, *Income, Poverty, and Health Insurance Coverage in the United States: 2008* (Washington, DC: U.S. Government Printing Office, 2009), various tables.

13.2 percent of the population, had incomes that were below the poverty level in 2008. The misery of poverty, however, was not evenly divided among the many groups of the population. The burden fell much more heavily on some than on others.

Race

The image of the poor in most people's minds is that of a minority group-member, generally African American. As can be seen from the data in Table 1, that image is both right and wrong. It is wrong in the sense that the largest number of the poor, nearly 44 percent, are non-Hispanic white. However, the image is correct in that a much greater proportion of minority group members fall below the poverty line. Fewer than one of every twelve non-Hispanic white people in this country is poor, compared with nearly one of four persons of African or Hispanic origin. Whites constitute the largest number of the poor only because such a great majority of the population is white.

Age

The popular image of a poor person is of an able-bodied young adult. The Census Bureau data show this image to be wrong. The largest single age group among the poor is, in fact, children who are too young to work and who thus cannot improve their own status (see Figure 1). As people move into the productive adult years, the percentage in poverty declines rapidly. The percentage increases once again as people move into the older segment of the population.

Region

The distribution of poverty across the country is fairly even. There is a little more poverty in the South and West and a little less in the Midwest and Northeast. However, these differences probably reflect the greater proportion of the population in the South and West who live in rural areas.

Nativity

With the high level of concern being placed on immigration policy, the Census Bureau has added the category of nativity to the income, poverty, and health insurance statistics. It is not surprising that a high proportion of noncitizens in the

Figure 1

Source: Copyright © 1987. Tribune Media Services. Reprinted with permission.

United States, 23.3 percent, fall below the poverty line. Because illegal residents tend to be below the government statistics radar screen, it is a pretty certain bet that the actual percentage is probably much higher than this. What is surprising, and somewhat encouraging, is that the poverty rate among naturalized citizens is more than 2 percentage points below the national rate. These statistics lend credence to the traditional American dream narrative, where immigrants enter the country (legally), are poor and struggling for several years, and after being acculturated, go on to bright and prosperous futures.

Family Type

As is discussed later in this chapter, researchers are finding a great deal of evidence that points to family type as the most important determinant of economic status. The basis for this line of thinking can be found in Table 1. Families that have both a husband and a wife have a poverty rate of only 5.5 percent. For families with a female head and no husband present, the rate is 28.7 percent, nearly six times that of married-couple families. Interestingly, single-person households appear to do rather poorly in economic life. The overall rate of poverty for single individuals is 20.8 percent; for single males, the rate is 18.9 percent, and for single females, it is 22.6 percent.

The Feminization of Poverty

You have probably noticed in all the data being reviewed that women appear to be doing poorly in relation to men. This is an accurate observation and one that has not gone unnoticed by researchers and policymakers in recent years. In fact, a term was coined in 1978 to describe this problem—*the feminization of poverty*[2]. This problem has become even more severe in recent years because of the rapid and steady increase in the number of families headed by women. The percentage of families headed by women increased from 10.1 percent in 1950 to 14 percent in 1976, an increase of almost 40 percent in only one generation. The number of households headed by women is currently 18.5 percent, and the number of families with children under 18 headed by women is 25 percent.[3] In our society, because the woman is generally the parent who provides the bulk of child care, this trend contributes to the great number of children living below the poverty line.

DIFFERENT TYPES OF POVERTY

Although the preceding data are useful for giving us a general description of the characteristics of the poor, these data are static. That is, they tell us what the population looks like at various points in time but say little, if anything, about differences other than demographic ones within the population. Sociologists have long known that the poverty population is not homogeneous, and recent studies, notably the Panel Study of Income Dynamics, have added greatly to our understanding of the many differences within the poverty population.

Three Levels of Poverty

In their classic study of poverty, Segalman and Basu posited the existence of three different segments in the poverty population: the transitional poor, the marginal poor, and the residual poor.[4] The transitional poor are those people whose experience of poverty is only temporary and is usually brief. Poverty for this group is generally the result of some life change or misfortune. Examples of situations likely to result in transitional poverty include a person returning to school to finish a degree and living on a bare-bones budget while doing it, a person unemployed because of a plant closing who is unable to find a new job and finally moves to a more economically prosperous area, a person who has an extended illness, and a widow for whom it takes a year or so to adjust to the new realities of her situation, including entering or reentering the job market. Segalman and Basu say that new immigrants generally go through a period of transitional poverty before learning the many things they need to know to compete in the job market. The key characteristics of transitional poverty are that it is brief, temporary, and generally related to specific events in the life of the person experiencing it.

The marginal poor are the group often referred to as the "working poor." They generally have jobs, but because of low educational levels and few skills, or because of discrimination, the jobs they have are low paying and insecure. These people are nearly always at the margin of the poverty line and, depending on luck and the economy, may be on one side or the other of that line. When the economic boom of the 1990s was at its peak, many of the marginal poor were earning near-middle-class incomes because of the great amount of work and overtime available. Now that the economy is in recession, many of these folks are falling back below the poverty line. The main difference between the transitional poor and the marginal poor is that the transitional poor are experiencing a brief episode of poverty, may never experience another, and may quickly rise well above the poverty line. For the marginal poor, rising out of poverty and sinking back into it constitute a long-term pattern, and it is doubtful for most that they will ever rise much above the poverty level.

For the marginal poor, rising out of poverty and sinking back into it constitutes a long-term pattern, and it is doubtful for most that they will ever rise much above the poverty level.

The residual poor are a group who remain in poverty over an extended period of time. They are generally dependent on welfare benefits for their daily living, and their poverty may well be intergenerational. This group has received a good deal of attention in recent years, and they have come to be referred to as "the underclass."[5] Most media discussion of the problem of poverty in the United States, or of the corollary welfare problem, generally refers to the residual poor. This is the group that is hard to reach and that often seems almost immune to help; this group is thus frustrating to a society that likes to find rapid solutions to problems.

Data on Different Types of Poverty and Poverty Patterns

The preceding discussion of different types of poverty is based on Census Bureau data, which are of somewhat limited usefulness because they consist of statistical "snapshots" taken at various points in time. The data do not answer questions related to the proportion of the poor that is residual, the experience of poverty across the life cycle, the extent to which families and individuals move out of or remain in poverty, and consequently, the factors that are related to escaping poverty. To make up for this deficiency, several longitudinal (meaning "over time") data sets have been developed. Called *panel studies* because they follow a panel of respondents for a number of years, these include the National Longitudinal Survey of Youth (NLSY), the Survey of Income and Program Participation (SIPP), and the most useful for our purposes, the Panel Study of Income Dynamics (PSID). The PSID was developed in 1968 by a group of social scientists at the Survey Research Center at the University of Michigan.[6] For this study, the researchers selected a random sample of more than five thousand families, and repeated annual interviews have been conducted with the families each year since 1968. There are now thirty-five years of data on these families. In this section we summarize some of the major findings of the longitudinal studies. In the following section we use these data to examine some of the major theories on causes of poverty.

The official poverty rate in the United States remains fairly steady at between 11 and 15 percent; the rate in 2008 was 13.2 percent. With regard to this rate, the PSID contains both bad news and good news. The bad news is that during the years analyzed by Rebecca Blank, 1979–91, the data indicate that a percentage of the population much larger than 11 to 15 percent was in a state of poverty for at least one year. Fully one-third of the population (33.6 percent) fell below the poverty line for at least one of the twelve years. Rank, Yoon, and Hirschl, in a more recent analysis, found an even more startling number—at age seventy-five, 58.8 percent of the population have experienced at least one year of poverty[7] (see Table 2). The group we have called the *residual poor*, or the *underclass*, is called the *persistently poor* by the PSID researchers and are defined here as being poor for ten of the twelve years covered by Blank's

| Table 2 | **The Cumulative Percent of Americans Experiencing Poverty across Adulthood** | | |

	Level of Poverty		
Age	Below 1.00 Poverty Line	Below 1.25 Poverty Line	Below 1.50 Poverty Line
20	10.6	15.0	19.1
25	21.6	27.8	34.3
30	27.1	34.1	41.3
35	31.4	39.0	46.9
40	35.6	43.6	51.7
45	38.8	46.7	55.0
50	41.8	49.6	57.9
55	45.0	52.8	61.0
60	48.2	56.1	64.2
65	51.4	59.7	67.5
70	55.0	63.6	71.8
75	58.5	68.0	76.0

Sources: Panel Study of Income Dynamics, authors' computations; Mark R. Rank, Hong-Sik Yoon, and Thomas A. Hirschl, "American Poverty as a Structural Failing: Evidence and Arguments," *Journal of Sociology and Social Welfare* 30 (December 2003): 3–29.

analysis. The good news is that only 4.9 percent of the population were found to be persistently poor. The group Segalman and Basu call the *marginal poor* is called the *intermittently poor* by the PSID researchers. This group of people is defined here as those who were poor four to nine of the twelve years analyzed, usually with no predictable pattern to the years. Blank found that 11.6 percent of the population fell into this category. A little over 17 percent of the population fell into the transitionally poor category, having incomes below the poverty line for one to three of the twelve-year period. Thus, to summarize, 4.9 percent of the population were found to be persistently poor, an additional 11.6 percent were intermittently poor, and an additional 17.1 percent were poor for only one to three years. These data are summarized in Figure 2.

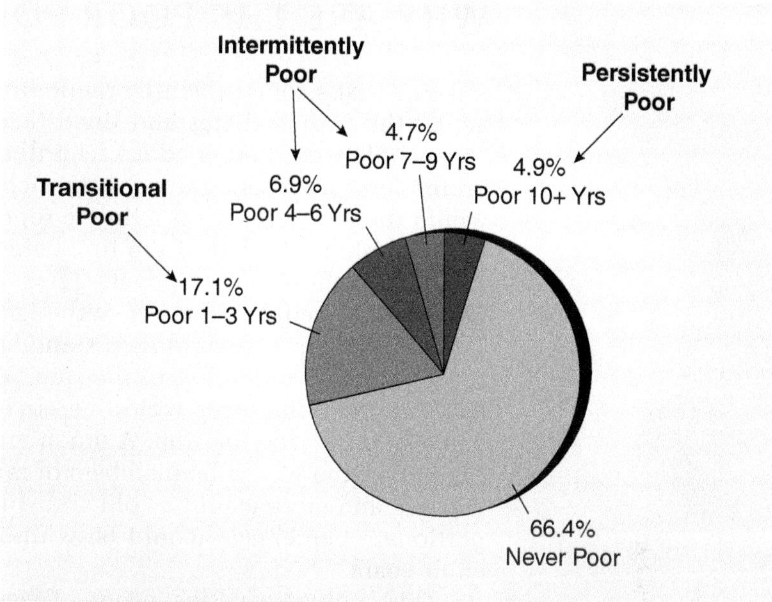

Figure 2

Extent of Poverty among Americans, 1979–1991.

Source: Rebecca M. Blank, *It Takes a Nation: A New Agenda for Fighting Poverty.* © 1997 Russell Sage Foundation, published by Princeton University Press. Reprinted by permission of Princeton University Press. Author's tabulations from the Panel Study of Income Dynamics.

Longitudinal data tend to show the same demographic differences as snapshot data, but they show the differences to be even more pronounced. Rank and Hirschl analyzed the PSID data to attempt to understand poverty across the life cycle. They divided the data into three age cohorts: twenty to forty (early adulthood), forty to sixty (middle adulthood), and sixty to eighty (later adulthood). Among their findings were that during early adulthood, 36.7 percent of the sample experienced at least one year in poverty, and 3.7 percent were in poverty for five or more years; during middle adulthood, 22.7 percent experienced at least one year in poverty, and 2.1 percent were poor for more than five years; during later adulthood, the figures were 28.8 percent experiencing one year in poverty and 2.2 percent falling below the poverty line for five or more years. This confirms the snapshot data that poverty is a greater problem for the young and the old than for those in the middle years. Rank and Hirschl conclude:

> Several patterns are apparent across all three panels. First, race, education, and gender exert an influence upon the odds of experiencing poverty during each of the three stages of adulthood. Specifically, being black, having less than 12 years of education, and being female all increase the chances of encountering at least one year of poverty during adulthood. Overall, race tends to exert the largest effect, followed by education, and then by gender. In combination, these characteristics dramatically alter the risk of poverty. For example, while 26.4 percent of white males with 12 or more years education will experience poverty between the ages of 20 and 40, 79.2 percent of black females with less than 12 years of education will be touched by poverty during the same span.[8]

First, race, education, and gender exert an influence upon the odds of experiencing poverty during each of the three stages of adulthood.

Blank's analysis of the PSID data yielded similar results.

WHY ARE THE POOR POOR?

Imagine that a social scientist randomly sampled one thousand people from across the United States and lined them all up along a long, straight road. The people would be lined up according to income, with the poorest people on the left, progressing toward the richest on the right. The social scientist would then actually paint a line to represent where the poverty level began, with people to the left of the line being those in poverty and people to the right being those out of poverty. Assuming that the poverty rate was 12.6 percent, 126 people would be to the left of the line and 874 to the right of it. The social scientist would then stand back and ask, "What is different about the 126 people to the left of the line? Why are *they* there and not the other 874?" Some differences would be obvious to the social scientist or to anyone else observing the line. A much greater percentage of the people to the left of the line would be members of minority groups, many more would be women, and more would be old and young. To the right of the line, a disproportionate percentage would be white, male, and in the early and middle adult years.

This simple visual inspection of the people would give us a hint as to the causes of poverty—they have something to do with race, sex, and age—but it would not give us a complete answer because of two broad questions. The first question has to do with what statisticians call *between-group variance.* We can see that more members of the female group than of the male group are poor. However, we do not know the source of this variance. Are more women poor because there is something in our society that systematically discriminates against them and bars them from an equal chance at well-paying jobs? This is known as a *structural explanation*; in other words, the source of the problem is in the social structure. Or are more women poor because there are genetic or cultural factors that make women less competitive in the job market, factors such as desire to stay home and have children or fear of competition? This is known as an *individual explanation.*

The second broad question has to do with what statisticians call *within-group variance.* This question addresses the fact that although a disproportionate number of women and African Americans are in poverty, not all are, and although most whites are not in poverty, some are. What are the differences among the members within these groups?

The question of the causes of poverty is complex and controversial, and answers are incomplete. And yet the question is extremely important. Proposed solutions to poverty based on different explanations often will be diametrically opposed. If you propose a program based on a structural explanation, the focus of the program will be on changing society. If you propose a program based on individual explanations, the focus will be on changing individuals. If we implement an antipoverty program that seeks to change individuals, and the causes of poverty are more structural, we have wasted our time and money. Conversely, if we implement an antipoverty strategy that seeks to change the social structure, and the causes of poverty are within the individual, we have also wasted our time and money. In this section we take a close look at three different broad explanations of poverty. The first explanation views poverty as being the result of individual characteristics. The second views poverty as the result of poor people holding values fundamentally different from those of the rest of society, values that prevent them from escaping poverty and make it likely that their children will follow them into lives of poverty—an explanation known as the *culture*

The question of the causes of poverty is complex and controversial, and answers are incomplete.

of poverty thesis. The third explanation sees the poor as victims of society and attributes their poverty to impersonal economic forces or to discrimination and oppression, which are mainly institutional; these are the structural explanations referred to earlier.

Poverty as the Result of Individual Characteristics

In previous chapters we discussed the belief among people in the United States, especially among conservatives, in individualism. The aspect of this belief most important for an understanding of social welfare is that it tends to attribute the cause of problems to the individuals affected by the problems. Thus it is natural in our society to assume that the primary cause of poverty is to be found in some defect in the individuals affected. Holman notes that "the analyses do not necessarily allocate blame to individuals who are poor, but they do regard poverty as stemming from the limitations, maladjustments or deficiencies of individuals."[9]

Individualistic explanations of poverty can be divided into three main types, which have emerged in rough chronological order. The explanation with the longest history is that people are poor because of inferior genetic quality, especially, but not limited to, intellectual ability. In earlier editions of this book we stated that this explanation had been largely discredited but was still expounded occasionally. In 1994, the genetic inferiority explanation reappeared with a bang in the best-selling book *The Bell Curve*, by psychologist Richard Herrnstein and political scientist Charles Murray. Another popular explanation of poverty as being due to individual characteristics is one that argues that the poor are not necessarily genetically inferior but that they suffer from psychological problems that inhibit their ability to compete for good jobs. This view continues to have some influence; in its most recent form it is known as the *expectancy model.* Finally, the current influential theory of those who insist on individual explanations of poverty is known as *human capital theory.* This is the notion that poor people do not have the knowledge, skills, and attributes (human capital) that make them valuable to employers. These three individualistic explanations are discussed in detail next.

Genetic Inferiority

People in the United States at one time attributed poverty almost entirely to genetics. Behavior often was described as being "in the blood." The Irish immigrants were poor because they drank heavily and had bad tempers; the Italians were hot-blooded Mediterraneans; African Americans were fun-loving and childlike. All were suspected of having low intelligence. As various groups have entered the mainstream of American life and competed successfully for jobs and income, these theories of innate genetic inferiority generally have been dropped. They have been replaced by a much more sophisticated theory based on the science of psychological measurement, specifically the development of the IQ test. This theory argues that intelligence is inherited (that is, it is genetically determined) and that economic success is closely related to intelligence.

The originator of the IQ test and of the idea that intelligence was a measurable quality was French psychologist Alfred Binet. Binet developed a test in the early 1900s for the use of Paris public school administrators who desired a way to identify children in need of special education. Binet's test served this purpose, and he was quite specific about its limitations. He insisted that the test should be used only to identify children in need of special help and should

Critical Thinking Question

The chapter cites a number of complex and controversial rationales for poverty in the United States What do you think are the causes of poverty? Why?

not be used to classify normal children. Binet strongly asserted that the test did not measure anything innate or permanent, writing in 1909 that

> some recent philosophers appear to have given their moral support to the deplorable verdict that the intelligence of an individual is a fixed quantity. We must protest and act against this brutal pessimism. A child's mind is like a field, for which an expert farmer has advised a change in the method of cultivation, with the result that, in place of desert land, we now have a harvest.[10]

Binet's ideas of testing intelligence were quickly snapped up by H. H. Goddard and Lewis M. Terman in the United States and by Sir Cyril Burt in England. These psychologists chose to ignore Binet's statements about the limitations of intelligence tests; in fact, they advanced quite the opposite idea. They insisted that intelligence was heritable (passed down from generation to generation) and immutable (unable to be changed). Therefore, a person who is born to parents with low intelligence is doomed to a life of failure and probably misery. The result of the work of these men and a number of similar thinkers was what has come to be called the *eugenics movement*. This movement was based on the idea that not only is intelligence genetic but also that those with low intelligence (at that time called the *feeble-minded*) reproduce at rates far greater than the more intelligent segments of the population. Thus the human race was seen as being in danger of becoming overrun by people of low intelligence.[11]

Although eugenics fell into disrepute following World War II, the notion that intelligence is hereditary and that poverty can be explained largely by inherited low intelligence has persisted. The most influential modern advocate of the notion that intelligence is an innate quality and is inherited is the Berkeley psychologist Arthur Jensen.[12] Jensen argues that modern genetic research has firmly established that about 49 percent of the variance in IQ scores can be explained by heritability. After reviewing the work of seventeen geneticists and behavioral geneticists, Jensen concludes, "With such general agreement among scientists, it is all the more amazing how the popular media have so often promoted the notion that the genetic inheritance of intelligence is a highly controversial issue."[13]

The most influential modern exponents of the idea that socioeconomic class, and by extension, poverty, is related to inherited intelligence are Charles Murray and the late Richard Herrnstein. Although Herrnstein reported his ideas in many publications in the past, they became popularized through *The Bell Curve,* coauthored with Murray, a well-known conservative critic of social programs.[14] In this book, Herrnstein and Murray argue that

1. Differences in mental ability are largely inherited.
2. Success requires high mental ability.
3. Earnings and prestige depend on success.
4. Thus social standing (which reflects earnings and prestige) will be based to a large degree on inherited differences among people.

Herrnstein and Murray argue that the differences in intellectual ability between social classes are becoming greater as barriers to the upward mobility of gifted people are removed, thus removing them from the gene pool of the lower classes. The trend for an increasing proportion of people to marry within their social class has been confirmed by recent research. Schwartz and Mare found that the odds of a high school graduate marrying someone with a college degree declined by 43 percent between 1940 and the late 1970s. Sweeney and Cancian found an increasingly strong association between women's wages before marriage and the occupational status and future earnings prospects of the men they married.[15] Based on his belief in the heritability of intelligence, Herrnstein concludes, "The biological stratification of society looms."[16]

The idea that intelligence is an inherited trait and that success is the result of high intelligence and lack of success the result of low intelligence has been the subject of severe, and often emotional, criticism. The arguments are technical and complex, and we do not have room to go into them in detail. However, basically the critics of Jensen, and of Herrnstein and Murray, argue that we do not really know what intelligence is and that whatever it is, it is doubtful that intelligence tests measure it. Critics argue that the tests are culturally biased. That is, items selected for the tests are based on what is familiar to white and middle-class people, so minorities and lower-class people are less likely to be familiar with them.

Fischer and his colleagues, in a lengthy and reasoned refutation of Herrnstein and Murray, argue that "scholars long ago established that scores on IQ and IQ-like tests were only of modest importance compared with social context in explaining individual attainment." They demonstrate that the test Herrnstein and Murray used as an indication of intelligence, the Armed Forces Qualification Test, is really a measure of education, not of native intelligence. Of the major argument of Herrnstein and Murray, Fischer and colleagues assert

> At its base it is a philosophy ages old: human misery is natural and beyond human redemption; inequality is fated; and people deserve, by virtue of their native talents, the positions they have in society. ... The political implications [are] clear: If inequality is natural, then governmental intervention to moderate it is at best wrongheaded and at worst destructive.[17]

Poverty as a Result of Psychological Problems

The idea that a large proportion of the poor are that way because they are suffering from some psychological problem gained popularity throughout the 1950s, peaked and even gained legislative support during the 1960s, and then rapidly lost influence. Especially popular was the idea that the poor live in "multiproblem families" that have an almost insatiable appetite for social services. Buell, for example, in a study of social services in St. Paul, Minnesota, found that 6 percent of families receiving services consumed more than half the total services provided.[18] The basic idea of this theory is that poor people do not have their developmental needs met as children; as a result, they are immature, and consequently, they are unable to meet the needs of their own children—who then grow up immature, and the cycle goes on and on. Curran has studied the social work profession's contribution to this theory of poverty, saying

> In line with the profession's psychiatric outlook, many postwar social work scholars claimed that psychopathology plagued ADC recipients. A 1954 *Social Service Review* article expressed popular social work sentiment in describing ADC recipients as frequently "ill in body and mind." Social work research suggested that a significant portion of ADC clients had mental health problems. For instance, Kermit Wiltse, a leading proponent of the psychological model and a faculty member of the

University of California's School of Social Work, "found a kind of pseudo or subclinical depression in many of our [ADC] clients, particularly in the early phase of contact." The widely circulated 1960 study of the ADC program in Cook County, Illinois, *Facts, Fallacies, and Future,* also found that approximately one-third of the families suffered from a diagnosed or suspected mental disorder. Psychiatric disorders topped the list of psychosocial issues faced by "multi-problem" families, the term postwar social workers coined to describe long-term ADC users. One author working with multi-problem families noted, "The psychiatric diagnosis of the parent or parents have [sic] ranged from psychosis to borderline character disorders."[19]

The theory that poverty is largely caused by psychological problems among the poor hit its high point in 1962, when it was incorporated into the amendments to the Social Security Act popularly known as the "social service amendments." These amendments were based on the idea that the poor "needed not just, or even primarily, financial aid but rather psychological assistance and other forms of counseling; they had to 'adjust' to being single parents or to life in the city; they needed instruction on how to keep house and manage their meager resources in order to make ends meet; they needed to learn how to make friendships and develop self-esteem."[20] The amendments provided a large sum of money to enable states to hire social workers trained in psychological techniques to help people solve psychological problems that were preventing them from being self-supporting.

The social service amendments proved to be the undoing of the theory that psychological maladjustment was a major dynamic in poverty. Social workers went out armed with new therapeutic skills and quickly discovered that these had little relevance for dealing with the harsh realities of impoverished families. Congress also quickly lost its enthusiasm for this approach when the welfare rolls did not go down. In fact, just the opposite happened; following passage of the social service amendments, the welfare caseloads skyrocketed.

The fact that social workers for a time embraced an individual, psychological explanation of poverty generally has been attributed to the professions' desire to achieve status in the years following World War II as a psychotherapeutic profession. Curran offers another explanation, one more in keeping with the social change and advocacy tradition of the profession. She says

> Faced with a popular and legislative backlash against Aid to Dependent Children (ADC), the public assistance program for single mothers and their children, postwar social work researchers, educators, and clinical theorists increasingly turned to fashionable psychological and psychoanalytic paradigms to explain and justify welfare use. The profession's portrayal of welfare recipients as victims of psychologically abusive pasts stood in contrast to a hostile popular and legislative discourse that cast ADC recipients as unscrupulous chiselers and immoral cheats.[21]

The idea that psychopathology provides at least part of the explanation for long-term poverty has resurfaced recently in conservative thinking on the subject. Lawrence Mead recognizes that this explanation was discredited previously because of a lack of empirical verification—that is, that research failed to find more psychological problems among the poor than among the nonpoor. However, he argues that there is evidence that the poor have become significantly more dysfunctional since the mid-1970s:

Critical Thinking Question

What contributions has the profession of social work made toward the explanation of poverty?

Signs include the drug epidemic, the explosion of foster care in major cities, and the growth in the homeless population, two-thirds of which has been in prison or institutionalized for mental illness or substance abuse. Significant portions of the long-term poor may suffer from depression, posttraumatic stress disorder, or antisocial personality. Such impairments may be immediate causes of poverty, even if the ultimate causes lie in society.[22]

A newer version of the psychological explanation of poverty has emerged that does not assume pathology but rather explains the problem of poverty in social psychological terms. This theory is called the *expectancy model.* This model is based on the theory that there is a relationship between confidence, sense of control, and success. Those who are successful gain confidence, and this leads to a sense of control over their lives, which in turn results in more success. On the other hand, those who fail lose confidence and begin to feel out of control of their lives, and this leads to further failure. Poverty results when people lose a sense of control over their lives, when they begin to expect failure, and when they cease to believe that they can ever escape poverty. Ellwood observes that "people who are frustrated by their lack of control may be observed to exhibit two almost opposite kinds of responses: either an aggressive and potentially antagonistic response or a very passive and sedate one. People become overwhelmed by their situation and lose the capacity to seek out and use the opportunities available."[23]

The Human Capital Approach

This is an economist's approach to explaining the individual's contribution to his or her own poverty. *Human capital* is defined by Thurow as "an individual's productive skills, talents, and knowledge. It is *measured* in terms of the value (price multiplied by quantity) of goods and services produced."[24] In other words, the human capital approach looks at how much an individual's labor is worth. People who have a large amount of skill obtained by experience, education, and training are going to be worth more on the labor market than those who have not invested in these things. Some aspects of the value of human capital are, of course, natural abilities that cannot be acquired. Most aspects, however, are acquired or enhanced by human actions.

The human capital approach views poverty as the result of individuals having low amounts of human capital. Thurow notes

> Efforts to eliminate poverty and the income gap between white and black have focused attention on the factors that produce individual incomes of human capital. . . . If individuals are paid according to their productivity, then individual skills, talents, and knowledge determine earnings. A wide dispersion in the distribution of human capital creates a wide dispersion in the distribution of earnings. Many factors, such as discrimination, play a role in determining the shape of the income distribution, but the distribution of productive investments is certainly one determinant.[25]

Recently, the human capital approach has been expanded to include the concept of social capital. *Social capital* has been defined by Putnam as "the connections among individuals—social networks and the norms of reciprocity and trustworthiness that arise from them." In other words, social capital is the network of friends and colleagues that a person has that provides support for the person, as well as providing ties that act as social bridges that help the person get ahead.[26]

The human capital approach is a straightforward approach to poverty. It says, in essence, that people are poor because they lack the knowledge and skills necessary to get good jobs that will provide above-poverty-level incomes. There is no doubt that this lack is one factor in poverty. However, the human capital approach does not account for several other factors, including discrimination. Traditionally female jobs requiring a college degree (in other words, a large amount of human capital), such as elementary school teaching, often will pay much less than jobs traditionally held by men and requiring much less human capital—for example, the job of electrician. Be that as it may, for our purposes, the human capital approach merely substitutes one definition of poverty for another. Thurow says, "One of the advantages of thinking in terms of human capital is that it immediately focuses attention on the production problem. What factors create human capital? What is the most efficient method of combining these factors?"[27] The human capital approach merely substitutes the question, "Why do some people possess low amounts of human capital?" for the question, "Why are some people poor?" And this takes us back to the question with which we began this chapter.

Cultural Explanations of Poverty

The preceding individual explanations of poverty tend to appeal to conservatives because of the conservative focus on the individual's responsibility for his or her own situation. Structural explanations, which are discussed in the next section, locate major responsibility for personal problems within the social structure in which the individual finds himself or herself. Liberals and radicals tend to favor these explanations because of their belief in the strength of the environment in shaping individuals' lives. Between these two types of explanations are the cultural explanations. These have been and continue to be influential because they mix individual and structural factors in such a way that both conservatives and liberals feel comfortable subscribing to them.

Cultural explanations, like individualistic explanations, locate the proximate cause of poverty as being individual characteristics. Individuals who are poor are seen as being in this situation because they are not motivated to succeed, they do not value work, they demand immediate gratification of their needs, and they do not value marriage or education. Unlike individualistic explanations, however, cultural explanations do not view these individual characteristics as being caused by any innate quality of the individual affected, such as low intelligence or some form of psychopathology. Instead, individuals are viewed as possessing these characteristics because of the social situations they were born into and in which they were reared and educated. Thus cultural explanations are more hopeful than individual explanations because these factors are more easily "corrected" than low intelligence or psychological disorders. There are two slightly different versions of cultural explanations: the culture of poverty theory and the cultural deprivation theory.

Culture of Poverty

The concept of a *culture of poverty* was first suggested by anthropologist Oscar Lewis in his 1959 book *Five Families: Mexican Case Studies in the Culture of Poverty*[28]. The concept won almost immediate acceptance by social scientists, journalists, and policymakers who were struggling with ways to deal with poverty in the 1960s. Michael Harrington made extensive use of the concept in his 1962 book *The Other America,* Frank Riessman related the concept to education in his 1962 book *The Culturally Deprived Child,* and Daniel Patrick Moynihan used the concept in his controversial but influential Department of Labor report *The Negro Family*[29]. The massive antipoverty programs of the Kennedy administration and Lyndon Johnson's War on Poverty programs were greatly influenced by the culture of poverty idea.

Lewis set out to apply basic ideas of anthropology to the study of poverty. He looked at poverty as a "subculture with its own structure and rationale, as a way of life which is passed down from generation to generation along family lines." He proposed that poverty was not only something negative—want and deprivation—but that it also included positive aspects, some rewards without which the poor could not carry on. The culture of poverty develops, according to Lewis, as a reaction by the poor to their marginal position in society; and it "represents an effort to cope with feelings of hopelessness and despair which develop from the realization of the improbability of achieving success."[30]

The culture of poverty, according to this theory, consists of a set of values, behavior patterns, and beliefs among the poor that are different from those of the larger society. Lewis identified seventy separate elements of the culture of poverty, which he lumped into four groups. The first group includes characteristics related to the fact that the poor are not effectively integrated into the major institutions of the larger society. For example, they do not participate in unions, political parties, or voluntary groups. In fact, they show a fundamental distrust of many of the basic institutions of society—the police, government offices, and even the church. They are poorly integrated into the job market, and this is a main reason that they control very little wealth. Banfield, a popularizer of the culture of poverty theory whose version is much more conservative than that of its originator, comments that the poor person "feels no attachment to community, neighbors, or friends, . . . resents all authority (for example, that of policemen, social workers, teachers, landlords, employers), and is apt to think that he has been 'railroaded' and to want to 'get even.'"[31]

The second group of elements of the culture of poverty is related to the communities in which poor people live. In these communities, there is little organization beyond the level of the extended family. Occasionally, temporary groupings and voluntary organizations emerge, and sometimes even a sense of community, but this does not last long.

The third group of elements of the culture of poverty related to the family. According to Lewis, major traits of family life are

> absence of childhood as a specially prolonged and protected stage in the life cycle, early initiation into sex, free unions or consensual marriages, a relatively high incidence of the abandonment of wives and children, a trend toward female- or mother-centered families and consequently a much greater knowledge of maternal relatives, a strong predisposition to authoritarianism, lack of privacy, verbal emphasis upon family solidarity which is only rarely achieved because of sibling rivalry, and competition for limited goods and maternal affection.[32]

Banfield asserts that the child-rearing style of the mother is impulsive, and once children have passed infancy, they are likely to be neglected or abused.[33]

Finally, there are those elements related to the individual. People in the culture of poverty supposedly have strong feelings of marginality; that is, they do not feel they really belong to anything in society. They are also characterized as having strong feelings of helplessness, dependence, and inferiority. There is a high incidence of maternal deprivation, weak ego structure, and confused sexual identity. Poor people are viewed as having poor impulse control, a strong present-time orientation with little ability to defer gratification and to plan for the future, and a corresponding sense of resignation and fatalism. Banfield says, "At the present-oriented end of the scale, the lower-class individual lives from moment to moment. If he has any awareness of a future, it is of something fixed, fated, beyond his control: things happen to him, he does not *make* them happen. . . . [W]hatever he cannot use immediately he considers valueless."[34]

Lewis argues that these elements represent characteristics of a culture or, more accurately, of a subculture. They are social, psychological, and economic traits that are passed on from one generation to another. They represent beliefs, attitudes, and values that are fundamentally different from those of the larger society. Lewis says

> People with a culture of poverty are aware of middle-class values, talk about them and even claim some of them as their own, but on the whole they do not live by them. Thus it is important to distinguish between what they say and what they do. For example, many will tell you that marriage by law, by the church, or by both, is the ideal form of marriage, but few will marry.

A key argument is that these cultural elements survive and are passed down from generation to generation because they are functional for people living within a poverty situation. Lewis continues the example on marriage: "To men who have no steady jobs or other sources of income . . . free unions and consensual marriage makes a lot of sense. Women will often turn down offers of marriage because they feel it ties them down to men who are immature, punishing and generally unreliable."[35]

According to culture of poverty theorists, these characteristics of the poor make it unlikely that they will be able to escape their poverty. To get out of poverty, one has to participate in social institutions, especially school; one has to form stable relationships, mainly two-parent families; and perhaps most important of all, one must be willing to defer gratification of immediate wants in order to gain greater rewards at a future date. For example, we all realize that going to college requires that a young person delay a large number of desires. It generally involves putting off buying a nice car, getting married, and traveling for at least four years. Going to college costs a lot in terms of deferred pleasures. However, most people realize that if they put these things off for four years, there is a higher likelihood that they will reap large rewards over the remainder of their lifetime. Culture of poverty theorists assert that poor people are unable to see this far ahead and so do not defer gratification in order to get an education, among other things; thus they hurt or destroy their chances to escape poverty.

Three additional points need to be made about the culture of poverty theory. The first is that this theory is not meant to apply to all poor people. The group being discussed is the group we identified earlier as the residual poor—the persistently poor. People in this group represent only a small

Critical Thinking Question

Do cultural explanations of poverty discriminate against certain races and ethnicities, or are the reasons given legitimate elements of poverty? What evidence is there to support your answer?

percentage of the poor, but they receive much attention because of the seemingly intractable nature of their poverty. The second point is that culture of poverty theory views the lives of the residual poor as containing a kind of an irony. That is, the beliefs, attitudes, and behavior patterns that help make life in poverty bearable are the same patterns that prevent people from escaping poverty. For example, for a teenage boy in the ghetto, belonging to a gang and selling drugs are going to provide much more pleasure and status among his peers than being on the honor roll and working afternoons at McDonald's for minimum wage. Yet going to school and working at a straight job are likely to be a route out of poverty, whereas belonging to a gang and selling drugs are probably going to eventually result in disaster. The third point is that because poverty constitutes a subculture, it involves more than money. According to this theory, even if members of the poverty culture were given enough money to meet all their needs, they would not change their lives. They would most likely "squander the money" to gratify immediate needs and wants, and they would end up just as miserable as before.

Cultural Deprivation

Whereas culture of poverty theory is based on research in anthropology and focuses on the concept of culture, cultural deprivation theory is based on research in education and focuses on the concept of socialization. Cultural deprivation theory does not assert that the poor have *different* values, beliefs, and knowledge from the nonpoor; it posits that they are deprived of

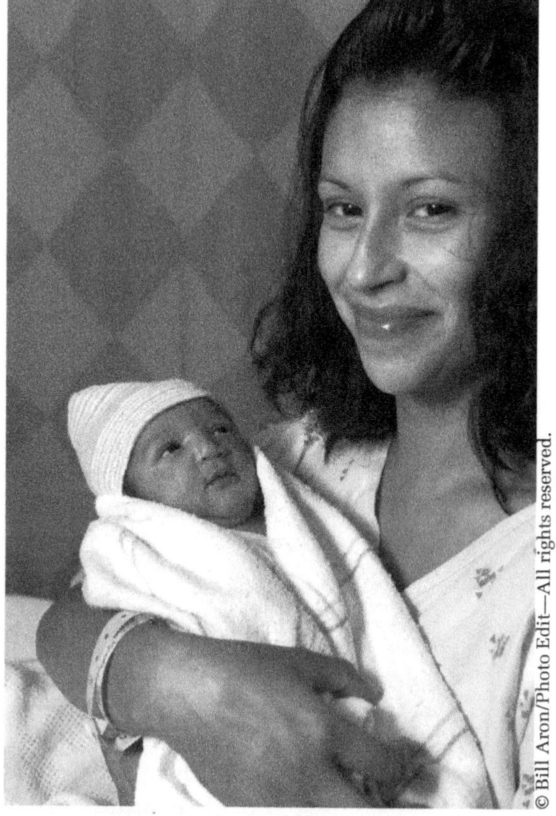

Culture of poverty theory asserts that people are poor and remain poor because they do not share major American values essential for success, such as deferral of gratification and marriage before parenthood.

the opportunity to develop the knowledge, beliefs, and values of the larger society. Cultural deprivation theory has focused mainly on low educational achievement among poor children, which in turn results in poor life chances. The theory argues that differences in educational achievement between poor and nonpoor children are explained by differences in home background. Ryan, a critic of this approach, summarizes it as follows: "Uneducated parents, crowded living quarters, absence of books, family disinterest in education—all combine to handicap the poor black child as he enters the school system. There is a specific denial of any innate inferiority; rather there is perceived a *functional* inferiority that is attributable to the depressing and stultifying effects of living in poverty, which is, of course, condemned as bad and unjust."[36] According to cultural deprivation theory, poor children do not *dis*value education; they simply have never been taught (or, more accurately, socialized) to value it. According to Holman, "If the child-rearing practices are deficient, then the children will not develop into adults who can fit into the prevailing culture with all its opportunities for education and advancement. (Again, a contrast can be made with the culture of poverty thesis in which the children are adequately socialized but into a culture which accepts poverty.)"[37]

Critique of Cultural Explanations

Cultural explanations of poverty are extremely popular for two major reasons. The first is that they appeal to both liberals and conservatives. The second reason is that to the average person on the street, as well as to academics and professionals, these theories just seem to make so much sense. When subjected to close scrutiny, however, cultural explanations do not make nearly as much sense. There are several criticisms of cultural theories, mainly directed at the more influential culture of poverty theory and its intellectual heir, underclass theory. The first criticism is directed at the research on which the theory is based, and the second stems from other research that has failed to support major aspects of the theory. The third, aimed at the recent popular interest in the underclass, asserts that cultural explanations of poverty are really a modern attempt to define a portion of the poor as "undeserving." In this section we briefly address these critiques, discuss a major and influential theory called *blaming the victim* that rejects cultural explanations, and look at alternative explanations of the characteristics of the poor that have been attributed to cultural differences.

Culture of Poverty Theory is Based on Methodologically Flawed Research

Although culture of poverty theory has been expounded by an enormous number of authors, few have conducted original research to test whether the theory is correct. Nearly all applications of the theory are based on the anthropological studies of Oscar Lewis, notably *Five Families: Mexican Case Studies in the Culture of Poverty, The Children of Sanchez,* and *La Vida: A Puerto Rican Family in the Culture of Poverty—San Juan and New York* The method Lewis used in writing these books is simple and straightforward. He begins with a description of the attributes of the culture of poverty, as discussed previously. He then records an immense quantity of biographic data about people whom he believes characterize the culture of poverty. According to one of his critics, Charles Valentine, "The principal purpose of this design is evidently to convey the impression that the biographical evidence supports and validates the theoretical abstraction which is labeled the 'culture of poverty.'" Valentine argues that Lewis's research does not validate the culture of poverty concept because of the following flaws:

- Lewis met with the subjects of his research in his office rather than in their own environment.
- Lewis employed a "directive" approach, guiding the respondents to material he wanted them to cover.
- Lewis edited the material and, according to Valentine, "often reorganized the material, selected some portions of the testimony, and eliminated others."

The most serious flaw, according to Valentine, is that the subjects selected may not have been representative of the group being studied. For example, in the Rios family, the subjects of *La Vida,* prostitution is very important in the lives of the women. This is not typical of poor Puerto Rican families and indicates that the family is an unreliable basis for generalization.[38]

Valentine concludes that "the scientific status of the 'culture of poverty' remains essentially a series of undemonstrated hypotheses. With respect to many or most of these hypotheses, alternative propositions are theoretically more convincing and are supported by more available evidence."[39] These alternative propositions are discussed later in this section.

Cultural Definitions Really Refer to the "Undeserving Poor"

The well-known sociologist and urban planner Herbert Gans points out that the original use of the term *underclass* was as a purely economic concept to describe people who were chronically unemployed or underemployed as a result of the emerging postindustrial economy. These people were poor for purely structural reasons. In recent years, however, there has been a gradual change in the use of the term. *Underclass* has come to refer more and more to people who are viewed as attitudinally and behaviorally deviant. Gans believes that it is not coincidental that those defined as members of the underclass are almost entirely African American and Latino. Thus, according to Gans, the term has become a code word for the old concept of the *undeserving poor* It has become the most recent in a long line of concepts that permit us to maintain harsh attitudes and hard hearts toward the poor by defining their poverty as their own fault. Gans says

> The *first* danger of the term is its unusual power as a buzzword. It is a handy euphemism; while it seems inoffensively technical on the surface, it hides within it all the moral opprobrium Americans have long felt toward those poor people who have been judged to be undeserving. Even when it is being used by journalists, scholars, and others as a technical term, it carries with it this judgmental baggage. ... A *second* and related danger of the term is its use as a racial codeword that subtly hides anti-black and anti-Hispanic feelings.[40]

Research Fails to Support Elements of Cultural Explanations

Criticisms of weakness in Lewis's research design are supported by the fact that studies looking at various characteristics of people who are supposedly members of the culture of poverty have almost uniformly failed to verify the existence of these characteristics. Culture of poverty theory asserts, for example, that one of the reasons poor people do badly in the job market is that they do not value work. Two studies by Goodwin, based on a sample of more than four thousand adults, found just the opposite to be true. These studies found that work was just as essential to the self-esteem of poor people as it was to the nonpoor.[41] Ethnographic studies by anthropologists have arrived at the same conclusion—the poor want to work, just like the middle class; that is, there is no cultural difference on this variable.[42] A 2001 study by Barnes found not only that members of the underclass want to work but also that the majority are in fact working. Their jobs, however, are often not counted in employment statistics because the poor often "earn money by performing informal jobs such as lawn care, home child care, selling products, and day labor."[43] A recent ethnographic study by Edin and Kefalas of 162 women with incomes below \$16,000 found a similarity in values and attitudes about marriage and parenthood between poor and middle-class women.[44]

A cornerstone of cultural theories, particularly cultural deprivation theory, is that the poor do not value education and so are not motivated to strive for an education. The research evidence also casts doubt on this proposition. A study by Sears, Maccoby, and Levin found that the poor were even more concerned that their children do well in school than were middle-class parents.[45] Similarly, Riessman found that lower-class parents regretted their own lack of education and were strongly motivated to see that their children did better.[46] Similarly, Barnes's data revealed education to be "very important to [underclass] respondents."[47]

In the years since the original cultural deprivation studies, research has been conducted that presents another explanation for poor school performance by poor children. Psychologists Betty Hart and Todd Risley compared the development of forty-two children for three years. They found a marked difference in vocabulary development between middle-class and poor children. By age three, the children whose parents were professionals had vocabularies of about 1,100 words, whereas the children whose parents were on welfare had vocabularies of only about 525 words. The children's IQs correlated closely with their vocabularies, with the average IQ among the middle class children being 117, and the welfare children's average being 79. Hart and Risley's explanation of this difference had nothing to do with values but rather with the verbal behavior of the parents. They found that in professional homes the parents directed an average of 487 "utterances" toward the child per hour, whereas in the welfare homes the number was only 178. In addition, they found that among the professional parents, the communications tended to be mainly positive, words of praise and approval, whereas in the poor homes, communications tended to be more commonly words of disapproval. Anthropologist Annette Lareau also has looked at the achievement gap between middle-class children and poor children and found that much of the difference can be explained by parental resources. Middle-class parents tend to schedule countless activities for their children—music lessons, clubs, soccer games, trips to the museum or the zoo—things that poor parents have neither the time nor the money to provide for their children. These "cultural differences translate into a distinct advantage for middle-class children in school, on standardized achievement tests, and later in life, in the workplace."[48]

We could go on and on discussing research that casts doubt on cultural explanations of poverty. However, there is still one problem: Even though research has demonstrated that the poor do not really hold values significantly different from those of the rest of the population—that is, they do not have a separate culture—there are still some differences in their lifeways that must be explained if cultural explanations are to be rejected. For example, it has been demonstrated that the poor are less likely to defer gratification than the middle class, poor kids are less likely to continue their educations, and poor women are more likely than nonpoor women to have children outside of marriage. How do we explain these things?

Alternative Explanation for the Lifeways of the Poor

At the risk of seeming repetitive, we need to emphasize that the main idea of the cultural explanations of poverty is that the lifeways, or behaviors, of the poor are caused by a set of *values* existing among poor people that are fundamentally different from those of the larger society. Poor people often have children out of wedlock because, supposedly, they do not value marriage; poor people do not work, the theory contends, because they do not value work and do not feel any stigma from being supported by welfare; poor children do not do well in school, it is argued, because they have not been taught to value education and its related components, such as paying attention and reading books. But there is a different explanation for these lifeways of poor people. That is, poor people have the same values as the rest of society (this has been supported by the research cited earlier), but they behave differently because within the limited range of choices available to them, those behaviors are the ones that make the most sense. Sociologists refer to this as the *situational adaptation interpretation,* and economists call it the *choice model.*[49]

Let's illustrate this interpretation with an example of two young couples: James and Vivian and Cindy and Dave. Each couple has had a relationship for about one year. Vivian and Cindy each become pregnant, and both are strongly opposed to abortion as a solution. Here the similarity ends.

James and Vivian have grown up in the ghetto, and they are the children of welfare mothers. Vivian finished the eleventh grade and then dropped out of high school. She has worked fairly steadily in a series of minimum-wage jobs, mainly in fast-food restaurants. James dropped out of school in his senior year when the high school graduation exam revealed that he could barely read or write, and school personnel said that he would be required to take remedial work before he could earn his diploma. Since leaving school, he has worked only sporadically, usually in temporary manual labor jobs.

In contrast, Cindy and Dave are both juniors at a large state university. They grew up in the suburbs, and they are the children of middle-class professional parents. Dave is majoring in engineering and is an officer candidate in army ROTC. Cindy is majoring in accounting.

On learning of their respective pregnancies, what do the two couples do? James and Vivian do not even consider marriage. Vivian applies for welfare and food stamps shortly after the baby is born; she has quit her job because she could not afford day care on the salary she was earning. James hangs around for a few months and contributes whatever money he can for the baby's support, but eventually he drifts away. Vivian basically reproduces her own childhood for her baby.

Dave and Cindy approach the situation differently. When they learn that Cindy is pregnant, they immediately decide to get married. They both take part-time jobs, and this income, combined with Dave's ROTC stipend plus some help from their families, provides enough income for them to survive until Dave graduates and is commissioned a second lieutenant in the army. Cindy takes a year off to be with the baby and then goes back to school, earns her degree, and begins a career with a large accounting firm.

How do we explain the different behaviors of these two couples? Cultural theorists would say that their behaviors reflect the fundamentally different values the two couples have learned in their respective social environments. James and Vivian come from environments that have taught them that single parenthood is acceptable, perhaps even preferable, to marriage. They do not really value work and achievement and so view welfare as an acceptable way to rear their child. Fathers are not considered to be important to the well-being of children, so no one is too concerned when James drifts away. Cindy and Dave hold different values. For them, it is of paramount importance that a child have parents who are married; the concepts of work and self-support are also extremely important to them.

The situational adaptation interpretation provides a different explanation. This perspective argues that the two couples probably have similar values but are existing in very different situations that make their choices different. Both couples value marriage and work, but these are realistic choices only for Cindy and Dave. James and Vivian realize that there is no bright future for them as a couple. There is no commission in the army followed by a good engineering job for James, and there is no period of full-time motherhood followed by a professional career with good day care for Vivian. Instead, what lies in their future is a series of low-paying jobs interspersed by long periods of unemployment. To make matters worse, by getting married, Vivian would lose eligibility for some types of aid. Thus both couples are making rational choices based on the opportunities available to them. The difference is that the opportunities available to Cindy and Dave are in line with traditional American values—marriage, job, and a two-parent family. For James and Vivian, violating these norms makes far more sense: As a single mother, at least Vivian will not be tied to an unemployed man, and James will not be constantly frustrated by obligations he has no way of fulfilling.

If poor people like James and Vivian hold basically the same values as the rest of society but are forced to violate these values in order to make rational decisions, how do they cope with the frustration that must result? Rodman argues that they do this through a process he calls the "lower class value stretch." This is a process through which poor people "come to tolerate and eventually evaluate favorably certain deviations from middle class values."[50] This process is closely related to what psychologists call *rationalization* or the "sweet lemon effect." For example, when Vivian and James do not get married, one might very well hear Vivian saying something like, "I don't want to be tied down to one man anyway. This way I can be a mother and still be able to party and have fun." When James can secure only manual labor jobs, he may say something like, "I'd really hate to be cooped up in an office all day and be forced to wear a tie. Only suckers do that. I want to be working outside with the real men. Sure, the boss can fire me anytime he likes because my job is only temporary, but the other side of that coin is that anytime I want I can tell him to take this job and shove it. I don't have to take grief from anyone!" The point Rodman emphasizes is that poor people share the same basic values as the rest of society but that because of their limited opportunity to make these values work for them, they "stretch" the values to fit the opportunities they do have.

With all the criticisms of the cultural theories, why do they continue to exert so much influence? These theories were first formulated and exerted tremendous influence in the 1950s and 1960s. They largely went out of vogue in the 1970s with the landslide of contradictory data. Like the mythological phoenix, they have risen from the ashes and once again have a grip on our collective imagination, this time under the new and catchy label "the underclass." The reemergence of cultural theories is in no way related to any new data, but this appears to bother only a few people. One of these is economist David Ellwood, who sees value in cultural theories but recognizes that they remain largely untested. Even Ellwood, a hard-nosed, empirically oriented (and incidentally liberal) economist, is willing to give some credence to cultural theories; he argues that the fact "that [cultural] theories are hard to test and interpret is not a legitimate basis for ignoring them in empirical work or policy discussion. The way welfare recipients are treated, the way they perceive the world, and the way the world interacts with them must have profound influences."[51] Why do cultural theories continue to exert so much influence in the face of so little solid empirical support? And why have people shown so little inclination to seek empirical support, instead relying on the assumption that these theories are valid? The answer, perhaps, lies in a tendency in U.S. society that psychologist William Ryan calls *blaming the victim*.[52]

Blaming the Victim

Because of our strong belief in individualism, we tend to place responsibility for problems, as well as credit for successes, squarely on the shoulders of the individual affected. This approach sometimes makes perfectly good sense, but we often carry it to ridiculous extremes. A woman is raped, and some people will ask, "Why was she wearing such suggestive clothes? Had she been drinking? What was she doing unescorted in a bar? Had she been flirting with her attacker?" The implication of these questions is that she somehow was responsible for the attack on her. This tendency is so deeply ingrained that we even do it to ourselves. When a person's car is stolen, you will often hear him or her saying things like, "I should have known better than to park it in that lot" or "I knew I should have ridden the bus to work; this neighborhood is no place to leave a car." The point is that the woman did not rape herself and the person did not steal his or her own car. These things were done to them, yet we still tend to place much of the blame on the person who was victimized.

Ryan asserts that because of our tendency to blame people for their own problems, we naturally look for reasons why the poor are responsible for their own poverty. The earliest explanations were that the poor were in some way morally or genetically inferior. However, these explanations always seemed harsh, at least to liberals, and they did not last long against the weight of experience with the poor. So, according to Ryan, we developed new theories that still placed the responsibility for poverty on the poor themselves but that seemed to be more scientific and more humanitarian. When trying to explain why poor children do not do as well as middle-class children in school, we ask, says Ryan,

> What is wrong with the victim? . . . The shorthand phrase is "cultural deprivation," which, to those in the know, conveys what they allege to be inside information: that the poor child carries a scanty pack of cultural baggage as he enters school. He doesn't know about books and magazines and newspapers. . . . They say that if he talks at all . . . he certainly doesn't talk correctly. . . . If you can get him to sit in a chair, they say, he squirms and looks out the window. . . . In a word he is "disadvantaged" and "socially deprived," they say, and this of course, accounts for *his* failure (his failure, they say) to learn much in school. . . . In pursuing this logic, no one remembers to ask questions about the collapsing buildings and torn textbooks, the frightened, insensitive teachers, the six additional desks in the room, the blustering frightened principals, the relentless segregation, the callous administrator, the irrelevant curriculum, the bigoted or cowardly members of the school board, the insulting history book, the stingy taxpayers, the fairy tale readers, or the self-serving faculty of the local teachers' college. We are encouraged to confine our attention to the child and to dwell on his alleged defects.[53]

Ryan argues that cultural explanations of poverty are so powerful and have lasted so long precisely because they allow us to continue to explain problems as being the fault of the individuals affected, but to do so under the cloak of liberal humanitarianism and concern. The old conservative notion of intrinsic or hereditary defect is replaced by an emphasis on environmental causation:

> The new ideology attributes defect and inadequacy to the malignant nature of poverty, injustice, slum life, and racial difficulties. . . . But the stigma, the defect, the fatal difference—though derived in the past from environmental forces—is still located *within* the victim, inside his skin. With such an elegant formulation, the humanitarian can have it both ways. He can, all at the same time, concentrate his charitable interest on the defects of the victim, condemn the vague social and environmental stresses that produced the defect (some time ago), and ignore the continuing effect of victimizing social forces (right now). It is a brilliant ideology for justifying a perverse form of social action designed to change, not society, as one might expect, but rather society's victim.[54]

Ryan's belief is, of course, that the individual is not responsible for his or her own poverty and that cultural explanations are just sophisticated attempts to cover up the real reasons for poverty. These reasons are not defects in the individual but defects in the structure of society. It is to this explanation of poverty that we now turn.

Structural Explanations of Poverty—Liberal Version

Structural explanations argue that poverty is not a result of individual or cultural factors that we can change by working with individuals on a one-to-one basis. Rather, poverty is viewed as the result of social factors that act on individuals, causing them to exhibit the characteristics that the other theories state are the result of individual or cultural shortcomings. To reduce poverty significantly, according to the structural perspective, the basic fabric of society will need to change. Obviously, this is a perspective that appeals to liberals and radicals and one that conservatives traditionally have opposed. In recent years, however, conservatives have developed their own structural theory, albeit one that is quite different from that espoused by liberals and radicals.

What are these structural factors purported to have so much influence over the life chances of people? One of the clearest explanations of these factors from the liberal perspective is presented by the sociologist Leonard Beeghley. Beeghley classifies structural factors that contribute to poverty into four main groups:

- The way in which the correlates of poverty create a vicious circle that often traps the poor and prevents them from changing their situation.
- The way the class system reproduces itself over time.
- The organization of the economy.
- The continuation of institutionalized discrimination against African Americans and women.[55]

Sociologists and psychologists have recently added structural explanations of poverty from the perspectives of their respective fields. Sociologist William Julius Wilson argues that poverty is a result of the increasing social isolation of inner city neighborhoods. Psychologist Bernice Lott argues that much of poverty is a result of classism, operationally defined as upper social classes distancing themselves from the poor.[56]

These six factors are discussed next.

Poverty as a Vicious Circle

Once people are caught in poverty, it becomes a trap from which it is very difficult to escape. There are many elements to this poverty trap. The first is the public assistance system, which, although it seeks to make people self-supporting, often perversely contributes to their inability to escape welfare and poverty. One aspect of the welfare system that traps people in poverty is the fact that people must be so destitute before they become eligible for assistance that they no longer have the resources to obtain employment. Before people can get welfare, they have often lost their home, furniture, and car, and their clothes are old and worn. Obviously, if you don't have a nice outfit to wear to a job interview, if you can't afford to take a trip to another town to look for work where the opportunities may be better, if you don't have a phone for prospective employers to call or an email address to which they can write, and if you do not have a dependable car to commute in, your chances of obtaining a good job and escaping poverty are slim.

Another element of the vicious circle is crime and the criminal justice system. Poor people are much more likely to be the victims of crime than are people in higher income brackets. They must spend much more time and energy defending themselves against crime than other citizens, time and energy that otherwise might be devoted to escaping poverty. One of the authors once worked in a community school in the inner-city area of St. Louis. The school provided educational programs to help people develop marketable job skills, but many people did not take advantage of the courses because they were at night and the people were afraid to walk in that neighborhood after dark. In a very real sense, these folks were trapped in their own homes by their poverty. The other side of this element is what happens to poor people when, as defendants, they come in contact with the criminal justice system. When higher-income people are arrested for a crime, they post bail and go about their lives more or less as usual. When tried, they are represented by competent lawyers who often can strike a bargain for them that allows them to stay out of jail. By contrast, poor people often will be unable to afford bail. Thus, when arrested, they will stay in jail, which means they will lose their jobs, be evicted from their homes or apartments, and lose anything they are making payments on. When a poor person goes on trial, he or she probably will not be able to afford the best lawyer, will have no influence with the judge, and probably will be given a prison term with all its predictable economic consequences.

The next element in the vicious circle of poverty is ill health and the health care system. By almost any measure available, the health of the poor is significantly worse than that of the population in general.[57] Poor health is both a cause and an effect of poverty. If a person has a health problem, particularly a chronic one, it is going to adversely affect that person's ability to make a living. Once a person is poor, his or her access to healthy living conditions becomes limited. Poor people cannot afford to eat the most healthy foods, they may live in conditions that are hot in the summer and cold in the winter, and their homes are more prone to infestations by disease-carrying pests such as rats. Illness also has a more immediate economic effect on the poor than on the general population. When poor people become ill for more than a few days, it is very likely that they will lose their jobs, and it is very unlikely that they will have insurance to cover either the cost of medical care or the lost income from missed work. The health care system in the United States, as we discuss in a later chapter, is designed primarily to serve the middle class, and it does not do a good job of serving the health care needs of the poor. Thus, once poor people become sick, they most likely will have a hard time obtaining efficient, high-quality medical care.

There is an old saying that it takes money to make money. A corollary of this saying, related to the vicious circle of poverty, is that it takes money to save money. It is a hard fact of economic life that the poor pay more. If poor people need to borrow money, they pay much higher interest rates than the nonpoor. Stores in ghetto areas charge higher prices than stores in the suburbs. You must have extra money to take full advantage of sales. For example, middle-income parents often refuse to buy disposable diapers at regular price. They wait until diapers go on sale, at discounts of as much as two or three dollars a box, and then they stock up on several weeks' or even months' worth of diapers. Poor parents who do not have the extra cash to take advantage of the sale end up paying more than the higher-income parents for the same diapers.

We could discuss numerous other elements of the vicious circle of poverty. The poor lack political power, so they rarely get their way when decisions are being made that could benefit them. Low-income people tend to get married earlier and have children earlier; they thereby increase the chance that their children will grow up poor and in turn marry early and have children early. The educational system tends to define poor children as low achievers, to put them into remedial classes, and thereby to increase the probability of this becoming a self-fulfilling prophecy. The main point is that the very condition of being in poverty decreases a person's chances of getting out of poverty. Over time, these conditions tend to wear a person down and cause many of the characteristics that Lewis identified as the culture of poverty.

Does the Class System Reproduce Itself?

Beeghley, among others, argues that one of the causes of poverty is that the class system tends to reproduce itself. He discusses the status attainment process in the United States and concludes, "The result is that the class structure reproduces itself over time and a stratum of impoverished persons is continually recreated."[58] What he means is that the children of wealthy parents, through various mechanisms such as inheritance and family connections, themselves grow into wealthy adults; children of middle-class parents become middle-class adults; and children of poor parents, as a result of the socially disadvantaged position into which they are born, are almost automatically doomed to lives of poverty. Does this actually happen? The answer is that no, the class system does not totally reproduce itself, but yes, the lowest and highest classes do.

Research on stratification and social mobility is one of the most highly developed areas in contemporary sociology.[59] This research seeks to understand how people obtain and change their positions in the social structure. We all like to believe that the United States is the land of opportunity, that our class structure is open, and that people often rise out of poverty into wealth, as in the famous Horatio Alger stories. And indeed, research results indicate that the class system in the United States is open for most people; that is, parents' status has relatively little effect on the status of their children.[60]

Recent research indicates that while the class system may be fluid for most of the population, it is not for lower-income Americans. Nam, using data from the PSID, compared two cohorts of fathers and sons (sons who were eleven to fifteen years old in 1969 compared with sons who were the same age in 1979). He analyzed the economic positions of the two groups of children when they reached adulthood, between twenty-five and twenty-seven years of age. His data indicated that high-income status increased between the two cohorts, but low-income status stayed the same—it had become easier for high-income sons to maintain their economically advantaged status over time, but low income sons' fortunes had not improved. Nam concludes that "These findings imply that America is not becoming more equal for its children, at least in terms of the intergenerational transmission of low-income status."[61] Thus, the American dream is alive and well for most people in the country; but for poor people, being born into poverty generally means living out life in poverty. For the poor, the class structure does indeed reproduce itself.

The Organization of the Economy

This element of the structural explanation of poverty asserts that the organization of the economy is such that some people are forced into poverty. There are two versions of this explanation, the radical version and the liberal version. The radical version is derived from the work of Marx and Engels and claims, basically, that the labor market of capitalist economies cannot provide sufficient employment at above-poverty-line wages to prevent poverty. Behind this problem is the assertion that capitalist economies are organized so that the owners of the means of production (the capitalists) get wealthy by exploiting the workers.[62] This perspective further asserts that the welfare system is designed to force people into starvation-level jobs when they are available but to provide enough support when jobs are not available to prevent workers from organizing and overthrowing the capitalist system.[63] The basic contention is that in capitalist economies, poor people are poor because this is a necessary condition for others to be rich. In other words, poverty is intentional; it is designed into the fabric of the economy.

The second version of the assertion that the organization of the economy forces people into poverty is the liberal version. This version claims that there are two labor markets operating in our society, the primary and the secondary labor markets, sometimes called the *core* and the *periphery* The primary, or core, labor market is the one in which most people in the United States work. Jobs in this labor market pay well; they include benefits such as health coverage, sick leave, a retirement plan, and paid vacation; and they are often fairly secure.

However, owing to the way the economy is organized, there are not enough jobs in the primary labor market for everyone. Economists discuss what they call the *natural level of unemployment,* which means that a certain percent of the labor force must be unemployed, or underemployed, so that businesses will have workers available when they need to expand. Rank reports that over the past forty years, the natural unemployment rate has run between 4 and 10 percent.[64] These people who cannot find jobs in the primary labor market are forced into the secondary labor market. The secondary, or peripheral, job market is made up of jobs that do not pay well; they generally include few benefits; and they offer little security. Jobs in the primary labor market are found in government and in industries dominated by large, capital-intensive, oligopolistic firms. Jobs in the secondary labor market are found in small, labor-intensive, highly

competitive firms. These are businesses that unions have not been able to organize because of their small size, that cannot pay well because they have to keep
costs down to remain competitive and do not offer benefits for the same reason,
and that do not offer job security because of the basic instability of their position in the market. The job skills and training (human capital) of workers in the
secondary labor market are not much different from those of workers in the primary labor market. It is often just a matter of luck and sometimes geographic
location that determine whether a person gets well-paid and secure employment
or spends life in a series of minimum-wage jobs at fast-food restaurants or discount stores.[65] Beeghley says, "Regardless of the skills people have, the nature
of the jobs available to them decisively influences the likelihood of their living
poorly."[66]

Racial, Sexual, and Age Discrimination

Prejudice and discrimination appear to be a major structural component of
poverty. As the data reviewed earlier clearly indicate, a disproportionate number of minorities, women, and the elderly are found among the ranks of the
poor. Beeghley identifies three mechanisms that he believes account for the
large proportion of minorities and women among the poor. First, recruitment
procedures used by employers work to the advantage of white males and to the
disadvantage of other groups. Second, divorce laws usually grant custody of
children to the mother but often do not grant enough child support to provide
for them, or if adequate child support is ordered, the courts do not strongly
enforce its payment. Third, child-rearing patterns tend to guide women into
lower-paying careers or to create the expectation that a woman should be
dependent on a husband, thus putting a woman in a bad position when her
marriage breaks down and she has to support herself.

The Increasing Social Isolation of the Ghetto

A recent structural explanation of poverty that is gaining a wide following is
the social isolation hypothesis of Harvard University sociologist William Julius
Wilson. This explanation is especially popular among liberals who are anxious
for an alternative to the extreme culture of poverty interpretation of conservatives such as Edward Banfield. Wilson argues that much of poverty in the
United States can be explained by the fact that poor people are geographically
and, consequently, socially isolated. That is, poor people are largely confined
to housing projects and inner-city ghettos where they are denied contact with
the wide variety of influences and opportunities the rest of society enjoys.

Wilson contends that the rapid increase in poverty, particularly among
inner-city blacks, and the growth of what is now referred to as the underclass
have been ironic by products of the success of the civil rights movement. The
ghetto, Wilson states, used to be characterized by vertical integration of different segments of the urban African-American population. Lower-, middle-, and
upper-class African Americans used to live in the same communities largely
because neighborhood segregation provided few options for the higher-income
groups. The presence of these economically better off segments of the population resulted in a high degree of social organization in the neighborhoods. By
social organization, Wilson means "(1) the prevalence, strength, and interdependence of social networks; (2) the extent of collective supervision that the
residents exercise and the degree of personal responsibility they assume in
addressing neighborhood problems; and (3) the rate of resident participation in
voluntary and formal organizations."[67]

Today, however, because of the success of the civil rights movement, middle- and upper-class African-American professionals have moved out of black inner-city neighbor-hoods, leaving many of these areas almost totally populated by the unemployed, welfare recipients, drug addicts and alcoholics, the mentally disabled, and other problem-ridden segments of the population. The results have been that these communities have lost their stability, crime and violence have increased, unemployment has increased, female-headed families have become the norm, welfare is the standard form of support, leadership has disappeared, children have few role models, and the inner city has become characterized by a tangle of pathology.

Social isolation means several things to the residents of inner-city neighborhoods. First, it means that these communities are characterized by a high concentration of poverty and its associated problems, which Wilson refers to as *concentration effects.* It also means that the residents lack contact or sustained interaction with individuals or institutions that represent mainstream society; Wilson refers to this as a *social buffer.* Because of this social buffer, the residents of these areas are unlikely to develop good work habits—if you don't know anyone who gets up each morning to go to work, it is unlikely that you will develop this habit yourself. Also, because businesses often leave inner-city areas along with the higher-income residents who were their best customers, very few jobs are left; the only ones available are generally undesirable and likely to alienate the people who do them. According to Wilson, "the combination of unattractive jobs and lack of community norms to reinforce work increases the likelihood that individuals will turn to either underground illegal activity or idleness or both."[68]

The results of social isolation look very much like the attributes of the poor that culture of poverty theorists attempt to explain—low work ethic, a high degree and favorable evaluation of welfare dependency, female-headed families, and inability to defer gratification. Wilson admits that these cultural traits exist, but he contends, in opposition to culture of poverty theorists, that they do not result from unique, ghetto-specific values. Culture of poverty theory "places strong emphasis on the autonomous character of the cultural traits once they come into existence. In other words, these traits assume a 'life of their own' and continue to influence behavior even if opportunities for social mobility improve." By contrast, "social isolation does not mean that cultural traits are irrelevant in understanding behavior in highly concentrated poverty areas; rather it highlights the fact that culture is a response to social structural constraints and opportunities."[69]

Wilson's social isolation hypothesis is similar to the situational adaptation thesis and the choice model discussed earlier. You will recall that these theories contend that the differences in behavior between poor and nonpoor people are not a result of different values but rather are caused by the different situations in which people find themselves. The value of marriage is functional for two people who have reasonable expectations of a secure future; it makes much less sense for people who know that life will be hard enough on their own and who expect that for a married couple it will only be harder. Wilson's hypothesis deals with the rapid rise of inner-city poverty in recent years and contends that the situation to which poor people have to adapt has gotten quite a lot worse for a large number of people because of social isolation, concentration effects, and social buffering.

A great deal of research has been done since Wilson first proposed the social isolation hypothesis in the mid-1980s. Chow, Johnson, and Austin reviewed the

What Americans Believe

In this chapter we review various theories and data about the causes of poverty that have been presented by policymakers, social scientists, and social theorists. It is the average citizen, however, who gives money to antipoverty agencies and who votes candidates into office based on the candidate's perceived beliefs and values. It is thus important for social workers, and other antipoverty activists, to have some idea of what the average citizen believes are the causes of poverty.

The General Social Survey from 1988 to 1991 included four questions (actually one question with four parts) related to beliefs about the causation of poverty. The question was, "Now I will present a list of reasons some people give to explain why there are poor people in this country. Please tell me whether you feel each of these is very important, somewhat important, or not important in explaining why there are poor people in this country." The list included two structural explanations, "Failure of society to provide good schools for many Americans" and "Failure of industry to provide enough jobs," and two individual explanations, "Loose morals and drunkenness" and "Lack of effort by the poor themselves." The responses to these questions are summarized in Table 3.

Most respondents identified all of these factors as important, although with individual explanations given the most credence. It is interesting that of the two individual explanations people could choose, the one that placed responsibility on lack of effort exceeded by far the loose morals explanation. Apparently the average citizen feels that poor people are not bad people, but they believe that America is indeed the land of opportunity, and so if people are not succeeding it must clearly be due to a lack of effort on their part.

We combined the responses to the two individual explanation factors (loose morals and drunkenness, and lack of effort by the poor themselves) and the two structural factors (failure of society to provide good schools, and failure of industry to provide enough jobs). We cross-tabulated these with the item asking for the political orientation of the respondent. The results of these cross tabulations are shown in Tables 4 and 5. The results of these calculations are not surprising and reinforce our discussions about political perspectives and opinions regarding social welfare issues. A significantly greater number of liberals subscribed to structural explanations than did those identifying themselves as conservatives. Conversely, a significantly greater number of conservatives supported individual explanations of poverty than did those identifying themselves as liberals.[70]

Table 3	Importance of Various Factors in Explaining Why Some People Are Poor			
	Failure of Society to Provide Good Schools	Failure of Industry to Provide Enough Jobs	Loose Morals and Drunkenness by the Poor Themselves	Lack of Effort by the Poor Themselves
Very important	36.6%	35.6%	39.5%	46.4%
Somewhat important	39.4%	42.9%	34.9%	45.0%
Not important	24.2%	21.4%	25.6%	8.6%

Table 4	How Important Are Structural Factors in Explaining Poverty? (Poor Schools and Not Enough Jobs)		
	Liberal	Moderate	Conservative
Very	45.2%	34.4%	26.0%
Somewhat	36.4%	43.0%	36.8%
Not important	18.5%	22.5%	37.2%

Table 5	**How Important Are Individual Factors in Explaining Poverty? (Loose Morals and Drunkenness; Lack of Effort by the Poor Themselves)**		
	Liberal	Moderate	Conservative
Very	34.4%	43.7%	47.6%
Somewhat	40.8%	40.5%	38.7%
Not important	24.6%	15.8%	13.7%

literature and report that since the mid-1990s, over a hundred studies of neighborhood effects are being published per year. They report that the main findings of this huge group of studies are

- Considerable social inequality exists among U.S. neighborhoods in terms of socioeconomic and racial segregation.
- Social problems tend to come bundled together at the neighborhood level in geographic "hot spots."
- Neighborhood predictors common to many social problems and child and adolescent outcomes tend to be related and include the concentration of poverty, racial isolation, single-parent families, low rate of home ownership, and short length of tenure of residents.
- Place matters, regardless of factors such as social class, race, and family status.
- The concentration of poverty appears to have increased significantly during recent decades in concert with the concentration of affluence at the opposite end of the income scale.
- Other social-ecologic factors besides disadvantage may play a role in well-being, including residential stability, home ownership, density, ethnic heterogeneity, and life cycle status.[71]

Wilson's social isolation hypothesis has great implications for social policy regarding inner-city poverty. Using this approach instead of the currently prevailing cultural explanations would mean shifting the focus of our policies and programs from attempting to change subcultural traits (by means of classes on family life for teenagers in poverty, counseling sessions aimed at developing an appreciation of the benefits of deferring gratification, and work habits classes) to attempting to change the structure of constraints and opportunities in which inner-city dwellers find themselves. In other words, the social isolation approach to inner-city poverty would involve changing social structures rather than changing individuals.

A Psychological Structural Explanation

As reviewed earlier, explanations of poverty advanced by the discipline of psychology have tended to focus on individual deficiencies. This has recently begun to change as psychologists have looked at external factors impacting individuals and contributing to their low economic status. This approach was furthered in 2000 by the American Psychological Association when they adopted the Resolution on Poverty and Economic Status that argued for the primacy of social environmental causes of poverty and ended with the promise of advocacy for research, education, and training, and public policy in the interest of low income people. An example of the new psychological structural explanation of poverty is the theory of social distancing advanced by social psychologist Bernice Lott. Lott argues that a major contributor to poverty is classism, operationalized by members of upper classes creating distance between themselves and their poorer fellow citizens. Based on a review of the research evidence, Lott categorized distancing into three types:

- Cognitive distancing. This refers to better off members of society holding negative stereotypes of characteristics and behaviors of the poor that explain poverty as a result of individual shortcomings and failure. Examples are beliefs that poor people are dishonest, lazy, dependent, not interested in education, and sexually promiscuous.
- Institutional distancing. This refers to social barriers that exclude the poor from full social participation. Examples include inferior schools for poor children; low quality and inaccessible health care for the poor; and longer prison sentences and a greater chance of capital punishment for the poor. Institutional distancing may be deliberate and obvious or it may be subtle and indirect, but the result is to reduce opportunities for the poor to improve their position in society.
- Interpersonal distancing. This refers to the face-to-face classist discrimination that poor people often encounter in their daily activities. Examples are a shopkeeper who closely follows a poor customer obviously suspicious that the person might try to steal something; a grocery store clerk who expresses disapproval over what she sees as extravagant purchases by a customer paying with a Supplemental Nutritional Assistance Program (food stamps) card; and a thrift store volunteer who refers to a customer as "girl."[72]

The new psychological structural explanation of poverty is not significant for discovering anything new. After reading this chapter you should recognize that these are all factors that social workers and sociologists have been discussing for years. What is significant about this perspective is that the psychological profession, a profession defined by its focus on individual behavior, is now recognizing structural factors as having a primary impact on the social and economic condition of individuals.

Critique of Liberal Structural Explanations

As you might imagine, structural explanations of poverty are not well received by conservatives. These explanations are diametrically opposed to nearly all the major components of the conservative belief system discussed in Chapter 1. Conservatives believe in individual responsibility; the structural perspective rejects this and says the social and economic environment is largely responsible for poverty. Conservatives believe in minimum government; the structural perspective logically leads to the conclusion that government intervention is necessary to correct the structural flaws that are causing poverty. Conservatives believe in the free market; the structural perspective argues that the market is not really free. Thus it is obvious that conservatives will be critical of this perspective.

Probably the most influential critique of the structural perspective is that presented in *Losing Ground* by Charles Murray. Murray argues that the huge growth of social programs that occurred during the 1960s was based on a structural explanation of poverty. He says that, according to the designers of the antipoverty programs, "Poverty was not a consequence of indolence or vice. It was not the just deserts of people who didn't try hard enough. It was produced by conditions that had nothing to do with individual virtue or effort. *Poverty was not the fault of the individual but of the system*"[73]. But Murray believes that poverty is indeed caused by all the individual failings structural explanations reject. He reviews what he believes to be the catastrophic failure of the social programs that have been implemented in the last quarter-century and lays the blame for this failure squarely at the feet of structural explanations of poverty. Murray argues that the result of structural explanations has been to remove responsibility for self-support from individuals and to make it more profitable to be on welfare than to work; this in general has made it "profitable for the poor to behave in the short term in ways that were destructive in the long term."[74]

Murray's critique of structural explanations of poverty can itself be criticized on several points. There have been responses that criticize Murray's use and interpretation of data, as well as the logic of his arguments.[75] Murray cites a great deal of research that he claims demonstrates that programs were failures, but he fails even to mention research that did not reach these conclusions.[76] The most serious shortcoming of Murray's argument, however, is that very few people have ever believed that the social programs developed during the 1960s were based on a structural explanation of poverty. Most, even Murray's fellow conservatives such as Butler and Kondratas, have interpreted the programs as being based on the culture of poverty theory. This theory, as reviewed previously, gives lip service to structural factors but still lays responsibility for poverty at the feet of the poor person. Thus, as a critique of structural explanations of poverty, Murray's argument is really of the straw man variety.

Structural Explanations of Poverty—Conservative Version

In recent years, a new conservative explanation of structurally caused poverty has emerged. This theory is referred to as *new structural poverty*. Basically this explanation contends that "overly generous" government welfare programs encourage able-bodied working-age persons to sink into a lifestyle of welfare dependency and consequently permanent poverty. Basically, according to this theory, poor people make a rational choice that a combination of welfare program benefits will produce higher income than they can get from employment earnings. Advocates of this perspective argue additionally that welfare payments to poor female-headed families undermine the traditional role of the male breadwinner, for whom the state unintentionally becomes a surrogate.[77]

To the chagrin of liberals, conservatives have some empirical data with which to back up this theory. From 1967 until 1977, the government financed a series of studies that looked at increased benefits and liberalized policies for public assistance recipients. The studies were the New Jersey Guaranteed Income Experiment, which began in 1967; the Rural (1968) and Gary (1969) Guaranteed Income Experiments; and finally, the largest, the Seattle–Denver Income Maintenance Experiments (Sime/Dime), which began in 1970. In these studies, more than five thousand families were randomly assigned to experimental and control groups. The experimental groups were placed on what is known as a "negative income tax," or "guaranteed annual income"; in addition, some received labor market counseling and training. The control groups received traditional welfare support. After various periods of time, the families were evaluated to see whether there were any differences in the amount of labor force participation (Were participants in the more generous guaranteed annual income program less motivated to work?), whether labor market counseling affected labor market participation, and what the effects of the experimental program were on marital stability. The study found that the program did have some (although there is debate as to just how much) negative effect on labor market participation. It also found that the more generous benefits and liberalized policies did not have the anticipated effect of reducing marital breakup among recipients. Conservatives point to these studies as evidence that more generous welfare programs will have a result just the opposite of that intended; that is, they will increase poverty and dependency rather than reduce it.

Critique of Conservative Explanations

Although liberals will admit that the guaranteed income experiments demonstrated that generous welfare programs provide some work disincentives, they consider these effects to be minor when compared with the poverty-reducing results of the increased benefits. They argue that generous welfare benefits help families maintain basic financial and health care standards they would not otherwise enjoy. These benefits, besides making the lives of the poor more tolerable, also function to prevent temporary hardships from escalating into such sustained and severe difficulties that the family is never able to recover.

Liberals argue that the conservative structural explanation of poverty is really an old idea that has been brought out and dusted off not in response to any new data but rather because the political atmosphere is once again receptive. When the Elizabethan Poor Law was passed in England in 1601, one of the major fears of its critics was that the law would result in "pauperization" of the poor. By this, the critics meant that once people learned they could survive without working, they would be forevermore rendered useless for socially beneficial work. Liberals argue that the new structural poverty theory is simply a restatement of this idea, and as Sanders notes, "the attraction of [conservative] arguments may derive more from the 'hands-off' governmental approach and the potential for lower taxes it implies."[78]

CONCLUSION

If you find the preceding discussion a little confusing, do not be surprised, because it is. Obviously, there is no consensus on what causes poverty, and so, as we discuss in the next chapter, there is no agreement on what to do about it. Your view of what causes poverty is heavily influenced by your political perspective. If you are conservative, you are likely to believe either in individual factors or in the individual components of cultural factors. If you are liberal, you most likely will believe in structural explanations and/or in the social components of the cultural explanations. If you are radical, you will concentrate on structural factors.

How do we make sense out of all this uncertainty? The first thing we need to do is to recognize the complexity of poverty. Anyone searching for a simple, single-variable explanation of poverty is going to be frustrated. To say poverty is a multivariate problem is to understate the situation. Each individual case of poverty involves hundreds of variables, including age, gender, race, health, geographic location, family background, friends, and luck—the list goes on and on. When you multiply these variables by millions of individuals, you see the complexity of the situation. There are some commonalities among individuals, however, and so it is possible to discover some generalizations, even though they are imperfect.

If you recall, at the beginning of this chapter we spoke of within-group variance and between-group variance. We think that it is probably safe to say that different types of explanations probably better explain the different types of variation. For example, if you take a sample of people who are carefully matched on as many characteristics as possible—they are all of the same race, gender, and social class background and from the same geographic location—and then compare the members of that group on the variable of economic status, it would be a good hypothesis that economic differences were caused largely by individual characteristics. Those who were more intelligent, energetic, focused, and motivated probably would be found to be doing better. However, the statistics reviewed earlier reveal that a large part of poverty falls into the between-group variance. Being a minority, old or young, female, a member of a single-parent family, rural, or an inner-city dweller all greatly increase the likelihood of being in poverty. It is very difficult to explain poverty related to these between-group variations using anything but a structural explanation.

Log onto **MySocialWorkLab** to access a wealth of case studies, videos, and assessment. (*If you did not receive an access code* to **MySocialWorkLab** *with this text and wish to purchase access online, please visit* www.mysocialworklab.com.)

1. **Read the case:** *Community Practice: Organizing Social Work in the Republic of Armenia,* Part II. A number of complex issues have impacted the poverty in Republic of Armenia. What do you think are some of the causes of poverty?

2. **Watch the Research Based Practice video:** *Social and Economic Justice: Understanding Forms of Oppression and Discrimination.* What theories of poverty could have possibly informed the social worker's approach with the recently homeless client?

PRACTICE TEST The following questions will test your knowledge of the content found within this chapter. For additional assessment, including licensing-exam type questions on applying chapter content to practice, visit **MySocialWorkLab**.

Policy Practice

1. Statistical descriptions of poverty rely mostly on:
   a. longitudinal data.
   b. snapshot data.
   c. census data.
   d. demographic data.

2. The transitional poor are those people whose experience of poverty is:
   a. extended and possibly intergenerational.
   b. a long-term pattern of rising out of poverty and sinking back into it.
   c. generally positive as a means to an end.
   d. brief, temporary, and related to specific life events.

3. The residual poor are those people whose experience of poverty is:
   a. extended and possibly intergenerational.
   b. a long-term pattern of rising out of poverty and sinking back into it.
   c. generally positive as a means to an end.
   d. brief, temporary, and related to specific life events.

4. According to Rank and Hirschl, which three factors influence the odds of experiencing poverty during each of the three stages of adulthood?
   a. Level of education, gender, and region of residence
   b. Race, level of education, and region of residence
   c. Race, level of education, and gender
   d. Race, gender, and region of residence

5. What best describes the *human capital theory* of how individual characteristics affect poverty?
   a. Inferior genetics leads to a lack of intelligence, among other issues.
   b. Poor people suffer from psychological problems that inhibit their ability to compete for good jobs.
   c. Poor people do not have the knowledge, skills, or attributes that make them valuable to employers.
   d. Poor people are reared and educated in social situations that obstruct their advancement.

Human Behavior

6. The *culture of poverty* views poverty as:
   a. the result of a person's psychological inability to resolve their personal problems within the social structure.
   b. a subculture with its own structure and rationale; a way of life passed down along family lines.
   c. a subculture of isolated individuals whose innate lack of employable skills prevents them from obtaining work.
   d. the result of the feminization of the underclass and working poor.

7. Cultural deprivation theory asserts that:
   a. the poor are deprived of the opportunity to develop the knowledge, beliefs, and values of the larger society.
   b. the poor exist in a subculture with its own structure and rationale.
   c. the poor have different values, beliefs, and knowledge than those of the larger society.
   d. the poor are innately inferior to the larger society, both genetically and psychologically.

8. Which is not a critique of cultural explanations for poverty?
   a. Culture of poverty theory is based on methodologically flawed research
   b. Cultural definitions really refer to the "undeserving poor"
   c. Other research in fails to support major aspects of culture theories
   d. Culture definitions remove responsibility for self-support from the individual

Log onto **MySocialWorkLab** once you have completed the Practice Test above to access additional study tools and assessment.

Answers:

Key: 1) b 2) d 3) a 4) c 5) c 6) c 7) b 8) d

NOTES

1. Carman DeNavas-Walt, Bernadette D. Proctor, and Jessica C. Smith, U.S. Bureau Census Bureau, Current Population Reports, P60-236, *Income, Poverty, and Health Insurance Coverage in the United States: 2008* (Washington, DC: U.S. Government Printing Office, 2009), www.census.gov.

2. Diana Pearce, "The Feminization of Poverty: Women, Work, and Welfare," *Urban and Social Change Review* 11 (February 1978): 28–36.

3. Pearce, "The Feminization of Poverty," 29; U.S. Bureau of the Census, *The 2010 Statistical Abstract of the United States*, Table 67 "Family Groups with Children Under 18 Years Old" (Washington, DC: U.S. Government Printing Office, 2001).

4. Ralph Segalman and Asoke Basu, *Poverty in America: The Welfare Dilemma* (Westport, CT: Greenwood Press, 1981), 10–12.

5. Gunnar Myrdal, *The Challenge of World Poverty* (New York: Vintage, 1970); Ken Auletta, *The Underclass* (New York: Random House, 1982); Christopher Jencks and Paul E. Peterson, eds., *The Urban Underclass* (Washington, DC: Brookings Institution, 1990).

6. The Panel Study of Income Dynamics has resulted in numerous publications. Information in this chapter, unless otherwise noted, comes from Greg J. Duncan et al., *Years of Poverty, Years of Plenty: The Changing Economic Fortunes of American Workers and Families* (Ann Arbor, MI: Survey Research Center–Institute for Social Research, University of Michigan, 1984), and Rebecca M. Blank, *It Takes a Nation: A New Agenda for Fighting Poverty* (Princeton, NJ: Princeton UP, 1997); data from the SIPP comes from John Iceland, U.S. Census Bureau, Household Economic Studies, *Dynamics of Economic Well-Being: Poverty 1996–1999* (Washington, DC: U.S. Government Printing Office, 2003).

7. Mark R. Rank, Hong-Sik Yoon, and Thomas A. Hirschl, "American Poverty as a Structural Failing: Evidence and Arguments," *Journal of Sociology and Social Welfare* 30 (December 2003), 3–29.

8. Mark R. Rank and Thomas A. Hirschl, "The Occurrence of Poverty across the Life Cycle: Evidence from the PSID," *Journal of Policy Analysis and Management* 20, no. 4 (2001): 737–55.

9. Robert Holman, *Poverty: Explanations of Social Deprivation* (New York: St. Martin's, 1978), 54–55.

10. Quoted on National Public Radio, "Morning Edition," October 31, 1994, transcript 1466–68.

11. Edwin Black, *War against the Weak: Eugenics and America's Campaign to Create a Master Race* (New York: Four Walls Eight Windows, 2003).

12. Arthur R. Jensen, "How Much Can We Boost IQ and Scholastic Achievement?" *Harvard Education Review* 33 (1969): 1–123; Arthur R. Jensen, *Bias in Mental Testing* (New York: Free Press, 1979); Arthur R. Jensen, *Straight Talk about Mental Tests* (New York: Free Press, 1981).

13. Jensen, *Straight Talk about Mental Tests*, 103, 105.

14. Richard Herrnstein and Charles Murray, *The Bell Curve* (New York: Free Press, 1995).

15. Christine R. Schwartz and Robert D. Mare, "Trends in Educational Assortive Marriage from 1940 to 2003," *Demography* 42 (November 2005): 621–46; Megan M. Sweeney and Maria Cancian, "The Changing Importance of White Women's Prospects for Assortative Mating," *Journal of Marriage and Family* 66 (November 2004): 1015–28.

16. Richard J. Herrnstein, *I.Q. in the Meritocracy* (Boston: Little, Brown, 1971), 197–98, 221.

17. Claude S. Fischer, Michael Hout, Martin Sanchez Jankowski, Samuel R. Lucas, Ann Swidler, and Kim Voss, *Inequality by Design; Cracking the Bell Curve Myth* (Princeton, NJ: Princeton UP, 1996), 11–12.

18. Bradley Buell et al., *Community Planning for Human Services* (New York: Columbia UP, 1952).

19. Laura Curran, "The Psychology of Poverty: Professional Social Work and Aid to Dependent Children in Postwar America, 1946–1963," *Social Service Review* 76 (September 2002): 371.

20. Walter Trattner, *From Poor Law to Welfare State: A History of Social Welfare in America*, 6th ed. (New York: Free Press, 1999), 320.

21. Laura Curran, "The Psychology of Poverty," 365.

22. Lawrence M. Mead, "Poverty: How Little We Know," *Social Service Review* 68 (September 1994): 339.

23. David T. Ellwood, "The Origins of 'Dependency': Choices, Confidence, or Culture?" *Focus* 12 (1989): 9.

24. Lester C. Thurow, *Investment in Human Capital* (Belmont, CA: Wadsworth, 1970), 20.

25. Thurow, *Investment in Human Capital*, 11–12.

26. Alexandra M. Curley, "Theories of Urban Poverty and Implications for Public Housing Policy," *Journal of Sociology and Social Welfare* 32 (June 2005): 97–119.
27. Thurow, *Investment in Human Capital*, 13.
28. Oscar Lewis, *Five Families: Mexican Case Studies in the Culture of Poverty* (New York: Basic Books, 1959).
29. Michael Harrington, *The Other America: Poverty in the United States* (New York: Penguin, 1962); Frank Riessman, *The Culturally Deprived Child* (New York: Harper & Row, 1962); Daniel Patrick Moynihan, *The Negro Family* (Washington, DC: U.S. Department of Labor, 1965).
30. Oscar Lewis, *La Vida: A Puerto Rican Family in the Culture of Poverty—San Juan and New York* (New York: Random House, 1965), xliii–xliv.
31. Edward C. Banfield, *The Unheavenly City Revisited* (Boston: Little, Brown, 1974), 62.
32. Lewis, *La Vida*, xlvii.
33. Banfield, *The Unheavenly City Revisited*, 62.
34. Banfield, *The Unheavenly City Revisited*, 61.
35. Lewis, *La Vida*, xlvi.
36. William Ryan, *Blaming the Victim* (New York: Pantheon, 1971). Copyright 1971 Pantheon Books, a Division of Random House, Inc.
37. Robert Holman, *Poverty: Explanations of Social Deprivation*, 112.
38. Charles A. Valentine, "The 'Culture of Poverty': Its Scientific Significance and Its Implications for Action," in Eleanor Burke Leacock, ed., *The Culture of Poverty: A Critique* (New York: Simon & Schuster, 1971), 194–97.
39. Valentine, "The 'Culture of Poverty': Its Scientific Significance and Its Implications for Action," 193.
40. Herbert J. Gans, "Deconstructing the Underclass: The Term's Danger as a Planning Concept," *APA Journal* 56 (Summer 1990): 271–77.
41. Leonard Goodwin, *Do the Poor Want to Work?* (Washington, DC: Brookings Institution, 1972); Leonard Goodwin, "How Suburban Families View the Work Orientations of the Welfare Poor," *Social Problems* 19 (1972): 337–48.
42. See, for example, Elliot Liebow, *Tally's Corner* (Boston: Little, Brown, 1967); Joseph T. Howell, *Hard Living on Clay Street* (New York: Anchor Books, 1973).
43. Sandra L. Barnes, "Debunking Deficiency Theories: Evaluating Non-Traditional Attitudes and Behavior among Residents in Poor Urban Neighborhoods," *Journal of Poverty* 5 (January 2001): 51.
44. Kathryn Edin and Maria Kefalas, *Promises I Can Keep: Why Poor Women Put Motherhood before Marriage* (Berkeley: University of California Press, 2005).
45. Robert Sears, Eleanor Maccoby, and Harry Levin, *Patterns of Child Rearing* (New York: Row Peterson, 1957).
46. Riessman, *The Culturally Deprived Child*.
47. Barnes, "Debunking Deficiency Theories: Evaluating Non-Traditional Attitudes and Behavior among Residents in Poor Urban Neighborhoods," 53.
48. Paul Tough, "What It Takes to Make a Student," *New York Times Magazine* (November 26, 2006): 44–52.
49. Leonard Beeghley, *Living Poorly in America* (New York: Praeger, 1983), 122; Ellwood, "The Origins of 'Dependency': Choices, Confidence, or Culture?" 6–9.
50. Hyman Rodman, "The Lower Class Value Stretch," *Social Forces* 42 (December 1963): 205–15.
51. Ellwood, "The Origins of 'Dependency': Choices, Confidence, or Culture?" 13.
52. William Ryan, *Blaming the Victim*. Copyright 1971 Pantheon Books, a Division of Random House, Inc.
53. Ryan, *Blaming the Victim*, 4. Copyright 1971 Pantheon Books, a Division of Random House, Inc.
54. Ryan, *Blaming the Victim*, 4. Copyright 1971 Pantheon Books, a Division of Random House, Inc.
55. Beeghley, *Living Poorly in America*, 133; William Julius Wilson, *When Work Disappears: The World of the New Urban Poor* (New York: Knopf, 1996).
56. William Julius Wilson, *The Truly Disadvantaged: The Inner City, the Underclass, and Public Policy* (Chicago: University of Chicago Press, 1987); Bernice Lott, "Connitive and Behavioral Distancing From the Poor," *American Psychologist* 57 (February 2002): 100–10.
57. Beeghley, *Living Poorly in America*, 108–15.
58. Beeghley, *Living Poorly in America*, 141.

59. David Featherman, "Stratification and Social Mobility: Two Decades of Cumulative Social Science," in James F. Short, Jr., ed., *The State of Sociology: Problems and Prospects* (San Francisco: Sage, 1981), 79–100.
60. David Featherman and Robert Hauser, *Opportunity and Change* (New York: Academic Press, 1978); Peter Blau and Otis D. Duncan, *The American Occupational Structure* (New York: Wiley, 1967).
61. Yunju Nam, "Is America Becoming More Equal for Children? Changes in the Intergenerational Transmission of Low- and High-Income Status," *Social Science Research* 33 (2004): 187–205.
62. Karl Marx and Friedrich Engels, *Manifesto of the Communist Party* (1848), reprinted in Lewis S. Feuer, ed., *Marx and Engels: Basic Writings on Politics and Philosophy* (Garden City, NY: Doubleday, 1959), 1–41.
63. Francis F. Piven and Richard A. Cloward, *Regulating the Poor: The Functions of Public Welfare* (New York: Pantheon, 1971).
64. Mark Rank, *One Nation Underprivileged: Why Poverty Affects Us All* (New York: Oxford UP, 2004).
65. E. M. Beck, Patrick M. Horan, and Charles M. Tolbert, "Stratification in a Dual Economy," *American Sociological Review* 43 (October 1978): 704–20.
66. Beeghley, *Living Poorly in America,* 155.
67. William Julius Wilson, *When Work Disappears,* 20.
68. William Julius Wilson, *The Truly Disadvantaged,* 3.
69. Wilson, *The Truly Disadvantaged,* 61, 137.
70. For a more detailed and very interesting discussion of the relationship of political perspectives to beliefs about the causes of poverty see James W. Robinson, "American Poverty Cause Beliefs and Structured Inequality Legitimation," *Sociological Spectrum* 29 (2009): 489–518.
71. Julian Chun-Chung Chow, Michelle A. Johnson, and Michael J. Austin, "The Status of Low-Income Neighborhoods in the Post-Welfare Reform Environment: Mapping the Relationship Between Poverty and Place," *Journal of Health and Social Policy* 21 (2005): 1–31.
72. Bernice Lott, "Cognitive and Behavioral Distancing From the Poor," *American Psychologist* 57, no. 2 (2002): 102–08; Bernice Lott and Heather E. Bullock, "Who Are The Poor," *Journal of Social Issues* 57, no. 2 (2001): 189–206.
73. Charles Murray, *Losing Ground: American Social Policy, 1950–1980* (New York: Basic Books, 1984), 29.
74. Murray, *Losing Ground,* 9.
75. See, for example, Rino Patti, Mimi Abramovitz, Steven Burkhardt, Michael Fabricant, Martha Haffey, and Rose Starr, *Gaining Perspective on Losing Ground* (New York: Lois and Samuel Silberman Fund, 1987).
76. See, for example, Sonia Wright, "Work Response to Income Maintenance: Economic, Sociological, and Cultural Perspectives," *Social Forces* 53 (June 1975): 553–62. Wright found that, contrary to "popular wisdom," no work disincentives were found.
77. Jimy M. Sanders, "'New' Structural Poverty?" *Sociological Quarterly* 32 (1991): 182; J.D. Kasarda and K. Ting, "Joblessness and Poverty in America's Central Cities: Causes and Policy Prescriptions," *Housing Policy Debate* 7, no. 2 (1996): 387–419.
78. Jimy M. Sanders, "'New' Structural Poverty?" 182.

Tax Policy and Income Distribution

Tax Policy and Income Distribution

© Melanie Stetson Freeman/Getty Images, Inc./Christian Science Monitor

*T*ax policy, the use of legislation to define how revenues are generated in order to achieve social objectives, is fundamental to the structure of social welfare in the United States. Although this function may seem prosaic, in fact tax policy has been the flash point of major historical events, as evident in the Boston "tea party" when colonists objected to taxation without representation. Recently, the massive tax cuts of the George W. Bush administration have provoked dire warnings by liberals and conservatives alike about the fiscal health of the republic. Although tax policy is an instrument of government, its influence is not limited solely to generating revenues for federal and state social programs: Through "tax expenditures," areas exempted from taxation, tax policy provides significant incentives not only for specific industries, as in "corporate welfare," but also for individual behavior, as in the mortgage interest deduction. For this reason tax policy is of increasing interest to advocates of social justice. As support for direct benefits through traditional social programs has waned, social advocates have turned to "targeted tax expenditures"—preferably, refundable tax credits—as a means to advance economic justice. As a vehicle for funding social programs, tax policy is also an important barometer for social equity; and indeed, policy analysts have long used income distribution—and more recently wealth distribution—as an indicator of how fair the economy has been for various groups. Changes in income and wealth over time influence the economic mobility of Americans, some of whom fare better than others.

History of U.S. Tax Policy

All governments levy taxes to meet their legislated obligations. Because taxation appropriates income from private parties—individuals and corporations—and puts it to public use, it has been controversial and, at times, volatile. Ever since the establishment of the republic, various groups have objected to government taxation, challenging the authority to appropriate private property. Such challenges have usually been sorted out through the courts, but on occasion they have led to violent armed confrontations, as in the Whiskey Rebellion that divided the nation shortly after its creation. Although tax policy has traditionally been of professional interest primarily to the "green-eyeshade" accountants at the Internal Revenue Service, the radical Right also have

a keen interest in it because it recognizes that tax money is the lifeblood that allows government to function. A precept of American conservatism has been minimal taxation. Speaking about the American colonies, Edmund Burke observed that taxes, by their very nature, tended to be imprudent: "To tax and to please, no more than to love and to be wise, is not given to men."

Progressives and liberals understood the relationship between taxes and social programs differently, citing Oliver Wendell Holmes: "Taxes are what we pay for civilized society." Ever since the creation of the welfare state with the passage of the Social Security Act of 1935, social program expenditures have grown; and all these programs have been paid for by increasing taxes. The optimal welfare state, as liberals conceived it, would provide essential benefits as a right of citizenship. These benefits would be funded by progressive taxes—taxes that derived their revenues disproportionately from the wealthy. Implicit in this vision was the political calculus that was captured by Harry Hopkins, whose synopsis has become part of welfare folklore: "Tax, tax; spend, spend; elect, elect!" For half a century, this strategy produced solid electoral support for liberal social programs: The wealthy were taxed at higher rates, the revenues were diverted to social benefits for the middle and working classes through social programs, and social program beneficiaries expressed their gratitude by voting Democratic. Ultimately, however, liberal Democratic hegemony in social policy foundered on the shoals of its own success. As working families rose into the middle class, they tended to individualize their achievements, discounting the role of social programs and, in the process, becoming more receptive to conservative proposals to reduce social programs and their tax burden. By the 1980s this scenario led to the election of Ronald Reagan, who had a visceral dislike for federal social programs. The Reagan presidency was revolutionary in several respects, one being profound changes in tax policy, increasing economic inequality.

While the Clinton interregnum restored a measure of fairness in tax policy, the presidency of George W. Bush has viewed tax cuts as the centerpiece of its domestic agenda, achieving one for each year of its first term. The intent of the Bush White House has been summarized by Grover Norquist, who as president of Americans for Tax Reform has proposed that the Bush White House implement annual tax cuts: "I don't want to abolish government. I simply want to reduce it to the size where I can drag it into the bathroom and drown it in the bathtub."[1] Accordingly, conservatives have viewed tax cuts as essential to rolling back social programs, "starving the beast." As Paul Krugman observed, "Starving-the-beasters believe that budget deficits will lead to spending cuts that will eventually achieve their true aim: shrinking the government's role back to what it was under Calvin Coolidge."[2] For intellectuals of the Right, tax reform is ultimately the vehicle for dismantling the U.S. welfare state. "Instead of sending taxes to Washington, straining them through bureaucracies and converting what remains into a muddle of services, subsidies, in-kind support, and cash hedged with restrictions and exceptions," argued Charles Murray, "just collect the taxes, divide them up, and send the money back in cash grants to all American adults." According to Murray, a $10,000 grant to each nonincarcerated U.S. citizen, of which $3,000 would be for health care, would cost $355 billion more than current expenditures. By 2011, however, Murray's thought experiment would be revenue neutral; by 2020 it would save a half trillion dollars.[3] How this dispute between social entitlements and tax revenues will be worked out has implications far beyond beneficiaries of social welfare programs. Issues, such as the federal deficit, global economic competition, and the fate of discretionary programs, make the resolution extraordinarily complex.

As a creation of the legislative process, tax policy is most visible in the passage of major bills. Over time these become the basis of the state and federal tax codes, those notoriously confounding labyrinths of accounting rules. Periodically, attempts to reform tax policy emerge, such as the 1986 federal tax reform, which simplified the tax code and eliminated—at least temporarily—provisions for special interests. Indeed, the lobbying around deletion of special tax provisions was so intense that the 1986 tax reform became known as the "showdown at Gucci gulch," after the impeccable dress of the professionals populating the lobbying firms on Washington's K Street.

As this overview suggests, tax policy is dense and at the same time dynamic. Historically, three tax policies have been central to U.S. social policy: the income tax, the withholding tax, and the earned income tax credit.

- The federal income tax was instituted after approval of the 16th Amendment to the Constitution in 1914. A *progressive tax*, in that the wealthy were taxed at a higher rate, the income tax was initially levied on less than 1 percent of the population and had a top rate of only 7 percent. On average, the income tax is 8.2 percent, but it is higher for upper-income families, 11.7 percent. Because a threshold on taxable income has been set, low-income families are exempt from paying the federal income tax.[4]

- The Social Security withholding tax, the payroll tax, was established in 1935. For employed workers, the withholding tax was initially set at 2 percent of the first $3,000 in wages, paid equally between employers and workers. Since then Social Security withholding has increased to 12.4 percent of the first $97,500 in wages in 2007, increasing to $102,000 in 2008. The wage cap was established at the outset, under the presumption that Social Security was a public pension plan for workers who would not have recourse to retirement provisions available to the wealthy.[5] The withholding tax is a regressive tax, in that lower-income workers pay the same rate as higher-wage employees. Most taxpayers now pay more in Social Security withholding than they do in income taxes.

- The **earned income tax credit (EITC)** was enacted in 1975 after the failure of a "negative income tax" plan advanced by the Nixon administration. A *refundable tax credit*, the EITC instructs the IRS to send a check to low-wage workers, especially those with children, who have earned income below a certain level. In 2003, for example, a worker with two children could receive a maximum refund of $4,204.[6] Since the creation of the EITC, other tax credits have been introduced: A child care tax credit allows low-wage workers to deduct the costs of day care, and 22 states and the District of Columbia have introduced tax credits for low-income workers, some of which are refundable.

The interaction of these basic tax policies is complex, as evident in Table 1. Although the top quintile claims over 60 percent of income, it also bears the weight of paying most of the income, payroll, corporate, and estate taxes. On the other hand, the effective tax rate of the top quintile—almost 26 percent—is considerably less than its share of income. The negative income tax entries for the lowest quintiles can be attributed to rebates paid them through the earned income tax credit, a negative income tax for low-wage families with children.

Tax provisions fund social programs that exist within an economy that is also shaped by economic

Table 1

Distribution of Federal Taxes by Quintiles, 2007

	Economic Income	Individual Income Tax	Payroll Tax	Corporate Income Tax	Estate Tax	All Federal Tax
			Share of Total			
Top quintile	61.1	96.7	51.2	84.9	94.2	73.0
Fourth quintile	19.5	13.1	25.5	7.8	0.8	17.0
Middle quintile	11.2	3.1	14.4	3.4	1.2	7.4
Second quintile	6.2	−1.7	6.7	2.2	0.1	2.1
Lowest quintile	2.4	−1.2	2.1	0.9	0.2	0.4
			Average Effective Tax Rate			
Top quintile		14.5	6.9	4.2	0.3	25.9
Fourth quintile		6.8	10.8	1.2	0.0	18.8
Middle quintile		2.8	10.7	0.9	0.0	14.4
Second quintile		−2.8	8.9	1.1	0.0	7.3
Lowest quintile		−5.0	7.3	1.2	0.0	3.4
All		10.2	9.3	3.0	0.2	21.7

Source: Adapted from "Current-Law Distribution of Federal Taxes by Economic Income Percentiles, 2007: Table T04-0093," Urban-Brookings Tax Policy Center, Microsimulation Model (Version 0304-2). Retrieved September 28, 2004, from www.taxpolicycenter.org. Used by permission.

policy; thus, economic policy, through tax policy, influences social programs. A classic example was the conservative enthusiasm about "supply-side economics" during the 1980s. As advocated by Arthur Laffer, optimal economic policy would consist of minimal taxation, so as not to impede capital formation and expansion. Given the relatively higher tax rates that preceded his presidency, Ronald Reagan endorsed tax reform that incorporated a one-third cut in the income tax, assuming that the cut would reinvigorate a sluggish economy.[7] But although the tax cut of 1981 jolted the economy out of recession, it also cut off tax revenues to the Treasury, which then had to sell bonds to service the federal debt. Soon the federal government plunged further into debt, the depth of which was unprecedented for peacetime. By 1983 the annual deficit was $207 billion, 6.3 percent of **gross national product,** and growing. Debt service on government bonds grew commensurately, so that by the end of the 1980s, annual interest payments on the debt were $150 billion, the second largest item in the federal budget.[8]

Annual debt service overshadowed domestic policy discussions during the early 1990s. The congressional response was to impose a cap on domestic spending, an effort to stem the hemorrhaging of cash leaving the Treasury during a period when inflowing revenues had been stemmed by tax cuts. Liberal Democrats insisted that entitlement spending for social programs be exempt from the spending cap, with the result that federal budget decisions subsequently penalized discretionary programs—those with fixed budgets that are subject to the appropriation process annually—disproportionately. Because discretionary programs include research and development, student loans, public transportation, and the entire defense budget, the spending cap created intense pressure between social entitlements and discretionary programs. Thus, several years after a sharp cut in federal taxes, the effects took the form of pressure to cut an array of discretionary programs.

Looming federal deficits cast a pall over the incoming Clinton administration. After campaigning on a platform that emphasized investments in human capital, President Clinton was confronted with the massive deficits left over from the Reagan and Bush administrations. Clinton's nascent liberal tendencies, evident in his support for public works and national health insurance, were redirected by Alan Greenspan, chair of the Federal Reserve. Greenspan argued that the economy in general, and financial markets in particular, would respond negatively to new social programs that carried high price tags, because such programs would either (1) worsen the federal debt or (2) require significant tax increases. Although Clinton balked at Greenspan's position, economic reality was making short work of the new president's campaign rhetoric. Cornered between forces that advocated social investments and groups demanding deficit reduction, Clinton blew up during a staff meeting, as Bob Woodward recounted in *The Agenda:*

> "Where are all the Democrats?" Clinton bellowed. "I hope you're all aware we're all Eisenhower Republicans," he said, his voice dripping with sarcasm. "We're Eisenhower Republicans here, and we are fighting the Reagan Republicans. We stand for lower deficits and free trade and the bond market. Isn't that great?"
>
> The room was silent once more.
>
> He erupted again, his voice severe and loud, "I don't have a goddamn Democratic budget until 1996. None of the investments, none of the things I campaigned on."[9]

Capitulating to Greenspan's insistence on deficit reduction, Clinton put his social investment plans on hold, a decision that contributed to an unprecedented economic expansion that promised to make possible the eventual elimination of the federal debt by generating a surplus projected at $2 trillion over 10 years.

After a hotly disputed 2000 presidential election, many anticipated that George W. Bush would govern in a bipartisan manner, yet this was not the case. With Republican control of Congress, the White House was positioned to move aggressively on domestic policy; among its primary concerns was tax policy. During its first term, four tax cuts were passed reducing federal revenues $1.9 trillion over 10 years. Because the federal government had to honor its obligation to social entitlements while increasing spending for national security and mounting a war on terrorism, the federal government not only spent the surplus inherited from the Clinton presidency but also slid rapidly back into debt. As a result, the federal debt skyrocketed. With passage of the 2004 tax cut, the federal debt was projected to increase from $4.3 trillion to $8 trillion by 2014.[10] Conservatives minimized the fiscal consequences of the federal deficit, noting that as a

percentage of gross domestic product the Bush deficit was only 1.8 percent in 2007 while the Reagan deficits were much higher, 6 percent.[11] Adherents to supply-side economics in the Bush White House bet that economic growth would shrink the deficit—in the words of Vice President Cheney: "Reagan proved that deficits don't matter." Liberals were less sanguine. "Bush's policies may, in fact, best be explained by another, more radical agenda. Extensive tax cuts will require Congress to limit the growth of social programs and public investment and undermine other programs altogether," argued Jeff Madrick, "Rising deficits will inevitably force Congress to starve those 'wasteful' social programs. The prospective high deficits may even make it imperative to privatize Social Security and Medicare eventually."[12] In 2008 the first of 77 million baby boomers began collecting Social Security, incurring future obligations that current social insurance programs will not be able to meet. The prospects would be to either trim social insurance benefits severely or convert them to public assistance programs, neither of which are desirable outcomes for liberals who have sought to extend social program coverage. The continuation of the Bush tax cuts past 2010, when they are scheduled to expire, looms as a critical fiscal issue; assuming continuation of tax cuts and contemporary expenditures, there will be insufficient revenues for Medicaid and Medicare by 2030; by 2040 Social Security will be underfunded and net interest on federal debt will approximate 15 percent of GDP.[13]

Tax Policy and Special Interests

Tax policy has always contained provisions that benefit specific interests. Bending the tax code in response to lobbying is a long-standing practice in the United States, though today it is most often associated with corporate influence. Actually, the exclusion of pension plans from taxation began in 1921, and these provisions have been updated to include provisions such as individual retirement accounts. Tax expenditures that benefit individuals have now grown to the point that they exceed allocations for many prominent social welfare programs. In 2003, for example, tax expenditures for pension contributions were projected to be $279.1 billion, for health insurance $561.9 billion, and for mortgage interest deductions $362.9 billion. By comparison, in 2002

spotlight 1

Tax Policy

The Tax Policy Center is a joint venture of the Urban Institute and the Brookings Institution. The center is comprised of nationally recognized experts in tax, budget, and social policy who have served at the highest levels of government. The center provides analysis and facts about tax policy to policymakers, journalists, citizens, and researchers. To learn more about this group, go to its website at **www.taxpolicycenter.org.**

allocations for Supplemental Security Income were $38.5 billion, Medicaid $258.2, and federal housing programs $25.7 billion. Even the largest tax credits available for low-income taxpayers for 2003 are dwarfed by middle-class tax expenditures: The EITC costs $34.4 billion, child care $44.1 billion, and housing $4.1 billion.[14]

Realizing that the tax code can be manipulated to serve the interests of the affluent, many social justice advocates have targeted "corporate welfare," or the special provisions directed at specific industries, for reform. The libertarian CATO Institute reported that the federal government spends $92 billion, directly and indirectly, to subsidize private sector activities.

This list might rankle many taxpayers, but efforts to downsize corporate welfare have been frustrating. As long as there is pork in politics, there is the opportunity to customize tax policy to serve the concerns of individual legislators—who, after all, are often influenced by constituent requests. Thus, tax policy is crafted both to meet the Appalachian Regional Commission's need for roads and to respond to Sonoma Valley vintners' desire to export their products to France.

Tax law also has a significant influence, directly and indirectly, on the revenues of nonprofit organizations. By allowing taxpayers to deduct charitable contributions from taxable income, tax law directly encourages support of philanthropy. Lower tax rates work indirectly, at least in theory, by leaving taxpayers with more discretionary income and assets that they may then donate to nonprofit causes. Comparatively, policy analysts are more confident

Corporate Welfare by Federal Agency

Department	2001 Outlays Millions	2006 Outlays Millions	% Change
Dept. of Agriculture	$44,103	$43,732	−.1
Dept. of Commerce	2,024	1,726	−14
Dept. of Defense	7,691	11,814	54
Dept. of Energy	1,930	1,875	−3
Dept. of Housing and Urban Development	5,988	5,116	−15
Dept. of State	4,310	4,610	7
Dept. of Transportation	2,849	5,749	102
Others	14,201	17,326	22
Total	83,096	91,967	11

Source: Stephen Slivinski, "The Corporate Welfare State," (Washington, DC: CATO Institution, 2007), Table 2.

about the effectiveness of direct support through tax deductions than about indirect support via lower taxation. In 1981, for example, taxpayers who did not itemize their tax deductions were allowed to deduct contributions to nonprofit organizations; at the same time significant reductions in income and estate taxes were instituted. In 1986 legislation removed the deduction for charitable contributions on the part of nonitemizers; concurrently, income and corporate tax rates were reduced sharply, although many tax shelters were also eliminated. The effects on charitable giving proved ambiguous. Despite his celebration of "compassionate conservatism," George W. Bush failed to change the tax code to allow nonitemizers to claim deductions for charitable contributions. As a result, fewer low-income families contribute less than do upper-income families. In 2004, 56.3 percent of families earning less than $50,000 contributed to charities while 93.3 percent of those with incomes above $100,000 did so. For lower-income families, the average annual contributions totaled $1,186, compared to $3,886 for wealthier families.[15] Yet the charitable impulse of Americans has continued despite changes in tax policy. "Giving as a percent of income has remained remarkably constant in the face of increases in the cost of giving," concluded tax policy analysts.[16]

The story on charitable giving as a function of tax reduction is less unilinear than conservatives might wish. The idea is that as taxes on individual and corporate income are lowered, private wealth increases, creating a larger pool of resources against which nonprofits can lay claim. This, of course, is a mantra that conservatives have chanted since the 1980s—indeed, to the point that some ideologues have proposed that private charity actually replace government activity in social welfare. Deep tax cuts introduced during the 1980s significantly reduced federal social welfare funding; and indeed, until the early 1990s, these were made up for by increases in charitable giving. During the 1990s, however, although both private giving and federal support of nonprofits increased significantly, these sources never compensated for the total revenue losses attributed to direct federal funding cuts. After the election of George W. Bush, conservatives proposed repeal of the estate tax, the consequence of which the Congressional Budget Office predicts would be between $13 billion and $25 billion in reduced charitable contributions because the wealthy would no longer count gifts against their tax obligations.[17]

Despite the mammoth size of the federal budget of the United States, it is predicated on a tax base that is minimal compared to those of other industrialized nations. As shown in Table 2, the 2002 tax burden of the United States was lower than that in most industrialized nations. Another way to assess the fairness of tax policy is to compare nations with respect to their income equality by use of the Gini index. This index calibrates the extent to which a nation's income distribution varies from a perfectly equal distribution; the closer the Gini index is to zero the greater the equality—higher values indicate greater inequality. Table 3 ranks the nations of the Organization for Economic Cooperation and Development (OECD), the most developed of national economies.

The relatively low tax rate of the United States largely accounts for the nation's skewed **income distribution.** A tenet of the welfare state has been the progressive taxation of income and its redistribution to the poor through social programs. By definition, a welfare state with a low tax rate is unable to generate revenues sufficient to level the differences between rich and poor; thus, the question of income distribution has become integral to the discussion of tax policy. Income distribution changes over time; most recently, wealthier families have benefited significantly.

Economic growth during the latter decades of the twentieth century exacerbated income inequality; while the lowest two quintiles treaded water with respect to family income, the top quintile fared significantly better. The fortunes of the wealthiest 20 percent of families were battened by the tax cuts during the presidency of George W. Bush, which favored the rich. By 2006 the top 10 percent of American families claimed almost half of family income, second only to that figure in 1929! By one calculation, the top 1 percent claimed 53 percent of the growth in income in 2004.[18] Significantly, the new rich are less likely to have inherited their wealth and more likely to be executives.

The evidence suggests that top income earners are not "rentiers" deriving their incomes from past wealth but rather are "working rich," highly paid employees or new entrepreneurs who have not yet accumulated fortunes comparable to those accumulated during the Gilded Age. Such a pattern might not last for very long. The possible repeal of

Changes in Family Income

Quintile	1973	1979	1989	2000	Percent Change		
					1973–79	1979–89	1989–2000
Highest	$92,160	$94,752	$107,925	$132,487	2.8	13.9	22.8
Fourth	52,696	53,715	56,068	59,657	1.9	4.4	6.4
Middle	35,980	35,563	35,861	36,576	−1.2	0.8	2.0
Second	21,408	21,256	20,979	21,567	−0.7	−1.3	2.8
Lowest	8,417	8,324	8,146	8,216	−1.1	−2.1	0.9

Source: Committee on Ways and Means, Overview of Entitlement Programs (Washington, DC: US GPO, 2004), p. H-19.

the federal tax on large estates in coming years would certainly accelerate the path toward the reconstitution of the great wealth concentration that existed in the U.S. economy before the Great Depression.[19]

Thus, the demise of the estate tax, cleverly called the "death tax" by its opponents, may reintroduce a degree of income inequality not seen in eight decades. Income is skewed according to gender, race, and ethnicity, although in ways that are sometimes unexpected. The following table shows changes in wages from 1989 to 2005.

White men earned more than any income group until they were eclipsed by Asian men at the beginning of the twenty-first century. Among male workers, Hispanics consistently earned least. The earnings of Asian women have not only exceeded other groups of female workers since at least 1989, but

Median Hourly Wages by Gender, Race/Ethnicity, 1989-2005 (2005 Dollars)

	1989	1995	2000	2005
Men				
White	$16.51	$15.88	$17.28	$17.42
Black	11.94	11.61	12.64	12.48
Hispanic	11.10	10.12	11.09	11.14
Asian	15.42	15.29	17.18	18.49
Women				
White	11.56	11.84	12.96	13.78
Black	10.30	10.18	11.33	11.22
Hispanic	9.19	9.00	9.58	9.99
Asian	11.96	12.18	13.81	14.49

Black and Hispanic men as well. Among all groups, Hispanic women had the lowest wages. At different points in time, the earnings of every one of these groups actually fell, except for White and Asian women whose incomes steadily increased. This would help explain how, between 1973 and 2005, the ratio of women's wages to those of men has increased from 63.1 to 82 percent.[20]

Yet, income is only one component of economic justice; another measure of affluence is assets. Although considered in discussions of social policy less often than income, assets are important insofar as they are an indication of real wealth. Consisting of savings, real estate, stocks and bonds, and related property, assets not only can be liquidated during periods of adversity, thus offering the owner a buffer against poverty, but also appreciate in value, thus generating additional wealth. The distribution of assets is even more skewed than income distribution, with the highest quintile owning more than 80 percent. By contrast, the wealth of the lowest quintile is negative, indicative of debt. As has been the case with income, the distribution of assets has become more skewed during recent decades, the wealthiest quintile controlling more wealth with the lowest remaining in debt. And as with income, the distribution of assets is relatively constant; moderate changes occur, but the distribution pattern remains essentially the same over time. Consider the period following the Great Society efforts of the mid-1960s: Despite a major expansion of social programs for the poor, the lowest quintile still showed negative wealth, remaining mired in debt. For these reasons, a critical examination of wealth is essential for assessing economic justice.[21] If income distribution is skewed in favor of the affluent, assets are even more so. Notably, the bottom quintile is chronically in debt, its obligations

Table 2

Tax Revenue of OECD* Countries as a Percent of GDP, 2002

Rank	Country	Total Tax Rate
1	Sweden	50.2
2	Denmark	48.9
3	Belgium	46.4
4	Finland	45.9
5	Austria	44.0
5	France	44.0
7	Norway	43.5
8	Italy	42.8
9	Luxembourg	41.8
10	Czech Republic	39.3
11	Netherlands	39.2
12	Hungary	38.3
13	Iceland	38.1
14	Germany	36.0
15	Greece	35.9
16	Spain	35.8
17	United Kingdom	35.6
18	New Zealand	34.9
19	Canada	33.9
19	Portugal	33.9
21	Slovak Republic	33.1
22	Poland	32.8
23	Australia	31.5
24	Turkey	31.1
25	Switzerland	30.3
26	Ireland	28.4
27	United States	26.4
28	Japan	25.8
29	Korea	24.4
30	Mexico	18.1
	European Union	40.6
	OECD	36.3

*Organization for Economic Cooperation and Development

Table 3

Gini Index of OECD Member Nations

Rank	Nation	Gini Index
1	Denmark	24.7
2	Japan	24.9
3.5	Belgium	25.0
3.5	Sweden	25.0
5	Finland	25.6
6	Norway	25.8
7	Austria	30.5
8	Canada	31.5
9	Spain	32.5
10	Netherlands	32.6
11	France	32.7
12	Switzerland	33.1
13	Australia	35.2
14	Ireland	35.9
15.5	Italy	36.0
15.5	United Kingdom	36.0
17	New Zealand	36.2
18	Germany	38.2
19	Portugal	38.5
20	United States	40.8

Source: Adapted from United Nations Development Program, *Human Development Report, 2003* (New York: Oxford, 2003), p. 282.

exceeding its assets. Wealth is also skewed in relation to race and ethnicity. Between 1996 and 2002, the wealth of African Americans fell 16.1 percent, while that of Hispanics increased 14 percent (compared to an increase of 17.4 percent for non-Hispanic whites).[22]

The fact that assets are consistently negative for the lowest quintile reflects the difficulty of poorer families to buffer themselves from economic shocks. Thus, asset poverty, the wealth needed to survive for three months at the poverty level, exceeds income-based poverty. In 1999 the official poverty level was 11.8 percent, and the asset poverty rate was 27.9 percent; however, the asset poverty rate for minorities was much higher, for blacks 57.6 percent and Hispanics 52.3 percent.[23] In 2000 the asset poverty rate was 25.5 percent, twice the conventional poverty level, 12.7 percent.[24] The consequences of the tax cuts engineered during the second Bush presidency would be expected to widen the chasm between rich and poor.

Changes in the Distribution of Wealth (Household Assets Minus Debts), 1962–2004

Quintile	1962	1983	1989	2001	2004	Percent Change			
						1962–83	1983–89	1989–2001	2001–2004
Highest	81.0%	81.3%	83.5%	84.4%	84.7%	0.4	2.2	0.9	0.2
Fourth	13.4	12.6	12.3	11.3	11.3	−0.8	−0.3	−1.0	0.0
Middle	5.4	5.2	4.8	3.9	3.8	−0.2	−0.4	−0.9	−0.1
Second	1.0	1.2	0.8	0.7	0.7	0.2	−0.3	−0.1	0.0
Lowest	−0.7	−0.3	−1.5	−0.4	−0.5	0.4	−1.2	1.1	−0.1

Change in Average Wealth (Thousands of 2004 dollars)						Annualized Growth			
Top	$680.8	$1,001.9	$1,178.7	$1,711.6	$1,822.6	1.8	2.7	3.2	2.1
Fourth	112.7	154.8	173.9	229.6	243.6	1.5	1.9	2.3	2.0
Middle	45.7	64.3	68.2	80.0	81.9	1.6	1.0	1.3	0.8
Second	8.0	14.5	11.9	14.9	14.4	2.9	−3.3	1.9	−1.0
Lowest	−6.1	−3.7	−21.3	−8.7	−11.4	2.4	−33.9	7.2	−9.2

Source: Lawrence Mishel, Jared Bernstein, and Sylvia Allegretto, The State of Working America 2006–2007 (Washington, DC: Economic Policy Institute, 2007), pp. 254–55.

State Tax Policy and the Poor

Federal taxes are important in social welfare policy because they subsidize the major social entitlements, but states also levy taxes in order to meet their legislative obligations. Historically, states have held major responsibility in social programs, areas such as mental health, child welfare, and corrections; and to a great degree the adequacy of a state's social programs depends on its tax collections. Unlike federal taxation, which is uniform across the nation, state tax policy varies significantly. By way of illustration, consider the income tax. Whereas the federal income tax is uniform nationwide, 43 states have income taxes, but 7 do not (Florida, Nevada, South Dakota, Tennessee, Texas, Washington, and Wyoming). State income taxes provide general revenues that can be used for a range of social programs, but this is not the only reason that state tax policy is important. State tax policy can establish an income floor for taxation or exempt low-income families from any tax liability altogether, thus allowing them to keep more of their income. Disparities among states are striking; in 2006, the state income threshold in Alabama was only $4,600, for example, while that of California was $44,700. Of states that levy an income tax, the more progressive jurisdictions actually provide a rebate, similar to the federal Earned Income Tax Credit. As Table 4 on the next page indicates, some states have been much more generous with respect to low-income families, while others have been downright punitive.

The Efficiency of Tax Policy in Reducing Poverty

In the larger context of social policy, tax policy is one of several strategies that apportion societal resources. Within social welfare, more traditional benefits have consisted of social insurance such as Social Security, cash public assistance (means-tested cash benefits) such as Temporary Assistance for Needy Families (TANF), in-kind public assistance (means-tested noncash benefits) such as Food Stamps, and the Earned Income Tax Credit (tax rebates). These different strategies vary in terms of their efficiency in poverty reduction over time. For elders, social insurance—compulsory contributions to social programs like Social Security and

Table 4

State Income Tax at Poverty Line of $20,615 for Two-Parent Families of Four, 2002

Rank	State	Tax	Rank	State	Tax
1	Alabama	$573	20	Colorado	$0
2	Hawaii	546	20	Connecticut	0
3	Arkansas	427	20	Delaware	0
4	West Virginia	406	20	Idaho	0
5	Oregon	319	20	Maine	0
6	Michigan	242	20	North Dakota	0
7	Indiana	239	20	Pennsylvania	0
8	Iowa	236	20	South Carolina	0
9	New Jersey	219	20	Utah	0
10	Montana	211	20	Virginia	0
11	Illinois	192	32	New Mexico	(40)
12	Louisiana	169	33	Rhode Island	(140)
13	Georgia	160	34	Nebraska	(299)
14	Ohio	159	35	Kansas	(363)
15	Oklahoma	139	36	Wisconsin	(373)
16	Missouri	83	37	Maryland	(423)
17	Kentucky	82	38	Massachusetts	(447)
18	North Carolina	78	39	District of Columbia	(708)
19	Mississippi	30	40	Vermont	(1,195)
20	Arizona	0	41	New York	(1,436)
20	California	0	42	Minnesota	(1,587)

Source: Adapted from Jason Levitis, *The Impact of State Income Taxes on Low-Income Families in 2006* (Washington, DC: Center on Budget and Policy Priorities, 2007), p. 17.

Medicare—makes the biggest dent in poverty, and means-tested in-kind benefits and tax policies are more important for children and families. Regardless, more than twice the number of elders are removed from poverty than are children and families by these different strategies (see Table 5).

Tax Expenditures as Poverty Policy

The use of federal tax policy to alleviate poverty and the increase in states' use of tax policy to augment the income of poor families are relatively new features of U.S. social policy. In the past quarter centu-ry, a significant shift in social welfare policy has been witnessed: gradually, direct welfare transfers are being augmented with indirect expenditures through tax credits. While the family welfare alloca-tion was restricted to $16.5 billion when AFDC was replaced by TANF, the EITC expanded to over $34 billion. This created a major disconnect in poverty policy insofar as many of the families transitioning from welfare to work do not claim EITC benefits even though they would be eligible for them. In 1999, 61.6 percent of TANF/AFDC families had heard of the EITC, but only 33.3 percent had received an EITC refund.[25] If welfare departments were truly concerned about poverty, as opposed to simply distributing public assistance benefits, they would make certain that all families with earned income claimed the EITC, but few welfare workers

Table 5

Impact of Safety Net on Poverty Reduction, 2002

Category	Individuals, over 65 (in thousands)	Percent over 65	Children under 18 (in thousands)	Percent under 18	Persons in Unmarried Households (in thousands)	Percent in Unmarried Households
Number of poor	17,082		14,314		14,425	
Number removed due to:						
Social Insurance	13,133	76.9	1,676	11.7	535	3.7
Means-tested cash benefits	373	2.2	505	3.5	1,103	7.6
Means-tested in-kind	508	3.0	1,392	9.7	546	3.8
Federal taxes and refunds	−10	−0.1	1,565	10.9	1,544	10.7
Total removed	14,004	82	5,138	35.9	1,573	36.8

Source: House Ways and Means Committee, Overview of Entitlement Programs (Washington, DC: U.S. GPO, 2004), adapted from Tables H-19, H-20, and H-21.

are familiar with the program. As a result, it is underutilized by the welfare poor.

Tax expenditures in the form of deductions for families' housing and health insurance costs have been enjoyed by the middle class for more than a half century, but it has not been until relatively recently that tax expenditures have been targeted for low-income families. The list of tax credits available to the poor has grown to include credits for earned income, child care, the welfare-to-work transition, care for the elderly and disabled, and adoption expenses. As the number of tax credits targeted to the poor has increased, tax credits have emerged as a contender to replace, at least partially, direct income transfers to aid the poor.

Although promises of federal tax credits for low-income families were conspicuous during the 2000 presidential campaign, many advocates of social justice had already enjoyed success lobbying state legislatures. Because many state legislatures were controlled by conservatives, a tax credit strategy proved more effective than a traditional appeal for increases in welfare transfers. By 2000 almost a dozen states had complemented the federal EITC with comparable state programs, and several had introduced other tax credits. Notably, Minnesota enacted a state EITC, a refundable child care credit, a property tax credit for renters, and a subsidized health insurance program. Paul Wilson and Robert

Cline note that 27 percent of Minnesotans take advantage of at least one of these programs; the Minnesota array of tax credits thus extends important income and health assistance to families ranging from the welfare poor to the working poor.[26]

As might be expected by a transition of such magnitude, the replacement of welfare transfers with tax credits raises several policy issues:

- Tax and revenue agencies replace welfare departments as the source of benefits, a role that many departments of social services are either unprepared for or may resist outright.
- Beneficiaries of tax credits must participate in the tax system in order to claim benefits, a status that is unfamiliar for many.
- Because much tax preparation is done by commercial firms, low-income workers may fall prey to unscrupulous preparers, particularly those advancing a refund as a loan.
- Tax credit refunds are almost always paid after the fact, requiring the recipient's willingness to wait, unlike traditional welfare that arrives monthly.
- As tax expenditures, tax credits are no less consequential for the federal and state treasuries than are traditional welfare transfers.

An important advantage of tax credits is that their allocations are not fixed; like open-ended entitlements, the amount awarded is determined by the volume of valid claims.

Tax credits offer new opportunities in areas historically understood as "welfare." In order to accelerate the upward mobility of the poor, for example, tax credits could be connected directly to asset-accrual strategies, such as individual development accounts, by encouraging low-income taxpayers to split their refund, directing a portion to a savings instrument. The tax preparation necessary for people to access tax credits could be one of several basic services—checking, savings, financial planning—offered by community financial services that could replace current welfare departments and serve as alternatives to marginal financial outfits that exploit the poor. Integrated with other capital formation strategies such as electronic benefit transfer, deposits by commercial banks to meet their Community Reinvestment Act obligations, and deposits by government and nonprofit agencies, tax credits could be part of a broad community development initiative that would finance projects in poor neighborhoods, thereby providing jobs to residents. In this respect, tax credits may not only begin to replace traditional welfare transfers, but in so doing may well introduce a new era of basic supports for poor families.[27]

Other tax credits have been proposed to augment poverty policy. Martha Ozawa and Baeg-Eui Hong suggested using the EITC to establish a $1,000 income floor for poor children and adjusting the benefit according to family size. "The modified EITC and children's allowances combined would improve the income status of all EITC-recipient children by 23.6 percent, with black and Hispanic children benefiting more than white children," Ozawa and Hong concluded.[28] Robert Cherry and Max Sawicky proposed a universal unified child credit that would augment the EITC and child care tax credit with an additional child credit.[29] Thus, the integration of refundable tax credits and calibrating them according to family size could reduce poverty significantly.

The Anti-tax Movement

Proponents of publicly funded social programs assume that tax-generated revenues are prudent investments toward the public good. Within the larger policy context, there are differing views on this assumption, however. It is worth acknowledging that some of the most egregious violations of personal decency, to say nothing of civil rights, have occurred under the auspices of public programs—such as the sterilization of "feeble-minded" people during the eugenics movement, the Tuskegee

© Steven Rubin/JB Pictures Ltd./The Image Works

■ *Despite support for publicly funded social programs, there are some who believe that Americans should not pay any taxes.*

"experiment" on syphilitic African American men, and the warehousing of chronically mentally ill patients as well as of prison inmates.

For conservatives, particularly libertarians, government activities are likely to attenuate individual liberties, a likelihood encouraged by the fragmentation of modern society. The oppressive capacity of the state has long been a concern of political philosophers; in a recent statement of the issue, Jared Diamond noted that all societies try to balance the provision of essential services with measures aimed at thwarting the kleptocratic inclinations of those in power:

> These noble and selfish functions are inextricably linked, although some governments emphasize much more of one function than of the other. The difference between a kleptocrat and a wise statesman, between a robber baron and a public benefactor is merely one of degree: a matter of just how large a percentage of the tribute extracted from producers is retained by the elite, and how much the commoners like the public uses to which the redistributed tribute is put.[30]

To the extent that government enriches the powerful and mistreats citizens, a logical reform strategy is to de-fund the state by cutting off its tax revenues. By way of illustration, Michael Tanner of the Cato Institute calculates that $3.5 trillion has been spent on poverty programs since the Great Society period, yet with little success. "We are not going to solve our welfare problems by throwing more money at them," he concludes. "It is time to recognize that welfare cannot be reformed. It should be ended."[31]

An equally compelling critique of government taxation can be found in classic liberalism, a philosophic doctrine that emphasizes the freedom of individuals to act in their own best interests. Isaiah Berlin's distinction between "positive liberty" and "negative liberty" was framed within the context of twentieth-century state socialism, in an era when public programs were ascendant. Advocates of public programs justified them on the basis that they protected the vulnerable from poverty, idleness, and sickness, but Berlin noted that such "positive liberty" invariably strengthened the state. Berlin preferred "negative liberty," because it emphasized the ability of free citizens to act in their own interests.[32] Although dichotomies such as Berlin's may seem to be of limited application in social work practice or, worse, to be a rationale for gutting essential social programs, it is worth noting that a primary ethical value in social work is client self-determination.

The obvious question raised by conservatives is, why tax at all? Beyond central functions of the state, conservatives contend that citizens should be allowed to retain earned income and use it as they see fit. The liberal rebuttal to this suggestion has been that unregulated capitalism inevitably skews the distribution of resources and opportunities, leaving subgroups vulnerable to insecurity with respect to income, employment, and health. The result, liberals have contended, is that specific populations suffer disproportionate and protracted poverty, thus providing the rationale for social programs. For more than a half century, they note, social insurance and public assistance programs have buffered low-income families from poverty.

Conservative ambitions in domestic policy are to reverse liberal dominance of government in the lives of citizens and allow them to do more for themselves. At best, the Right contends, government consumes tax revenues that could be otherwise used for personal purposes; at worst, social programs inflict not only acute damage on individuals but long-term harm on society as well. The inverse relationship between citizen autonomy and government social programs is at the heart of the conservative social policy strategy. By favoring autonomy, tax cuts provide individuals with discretionary income with which they can choose the services they desire. This is shrewd politics, as Jonathan Rauch noted, "by repudiating the Washington-knows-best legacy of the New Deal, Republicans will empower the people, and the people will empower Republicans." And the consequences for welfare liberalism are equally profound:

> If the Democrats dig in their heels and fall back on stale rants against greed, inequality, and privatization, so much the better. The voters will know whom to thank for empowering choices that Republicans intend to give them. As for which is the "party of nostalgia," the voters will also remember who defended, until the last dog died, single-payer Medicare, one-size-fits-all Social Security, schools without accountability, bureaucratic government monopolies, static economics, and Mutually Assured Destruction.[33]

The success of the antitax movement seems evident with the relatively wide support that the Bush tax cuts have received, even if they benefit the wealthy disproportionately. In this respect, voter support of tax cuts can be interpreted as a referendum on the welfare state; given the choice, rather than divert income to public programs through taxes, many voters prefer to keep their income for themselves.

Having seized on the strategy, the Right has been ruthless in its application. Movement conservatives, such as Grover Norquist, hoped to pass a new tax cut every year of George W. Bush's presidency.[34] Ultimately, conservatives intend to amplify the strategy through control of state and federal legislatures, eventually securing "an era of Republican dominance."[35] In all this, the second Bush administration had not only veered farther to the Right but had shown more organizational discipline in pursuing its objectives than even the avatar of contemporary conservatism, Ronald Reagan.[36]

Upward Mobility

If people kept more of their income instead of having it taxed to support social programs, would this be prudent public policy? Obviously, there are events that afflict individuals, communities, and societies that, being unexpected, warrant a governmental safety net; but, beyond such circumstances, can people be expected to act in their own best interests economically?

Recently, economists have approached these questions through examining the concept of "social mobility." Their research has raised profound questions about the embeddedness of poverty as well as the permanence of being poor. The policy issue is simple: To the extent that poor people of working age are upwardly mobile, the case for social programs is weakened. Brad Schiller, the author of a standard text on poverty and discrimination, examined the upward mobility of the poorest Americans and, in its absence, the intractability of the underclass. Using a national data set, Schiller examined the experience of young workers earning the minimum wage and their subsequent earnings, finding that one-third of minimum wage workers had received a raise within a year and that 60 percent were beyond the minimum wage within two years. Of those who entered the labor market in 1980, a recession year, only 15 percent continued earning the minimum wage after three years.[37] Furthermore,

> . . . the available perceptions of minimum-wage youth seem to dispel the notion that minimum-wage jobs offer low wages and nothing more. Over 85 percent of the minimum-wage entrants stated that they liked their jobs, and over 60 percent felt that they were earning skills that would be valuable in attaining better jobs. Only one out of eight minimum-wage youth perceived a total lack of on-the-job training—a condition compatible with the notion of "dead-end" jobs. Over half (56 percent) of the minimum-wage workers perceived opportunities for promotion with the same employer.[38]

Seven years after beginning a minimum wage job, the average worker had seen an increase in his or her wages of 154 percent, about 15 percent per year. Although non-minimum-wage job entrants were earning more, the minimum wage entrants had closed the gap significantly. Notably, Schiller concluded that race did not appear to retard the wage increases of youth. "The longitudinal experiences of minimum-wage youth . . . refute the notion of a 'minimum-wage trap,'" concluded Schiller. "Youth who started at the minimum wage in 1980 recorded impressive wage gains over the subsequent seven years both in absolute and relative terms."[39]

The upward mobility of low-wage workers thus parallels that of the general population. Daniel McMurer and Isabel Sawhill noted that upward mobility is more pronounced than data on a stagnating income distribution would suggest. Mobility in the United States is substantial, according to the evidence. Large portions of the population move into a new income quintile, with estimates ranging from about 25 to 40 percent in a single year. As one would expect, the mobility rate is even higher over longer periods—it averages about 45 percent over a 5-year period and about 60 percent over both 9-year and 17-year periods.[40]

Mobility is also pronounced among the poor. Reporting on data from the mid-1990s, the U.S. Census Bureau found that although 30.3 percent of Americans lived below the poverty line for at least two months during a three-year span, only 5.3 percent were poor continuously for two years. On average, families were below the poverty line for four and a half months.[41] Using data from the Panel Survey on Income Dynamics, W. Michael Cox and Richard Alm conclude that upward mobility, even of the poorest Americans, is striking:

> Only 5 percent of those in the bottom fifth in 1975 were still there in 1991. Where did they end up? A majority made it to the top three-fifths of the income distribution—middle class or better. But most amazing of all, almost 3 out of 10 of the low-income earners from 1975 had risen to the uppermost 20 percent by 1991. More than three-quarters found their way into the two highest tiers of income earners for at least one year by 1991.[42]

Family Income Mobility Over Three Decades

Quintile in 1979

Quintile in 1969	Top	Fourth	Middle	Second	Lowest
Top	49.1	23.7	13.2	9.0	5.0
Fourth	23.7	27.4	24.1	15.0	9.9
Middle	18.7	23.0	24.8	23.4	10.2
Second	7.7	16.2	25.2	27.8	23.2
Lowest	3.3	9.1	13.8	24.5	49.4

Quintile in 1989

Quintile in 1979	Top	Fourth	Middle	Second	Lowest
Top	50.9	26.1	13.4	5.4	4.2
Fourth	25.3	27.6	24.3	16.1	6.8
Middle	15.0	24.6	25.0	23.3	12.1
Second	7.6	15.8	23.8	31.5	21.3
Lowest	3.2	7.4	15.0	24.1	50.4

Quintile in 1998

Quintile in 1989	Top	Fourth	Middle	Second	Lowest
Top	53.2	23.2	14.9	5.7	3.0
Fourth	25.8	31.1	23.7	12.9	6.5
Middle	12.6	27.5	28.3	20.7	10.9
Second	4.3	11.0	22.6	36.3	25.7
Lowest	4.3	6.4	12.4	23.6	53.3

Source: Adapted from Lawrence Mishel, Jared Bernstein, and Sylvia Allegretto, *The State of Working America 2006–2007* (Washington, DC: Economic Policy Institute, 2007), p. 106.

On average, children tend to have higher income than their families of origin with those at the bottom of the income distribution doing better. Of all children, 67 percent have higher incomes than their parents' families; but that was true for only 43 percent of children in the top quintile, compared to 82 percent in the bottom quintile.[43] Despite increased income across generations, economic mobility slowed during the last quarter of the twentieth century.

During the last decades of the twentieth century a larger number of individuals in the top quintile remained in place as did those in the bottom quintile. Had the nation experienced more upward mobility economically, the opposite would have occurred: The percent of people in the top quintile would have dropped and those in the lowest quintile would have risen. Yet, the table also reveals an anomaly: Of those in the lowest quintile in 1969, 3.3 percent rose to the top quintile by the end of the decade, a figure that lagged a bit 10 years later and then increased to 4.3 percent in 1998.

An artifact of segregation, race adversely affects economic mobility. If economic mobility has stagnated for all families, the mobility of African American families has actually worsened (see Table 6 on the next page). While middle income status protects white families from downward, this does not occur with African American families. "Startlingly, almost half (45 percent) of black children whose parents were solidly middle class end up falling to the bottom of the income distribution compared to only 16 percent of white children." Over half of all African American children born to families in the bottom quintile (54 percent) stay there.[44]

The research on economic mobility suggests that if the American dream is to be valid for all, strategies are necessary to accelerate the upward mobility of low-income families. These not only include methods for augmenting earned income, such as the minimum wage, but also strategies for accruing assets, such as Individual Development Accounts. The 1995 Assets for Independence Act allocated $125 million over five years to encourage poor families to save for specific activities, yet the amount budgeted was miniscule compared to tax expenditures that favor wealthier families. Still, initiatives such as the SEED (Saving for Education, Entrepreneurship, and Downpayment) Initiative, which encourages low-income families to build assets, illustrate how the tax code can be an instrument of economic justice.[45]

Conclusion

Tax policy, often undervalued in discussions of social welfare, serves a vital function because it provides the revenues through which public programs operate. Increasing fluency in tax policy has significant benefits for advocates of social justice. At the national level, for example, introducing progressive features to the Social Security withholding tax, adjusting the tax rate for income, and lifting the cap on taxable income, would generate significant new

Table 6

Parents' Income of Children by Race

Percent of Children Living in Each Income Quintile		
Quintile	White	African American
Parents in top quintile, $81,200	23	*
Parents in fourth quintile, $65,100–$81,200	23	7**
Parents in middle quintile, $48,800–$65,100	22	8
Parents in second quintile, $33,800–48,800	19	23
Parents in lowest quintile, $0–$33,800	13	62

*Too few observations to report entry.
**Treat data with caution due to small sample size.

Source: Julia Isaacs, *Economic Mobility of Black and White Families* (Washington, DC: Brookings Institution, 2007), p. 4.

revenues that could make minimal Social Security benefits more adequate. This could serve a strategic purpose, as well, by providing a counterpoint to conservative contentions that Social Security should be privatized.

Leveraging tax policy to advance social justice requires sophistication in social policy, however. Historically, two streams of poverty policy have evolved in the United States. The first—public welfare—was legislated through the Social Security Act of 1935 and consists of TANF, SSI, Medicaid, Food Stamps, and the like. Much of public welfare is managed by HHS and parallel agencies at the state level. The second—Bootstrap Capitalism[46]—was enacted through the 1975 Earned Income Tax Credit and consists of an array of tax credits for individuals as well as businesses. Bootstrap Capitalism is operated by the Treasury Department and the Federal Reserve System. By understanding poverty policy exclusively through the public welfare paradigm, human service professionals omit from the realm of possibility a set of policy options that have enormous promise. Thus, if social welfare professionals are to enhance their role in the domestic policy debate, they will have to master the financial, procedural, and accounting nuances of tax policy. These are daunting fields, to be sure, but the potential payoff makes the effort worthwhile.

Discussion Questions

1. Click on the "Student Section" link of the policyAmerica website (http://capwiz.com/policyamerica/index.html) and explore tax cuts that have passed during the Bush administration. Who have they benefited? Who has been disadvantaged? What changes in tax policy could advance economic justice?

2. Why has Harry Hopkins's political calculus, "Tax, tax, spend, spend, elect, elect!" lost its political currency in more recent times?

3. Should the federal government expand its spending on social programs despite the large and ongoing federal debt? What are the effects of increased spending, and what are the effects of stable or even decreasing spending, on social programs?

4. What are the positive and negative effects of increasing corporate taxation? How would it affect the poor in both the short term and the long term?

5. Should nonprofit human service corporations be required to pay taxes just as for-profit firms do? What would be the possible consequences of restructuring the tax code to mandate that nonprofits lose their nonprofit tax status?

6. Should the altruism of Americans be rewarded by tax codes that permit charitable contributions, cash as well as in-kind, to be deducted from

taxes? Do the long-term effects of this tax deduction encourage or discourage real altruism?

7. Some welfare advocates concerned with income inequality argue that the function of the welfare state is to equalize incomes and assets through social welfare programs. Others believe it is unrealistic to expect that welfare state programs can do more than alleviate human suffering by providing resources to those in need. Should the goal of social welfare programs be to reduce income and asset inequality, or should that function be relegated to tax and labor policy?

8. Has the social work profession been successful in lobbying efforts and in promoting a more just society? If not, why? What strategies should social workers employ to move society toward more equitable income and asset redistribution?

Notes

1. Paul Krugman, "Duped and Betrayed," *New York Times* (July 6, 2003), p. A31.

2. Paul Krugman, "The Tax-Cut Zombies," *New York Times* (December 23, 2005), p. A27.

3. Charles Murray, "A Plan to Replace the Welfare State," *Focus* 24, 2 (Spring–Summer 2006), p. 2.

4. Thomas Dye, *Understanding Public Policy*, 9th ed. (Upper Saddle River, NJ: Prentice Hall, 1998), pp. 242–243.

5. That part of the withholding tax dedicated to Medicare Health Insurance is levied on all income, though that for Social Security has a cap on taxable income. Committee on Ways and Means, *Overview of Entitlement Programs* (Washington, DC: U.S. GPO, 1998), p. 58.

6. Committee on Ways and Means, *Overview of Entitlement Programs* (Washington, DC: U.S. GPO, 2004), pp. 13–36.

7. Reynolds Farley, *The New American Reality* (New York: Russell Sage Foundation, 1996), p. 85.

8. *The Economic and Budget Outlook: Fiscal Years, 1991–1995* (Washington, DC: CBO, 1990), pp. 112, 122.

9. Bob Woodward, *The Agenda* (New York: Simon & Schuster, 1994), p. 165.

10. Jonathan Weisman, "Congress Votes to Extend Tax Cuts," *Washington Post* (September 24, 2004), p. A7.

11. Lori Montgomery and Nell Henderson, "Burden Set to Shift on Balanced Budget," *Washington Post* (January 16, 2007), p. A1.

12. Jeff Madrick, "The Iraqi Time Bomb," *New York Times Magazine* (April 6, 2003), p. 50.

13. "The Bottom Line: Today's Fiscal Policy Remains Unsustainable" (Washington, DC: Government Accountability Office, September 2006).

14. Committee on Ways and Means, *Overview of Entitlement Programs* (Washington, DC: U.S. GPO, 2004), pp. 13-4–13-5.

15. "Key Findings Center on Philanthropy Study" (Indianapolis, IN: Center on Philanthropy, 2005), pp. 6–7.

16. Alan Abramson, Lester Salamon, and C. Eugene Steuerle, "The Nonprofit Sector and the Federal Budget," in Elizabeth Boris and C. Eugene Steuerle (eds.), *Nonprofits and Government* (Washington, DC: Urban Institute, 1999), p. 122.

17. David Kamin, "New CBO Study Finds That Estate Tax Repeal Would Substantially Reduce Charitable Giving," (Washington, DC: Center on Budget and Policy Priorities, 2004), p. 1.

18. Aviva Aron-Dine and Isaac Shapiro, "New Data Show Extraordinary Jump in Income Concentration in 2004" (Washington, DC: Center on Budget and Policy Priorities, 2007), p. 3.

19. Emmanuel Saez, "Striking It Richer," *Pathways* (Winter 2008), p. 7.

20. Lawrence Mishel, Jared Bernstein, and Sylvia Allegretto, *The State of Working America, 2006–2007* (Washington, DC: Economic Policy Insitute, 2007), pp. 163–164.

21. Thomas Shapiro and Edward Wolff (eds.), *Assets for the Poor* (New York: Russell Sage Foundation, 2001).

22. Rakesh Kochhar, "The Wealth of Hispanic Households: 1996–2002" (Washington, DC: Pew Hispanic Center, 2004), p. 5.

23. Asena Caner and Edward Wolff, "Asset Poverty in the United States," *Public Policy Brief* 76A (Annandale-on-Hudson, New York: Jerome Levy Economics Institute, 2004), p. 4.

24. Ray Boshara (ed.), *Building Assets* (Washington, DC: Corporation for Enterprise Development, 2001), p. 2008.

25. Katherin Phillips, "Who Knows about the Earned Income Tax Credit?" (Washington, DC: Urban Institute, January 2001).

26. Paul Wilson and Robert Cline, "State Welfare Reform: Integrating Tax Credits and Income Transfers." Paper presented at the 1994 National Tax Symposium, Washington, DC, May 24, 1994.

27. David Stoesz and David Saunders, "Welfare Capitalism," *Social Service Review* (September 1999).

28. Martha Ozawa and Baeg-Eui Hong, "The Effects of EITC and Children';s Allowances on the Economic

Well-Being of Children," *Social Work* 27, no. 3 (September 2003), p. 171.

29. Robert Cherry and Max Sawicky, "Giving Tax Credit Where Credit Is Due," (Washington, DC: Economic Policy Institute, n.d.).

30. Jared Diamond, *Guns, Germs, and Steel* (New York: Norton, 1997), p. 276.

31. Michael Tanner, "Ending Welfare as We Know It" (Washington, DC: Cato Institute, 1994), p. 24.

32. Michael Ignatieff, *Isaiah Berlin* (New York: Henry Holt, 1998), pp. 202–203.

33. Jonathan Rauch, "The Accidental Radical," *The National Journal* 35, no. 30 (July 26, 2003).

34. Dana Milbank and Dan Balz, "GOP Eyes Tax Cuts as Annual Events," *Washington Post* (May 11, 2003), A1.

35. Adam Clymer, "Buoyed by Resurgence, G.O.P. Strives for an Era of Dominance," *New York Times* (May 25, 2003), p. A1.

36. Bill Keller, "Reagan's Son," *New York Times Magazine* (January 26, 2003).

37. Bradley Schiller, "Moving Up: The Training and Wage Gains of Minimum-Wage Entrants," *Social Science Quarterly* 75, no. 3 (September 1994), p. 629.

38. Ibid., p. 627.

39. Ibid., p. 634.

40. Daniel McMurer and Isabel Sawhill, *Getting Ahead* (Washington, DC: Urban Institute, 1998), p. 33.

41. "Poverty Short-Lived for Most, Study Finds," *Richmond Times Dispatch* (August 10, 1998), p. A3.

42. W. Michael Cox and Richard Alm, *Myths of Rich and Poor* (New York: Basic Books, 1999), p. 73.

43. "Economic Mobility of Families across Generations," (Washington, DC: Brookings Institution, 2007), p. 3.

44. Julia Isaacs, "Economic Mobility of Black and White Families" (Washington, DC: Brookings Institution, 2007), p. 2.

45. "Banking on SEED: Lessons from Financial Institutions in the SEED Initiative" (Washington, DC: Corporation for Enterprise Development, 2007).

46. David Stoesz, "Bootstrap Capitalism," *Families in Society*, 88, 3 (July–September 2007), pp. 375–379.

Social Security and Public Welfare

Core Competencies in this Chapter (Check marks indicate which competencies are covered in depth)				
Professional Identity	Ethical Practice	Critical Thinking	Diversity in Practice	Human Rights & Justice
✓ Research-Based Practice	Human Behavior	Policy Practice	✓ Practice Contexts	✓ Engage, Assess, Intervene, Evaluate

From Chapter 12 of *Introduction to Social Work*, Twelfth Edition. O. William Farley, Larry Lorenzo Smith, Scott W. Boyle.

Practice Contexts

Critical Thinking Question: How can a single mother with two children benefit from TANF?

A 26-year-old mother of two little children was alone when she arrived in New York City. When she couldn't find work, she applied for welfare assistance and was enrolled in Temporary Assistance for Needy Families (TANF). She soon opted for "self-sufficiency" training under TANF guidelines. The "self-sufficiency" worker at the agency steered her into a program where she could learn a skill. She chose a computer operation program at the local technical college. Her TANF allowance and food stamps met her basic needs, and the TANF worker helped her apply for subsidized housing.

At the end of her two-year program, she graduated with honors and found work with a large company. As her financial situation improved, she was allowed to remain in subsidized housing, and she continued to receive limited assistance until she became totally self-sufficient. By the end of the third year, she was able to provide for herself and her two little children without any further help from TANF.[1]

***

What is public welfare? Public welfare means different things to differ- ent people, and what it means depends somewhat on who these people are and through what lens they view the picture.

What is public welfare? Public welfare means different things to different peo- ple, and what it means depends somewhat on who these people are and through what lens they view the picture.

To some, public welfare is the "garbage heap" for human wreckage—the idle, the shiftless, the unemployable, the sick and decrepit, the transient, loafers, malingerers, beggars, and certain ne'er-do-wells. In the minds of many, public welfare is income, medical and dental care, and commodities: support to those who are widowed, blind, or disabled; dependent children with dis- abilities; and people who are sick and unable to cope without help in a com- plex, ever-changing society.

Individuals see public welfare in different ways. Most see public welfare as a collection of distinct agencies where each agency operates independently. Others see public welfare as a single entity where the individual parts serve the whole.[2]

Public welfare includes income and health maintenance programs for indi- viduals who are aging, blind, or disabled; aid to families for care of dependent children; medical care to low-income and older persons; and various social rehabilitation services to eligible children, families, and single adults.

GOVERNMENT'S RESPONSIBILITY FOR WELFARE

Basic responsibility of government for welfare was established in England with the Elizabethan Poor Laws, and relief under the provisions of those laws was a local matter, limited to specialized kinds of need and extending only to those whose claims of settlement could not be disputed legally.

Residual elements of relief in kind, means test approaches, public respon- sibility for only certain kinds of need, work and residence requirements, and characteristics of colonial relief still are found in various services and assis- tance provisions, particularly at the state and local levels of government. Although many of these measures are repressive and intended to discourage their use, remember that they do, nevertheless, affirm the principle of govern- mental responsibility.

The *federal* government's responsibility for welfare started in the earliest days of the republic when in 1785 Congress made grants of public lands to states for schools. Other responsibilities were extended when the people, through their elected representatives, added other agencies such as the Federal Office of Education, the Children's Bureau, and the Vocational Rehabilitation Administration; but a comprehensive plan for the protection of citizens against income risks did not become an *enduring* principle of federal responsibility for welfare until 1935 with the passage of the Social Security Act. Reinforcement of this principle has been a clear result of the many amendments to the act legislated by Congress.

The Department of Health, Education, and Welfare (HEW), created in 1953 with cabinet status, is an outgrowth of a widely held view that the federal government has a responsibility for the *general welfare.* In 1980, HEW was divided into two cabinet-level departments: the Department of Education and the Department of Health and Human Services.

The federal government now assumes responsibility to insure virtually all American workers and their families against the loss of income from retirement and disability. Survivors of insured workers also are protected. Risks to employed workers from unemployment for a specified period of time are assumed as a federal–state responsibility. A system is yet to be developed to protect workers for long periods of unemployment and various work stoppages.

An expanded health care system, the "largest human service system" in the history of the United States, further affirms the role of government as an instrument of social policy. Medical care under Social Security protects retired workers, their families, and certain persons with disabilities. A comprehensive national health plan has not been adopted but has been widely debated in congressional committees. The Clinton administration proposed a health care reform plan in 1993, but the plan was defeated by Congress a year later.

The federal government assumes financial responsibility for persons who are aging, blind, and disabled under the Supplemental Security Income (SSI) program, and in cooperation with the states, the federal government also extends protection to families covered under the Aid to Families with Dependent Children (AFDC) program and to other citizens who qualify for assistance under other provisions of the Social Security Act as a statutory right, including medical care to indigent recipients of public assistance (Medicaid), and to older persons whose income is too low to provide this care.

With the presidency of Ronald Reagan, there was a shift in the thinking about government's responsibility for welfare. It is sometimes asked, will the thinking of former President Reagan become a trend, implemented in policy and a new approach to welfare, or will the people and Congress resist more than cosmetic changes? This trend continued into the Bush presidency with even more emphasis placed on self-sufficiency programs. During the Obama presidency, welfare reform again became a national priority although change has been slow. Much of the national debate centered on the role federal and state government should play in welfare programs and the viability of self-sufficiency programs versus more traditional welfare assistance.

President Ronald Reagan's Ideology

Ronald Reagan "redrew the ideological landscape." His political and fiscal philosophy and his views on the role of government were in sharp contrast to Franklin Roosevelt's *New Deal* and Lyndon Johnson's *Great Society.*

As governor of California and as president, Reagan preached a limited role for government—it should do only what people could not do for themselves. He argued for fewer, not more, government regulations and for citizens to have greater freedom in the management of their lives and their money. He slashed taxes and urged the paring back of government programs, including those for poor and disadvantaged people, insisting that these should remain at the state and local levels. Reagan believed that people should get help when needed from families, neighborhoods, and local charitable, religious, and governmental entities and that power concentrated in Washington made serious inroads on individual freedom.

Reagan's philosophy impacted social legislation and continues to be debated in the halls of Congress. The jury, however, is still out and what to do about health and welfare is hotly debated. That these issues and problems are at the front of national concern where policy decisions are made is very much in the country's interest. It is hoped that individuals who are poor, disadvantaged, homeless, and ill will be served by governmental and nongovernmental agencies seeking solutions to these most difficult social problems.

THE SOCIAL SECURITY ACT

Research-Based Practice

Critical Thinking Question: Why was the Social Security Act such an important piece of legislation?

The cornerstone of public welfare in the United States is the Social Security Act, passed August 14, 1935.

In general, this act, with its many amendments, is the chief means by which government at the local, state, and national levels provides income security to citizens.

Discussion in this chapter centers on provisions under old age, survivors, disability, and health insurance (OASDHI); unemployment compensation; old-age assistance; AFDC; aid to blind persons; aid to disabled persons; and social services.

Old Age, Survivors, Disability, and Health Insurance

The national OASDHI, popularly referred to as Social Security and administered by the federal government, is the largest and most important of the income and health insurance programs in the United States. Cash benefits from this program are designed to partially replace income lost when a worker retires or becomes disabled. Cash benefits also are paid to survivors of "insured" workers.

The program also provides partial health care benefits for old age and disability under Medicare. Amendments to the Social Security Act in 1965 set up a contributory health insurance plan for nearly all people aged 65 and over: a compulsory program of hospital insurance (HI) and a voluntary supplementary medical insurance (SMI) to pay for health services. Other amendments also extended coverage to certain severely disabled persons under age 65, including disabled workers, disabled widows and widowers, and childhood disability beneficiaries.

Since its inception, Social Security has extended its benefits so OASDHI coverage approaches universal dimensions.

OASDHI is a contributory system. It is not to be confused with insurance in the private sector; it is *social* insurance. Payments to beneficiaries are based on previous earnings; equity can be claimed for the system. Beneficiaries of OASDHI are not subject to investigation or a test of means to establish eligibility. They do not have to prove they are poor to receive benefits. Records are maintained accurately and "claims" are processed and paid with technological efficiency. The system's administration is handled efficiently and is nonjudgmental. Other retirement income and income derived from interest on savings, stocks, and bonds, rental property, and annuities—regardless of the amount—do not limit payments. On the other hand, limits *are* placed on the amount of income retired workers can earn from employment while receiving Social Security payments.[3] To understand this constraint, it may be helpful to recall that the Social Security Act was passed in 1935 when the country was experiencing the Great Depression. Many workers were unemployed. Retirement was written into the law to encourage workers aged 65 and older to retire to make way on the labor market for younger, unemployed men and women. In times of high employment or labor shortage, the act might well have to be changed to induce workers not to retire but to continue in the labor force. Incentives for workers to continue employment now exist without losing payment benefits.

Taxes, under the provision of the Federal Insurance Contribution Act (FICA), are collected from the employee and employer during the productive working life of the worker to pay for OASDHI. Self-employed workers pay the full amount of the tax. In 1935, the tax was 1 percent each for the employee and the employer on an income base of $3,000 per year. In 2009, the tax base has been raised to $106,800.

In adopting OASDHI, the United States radically departed from reliance on the family, the church, private philanthropy, local government, and unending emergency measures to provide a bulwark against want and income need. Many believe that such a departure was warranted and that, for retired and disabled workers and survivors of insured workers, OASDHI offers greater security and financial independence than they previously knew. Five and one-half million persons were receiving Social Security in 1953.

At the end of August 1991, a total of $22 billion in monthly cash benefits was paid to 40,307,337 beneficiaries. Sixty-two percent of all OASDHI beneficiaries were retired workers. Disabled worker beneficiaries numbered 3,124,129. These numbers are continuing to increase in the twenty-first century.

The concern raised about financing Social Security has to do with Medicare, not retirement and survivors' insurance. Authorities appear to be somewhat agreed that we can count on OASDHI being paid until 2020. To provide this assurance, the tax on earnings has been increased on an income base of $106,800 in 2009 with provisions for further increases in the years ahead.

The spiraling costs of medical care pose a threat to the solvency of the system. This problem is being addressed, and we can be assured that steps will be taken such as caps on what the system will pay for medical procedures, limits the system will pay hospitals, higher costs to consumers in premiums, or some universal system of health care for everyone. Beginning in 1992, the base income taxed for Medicare had risen to $130,000. This is 1.45 percent for employers and employees each, and 2.9 percent for self-employed people.

When Social Security was enacted, only workers in commerce and industry were covered. Since then, major changes have been legislated, and today, about 95 percent of the jobs in this country are covered. Medicare was expanded in 1972. The Medicare Catastrophic Coverage Act of 1988 is an example of government wanting to further reduce the financial risk on the elderly for prolonged health care and costly medical procedures; however, the major provisions of the act were repealed in 1989. The elderly themselves objected to the increase in their income taxes and lobbied Congress to repeal the legislation.

Under the provisions of this act, taxes on income of the nation's elderly would have paid for medical care. Some argued that the tax was fair, and that those receiving the benefits should pay for them. Others argued against it, using the logic that the elderly, who don't go to school, are nevertheless taxed to help pay the cost of educating youth. There seems to be a growing consensus that the costs of common human needs should be equitably shared and socially distributed. Additional expansion covering the health care field can be reasonably predicted in the years ahead.

In times of recession and high unemployment, the number of workers paying into Social Security is decreased, thus reducing the money available to pay beneficiaries. Also, inflation forces upward adjustments of payments, making heavier demands on the Social Security tax. The decline in the birth rate, not a major concern in the 1980s, may become so in the years ahead when the retired population will be disproportionately large compared to the younger working population.

An alternative to government management would be to privatize the system in part or in full. Many believe that this would provide more generous retirement and cut back on the burden to the taxpayer. One objection to this approach is that those most likely to benefit would be the younger, more affluent, who also would not be contributing to the less affluent.

Basically, the system is a pay-as-you-go arrangement. Wage earners are taxed to pay benefits to retired and disabled workers and their dependents. Resistance to the system might be expected as taxes increase causing paychecks to shrink. Also, an increasing number of workers believe that the private sector can offer greater benefits than Social Security. Some experts are even suggesting that wage earners should be able to invest and manage their own Social Security taxes in various brokerage and financial accounts. Although this is undoubtedly true for some workers, for the vast majority of the population, Social Security offers more income security for retired and disabled workers and their survivors. Social Security is a form of *social* insurance and a reasonably well-accepted mechanism for sharing costs and transferring income.

Congress appears unwilling to make the changes in Social Security that many believe necessary for the system to continue to be viable well into this century. Scholars and analysts agree that the demographics of today are different from when the system was enacted and that the world for which it was designed no longer exists. For example, in 1950, there were sixteen workers paying taxes for every retiree. In 1995, only three taxpayers support each retiree. By 2030, two workers will support each person receiving benefits. Taxes on workers have increased from 3 percent on $3,000 in 1950 to 12.4 percent for workers and employers on $61,200 in 1995. As we move into the year 2011, it is estimated that for the system to remain solvent, taxes will have to be raised to 17 or 18 percent, a figure that appears to be detrimental to continued economic growth.

Most scholars and economists agree that changes can and should be made. For example:

1. An increase in the age of retirees to reflect the changes in demographics; men and women are living years longer.

2. The formula used today to increase benefits based on cost-of-living index should be more in line with private pensions.

3. Retirees independently wealthy and those with large incomes would receive less Social Security, if any.

4. Raise taxes.

5. A combination of the above and possibly other changes as well.

Social work basically supports Social Security as a method of income transfer. It approaches universality in application. It is nondeterrent. It is a contributory system that makes it more acceptable to recipients as it is compatible with the ethic of "working for what you get." It is *social* as distinguished from regular insurance, suggesting a role of government in the welfare domain. Some central system of income maintenance for the retired and disabled workers and their survivors is essential.

Unemployment Insurance

OASDHI and unemployment insurance are the two insurance provisions of the Social Security Act. Unemployment insurance cushions workers whose income is interrupted by work stoppages and layoffs. Most states will pay unemployment compensation for a maximum of twenty-six weeks. In 1970, extended benefits became a "temporary" measure of a federal–state program for workers who had exhausted their entitlements in periods of high unemployment. The extended benefit provided for a 50 percent increase in benefit duration up to a maximum of thirteen weeks or a total of thirty-nine weeks of regular and extended benefits. Extensions of benefit periods were approved by Congress in 1974 and again in 1975. Extended benefits, in times of recession or periods of high rates of unemployment, may be "triggered" by the states or by the federal government up to an additional thirteen weeks, or for as many as two extended periods of thirteen weeks each. The maximum for which any insured worker has been covered is sixty-five weeks.

Unemployment insurance is no protection of income against strikes or long periods of unemployment resulting from economic recession and depression. The American system makes no income provisions for prolonged unemployment except to a few workers who can qualify for AFDC or residual general assistance.

Unemployment compensation is a *nondeterrent*[4] *insurance* rather than a public assistance program. To be eligible to receive this compensation, in most states a person must

1. demonstrate attachment to the labor force by a specified amount of recent work in covered employment;

2. be ready, able, and willing to work;

3. be registered for work in a public employment office and file a claim for benefits;

4. not be disqualified for benefits by some act that would indicate he or she was responsible for his or her unemployment;

5. demonstrate that unemployment is due to a lack of work for which the employee is qualified;

6. not be unemployed because of a labor dispute or refusal to accept suitable employment.

Unemployment insurance is financed almost completely by a tax on employers. The employer pays the tax but to show a profit may pass this tax on to the consumer in higher costs of goods and services, or on to the employee in lower wages, or both. Workers, as consumers, also pay for unemployment insurance in higher costs of consumer goods and services. Extended benefits, those paid to workers beyond the period provided in their state plans, are financed equally by federal and state funds.

Public Assistance

Public assistance is an income-maintenance system that should not be confused with the insurance provisions of the Social Security Act. Four main categories of clients are classified under this system: aged, blind, disabled, and families of dependent children.

Supplemental Security Income

Under the SSI program, the federal government pays monthly checks to people in need at 65 years of age and older and to the blind and disabled at any age. People who qualify for these payments are those who have little or no regular cash income, who own little, if any, property, or who have little cash or few assets that can be turned into cash, such as stocks and bonds, jewelry, or other valuables.

Payments under SSI, managed by the Social Security Administration, are based on the recipient's assets and income. States have the option of supplementing the payments. Financed from general revenues, not from Social Security contributions, SSI is not a contributory system; that is, no payments have been previously made by the recipient or the recipient's employer. Benefits are not presumed to have been "earned."

AID TO FAMILIES WITH DEPENDENT CHILDREN

Engage, Assess, Intervene, Evaluate

Critical Thinking Question: What were some of the requirements that families needed to meet to qualify for AFDC?

Income through AFDC is available to those who qualify under provisions of the Social Security Act.

For example, AFDC families must satisfy such requirements as:

1. The child must be under 18 years of age (21 if attending school or training full time).
2. The family must reside in the United States and be citizens or otherwise permanently residing here under legal provisions.
3. No limits are placed on ownership of a home occupied by the family. Other personal and real property is limited to a net value of some specified amount.

AFDC is the most controversial of the welfare programs and is the concern of economists as well as politicians. It is a program that needs strong advocates, for the children involved are unable to speak for themselves. But at the rate it is growing, it is clear that some changes need to be made.

In the year 2000, some 7.2 million Americans were on AFDC, down 6.3 million from a high of 13.5 million in 1992. Sixty percent of poor families with children are headed by women. The amount of money the recipients receive varies by states. In addition to AFDC grants, recipients also receive food stamps and Medicaid, which may bring their total income higher than those who are working in low-paying jobs.

A major overhaul of the AFDC system was made in 1988 with the Family Support Act, which sought to modify the handling of grants. These new options are a step in the right direction. However, changes do not come quickly, and some of these need more time and study.

Highlights of the reform are as follows:

1. Beginning in January 1994, states are required to withhold court-ordered child-support payments.

2. States are required to meet federal standards in establishing paternity.

3. States are mandated to establish a Job Opportunities and Basic Skills (JOBS) program to provide education, training, and employment, with the objective of helping people leave the welfare rolls.

4. Most adult clients will be enrolled in JOBS, with exemptions for parents with children under the age of 3.

5. Child care, transportation, and work expenses will be provided, and wage rates will be not less than minimum rates.

6. Beginning in 1994, an unemployed parent will be required to work a minimum of sixteen hours per week.

Although these work incentives sound good, there has not been a rush to enroll in JOBS. This program depends on state funds, and some states have not fully implemented the plan because of budget problems. Also, the definition for "exemptions," "participation," and "able-bodied" are so imprecise that those who do not want to be a part of the program can easily find a way to circumvent it.

With the enormous financial drain on federal and state budgets, and the wasting of the young men and women in our country, there is clearly a need to replace or reform the welfare system. Politicians, economists, and other leaders suggest solutions to this problem. Some of their suggestions include the following:

1. All able-bodied recipients are to be off the AFDC rolls after two years. They will be provided with child care, medical care, and job training while on the rolls.

2. To able-bodied recipients, 25 percent of the aid will be cut after six months.

3. No additional money will be given for any babies born while the mother is receiving AFDC.

4. Recipients are required to work toward self-sufficiency while receiving benefits.

5. Stricter discipline will be set for those receiving aid: parents must be in training and children in school.

6. Public-works-type jobs will be available for those able to work.

President Obama has promised change. Among the changes proposed for AFDC were several of the previously mentioned and others: work requirements for the able-bodied, training and education for high-tech jobs, and public works for the homeless and those who may not be trainable.

In their Contract with America, the House Republicans stated that their goal by 2003 was to have half the adults on AFDC—91 percent of whom are women—in the workforce, working a minimum of thirty-five hours per week.

Although all the suggested solutions sound feasible, they do not take into account the reality of the situation of welfare clients. The reason that many AFDC parents cannot be put to work and taken off welfare rolls is that they are not employable. They lack education and aptitude. Two-thirds of recipients on the rolls for two years or more have not graduated from high school; their reading and math skills are so low that they cannot solve even basic problems. A majority have no work experience and no work ethic. Because of low self-esteem, many become depressed. One-third of AFDC mothers are disabled or have a disabled child. A large number of welfare mothers are in an abusive relationship with a spouse or boyfriend. Many of them refuse to leave their children in day care because they fear the children will be abused.

A Health and Human Services study in 1994 found that 16 percent of welfare mothers have substance abuse problems that require treatment before they can succeed in the job market.

With more unwed teenage mothers keeping their babies, the welfare rolls continue to rise. The Contract with America would not provide money or housing for mothers under age 18 if they had children out of wedlock. Yet, often the parental home of the mother is unsuitable for the teenager and the baby. Teens, often without schooling or marketable skills and without family support, develop welfare dependency as a way of life. Special programs for them are indicated if the cycle of pregnancy and dependency on AFDC is to be broken.

The Family Support Act sets up the JOBS program, which provides training for a place in the workforce. This, with various state-operated job club opportunities, is producing some results. It is possible to make some improvements. Some governors are asking for more leeway in administering the funds, stressing that social workers can deal more effectively at the state and local levels rather than at the federal level. They can work with individuals in job training and education to make the clients become employable. Programs in some states and communities show progress, but it is slow.

It is a challenge to planners to find ways for single mothers to climb out of poverty so that they and their children have sufficient means to live a decent life.[5]

The perfect solution has not yet been found, and there is not just one answer to this overwhelming problem. However, pilot programs in small areas both in inner-city ghettos and in middle-class communities have provided new insights into what works and what does not. People become dependent on welfare for many reasons, and they resist giving up the security of a regular paycheck to an unknown job where performance is a determining factor as to whether the money will continue to arrive.

Welfare Reform (TANF)

In 1996, President Clinton signed the Personal Responsibility and Work Opportunity Reconciliation Act that created the program commonly referred to as TANF. This new act replaced the former AFDC program that assisted children and families. This legislation ushered in dramatic changes to the nation's public welfare system. These changes included the loss of individual entitlement and the elimination of the economic safety net for children and their families. The act provided assistance to families in need with children by promoting job preparation, work, and marriage. States were required to develop programs to prevent out-of-wedlock pregnancies and encourage the formation of two-parent families. Adults in families receiving assistance were required to participate in work activities after receiving assistance for twenty-four months.

No state has embraced work and self-sufficiency programs more than the state of Wisconsin where the number of welfare recipients has been slashed by 85 percent since 1987. The state's approach has been simple—if you don't work, you don't get assistance. On April 1, 1998, Wisconsin became the first state to eliminate the old public welfare system that paid poor families to stay home. Instead, every adult able to work will be cut off welfare if he or she doesn't work. Only single mothers with children under 12 weeks will be given a reprieve. Other states will be implementing similar plans, although most are two to four years behind Wisconsin. Will work and self-sufficiency programs succeed in Wisconsin?[6] After twelve years of incorporating the TANF program, the state of Wisconsin has reported favorable outcomes.

On April 10, 1999, President Clinton announced that welfare caseloads made up of families with children on welfare had dropped by 50 percent or more in twenty-nine states and by about half nationwide.[7] This decline in welfare caseloads has permitted many states to reevaluate their welfare policies. States such as California and New York have rethought their long-term strategies and made some interesting changes.

In California, for example, working welfare recipients are now allowed to keep a larger portion of their welfare benefits as their earnings increase. This was necessary because the state offers relatively high welfare benefits to begin with and a higher adjustment was needed to increase participation in the program. The California experience with welfare reform also suggests that during a downturn in the economy the federal time limit for receiving welfare payments should be extended from twenty-four months to as many as sixty months.

It is also clear that welfare reform works best when states expand their employment and job training opportunities for welfare recipients. California and New York are now refocusing their long-term welfare plans and identifying those welfare recipients who have the greatest employment barriers. Once they are identified, employment and job training opportunities and programs are implemented to make them economically self-sufficient.

In 1996, President Clinton signed the Personal Responsibility and Work Opportunity Reconciliation Act that created the program commonly referred to as TANF.

Poverty

Poverty continues to be a reality for many Americans. It has been reported that poverty rates in this country reached a seventeen-year high in the recession year of 1982, and the Census Bureau reported increasing numbers of people below the poverty line even in 2010. Income maintenance systems and such programs as work relief, food stamps, school lunches, and Medicaid haven't done the job. The rolls of poverty have not been reduced and there is no end in sight.

Many taxpayers are convinced that the system is ineffective and should be dismantled. Some say it provides too many disincentives, and that it favors those who don't work over those who can't. It is criticized because it is fragmented into a patchwork of overlapping out-of-control programs. While recognizing the cost to the country in a loss of productivity (people have little or no incentive to work because of the alternative—unemployment compensation, food stamps, etc.), some still believe the gains of the "welfare state" offset its losses.

Americans who address themselves seriously to the problems of poverty seem to agree on one thing: There are no easy victories where poverty and need are concerned. Perhaps offering as much hope as anything are those efforts that (1) recognize the existence of a problem of major proportions; (2) attempt to mobilize the talents of interested, capable men and women to work on the problem; and (3) recognize that a concerted, consistent, and independent pressure must be maintained to deal with the problems of poverty and material deprivation. Social work is one of the professions that, because of its value system, knowledge base, and methodology, helps find solutions to these serious problems. Increasingly, social work expects to provide some of the answers—both ameliorative and preventive—to problems resulting from poverty and economic deprivation.

The efforts and resources of the total community will have to be mobilized to make inroads on this problem. If the Great Society of the Lyndon Johnson administration proved anything, it was that resources alone will not do the job. Leadership is needed. Commitment and dedication are needed. Teamwork involving the sustained and united efforts of society's major institutions—political, educational, industrial, professional, governmental, and religious—is the best hope for the prevention and "cure" of poverty.

Women in Poverty

In 2010, the number of persons living in poverty reached the highest level in this country since 1982. Although the economic recession of the early 1980s has pushed more working adults in general into poverty, the number of poor female-headed families has risen more rapidly than other segments of the poor. Since the late 1960s, as the number of births to unmarried women and the divorce and separation rates have increased, the number of female-headed families has grown tremendously, and the rate of increase is greater for blacks than it is for whites. The number of female-headed families has more than doubled since 1970, and their proportion within the poverty population has also increased. Although more single mothers are entering the labor force, their earnings are far lower than those of single males. The substantial income gap between female-headed families and husband–wife families is greater than it was in 1960. The plight of female-headed families among the working poor, therefore, must be a major focus of national concern.[8]

Women who find themselves single after marriage—whether through death of a husband or through divorce—learn that being the "head of a household" brings with it a set of special problems. If there are children still living at home, problems are compounded. In addition to the distress, loneliness, sense of loss, and often a loss of self-esteem, there are other problems such as facing financial obligations.

A woman who has been emotionally and financially dependent on a husband may be unable to cope with the heavy load of responsibility. Widows in their 40s or 50s are too young for Social Security and may be left with mortgages, medical bills, and limited savings. Divorcees face similar circumstances and are often displaced from their homes and find that the courts have awarded inadequate child support payments and limited, often temporary, alimony. Divorce almost always has the greatest impact on women because it causes a bigger change in their lives than in the lives of the men involved. Women most often are given custody of the children, and although this attachment is satisfying, it also adds problems. These women must get jobs, but many do not have marketable skills or requisite knowledge.

As more and more women work in business, industry, and the professions and early in life become career-oriented, this will be less of a problem. But for the millions of women who face this problem now, it can be overwhelming. They need time to deal with their loss because until they come to grips with personal problems, they cannot cope with a job. Usually, an employer will recognize the applicant who is not in control and will not trust her to perform. Mothers have to deal not only with their own personal problems but also with the anxiety expressed by their children. Time, patience, and understanding are required.

Responding to the needs of these women, displaced homemaker centers are in operation in virtually every city. Here women, often with the help of social workers, are able to become independent. Through individual and group counseling, they work through their grief and sense of loss to find their true identity and to define their values. Through guidance, women learn to assess their potential and find self-confidence and self-worth.

Displaced homemaker services, operating under a variety of names, are sometimes associated with colleges and universities. Others are independently operated or are under city, county, or state support. They offer women help in becoming independent and give them an opportunity to discuss their problems and vent their anger and feelings of hopelessness. They also act as referral agencies to those who need immediate psychological, financial, or legal advice. Often they are staffed with single women who have faced the problems their clients face and who have successfully made the transition from dependence to independence.

Usually, the next big problem is to become employable. Wives and mothers who have efficiently cared for their homes and families and who have been involved in community activities may find that they have skills that lead them into employment without further training. Others need varying amounts of education or training. Counselors help them focus their energy toward a job and at the same time provide information where they can get the education they need.

Single women find that they can climb from the bottom to find a new life with security and independence and on the way find new friends, interests, skills, and self-confidence in learning to cope with their individual problems.

General Assistance

General Assistance (GA), residual to OASDHI, is intended to aid those who cannot qualify under the federally financed SSI program for aged, blind, or disabled persons, or AFDC, or who are not covered by social insurance. There were 1,221,625 recipients of GA reported in the United States in September 1990, and in 2008, the number rose to 1,540,000.

GA is not a popular program, from the standpoint of both the administration and the beneficiary. Because taxes for it must be raised at the state and local levels, the program usually is poorly funded as local taxes may not yield enough revenue. Payments tend to be minimal and are grudgingly made to discourage people from applying or becoming dependent on welfare. Subject to such unpopular practices as voucher payments and giving assistance in kind, this form of aid carries with it the presumption that those who receive it are incapable of managing their own affairs. Other rules some states insist upon require the recipient to work for low wages at menial jobs, be reevaluated often, have payments so low that it discourages applicants, and other requirements that are unacceptable to those who are in need. The GA program in some parts of the country is demoralizing, a disgrace to the community, and has much in common with the poor relief of the Elizabethan period.

Able employable men and women are sometimes found in the ranks of GA, and there exists a strong aversion to their receiving public "handouts." Also on GA are those whom Gladwin has labeled the "undeserving poor."

> It is not that these people are dirty, or dishonest, or unfaithful in marriage. We have no trouble in respecting the natives of other lands who never bathe, and at least some crooks, and the majority of movie stars. The real reason, in my opinion, is that they are unwilling to undertake responsibility on their own behalf. We like to help people who are trying to help themselves. However pitiful the individual, or unsavory his circumstances, if he is really trying to improve his lot we will help him, and we will respect him for trying.
>
> The people with whom we are here concerned do not try. Some of us, certainly most social workers, may be able rationally to understand that in their unhappy environment these people have never learned to try; or, perhaps, even learned that it is better *not* to try. Nevertheless, our objective judgment that their apathy is not their fault seems to help even us professionals very little to persuade our subjective selves that we should accord them real respect. These are, in the immortal phrase of Alfred P. Doolittle in George Bernard Shaw's *Pygmalion,* the undeserving poor.[9]

Social work as a profession identifies with those in society who favor more constructive measures and interpretations, which include the following:

1. Provide an income floor for all citizens and the elimination of hunger and destitution, or their threat, as an instrument of social policy.

2. Extend relief to applicants who can qualify under eligibility requirements; that is, remove it from subjective, biased, and capricious considerations. Relief should be based on need as it is determined to exist by objective, rather than subjective, criteria and as a legally determined right.

3. It is assumed that workers, generally, prefer income from employment to public welfare and that motivations to work are built into the economy in the form of social, cultural, and economic advantages to the employed man or woman.

4. Psychological and social barriers sometimes stand in the way of rehabilitation and employment. Counseling and other services may be needed to restore certain individuals to economic and social self-sufficiency.

5. Preservation of the independence and self-respect of the applicant for assistance is a prime consideration in the administration of programs of relief.

6. A punitive approach defeats the purpose for which assistance is used, namely, the restoration of the individual to normal functioning; it deepens feelings of inadequacy and dependency, causes embarrassment and humiliation, and brings destructive psychological defenses into play.

7. There are many pulls in society that tend to make work more appealing than public welfare—a higher standard of living, the prestige and sense of importance one receives from work, tenure, the emoluments of society, and others.

Homelessness

Home! The word conjures up images of warmth, comfort, food, a bed, and love—the American dream. But for a growing number of men, women, and children, it is *only* a dream, for they are the homeless. Although experts argue over the number, estimates range from a low of 600,000 to a high of 6 million Americans who are without shelter in a place of their own.

Caring for these people takes more than just providing a house or apartment, for their problems are many and varied. Some are homeless because housing costs increased up to three times faster than income. Even though many of them have jobs, they are unable to find housing that they can pay for on their minimum wages. Each year, as many as 2.5 million people are displaced by rent inflation, economic development plans, condominium development, abandonment, and arson. Besides housing, many need much more help to solve their problems. Large numbers of homeless parents are minorities with few job skills and little experience in the work place. Many subsist on welfare.

A growing number of single women, often in their teens or early 20s with small children, are joining the ranks of the homeless. They, too, are without job training. Estimates place this group at about one-fourth of those in shelters or on the streets. Often, they are driven from their homes by violence—which presents yet another special need.

School-age children (perhaps as many as 700,000) who move from shelter to shelter change schools frequently. They not only have a difficult time academically but also have more chronic illnesses and need the services of mental health specialists more often than children who live in their own homes.

Homeless individuals often have serious personal problems. Approximately one-third of the adults are alcoholics, one-fourth are drug abusers, and another one-fourth have had a felony conviction or have served time in a state or federal prison. A smaller number are mentally ill. (Many fit more than one category.)

In 1989, the NASW (National Association of Social Workers) launched a campaign "There's No Place Like Home" designed to show how homelessness affects families and children. Its goal was to bring greater understanding to the American public of the magnitude of the problem and to suggest solutions through cooperation between the public and private sectors in providing better employment, better distribution of funds, and adequate housing. Through the efforts of social workers in their communities, services for the homeless, legislative reforms, and more involvement by volunteers have taken place.

People standing in line for
unemployment

Jim West/Alamy

Medicare

In 1965, Congress legislated health insurance for aged and disabled individuals under the provision of the Social Security Act, thus establishing the principle of a nonmeans test approach to health care.

Medicare is a compulsory HI plan and a voluntary SMI. HI, without the payment of monthly premiums, is for everyone aged 65 or over entitled to Social Security or railroad retirement. Others over age 65 may enroll for HI by paying monthly premiums. HI *helps* pay such costs as inpatient hospital care, nursing home care, and various services. SMI *helps* pay for physicians' services, outpatient hospital services, home "health" visits under certain conditions, outpatient physical therapy, and certain other prescribed services.

Title XVIII, an amendment to the Social Security Act, is the authority for Medicare. The action by Congress to provide Medicare hailed the beginning of what many leaders predict eventually will become a national health insurance program providing "coverage" for virtually all Americans. It can be assumed that some plan to underwrite some, if not most, of the cost of medical care and hospitalization will be legislated. Under Title XVIII, the federal government has accepted in principle the centralized mechanism of support for medical care, by borrowing a funding arrangement—namely, the tax on payroll—from Social Security income maintenance.

Social Security as a "universal" income-maintenance program has been maturing as an enduring principle for workers and their families for more than fifty years. Social insurance appeals to Americans' sense of independence and justice. Provisions for health care should benefit from the nation's experience with the Social Security system. Nevertheless, it can be predicted that proponents and opponents will hotly debate the issues, with emerging patterns clearly showing the results of compromise.

Medicare was expanded by the 1972 amendments to extend the coverage to certain workers, widows, and widowers who are disabled, and childhood disability beneficiaries. Workers and their employers, including the self-employed, are taxed to pay for health insurance. As coverage is extended, the tax increases and results in the transfer of income from one group to another. How much and whose income will be transferred are political issues. How much of the total cost will be paid from a payroll tax is also a political decision. Some leaders argue for general taxation and universal coverage, suggesting that eligibility should not be subjected to the payroll tax, which in the opinion of many fails to meet tests of equity or universality. Others argue that the payroll tax is more acceptable to vast numbers of Americans who want to "pay their own way." However, as benefits are extended and costs climb, a growing resistance to the payroll tax can be expected.

Congress is planning a rate of growth that is not to exceed the current rate of inflation. Proponents argue that it will not be possible to balance the budget unless proposed cuts are made in both Medicare and Medicaid. Opponents to cuts in these programs argue that proposals now being offered will be too painful, particularly to the elderly in case of Medicare and to the poor in case of Medicaid.

Medicare Reform

Senior citizens are anxiously awaiting a number of proposed reforms to the Medicare program. None is more anticipated or more debated than a universal Medicare prescription drug benefit that would be affordable to both taxpayers and beneficiaries. According to the Congressional Budget Office, $1.5 trillion will be spent on prescription drugs by the Medicare population over the next ten years.[10] The new Obama health care plan will be addressing this precipitous increase in prescription drugs. The cost of prescription medications has become an onerous burden for many senior citizens, with some spending one-third or more of their disposal income on medications. Many senior citizens struggle each day with an unsolvable dilemma: either purchase the medications they need and cut back on food, clothing, and other necessities or go without prescription medications and risk serious medical complications. A prescription drug plan was passed by the Bush administration in 2004 as a stopgap measure. It has attempted to alleviate the problems of high drug costs but it has not done so. New prescription drug funding is an important part of the new Obama health care plan, which has not yet been implemented.

Another pressing issue that concerns senior citizens is the spiraling cost of nursing home care and the limited coverage provided by Medicare. At the present time, the Medicare program covers only the costs of skilled nursing home care and even that coverage is limited to so many nursing home days a year. Senior citizens who are being cared for in semiskilled or assisted living homes have no Medicare benefits. This poses significant personal expense to senior citizens who can't take care of themselves but who do not require skilled nursing home care. The cost of maintaining a senior citizen with Alzheimer's disease in a semiskilled nursing home can cost $4,000 or more a month. Because the senior citizen doesn't require skilled nursing home care, the costs must be assumed by the senior citizen and his or her family. This personal liability continues until the senior citizen has "paid down" his or her assets to a certain level, at which time he or she is then eligible for Medicaid benefits. Many senior citizen groups, including American Association of Retired Persons (AARP), are lobbying Congress to close or at least modify this Medicare gap in nursing home coverage.

Another issue that will have a significant effect on Medicare is the health care reform package that Congress passed and President Obama signed into law on March 23, 2010. One of the main problems that health care reform must confront is how to insure the 40 million Americans who currently have no health care coverage. Different options are being discussed including a government health care insurance option that will compete with the private health care insurance giants in an attempt to lower costs while insuring those Americans who do not have health care coverage. Will this government-sponsored health care option only include hospital and physician coverage or will it also include long-term nursing home care? Will the government-sponsored health care program only be offered to the 40 million Americans who are currently uninsured or will the program also be available to those Americans who want to switch from a more expensive private health care insurance plan to the government-sponsored option?

A series of questions focus on how we will pay for this new government-sponsored health care option or whatever other program that becomes the basis of the new health care reform package. One proposal that has already been rejected included taking part of the current Medicare budget to pay for the new program. Another proposal includes imposing a special health care reform tax on Americans who make more than $1 million a year while yet another proposal shifts the financial burden to large corporations and increased business taxes. These and other options are being rigorously debated at the same time America suffers from an economic downturn that is second only to the Great Depression. Other critics are warning that there is not enough money in the federal coffers to fund health care reform while also maintaining current funding for the Medicare program. When the wars in Iraq and Afghanistan are added to this mix, the financial burden does appear to be almost impossible to bear.

Medicare Drug Prescription Program

Beginning January 1, 2006, Medicare started providing insurance for prescription drugs. The Medicare Prescription Drug Program, known as Part D, emphasized the following: (1) everyone on Medicare can get drug coverage regardless of income or health; (2) you are not required to sign up; (3) to get drug coverage, you must choose one of the many private drug companies Medicare has approved; (4) if you have limited income and can qualify for the "Extra Help" program, you will pay very little; (5) if your drug costs are high, Medicare will pay 95 percent of your costs beyond a certain amount in any one year; and (6) if you already have drug coverage, you won't need the new program unless you choose to enroll. If you wanted to participate in the Medicare drug program, people on Medicare had to apply by May 15, 2006. A late fee was charged for anyone who applied after that date. A premium of about $32 a month was charged for the Medicare drug program with a $250 annual deductible on drug costs before coverage began.[11]

Experts agree that the Medicare Prescription Drug Program has lowered the drug costs for most of the 23 million Americans who have enrolled in the program. The AARP, a strong supporter of the program, believes that "prescription-drug coverage was an important benefit missing from Medicare."[12] To date, the greatest criticism of the program involves what is called "the doughnut hole." Under Part D, initial drug coverage is limited for most enrollees to $2,250 per year. After that amount is exceeded, the Medicare enrollee must pay $3,600 out-of-pocket drug expenses before the gap or doughnut hole is closed. After $3,600 in out-of-pocket expenses is paid, the Medicare coverage automatically returns to the catastrophic level with low co-payments. Estimates suggest that from 24 to 38 percent of all enrollees fall into this gap or doughnut hole and are required to spend $3,600 in out-of-pocket expenses before the catastrophic level of Part D goes into effect.[13] Congress will no doubt look into this gap or doughnut hole and possibly change the law. Even with this setback, most Americans who have enrolled in Medicare Part D have seen their drug costs lowered.

Medicaid

Medical care for low-income people (Medicaid) is administered by the states. Direct payments are made to providers of services. Those persons who qualify for assistance under the federally financed income-maintenance program, SSI, are eligible for Medicaid. In addition, states have the option to include persons who are able to provide for their own daily living but whose income and resources are not sufficient to meet all of their medical costs.

Families who have larger incomes may be eligible for Medicaid, provided their income, after they deduct for medical expenses, is within the limits set by the state for meeting maintenance expenses.

Under the 1972 amendments, states are required to make family planning available on a confidential and voluntary basis to recipients of Medicaid.

Under provisions of both Medicare and Medicaid, hospital and nursing homes are required to use review committees and procedures (peer review organization) established to provide assurance of appropriateness, necessity, and quality of medical and nursing care.

The main advantages of Medicaid are that it may be used to provide hospital and medical care for very-low-income people who have no regular income from employment, and it may be used for others whose income is so low that they are unable to pay the high cost of medical and health care for themselves and their families. The limitations are those of a means test system—namely, poverty has to be proved, the system lacks uniformity of application, availability to people in need depends on a wide range of interpretations of the law and its intent, and applicants for health care who have not "earned the right" to medical care may be made to feel they are objects of charity.

The Social Security Crisis

Every year, the Social Security Administration sends a report to American workers advising them of what is happening to the Social Security program. On February 12, 2004, American workers enrolled in the Social Security program were sent the following ominous message:

> Social Security is a compact between generations. For more than 60 years, America has kept the promise of security for its workers and their families. But now, the Social Security system is facing serious future financial problems, and action is needed soon to make sure that the system is sound when today's younger workers are ready for retirement.

Today there are almost 36 million Americans age 65 or older. Their Social Security retirement benefits are funded by today's workers and their employers who jointly pay Social Security taxes—just as the money they paid into Social Security was used to pay benefits to those who retired before them. Unless action is taken soon to strengthen Social Security, in just 15 years we will begin paying more in benefits than we collect in taxes. Without changes, by 2042 the Social Security Trust Fund will be exhausted. By then, the number of Americans 65 or older is expected to have doubled. There won't be enough younger people working to pay all of the benefits owed to those who are retiring. At that point, there will be enough money to pay only 73 cents for each dollar of scheduled benefits. We will need to resolve these issues soon to make sure Social Security continues to provide a foundation of protection for future generations as it has done in the past.[14]

This terse and blunt statement about the future of the Social Security program should cause alarm for all Americans, especially those who have not yet applied for retirement benefits. In a way, the problem is both simple and complex. Simple because our population growth is declining and fewer Americans are paying into the Social Security system and complex because so many different "solutions" are being proposed to fix the problem. Some of these "solutions" include:

1. Gradually raising the retirement age from 65 to 70 as the number of American workers declines.

2. Increasing taxes on other retirement programs such as IRAs (individual retirement accounts) and 401(k)s.

3. Permitting Americans who are currently paying into the Social Security system to invest as much as 25 percent of their Social Security taxes into other equity programs such as stocks, bonds, and mutual funds.

4. Decreasing the monthly cash benefit currently being paid to retirees.

5. Reducing the benefits of other parts of the Social Security program (i.e., Medicare, Survivors, and Disability).

6. Reducing federal spending in other areas such as defense and education.

To complicate matters further, in December 2003, the Congress passed, and President George W. Bush signed, a new $400 billion Medicare drug legislation bill that went into full effect in 2006. Critics and pundits alike are asking how America can afford such expenditure and how this new $400 billion program can help an already faltering Social Security program. What concerns a lot of seniors is that one-third of the program's $400 billion cost will subsidize drugs for very-low-income people, with most seniors benefiting very little from the program.[15] Some critics are even saying that the new Medicare drug program will bankrupt the Social Security system within ten to fifteen years. Social Security reform continues to be a major political concern in the United States today. It will take our best minds and a united citizenry to fix what appears to be a problem that can't be fixed.

Social Services and Social Work

Public services, as distinguished from assistance payments under the broad provisions of the Social Security Act, are available to certain categories of the population. These services provide for children, families, and certain adults.

Social workers play a major role in the administering of services and as providers. Service programs are financed under state–federal financial arrangements and are administered by the states and local communities. The particular service modality varies widely.

Until 1972, service and assistance were combined under one administration. Generally, it was assumed that services were needed for purposes of rehabilitation. In the minds of many, rehabilitation meant becoming independent of assistance. What has not been generally accepted is that assistance payments are made mainly for the benefit of dependent children; their parents (usually an unemployed mother); persons who are aged, disabled, or blind; a few employable males; and mothers needed at home to provide for their children.

Administered at the local level, service patterns are widely diverse. Nevertheless, services have received acceptance in many places as their need has been demonstrated, and although there is much criticism of service programs, studies in some places show that the public generally supports these services.

Under Title XX, each state develops its own Comprehensive Annual Services Program (CASP) plan. The services to be provided are spelled out in each state plan. Fifty states and the District of Columbia listed 1,313 services reported in Social Services U.S.A.[16] Table 1 summarizes the kinds of services offered to children and adults for the quarter ending June 1978.

Table 1   **Services to Children and Adults**

Adoption Services	Foster Care—Children	Unmarried Parent Services
Case Management Services	Foster Care—Various	Socialization Services
Chore Services	Health-Related Services	Special Services—Alcohol
Counseling Services	Home Delivery Congregate	and Drug
Day Care—Adults	Meals	Special Services—Blind
Day Care—Children	Homemaker Services	Special Services—Child and
Day Care—Various	Home Management	Youth
Diagnostic and Evaluative	Housing Improvement	Special Services—Disabled
Services	Information and Referral	Special Services—Juvenile
Education and Training Services	Legal Services	Delinquents
Emergency Services	Placement Services	Transitional Services
Employment-Related Medical	Protective Services—Adults	Transportation
Services	Protective Services—Children	Vocational Rehabilitation
Employment Services	Protective Services—Various	Work Incentive (WIN) Medical
Family Planning	Recreational Services	Examinations
Foster Care—Adults	Residential Care and Treatment	Other

GOVERNMENT AND PUBLIC WELFARE

There is a growing realization that government cannot solve all problems. Failures of the Great Society (President Lyndon Johnson's war on poverty) did not result entirely from a lack of resources. In some ways, these failures resulted from a lack of leadership. Community action programs and the Model Cities program failed because power was given to some groups not ready to use it and because it was not recognized that great social changes cannot be mandated or brought about overnight. Change must be an extension of the past, and the war on poverty appeared to lack the impulse necessary for its survival.

The largest nondefense program, Social Security, expanded rapidly after 1965 into a set of programs. The question is raised: Has it promised too much to too many? It is a fallacy to assume (1) the nation has unlimited resources and (2) *only* money is needed to solve personal and family problems. The fact is that resources do not exist to provide all things for all people. Choices from alternatives will have to be made. A nation that invests in general health care may be unable to provide good pensions, and the assumption of resources that do not exist can lead to colossal failure in national policy.

With their vast experience in working with troubled families and individuals, social workers know that some problems defy complete solution and that money is needed, but so are understanding and compassionate regard. Money cannot provide these, nor is mere desire to help enough. Someone has described social work education as a "pasteurization process for taking the bugs out of the milk of human kindness." Robert Frost, speaking to the Israelis, justified education because it "raised human pain and suffering to a higher plane of regard." The solution to many human problems calls for widespread regard for the worth of the individual, and this cherished value cannot be legislated or purchased. Social work can help.

It is true that the voluntary social work field is experiencing some extremely difficult periods and that some national agencies are in trouble. However, voluntary agencies most likely will continue to play an important role in "public" welfare in the future. Some people have observed that centralized, computerized federal programs, including Social Security, often are not responsive to the special needs of individuals and localities. A tenet of social work is that the smaller private agencies have the edge on larger computerized governmental systems in regard to unmet, unplanned for, and unanticipated needs. Volunteerism in general is needed today as never before, particularly in the human service area.

Since 1935 and the passage of the Social Security Act, the federal government has increasingly assumed responsibility for the protection of citizens against want as an *enduring* principle.

Fifty years later, Ronald Reagan strongly argued for less government, greater local control of welfare, and a *market* economy. These sentiments have carried over to the H. W. Bush, Clinton, Bush, and Obama administrations, especially in relation to welfare reform.

Government responsibility for welfare has become an enduring principle with the passage of the Social Security Act of 1935.

SUMMARY

Government responsibility for welfare has become an *enduring* principle with the passage of the Social Security Act of 1935.

A shift in thinking about welfare marked the administration of Ronald Reagan. It has been asked, will the Reagan views about welfare shape policy in the future and become a trend? Are the costs of state-funded welfare programs becoming greater than the country can bear or is willing to afford, and will Congress make the hard choices and reduce spending on such programs as income for the elderly, Medicare, and Medicaid? The debate continues into the Obama administration.

SSI and TANF programs are the main *public assistance* programs. TANF is criticized for the increasing numbers of young women who seem to rely on it as a way of life. Teenagers, becoming pregnant out of wedlock and unable to provide for themselves, are at the heart of the debate in Congress over what to do with our welfare system.

Poverty and the feminization of poverty continue to be major social problems, notwithstanding the gains that have been made toward the equalization of opportunities for women in industry and in the professions.

GA is a public response to those in need who don't qualify for federally financed help. This assistance is paid for from taxes by local entities and is often barely adequate to provide for the needs of these recipients.

Medicare and Medicaid provide for the health care of the aged and others in need of doctor's care and hospitalization. Hospitals and doctors are available to covered workers under the provision of OASDHI. Medicaid provides care for low-income families who are not covered by the insurance provisions of Social Security.

Social services to children and adults, provided to certain categories of recipients, are generally seen as needed for purposes of rehabilitation.

Income needs are but a part of the problems people face. Values and ethics provide guidelines for practice, and a concerted effort of many elements of society is needed to solve complex social welfare problems.

Succeed with 

Log onto **www.mysocialworklab.com** and answer the questions below. (*If you did not receive an access code to* **MySocialWorkLab** *with this text and wish to purchase access online, please visit* www.mysocialworklab.com.)

1. Watch the core competency video dealing with human rights and justice, "Social and Economic Justice...." What are some of the stigmas associated with homelessness?

2. How can the social worker avoid shaming the client while still advocating for him or her?

PRACTICE TEST The following questions will test your knowledge of the content found within this chapter. For additional assessment, including licensing-exam type questions on applying chapter content to practice, visit **MySocialWorkLab**.

1. America's first social welfare system was modeled in part on England's program for public welfare that began in the early 1600s. This earlier English program is usually referred to as the:
   a. Edwardian Poor Laws.
   b. Elizabethan Poor Laws.
   c. Henry VIII Welfare Act.
   d. English Workhouse Act.

2. In 1965, Congress legislated health insurance for aged and disabled individuals under the Social Security Act. This federally funded program is called:
   a. Medicare.
   b. Medicaid.
   c. TANF.
   d. SSA/SSI.

3. The federally funded and managed retirement program that most Americans are enrolled in recently changed the age when people can receive full retirement benefits from age 65 to age:
   a. 66.
   b. 67.
   c. 68.
   d. 69.

4. This federally funded and state-managed program provides health care benefits to the medically indigent who can meet stringent financial requirements.
   a. Medicare.
   b. Medicaid.
   c. TANF.
   d. SSA/SSI.

5. Discuss the differences between the Medicare and Medicaid programs.

ASSESS YOUR COMPETENCE Use the following scale to rate your current level of achievement on the following concepts or skills associated with each competency presented in the chapter:

1	2	3
I can accurately describe the concept or skill	I can consistently identify the concept or skill when observing and analyzing practice activities	I can competently implement the concept or skill in my own practice

______ Describe the key elements of the Social Security Act of 1935.

______ Differentiate between the AFDC and TANF programs.

______ Delineate the differences between Medicare and Medicaid.

NOTES

1. Case material provided by Phyllis N. Johnson, MSW, self-sufficiency coordinator at Utah Issues, a nonprofit referral system advocacy for low-income people of Utah.

2. Elizabeth Wickenden and Winifred Bell, "Public Welfare, Time for Change," a report of the Project on Public Services for Families and Children (New York: New York School of Social Work, Columbia University, 1961), p. 13.

3. No limits are placed on the income a person can earn after he or she turns 66.

4. Nondeterrent systems, as opposed to deterrent *means test* programs, eliminate tests of need. Beneficiaries are not "investigated," they do not have to be indigent to be eligible, and it is presumed that benefits are earned by the worker. Not only are repressive measures not employed, but also the OASDHI actively tries to locate workers eligible for benefits who have not filed claims.

5. David Whitman, Dorian Friedman, Mike Tharp, and Kate Griffin, "Welfare: The Myth of Reform," *U.S. News and World Report*, January 16, 1995, pp. 30–39.

6. Richard Wolf, "'Wisconsin Works'—or Else Gets Cut Off." *USA Today,* March 11, 1998, p. 9A.

7. Vicky N. Albert, "The Role of the Economy and Welfare Policies in Shaping Welfare Caseload: The California Experience," *Social Work Research*, 24 (December 2000), p. 197.

8. John S. Wodarski, T. M. Jim Parharm, Elizabeth W. Lindsey, and Barry W. Blackburn, "Reagan's AFDC Policy Changes: The Georgia Experience," *Social Work,* 31 (July/August 1986), p. 273.

9. Thomas Gladwin, "The Anthropologist's View of Poverty," in *The Social Welfare Forum, 1961* (New York: National Conference on Social Welfare, 1961), pp. 76–77.

10. Patricia Barry, "Costs, Politics Cloud Drug Benefit," *AARP Bulletin*, 42 (May 2001), p. 4.

11. Patricia Barry, "Medicare Drug Coverage: The Basics," *AARP The Magazine*, January/February 2006, pp. 61–63.

12. Erik D. Olsen, "Ask Erik," *AARP The Magazine*, September/October 2006, p. 156.

13. Patricia Barry, "In and Out of the Doughnut Hole," *AARP Bulletin*, 47 (June 2006), pp. 16–17.

14. "What Social Security Means to You," in *Your Social Security Statement* (Washington, DC: Social Security Administration, February 12, 2004), p. 1.

15. Jane Bryant Quinn, "The Drug Bill's Hidden Costs," *Newsweek*, December 22, 2003, p. 37.

16. *Social Services U.S.A.: Third Quarter Report, FY1978* (Washington, DC: U.S. Department of Health and Human Services, 1978), p. 38.

The American Health Care System

The American Health Care System

© Gary Kazanjian/AP Wide World Photos

*F*ifty-five percent of Americans surveyed in February 2007 said that the most important domestic policy for the President and Congress to focus on is making health insurance available for everyone. In the same survey, 90 percent said that the present health care system requires fundamental changes or needs to be completely rebuilt.[1] This chapter examines the U.S. health care system—specifically, the organization of medical services; key governmental health programs such as Medicare and Medicaid; the crisis in health care, including attempts to curb health care costs; the large numbers of uninsured people; the impact of the American Medical Association on health care; the growing role of managed care; and the ramifications of the AIDS epidemic in the health care system. The chapter also surveys various proposals designed to ameliorate the problems in U.S. health care and considers how medical services are organized in Great Britain and Canada.

The Uninsured

Health care in the United States is marked by several contradictions. According to Census Bureau data, the number of people *with* health insurance rose to 249.8 million in 2006, up from 240.1 million in 2000. The number *without* such coverage rose from 38.4 million to 47 million in the same period. The percentage of the nation's population without health care coverage was 15.8 percent in 2006, and the percentage of people covered by government health insurance programs (Medicaid and Medicare) was 27 percent. The proportion of uninsured children in 2006 was 11.7 percent of all children, or 8.7 million.[2] Although the vast majority of Americans have easy access to a wide range of health care services through employment-based or public insurance programs, more than 47 million people remain without coverage. The medically uninsured have the following characteristics:

- Children under age 18 in poverty were more likely to be uninsured—19.3 percent in 2006 compared to 11.7 percent of all children. Adults between the ages of 18 and 44 made up three-quarters (76 percent) of the uninsured.
- Young adults (18 to 24 years old) were the least likely of any age group to have health insurance in 2006. Nearly 30 percent of uninsured persons were in this six-year age bracket.
- The poor are three times more likely to be uninsured as those who are not poor. One-quarter of people in households with annual incomes under $25,000 had no health insurance in 2006 compared with only 8.5 percent for those with incomes over $75,000.

spotlight 1

The National Center for Health Statistics

The National Center for Health Statistics (NCHS) is a key resource of information about the health of Americans. As the principal health statistics agency in the United States, the organization compiles statistical information to guide action and policies to improve the health of people living within the United States. The information provided by NCHS helps to do the following:

- Document the health status of the population and of important subgroups
- Identify disparities in health status and use of health care by race/ethnicity, socioeconomic status, region, and other population characteristics
- Describe various experiences with the health care system
- Monitor trends in health status and health care delivery
- Identify health problems
- Support biomedical and health services research
- Provide information for making changes in public policies and programs
- Evaluate the impact of health policies and programs

To learn more about NCHS, go to its website at **www.cdc.gov/nchs.**

- The uninsured rate for African Americans in 2006 was 20.5 percent; for Asians, 15.5 percent; for whites, 10.8 percent; for Hispanics 34.1 percent; and for American Indians or Alaska Natives it was 31.4 percent.
- The proportion of the foreign-born population without health insurance (33.8 percent) was about two-and-a-half times that of the native population (13.2 percent) in 2006.
- The South (19 percent) and West (17.9 percent) have a higher uninsured rate than either the Northeast (12.3 percent) or the Midwest (11.4 percent).
- The number of people who received health insurance coverage through their employers fell slightly from 60.2 percent in 2005 to 59.7 percent in 2006, while the number of people covered by government health insurance programs (e.g., Medicare and Medicaid) was 80.3 million or 27 percent.[3]

The relatively high number of uninsured Americans is not surprising, given that family health insurance premiums cost on average $9,320 annually in 2004—a high cost for a family trying to make ends meet.[4] In 35 states average premium costs for workers rose three times faster than average earnings from 2000 to 2004. Purchasing affordable, accessible insurance is a particular challenge for many older people, for workers in transition between jobs, and for small businesses and their employees. For example, premiums for **COBRA** (transitional health insurance allowed a worker when they terminate employment) average almost $700 a month for family coverage and $250 for individual coverage, a huge expenditure given the average $1,100 monthly unemployment check.[5]

The uninsured are three times more likely than the privately insured not to receive needed medical care, 50 to 70 percent more likely to need hospitalization for avoidable acute conditions like pneumonia or uncontrolled diabetes, and four times more likely to rely on an emergency room or to have no regular source of care.[6] At least one million Americans seeking medical care are turned away each year because they cannot pay, and millions more forgo preventive services.[7] This exists even though every major city has at least one major medical center.[8] The uninsured face other problems:

- Uninsured children have a higher incidence of developmental delays than those with health coverage.

- They are more likely to put off seeking care; to not receive care when needed; and to not fill a prescription or get a recommended treatment because of the expense.
- They are more likely to have problems paying their medical bills, and to be contacted by a collection agency.
- Uninsured adults hospitalized for heart attacks are 25 percent more likely to die while in the hospital than privately insured adults.
- Even after controlling for the severity of the injury, uninsured adults hospitalized for a traumatic injury are more than twice as likely to die in the hospital as insured adults.
- The diagnosis of a serious new health condition, including cancer, diabetes, heart attack, chronic lung disease, or stroke, reduced the wealth of uninsured households by 20 percent. Insured households with a similar diagnosis suffered a 2 percent decline in overall wealth.
- Insured households paid about $26,957 in total medical spending after the diagnosis of a serious new health condition; uninsured households paid $42,166.
- Americans who lack health insurance cost the economy between $65 and $130 billion a year in lost productivity.[9]
- The cost of medical care for the uninsured totaled around $125 billion in 2004.[10]

The Organization of Medical Services

Most health care costs in the United States are paid for by private insurers, public plans, and the direct public provision of health care. Only about 25 percent of health care costs are paid for directly by consumers. The dominant form of health care coverage in the United States is private insurance, which covers about 70 percent of the population (of whom three-quarters are covered by employer-based plans). Many elderly people use private health insurance plans to supplement the coverage offered by Medicare. Medical services in the United States consist of six major components:

1. Physicians in solo practice. These are typically the traditional physicians who may employ a nurse and receptionist. This form of medical

organization is becoming increasingly rare in an age of group practices and managed care.

2. Group outpatient settings, including groups of physicians sharing facilities. This setting is becoming common as physicians are forced to pool resources—capital, equipment, office staff, and so forth—in order to compete in an increasingly difficult health care marketplace. Group outpatient settings may also include health maintenance organizations (HMOs), physicians in industrial Employee Assistance Plan (EAP) settings, or doctors operating under university auspices. During the past few decades, physicians have increasingly worked in group practices or other organized settings.[11]

3. Physicians employed in corporate-owned for-profit clinics or in nonprofit clinics.

4. Hospitals—private, nonprofit, or public.

5. Public health services delivered on the state, local, regional, national, or international level. These services include health counseling; family planning; prenatal and postnatal care; school health services; disease prevention and control; immunization; referral agencies; STD (sexually transmitted diseases) services; environmental sanitation; health education; and maintenance of indexes on births, deaths, and communicable diseases. Government-sponsored health services include the Veterans Administration Hospitals (the largest network of hospitals in the United States); Community and Migrant Health Centers; services provided under the Title V Maternal and Child Health Block Grant; and the Title X Family Planning Program.

6. Sundry and corollary health services. This category includes home health services, physical rehabilitation, group homes, nursing homes, and so forth.

Major Public Health Programs: Medicare, Medicaid, and SCHIP

Health care spending is the second fastest-growing component of the federal budget, overshadowed only by the growth in the public debt. Overall, health care spending accounts for about one-fifth of total governmental expenditures at the state and federal levels. In 2006, 40.3 million people were covered by Medicare (13.6 percent) and 38.3 million (12.9 percent) were covered by Medicaid.[12]

Medicare

After Social Security, Medicare is the largest social insurance program in the United States with expenditures of $408.3 billion in 2006. It is also the largest public payer of health care, financing close to 20 percent of all health care spending. When Medicare began in July 1966, approximately 19 million people were enrolled; by 2007 more than 44 million people were enrolled in one or both of Parts A and B, and 8 million chose to participate in the Medicare+Choice (renamed Medicare Advantage) plan. In 2006, HI benefits totaled $189 billion.[13]

Medicare was added to the Social Security Act in 1965 and was designed to provide elderly people with prepaid hospital and optional medical insurance. The modern Medicare system is composed of four parts: compulsory Hospital Insurance (HI), known as Part A; Supplemental Medical Insurance (SMI), known as Part B; the Medicare Advantage program, known as Part C; and the Medicare Prescription Drug, Improvement, and Modernization Act of 2003, known as MMA or Part D. Although traditionally consisting of two parts (HI and SMI), Part C (established by the Balanced Budget Act of 1997) expanded beneficiaries' options for participation in private sector health care plans. The MMA or Part D was added in 2003.

Surrounded by controversy, the MMA was signed into law in 2003. As a 700-page document, this complex bill proved difficult for Medicare beneficiaries to understand. Apart from prescription drug coverage, Part D also includes changes for beneficiaries such as increases in the Part B deductible, increased income standards relating to the Part B premium, and new preventive health benefits. Like SMI, participation in the MMA is voluntary.

From mid-2004, beneficiaries had access to Medicare-endorsed drug discount cards estimated to save consumers 10 to 15 percent. For beneficiaries with incomes below 135 percent of poverty, the federal government provided $600 a year toward drug expenses plus the annual enrollment fee. This temporary plan was phased out in 2006. Part D now provides subsidized access to prescription drug insurance coverage on a voluntary basis, upon payment of a premium, to individuals entitled to Part A or enrolled in Part B. Premium and cost-sharing subsidies are available for low-income enrollees. People may enroll in either a stand-alone prescription drug plan (PDP) or an integrated Medicare Advantage plan that offers Part D coverage.[14]

The standard benefits for the MMA include the following:

• Beneficiaries pay about $25 a month in premiums for basic drug coverage (these are likely to vary across plans) in addition to the Part B premium. They also pay a $180 to $265 annual deductible and 25 percent (or approximate flat copayment) of full drug costs up to $2,400. After the initial coverage limit of $2,400 is met, a "doughnut hole" begins where the beneficiary may be responsible for up to the full amount of his or her drug costs. The "doughnut hole" ends once the beneficiary has met an out-of-pocket expense of $3,850. In the final post–"doughnut hole phase," enrollees pay only 5 percent of their total drug costs.

• Beneficiaries are required to find a private prescription drug plan that has contracted with the Medicare program. Managed care plans, like those currently in Medicare Advantage, may also provide the drug benefit. In areas where only one (or no) private plan exists, the government will provide a "fall-back" plan that provides the standard benefit.

• Medicare beneficiaries receive preventive benefits, including an initial routine physical examination, cardiovascular blood screening tests, and diabetes screening tests and services.

• The deductible, the size of the "doughnut hole," and catastrophic thresholds grow each year based on increased MMA spending. Thus, if Medicare drug costs skyrocket, the deductible and the "doughnut hole" will increase. For example, the benefit gap is projected to be $5,066 in 2013 and the annual premium is expected to jump to $696 by 2013. Because drug costs rise faster than inflation— and are projected to continue to do so—most Medicare beneficiaries will see their drug costs rise faster than their income. In the end, it is estimated that the MMA will only pay for about 25 percent of seniors' drug costs.

• Medicare will provide additional assistance to beneficiaries who qualify based on low incomes and limited assets. There are multiple levels of low-income assistance. For example, beneficiaries with incomes below 135 percent of the poverty line and assets under $6,000 for an individual or $9,000 for a couple (not including the value of a home or car), will be eligible to get drugs at $1 to $2 per generic prescription and $3 to $5 per brand-name prescription. Many of these six million people (called dual

eligibles) will have to pay higher copayments for prescription drugs. This is compounded by the fact that, unlike Medicare, there are no due process clauses for lodging complaints.

• MMA plan providers are permitted to offer an alternative benefit design provided it is actuarially equivalent and does not raise the Part D deductible or out-of-pocket limit. Plan providers are also required to provide drugs in each therapeutic category but have flexibility to establish preferred drug lists. In addition, companies offering drug plans can change formularies at any time, while a beneficiary can only change cards once a year. Plans may utilize a preferred network of pharmacies to reduce beneficiary cost-sharing. They may also offer supplemental benefits for an additional premium. Medicare has guidelines for the type of drugs plans must cover, but they do not require that all plans offer the same drugs. Beneficiaries will be required to ascertain whether the plan they enroll in covers the drugs they need.

Critics charge that the MMA does not curb skyrocketing drug costs. In fact, the MMA may actually increase costs by prohibiting Medicare from using its purchasing power to negotiate lower drug prices for beneficiaries. Private plan providers seek discounts for enrollees, but they lack Medicare's purchasing power. This stands in contrast to the Veterans Administration which has successfully negotiated lower prices with drug companies. In effect, the "no negotiation" clause increases program costs, which in turn adds to the deficit. The one-sided bill also prohibits consumers from buying cheaper drugs from Canada or Mexico. Under the Medicare legislation, drugs can only be reimported from Canada, and then only if the Secretary of Health and Human Services certifies that the reimportation is safe and would significantly reduce costs.

Drug companies and the managed care industry stand to reap huge profits from this legislation. Not only are there no mechanisms to effectively control rising drug costs, but the new drug benefit means much larger sales volume. Private insurance companies that participate in the Medicare program also realize windfall profits as they attempt to enroll the healthiest and youngest seniors, thereby lowering their costs. The MMA also includes an opportunity for private providers to gain more ground by allowing demonstration programs that lay the groundwork for privatizing Medicare. For instance, in 2010 Medicare will begin a demonstration project in six metropolitan areas in which traditional fee-for-service Medicare will bid competitively against private plans. Because traditional Medicare serves an older, sicker, and more expensive population, its costs will undoubtedly be higher.[15]

The Medicare bill was passed under a cloud of impropriety. In July 2004, Medicare administrator Thomas Scully admitted to ordering Richard Foster, a Medicare actuary, to withhold information from Congress. Foster had projected that the bill would cost at least $139 billion dollars more than the White House was claiming.[16] Even that estimate would climb as the costs of the MMA are expected to rise 11.5 percent a year until 2015.[17]

Perhaps the most important part of the MMA has nothing to do with Medicare. It is a little-noticed component called health savings accounts (HSAs) that could cost the federal government $6.4 billion over the next decade. Basically, the HSAs offer a tax-free shelter for those with high-deductible insurance. When a person puts money into the account it is not taxed. Nor is it taxed when the money is removed to pay for medical costs. Critics argue that this adds to the federal budget deficit. Moreover, this plan removes the owners of these accounts from the shared risk that is at the core of the health insurance system. Conservatives claim health savings accounts will encourage people to more closely monitor their health care spending and bring down medical costs. Critics call the accounts a tax shelter that benefits the wealthy and draws young, healthy workers out of health care plans, potentially doubling the cost of insurance for everyone else. For conservatives, a key selling point of health savings accounts is its potential effect on the future of health care. Specifically, polls show that two-thirds of Americans support government-run, universal health care. By giving a large segment of the population the option to withdraw from the health insurance system, health savings accounts can serve to prevent another Clinton-style health care reform proposal. Simply put, it would be hard to reform the health care system if a large number of people opted out and were self-insured.[18]

Medicare Coverage HI or Part A is provided free to persons aged 65 or over who are eligible for Social Security or Railroad Retirement benefits. It is a compulsory **inpatient care** (hospital) insurance plan (it also includes some nursing and home health care) with premiums coming out of a payroll tax that is part of the Social Security deductions. Most Americans 65 or older are automatically entitled to

Part A, and workers and their spouses with a sufficient period of Medicare-only coverage in federal, state, or local government employment are also eligible beginning at age 65. In addition, HI coverage is provided to insured workers (and spouses and children) with end-stage renal disease (ESRD), and to some otherwise ineligible aged and disabled beneficiaries who voluntarily pay a monthly premium. In 2006 the HI program covered about 43 million people (36 million aged and 7 million disabled enrollees).[19] The following health care services are covered under Medicare's HI program:

- Inpatient hospital care includes the costs of a semi-private room, meals, regular nursing services, operating and recovery rooms, intensive care, inpatient prescription drugs, laboratory tests, X-rays, inpatient rehabilitation, long-term care hospitalization, and all other medically necessary services and supplies.
- Skilled nursing facility (SNF) care is covered only if it follows within 30 days of a hospitalization of three days or more and is certified as medically necessary. Covered services are similar to those for hospitalized patients but also include rehabilitation services and medical appliances.
- Home health agency (HHA) care may be provided for a home-bound beneficiary if deemed medically necessary. Certain medical supplies and durable medical equipment may also be provided but require a copayment. Full-time nursing care, food, blood, and drugs are not provided as HHA services. Home health agency (HHA) care is covered by both HI and SMI and requires no copayment or deductible.
- Hospice care is available to terminally ill persons with life expectancies of six months or less who forego the standard Medicare benefits. Such care includes pain relief, supportive medical and social services, physical therapy, nursing services, and symptom management. If a hospice patient requires treatment for a condition not related to the terminal illness, Medicare will pay for all covered services necessary for that condition. Beneficiaries pay no deductible for the hospice program but do pay a small coinsurance for drugs and inpatient respite care.[20]

By paying a monthly premium, U.S. citizens (and certain legal aliens) over age 65 and all disabled persons entitled to HI are eligible to enroll in the SMI program. Almost all persons entitled to HI enroll in SMI. In 2006 the SMI program covered about 40 million (34 million aged and 6 million disabled) people with benefits totaling $165.9 billion.[21] The SMI program covers the following:

- Physicians' and surgeons' services, including some covered services furnished by chiropractors, podiatrists, dentists, and optometrists; also covered are services provided by nonphysician Medicare-approved practitioners, such as nurse practitioners in collaboration with a physician, clinical psychologists, clinical social workers (other than in a hospital or skilled nursing facility), and physician assistants.
- Services in an emergency room or outpatient clinic, including same-day surgery, and ambulance services
- Home health care not covered under HI
- Laboratory tests, X-rays, and other diagnostic radiology services, as well as certain preventive care screening tests
- Ambulatory surgical center services in a Medicare-approved facility
- Most physical and occupational therapy and speech pathology services
- Comprehensive outpatient rehabilitation facility services, and mental health treatment in a partial hospitalization psychiatric program
- Radiation therapy, renal dialysis, and certain (e.g., heart, lung, liver, pancreas, bone marrow, kidney, and intestinal) transplants
- Approved durable medical equipment for home use, such as oxygen equipment, wheelchairs, prosthetic devices, and surgical dressings, splints, and casts
- Drugs that cannot be self-administered[22]

Funding Medicare finances are handled by two trust funds in the U.S. Treasury, one for the HI program and the other for SMI. The HI program is financed primarily through a mandatory payroll tax. Almost all employees and self-employed persons pay taxes to support benefits for aged and disabled beneficiaries. In 2008 the HI tax rate was 1.45 percent of earnings (paid by each employee with a matching amount paid by the employer) and 2.90 percent for self-employed persons. Unlike Social Security, there is no earnings cap on taxable wages.

The SMI program is financed by beneficiary payments ($96.40 a month in 2008) and contributions from general tax revenues. Beneficiary premiums are generally set at a level that covers 25 percent of the average expenditures for aged beneficiaries. As such, the contribution from general tax revenues is the largest source income for the SMI program. Beneficiary premiums and general fund payments are determined annually to match estimated program costs for the following year. Capitation payments to Medicare Advantage plans are financed from the HI and SMI trust funds.

Gaps in Medicare Coverage Fee-for-service beneficiaries pay for charges not covered by Medicare and for various cost-sharing aspects of both HI and SMI. These liabilities may be paid by beneficiaries out-of-pocket, by a third party (an employer-sponsored retiree health plan or private "Medigap" insurance), or by Medicaid (if the person is eligible). "Medigap" insurance refers to private insurance plans that pay most of the charges not covered by Medicare. For beneficiaries enrolled in Medicare Advantage plans, the beneficiary's payment share is based on the cost-sharing structure of the specific plan selected by the beneficiary. Most plans have lower deductibles and coinsurance than that required for fee-for-service beneficiaries. Beneficiaries pay the monthly Part B premium and may pay an additional plan premium.

For HI hospital care, a fee-for-service beneficiary's payment share includes a one-time deductible at the beginning of each benefit period ($1,024 in 2008). This deductible covers the beneficiary's part of the first 60 days of each instance of inpatient hospital care. If continued inpatient care is needed beyond the 60 days, additional coinsurance payments ($256 a day in 2008) are required through the 90th day of a benefit period. Each HI beneficiary also has a lifetime reserve of 60 additional hospital days that may be used when the covered days within a benefit period have been exhausted. Lifetime reserve days may be used only once, and coinsurance payments are required.

Medicare covers the first 20 days of skilled nursing care (SNF) in a benefit period. But a copayment is required ($128 a day in 2008) for days 21 through 100. Medicare's obligation ends after 100 days of SNF care per benefit period. Home health care has no deductible or coinsurance payment.

For SMI, the beneficiary's payment share includes one annual deductible ($135 in 2008), the monthly premiums, the coinsurance payments for

SMI services (usually 20 percent of the medically allowed charges), a deductible for blood, certain charges above the Medicare-allowed charge, and payment for any services not covered by Medicare. The beneficiary is liable for 50 percent of the approved charges for outpatient mental health treatment services.

Reimbursements to Providers Medicare payments for most inpatient hospital services are made under a reimbursement mechanism known as the prospective payment system (PPS). Under PPS, a predetermined amount is paid for each inpatient hospital stay based on a diagnosis-related group classification. In some cases the payment to the hospital is less than the actual costs, while in other cases it is more. The hospital absorbs the loss or makes a profit. Adjustments are made for unusual or costly hospital stays. Payments for skilled nursing care, home health care, inpatient rehabilitation, and long-term hospital care are made under separate PPSs.[23]

If a doctor or medical supplier agrees to accept the Medicare-approved rate as payment in full, they may not request any additional payments from the beneficiary. If the provider does not take assignment, the beneficiary is charged for the excess (sometimes paid by Medigap insurance). Limits exist on the excess that doctors or suppliers can charge. Medicare reimbursements to health care providers are subject to maximum payments by level of service, which are often less than some physicians will accept. In these cases, patients pay the difference between the physician's charge and the Medicare reimbursement. Because of paperwork and limited reimbursement, many physicians choose not to participate in Medicare.

Medicare payments to Medicare Advantage plans are based on a blend of local and national capitated rates. Actual payments to plans vary depending on the demographic characteristics of the enrolled population. Although Medicare provides important services, the gaps in coverage are extensive, which is why many beneficiaries opt for HMOs or supplement Medicare with private **Medigap** insurance.

Since 1980 Medicare costs have risen about 10 percent a year. Total Medicare expenditures more than doubled from 1989 to 1998, and they are rising faster than the wages on which the payroll tax is based. Medicare's annual costs in 2007 equaled

3.2 percent of the gross domestic product (GDP) but are expected to reach almost 10.8 percent by 2082. In turn, the projected date of the HI trust fund exhaustion is 2019. Part B of the SMI trust fund and the MMA are both expected to remain adequately funded into the future because current law automatically sets financing to meet the next year's expected costs (something not true for the HI program). The Medicare program is expected to experience even greater hardships when the baby boom generation begins retiring around 2010 (see Figure 1).[24]

Medicaid

Before 1965, medical care for those unable to afford it was primarily a responsibility of charitable institutions and state and local governments. In 1950 the federal government authorized states to use federal/state funds under the Social Security Act of 1935 to provide medical care for the indigent. In 1957 the Kerr-Mills Act provided for a federal/state matching program to provide health care for the elderly and the poor. However, Kerr-Mills was not

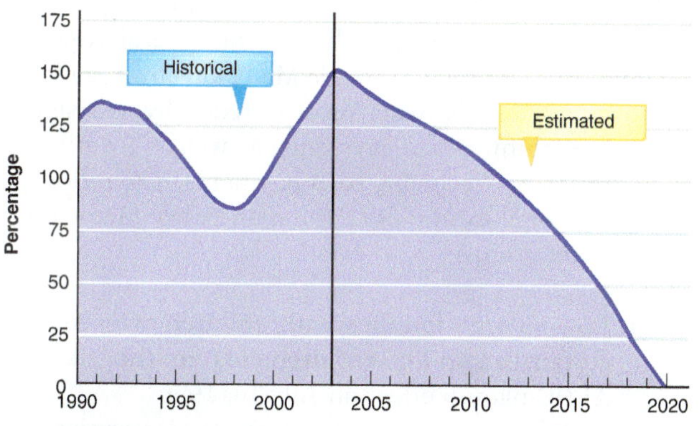

Figure 1

Hospital Insurance Trust Funds Assets (assets at beginning of year as percentage of annual expenditures)

Source: House Committee on Ways and Means, Statement of Rick Foster, Chief Actuary, Centers for Medicare and Medicaid Services, Testimony before the House Committee on Ways and Means, March 24, 2004.

mandatory, and many states chose not to participate. As a compromise to ward off more far-reaching health policies, President Lyndon Johnson signed the Medicaid and Medicare programs into law in 1965.[25] Replacing all previous governmental health programs, Medicaid became the largest public assistance program in the nation. In 2006 Medicaid served about one in every six people at a combined federal and state cost of $319.6 billion.[26]

Medicaid is a means-tested public assistance program. Eligible persons receive services from physicians who accept Medicaid patients (in many places a minority of physicians) and other health care providers. These providers are reimbursed by the federal government on a per-patient basis. Alternatively, several states require Medicaid recipients to enroll in state-contracted HMOs.

Medicaid is a federal/state program. States determine eligibility within broad federal guidelines. For instance, each state establishes its own eligibility standards; determines the type, amount, duration, and scope of services; sets the rate of payment for services; and administers its own program. Medicaid policies can be complex and vary widely among states. For instance, a person eligible for Medicaid in one state may be ineligible in another, and the services provided by one state may differ in the amount, duration, or scope of services compared to other states. State legislatures may change Medicaid eligibility, services, or reimbursement during the year. To be eligible for federal funds, states are required to provide Medicaid coverage for most individuals who receive federally assisted income maintenance payments, as well as for related groups not receiving cash payments. The following are some examples of the mandatory Medicaid eligibility groups:

- Low-income families with children who meet certain eligibility requirements in the state's AFDC plan in effect on July 16, 1996
- Supplemental Security Income (SSI) recipients
- Infants born to Medicaid-eligible pregnant women. Medicaid eligibility continues throughout the first year of life, as long as the infant remains in the mother's household and she remains eligible, or would be eligible if she were still pregnant.
- Children under age 6 and pregnant women whose family income is at or below 133 percent of the federal poverty level. The maximum mandatory income level for pregnant women

and infants in certain states may be higher than 133 percent if the state has established a higher percentage for covering those groups. All poor children under age 19 are covered.

- Recipients of adoption assistance and foster care under Title IV-E of the Social Security Act
- Certain Medicare beneficiaries and special protected groups; for example, those who lose SSI payments due to earnings from work or increased Social Security benefits
- Other "categorically needy" groups as decided by the state. These optional groups share characteristics of the mandatory groups, but the eligibility criteria are somewhat more liberally defined. Examples of these optional groups are (1) infants up to age 1 and pregnant women not covered under the mandatory rules whose family income is below 185 percent of the federal poverty level; (2) certain targeted low-income children; (3) certain elderly, blind, or disabled adults who have incomes above those requiring mandatory coverage but below the federal poverty level; (4) children under age 21 who meet income and resources requirements for Temporary Assistance for Needy Families (TANF) but who otherwise are not eligible for TANF; (5) institutionalized individuals with income and resources below specified limits; (6) persons who would be eligible if institutionalized but are receiving care under home- and community-based services waivers; (7) recipients of state supplementary payments; and (8) tuberculosis (TB)-infected persons who would be financially eligible for Medicaid at the SSI level.[27] (Table 1 shows the numbers and eligibility categories of the Medicaid population.)

The medically needy (MN) option allows states to extend Medicaid eligibility to additional persons. These persons would be eligible for Medicaid under one of the mandatory or optional groups, except that their income or resources are above the eligibility level set by their state. Persons may qualify immediately or may "spend down" by incurring medical expenses that reduce their income to or below their state's medically needy level. By 2008, 24 states had elected to have a medically needy program. All remaining states utilize the "special income level" option to extend Medicaid to the "near poor" in medical institutional settings.

Table 1

Medicaid Recipients by Category, 1985–2005, Selected Years (in thousands)

Year	Total	Age 65 or Older	Blind/Disabled	Children	Adults	Other
1985	21,814	3,061	3,017	9,757	5,518	1,214
1988	22,907	3,159	3,487	10,037	5,503	1,343
1990	25,255	3,202	3,718	11,220	6,010	1,105
1993	33,432	3,863	5,016	16,285	7,505	763
1997	34,872	3,955	6,129	15,791	6,803	2,195
2000	42,886	4,289	7,479	21,086	10,543	862
2005	57,643	4,396	8,210	26,337	12,529	6,171

Source: Social Security Administration, "Unduplicated Number of Recipients, Total Vendor Payments, and Average Payment by Type of Eligibility Category, Fiscal Years 1985–2005" *Annual Statistical Supplement, 2007.* Retrieved July 2008, from www.socialsecurity .gov/policy/docs/statcomps/supplement/2007/8e.pdf

Medicaid is funded by federal/state matching funds. In every state the federal government pays at least half, and in some states far more, of state Medicaid spending. Title XIX of the Social Security Act allows considerable flexibility within the states' Medicaid plans. However, some federal services are mandatory if matching funds are to be received:

- Inpatient hospital services
- Outpatient hospital services
- Prenatal care
- Vaccines for children
- Physician services
- Nursing facility services for persons aged 21 or older
- Family planning services and supplies
- Rural health clinic services
- Home health care for persons eligible for skilled-nursing services
- Laboratory and X-ray services
- Pediatric and family nurse practitioner services
- Nurse midwife services
- Federally qualified health center (FQHC) services, and ambulatory services of an FQHC that would be available in other settings
- Early and periodic screening, diagnostic, and treatment (EPSDT) services for children under 21 years[28]

States may also receive federal matching funds to provide certain optional services:

- Diagnostic services
- Clinic services
- Intermediate care facilities for the mentally retarded (ICFs/MR)
- Prescribed drugs and prosthetic devices
- Optometrist services and eyeglasses
- Nursing facility services for children under age 21
- Transportation services
- Rehabilitation and physical therapy services
- Home- and community-based care to certain persons with chronic impairments[29]

Medicaid was designed as a federal/state program to pay for health care for low-income and disabled citizens. On average Medicaid pays for about one-third of all births in the United States and, in some states, pays as much as 55 percent. Almost half of Medicaid recipients are children. Despite this number, the greatest single outlay of Medicaid funds goes to the elderly. For example, in 2004, Medicaid payments for services for 4.7 million aged, who constituted 8 percent of all Medicaid beneficiaries, was about $13,295 per person compared to the average 4,640 per person.[30] Payment for long-term nursing home care alone accounted for 37 percent of the Medicaid budget. Of the almost 1.8 million nursing home beds in the United States in 2004, 1.33 million were certified as Medicare/Medicaid beds, and 286,000 were certified as Medicaid only.[31] Although Medicaid pays only 48 percent of the cost of nursing home care nationally, the program covers 70 percent of nursing home residents and it pays something toward the cost of nearly 80 percent of all patient days.[32] Not surprisingly, the growth of the nursing home industry parallels the creation of Medicaid. From 1965 (the year Medicaid was created) to 1970, the number of nursing home residents rose by 18 percent. From 1970 to 1975 that number rose another 17 percent; from 1975 to 1980 it rose 14 percent; and from 1980 to 1985 it rose about 12 percent. Because 75 percent of nursing homes are for-profit facilities, Medicaid functions as a de facto subsidy for the nursing home industry. Medicaid also functions as a subsidy for the middle class. Namely, when elderly parents of today's middle class spend down their assets they become eligible for Medicaid. Without Medicaid the children of elderly parents would be responsible for paying the average national rate of $150 a day for nursing home care. A nursing home resident lives on average 2.4 years, so the total cost to a middle-class family would be more than $128,000. If their elderly parents lived in Alaska, Connecticut, District of Columbia, Hawaii, Massachusetts, New Jersey, or New York, they would pay from $189,000 to $381,000 for the nursing home care of their parents.[33]

Despite federal guidelines, four important gaps exist in Medicaid coverage: (1) the low eligibility limits set for Medicaid; (2) the refusal of many states to adopt most or all of the Medicaid options; (3) the gaps in coverage for the elderly and disabled; (4) the general ineligibility of poor single persons and childless couples for Medicaid unless they are elderly or disabled; and (5) state cutbacks in Medicaid coverage because of lower state revenues. Even though Medicaid covered about one in every six people in 2006, it does not provide health care services even for some very poor persons unless they are in a designated group.[34]

For all its shortcomings, the Medicaid program has led to important gains in the nation's health. In 1963, 54 percent of poor people did not see a physician and only 63 percent of poor pregnant women received prenatal care (by 1976 that number had increased to 76 percent). Between 1964 and 1975 the use of physicians' services by poor children increased 74 percent. The increased health care utilization helped bring about a 49 percent drop in infant mortality between 1965 and 1988. For African American infants the drop in mortality was even sharper: Infant mortality dropped by only 5 percent in the 15 years before Medicaid, but it dropped by 49 percent in the 15 years after the program began. Ongoing preventive care also cut program costs for Medicaid-eligible children by 10 percent.[35] Medicaid is one of the most important governmental health programs in the United States.

The State Children's Health Insurance Program (SCHIP)

As part of the Balanced Budget Act of 1997, Congress created the State Children's Health Insurance Program (SCHIP), a federal–state partnership that allocated $48 billion over 10 years to expand health care coverage to uninsured children under age 19 who are ineligible for Medicaid or are not covered by private insurance. In 2007, $6.04 billion was spent on SCHIPs and 4.4 million children were enrolled (as at June 2007).[36] The SCHIP program gives states three options for covering uninsured children: designing a new children's health insurance program, expanding current Medicaid programs, or a combination of both strategies. By 2007, 19 states had chosen to implement a separate SCHIP program, 18 states had a combined SCHIP and Medicaid program, and the remainder expanded their Medicaid program. SCHIP is a block grant program financed by federal/state matching funds. Each state with an approved plan receives enhanced federal matching payments for its SCHIP expenditures up to a fixed state allotment. However, the largest share of SCHIP funds come from the federal government, and in 2007, the federal share accounted for 65 percent of the program's funding.[37] SCHIP allows states to charge premiums and copayments and covers a more limited set of benefits than Medicaid.

Before SCHIP, Medicaid eligibility was largely linked to welfare receipt. In large measure, Medicaid-eligible children had to be in an SSI or a TANF family. Perhaps the most important policy change in SCHIP is that it delinked state-subsidized child health care from welfare receipt. Before SCHIP only four states covered children whose family incomes were at least 200 percent of the federal poverty line. Now, SCHIP enables states to insure children from working families with incomes too high to qualify for Medicaid but too low to afford private health insurance. In 2008, 44 states including the District of Columbia covered children in families with incomes up to 200 percent of the federal poverty line ($42,400 per year for a family of four in 2008) or higher. Of the 38 states with separate SCHIP programs, nearly two-thirds (25 states) apply at least one type of disregard when determining eligibility.[38]

The Tobacco Settlement

Public policy is occasionally made by the court system rather than the legislature. This was the case in the 1998 tobacco industry settlement. For 40 years tobacco companies had won every lawsuit brought against them. The long march toward a national tobacco settlement began in April 1994, when representatives from seven of the leading American tobacco companies stood before Congress and swore that nicotine was not an addictive substance. The presentation was astounding even in the eyes of many people who were neutral toward cigarette companies. In 1998 the tobacco companies were forced to accept a 600-page Master Settlement Agreement (MSA) requiring them to pay $206 billion to 46 states over a 25-year period. (That amount did not include $40 billion in separate settlements reached by four other states.) From 2000 to 2004, states realized $37.5 billion in tobacco company payments. The MSA was the largest civil settlement in U.S. history. Payments are based on states' shares of the cost of smoking-related illnesses paid for through the Medicaid program. In exchange for the fine levied by the MSA, 39 states with pending individual lawsuits agreed to drop their cases. Following are some highlights of the MSA:

• Public health initiatives prohibit youth targeting in advertising and promotion; ban the use of cartoon characters in advertising, promotion, packaging, and labeling; restrict sponsorship by brand names; ban outdoor advertising; ban sales of merchandise with tobacco brand names; ban free samples to youth; and set minimum pack size at 20 cigarettes.

• Tobacco companies must develop corporate principles committed to compliance with the MSA, such as reducing youth smoking, designating an executive manager to identify ways to reduce youth access, and encouraging employees to identify alternative methods to reduce youth access.

• The MSA disbands tobacco trade associations, including the Council for Tobacco Research, the Tobacco Institute, and the Council for Indoor Air Research. It creates regulations and oversight for any new trade organizations.

• The settlement limits industry lobbying by prohibiting tobacco companies from opposing legislation aimed at restricting youth access and reducing consumption, specifically at the state and local levels.

• It includes the creation of a $1.45 billion public education fund to carry out a sustained nationwide advertising and education program to counter youth tobacco use and educate consumers about tobacco-related disease.[39]

States accrued significant revenues from the tobacco settlement: $6.4 billion in 2000, $6.9 billion in 2001, $8.3 billion in 2002, and $8.4 billion in 2003. Contrary to the hopes of many public health advocates, there are no restrictions on the use of MSA funds by the states. Some criticism of the tobacco settlement has centered on the following issues:

• The tobacco settlement did not require the money be spent on antismoking or health care programs. In 2003, 31 states used their tobacco settlement funds to fill budget gaps for 2004. Only a handful of states spent all of their tobacco money for health purposes in 2003. Only six states earned "A" grades from the American Lung Association in its 2004 report card for their antismoking programs. By 2008 states spent $717 million in tobacco prevention and cessation. Even though this is the highest figure in six years, it is less than half of what the Centers for Disease Control and Prevention (CDC) recommend.

• California, Connecticut, New Jersey, New York, Oregon, Rhode Island, Washington, and Wisconsin have cashed in a big chunk of their share of the settlement, selling future tobacco payments to investors for an upfront lump sum, known as securitization.

• Fewer people are smoking and hence states receive less because their yearly allotment from the settlement fund is based on the number of cigarettes sold in the state. Nationwide, the number of smokers has dropped to 13 percent of adults, down from about 50 percent 40 years ago. State allotments also will go down as smokers turn to cigarettes from off-brand manufacturers and online retailers that do not pay into the settlement fund. Given the fiscal crunch experienced by states, many are turning to raising cigarette taxes because studies have shown that this often causes people to stop smoking. Instead of curbing advertising, the tobacco industry actually raised its marketing budget to a record $14 billion from 1998 to 2004.[40]

(For some facts on the U.S. tobacco industry, see Figure 2 on the next page.)

Cigarettes account for over 90 percent of spending on tobacco products in the United States; in 1998 Americans smoked 24 billion packs. In 1995 U.S. spending for all tobacco products totaled about $49 billion.

Five American companies–Philip Morris, R.J. Reynolds, Brown and Williamson, Lorillard, and Liggett–produce almost all of the cigarettes sold in the United States. Two companies, Philip Morris and R.J. Reynolds, account for more than 70 percent of industry sales. About 36 billion packs of cigarettes were produced by U.S. firms in 1997; about 12 billion packs were exported to other countries and about 280 million shipped to U.S. territories and to U.S. armed forces stationed overseas. The rest were consumed by domestic smokers. Smokeless tobacco products are also produced by only five domestic manufacturers: U.S. Tobacco, Conwood, Pinkerton, National, and Swisher. Over 120 million pounds of chewing tobacco and snuff were produced in the United States in 1996; in 1995, smokeless tobacco companies posted revenues of $1.7 billion. About 2.5 billion large cigars and cigarillos and 14.2 million pounds of pipe and roll-your-own tobacco were produced by U.S. companies in 1995.

The United States is the second largest tobacco producer in the world, well below China. In 1996 tobacco was grown on over 124,000 U.S. farms, with a crop value of $2.9 billion. The tobacco industry supports more than 600,000 jobs.

Figure 2

Tobacco at a Glance

Source: CNN, "A Brief History of Tobacco." Retrieved 2001, from www.cnn.com/US/9705/tobacco/history/index.html

The Health Care Crisis

Health care in the United States is plagued with problems such as eroding coverage, rising costs, cost shifting, and an increasing number of anxious citizens. This and the following sections will explore some parameters of the health care crisis, including health care spending and cost efficiency, the effectiveness of the U.S. health care system, attempts at cost cutting, the growing role of managed care, and the impact of AIDS on the health care budget.

Overview of U.S. Health Care Expenditures

U.S. health care cost $2.26 trillion in 2007, up from $73 billion in 1970. This translates into about 16 percent of the total gross domestic product (GDP). (Health expenditures as a percentage of the GDP measure the proportion of all resources devoted to health care.) It is projected that by 2013 health care spending will rise to $3.4 trillion and make up 18.4 percent of the GDP. In comparison, health care spending in 1970 was only 7.1 percent of the GDP. From 1970 to 2007, per capita health care costs rose from $341 to $7,439, an increase of more than 2,000 percent (see Figure 3).

Health care spending accounted for about 14 percent of the GDP in 2001 compared to education which was only 4.8 percent. Moreover, the costs of providing health care have risen faster than the rate of inflation. From 1980 to 1992, annual increases in per capita expenditures on health care were approximately five points above the yearly inflation rate. The growth rate in health care expenditures decelerated somewhat in 1992 (registering less than three points above the rate of inflation)[41]—but it accelerated again in the late 1990s. In 2002 health care expenditures rose by 9.5 percent or more than four times the rate of inflation.

When health care expenditures are broken down, the largest share (31 percent) goes to hospitals.[42] (See Figure 4.) An increase in the cost of hospital care has been a key factor in driving up health care costs, and in 2004 that rose 6.5 percent which outpaced overall inflation. By comparison, in 1965 the average daily hospital room charge was $41; by

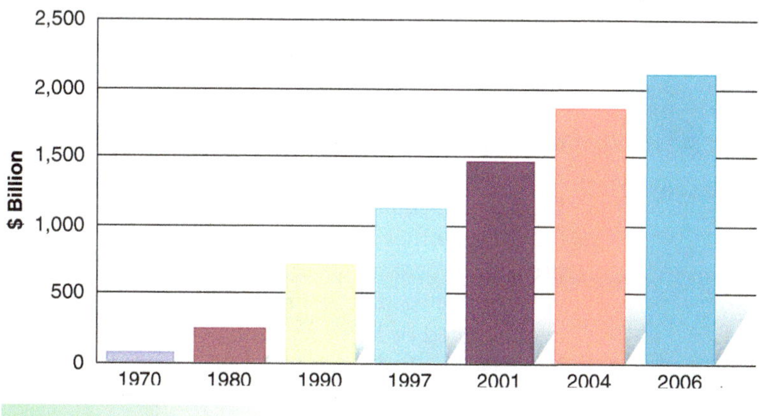

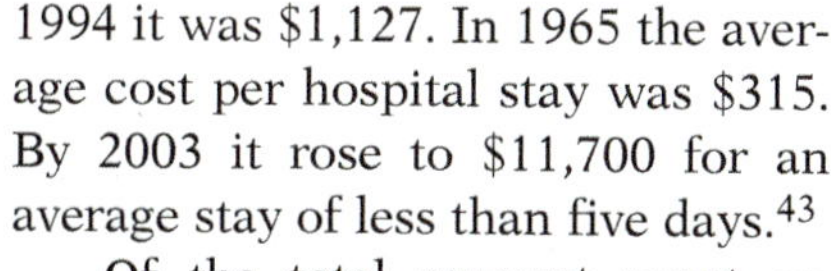

Figure 3

National Health Care Expenditures Selected Years, 1970–2006 (dollar amount in billions)

Source: HHS, Centers for Medicare & Medicaid Services, "National Health Expenditures Aggregate, Per Capita Amounts, Percent Distribution, and Average Annual Percent Growth, by Source of Funds: Selected Calendar Years 1960–2006". Retrieved July 2008, from www.cms.hhs.gov/NationalHealth ExpendData/downloads/tables.pdf

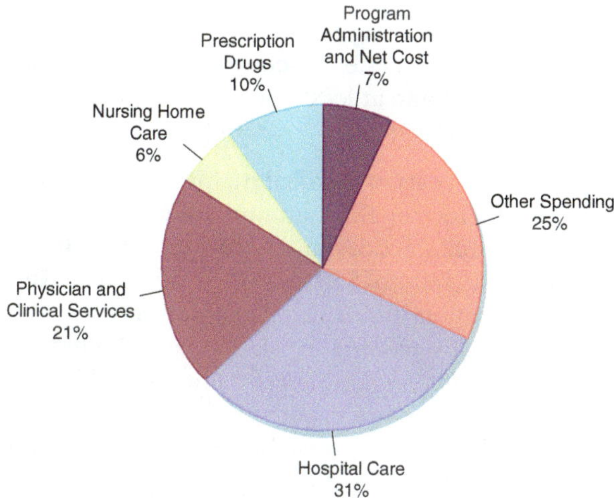

Figure 4

The Nation's Health Dollar, Calendar Year 2006: Where It Went

Note: "Other Spending" includes dental services, other professional services, home health, durable medical products, over-the-counter medicines and sundries, public health, other personal health care, research and structures, and equipment.

Source: HHS, Centers for Medicare & Medicaid Services. Retrieved July 2008, from www.cms.hhs.gov/National HealthExpendData/downloads/PieChartSourcesExpendit ures2006.pdf

1994 it was $1,127. In 1965 the average cost per hospital stay was $315. By 2003 it rose to $11,700 for an average stay of less than five days.[43]

Of the total amount spent on health in 2006, 34 percent came from private insurance, 19 percent from Medicare, 15 percent from Medicaid and SCHIP, and 12 percent from out-of-pocket expenses. The remaining 19 percent came from other public (workers' compensation, Department of Defense, etc.) and other private (including philanthropy) sources.[44] Premiums increased only 2 percent yearly from 1994 to 1998, but then jumped to 8.2 percent in 1998. In 2002 premiums shot up by 11.4 percent and then dropped to about 7.1 percent in 2004.[45]

U.S. Health Care in International Perspective

Health care costs are higher in the United States than in any other industrialized nation.[46] The United States spends more than other countries on health care, both in absolute dollars and in the share of total economic activity. Health spending per capita in the United States was almost $7,500 in 2007, more than twice the average for the other industrial nations in the Organization for Economic Cooperation and Development (OECD). Specifically, health spending in the United States in 2006 was 15.3 percent of the gross domestic product, nearly twice the percentage of Australia and the United Kingdom and by far the highest of 30 OECD countries.[47] (See Table 2 on the next page.) Although high expenditures are often equated with excellent medical treatment, the health of the average American—as measured by life expectancy and infant mortality—is below that of other major industrialized nations. More specifically, despite the high costs of U.S. medical care, life expectancy ranks only in the middle of the 30 OECD nations. This is due to a variety of factors, including diet, low levels of physical activity, births to teenage mothers, and the high number of violent deaths.[48]

The data clearly suggest that the U.S. health care system does not perform as well as health care systems in other industrialized countries. For one,

Table 2

Total Health Care Expenditures as a Percentage of GDP

Country	1975	2006	Percentage Point Change
United States	7.9	15.3	7.4
France	6.4	11.1	4.7
New Zealand	6.7	9.3	2.6
Germany	8.4	10.6	2.2
Canada	7.0	10.0	3.0
Australia	6.5	8.8 (2005)	2.3
United Kingdom	5.5	8.4	2.9

Source: OECD Health Data 2008, www.oecd.org

the United States is the only major industrialized country that fails to provide health coverage for all its citizens, yet spending on health is extremely high compared to other nations. The United States emphasizes private markets as a strategy for cost containment, yet health care costs are growing rapidly. Private spending as a share of total health care expenditures is far higher in the United States than in other industrialized nations. Moreover, out-of-pocket per capita health care spending in the United States was $707 in 2000, more than twice ($328) that of other industrialized nations.[49]

A common perception is that other industrialized countries control costs by rationing patient care. In fact, Americans receive fewer days of hospital care than residents of other industrialized nations and have about the same amount of physician visits. Americans are, however, more likely to undergo specialized medical procedures.[50]

According to the Commonwealth Fund, the United States falls short in access to needed services. The Fund ranked the United States last among five English-speaking countries on measures of equity and first for access problems due to costs. Americans are much more likely than their counterparts in other countries to say they did not visit a physician, fill a prescription, or get a recommended test, treatment, or follow-up care because of costs. Disparities between people in above-average and below-average income groups were greatest in the United States and the uninsured were much more likely to report problems in obtaining needed care.[51]

Infant mortality rates also illustrate troubling trends. In 2002 the United States had one of the highest infant mortality rates among OECD countries (6.69 per 1,000 live births). This compared unfavorably to Greece (6.25), New Zealand (6.18), Portugal (5.84), Italy (5.76), Czech Republic (5.46), United Kingdom (5.45), Ireland (5.43), Canada (4.95), and other nations. Another health indicator is premature deaths, or deaths that would have been preventable had appropriate medical knowledge been applied or had risky behavior been less prevalent. The United States had the most preventable deaths per 100,000 people, with Japan having the least.[52] In short, Americans are neither healthier nor live longer than people in similar industrial nations where health care spending is 50 percent lower.[53]

Explaining the High Cost of U.S. Health Care

Although accounting for the enormous costs of the U.S. health care system is complicated, some policy analysts attribute at least some of these costs to the following factors:

- High costs of medical malpractice.
- The former Bush administration argued that medical malpractice suits drove up health care costs from $60 to $80 billion a year. The Bush Administration maintains that this waste could be eliminated by passing legislation that limited (i.e., up to $250,000) what injured patients could collect in lawsuits. In contrast, both the General Accounting Office and the Congressional Budget Office criticized the 1996 study the Bush administration used as their main support, instead maintaining that any savings would be relatively small.[54]
- The United States leads the world in the development and use of medical technology, but these advances have come at a high price. For example, between 1980 and 1991, the number of coronary bypass operations for men increased from 108,000 to 206,000. By 2006, the number of bypass operations had reached 365,000 and the number of "stent" operations (an alternative to bypasses) had soared to nearly one million.[55] The treatment is now available for some diseases that were formerly untreatable, albeit at a high price. For example, some technologies are introduced before being

sufficiently tested to determine their cost effectiveness and superiority to existing technologies.

• The administrative costs involved in processing millions of insurance claims also add to rising health care expenditures. Harvard Medical School researchers reported in 2004 that the United States spent $399 billion a year on its health care bureaucracy, essentially the administrative costs of insurers, hospitals, doctors, nursing homes, and other institutions. In California, $45 billion of the $163 billion spent on health care (28 percent) went to administration.[56]

Hospital Costs

As noted earlier, 31.7 percent of all health care expenditures go toward hospital costs. The total costs of hospital care reached $648 billion in 2006, up from $28 billion in 1970. Since 2000, spending on hospital services has grown by over 7 percent each year. [57] According to the American Hospital Association, nearly 60 percent of hospital costs go to wages and benefits of caregivers and others. Labor costs account for the largest share of spending growth for hospital services from 2001 to 2003. In addition, the costs of technology, construction, and regulatory compliance account for a growing share of hospital costs. Predictions from the Centers for Medicare and Medicaid Services suggest that hospitals' share of national health expenditures will decline to less than 28 percent in 2012. However, much of this decline may be attributable to cuts in federal and state health programs.[58]

Physicians' Salaries

The second largest health care expenditure is for physicians' services. From 1970 to 1999, the cost of physicians' services rose by almost 1,800 percent. From 1980 to 1990 alone, the cost of physicians' services rose by 300 percent.[59] By 2008 the average salary for a number of specialist physicians was approaching $400,000 (see Table 3 on the next page).

Physician organizations argue that high salaries are necessary to repay the high debts incurred by medical students. In 2003, medical students graduated with 4.5 times more debt than in 1984. Moreover, in that same year the median debt was $100,000 and $135,000 for public school and private medical school graduates, respectively.[60] Despite this debt, the American Medical Association claims that "Even though the cost of medical school has risen faster than physician salaries, physicians still earn a decent return on their investment, roughly 6% for the $1.2 million a physician bears for the assorted costs of a public education and the wages lost while in school. Also, becoming a doctor is typically a higher paying investment when comparing average educational costs and salaries of business and law school graduates."[61]

The problem of high physician salaries is aggravated by the growth in the number of expensive medical specialists. Beginning in 1997 fewer medical students chose **primary care** tracks.

The increasing costs of malpractice suits against health care providers are felt most directly by consumers, who must pay higher medical costs to offset these suits.

Table 3

Average Salaries of Selected U.S. Practicing Physicians, 2008

Specialty	Salary
Orthopedic surgery	$439,000
Anesthesiology	336,000
Urology	387,000
Gastroenterology	379,000
Otolaryngology	362,000
General surgery	321,000
CRNA	185,000

Source: ASC Review, "Average Salaries for Top Recruited Specialties," June 27, 2008. Retrieved July 2008, from www.beckersasc.com/healthcare-business/healthcare-business-issues/average-salaries-for-top-recruited-specialties.html

By 2002, 20 percent fewer medical students were in a primary care track compared to 1997. For example, from 2000 to 2001 the number of medical students pursuing a family practice track dropped by 9.1 percent and the number of those pursuing internal medicine dropped by 2 percent. On the other hand, students pursuing neurological surgery increased by 36 percent, pathology by almost 27 percent, anesthesiology by almost 14 percent, and diagnostic radiology by 10 percent.[62] By 2005, approximately 60 percent of physicians were specialists and 40 percent primary care (12.3 percent in family medicine and general practice)—a reversal of the ratio that existed 30 years ago.[63]

The Pharmaceutical Industry

The high cost of prescription drugs is also driving up health care costs. Over the past decade, the share of health expenditures spent on pharmaceuticals in the United States increased from 8.9 percent of total health spending in 1995 to 12.6 percent in 2006. Consumers pay more for medicine in the United States than in any other country. The United States was the top spender on pharmaceuticals in 2006, with spending of $843 per person, followed by Canada, Belgium, and France.[64] Two-thirds of doctor visits result in a drug being prescribed, and overreliance on drugs is a major factor contributing to medical care being the third leading cause of death in the United States. Many of these people are exposed to financial catastrophe as a result of highly inflated drug prices. In contrast, manufacturers of the top 20 drugs have increased their profits at rates much higher than the average rate of Fortune 500 companies.[65]

Harvard physician Marcia Angell disputes the drug industry's reputation as an "engine of innovation," arguing that the top U.S. drug makers spend 2.5 times as much on marketing and administration as they do on research. According to Angell, at least a third of the drugs marketed by the industry were discovered by universities or small biotech companies but are sold to the public at inflated prices. Angell cites Taxol, the cancer drug discovered by the National Institutes of Health but sold by Bristol Myers Squibb for $20,000 a year, reportedly 20 times the manufacturing cost. Angell attacks the pharmaceutical industry—whose top ten companies make more in profits than the rest of the Fortune 500 combined—for using free market rhetoric while opposing competition.[66]

Though advertising prescription drugs has been legal for years, Food and Drug Administration (FDA) guidelines released in 1997 clarified the rules for advertising directly to consumers. Since the mid-1990s, pharmaceutical companies have tripled the amount of money spent on advertising prescription drugs directly to consumers. From 1996 to 2000, spending on these ads more than tripled, rising from $791 million to nearly $2.5 billion.[67]

In 1999 the drug industry spent $8.3 billion promoting its products—nearly half as much as the $17 billion it spent on research and development. Direct consumer advertising accounted for $1.3 billion of the total, with the rest being aimed at medical professionals. The advertising paid off. Posting huge increases in sales between 1993 and 1998 were heavily advertised drugs that included antihistamines (sales increases of $1.9 billion), antidepressants ($5 billion), cholesterol reducers ($3.4 billion), and anti-ulcer drugs ($2.7 billion).[68] Health care costs almost doubled in a decade, and prescription drug prices increased by 152 percent.[69]

Cutting Health Care Costs

There are two aspects to cutting health care costs. The first involves cutting costs for governmental health care programs; the second involves lowering overall medical costs.[70] The rising costs of Medicare have led the federal government to seek alternative ways to lower hospital costs, including the Diagnostic Related Group system (DRG). In 1983 Congress enacted the DRG form of medical payment. Although earlier Medicare rules had restricted the fees hospitals could charge, the government generally reimbursed them for the entire bill. This style of reimbursement was called retrospective (after-the-fact) payment. By contrast, DRGs are a form of **prospective payment system**, or payment before the fact, whereby the federal government specifies in advance what it will pay for the treatment of 468 classified illnesses or diagnosis-related groups.[71]

Developed by health researchers at the Yale-New Haven Hospital, the DRG system was designed to enforce economy by defining expected lengths of hospital stays. This system provides a treatment and diagnostic classification scheme, using the patient's medical diagnosis, prescribed treatment, and age as a means for categorizing and defining hospital services. In other words, the DRG system determines the length of a typical patient's hospital stay and reimburses hospitals only for that period of time. (Exceptions to the DRG classification system are made for long hospital stays, certain kinds of hospital facilities, hospitals that are the only facility in a community, and hospitals that serve large numbers of poor people.) Additional costs beyond the DRG allotment must be borne by the hospital. Conversely, if a patient requires less hospitalization than the maximum DRG allocation, the hospital keeps the difference. Hence, patients not yet ready for discharge (e.g., patients who do not have appropriate aftercare services available) may be discharged—a situation that can result in patient dumping.

Managed Care

Managed care became a household word in the 1990s. By 2008 more than 70 million Americans were enrolled in HMOs, up from 33.3 million in 1990. An estimated 90 million more are enrolled in PPOs, which cost more but allow patients more flexibility. Managed care and HMOs have been touted by the nation's large employers as a way to control health care costs. However, while managed care cut costs for most of the 1990s, by the end of the decade costs started climbing again, increasing by more than 7 percent in 2000.[72] From 2002 to 2004 managed care costs rose from 7 to 10 percent.

Paul Schmolling Jr., Merrill Youkeles, and William Burger define **managed care** as "an umbrella for health care insurance systems that contract with

a network of hospitals, clinics, and doctors who agree to accept fees for each service or flat payments per patient. The advantage to providers is that they are given a ready source of referrals."[73] Figure 5 on the next page lists various types of managed care systems.

Proponents of managed care argue that the system has effectively lowered health care costs without reducing the quality of health care services. They maintain that the system encourages more efficient and less expensive medical care and that it can stress prevention over treatment. Because doctors reimbursed by managed care organizations have little incentive to overtreat patients or recommend unnecessary medical care, the health care system is expected to be more efficient. This suggests that in some degree the proponents are correct. For example:

- The per capita growth in health care expenditures was 2.7 percent in 1994, dropping from 5 percent in the 1980s and early 1990s (before managed care had gained a strong foothold). Per capita national expenditures on health care were $3,510 in 1994, only $100 more than in 1993 and half the increase of 1992 to 1993.
- Physicians' salaries dropped 3.6 percent from 1993 to 1994—the first recorded drop in the history of the American Medical Association.[74]

Managed care is clearly shaping U.S. medicine. According to the AMA, the percentage of doctors who had contracts with managed-care plans increased from 61 percent in 1990 to 92 percent by 1997. Among doctors with such contracts, the proportion of their income resulting from those plans rose from 35 percent to 40 percent between 1996 and 1997.[75] Broadly defined, private managed plans now cover two-thirds of all privately insured Americans. Jumping on the bandwagon, the federal and many state governments have encouraged (and, in some states, required) Medicare and Medicaid beneficiaries to join managed care plans. By 2003, there were 179 Medicare plans with 5 million members, 1 million less than five years previously because of HMOs dropping elderly consumers.[76] Insurers have charged that the federal government's Medicare reimbursement rate is too low to keep pace with medical inflation and thus ensure the financial solvency of Medicare HMOs.[77]

Critics of managed care (including HMOs) maintain that they are plagued with serious problems.[78] Indeed, managed care has not won the hearts and minds of the public. In a 1999 survey, only 46 percent of Americans said they were very confident their treatment would be based on their

- **Health Maintenance Organizations (HMO)**—a prepaid or capitated insurance plan in which individuals or their employers pay a fixed monthly fee for services rather than a separate charge for each visit or service.

- **Preferred Provider Organizations (PPO)**—a type of HMO whereby an employer or insurance company contracts with a selected group of health care delivery providers for services at preestablished reimbursement rates. Consumers have the choice of who to contact to provide the service. If a doctor is not on the provider list, higher out of pocket expenses will result.

- **Exclusive Provider Organization (EPO)**—a type of HMO where members must get care only from the EPO doctors who may only treat members of the plan.

- **The Independent Practice Association (IPA)**—a type of HMO which has large numbers of independent doctors in private practice. Physicians are paid a fixed fee for treating IPA members but also can treat patients who are not members of the plan.

- **The Network Model**—multispecialty groups of doctors who have contracts with more than one HMO. Doctors work out of their own offices.

- **Point of Service (POS)**—an option that can be offered by any type of HMO. If patients use doctors in their HMO network, and if referrals are made only by the primary care physician, only nominal fees are charged. If patients use doctors outside their HMO network the cost is higher.

- **Physician–Hospital Organization (PHO)**—organized groups of doctors affiliated with a particular hospital who provide services to patients enrolled in their plan as they would in an HMO.

Figure 5

Types of Managed Care Plans

Source: Naomi Brill and Joanne Levine, *Working With People*, 7th ed. (Boston: Allyn & Bacon, 2001).

health care needs rather than on the cost of their care. Another national poll found that 61 percent of Americans agreed with the statement "I'm frustrated and angry about the state of the health care system in this country." In addition, only a third of people who had been ill in the previous year said they were completely happy or very happy about the care they received through their HMO.[79]

Many physicians believe the quality of care has gotten worse under managed care. Some physicians have joined unions, and others have formed networks to negotiate contracts with managed care. Still others have stopped taking HMO patients. Hospitals say they are squeezed by slow and low payments from HMOs and cuts to Medicare. Many have had to cut staff. Nurses say that hospitals often are so short staffed that patient care is seriously compromised. One study found that nearly 70 percent of nurses worry about inadequate staffing levels.[80]

Managed care plans generally gate-keep the access to specialists for consumers. These plans do this by pressuring primary physicians to not refer or by limiting specialist care to one or two visits. Some managed care plans are reluctant to cover costly procedures or experimental treatments, especially those relating to cancer. Still other plans refuse to pay for medical care clients receive while out of state, even if it was required in an emergency. Some enrollees complain that managed care forces them to use only primary care physicians, hospitals, and specialists that are on an approved list, which restricts their freedom of choice. And some managed care operations do not provide the same level of benefits as Medicare, especially when it comes to home health care, physical therapy, and nursing home care.[81] Critics also note that the size of managed care operations has led to greater bureaucratization and impersonality.[82]

During the late 1990s many HMOs were in financial trouble and the industry posted $1.25 billion in net losses in 1998. To compensate, HMOs raised premiums, cut services, or many left the business. Several large managed care companies across the country went bankrupt, leaving state officials and consumers scrambling to find replacement coverage. From the mid-1990s onward the health insurance market consolidated at a rapid pace. Between 1995 and 2001 there were over 350 mergers involving health insurers and managed care organizations. The result is that more than half of all commercially insured Americans are now covered by the 10 largest health insurers. In many parts of the country health insurance markets are dominated by a few companies that have significant power over the marketplace. According to one AMA study, there is at least one insurer with a market share in excess of 30 percent in 89 percent of highly concentrated metropolitan areas. In 40 percent of these markets a single insurer has a market share in excess of 50 percent; and in 15 percent they have a market share of more than 70 percent.[83] This trend has resulted in the profit margins of health insurers rising, albeit in fits and starts.[84]

Managed care companies are boxed in to a degree. Specifically, HMOs cannot reprise their 1990s role as gatekeepers that restrict care to boost the bottom line. Regulations on the state and federal level have dampened that idea, and after bad publicity in the 1990s, managed care companies became somewhat more lenient and paid for more care. Instead of gate-keeping, these companies simply passed along premium hikes plus a few percent for profits. In short, instead of cutting costs, managed care companies simply pass on rate hikes. On the other hand, managed care companies cannot survive by simply passing along high rate hikes each year. Their role of belt-tightening has been lost, and with it, their justification for providing affordable health care.

The Underinsured

The U.S. medical system provides high-quality care for most people in the upper and upper-middle classes, who are protected by adequate health insurance. Although most Americans are covered by private insurance plans,[85] gaps in private health insurance may include high deductibles and copayments, limits on the length of hospital stays, dollar limits on payments to hospitals and physicians, exclusion of certain laboratory tests, refusal of coverage for office visits and routine health care, noncoverage for mental health services, refusal of coverage to persons who are found to be in poor health when applying for insurance, and a lack of coverage for dental and eye care. Because privately purchased health insurance has become almost unaffordable, the availability of health insurance may be a major factor in an individual's job search or decision to continue in a job.[86] Moreover, employers may be reluctant to hire people with high-risk conditions, because of the negative effect on their insurance premiums. Finally, one of the most dramatic gaps is the frequent failure of some private health insurance plans to cover catastrophic medical costs—those costs that could reduce a middle-class family to "medically indigent" status within only a few months.

AIDS and Health Care

The U.S. health care crisis is aggravated by the AIDS epidemic that first surfaced during the presidency of Ronald Reagan. The Reagan administration initially saw the AIDS problem as being of little consequence. Indeed, expressing public concern for the suffering of homosexuals was a political liability—especially given that the Republican Party was actively courting the religious right, some of whose leaders saw AIDS as a divine punishment for the sin of homosexuality.[87] Unlike the Reagan and Bush administrations, the Clinton administration was unafraid to address the AIDS crisis head-on. President Clinton pushed for full funding for the Ryan White Care Act, created the National Task Force on AIDS Drug Development, strengthened the Office of AIDS Research at the National Institutes of Health, and placed HIV/AIDS victims under the protection of the Americans with Disabilities Act.

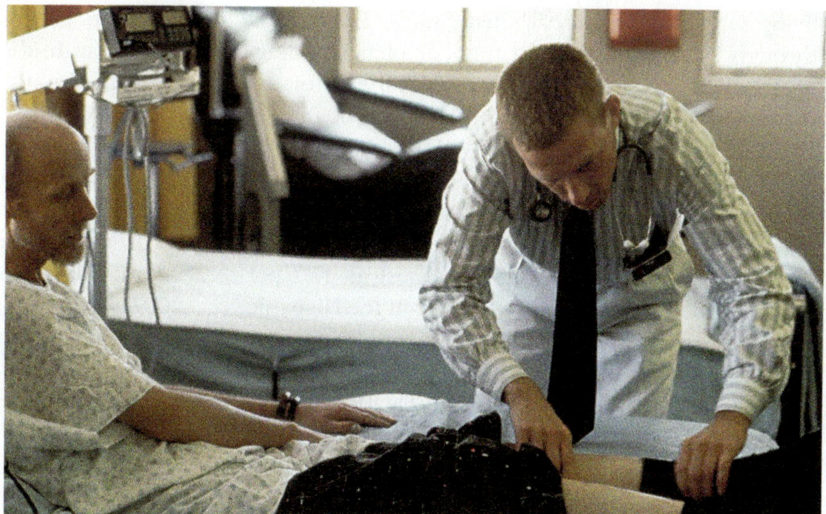

■ *According to a Rand study, not all people with HIV are treated equally. Among adults with HIV, women receive inferior care compared to men, as do African Americans and Hispanics compared to non-Hispanic whites.*

Table 4

Characteristics of Male and Female Adults/Adolescents Living with AIDS in the U.S., 2006

Exposure Category	White (not Hispanic)		African American (not Hispanic)		Hispanic	
	Male	Female	Male	Female	Male	Female
Sex between men	101,299	NA	57,520	NA	36,087	NA
Injecting drug use	13,168	7,407	33,911	18,531	14,795	5,025
Sex between men and injecting drugs	12,393	NA	10,121	NA	4,352	NA
High risk heterosexual contact	6,081	11,350	24,205	41,741	7,816	11,092
Other	1,743	508	1,602	1,456	574	413
Total	134,684	19,265	127,359	61,728	63,624	16,530

Source: Centers for Disease Control and Prevention, "Estimated Numbers of Persons Living with AIDS at the End of 2006, by Race/Ethnicity, Sex, and Transmission category—50 States and the District of Columbia," Basic Statistics, HIV/AIDS Surveillance Report. Retrieved July 2008, from www.cdc.gov/hiv/topics/surveillance/resources/reports/2006report/pdf/2006SurveillanceReport.pdf

The epidemiological data on AIDS are striking. At the end of 2006, the prevalence rate of AIDS among adults and adolescents in the United States was estimated at 178.6 per 100,000. Among male adults and adolescents, male-to-male sexual contact is a key characteristic for people living with AIDS (nearly 200,000) and for African American females, heterosexual contact (over 40,000) (see Table 4).[88] Marked declines in AIDS deaths began in 1996 because of the widespread use of potent combination antiretroviral therapies. By 2002 AIDS prevalence was continuing to rise, with almost 400,000 persons living with AIDS in the United States. From 2002 through 2006 the estimated number of newly diagnosed AIDS cases remained stable with the estimated rate of AIDS cases in 2006 being 12.3 per 100,000.[89]

The prevalence of HIV/AIDS in African Americans and Hispanics is much higher than for other groups. In 2006, African Americans accounted for 49 percent of all HIV/AIDS cases diagnosed, and their rate of HIV/AIDS was the highest at 67.7 per 100,000, followed by 25.5 per 100,000 in the Hispanic population, 8.8 per 100,000 for American Indians/Alaska Natives, 8.2 per 100,000 for whites, and 6.7 per 100,000 for the Asian/Pacific Islander population. From 2003 through 2006, the estimated number of HIV/AIDS cases increased approximately 5 percent among males and decreased 6 percent for females. In 2006, males accounted for 74 percent of all HIV/AIDS cases among adults and adolescents. From 2002 through 2006, the estimated number of

AIDS cases decreased 10 percent in the West, 6 percent in the Northeast, and remained stable in the South and the Midwest.[90]

According to a recent Rand study, not all people with HIV are treated equally. Among adults with HIV in the United States, women receive inferior care compared to men, as do African Americans and Hispanics compared to non-Hispanic whites. Uninsured and Medicaid-insured HIV victims receive inferior care compared to the privately insured. Patients infected through heterosexual, gay, or bisexual contacts receive superior care compared to patients infected through injection drug use. In sum, disparities in HIV care are frequently associated with insurance status, gender, race, ethnicity, exposure group, income, education, age, and even geographical region.[91]

HIV/AIDS has spread at an alarming rate over the past few decades, although it has slowed slightly in recent years (see Table 5). In 2007, about 2.5 million people were newly infected with HIV. In 2007, around 2.1 million people died from AIDS (over 30 million have died since the first cases of AIDS were identified in 1981). According to the World Health Organization, about 33 million people were living with HIV/AIDS worldwide in 2007.[92]

Nowhere has the impact of HIV/AIDS been more severe than in sub-Saharan Africa:

- HIV/AIDS has reduced life expectancy by more than 20 years in Botswana, Lesotho, Swaziland,

Table 5

Regional HIV/AIDS Statistics, 2007

Region	Adults and Children Living with HIV/AIDS	Adults and Children Newly Infected with HIV	Adult Prevalence Rate
Sub-Saharan Africa	20.9–24.3 million	1.4–2.4 million	4.6–5.5%
North Africa and the Middle East	270,000–500,000	16,000–65,000	0.2–0.4%
South and Southeast Asia	3.3–5.1 million	180,000–740,000	0.2–0.4%
East Asia	620,000–960,000	21,000–220,000	< 0.2%
Oceania	53,000–120,000	11,000–26,000	0.3–0.7%
Latin America	1.4–1.9 million	47,000–220,000	0.4–0.6%
Caribbean	210,000–270,000	15,000–23,000	0.9–1.2%
Eastern Europe and Central Asia	1.2– 2.1 million	70,000–290,000	0.7–1.2%
Western and Central Europe	600,000–1.1 million	19,000–86,000	0.2–0.4%
North America	480,000–1.9 million	38,000–68,000	0.5–0.9%
Total	33.2 million	2.5 million	0.8%
	(30.6–36.1 million)	(1.8–4.1 million)	(0.7–0.9%)

Source: UNAIDS/WHO, "AIDS Epidemic Update," December 2007. Retrieved July 2008, from http://data.unaids.org/pub/EPISlides/2007/2007_epiupdate_en.pdf

and Zimbabwe. By 2015 the disease will have reduced populations of the 38 most affected countries by 10 percent or some 91 million people.

- Young adults aged 15 to 24 account for half of all new HIV cases; the majority are women.
- Women are biologically two to four times more likely to contract HIV during unprotected sex than men, and teenagers are even more biologically vulnerable.
- AIDS has orphaned at least 14 million children. By 2010 a number expected to double.
- AIDS is directly or indirectly responsible for up to 60 percent of all child deaths in Africa.
- Fewer than 5 percent of all the people with HIV/AIDS in the developing world have access to lifesaving antiretroviral (ARV) therapy.[93]

Reforming U.S. Health Care

The Business Roundtable is a Washington, DC–based organization of the Chief Executive Officers of leading U.S. corporations. Together they represent more than 10 million employees and $4.6 trillion in annual revenues.[94] On January 16, 2007, Business Roundtable joined with AARP and the Service Employees International Union (SEIU) to create the Divided We Fail partnership.[95] Among other things, the Divided We Fail platform includes, "All Americans should have access to affordable health care, including prescription drugs, and these costs should not burden future generations."[96] The U.S. Chamber of Commerce, the world's largest association of businesses with more than 3 million corporate members, echoes this sentiment in their Policy Priorities for 2004 that include "passage of legislation to help business continue to provide affordable coverage for their employees."[97] Even the National Agenda of the smaller National Federation of Independent Businesses, traditionally an opponent of attempts to expand mandatory health insurance coverage, states that "finding and affording quality health insurance is a top concern of small-business owners."[98] In the past there has been a large gap between access/affordability and universal coverage; however, there are signs that this gap is narrowing.

In 2007 Andy Stern, President of SEIU, and Lee Scott, CEO of Wal-Mart, together announced the good of universal health care coverage by 2012.[99] Prior to that in December 2006, Steve

Burd, chairman and CEO of Safeway, stood with Senator Ron Wyden and Andy Stern to advocate for universal coverage. Burd even announced the creation of a new advocacy group composed of businesses to be called the Coalition to Advance Health Care Reform.[100] What Burd came to realize is that access to affordable health care cannot be achieved without universal participation. Universal health care is not simply a moral issue. It represents a major cost in operating a business and has a significant impact on international competitiveness. For potential employees it is a jobs issue, with escalating health costs impacting the ability of the business sector to create and sustain new jobs.

In January 2004, a coalition of associations representing medical providers, pharmaceutical companies, insurance companies, businesses, and leading nonprofits began working to see if they could come to a consensus on how to reform health care. On January 18, 2007, this new Health Coverage Coalition for the Uninsured (HCCU) (www.coalitionfortheuninsured.org) issued "Expanding Health Care Coverage in the United States: A Historic Agreement."[101] The policy recommendations advocated by HCCU have the goal "to expand health coverage to as many people as possible as soon as possible."[102] The specific proposals rely heavily on tax credits to fund the cost of health insurance. Signatories to this agreement include the American Medical Association, the American Hospital Association, America's Health Insurance Plans, Kaiser Permanente, Pfizer, and the U.S. Chamber of Commerce. The policy proposals by HCCU are more incremental than the universal coverage being advocated by Burd, yet the mere existence of a policy consensus by associations this diverse suggests that some form of health care reform cannot be too far away, and HCCU does have the same goal as Burd—coverage for everyone.

The U.S. health care system is driven by a combination of ideological and fiscal variables. Primary among these is whether **health care access** should be a right or a privilege. Conservatives generally believe that access to medical care is a privilege that must be earned through past or present labor force participation. Democrats, in turn, believe that health care should be a right that is somehow tied to labor force participation, except in instances in which people are not linked to the workforce. Progressive thinkers, grounded in a European tradition, argue that health care is a right that should be bestowed upon each individual at birth.

Another issue in the health care debate is the role of the private marketplace in the provision of medical care. Conservatives support the **commodification** of health care and believe that medical care should be lodged squarely in the private marketplace. Conservatives argue that medical institutions and drug companies should be free to establish the prices of health care and medical goods. They believe that in medical care, as with other commodities, increased competition lowers the price of goods and increases quality. Government regulation of the health care market is therefore seen as leading to more inefficiencies, lower quality or poorer service, and higher prices. Some liberals believe the private marketplace is the proper venue for the delivery of health care, but they also recognize that health care is a commodity that does not respond to market conditions in the same way as other commodities. For example, if a person is immobilized by cardiac arrest, it is unlikely that he or she will shop around for the cheapest cardiac care prices. Likewise, most patients facing serious surgery will not choose a surgeon based on price point. These conservatives believe that the health care marketplace must be somewhat regulated by government to ensure quality, price, and access.

More progressive thinkers argue that health care is too important to be left to the vicissitudes of the marketplace. For them, health care should be removed from the context of a market in which decisions are made solely on economic precepts. Health care must therefore be free or heavily subsidized at the point of access, universal in its coverage, and administered and controlled by government.

During the past 30 years, most proposals designed to reform or transform health care in the United States fall into three basic categories: (1) removing health care from the marketplace, (2) maintaining the private health care system while providing universal coverage through national health insurance, and (3) incremental reforms designed to soften the harder features of the U.S. health care system.

National Health Service

The most radical proposal for reforming the U.S. health care system involved the creation of a National Health Service (NHS). Proposed in the mid-1970s by left-wing health planners and members of Congress, the plan was promoted by Congressman Ronald Dellums (a social worker). The NHS would have established health care as a right of citizenship. Similar to the British model, it would have provided free (no fee at the point of access and no payments from third-party vendors) and comprehensive health care coverage, including diagnostic, therapeutic, preventive, rehabilitative, environmental, and occupational health services. To improve the maldistribution of medical services, the NHS would have provided free medical education in return for required periods of service in medically underserved areas.[103] The goal of the NHS was the elimination of private profit in the health care system.

Supporters argue that socialized health care would allow for the coordination of health services and reduce profiteering by professionals and corporations. Moreover, they contend that the experience of other countries illustrates that a system incorporating strict budgeting, nationalization, and the elimination of the profit motive arrests the growth of health care costs and, in the end, will prove less expensive than the current privatized system.

National Health Insurance

Single Payer System Another proposal for restructuring U.S. health care as a **single-payer system** was the National Health Care Act of 1992. As in the Canadian model, states would have had responsibility for ensuring the delivery of health services, for paying all providers, and for planning in accordance with federal guidelines. Although this plan would have allowed the practice of private medicine, the act would have discontinued private health insurance coverage.[104] Supporters of this bill claimed that it would immediately reduce health care spending by 18 percent, and that a single payer approach would reduce the fraud endemic to a multiple-payer system.[105]

Another strategy to restructure the U.S. health care system is **national health insurance (NHI).** According to Paul Starr, the United States was on the brink of establishing national health insurance several times during the twentieth century, but each time factors unique to the country's political and social institutions prevented its adoption.[106] In the 1930s, for example, NHI plans began to proliferate as part of Roosevelt's New Deal; but the idea was abandoned because of the strident opposition of the AMA—originally a supporter of NHI—and the fear that NHI's inclusion would jeopardize passage of the 1935 Social Security Act. President Harry Truman took up the NHI banner in the days

following World War II, but by that time most middle-class and unionized workers were covered by private insurance plans. Moreover, the AMA again set its powerful lobbying machine into motion, this time equating national health insurance with socialized medicine and with Communism.[107]

The most recent incarnation of NHI occurred in the Health Security Act (HSA) proposed by former President Bill Clinton in 1993. Although the HSA was not a NHI per se, it contained important components of national insurance. Clinton's bill was based partly on the ideas of the Jackson Hole Group, who reiterated the need for cost consciousness in health care and the need for substantial investment in outcome and evaluation research.[108]

To formulate the health care bill, Hillary Clinton and Ira Magaziner led a 500-person task force charged with (1) extending medical insurance to the uninsured at a reasonable cost; (2) guaranteeing continued coverage when workers change jobs or get sick; (3) curbing and controlling steadily rising health care costs by developing health care networks; (4) addressing the problems of the insurance industry; (5) stopping drug companies from inflating drug prices; (6) developing a basic benefits package for every American; and (7) providing universal health care coverage. The result of this task force was the 1,342-page Health Security Act.

The HSA would have worked in the following manner: All citizens and legal immigrants would get a card guaranteeing them a comprehensive lifelong package of health care benefits, including inpatient and outpatient medical care, prescription drugs, dental and vision care, long-term care, mental health services, and substance abuse treatment. Coverage would be continuous regardless of employment status. All participants would buy into large purchasing pools called Health Care Alliances. Each alliance would offer separate plans for consumers: (1) a **fee-for-service** option allowing consumers to choose their doctors; (2) a plan based on joining a network of doctors and hospitals; and (3) the choice of an HMO. Charges for low-income self-insurers would be based on a sliding scale. Those on public assistance would have their fees paid by Medicaid. Employers would pay 80 percent of the premium of the standard benefit package and workers would pay the additional 20 percent.

Despite a promising start, the HSA bill faltered almost from the moment of its inception. Opposition came from several quarters. Smaller health insurers felt they were being maneuvered out of the industry and took to the airwaves. Almost immediately, the Health Insurance Association of America (HIAA) broadcast $2 million worth of "Harry and Louise" commercials attacking the HSA as rationing health care under socialized medicine.[109] Within days HIAA claimed that more than 40,000 callers had phoned their 800 number to register complaints about health care reform.[110] On the congressional side, small business lobbyists argued that the costs of the employer mandate would bankrupt thousands of small companies. Within weeks, dozens of lobbyists from such groups as pharmaceutical companies, tobacco companies, restaurants, and labor unions besieged Congress. Anticipating the 1994 elections, health industry interest groups contributed $26 million to congressional campaigns.[111] Observers put the price tag on defeating the HSA at $100 million.[112] The conservative 104th Congress of 1994 killed the possibility of comprehensive health care reform.

Critics of NHI plans charge that they would modify payment mechanisms rather than encourage major changes in the health care system. Although NHI schemes would equalize the ability of patients to pay, they would not improve the accessibility or the quality of services. Furthermore, most NHI proposals call for coinsurance (copayments) in amounts that many poor people could not afford.[113] Contrary to what some critics claim, NHI schemes are not socialized medicine: Hospitals would remain private, doctors would continue to be private practitioners, and most NHI plans reserve a major role for private insurance companies.

Incremental Reform

Incremental health care reform has proved more acceptable to the general public and policymakers than sweeping reforms. This approach has generally focused on remedying the more troubling aspects of the private health care system and on fine-tuning public health care programs.

A conservative approach to incremental health care reform is based on the concept of the individual medical savings account (MSA). The MSA is a form of self-insurance whereby individuals can purchase high-deductible health insurance while setting aside pretax dollars to pay for medical expenses. Opponents of MSAs fear, however, that these plans would benefit only the healthy and wealthy, leaving those with less money and more health problems behind in an increasingly costly insurance pool.

Congress also passed legislation in 1996 to require insurers to pay for a 48-hour hospital stay following a vaginal birth and a 96-hour stay after a cesarean section. In addition, Congress passed an amendment designed to create some level of parity between mental health and physical health benefits. The amendment requires insurers to set the same levels for annual and lifetime caps on mental health benefits as on physical health benefits. However, the bill stipulates that plans are not prohibited from requiring preadmission screening before authorization of services; nor are they prohibited from restricting mental health coverage to only those services that are medically necessary.[114]

Other reforms have been enacted on state levels. In Hawaii, employers are required to insure employees who work more than 20 hours a week.[115] A Health Rights program in Minnesota extends health care coverage to all noncovered low-income residents and charges them on a sliding-scale basis.[116]

Barack Obama's health care plan fits squarely under the category of incremental reform. Building on the existing system, Obama's plan is based on using current providers, doctors, and insurance plans. Under this plan, those who liked their health insurance would keep it with no changes except lower premiums. The 40 million plus Americans without health insurance would have a choice of health insurance options. Obama's plan would:

- Require insurance companies to cover pre-existing conditions.
- Create a new Small Business Health Tax Credit to help small businesses provide health insurance to their employees.
- Lower business costs by covering a portion of the catastrophic health costs they pay in return for lower employee premiums.
- Prohibit insurers from overcharging doctors for malpractice insurance.
- Make employer contributions fairer by requiring large employers not offering health insurance to contribute a percentage of payroll costs toward employee health care.
- Establish a National Health Insurance Exchange allowing individuals and small businesses to buy affordable health coverage.
- Allow cheaper medicines from abroad, increase the use of generic drugs in public programs, and take on drug companies that block generic medicines from the market.

Obama proposed to pay for his $50 to $65 billion health care reform by ending the Bush tax cuts for those earning more than $250,000 per year and retaining the estate tax at its 2009 level.[117]

Comparative Analysis: Health Care in Canada and Britain

Americans often fail to look at what is happening in other parts of the world. This section briefly explores medical systems in Canada (a single-payer system), Great Britain (National Health Service), and Australia which has a hybrid public–private system.

The Canadian Health Care System

The current Canadian health care system began less than 50 years ago when a hospital insurance plan in Saskatchewan evolved into a network of plans developed by Canada's 10 provinces and 2 territories.[118] In 1966 Canada passed the Medical Care Act (Medicare), which instituted a nationwide federal/provincial health insurance system that is publicly funded, privately delivered, and free at the point of access.[119] Each province is responsible for administering its own health care plan.[120] Although each of the 10 provinces and 2 territories has its own unique plan, all plans are essentially universal and comprehensive, covering all residents for inpatient and outpatient hospital and physician services. To receive federal funds, every plan must meet basic national eligibility standards:

1. *Universal coverage.* Every provincial resident must be covered under uniform terms and conditions.
2. *Portability.* Plans must be portable, in that they must cover residents who are temporarily away from home or who have moved to another province.
3. *Comprehensiveness.* All approved hospital and physicians' services must be covered, including medical and hospital care, mental health services, and prescription drugs for those over 65 and for those with catastrophic illnesses.
4. *No cost to patient at point of access.* Services must be free at point of access and include no financial barriers to care.
5. *Nonprofit administration.* Plans must be nonprofit and publicly administered.
6. *Freedom of choice.* Each Canadian is free to choose his or her provider.[121]

Unlike the U.S. system, the Canadian system is grounded in universal entitlement rather than linked to employment. Accordingly, all of Canada's 33 million residents are eligible for provincial health insurance, regardless of their employment status, except for people covered by other federal programs such as the military.[122] Questions arose in the 1980s about direct charges made to patients beyond the level paid by the provincial health care plan. The 1984 Canada Health Act eliminated all extra billing and user charges. Today virtually every Canadian is covered by a comprehensive medical and hospital plan with no copayment.[123]

General practitioners (GPs) make up the majority of physicians in Canada and provide most of the nation's health care. Specialists can be used only if a referral is received from the GP. Although patients may choose their primary care physician, the choice is contingent upon whether the physician has openings for new patients. Patients also use the hospital in which the physician has admitting privileges. In addition to providing free physician and hospital care, most provinces cover the cost of travel and medical services if the treatment cannot be obtained in the area where the patient resides. Although covered health care is free at the point of access, some elements not covered include out-of-hospital drugs, dental care, eyeglasses, physical therapy, and chiropractic care not ordered by a medical doctor.[124]

Contrary to some misconceptions, the Canadian health care system is not a form of socialized medicine; instead, it is a social insurance model that mixes public funds with private health care delivery. Canada's single-payer model is based on the idea that provincial governments function as single-source payers of health care with a centralized locus of control. As such, Canada's provincial governments reimburse both hospitals and physicians on a prospective budgeting basis. Specifically, private physicians' fees are negotiated between the provincial governments and the medical associations. Reimbursements for physicians are on a fee-for-service basis. The salaries of physicians in Canada are generally lower than those of their U.S. counterparts. Because of budgetary problems, several provinces have limited payments to physicians who earn above a certain income by lowering the reimbursement rates.[125]

There are more than 1,250 hospitals in Canada, of which 57 percent are run by religious orders or nonprofit organizations. Hospital reimbursements are made on a global prospective basis. In other words, hospitals operate on a negotiated but fixed yearly budget. As such, they must stay within the budgetary allotment granted by the province regardless of the number of patients seen in a year.[126]

Canada's Medicare system is paid for with a mixture of federal and provincial funds. Federal funds go to the provinces in the form of block grants and transfer payments. The provinces obtain funds to operate the medical system from general revenue taxes and, in the case of Alberta and British Columbia, from insurance premiums paid for by employers. Provinces that charge such premiums provide exemptions or subsidies for the aged, the unemployed, and the indigent.[127]

Critics of Canadian health care point to numerous problems facing the system. One of the most important is the question of funding. Cutbacks in government spending (from 1981 to 1992 the Canadian government cut transfer payments to the provinces by almost $8 billion), increasing demands for services, and the high cost of technology have made controlling costs the number one issue facing the Canadian health care system.

Some critics have charged that Canada's prospective global budgeting system for hospitals has caused health care rationing. These critics argue that to cope with budgetary constraints, Canadian hospitals are closing down hospital wards during certain times of the year; filling up one-third of hospital beds with long-term elderly patients to keep high-volume (and expensive) traffic down; using cheaper medical materials; rushing medical procedures and thus jeopardizing accuracy; providing substandard hospital care; not investing in technology or capital improvements; and prioritizing illnesses into "urgent," "emergent," and "elective" categories, thereby causing artificial queues for treatment.[128] According to these critics, health care rationing is having a dramatic effect on Canada's medical system.[129]

Some health care analysts have suggested that the United States adopt a health care reform plan similar to the Canadian model.[130] They argue that a single-payer system allows for greater control of systemwide health care capacity—that is, supply, distribution, and costs—than does a fragmented insurance system in which no party has the overall authority for controlling the production and distribution of medical goods and services. Health care analysts also point to the uneven coverage provided to Americans under the current patchwork of private and public health insurance plans. In comparison to the universal, comprehensive, and publicly funded health care system that Canadians enjoy, most Americans are forced to purchase employer-based health insurance offering coverage that ranges from minimal to comprehensive, depending on the type of policy. Moreover, a significant number of Americans fall through the cracks in health insurance: They receive no employment-based health insurance, they cannot afford to insure themselves, and they are ineligible for Medicaid or Medicare. Critics claim that a Canadian-style universal health care policy would ensure all Americans adequate medical care without regard to their ability to pay or the generosity of their employers.

Perhaps the most formidable argument for the United States adopting a Canadian-style health care system is provided by an examination of leading health indicators and per capita health care spending. Before the Canadian Medicare system became operational in 1971, Canada lagged behind the United States in the important indicators of infant mortality and life expectancy. Impressive gains now place Canada ahead of the United States on both health indicators. Moreover, Canada has been able to achieve those gains while spending less of its GNP on health care than the United States. Although health care costs are rising in Canada, they are doing so at a slower rate than in the United States.[131]

Factors that influence lower health care costs in Canada include lower physician and administrative costs and less concern with malpractice litigation. According to the *Journal of the American Medical Association*, the higher per capita expenditure in the United States is explained entirely by higher fees, because the per capita number of physician visits is actually lower in the United States than in Canada. Fees for procedures in the United States are more than three times as high as in Canada.

In addition, fees for evaluation and management services are about 80 percent lower in Canada. Part of the difference in fee structures may be related to the lower rates of malpractice litigation in Canada. Also, because Canadian health care is based on a single-payer system, overhead costs are lower.[132] In part, this is due to the significant portion of the U.S. health care budget that is spent on advertising and billing.[133] The single-payer system also lessens the paperwork load on physicians, thereby freeing them up to see more patients. One indicator of the success of Canada's health care system is that the majority of Canadians are generally satisfied with it and show no inclination of giving it up.[134]

Britain's National Health Service

The National Health Service (NHS) is the most enduring aspect of the British Labour Party's postwar welfare state. The direct inspiration for the NHS was a 1944 white paper written for the wartime coalition government by Sir William Beveridge. The Beveridge Report maintained that a "comprehensive system of health care was essential to any scheme for improving living standards."[135]

After initial resistance from the British Medical Association, the National Health Service Act was passed in 1946 and took effect in 1948. In the words of the act, the aim was to promote "the establishment of a comprehensive health service designed to secure improvement in the physical and mental health of the people . . . and the prevention, diagnosis and treatment of illness."[136] The principle of freedom of choice was upheld in that people could either use the NHS or seek outside doctors. Doctors were guaranteed that there would be no interference in their clinical judgment, and they were free to take private patients while participating in the service. The main goal of the NHS was to provide free medical service to anyone in need. The NHS Act was based on a tripartite system: (1) hospital service with specialists; (2) general medical doctors, dentists, and eye doctors, maintained on a contractual basis; and (3) prevention and support systems, provided by local health departments.

Under the leadership of Minister of Health Anuerin Bevan, all Britain's hospitals were nationalized. Because most hospitals were owned by local governments or were heavily subsidized nonprofit institutions, nationalization was not difficult. General medical practitioners were brought into a new governmentally subsidized plan that provided universal basic medical care that was free at the point of access. This was not a major change, as physicians' services had been subsidized for industrial workers since before World War II. The NHS Act simply extended this coverage to the whole population. British physicians generally came to support the act because it guaranteed a steady income.

The NHS Act does not eliminate private medicine, and a small percentage of NHS hospital beds are reserved for private patients. As mentioned, general practitioners (GPs) and specialists are permitted to treat private patients while working in the NHS. Moreover, affluent patients are permitted to purchase private health insurance and private care. The major advantages of private care are more attractive hospital rooms and quicker service for elective surgery. About 15 percent of Britons currently have private health insurance, which businesses often provide as a fringe benefit for upper-level management.

The backbone of the NHS is the GP. Every patient in Britain is registered with a GP who provides family care. Patients may change their GPs unless they are diagnosed with a chronic illness such as AIDS. GPs are paid by the NHS on the basis of an annual **capitation** fee (per-person fee) for each registered patient. Roughly half of a GP's income comes from capitation payments, with the rest made up by allowances for services such as contraceptive advice and immunization. The role of the GP is to provide primary medical care; GPs are forbidden to restrict their practice to any special client group. Individuals can register with any GP provided he or she is willing to accept them. GPs see almost 75 percent of their registered patients at least once a year; and, because mobility is relatively low in Britain, many people retain the same GP for a considerable period of time.[137]

The GP has wide professional latitude and equips his or her own office, hires staff, and may choose to work singly, in pairs, in groups, or in a government health center. Close to 50 percent of all GPs practice in groups of three or more. Health centers, part of the original National Health Service Act, mushroomed in the late 1960s and 1970s, and by 1975 there were 600 nationally. Sweeping changes in 1967 gave GPs increased benefits, including a higher capitation rate if they had a patient load of 2,500 to 3,500. In addition, extra remuneration was provided for each person on a doctor's list who was over 65, for night calls, for transients, for maternity care, for family planning services, and for certain preventive measures. GPs also receive partial reimbursement for secretaries, receptionists, and nurses, as well as for the rental costs of their offices. Extra payments are also provided for seniority, postgraduate education, and vocational training; for working in groups of three or more; and for practicing in underdoctored areas.[138]

The second tier of the British health care system is the physician consultant (specialist). Most referrals to consultants—except for accidents or emergency care—are made through GPs. Although employed by the government and under contract to a public hospital, a physician specialist is allowed a small private practice. In effect, patients in the community are served by GPs, whereas in the hospital they are under the care of specialists. As in the U.S. health care system, physician specialists are accorded greater prestige and remuneration.[139]

The NHS is funded from general taxes, with the proceeds divided among regional health authorities that plan local health services. The regions, in turn, divide their money among districts that pay for hospitals through global prospective budgets.[140] Health services under the NHS are relatively comprehensive, with hospital and primary medical care being free. However, there are significant patient charges for adult dentistry and eyeglasses and a small charge for prescriptions. Drug prices are agreed upon between the health department and the pharmaceutical industry according to a specific pricing formula based on company profits. In addition, government subsidies for medical education mean that students' direct educational costs are low.[141]

Critics complain that NHS hospital funds are dispersed in a haphazard manner. One reform suggested a way to remedy this problem was to create "internal markets," whereby the distribution of NHS money would follow patients rather than the other way around. Another important problem was that hospitals received nothing extra for efficiently treating more patients at less cost; as a result hospitals had little incentive to improve efficiency.[142]

Another criticism of the NHS is that its funding is based not on the medical needs of consumers, but rather on how much the British treasury believes it can afford to spend on health care. The result is de facto health care rationing and long waiting lists for elective procedures—caused not by inefficiencies in the system but by limited resources. In addition, consumers complain of long waits in GP offices and of hospital buildings that are often in poor repair. There are also long waiting lists for elective surgeries such as hip replacements, routine treatment of varicose veins, and repairs of hernias. (There is believed to be little wait for urgent surgery.) Long waiting lists can be misleading to some extent because they sometimes include people who have died, have moved, have already had their operations, or who have been kept waiting by consultants who want to secure more resources or private patients.[143]

Other critics charge that despite government efforts, there are serious shortages of doctors in certain parts of Britain. In addition, expenditures and resources under the NHS seem to be slanted toward hospitalization rather than toward primary, first-level care. Critics also complain about the lack of accountability of doctors and about strong unions that have supported restrictive practices and fought attempts to privatize support services.[144] Finally, other critics charge that the inequality in the British health system has resulted in higher disease and mortality rates for lower socioeconomic groups.

Under the original NHS Act, Parliament allocated money and power to local health authorities that managed the hospitals and contracted with specialists for services.[145] Passed in 1990, the National Health and Community Care Act was designed to reduce the long queues for the treatment of nonacute illnesses and procedures by introducing market efficiencies. Loosening the knot between funders and providers, this bill permitted some hospitals (called *trust hospitals*) to operate independently of the local health authority in setting fees, managing budgets, developing personnel packages, and purchasing goods. The theory was that independently managed hospitals would be more efficient than centrally planned ones. To further encourage efficiency, these trust hospitals were allowed to sell their services to any local health authority, private patients, or to private insurance companies. In addition, GPs with large practices were permitted to become fundholders of NHS grants from which they could purchase hospital or specialized services for their clients. It was expected that GPs would refer their patients to those hospitals or specialists that were the most efficient. Inefficient hospitals would get fewer referrals and thus would be forced to increase their quality of care while reducing costs.[146] Unfortunately, the hoped-for results have not been achieved.

Much of the reporting on the NHS in the U.S. press has tended to emphasize its flaws. Although some GPs express dissatisfaction with the system, the British people continue to use it in large numbers. For example, although 15 percent of Britons have private insurance, most use it as a supplement rather than as a substitute for the NHS.[147] Despite the criticisms, the NHS appears to be serving the majority of the British population as well as, and in some ways better than, the U.S. health care system. For instance, in 2005 per capita health care expenditures were only 8.3 percent of Britain's GDP compared to 15.3 percent for the United States.[148] Much of this lower cost is attributable to the success of GPs in keeping down hospital admission rates and to the relatively low administrative costs of the NHS. Notwithstanding the lower cost of the British health care system, most health indicators, such as life expectancy and infant mortality rates, are equivalent to or better than those found in the costlier U.S. health care system. Enoch Powell, a former British health minister, summed up the contradictions of the NHS: "One of the most striking features of the NHS is the continual, deafening chorus of complaints which rises day and night from every part of it, a chorus only interrupted when someone suggests that a different system altogether might be preferable . . . it presents what must be a unique spectacle of an undertaking that is run down by everyone engaged in it."

The Australian Health Care System

The current Australian health care system is a hybrid public–private system. Introduced in 1984, Medicare provides Australia's residents with high-quality universal health care. The Medicare system was predicated on the idea that all Australians should contribute to the cost of health care according to their ability to pay. As such, it is financed by a progressive income tax and an income-related Medicare levy. As a supplement to Medicare, Australians are strongly encouraged to purchase private health insurance, which in 2008 cost up to $250 a month for a family to get top-level coverage.[149]

Medicare provides comprehensive benefits such as consultation fees for doctors, including specialists; medical tests like X-rays, MRIs, and pathology tests; eye tests performed by optometrists; most surgical and therapeutic procedures performed by doctors; and some surgical procedures performed by approved dentists. From 2006 mental health services paid for by Medicare have broadened to include services to families and schools. The Australian Government's Better Access to Psychiatrists, Psychologists and General Practitioners program through the Medicare Benefits Schedule initiative is slated to cost $538 million over five years.[150]

One can enter an Australian hospital either as a public or private pay (using health insurance) patient. Public hospital patients are not charged for care and treatment by attending physicians or specialists, or aftercare by the treating doctor. However, the treatment they receive is from doctors and specialists nominated by the hospital. Those admitted to a public or private hospital as a private patient (i.e., using private health insurance) have a choice of doctors to treat them. Medicare pays 75 percent of the Medicare Schedule fee for services and procedures provided by the treating doctor. With private health insurance, some or all of the outstanding balance is covered. Private patients are charged for hospital accommodation and items such as surgery and medicines, which are often covered by private health insurance.[151]

Medicare does not cover private patient hospital costs (e.g., surgery or accommodation); most dental examinations and treatment; ambulance services; home nursing; acupuncture (unless part of a doctor's consultation); glasses and contact lenses; hearing aids and other appliances; prostheses; medicines (except those subsidized by the Pharmaceutical Benefits Scheme which covers most classes of medicines); and cosmetic surgery.

Criticism leveled against Medicare is similar to that directed at the British NHS. Namely, long waits for elective surgery as a public patient (private patients have no wait); inefficiencies, staff shortages, and underfunding. The new Labor government under Kevin Rudd has promised to significantly increase funding for public hospitals and medical services. Other criticisms involve copayments and gaps in services, such as dental. All told, Australians seem to be relatively pleased with their system.[152]

It is difficult to compare the quality of the Canadian, British, and Australian health care systems with that of the United States. For affluent or middle-class Americans with good health insurance, the U.S. system of health care may well provide the best medical care in the world; and for complex medical procedures involving sophisticated equipment and technology, U.S. health care is unequaled. Moreover, unlike the long queues characteristic of the UK and Canadian systems, the waiting period for surgery, tests, and other procedures is relatively short in the United States. Finally, physicians in this country are among the best trained in the world. However, the emphasis on costly equipment and technology is not without a price. A medical approach that emphasizes specific diseases over primary care and preventive medicine usually results in good care, but for fewer people. Health care systems that emphasize personal and primary care, accessibility, and free or inexpensive services often reach more people. Given that, the health care systems of Canada, Britain, and Australia appear to distribute health resources more equitably than does the U.S. health care system.

Conclusion

The examination of health care in the United States raises important questions. What is this nation's responsibility for providing health care to all its citizens? How much high-tech medicine can our society realistically afford? How should U.S. medical resources be allocated? What, if any, limitations on personal freedom are permissible in the name of promoting health and preventing disease? These and other questions require urgent answers.

The U.S. health care system is facing an acute crisis. This crisis is grounded in the failure of the marketplace to curb health care expenditures, the system's overreliance on medical technology at the expense of providing primary health care services, the huge amount spent on growth, health care administrative costs, and the large numbers of working people and their families who cannot afford health care coverage. Moreover, compared to industrialized countries with less-costly health care systems, the higher-cost U.S. health care system is not producing greater longevity, lower rates of infant mortality, or other indicators of improved public health.

The United States is one of the few industrialized countries without a national health insurance system. Moreover, it is also one of the few industrialized nations where medical expenses can cause poverty. Terri Combs-Orme suggests that a progressive reconstruction of the U.S. health care system must be grounded in the following principles:

1. Accessible health care should be a universal right of all Americans, not a privilege to be purchased or earned.
2. The quantity, quality, and accessibility of health care should be equal for all, not dependent on income or categorical status. No health care system should result in differential quantity, quality, or accessibility of care based on income, gender, age, or any other criterion.
3. Health care should not be linked to employment. A majority of Americans purchase health care insurance through their place of employment, but the fear of job loss or other issues not under their control undermines the security of this arrangement and limits their job mobility.
4. The quality, quantity, and accessibility of health care should not vary on a state-by-state basis.
5. A progressive health care system must balance the needs and rights of children and the elderly in a fair and rational way.
6. A comprehensive health care system should include coverage for and accessibility to long-term care for the elderly.[153]

If commodification and high costs are left unchecked, health care in the United States may someday be out of reach for the majority of citizens. Although the likely outcome of the U.S. health care crisis is unknown, left solely to the caprice of the marketplace, the problems will undoubtedly worsen.

Discussion Questions

1. In 2008 U.S. health care expenditures were more than $2 trillion a year. This cost has risen dramatically over the past 25 years in terms of the amount spent, the percentage of the GDP used for health care, and the per capita costs of health care. What are the main factors that have driven up health care costs? How can these factors be controlled?
2. Medicare has experienced large increases in costs. What are the major factors contributing to the steep rise in Medicare costs? What can be done to slow these rises?
3. Some critics believe that the costs of Medicare and Medicaid cannot be brought under control without radically reforming the entire health care system. They argue that incremental reforms in the Medicare and Medicaid programs have only a minuscule impact on the rise in federal and state expenditures for health care. Are these critics correct?

4. Evidence of the effectiveness of cost-controlling mechanisms such as DRGs has been mixed. Critics charge that not only has the DRG system failed to substantially reduce health care costs, but it has also led to a reduced level of patient care. Is the DRG system successful? If so, should it be a model for future health care reforms?

5. Many critics argue that there is a serious health care crisis in the United States. Describe the main characteristics of that crisis (e.g., health care costs, accessibility issues, uninsured populations, U.S. health indicators compared with those of other nations).

6. The AIDS epidemic is one of the most important public health issues facing the global community. Some critics insist that more money should be spent on basic AIDS research, outreach, and treatment. Other critics argue that AIDS is only one of many health care problems facing the United States and other countries around the world. They argue that the money spent on AIDS research should be in proportion to the numbers of people affected by the disease, which, in the United States, are relatively small compared to the numbers of people suffering from cancer and heart disease. Is AIDS a significantly more important public health problem in the United States than cancer, heart disease, or the effects of drugs, alcohol, and tobacco? Should the federal government spend proportionally more on AIDS research than on other diseases?

7. Some health care analysts are calling for radical reform in the U.S. health care system. Many of them insist that the nation's free market health care system should be replaced by a more cost-effective and comprehensive system. Assuming that these health care analysts are correct, which of the health care systems described in this chapter would be the best model for the United States to emulate? Why?

8. Why has the United States not developed a health care system that is universal and publicly funded, like those of its industrial counterparts? What, if anything, can be done to reform or radically transform U.S. health care?

Notes

1. "New York Times/CBS News Poll," February 23–27, 2007.

2. U.S. Census Bureau, "Income, Poverty, and Health Insurance Coverage in the United States: 2006," Economics and Statistics Administration, issued August 2007. Retrieved July 2008, from www.census.gov/prod/2007pubs/p60-233.pdf

3. Ibid.

4. C. P. Pandya, "Study: Health Insurance Premiums Rising Much Faster Than Average Wages," *The New Standard* (September 28, 2004), p. 3.

5. National Coalition on Health Care, "Health Insurance Coverage."

6. Health Care Financing Administration, "President Clinton Announces Approximately 2.5 Million Children Have Enrolled in the State Children's Health Insurance Program, Praises the Decline in Uninsured, Urges Congress to Expand Coverage, Unveils New Funds for Outreach" (Washington, DC: Health Care Financing Administration, 2000).

7. Terri Combs-Orme, "Should the Federal Government Finance Health Care for All Americans?: Yes," in Howard Jacob Karger and James Midgley (eds.), *Controversial Issues in Social Policy* (Boston: Allyn & Bacon, 1993).

8. Irving J. Lewis and Cecil G. Sheps, *The Sick Citadel* (Boston: Oelgeschlager, Gunn, and Hain, 1983), p. 16.

9. National Coalition on Health Care, "Health Insurance Coverage."

10. J. Hadley and J. Holahan, "The Cost of Care for the Uninsured: What Do We Spend, Who Pays, and What Would Full Coverage Add to Medical Spending?", 2004. Retrieved July 2008, from www.kff.org/uninsured/upload/The-Cost-of-Care-for-the-Uninsured-What-Do-We-Spend-Who-Pays-and-What-Would-Full-Coverage-Add-to-Medical-Spending.pdf

11. Sumner A. Rosen, David Fanshel, and Mary E. Lutz (eds.), *Face of the Nation 1987* (Silver Spring, MD: NASW, 1987), p. 75.

12. U.S. Census Bureau, "Income, Poverty, and Health Insurance Coverage in the United States: 2006."

13. Centers for Medicare & Medicaid Services, "Brief Summaries of Medicare and Medicaid," November 1, 2007. Retrieved July 2008, from www.cms.hhs.gov/MedicareMedicaidStatSupp/downloads/07BriefSummaries.pdf

14. Ibid.

15. See Families USA, "Understanding the New Medicare Prescription Drug Benefit," The Medicare Road

Show, Washington, DC, Spring 2004; Kaiser Family Foundation, "The Medicare Prescription Drug Law," March 2004, retrieved November 2004, from www.kff.org/medicare/loader.cfm?url=/commonspot/security/getfile.cfm&PageID=33325; and Egyptian Area Agency on Aging, "Medicare Prescription Drug Benefit," Cartersville, IL, May 20, 2004, retrieved November 2004, from www.egyptianaaa.org/MedicareDrugBill.htm.

16. Ceci Connolly, "OMB Says Medicare Drug Law Could Cost Still More, White House Estimates Show a $42 Billion Increase over 10 Years," *Washington Post* (September 19, 2004), p. A04.

17. Ibid.

18. Michael Scherer, "Medicare's Hidden Bonanza," *Mother Jones* (March/April 2004), p. 11.

19. Centers for Medicare & Medicaid Services, "Brief Summaries of Medicare and Medicaid."

20. Centers for Medicare & Medicaid Services, "Medicaid: A Brief Summary," September 16, 2004. Retrieved October 2004, from www.cms.hhs.gov/-publications/overview-medicare-medicaid/default4.asp

21. Centers for Medicare & Medicaid Services, "Brief Summaries of Medicare and Medicaid."

22. Centers for Medicare & Medicaid Services, "Medicaid: A Brief Summary."

23. Ibid.

24. David E. Rosenbaum, "Gloomy Forecast Touches off Feud on Medicare Fund," *New York Times* (June 6, 1996), pp. A1 and B14.

25. For a good historical analysis of the Medicare program, see Theodore R. Marmor, *The Politics of Medicare* (Chicago: Aldine, 1973).

26. Centers for Medicare & Medicaid Services, "Brief Summaries of Medicare and Medicaid."

27. Health Care Financing Administration, "Medicaid Eligibility." Retrieved 2001, from www.hcfa.gov/medicaid/meligib.htm

28. Centers for Medicare & Medicaid Services, "Medicaid: A Brief Summary."

29. Ibid.

30. Social Security Administration, "Medicaid," *Annual Statistical Supplement, 2007.* Retrieved July 2008, from www.socialsecurity.gov/policy/docs/statcomps/supplement/2007/medicaid.pdf

31. American Health Care Association, "Nursing Facility Beds by Certification Type," June 2004. Retrieved November 2004, from www.ahca.org/research/oscar/rpt_certified_beds_200406.pdf

32. Stephen A. Moses, "Denial Is Not a River in Egypt," *Health Insurance Underwriter* 50, no. 11 (December 2002), pp. 36–40.

33. American Association of Retired Persons (AARP), "Average Daily Cost for Nursing Home Care by State, 2001," 2004. Retrieved November 2004, from www.aarp.org/bulletin/longterm/Articles/a2003-10-30-dailycost.html

34. Social Security Administration, "Medicaid."

35. See Children's Defense Fund, *A Children's Defense Budget*, p. 109; and Barbara Wolfe, "A Medicaid Primer," *Focus* 17, no. 3 (Spring 1996), pp. 1–6.

36. Kaiser Family Foundation, "State Health Facts." Retrieved July 2008, from www.statehealthfacts.org

37. Ibid.

38. Kaiser Family Foundation, "Determining Income Eligibility in Children's Health Coverage Programs: How States Use Disregards in Children's Medicaid and SCHIP," May 2008. Retrieved July 2008, from www.kff.org/medicaid/upload/7776.pdf

39. Kentucky Farm Bureau, "Summary of Master Tobacco Settlement," April 1, 1999. Retrieved 2001, from www.kyfb.org/FactTobSett040199.htm

40. See Andrew Garber, "Tobacco Settlement Gregoire Negotiated Not Popular with All," *Seattle Times* (October 4, 2004), p. A6; and Pamela M. Prah, "Smokers Help to Balance State Budgets," *Stateline*, March 3, 2004, retrieved November 2004, from www.stateline.org/stateline/?pa=story&sa=showStoryInfo&print=1&id=354303

41. U.S. House of Representatives, *Overview of Entitlement Programs: 1996 Green Book.*

42. U.S. House of Representatives, *1996 Green Book*, p. 995.

43. See Ibid.; and U.S. Bureau of the Census, *Statistical Abstract of the United States, 1991* (Washington, DC: U.S. Government Printing Office, 1991), p. 107.

44. HHS, Centers for Medicare & Medicaid, "The Nation's Health Dollar, Calendar Year 2006: Where It Came From." Retrieved July 2008, from www.cms.hhs.gov/NationalHealthExpendData/downloads/PieChartSourcesExpenditures2006.pdf

45. Julie Appleby, "What Happens after the Band-Aids Run Out?" *USA Today* (December 8–10, 2000), pp. 1–2.

46. See Health Care Financing Administration, "Actuarial Products, N.H.E. Projections, Table 1;" and G. J. Schieber and J. P. Poullier, "International Health Care Spending: Issues and Trends," *Health Affairs*, 10 (1991), p. 110.

47. OECD Health Data 2008, "How Does the United States Compare." Retrieved July 2008, from www.oecd.org/dataoecd/46/2/38980580.pdf"

48. Alliance for Health Reform, "Covering Health Issues: 2003, A Sourcebook for Journalists," January 2003. Retrieved November 2004, from www.allhealth.org/sourcebook2002/ch8_8.html

49. The Commonwealth 2003 Annual Report, "A Look in the Mirror," 2003. Retrieved November 2004, from www.cmwf.org/annreprt/2003/msg_pres02_lookinmirror.htm

50. Ibid.

51. Ibid.

52. Ibid.

53. Ibid.

54. Annenberg School of Communication, "President Uses Dubious Statistics on Costs of Malpractice Lawsuits, Two Congressional Agencies Dispute Findings That Caps on Damage Awards Produce Big Savings in Medical Costs," University of Pennsylvania, January 29, 2004. Retrieved November 2004, from www.factcheck.org/article133.html

55. Michael Clemens, "Rising Costs Reflect Many Instances," USA Today May 5, 1993, p. B2.; and Barnaby J. Feder, "Heart Specialists Reconsider the Bypass," February 25, 2007. Retrieved July 2008, from www.iht.com/articles/2007/02/25/news/surgery.php

56. Victoria Colliver, "In Critical Condition: Health Care in America," *San Francisco Chronicle* (October 11, 2004), p. A8.

57. HHS, Centers for Medicare & Medicaid Services, "National Health Expenditures Aggregate, Per Capita Amounts, Percent Distribution, and Average Annual Percent Growth, by Source of Funds: Selected Calendar Years 1960–2006." Retrieved July 2008, from www.cms.hhs.gov/NationalHealthExpendData/downloads/tables.pdf

58. American Hospital Association, "Rising Demand, Increasing Costs of Caring Fuel Hospital Spending," Press Release, February 19, 2003. Retrieved November 2004, from www.aha.org/aha/hospitalconnect/search/pressrelease.jsp?dcrpath=AHA/Press_Release/data/PR_030219_Costs&domain=AHA

59. Health Care Financing Administration, "Actuarial Products, N.H.E. Projections, Table 2." Retrieved 2001, from www.hcfa.gov/stats/NHE-Proj

60. Myrle Croasdale, "High Medical School Debt Steers Life Choices for Young Doctors," *AMA News* (May 17, 2004), pp. 2–5.

61. Ibid., p. 6.

62. Jay Greene, "Primary Care Matches Down Again; Fourth Year of Decline Worries Some," *AMA News* (April 9, 2001), p. 16.

63. Bureau of Labor Statistics, "Occupational Handbook Outlook 2008–9 Edition." Retrieved July 2008, from http://stats.bls.gov/OCO/OCOS074.HTM

64. OECD Health Data 2008, "How Does the United States Compare."

65. Katherine van Wormer, *Social Welfare: A World View* (Chicago: Nelson-Hall, 1997), p. 412.

66. Marcia Angell, *The Truth About the Drug Companies: How They Deceive Us and What to Do About It* (New York: Random House, 2004).

67. Meredith Rosenthal and John H. Foster, "Drug Ads Take Increasing—Though Still Small—Share of Pharmaceutical Promotion Budget," *The New England Journal of Medicine* (February 14, 2002), pp. 498–505.

68. Nancy McVicar, "Drug Costs Go Up but Coverage Comes Down," *Sun-Sentinel* (February 23, 2000). Retrieved 2001, from www.sun-sentinel.com/news/daily/detail/0,1136,27000000000116737,00.html

69. "Melinda Beck, "Doctors under the knife," *Newsweek* (April 5, 1993), p. 29.

70. John H. Goddeeris and Andrew J. Hogan, "Nature and Dimensions of the Problem." In John H. Goddeeris and Andrew J. Hogan (eds.), *Improving Access to Health Care: What Can the States Do?* (Kalamazoo, MI: W. E. Upjohn Institute for Employment Research, 1992), pp. 14–15.

71. Quoted in Marie A. Caputi and William A. Heiss, "The DRG Revolution," *Health and Social Work 3*, no. 6 (June 1984), p. 5.

72. McVicar, "Drug Costs Go Up but Coverage Comes Down."

73. Paul Schmolling, Merrill Youkeles, and William R. Burger, *Human Services in Contemporary America* (Pacific Grove, CA: Brooks/Cole Publishing Co., 1997), p. 54.

74. U.S. House of Representatives, *1996 Green Book.*

75. Amy Goldstein, "Cutting Health Costs Slices into Charity," *Washington Post* (April 5, 1999), p. A1.

76. Weiss Ratings Inc., "Consumers Continue to Choose Medicare HMOs Despite High Risk of Being Dropped," 2004. Retrieved November 2004, from www.weissratings.com/News/Ins_HMO/20021209 hmo.htm

77. Vicki Lankarge, "Seniors Dropped from Medicare HMOs Shouldn't Rejoin Others, Weiss Warns," *insure.com* (November 14, 2000). Retrieved 2001, from www.insure.com/health/medicare/fewoptions1100.html

78. Howard Waitzkin, *The Second Sickness: Contradictions of Capitalist Health Care* (New York: Free Press, 1983), p. 220.

79. Nancy McVicar, "Medical Care Is There—If You Can Afford It," *Sun-Sentinel* (February 24, 2000). Retrieved 2001, from www.sun-sentinel.com/news/daily/detail/0,1136,27500000000104840,00.html

80. Ibid.

81. Ellyn E. Spragins, "Simon Says, Join Us," *Newsweek* (June 19, 1995), pp. 55–58.

82. Thomas H. Ainsworth, *Live or Die* (New York: Macmillan, 1983), p. 89.

83. American Medical Association, *Competition in Health Insurance: A Comprehensive Study of U.S. Markets*, 2nd ed. (Chicago: American Medical Association, January 2003).

84. Ibid.

85. John M. Herrick and Joseph Papsidero, "Uncompensated Care: What States Are Doing," in Goddeeris and Hogan (eds.), *Improving Access to Health Care: What Can the States Do?* (Kalamazoo, MI: W.E. Upjohn Institute for Employment Research, 1992), pp. 139–140.

86. W. Greenberg, "Elimination of Employer-Based Health Insurance," in R. B. Helms (ed.), *American Health Policy: Critical Issues for Reform* (Washington, DC: AEI Press, October 1992), pp. 1–4.

87. Robert Searles Walker, *AIDS: Today, Tomorrow* (New Jersey: Humanities Press International, 1992), p. 134.

88. Centers for Disease Control and Prevention, "Cases of HIV infection and AIDS in the United States and Dependent Areas, 2006." Retrieved July 2008, from www.cdc.gov/hiv/topics/surveillance/resources/reports/2006report/pdf/2006SurveillanceReport.pdf

89. Ibid.

90. Ibid.

91. Martin Shapiro and Samuel Bozzette, "Privileged Treatment Inequities in HIV Care Demand Remedies for U.S. Health Care," 1999. Retrieved 2001, from www.rand.org/publications/RRR/RRRfall99/privilege.html

92. UNAIDS/WHO, "AIDS Epidemic Update," December 2007. Retrieved July 2008, from http://data.unaids.org/pub/EPISlides/2007/2007_epiupdate_en.pdf

93. World Health Organization, *The World Health Report 2003*, Geneva, 2003.

94. "About Business Roundtable." Retrieved April 2, 2007, from www.businessroundtable.org/aboutUs/index.aspx

95. "AARP, Business Roundtable, and SEIU Partner to Spur Action on Health Care, Long-Term Financial Security," January 16, 2007. Retrieved April 2, 2007, from www.businessroundtable.org//taskForces/taskforce/document.aspx?qs=7025BF159FC49514481138A74EA1851159169FEB56A37B2AC

96. "The Divided We Fail Platform." Retrieved April 2, 2007, from www.businessroundtable.org//taskForces/taskforce/document.aspx?qs=7025BF159FC49514481138A74EA1851159169FEB56A37B2AC

97. "U.S. Chamber Policy Priorities for 2007," U.S. Chamber of Commerce, p. 3. Retrieved April 2, 2007, from www.uschamber.com/NR/rdonlyres/ehu6b2fp4efxznrpxdt2jk3db22imtentbak7wuiyqhvfposezwtma4a7gh64w7rg5nyi55zup6xilm4wrrplkmldhf/0701priorities.pdf

98. "Health Care: Introduction." Retrieved April 2, 2007, from www.nfib.com/page/healthcare.html

99. Jonathan Cohn, "What's the One Thing Big Business and the Left Have in Common?" *New York Times*, April 1, 2007. Retrieved April 2, 2007, from www.nytimes.com/2007/04/01/magazine/01Healthcare.t.html?ref=health

100. Ibid.

101. "Expanding Health Care Coverage in the United States: A Historic Agreement," Health Coverage Coalition for the Uninsured, January 18, 2007. Retrieved April 2, 2007, from www.coalitionfortheuninsured.org/pdfs/agreement.pdf

102. Ibid, p. 1.

103. Ronald V. Dellums et al., *Health Services Act* (H. R. 2969) (Washington, DC: U.S. Government Printing Office, 1979). For a good summary of the act, see Waitzkin, *The Second Sickness*, pp. 222–226.

104. "Summary of S. 2817, The National Health Care Act of 1992," *NASW-LA News* 16, no. 5 (September/October 1992), p. 2.

105. Thomas Daschle, Rima Cohen, and Charles Rice, "Health Care Reform: Single-Payer Models," *American Psychologist* 48, no. 3 (March 1993), pp. 265–267.

106. Paul Starr, *The Social Transformation of American Medicine* (New York: Basic Books, 1984).

107. Ibid.

108. Jeff Bingaman, Robert G. Frank, and Carrie L. Billy, "Combining a Global Health Budget with a Market-Driven Delivery System," *American Psychologist* 48, no. 3 (March 1993), pp. 271–272.

109. Robin Toner, "'Harry and Louise' Ad Campaign Biggest Gun in Health Care Battle," *San Diego Union-Tribune* (April 7, 1994), p. A7.

110. Sara Fritz, "Ads Are Designed to Counter Health Care Proposals," *Los Angeles Times* (May 15, 1993), p. A16.

111. Dana Priest, "The Slow Death of Health Reform," *Washington Post Weekly* (September 5–11, 1994), p. 11.

112. Douglas Frantz, "Lobbyists, Interest Groups Begin Costly Health Care Battle," *Los Angeles Times* (May 24, 1993).

113. Waitzkin, *The Second Sickness*, p. 218.

114. C. Sabatino, "Kassebaum-Kennedy Health Insurance Bill Clears Congress: Medical Savings Accounts Limited to Demonstration Program," Families USA (Washington, DC: Families USA).

115. Wolfe, "Changing the U.S. Health Care System," p. 17.

116. Diane M. DiNitto, *Social Welfare: Politics and Public Policy* (Boston: Allyn & Bacon, 1995), p. 270.

117. Obama–Biden, "Health Care." Retrieved December 6, 2008, from www.barackobama.com/issues/healthcare

118. W. Barnhill, "Canadian Health Care: Would It Work Here?" *Arthritis Today* 6, no. 6 (November–December 1992), p. 8.

119. Elaine Vayda and R. B. Deber, "The Canadian Health Care System: An Overview," *Social Science and Medicine* 18, no. 3 (1984), pp. 191–197.

120. Callaway, "Canadian Health Care: The Good, the Bad, and the Ugly," *Health Insurance Underwriter* (October 1991), pp. 18–35.

121. See Tracy Falwell, Suzy Carter, Jodie Daigle, Renee Mills, Lissa Cameron, and Leticia Gonzalez-Castro, "International Health Care Systems Analysis: Canada, Britain, Germany, Sweden, France, Mexico and South Africa," unpublished paper, Graduate School of Social Work, University of Houston, Houston, TX, April 30, 1996; and T. Mizrahi, R. Fasan, and S. Dooha, "National Health Line," *Health and Social Work* 18, no. 1 (1993), pp. 7–12.

122. Jonathan S. Rakich, "The Canadian and U.S. Health Care Systems: Profiles and Policies," *Hospital and Health Services Administration* 36, no. 1 (Spring 1991), pp. 26–27.

123. Falwell et al., "International Health Care Systems Analysis."

124. Barnhill, "Canadian Health Care," p. 19.

125. Ibid.

126. Ibid.

127. Rakich, "The Canadian and U.S. Health Care Systems," p. 32.

128. See Barnhill, "Canadian Health Care;" I. Munro, "How Not to Improve Health Care," *Reader's Digest* (September 1992), p. 21; and B. Gilray, "Standing Up for American Health Care," *Health Insurance Underwriter* (February 1992), p. 10.

129. Robert E. Moffitt, "Should the Federal Government Finance Health Care for All Americans?: No," in Howard Jacob Karger and James Midgley (eds.), *Controversial Issues in Social Policy* (Boston: Allyn & Bacon, 1993).

130. For example, David Himmelstein and Steffie Woolhandler, "A National Health Care Program for the United States: A Physicians' Proposal," *The New England Journal of Medicine* 320 (January 12, 1989), pp. 102–108; and Combs-Orme, "Should the Federal Government Finance Health Care for All Americans?: Yes."

131. Combs-Orme, "Should the Federal Government Finance Health Care for All Americans?: Yes."

132. van Wormer, *Social Welfare*, p. 419.

133. See Combs-Orme, "Should the Federal Government Finance Health Care for All Americans?: Yes;" and "How Does Canada Do It?: A Comparison of Expenditures for Physicians' Services in the United States and Canada," *Journal of the American Medical Association* 265, no. 19 (May 15, 1991), p. 2474.

134. See W. Caragata, "Medicare Wars," *Maclean's* 108, no. 14 (1995), p. 4; and Leger Marketing, "Canadian Perceptions of Their Health Care System," Executive Report, Ottawa, June 2001. Retrieved November 2004, from www.legermarketing.com/documents/spclm/010709eng.pdf

135. Ruth Levitt, *The Reorganised National Health Service* (London: Croom Helm, 1979), p. 15.

136. Quoted in Ibid. p. 17.

137. Victor W. Sidel and Ruth Sidel, *A Healthy State* (New York: Pantheon Books, 1983), p. 144.

138. Ibid., pp. 144, 157–159.

139. Ibid., p. 172.

140. Ibid.

141. Ibid.

142. "Nye Bevan's Legacy," *The Economist* (July 6, 1992), p. 12.

143. Ibid.

144. Ibid.

145. Levitt, *The Reorganized National Health Service*, p. 27.

146. "Nye Bevan's Legacy."

147. Ibid., p. 12.

148. OECD, Health Data 2007.

149. See www.iselect.com.au.

150. Australian Government, Medicare Australia, About Medicare, 2008. Retrieved June 10, 2008, from www.medicareaustralia.gov.au/public/register/index.jsp

151. Ibid.

152. Ibid.

153. Combs-Orme, "Should the Federal Government Finance Health Care for All Americans?: Yes."

Index